"All I know as a political reporter is that Adlai Stevenson injected humor and happiness and sophistication into American political life, and you have to have spent half your life listening to the normal run of American politicians to really understand what a fantastic accomplishment that was."
Eric Sevareid

This first volume of *The Papers of Adlai E. Stevenson* marks the beginning of an important new project: an eight-volume series which, when complete, will constitute not only a documentary biography of Stevenson but, at the same time, a documentary history, in his own words, of the extraordinary and often bewildering changes that remolded the United States and the world during his lifetime — from 1900 to 1965.

Volume I, *Beginnings of Education, 1900-1941*, traces Stevenson's early development, his consistent effort to acquire a deeper understanding of his times. In letters, postcards and speeches, it reflects his belief that education is both a never-ending process and a personal responsibility — and reflects, as well, Stevenson's growing desire to participate in the affairs of government. From his childhood in Bloomington, Illinois, the papers continue through his years at Choate School and Princeton, and then Harvard and Northwestern law schools. They chronicle his beginning Chicago law practice in the mid-twenties, his emergence as a Chicago civic leader with the Chicago Council

ring of honesty, intelligence, and goodwill in the words of Adlai Stevenson."

Books by Walter Johnson

THE BATTLE AGAINST ISOLATION

WILLIAM ALLEN WHITE'S AMERICA

THE UNITED STATES: EXPERIMENT IN DEMOCRACY
(with Avery Craven)

HOW WE DRAFTED ADLAI STEVENSON

1600 PENNSYLVANIA AVENUE: PRESIDENTS AND THE PEOPLE, 1929–1959

THE FULBRIGHT PROGRAM: A HISTORY
(with Francis J. Colligan)

Edited by Walter Johnson

SELECTED LETTERS OF WILLIAM ALLEN WHITE

ROOSEVELT AND THE RUSSIANS: THE YALTA CONFERENCE
By Edward R. Stettinius, Jr.

TURBULENT ERA: A DIPLOMATIC RECORD OF FORTY YEARS, 1904–1945
By Joseph C. Grew

The Papers of Adlai E. Stevenson

WALTER JOHNSON, *Editor*

CAROL EVANS, *Assistant Editor*

The Papers of

Advisory Committee

Adlai E. Stevenson

VOLUME I

Beginnings of Education

1900–1941

LITTLE, BROWN *and* **COMPANY** • *Boston* • *Toronto*

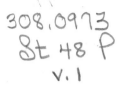

308.0973
St 48 P
v. 1

FIRST EDITION

T 09/72

cip in
Vol 2

The editors gratefully acknowledge the permission of the following authors, publishers, individuals and institutions to reprint selected materials as noted:

Edward E. Barthell, Jr., Noel F. Busch, The Choate School, The Curtis Publishing Company, the *Daily Pantagraph,* Kenneth S. Davis, Doubleday & Company, Inc., Arthur J. Goldberg, Harper & Row, Publishers, Robert M. Hutchins, Edward D. McDougal, Jr., Davis Merwin, Jr., Joe Alex Morris, Claude D. Pepper, G. P. Putnam's Sons, the *Quarterly Journal of Speech,* Random House, Inc., James A. Robinson, Arthur Schlesinger, Jr., Hermon D. Smith, the University of Chicago, Mrs. Clifton Utley, and Russel R. Windes for all items from their publications and writings as detailed in the footnotes.

Barron's Educational Series, Inc., for excerpts from *Adlai E. Stevenson — A Short Biography* by Stuart Gerry Brown. Copyright © 1965 by Barron's Educational Series, Inc.

Bulletin of the Atomic Scientists for quotations from the article "Adlai E. Stevenson, 1900–1965" by Eugene Rabinowitch, September, 1965. Copyright © 1965 by the Educational Foundation for Nuclear Science, Inc.

Chicago Bar Record for selections from the "Report of the Committee on Civil Rights" by Adlai E. Stevenson, Chairman. Copyright 1939 by the Chicago Bar Association.

Coward-McCann, Inc., for excerpts from *The Remnants of Power: The Tragic Last Years of Adlai Stevenson* by Richard J. Walton. Copyright © 1968 by Richard J. Walton.

Harper & Row, Publishers, for a selection from the chapter, "With A.E.S. in War and Politics" by George W. Ball, published in *As We Knew Adlai: The Stevenson Story by Twenty-two Friends,* Edited and with Preface by Edward P. Doyle. Copyright © 1966 by Harper & Row, Publishers, Inc.

Harper & Row, Publishers, for excerpts from *What I Think* by Adlai E. Stevenson. Copyright 1954, © 1955, 1956 by R. Keith Kane.

Mrs. Ernest L. Ives and William Morrow & Company, Inc., for excerpts from *My Brother Adlai* by Elizabeth Stevenson Ives and Hildegarde Dolson. Copyright © 1955, 1956 by Elizabeth Stevenson Ives.

Random House, Inc., for excerpts from *The Secret Search for Peace in Vietnam* by David Kraslow and Stuart H. Loory. Copyright © 1968 by David Kraslow and Stuart H. Loory.

*Published simultaneously in Canada
by Little, Brown & Company (Canada) Limited*

PRINTED IN THE UNITED STATES OF AMERICA

Foreword

After Adlai E. Stevenson died on July 14, 1965, Dr. Eugene Rabinowitch wrote in the September 1965, issue of the *Bulletin of the
Atomic Scientists:*

> He caught the imagination of intellectuals in America and
> abroad as a tolerant, rational, humble, and utterly civilized states-
> man.
> . . . The immense power of words in the affairs of man has
> been demonstrated in our times by the evil influence of Hitler's
> oratory, and by the spell of Winston Churchill's noble phrases. Of
> course, words can be empty, dishonest, and deceptive, and the po-
> litical air is full of such. But sincere and well-chosen words are the
> only paths by which ideas can spread from man to man and from
> nation to nation, and the light of understanding can break through
> the fog of suspicion and self-satisfaction. And somehow, not un-
> failingly and not at once, nations distinguish the ring of such words
> and respond to them. Men everywhere in the world heard the ring
> of honesty, intelligence, and goodwill in the words of Adlai Steven-
> son. . . . Whose voice will speak to the world for tolerance, for
> understanding, for reasonableness, in a time when continued in-
> tolerance, irrationality, and misunderstanding could mean the end
> of mankind?

Stevenson's own words — in letters, postcards, speeches, and his
abortive attempts at keeping a diary — are presented in the eight volumes of *The Papers of Adlai E. Stevenson.* These volumes are a documentary biography of Governor Stevenson and, at the same time, a
documentary history in his words of the extraordinary, and often bewildering, changes that remolded the United States and the world
during his lifetime from 1900 to 1965.

In 1954 Stevenson said:

[*vii*]

America's greatest contribution to human society has come not from her wealth or weapons or ambitions, but from her ideas; from the moral sentiments of human liberty and human welfare embodied in the Declaration of Independence and the Bill of Rights. We must cling to these truths, for these are everlasting and universal aspirations. In the words of Lincoln: "It was not the mere separation of the colonies from the motherland, but the sentiment in the Declaration of Independence which gave liberty not alone to the people of this country, but hope to all the world. It was that which gave promise that in due time the weights should be lifted from the shoulders of all men, and that all should have an equal chance." Throughout its history, America has given hope, comfort and inspiration to freedom's cause in all lands. The reservoir of good will and respect for America was not built up by American arms or intrigue; it was built upon our deep dedication to the cause of human liberty and human welfare.[1]

During the decade of the 1950's, Governor Stevenson sounded the tocsin against drift and complacency. He advocated a détente with the Soviet Union and an end to mindless anti-Communism. And, although he was warned that he would lose votes, he called in the 1956 campaign for unilateral suspension of nuclear testing in the atmosphere and an end to the inefficient and archaic Selective Service System. Sir Michael Foot observed after his death: "He was constantly trying to set standards and communicate ideas to raise the level of public life and, by Jove, he did so."

Stevenson wrote in his introduction to a volume of his 1952 campaign speeches:

For years I have listened to the nauseous nonsense, the pie-in-the-sky appeals to cupidity and greed, the cynical trifling with passion and prejudice and fear; the slander, fraudulent promises, and the all-things-to-all-men demagoguery that are too much a part of our political campaigns. Sometimes in the deafening clamor of political salesmanship, I've thought that the people might be better served if a party purchased a half hour of radio and TV silence during which the audience would be asked to think quietly for themselves.

Politicians all applaud and support public education as democracy's great monument and cornerstone, but does the politician, the agent and spokesman of democracy, have no responsibility for public education? Government by the consent of the governed is the most difficult system of all because it depends for its success

---

[1] *Call to Greatness* (New York: Harper, 1954), pp. 108–109.

and viability on the good judgments and wise decisions of so many of us. But judgment and decision depend on information and understanding. In matters of public policy, candidates then have the greatest responsibility of all to inform truthfully, so that the people will understand and will have the tools of good judgment and wise decision.

. . . I have no regrets about losing the election, except for the disappointment of so many dedicated supporters who share my hope of revitalizing a basic assumption of democracy: honest political leadership that despises the easy road to popularity and insists on focusing attention on reality and truth, however distasteful. Unless the great political parties and their spokesmen assume responsibility for educating and guiding the people with constant candor, how can we be sure that majority rule will meet the test of these searching times? [2]

Stevenson was the master of a distinguished writing style: witty, pungent, humorous, clear; and, when occasion demanded, effectively sharp. He was free of the pomposities of prose that make the pronouncements of some leaders sound like the suckings of leaky bilge pumps.

He was often given to depreciation of himself and occasional whimsy. In his famous message to the Illinois legislature in 1949, vetoing a bill that would have prevented cats from roaming at will, he can be seen at his lighthearted, refreshing, humane best:

> I cannot agree that it should be the declared public policy of Illinois that a cat visiting a neighbor's yard or crossing the highway is a public nuisance. It is in the nature of cats to do a certain amount of unescorted roaming. . . .
> We are all interested in protecting certain varieties of birds. That cats destroy some birds, I well know, but I believe this legislation would further but little the worthy cause to which its proponents give such unselfish effort. The problem of cat versus bird is as old as time. If we attempt to resolve it by legislation, who knows but what we may be called upon to take sides as well in the age-old problems of dog versus cat, bird versus bird, even bird versus worm. In my opinion, the state of Illinois and its local governing bodies already have enough to do without trying to control feline delinquency.[3]

The same man, however, was capable of a Cromwellian sternness despite his courtly manner. He was vigilant against freedom-constrict-

[2] *Major Campaign Speeches of Adlai E. Stevenson, 1952* (New York: Random House, 1953), pp. xxiv–xxv, xxx.
[3] See Volume III of *The Papers of Adlai E. Stevenson.*

ing pressures. In vetoing a bill in 1951 that, among other things, would have established an "anti-subversive squad" to police the state of Illinois, he wrote:

> We must fight traitors with laws. We already have the laws. We must fight falsehood and evil ideas with truth and better ideas. We have them in plenty. But we must not confuse the two. Laws infringing our rights and intimidating unoffending persons without enlarging our security will neither catch subversives nor win converts to our better ideas. And in the long run evil ideas can be counteracted and conquered not by law but only by better ideas. . . .
>
> I know that to veto this bill in this period of grave anxiety will be unpopular with many. But I must, in good conscience, protest against any unnecessary suppression of our ancient rights as free men. Moreover, we will win the contest of ideas that afflicts the world not by suppressing these rights, but by their triumph.[4]

He was quick to criticize reckless political statements and to challenge demagogues. Governor Stevenson said in Chicago on December 13, 1951:

> "McCarthyism" has become the trademark of a new breed of political demagogue who frightens the people with epithets, carelessly impugns the loyalty of patriotic men and shouts dire forebodings of a treacherous doom for America and all her cherished institutions. It is sad that America, at the height of her power, influence and well-being, should be ringing with slander, epithet, ill temper and the counsels of political desperation when all the world looks to us for dignity, sanity and confident leadership. . . .
>
> And there are some words uttered by the first Republican which reckless politicians could well ponder. Abraham Lincoln said: "In times like the present, men should utter nothing for which they would not willingly be responsible through time and eternity." Not only in times like the present, but at all times, we should do nothing for which we would not wish to be held accountable in the future. The responsibility for our moral standards rests heaviest upon the men and women in public life, because public confidence in the integrity of the government is indispensable to faith in democracy.[5]

Three years later, at the height of Senator Joseph McCarthy's "investigations," Governor Stevenson stated:

[4] Ibid.
[5] Ibid.

It is wicked and it is subversive for public officials to try deliberately to replace reason with passion; to substitute hatred for honest difference; to fulfill campaign promises by practicing deception; and to hide discord among Republicans by sowing the dragon's teeth of dissension among Americans.

The loyalty and patriotism of a whole political party of one-half of the nation has been indicted. Twenty years of bipartisan effort, highly intelligent and highly successful, have been called "Twenty Years of Treason" — under the auspices of the Republican National Committee.

When one party says that the other is the party of traitors who have deliberately conspired to betray America, to fill our government services with Communists and spies, to send our young men to unnecessary death in Korea, they violate not only the limits of partisanship, they offend not only the credulity of the people, but they stain the vision of America and of democracy for us and for the world we seek to lead.[6]

After Stevenson was nominated in 1952 as the Democratic candidate for President against his wishes, and was defeated by General Eisenhower, he devoted the next years of his life to preparing himself to *serve* in the presidency. (More expedient men in pursuit of power have concentrated on winning the presidency and devoted less thought than Stevenson did to what they might do once in the office.)

In 1953, as an illustration of how he prepared himself for national leadership, Stevenson embarked on a journey of education to Asia, the Middle East and Europe. At first hand he saw the revolution of rising expectations. He witnessed Asia and the Middle East in the throes of irrepressible change. He saw the death of Western colonialism and he understood the demand by the people in Asia that they be treated as equals by white Westerners.

Stevenson's 1952 campaign speeches impressed Asian leaders. His rational mind, his style, and his wit were refreshing to them. One day in Kashmir during the 1953 trip, a member of the cabinet started to explain what was wrong with American foreign policy. He emphasized that Americans were too impatient — that Americans expected easy and simplistic solutions when the complex problems required patience. Finally, Stevenson interjected, "I said all that in my campaign last fall." "I know," the cabinet member replied, "I'm just quoting them back to you." [7]

But it was not only his talking sense that impressed so many people.

[6] *What I Think* (New York: Harper, 1955), pp. 64–65.
[7] See Volume V of *The Papers of Adlai E. Stevenson.*

His humility was impressive as well. After he had been in a crash landing in the Malayan jungle in 1953, a reporter asked for his reactions. Stevenson replied, "I'm glad nobody reminded me that it was an American helicopter with an American engine." The next day a newspaper columnist in Singapore wrote:

> The last-but-one defeated Presidential candidate to visit Malaya, Mr. Thomas E. Dewey, created a bad impression so pronounced that the secret of Harry Truman's success was revealed in a blinding flash. His successor, Mr. Adlai Stevenson, has wiped out the belief that defeat at the hands of the great American public corrodes the soul. A more charming man it would be hard to find.
>
> Mr. Stevenson has busted rackets, too, but he must have been very nice about it. Mr. Dewey talked to Malayan pressmen as though he saw in every one a potential Lucky Luciano or Frank Costello. Mr. Stevenson talked to them as if he saw them as potential voters in 1956.
>
> Mr. Dewey could never have said, after a forced landing: "I'm glad nobody reminded me that it was an American helicopter with an American engine." He would probably have snapped that Malaya needed American know-how in order to service the thing properly.
>
> Mr. Stevenson has been touring Malaya in the capacity of a correspondent for a magazine. So did Mr. Dewey. So did Justice [William O.] Douglas. I have a hunch that Adlai is going to prove a better cub reporter than the other two.[8]

Weeks later in Israel, Stevenson's good friend, writer David L. Cohn, joined him for a few days. Cohn wrote in the Washington *Post:*

> Drifting around the halcyon shores of the Mediterranean where men sit in coffee houses and women are dancing girls — an admirable society we might well imitate — I ran into a man named Adlai Stevenson. . . . With but one digestive tract to give to his country, he had given it at dozens of official dinners. . . .
>
> A handicap of the Middle East is that its people have always lacked the refining influence of the DAR. Hence for 3,000 years they have been ready to fight at the drop of a dogma, making this a tough area to handle from Herod, 3 B.C., to John Foster Dulles, 1953 A.D. Here where vanished civilizations lie layer upon layer like wedges of a prize-winning county fair cake, Stevenson lunched one day on the Lake of Tiberias. Antiquity watching from the Galilean hills, perhaps he profited more from this moment than

---

[8] Ibid.

from all his briefings. For here a local man once wrote that where there is no vision the people perish; a good thing to know even at the cost of one's digestion.[9]

Governor Stevenson had more than charm and wit. He had, as his friend Barbara Ward observed, a zest for life and an "unspoilt freshness and directness." At times, in private discussions and in letters he could be devastatingly frank and critical. Sometimes these remarks found their way into print to his embarrassment.

There was no mistaking his Americanism, Barbara Ward pointed out — the energy ("chronic stamina"), the curiosity, the good spirits, and the frank good will. All this, she added, gave a special quality to his learning and manner. He had the eighteenth-century Enlightenment's belief in reason, the possibility of progress, fundamental optimism, and intellectual curiosity.[10]

Among the reasons that Adlai Stevenson was such a popular and reassuring figure abroad was that he advocated that American power be used generously, reasonably, and with a scrupulous concern for peace. He gave reassurance that American power would be used wisely and with due respect for the human community. And for this position he was attacked by those Americans who frightened the rest of the human race — the superpatriots, the Cold War warriors, the believers in unfettered, unilateral power. He found this America of national boasting, of saber-rattling and chest-thumping nauseating. He stood for the America dedicated to the proposition of liberty and equality of opportunity. It could still be, to him, "the last best hope" for a decent society for the whole human experiment.

Despite Governor Stevenson's emphasis on reason, on talking sense, on insisting that American power be used wisely and with due respect for the human community, some of his followers were disturbed by his support of American policy in Vietnam. Richard J. Walton, for instance, wrote that to "many of the intellectuals and the young and the idealistic, for whom he once had such enormous and unique appeal, he died not in esteem but in disgrace." [11]

As Walton saw it: "He could no longer speak the truth; he could only play the game. He was pained, perhaps even tormented, but he

[9] Ibid.

[10] "Affection and Always Respect," in *As We Knew Adlai: The Stevenson Story by Twenty-two Friends,* edited and with preface by Edward P. Doyle, foreword by Adlai E. Stevenson III (New York: Harper & Row, 1966), pp. 211–227.

[11] *The Remnants of Power: The Tragic Last Years of Adlai Stevenson* (New York: Coward-McCann, 1968), p. 236.

could not bring himself to put his loyalty to the nation he had served so well above his loyalty to Lyndon Baines Johnson as a member of the team." [12]

That Stevenson was frustrated and tormented the last years of his life is indisputable. That he wanted to influence policy from the inside is also indisputable — although one of his frustrations was his limited influence with both President Kennedy and President Johnson.

Stevenson turned out to be mistaken in thinking that because Johnson paid him greater deference than Kennedy had done, he could influence President Johnson on Vietnam. He believed that the peace initiatives undertaken by the Secretary General of the United Nations in the autumn of 1964 and the early winter of 1965 should have been pursued by Washington.

David Kraslow and Stuart H. Loory wrote: "Thant and Stevenson involved themselves deeply when hardly anyone with real authority in the United States government appeared much interested. The ordeal was to drive Thant to despair, and would nag at Stevenson's conscience until he dropped dead on a London street on July 14, 1965, just two weeks before President Johnson ordered large numbers of combat troops into Vietnam." [13]

When the overtures were not pursued, why did Stevenson not resign? Or why did he not resign a few weeks before his death when a group of writers and social critics called on him and asked him to resign and to publicly oppose the escalation of the war in Vietnam? [14] At the time of his death, Stevenson was working on a letter to one of his critics, Paul Goodman. The letter he left may not be what the final draft would have been, but it is revealing of Stevenson's position.[15]

He stated in the letter that the ultimate disaster of atomic conflict could be avoided only by the pursuit of two clear lines of policy: "The first is to establish a tacitly agreed frontier between Communist and non-Communist areas of influence on the understanding that neither

---

[12] Ibid., pp. 234–235.
[13] *The Secret Search for Peace in Vietnam* (New York: Random House, 1968), pp. 91–92, 98–101, 103–104. The coauthors wrote that the story of the peace initiative in places was "murky" (p. 98). After Stevenson's death President Johnson told U Thant that he had not been informed of the initiative. Secretary of State Rusk told the Secretary General that Stevenson had not been authorized to reject the Thant approach (p. 108). The editors of *The Papers of Adlai E. Stevenson* at the time of the writing of this Foreword have not completed their research on this question. It will appear in the concluding volume of the series, Volume VIII.
[14] For an analysis of this question see the review of Richard J. Walton's book by Stuart Gerry Brown in *Ethics: An International Journal of Social, Political and Legal Philosophy*, July, 1969, pp. 321–323.
[15] See Volume VIII of *The Papers of Adlai E. Stevenson*.

power system will use force to change the status quo." Stevenson explained that the years from 1947 to 1962 were largely occupied in fixing the postwar line with the Soviet Union, but that there was no such line with China.

Later in the letter he stated: "My hope in Viet Nam is that relatively small scale resistance now may establish the fact that changes in Asia are not to be precipitated by outside force. This was the point of the Korean War. This is the point of the conflict in Viet Nam. I believe Asia will be more stable if the outcome is the same in both — a negotiated line and a negotiated peace — this brings me to my second point — the hope of transcending the static policy of 'containment' and moving on to the more creative tasks of building a world security based on law and peaceful settlement."

And he added: "I believe that we must seek a negotiated peace in Viet Nam based upon the internationalization of the whole area's security, on a big effort to develop, under the U.N., the resources of the Mekong River and guarantees that Viet Nam, North and South, can choose, again under international supervision, the kind of governments, the form of association and, if so decree the type of reunification of the two states they genuinely want to establish.

"If we can achieve this, we begin to offer the small nations of the world an alternative to being within spheres of influence — we would begin to establish procedures by which local revolutionary movements such as the rising in the Dominican Republic, and for that matter Zanzibar, are *not* automatically a prey to outside intervention. . . ."

He then continued: "It is my conviction that American policy is groping its way towards this difficult but essential ideal, and this is the reason both for my support of the policy and for my continuance in a position which gives me some hope of assisting its advance in that direction."

The policy Stevenson felt the United States was groping its way toward was ignored in the ensuing debacle of attempting to solve by military means what was primarily a political problem.

Ambassador Stevenson was attempting — however ineffectually — to alter the course of American diplomacy and to move the United States and the world, as he wrote to Paul Goodman, from a "position of precarious stability toward agreed international procedures for settling differences, towards the building of an international juridical and policing system and toward a whole variety of policies designed to turn our small vulnerable planet into a genuine economic and social community."

Two days before his death, Stevenson had a lengthy and revealing talk with his good and trusted friend Eric Sevareid. "What he said that night," Sevareid reported later, "revealed a profound frustration, a certain resentment that stopped just short of bitterness." [16] Stevenson talked of U Thant's peace initiative, Washington's unenthusiastic reaction to it, and of his own inability to influence the course of American foreign policy.

After describing the conversation, Sevareid wrote: "Governor Stevenson died of exhaustion; he just wore himself out. I don't know how else to put it. Of course, the gathering frustration was part of this, but he did not die of a broken heart. If others regarded him as a 'tragic figure,' I don't think he thought of himself that way. Let others call his life a failure; I think it was a wonderful success. When he was 50 years old, almost nobody but his private friends knew his rare quality; when he died 15 years later, a million people cried. And he had this effect on the world of civilized people without using any of the instruments of power. He did it with words alone, and with that wry grin in his battered, lopsided face. . . .

"All I know as a political reporter," Sevareid concluded, "is that Adlai Stevenson injected humor and happiness and sophistication into American political life, and you have to have spent half your life listening to the normal run of American politicians to really understand what a fantastic accomplishment that was."

In selecting the papers to be published in *The Papers of Adlai E. Stevenson,* the editors decided to emphasize the material that helped answer such questions as: How did he educate himself? How did he become the man he became? What were the key influences in his life? How did he understand his times? How did he articulate the problems of his time?

Childhood in Bloomington, Illinois, preparatory school at Choate, undergraduate education at Princeton University, law school at Harvard University and Northwestern University, writing for the *Daily Pantagraph,* young lawyer in Chicago, legal work for the early New Deal in Washington, D.C., lawyer and emerging civic leader in Chicago from 1934 to 1941 are chronicled in Volume I. The letters, postcards, and speeches included in this volume delineate how he developed, how he was constantly learning and acquiring a deeper understanding of his times. Ignorance, a closed mind, and the refusal to educate oneself, he believed, were at the root of much of the trouble and sorrow in

[16] "Adlai Stevenson, His Final Troubled Hours," *Look,* November 30, 1965.

the world. Education, to him, was not only a never-ending process, it was a responsibility.

Stevenson's friend from childhood in Bloomington, Joseph F. Bohrer, wrote after his death:

> I must agree that nothing in his youth pointed out the role he was to play, but I also do know that he alone of all those fine friends I have had seemed to grow and learn every day of his life, constantly pushing outward the horizon of his knowledge of and concern for human beings and the world they occupy.[17]

Volume I also reflects Stevenson's growing desire to participate in the affairs of government. He grew up in a politically oriented family, politics was at the core of his existence, and after 1941 he was to be continuously involved in public service and political leadership.

Stevenson once told an old friend that a definitive biography could never be written of him since he had not kept notes. Nevertheless, a considerable number of his handwritten letters and postcards to his mother, father, and sister were saved, and carbon copies of some of his correspondence after he became a lawyer were preserved as were his newspaper articles and copies of his speeches.

We used nearly all the material available to us for Volume I. Governor Stevenson provided in his will that material about his governorship of Illinois be deposited in the Illinois State Historical Library and the remainder be deposited in the Princeton University Library. Stevenson's most important correspondence, drafts of speeches, and fragments of diary were at his home in Libertyville when he died. The editors selected some of the material for this volume from the material at Libertyville before the collection was divided between the two depositories. Some items are still in the possession of Adlai E. Stevenson III. We collected some handwritten letters and postcards from old friends. Governor Stevenson obviously enjoyed writing these letters and postcards. He must have. He wrote so many.

The editors of these volumes searched widely for handwritten documents. Some people, particularly before Stevenson became governor of Illinois, had failed to save them. Many people were most cooperative, placing all their Stevenson items at our disposal. Some preferred to send us only selections from their collections. A few refused to send us any material at all.[18] Some letters which would cause unnecessary

---

[17] "Boys In Bloomington," in *As We Knew Adlai*, p. 14.

[18] Katie Louchheim wrote: "These were [some of] the women who owned a share of Adlai's destiny." *By the Political Sea* (Garden City, New York: Doubleday, 1970), p. 108.

anguish to people still living, the editors have not included in these volumes or have made appropriate deletions within such letters. These deletions are indicated by ellipses. The location of handwritten letters, postcards, or originals of typewritten letters is given in the footnote references.

The editors indicate in the introduction to each part of Volume I or in footnotes to individual items the location of the material used. We have provided a brief summary of Stevenson's career in these introductions as well as a description of our editorial method. We have supplied editorial comment on any item where it was necessary for clarity or for continuity. We have included his signature on hand-written letters. In the case of typewritten letters we had to work from carbon copies. Whenever we have located the original letter, and he signed it Ad or Adlai, we have included the signature.

Whenever a statement in a letter was unclear, the editors, where possible, wrote to the recipient of the letter. The replies added greatly to the editorial information contained in these volumes. This research technique, when supplemented by interviews with those people most knowledgeable about a specific situation, furnished us with information that would be unavailable if *The Papers of Adlai E. Stevenson* were to be published only a long time after his death.[19]

The editors generally did not include letters written to Stevenson. Publishing letters written by people still alive or recently deceased requires permission — a time-consuming task. Instead, the editors summarized the contents of an incoming letter where it was necessary to make Stevenson's reply understandable.

Under the legal agreement between Walter Johnson and Adlai Stevenson III, Borden Stevenson, and John Fell Stevenson, Adlai III agreed to read each volume before publication. In the event of disagreement as to the inclusion of any item of his father's papers, the matter was to be referred to Judge Carl McGowan for final — and irrevocable — decision.

---

[19] The Oral History project at Columbia University has interviews with many people about Stevenson. The collection was closed when our volumes were prepared.

Contents

Illustrations

(*between pages 138 and 139*)

Part One

Childhood
1900–1916

*A*dlai E. Stevenson was born to politics and American history. His great-grandfather on his mother's side was Jesse Fell, a founder of the Republican party, close friend and one of the early Illinois advocates of Abraham Lincoln for the Republican nomination in 1860. His paternal grandfather, Adlai E. Stevenson, was elected Vice President with Grover Cleveland in 1892. He was nominated again with William Jennings Bryan in 1900 and in 1908 he lost the election for governor of Illinois by 22,000 votes. His father, Lewis G. Stevenson, served as secretary of state for Illinois, October, 1914 to January, 1917, and was active in national Democratic party affairs for many years.

Although his mother became a Democrat, her family remained staunchly Republican. As a result, he was "caught in a constant cross-ruffing of political controversy," he said in an interview years later. And, as a result of his family's prominence, he added, his "horizons were enlarged almost from birth by meeting famous people." "For as long as I can remember," he said, "I have been preoccupied with public affairs — probably at the expense of private affairs — I mean business and professional obligations." [1]

Adlai E. Stevenson's family had had a prominent part in making American history, and he had around him in his youth at Bloomington, Illinois, history-makers of his family, their friends who had shared great adventures with them, the books, records, souvenirs of several crowded decades of our national life. Nearly every Sunday the Lewis Stevensons had dinner at the home of the Vice President and Mrs. Stevenson. "He was a great raconteur, and no one ever tired of his tales — nor did he! His stories were apt, full of good humor and enriched with the Bible," his sister Elizabeth (now Mrs. Ernest Ives) has written.[2]

[1] Russel Windes, Jr., and James A. Robinson, "Public Address in the Career of Adlai E. Stevenson," *Quarterly Journal of Speech*, October, 1956, Vol. XLII, No. 3.
[2] Elizabeth Stevenson Ives and Hildegarde Dolson, *My Brother Adlai* (New York: Morrow, 1956), p. 14. There are excellent insights on their childhood and on their ancestors in this volume.

Adlai E. Stevenson was born in Los Angeles on February 5, 1900. His father was at that time managing estates for Mrs. Phoebe Hearst. Four years later Lewis Stevenson became assistant general manager of her son William Randolph Hearst's Los Angeles Examiner. *Although the father seemed to be heading toward a successful business and public career in California, he and his family returned to Bloomington, Illinois, in 1906. Deep family ties drew them back to the rich soil of central Illinois where Lewis became manager of the extensive farms of his Aunt Julia Scott.*

Bloomington and the adjoining community of Normal numbered some thirty thousand people when young Adlai Stevenson and his older sister Elizabeth (nicknamed Buffie by her brother) were brought there to live in a comfortable two-story house at 1316 East Washington Street. The Stevensons were well off and they were able to afford travel — summers at Charlevoix, Michigan, winters in the South — and private schools for their children.

Buffie and Adlai's parents were cultivated people whose family living room was a library. Their mother, Helen Davis Stevenson, believed in the custom of reading to the children from Greek mythology, the English classics, Hugo, Hawthorne, Emerson, Cooper, and the King James version of the Bible. Mrs. Ives later wrote "she gave us a magnificent variety." [3]

Near the end of his life, Adlai E. Stevenson remarked that his mother had formed his taste for literature and poetry. Such classic novelists as Thackeray, Dickens, Scott, the Brontës, and George Eliot were favorites from the days of his childhood. His mother, he added, was nervous, frequently ill, possessive and a stern disciplinarian. There was considerable tension in his family and as he was growing up he was the peacemaker. The tension pained him and throughout his lifetime he disliked family tensions and scenes.

He also observed that he had inherited his father's love of life, his vitality, and his lively sense of humor. His father traveled a good deal, particularly during Adlai's adolescence, and he envied his playmates who had a close relationship with their fathers. Adolescence was an extremely difficult time for him, he recalled. He was shy and self-conscious, and his mother preached to him about a clean mind and a clean body. His mother's little homilies, he added, had an inhibiting effect on him for years. He commented also that he was a pretty miserable student during these years. He was not an intellectual person but a physical one — he enjoyed sights, sounds, smells, tastes, and color.

[3] Ibid., p. 8.

[4]

The Stevenson family had a deep religious tradition of strict Presbyterianism. But the children were brought up in the tolerant, humanistic Unitarian faith of their mother. (The Fell-Davis side of the family were Quakers.) "Stevenson was spared the prejudice and intolerance that flourished on the common fundamentalism of rural America," Herbert J. Muller wrote.[4]

Grandfather W. O. Davis had married Jesse Fell's daughter, and he became sole editor and proprietor of the Daily Pantagraph (founded by Jesse Fell). Grandfather Davis and the Daily Pantagraph were as staunchly Republican as the Stevensons were Democratic. "Like all born editors and reporters, he had an enormous curiosity about everything and everybody," Mrs. Ives wrote. "When he'd say to Adlai and me, 'Tell me what you did today,' this was no social pleasantry. He expected a good, full account. . . . His eyes twinkled encouragement, and he listened so perceptively, not just with his ears but with his whole brilliant mind, that we sharpened our wits to please him." [5]

The handwritten letters and other material of Adlai E. Stevenson that follow are in the Elizabeth Stevenson Ives collection, the Illinois State Historical Library, Springfield, Illinois, unless indicated otherwise. The misspellings are reprinted as they are in the originals. (To have placed "sic" after each error would at times have made a letter extremely difficult to read.) The letters sometimes were dated and, if not, usually the envelopes with the postmark were saved. Where there was no date or envelope, the editors have placed the letter through internal evidence in its approximate place.

To Cora Galbraith [6]

February 4, 1906

Dear Codie: — I love you still. Codie this is a letter to you many happy birthdays to you this is my birthday. I got a heart filled with [candy?] and some "Buster Brown" stamps, a watch, a rose filled with candy. I had a party with many children. James & Richard etc. We had ice cream, a cake & candy & Douglas acted very badly. Codie, I had lots of fun, and I miss you very much dear Codie. On the other side you will [see?] how my "Buster B" stamp works. Buffie sends you lots of

[4] *Adlai Stevenson: A Study in Values* (New York: Harper & Row, 1967), p. 24.
[5] *My Brother Adlai*, p. 31.
[6] The nursemaid to Adlai and Buffie. She was in Illinois at this point and the Stevensons were still in Los Angeles. The letter is in the handwriting of Adlai's mother. How much the letter reflects the six-year-old boy or his mother is a reasonable question but difficult to answer.

love I wish you were here. I had a very nice Xmas and I hope you will like what I sent you.

ADLAI STEVENSON

To Lewis G. Stevenson [7]

New Year's Day, 1907

Dear Father

My pen is bad
My ink is pale
I hope you'll soon
Homeward sail!

Written in the dark
At Winter Park
I wish you would hurry,
We are all in a flurry.

As homeward we
Our trip did make,
We most ran over
A big bull snake.

The oranges are yellow,
As through the leaves are seen,
But I want to see a fellow
Whose middle name is Green.

Sherwin is my playmate —
Galey is his name,
He has to go to school now
But for that he's not to blame.

Buff has decorated
Our table this New Year,
We all deplore your absence,
And Adlai shed one tear. (crocodile tear)

There are alligato[r]s
In the water and yellow gaiters on the land

[7] This letter is in the handwriting of Helen D. Stevenson. The father was in Switzerland. Grandfather Davis had taken his daughter and the two Stevenson grandchildren to Winter Park, Florida, for the winter. Mrs. Ives stated that the poem was written by Grandfather Davis. Letter to Walter Johnson, September 17, 1968.

[6]

Automobiles rushing past us (nit)
And barefoot black boys in the sand.

Little boys out at play,
Shooting firecrackers
New Years Day!
Mama gentle rocking Adlai,
Lizbeth send her dearest wishes
Daddy also adds his gladly,
While Ag is busy washing dishes!

Your loving anxious little son,
Adlai Ewing Stevenson

To Lewis G. Stevenson [8]

March 1, 1907

Dear father
I hoped you will come home soon?
I will make you a pictire of a cow.

ADLAI E. STEVENSON

To Lewis G. Stevenson [9]

[sometime in 1907]
IALDA

Dear Father:

I hope you'll come home soon. So you can go up to B[loomington] with us. And I have so very much fun finding gun shells, Winchester, sure shot and shot guns.

I have a dozen of different kinds — I have so much fun feeding the horse and cow and getting down the hay and I wish you would come to see how much fun I have.

Come home, youve been gone a very long time and you can see the water works. There are 2 mother cats and one father and the lot of them have five kittens — four of them have there eyes open and I discovered them this morning — The 2 mother cats have one husband —

[8] This is the earliest extant letter in his own handwriting. Adlai drew a picture of himself seated on a cow with the caption: "This is Adlai on the cow."

[9] This letter is in his mother's handwriting. It was signed at the top by the author himself, with the name printed backwards as one might see it in a mirror. It was written from Florida or Augusta, Georgia, where they stopped en route to Bloomington.

[7]

the peach trees are in blossom. Last night all the lights went out. I saw two boys who had a handkerchief balloon.

Mama is writing this for me. Have you got the letter I wrote you all myself in W.P. [Winter Park, Florida]? One time we had the cow and horse out and they both ran away. I told Servis (the boy) that the halter was broken and we worked about 2 hrs. trying to get the horse in and at last we had to get a man. We have so much fun watching them milk the cow.

Adlai E. Stevenson's first published essay appeared in the Daily Panta-graph *in 1909:*

MY PET BUNNY [10]

When I was eight years old, my father brought me from his farm a wee bunny that seemed to me not more than three weeks old.

At first bunny was very much frightened. I got a large box for his home and fixed it up very comfortably, where bunny lived cosily for some time, never running away.

His box was kept in the upper hall during the night, and one morning when I went out to see how bunny was, I found he was gone. Then everyone in the house started to look for bunny, but nowhere was he to be found until the cook, coming into the dining room saw bunny sitting on a register as comfy as could be. This was only a taste of adventure for bunny, and every day he was in some new mischief. One bright day bunny was sunning himself on a window sill, when a thievish cat suddenly snatched him and ran away. I hunted everywhere, but I could not find him, and I never saw my pet bunny again.

ADLAI E. STEVENSON
Age 9 years old.

1316 East Washington Street

On January 27, 1910, Grandfather Davis took the two Stevenson grandchildren to New Orleans for the winter. Their mother joined them a few days later. Mrs. Ives wrote, "Adlai, who would rather travel, read and listen than anything else, often reminds me of Grandfather. My

---

[10] Reprinted in Ives and Dolson, *My Brother Adlai*, pp. 31–32. Mrs. Ives commented, "I suspect Grandfather or Uncle Bert [H. O. Davis, who became editor of the *Pantagraph* when his father died in 1911] fixed up the spelling before 'My Pet Bunny' went to press."

brother never had to be coerced, especially when it came to learning about trains. He dogged the footsteps of every conductor and porter, pestering them with questions, and he hopped off at each stop, to consult with his friends the brakemen, and bear up-to-the-minute reports to Grandfather." [11]

To Mrs. Lewis G. Stevenson

January 27, 1910

Dear Mother: —

We are on our way south we are about 200 mi. from Chicago. We will reach Neworleans in the morning at ten-fifteen.

The train is a very nice one and my sister and my selfe are having a fine time altho I did not wont to go at first.

There is very much to see and the land is very good for farming. I hope you are well and I would not be surprised if father has a sick headache. But I am well you beat I must say good by now

Yours trutey   AD STEV [12]

To Mrs. Stone [13]

Dear Mrs. Stone: —

I am going to school.
Buffie has a cold, and can't go to school.
We are coming home soon.
How is the weather there?
I wrote it myself.
With much love

ADLAI

To Mrs. Ira Allen Ransom [14]

December 15 [1910?]

Dear Mrs. Ransom

We have heard of the serious fire you have had.

[11] *My Brother Adlai*, p. 37.
[12] Below his signature he drew a sketch of a locomotive.
[13] This letter was written from New Orleans during the winter of 1910. There is a note at the bottom of it from the author's mother: "Please save this letter for me — it is Adlai's first! HDS." Mrs. Stevenson perhaps meant that this was the first letter that he wrote without her help, since the letter of March 1, 1907, to his father was in his handwriting. Mrs. Stone was the wife of a *Pantagraph* employee and stayed with Adlai and Buffie when their mother was away.
[14] The Ransoms had a summer cottage at Charlevoix, Michigan. Woody was Mrs. Ransom's grandson. Mildred Bromwell was the daughter of Mrs. Charles (Letty)

We are very sorry.
I am having a fine time going to school and coasting.
How is Woody?
Daddy has given mother a "Victor Victrola."
Buffy is going to visit Mildred Bromwell next week.
Davis Merwin is going to California soon.
With love to all,

Yours truly,
ADLAI E. STEVENSON

To Adlai E. Stevenson [15]

January 2, 1911

Dear Grandfather
I received your fine Christmas present and I thank you a thousand times!! I am going to put it in the bank and save it.
I hope you had a Merry Christmas and a happy New Year.
I have been too busy playing to write sooner, I hope you will pardon me.

With love to Grandmother and you — ADLAI

In December, 1911, the Stevensons sailed on the Lusitania *for Europe. Aboard ship Adlai wrote an essay:*

A LONELY DAY AT SEA

The sea is a leaden gray and as far as the eye can reach there is not a ship in sight; the sky is overcast and sullen; a storm is expected and the air is heavy and damp. All on board are depressed and irritable; the sailors are grumbling in groups togeather. Visions of home pass before the mind; of familiar faces of parents and friends; and of cheerful fires. Then the eye wanders around the deck and the mind comes slowly back to the dismal present.

The "Admiral Benbow" with all its horrors, of the Old Sea Dog would be a welcome sight, and he longs to be at home among green trees, blooming flours and singing birds. To him nothing could be more dreadful than a life at sea.

Bromwell, cousin of the Stevensons. Davis Merwin was Adlai's cousin and childhood playmate in Bloomington. The letter was written from Bloomington.

[15] This letter was written from New Orleans where Adlai, his mother, and sister spent the winter with W. O. Davis. It is in the possession of Mrs. Walter Baumgarten, Jr., of St. Louis, Missouri, a cousin of Elizabeth and Adlai.

In England the medieval armor in Windsor Castle and the armor and the dungeons in the Tower of London fascinated Adlai. "He had to see all the dungeons, and each joint of each piece of knight's armor, and ask a thousand questions," Mrs. Ives wrote. "I also have a mental picture of my brother, wearing a little gray flannel jacket and knee pants, standing sturdily in a vast cold corridor at Windsor Castle, announcing politely, 'But we haven't seen all the armor here yet.'" [16]

In Paris he developed a lasting enthusiasm for collecting postage stamps. As they toured France and Italy the castles and cathedrals stimulated in the twelve-year-old boy a fascinated interest in the Middle Ages. Years later he said: "It seemed wonderful to me that men, so long ago, could build such vast structures on hills. It still does. All through my early teens I reveled in historical novels about the Crusades, and the Hundred Years' War, and in histories of Joan of Arc and the whole medieval period. The 1912 trip had a lot to do with that." [17]

The family settled down at Lausanne for a time and Adlai attended a private school. Mrs. Ives wrote: "We were losing our insular notion that people in foreign countries were peculiar if they seemed different from Americans. It was good for two Midwestern children to learn that no one is a foreigner to friendship." [18]

To Sam White [19]

Dear Sam:

We are at Val d'illiez Switzerland. Val d'illiez is a verry little village at the foot of the Dent due Midi.

The Dent due Midi is one of the highest Swisse mountains it is all coverded with snow. The chalet that we live in is all of wood, everything is of wood. We hear French spoken all the time. We are the only people in the Village that speak English. Everybody that comes [here] comes for Mountain climbing. They carry a large sack for food and things. Also an alpine stick which is a pole with a pick and hatchet on one end, and a point at the other . . .

ADD

---

[16] *My Brother Adlai*, p. 65.

[17] Quoted in Kenneth S. Davis, *A Prophet in His Own Country: The Triumphs and Defeats of Adlai E. Stevenson* (New York: Doubleday, 1957), p. 64.

[18] *My Brother Adlai*, p. 69.

[19] The Stevensons' Negro houseman in Bloomington. At the top of the letter is a drawing of "Sam Driving the Auto" and being chased by a "Motorcycle Cop" who cries out, "Halt in the Name of the Law." (The Stevensons had one of the first automobiles in Bloomington.) At the bottom of the letter Adlai drew an alpenstock. The letter is not dated.

The following letter was written three weeks after a tragedy. On December 30, 1912, Buffie held a supper party at the family home in Bloomington. One of the boys present — Bob Whitmer — offered to demonstrate the manual of arms which he had learned at military school. Buffie called to Adlai, who was in his room, to get the old .22 rifle in the attic. Bob Whitmer examined the gun to make sure there were no bullets in the barrel or magazine. After he executed the manual of arms he gave the gun to Adlai. As Adlai left to return it to the attic, he imitated Whitmer's movements. The gun went off and Buffie's schoolmate and friend Ruth Merwin dropped dead.[20]

Adlai seemed utterly lost that night. Ruth's mother talked to him and explained that he must not blame himself. On the day of the funeral Helen Stevenson took Adlai and his cousin Dave (Davis) Merwin to Chicago and South Carolina. When they returned, the tragic event was not referred to, or ever mentioned again in the family or by Adlai, until a reporter questioned him about it in 1952.

To Lewis G. Stevenson [21]

January 20, 1913

Dear Father:

I was over at Dave [Merwin]'s house this afternoon. Betty Coolidge and Tip Frederick and Mary Frederick and Hester and Dave and I were there. We made pop corn balls, and had lots of fun in the attick.

We had consibrel snow to day it is freezing so I think we will have some coasting. When you called up from Urbana Mother and Aunt Jessie [Merwin] were at Normal in Aunt Jessie's electric. I made a big Wind Mill with my American Model builder, it works fine I am going to attach my motor and see how fast the fan will go round.

I am going to school to morrow and day after to-morrow they have the Geography test and I dont have to go because I dont have to take it.

I hope you are well,
yours
Truly
ADLAI E. STEVENSON

[20] Her father, Clarence, was a brother of L. B. Merwin (who had married Mrs. Stevenson's sister), so that Ruth was not actually related to the Stevensons. Letter, Mrs. Ernest L. Ives to Carol Evans, December, 1971. See Davis, *A Prophet in His Own Country*, pp. 69–71; Ives and Dolson, *My Brother Adlai*, pp. 72–73.

[21] The children mentioned in paragraph one were childhood playmates. In the right-hand corner of the letter there is a small drawing of a man which Adlai labeled "You."

In the autumn of 1913, Buffie attended University High School on Normal's college campus and Adlai entered the Metcalf Training School on the campus.

Before this he had attended the Bloomington public schools. His grade record for the first semester of the school year 1912–1913 was: Spelling, 83; Arithmetic, 79; Geography, 85; Writing, 80; Deportment, 95.

Buffie wrote in her diary: "We think Adlai has a lot of literary ability, and he is doing so well in his studies. He seems to have quite a talent for Latin. I wish he might become a great minister. It is such fun but pretty sad to watch Ad grow up, he begins to try to train his hair now, to brush his clothes altho' he is very untidy about his room and hanging his clothes in his closet — I suppose most boys are — Father certainly is." That year, Mrs. Ives wrote later, her brother was "trying more determinedly than ever to escape parental constraints." [22]

To Mrs. Lewis G. Stevenson [23]

September 15, 1913

Dear Mother: —

I wish!! you would not make me chang my studies as my english which comes in the morning is the best in the school, and I now every body in it. The other one is very large, *please, please! please!* dont make me change. I like normal very well except that I should have to change in the very beging of the term. Please dont make me change the class comes in the middle of the after noon and is very large.

Am playing golf most every afternoon. Am having a fine time except the thought of having to change hope I will not have to.

Your loving son
ADLAI

To Mrs. Lewis G. Stevenson

September 18, 1913

Dear Mother: —

Have changed studies so do not worry. I do not like the new english class as it is much larger and the teacher is not so nice.

Please telegraph father to let me play football as you said you would before I left Clifton, I have been deprived of that pleasur for so long you ought to let me play this year, as I have been asked to.

---

[22] *My Brother Adlai*, pp. 74–75.
[23] His mother was at a sanitarium at Clifton Springs, New York.

Hope you are better and will be home soon. I am having a fine time and like Normal pretty well. I have to write a thiem for this afternoon on one of the following subjects an houre in the assembly room an old bridge at sunset or old fashioned school house. As I know nothing about these it will be pretty hard. In Mr. Lancaster's class (that was the other one) he gave you storts to write — an there were all boys in his class.

With lots of love
ADLAI

P.S. Please dont forget about the football. Please.

To Mrs. Lewis G. Stevenson [24]

Dear Mother: —

I am writing this letter on the couch with my new fountain pen. Dave [Merwin] and I bought 2 dozen bottels of pop for 60 cents a few days ago. We made what we paid for it the first day. Father bought 3 bottels and Mr. Linn 4 Uncle 2. I started this letter last night and am finishing it this morning. Buffie got your letter this morning in which you said you would not let me play football for another year, that is what you and father have been telling me for so long, and anyway you promised me at Clifton you would let me play this fall. If I wait another year I will not be able to play. All doctors say its a bad game but all doctors havent played it, and more than that they didnot play like we play at Normal. Everybody these days have such terriable conceptions of football when they now nothing about it, just because they have read of accidents in for instance a *Harvard* and *Yale* game this is a third Normal team.

Everting all right at School I think Normal is easy.

!!! Lots of Love !!!
ADLAI

P.S. All the games you mencioned in your letter are out of season.[25]

A.E.S.

[24] This letter is postmarked September 20, 1913. On letterhead it is dated September 22.

[25] Mrs. Ives wrote: "In tackling the subject with Father, who was apt to answer with thunder and lightning, Adlai was as even-tempered as ever, but not to be cowed or sidetracked. He had a kind of unswerving reasonableness, in arguments, that made even parents think twice. He got permission to play on the third team." *My Brother Adlai*, p. 75.

To Lewis G. Stevenson [26]

Dear Father:

We are going to have a circus in Dave [Merwin]'s attick next Saturday. Last night I finished an incline delivery chute with my American-model-builder.

Mother is in bed with a bad cold. I saw your article in the Pantagraph this morning.

With love from

ADLAI E. STEVENSON JR.

A number of times during his lifetime, Adlai E. Stevenson attempted to keep a diary. Each attempt was abortive. In December 1913, his mother took her two children to Pasadena, California, for several months, where she received medical treatment at a clinic for a near nervous breakdown.

MY TRIP TO CALIFORNIA

I left Thrusday morning for Chicago on the 4:15 o'clock train. At eluven o'clock I met my sister at the Union Station. On leaving the station I had the pleasant expereance of finding a dollar. We did the shopping and, took the six o'clock train for Kansas City. When the train reached Bloomington Mother got on. At Kansas City next morning we met father and changed cars to the California Limited on the Santa Fe.

The first day we continued travelling thru Kansas, the scenery of which, was not very beautiful. It was rolling, with a few low hills. We passed many corn fields, which were almost burnt up by the hot weather in the summer.

The train was a very good one and we travelled quite fast. That night we went thru a corner of Colorado, as it was in the night I did not see much of it. All next day, Friday, we travelled thru New Mexico. The scenery was very beautiful and mountainous; there was snow on the ground all day. We kept asending until four o'clock when we began decending. We went thru many touns. At some, the train stopped and we got out. there were Indian women and men in front of the station selling crockery, bracelets, blanketes, and other things that they had made. They had bright-colored blankets throun over their shoulders and

[26] The only date on this letter reads Thursday 23, 1913.

they all wore many bracelets and trinkets even the babies. An Indian woman was weaving a blanket and her husband was making a bracelet and the children were combing wool. In the evening it began snowing very hard and the observation platform was covered with snow. At seven we reached Gallup, New Mexico which is 128 miles from the Arisona line; an Indian told us that it had been snowing there for a month. All night we went through Arisona. When I woke up in the morning we had just crossed the boarder and were in California. All morning we went thru the Majava desert. It was covered with a grouth of sage brush. We passed near the mouth of death valley where twenty mule team borax comes from. As we left the desert we passed thru the beautiful San Bernadinos mountains; we arrived at Pasadena at four.

Adlai wrote the following letter from Pasadena in schoolboy Latin to his father, on February 18, 1914. The translation is literal rather than literary. His father wrote on the bottom of the letter, "From the blessed Brute," his pet name for his son.

To Lewis G. Stevenson

February 18, 1914

If you are well, it is good. I also am well. I write this letter to you joyfully. I spent the winter in California with anxiety on advice of the doctor. While where you are snow falls everywhere, we see snow rarely here; the air is most clear; the sky smiles, as the poets say. Sometimes I stroll on the shore or wander in spacious gardens, for the grass and trees are green now. From this place I see the mountains, nearly the whole city, and the fair islands situated in the sea. I labor diligently on the Latin language every day. I am learning that language more easily than Greek. But now I shall make an end to my letter; soon I shall tell you everything in person.

Farewell my friend
ADLIEUS STEVENIUS

IVANHOE [27]

Ivanhoe is one of Sir Walter Scott's most popular novels.

The scene is laid in nothiren England, towards the end of the twelfth century, at about the time of King Richard's return from the Holy-land, where he had been on a crusade. Scott describes vividly and in excellent english the conditions at that time, he describes the

[27] This is the earliest extant school theme.

corrupt Norman nobles and their persecution of the Jews. He also describes the Saxons and compairs them with the Normans. The description of the tournement, which was the most popular amusement of the day, is very instructive. You also get a very good idea of the customs and manners of the Knight Templers and of Robin Hood and his band of outlaws. Also many good examples of the dissipation of the churchmen at that time. His descriptions of the appearance and character of the persons in the story are excellent.

English
May 6, 1914

Letitia Green Stevenson, the wife of the former Vice President, died in December, 1913. Six months later Adlai Ewing Stevenson was dead. Ten days after Grandfather Stevenson's funeral, the Archduke Franz Ferdinand was assassinated in Sarajevo. Soon Europe was at war and the nineteenth-century world that Vice President Stevenson had known disappeared forever.

In October, 1914, the secretary of state of Illinois committed suicide. On October 13, 1914, Governor F. Edward Dunne appointed Lewis G. Stevenson to fill out the term expiring in January, 1917. Dunne had appointed Adlai's father to the chairmanship of the Illinois State Board of Pardons in 1913. The appointment to secretary of state, the Governor announced, was because of "my personal observation of Mr. Stevenson's conduct of the Board of Pardons."

Lewis G. Stevenson moved to Springfield but his wife and children stayed in Bloomington to complete the school term. Then, early in 1915, they all moved into the home of former Governor Richard Yates. Their next-door neighbors were the Medill McCormicks. He was publisher of the Chicago Tribune and a state senator. The Stevensons were frequent guests at the Governor's Mansion, and political leaders, including Lieutenant Governor Barratt O'Hara, dined regularly at their home.

The Secretary of State presided over the House of Representatives when there was a bitter battle for five weeks over the election of the speaker. When the speaker was finally elected, the House members voted unanimously their thanks for the impartial and efficient manner in which Lewis G. Stevenson had performed his duties.

A frequent guest for dinner was the Springfield poet Vachel Lindsay. That spring of 1915 the town was quoting his new poem "Abraham Lincoln Walks at Midnight." Adlai was absorbed as Lindsay recited: "the quaint great figure . . . the prairie-lawyer, master of us all."

> *. . . on the well-worn stones*
> *He stalks until the dawn-stars hurry away. . . .*

> *He cannot rest until a spirit-dawn*
> *Shall come; — the shining hope of Europe free:*
> *The league of sober folk, the Workers' Earth,*
> *Bringing long peace to Cornland, Alp and Sea.*

Adlai's favorite partner at dances was Mary Douglas Hay. And, at her house, Adlai enjoyed hearing her father, Logan Hay, a leading Lincoln scholar and cousin of John Hay, talk about the martyred President. The great-grandson of Jesse Fell read and read about Lincoln and absorbed his ideas and stories.

Mrs. Ives wrote of their days in Springfield: "I realize now how much Adlai was absorbing — from poets as well as politicians — sitting with head slightly forward in what is still his typical 'listening post' look." [28]

THE COMING OF ARTHUR [29]

Arthur was the son of Ygine and King Uther. He was born the night of King Uther's death and was taken by the wise man, Merlin, who gave him to an old knight named Anton to be raised. When he was old enough to rule Merlin had him crowned. The Nobles of the country objected to this because they thought Arthur was not of Royal birth. After he had overcome the nobles he sent three messengers to the court of Leodogran to ask for the hand of Guinivere his daughter. After the three messengers and Arthur's half sister had explained his berth he consented and they were married amidst great pomp. He got his famous sword Excalibur from the Lady of the Lake and in twelve great battles he overcame the heathens and restored peace to the land.

In the summer of 1915, Adlai attended camp at Oxford, Maine, and his sister went to another camp in the same state. For a while their mother stayed at an inn near them.

To Mrs. Lewis G. Stevenson

July 25, 1915

Dear Mother:

When you telephoned me you said you might come over tomorrow or soon but I advise you not to as the weather is pretty bad.[30] Father wrote me and said that I should write him twice a week and if I did-

---

[28] *My Brother Adlai,* p. 80.

[29] This was a high school paper written March 26, 1915.

[30] Mrs. Ives wrote: "My brother had a boy's natural wariness of too many parental visits." *My Brother Adlai,* p. 82.

[18]

not he would write Prof [31] so I suppose I shall have to be real diligent and write him every Sunday and Wednesday.

I was very glad to hear that you had at last found a place that you like and was astonished to hear that Buff had gone to a camp and that she liked it. Our intermidate baseball team on which I play third base played Lake Pleasant Camp Friday and we beat them seven to five. I destinguished my self as a hitter and won considerable praze from the coach. I was chosen to play the singles in tennis against Camp Robert [?] the other day and was beaten only after three sets. The Kineo meet comes off in a few days and the swimming coach has me training for the plunge and high diving. I dont know wheather I have told you all this before but I have to think of something to say.

With lots of love
Adlai

To Mrs. Lewis G. Stevenson

August 1, 1915

Dear Mother:

I was awfully sorry to hear that the mesquitoes were so bad that you had to leave Denmark but I am sure that they are not as bad as they are here. I just filled my pen that is the reason for the change in ink. I hope you like your new location in Portland. Father says that he is having a law suit but he is sure that it will come out all right. Camp Oxford is not sending a team to Bridgeton this year so I am not sure wheath I shall see Buff Wensday or not. The subject of my editorail was the dissadvantages of the Hare and Hound race it will probably be read tonight. It has been raining slightly this afternoon but is clearing off now for a few hours I hope. Last Thursday we had the return game with Lake Pleasant camp and beat them seven to five. I played third base. Do you want me to start latin and if so do you want me to review the first year or go on from where I left of with Austin, Prof has the book? I was awfully glad to hear that Buff was liking her camp so well and that she had swam 175 feet. Yesterday we had the annual hare and hound race. A couple of fellows and myself cut off about five miles of the race by making a short cut to where we thought the hares would go. We were right and after the hares had passed we swam across the lake and got their bags then swam back and were the first hounds to return and the only ones that got bags and therefore got all the praise.

With lots of lov
Adlai

[31] Unable to identify.

To Elizabeth Stevenson

August 1, 1915

Dear Buff:

I was awfully glad to receive you[r] letters and you must excuse me for not having answered them sooner, but I have been so busy you know.

I am not sure wheather I will be at Bridgeton or not as Camp Oxford is not going to send a team this [year?]. But if I am over I will be there Wednesday and shall look you up. I was glad to hear that you had taken the canoe test and had done it. The canoe test here is a hundred yards with your clothes on but I didnot have to take it. I am glad you like your room mates although they are nuts. Last Thursday we had our return engagement with Lake Pleasant Camp and beat them seven to four. I played third base. I can see you playing baseball. Yesterday we had the annual hare and hound race. A couple of other fellows and myself cut off about five miles of the race by making a short cut to a place where we though[t] the hounds would go. We were right and after they had gone by we swam across the lake where they had hidden their bags got them and were the first hounds to return and the only ones to get bags and therefore got all the praise. I hope you are not suffering with the mosquetoes like we are.

Lots of love
ADLAI

Adlai's father wrote him a number of letters at camp. In one he told his son, "With the exception of a few words which were somewhat shady in spelling, the letter was splendid." In another letter, the father wrote: "I would rather you would tell me more about the boys. Who they are, where they come from, and what their different characteristics are. I want you to learn to observe people carefully; also to analyze them, and if you get into the practice of doing this early in life, it will be of immense value to you in later years." In another letter the father criticized Adlai for being too active in athletics. "I want you to stop this right away. . . . I want you to rest, lie around, read books, etc. for the balance of the summer, or come directly home. You simply shall not overdo, and come home all worn out, instead of in prime condition for the operation [tonsils] and your fall school work."

"Adlai's next letter to Mother proves he hadn't taken Father's impulsive ban on sports too literally," Mrs. Ives wrote.[32]

[32] *My Brother Adlai*, pp. 83–84.

To Mrs. Lewis G. Stevenson

August 16, 1915

Dear Mother:

When I got back yesterday afternoon I found your letters in which you didnot want me to go on the White Mountains hike, but I had already returned when I received them. I am certainly glad I went now. We left Monday morning, there were four of us in the bunch I was in. . . . There were fifteen that went all together in bunches of five. We walked four miles to the station where we caught the train to Bethel. The four of us left Bethel at half past eleven and got to Gorham that night a distance of twenty two miles. We slept in a railroad shop that night. The next morning we walked to the Glen house the next morning and rested near there for about two hours before climbing the mountain. Mount Washington is 6,300 feet hight and it is nine miles up the carrage road to the tiptop house. We reached there that afternoon after walking the last four miles in rain. The next day we waited until noon before we started down. We went down the Crawford trail and spent the night in a barn near the Crawford House. The next morning after walking about six miles an auto picked us up and gave us a twenty mile lift. We walked on and reached Bridgeton that night covering a distance of fifty two miles in one day. We slept in a barn that night and believe me we slept well. We reached home about three o'clock. The scenery was beautiful the whole trip and some of the views were magnificent.

Please write and tell me how you would like to have me come home. I would rather wait until the twenty fifth or sixth if possible.

With lots of love

ADLAI

P.S. Yesterday evening I swam the lake a distance of 2 miles in 1:16:21. Prof tells me you sprained your ankle. Tell me about it in your next letter.

Adlai's sister, now eighteen, was sent to Miss Wright's School for Young Ladies in Bryn Mawr, Pennsylvania. Her mother took her East in September, 1915.

To Elizabeth Stevenson

Saturday

Dear Buff:

Mother got home last night in good spirits although she was very distressed to see you go. We got your telegram and were glad to hear that you had arrived safely. Mother is resting now so I am writing you for her. She is not ill only tired from her trip which she says was very successful. Fathers rest is doing him a great deal of good as I suppose you know and he is fealing much better. The Rostrum [33] gave their roast last night, but I went to another one. The weather is bright but cool although it is much warmer today than it has been.

I hope you like you[r] school, and don't study to *hard*. Mother says that she saw cousin Letitia Bromwell and Mildred in Chicago.[34] I do not know wheather this was before you left or not. I got the second highest mark on my English History test in class.

Mother will write you soon.

With lots of love
ADLAI

Buffie wrote Adlai in response to his letter: "Don't let the Blessed be too homesick for me. Oh, Adlai, she's too wonderful to be our Mother!" Buffie described her roommate as a "sweet creature." (Adlai must have misread this as Sweed). Buffie wrote that their room was a "bleak, bare spot." Mr. and Mrs. Oberge — a Swedish family — were in charge of the "annex" where the girls lived. Buffie described him as "a character" and his wife as an inveterate talker.

To Elizabeth Stevenson

October 15, 1915

Dear *Friend* Buffie:

I received your *epistle* this morning and was very glad to hear that you were still alive. On receiving this letter dont be surprised becaus I will not write you again for two (2) months.

I was glad to hear that your room mate is a Sweed and docil, be cause Sweeds are, as a rule are simple (in the head), and poor dancers.

---

[33] A club at University High School.
[34] Letitia Bromwell was the sister of Mrs. Carl (Julia) Vrooman, of Bloomington. Mildred was her daughter.

Mr. Oberge must be a fool from your description and I hope that all the people there are not like the two you speak of in your letter.

I just got thru sending you a telegram regarding you[r] cold about which mother seems to be worried (although I am not). I just wrote the "old man" asking for fifty seeds (dollars) I am expecting a hot reply. I am going over to Decatur tomorrow with the football team. We are having a special car on the interurban (Notice: I did not know how to spell the last word, reason for curious figures at end). I hop[e] your cold will improve as it gets older, I mean better.

Lots of love

ADLAI

P.S. I have been working extreamly hard in school. This is what I will look like if I keep it up.[35]

To Elizabeth Stevenson

December 4, 1915

Dear Buff:

I had fully decided not to write you as you were coming home for the holidays so soon, but after considerable urging on mothers part I decided to take out my trus[t]y pen once more. Now comes the difficult task of saying something, I cant "sling the bull" like you can.

I was at a basket ball game this afternoon out at school, and we were beaten sad to relate by the little town of Lexington. Tonight I am going out to Normal to the Jesters play called the "Admirable Crighton." I am going to dancing school every week and am becoming some artist in the manily sport. I got a bid to the Iota B Φ dance the other day which comes off New Years Eve. Mother was out at school the other day and says that Dorothy Aldrich invited you. You had better hurry up and ask somebody before they are all taken, Weldon Funk for instance. Mother says that Mrs. Pasfield said that Charlott was going to ask us to Zeata B Y dance in Springfield. My Frat does not give a dance this winter as we are going to have the convention in Springfield next spring and have to save our money. But the dance next spring during the convention will be a peach. The old man is going to Washington today and wants me to go with him but I dont believe I will.

Lots of Love,

ADLAI

[35] A sketch follows of a bespectacled figure carrying books under each arm entitled "Professor Latin and Greek," "Degrees A.B., B.D., B.S., D.D., D.L." and "Me 20 years hence."

Part Two

Choate
1916–1918

Adlai's parents decided that their son should go East to college. Princeton University was the choice. There were family ties to Princeton. Adlai Osborne had graduated from there in 1764 and Great-grandfather Lewis Warner Green had studied at the Theological Seminary. Moreover, the Stevenson family's political idol, Woodrow Wilson, had been president of Princeton before he was elected governor of New Jersey in 1910. In August, 1912, Lewis G. Stevenson had taken son Adlai with him to call on the Democratic nominee for President. They spent an afternoon with Woodrow Wilson. He made a vivid impression on the twelve-year-old boy and became one of Adlai E. Stevenson's greatest heroes and a powerful influence molding his political values.

But Adlai failed to pass the three college entrance examinations in June, 1916. His father immediately entered his name at the Choate School, where Adlai's cousin Davis Merwin had studied. Since Adlai was deficient in French, he had to be tutored in the summer of 1916 before he was admitted to Choate.

Lewis G. Stevenson took Adlai and Buffie that summer to the national conventions of the Republican and Progressive parties which were meeting simultaneously in Chicago. At the Bull Moose convention Adlai met Harold L. Ickes and saw the collapse of this party when Theodore Roosevelt refused to run again as its presidential candidate. During the summer Adlai accompanied his father to Democratic rallies, passed out his father's cards and drove around the countryside tacking up posters to help his father's campaign for election as secretary of state. "At home, we talked, ate and dreamed politics," Mrs. Ives recalled.[1]

The Choate School at Wallingford, Connecticut, in 1916 had approxi-

[1] Elizabeth Stevenson Ives and Hildegarde Dolson, My Brother Adlai (New York: Morrow, 1956), p. 95.

mately two hundred boys. Dr. George Clair St. John, headmaster since 1908, tried to make sure that each individual boy received the type of liberal education that the British public schools provided for their governing class. Industry, efficiency, and an understanding of "the enduring values and of the spirit of public service" were instilled in the boys.[2]

Since Adlai E. Stevenson had been admitted to Choate late, he was assigned a single room. If he was isolated physically this way from the other boys, he was also isolated politically. Most of his classmates were drawn from wealthy Republican families who had resisted many of the reforms of Woodrow Wilson's New Freedom as an infringement on the "divine right" of property.

Adlai and two other boys were the only defenders of Wilson during the 1916 campaign. One of his classmates, Henry P. Stearns, said later: "We used to argue politics by the hour, but I never saw Ad lose his temper or act bitter."[3]

In 1936, Adlai E. Stevenson remarked:

My debt to Choate is formidable. Starting with something very fresh from the prairie and somewhat deficient in everything except appetite, the magic alchemy of Choate produced an accomplished actor, a promising writer and a passable athlete with revivalistic tendencies who sailed into college — on the wings of war — all in two years! All these things they did for me — and I enjoyed every minute of the operation. . . .

He then added:

Reflect for a moment that the boarding school is a boy's first impact with a compact, organized, social community of which he must at once become a self reliant, integral part. Mother isn't there to reflate his ego from time to time, father isn't there to help him with his lessons, even if he could; there are big boys, little boys, school heroes, masters, discipline, work and play and everything is organized and all competing relentlessly for consideration and evaluation by the astonishingly absorbent post adolescent mind. And this confusion of impressions is the perfect incubator of values — good and bad. I can imagine nothing much more difficult or precarious than the fine adjustments of emphasis which create in those impressionable school days a sensitive, discriminating taste for what's worthwhile and what isn't. I doubt if there's any prescription for this

[2] See Kenneth S. Davis, A Prophet in His Own Country: The Triumphs and Defeats of Adlai E. Stevenson (New York: Doubleday, 1957), pp. 91–98 for a discussion of Stevenson's two years at Choate.

[3] Quoted in Ives and Dolson, My Brother Adlai, p. 98.

quality in a school — Choate has it — thanks to the genius of its headmaster.[4]

The two years at the Choate School marked the first time that he was away from close parental supervision and overprotectiveness for an extended period. But whether Adlai knew it or not, both his mother and father kept the headmaster advised on how to educate and raise their son.

On January 2, 1917, his father wrote the headmaster: "Just at this age I believe the boy should have sufficient time to take a great deal of exercise. . . . I am going to urge you to see that he has a regular course of gymnastic exercises as well as out-of-door recreation. . . . When he reached home [for Christmas vacation] he seemed very tired . . . very much more stoop shouldered than when he went away . . . due to sitting the long hours at the uncomfortable desks."

His mother wrote the headmaster a few weeks later: "Adlai neglects to tell us if he is getting at least a couple of hours out of doors each afternoon. . . . Will you please look into the matter at once and so relieve our anxiety."

His father wrote the headmaster on May 4, 1917: "Without letting Adlai know that I have written you, will you please . . . have his eyes and throat examined. . . . He is very fond of the school, and especially of you, but, frankly, I am not at all satisfied with the progress he has made. I feel entirely too little individual attention has been given him."

On September 25, 1917, his father wrote the headmaster: "I do not feel he should go in for football seriously this Fall. . . . His work on the News . . . is quite enough to keep him as busy as we think safe. . . . It will be a relief to Mrs. Stevenson and me if you will send us an outline of the way his time is proportioned in study, recreation and extra work."

In December, 1917, his father wrote the headmaster: "Mrs. Stevenson and I do not think Adlai seemed entirely well when he was with us in Lakewood last week . . . thin, underweight, very nervous. . . . Frankly, I am worried about Adlai and unless his appearance is better when he comes home for Xmas I shall feel obliged to take him out of school."

[4] Stevenson delivered these remarks at a meeting of Choate alumni in Chicago in January, 1936, at which the headmaster, Dr. George St. John, was present. This handwritten speech is in the Stevenson papers at the Princeton University Library. On January 19, 1936, Dr. St. John wrote Stevenson: "A thousand thanks for the way you carried the Dinner. You were eloquent, delightful, amusing and to the point. And you make us all feel that you *liked* your old School." The Choate School Archives.

On June 16, 1918, his mother sent a telegram to the headmaster: "Distressed to hear of Adlai's illness. . . . He needs a rest. Should not remain for examinations unless entirely well."

These letters from Adlai's parents and Dr. George C. St. John's diplomatic replies are in the archives of the Choate School. Mrs. B. F. Sylvester, Jr., Choate's archivist, sent copies to the editors. Mrs. Sylvester has, in addition, assisted the editors in identifying the dates of a number of Adlai's letters. Miss Jessie Cushman, secretary to Dr. St. John, helped identify people mentioned in the letters. Usually Adlai wrote only the day of the week on the letter. Through checking the Choate News it was possible to date many of the letters from the sporting events or other activities mentioned in the letters. The dates determined this way are placed in brackets in the text.

The handwritten letters from Choate are in the Elizabeth Stevenson Ives collection at the Illinois State Historical Library. Adlai E. Stevenson's original spellings of certain words are printed as he wrote them — no "sic" has been added. We included all the letters we could locate written from Choate.

Only four letters that Adlai wrote during his first year at Choate were saved. Some of his mother's letters to him have been preserved and she continued to keep close track of his activities. When he was invited to a dance at a girls' school, his mother wrote: "I suppose after a few days you should write Jane a little note saying you had returned safely and thank her again for asking you, that you had greatly enjoyed the dance and the couple of days of freedom. Be careful that it is written well and properly spelled." Or when he was to play in a production of the Dramatic Club, she wrote: "The play will be of much benefit. I suppose the greatest thing for you, in the play, is to speak so you can be heard by all. Next try to be the part. Practise in your room aloud, and the gestures and the movements. Try to keep well so nothing will hold you back. And to keep your throat in good order for the play, you must gargle daily." [5]

To Lewis G. Stevenson

Tuesday night [6]

Dear Father:

I am writing you on a matter of great import, ie, import to me. You see the "News" competition ends this Saturday and I am now fourth

[5] Quoted in Ives and Dolson, *My Brother Adlai*, pp. 101–102.

[6] There is no date on this letter. It was written in mid-October, 1916. Adlai was "heeling" with eighteen other boys for a place on the board of the *Choate News*.

man on the competition, furthermore I think (and have been told so) that the board is only going to take on three men. Now an "ad" will help me greatly and I might possibly get taken on the board if I get a good one as they want them and I am so near to third place anyway. The "News" is considered the second biggest thing in school after football and Mr. St. J.[7] thinks it the first. Now, as I said before, an "ad" will help me consid[e]rably. Do you know of any firm, co. etc. that might advertize? If you do know of one please let me know immediately because the competition ends Saturday. Can you suggest any company to which I might write that would be likely to advertise?

Am feeling fine, everything O.K.

> Love to all,
> AD

R.S.V.P.

To Mrs. Lewis G. Stevenson

Sunday [January 21, 1917]

Dearest Mother

I just got back from church a few minutes ago. It certainly was a long sermon, believe me. Last night we had moving pictures here at school. We are going to have them every Sat, from now on. We saw Margurite Clark in "Prince and Pauper," it was very good however I have seen it before.

I got a letter from father the other day, he was in Washington then. I was glad to hear that the trip had not fallen thru.[8] But where will you be when they are floating around the world.

I received the glasses and the Pantagraph. I am out of second hall again this week but not first.

Yesterday afternoon we beat Bridgeport high in hockey.

How are you felling these days I didnot get a letter from you all last week. I go skating most every afternoon and am getting quite good at it.

A week after the letter was written he won a place on the board. *Choate News,* October 27, 1916. On May 25, 1917, he was elected business manager of the *Choate News.*

His mother wrote him about his work on the school paper: "I think it is a splendid experience for you. You will learn how to handle men etc. etc. and above all else I hope it will show you how necessary it is to gauge your strength, to allot your time, and not to give of both too ceaselessly." Quoted in Ives and Dolson, *My Brother Adlai,* p. 101.

[7] The headmaster, George St. John.

[8] The trip referred to was to have occurred in April, 1917, but American entrance into the Great War precluded it.

Well it is time for dinne[r] so I must close. Will write soon.

Love

A<small>D</small>.

The March, 1917, issue of the Choate Literary Magazine *printed the following short story by Adlai E. Stevenson.*

THE SECOND GAME

Jean Rouselle, a famous French gambler, lay one morning on his luxurious bed, a little longer than was his usual routine. He recalled the events of the previous night, and a sign of satisfaction seemed to cross his features, when the picture of the table, the circle of men gathered around, and the tense expression of his opponent at the other side flashed through his mind. This expression changed to one of unfeigned mirth, when he recalled the utter despondency of his opponent after they had finished. With a smile of complete satisfaction he reached for a small pocketbook lying on a nearby table. Opening it, he took out a coin, which he fondled as though it were the most precious thing in all the world. He thought of the many thousands of francs that this little coin had won for him. From these recollections his thoughts passed over the years to the springtime of his life. He recalled the circumstances under which he had come into possession of it.

His father had been exploring French possessions in the East Indies, and on one occasion had taken his son with him. He remembered the long sea voyage, the small island set like an emerald in the broad, blue expanse of that great south sea. The events of the trip to an ancient inland village passed before him. He recalled the very old and ugly sorceress, who had so terrified him with her dried skulls and other hideous trinkets. Her he considered the source of his present prosperity; it was she who had given him this coin, charging him to cherish it and to keep it with him all the rest of his life, for so it would bring him luck. It had been given her many, many years ago, by a great head hunter, who had told her that there were but two things that could break its spell, and one of those having crossed his path, he said that he would rather give the coin to her than let it fall into the hands of his enemies. That morning, the old woman had had a similar misfortune and gave the coin to this boy. As the years had passed, Rouselle had used this charm in cards; he usually won, but now and then he lost. And he discovered that every time he had lost, one or the other of two objects had lain in his path at some time during the day of such losses — objects that had come to take on the greatest horror.

Awakening from this pleasant and unpleasant reverie, he realized that he had not as yet received his morning mail, so he rang a bell at his bedside, and a valet, carrying a small silver tray with several letters upon it, entered immediately. Glancing at the letters carelessly, he laid them aside, except one bearing an American stamp which attracted his attention. He quickly opened the envelope, and while reading, the expression of his features changed from one of interest to that of deep concern and worry.

Many years previous to this time Rouselle had known a young American student in Paris, and, as he thought then, he had financially ruined him. But the young American swore that he would be avenged. He made Rouselle promise that if he ever returned he would play for the same stakes that they had then played for.

The fact that this old acquaintance was in Paris and had come all the way from America to be avenged on the man that had ruined him in youth caused Rouselle no little concern. His conscience hurt him. He passed over, in his mind, the occurrences of that previous meeting, and the more he thought about it the more troubled he became. He had not believed that this man would ever return for revenge. Moreover, he did not like the idea of playing for such large stakes, especially with a man whom he had so thoroughly beaten before. It seemed to him like some one rising from the dead to be revenged on his destroyer. Yet, he must play or else lose his reputation and honor. And, after all, he would surely win; the coin had never forsaken him when most he needed it.

As it neared five o'clock, the time set for the meeting, Rouselle dressed uneasily, always fondling his coin. On the way to the club — the very club where he had formerly ruined his opponent — he hastily bought a paper, but instead of the newsboy's handing him the journal, the urchin asked him to take one out of the bundle. Rouselle did so. But suddenly horror was upon him, for the boy was armless, and a maimed child had shattered the charm and her luck for the South Sea island sorceress. Completely unnerved, he hurried on, hesitating only on the club-house steps — the one-armed boy in his mind.

On entering he saw a group of his friends gathered around one of the tables. The group gave way, and before him sat a man whom he recognized immediately as the young American of many years ago — but the young no more, for he had grown from a young man to an old man, while Rouselle had grown from a youth to middle age.

[33]

"You received my letter?" said the American, rising.

"I did."

"You remember an agreement we had some years ago?"

"I believe I recollect it," said Rouselle, as he took a seat at the other side of the table.

Something about the eyes and expression of the man before him disturbed the Frenchman. This man had a vague, far away look in his eyes. He seemed to peer over the rough and broken path of his existence into the past.

"Will you shuffle?" he inquired, passing the cards over to Rouselle.

Rouselle shuffled and dealt, quickly and nervously, contrary to his usual slow, deliberate method. A young man standing back of the American, whom he had not noticed before, picked up the cards.

"May I ask the name of the young gentleman holding your cards?" said Rouselle.

"I beg your pardon, monsieur, for not having introduced my son to you before. I was stricken blind some years ago, and if you do not object, my son will read my hand to me."

Rouselle sank back into his chair livid and trembling. The far-seeing but sightless eyes remained motionless. He shuddered as he thought of the great head hunter, on that far-away island who gave himself up for lost when fate had set him against the blind. Here was the inexorable misfortune. The coin was twice thwarted in one day — first the maimed, now the blind.

Suddenly Rouselle laid his cards upon the table.

"If I pay you one-half of the amount for which we are now playing will you call it square, without finishing the hand?" he exclaimed.

Surprise crossed the face of the American.

"I believe, monsieur, that I would rather finish the hand."

The Frenchman displayed great agitation.

"Certainly, monsieur, you would not let an offer of two-thirds of the amount pass? You remember, I seldom lose a hand on such large stakes."

"Thank you for your kind offer, monsieur; however, I prefer to finish the hand."

The Frenchman sank again into his chair. His hand trembled violently, the cards slipped out and fell to the floor. He made no effort to regain them.

"Surely, my friend, you cannot know what a great offer I have made you, or you would not let it pass. Your chances of winning are slight, and the stakes are large. Think again!"

"Monsieur Rouselle, I have been thinking of this sum for many years past. I ask you to play."

The indescribable eyes remained motionless. The one-armed boy again flashed into Rouselle's memory. The enemies of his luck were arrayed in full force against him.

"Frenchman, the tide has turned. On our previous meeting it was I who begged for money, but you gave me none. Now it is you, and likewise you shall have none. I ask you once more to play."

Rouselle tried to pick up the cards, but could not. After all, what was the use? He simply prolonged his agony. He gave up, paid the stakes in full and left the room. The American took the money and closed his hands upon it as though it were the very prize of life. His son picked up the Frenchman's cards and glanced at them.

"He would have won, father," said he, and dropped them upon the table.

To Mrs. Lewis G. Stevenson

Sunday [June 15, 1917]

Dearest Mum:

Just 10 more days, and I will be on the road to "home sweet home."

This is a rotten day, the worst we have had for some time. We had a sermon, at church this morning by an officer of the Conn. Anti Saloon League. Very interesting.

The last two weeks and the week to come are about the hardest of the whole year, we work night and day preparing for the college exams. The school exams come this week and the next week come the board exams.[9] I got two recommendations and three consents and no checks for my college exams, that is considered pretty good. I got consented in Cicero and did not expect that Mr. Wheeler [10] would let me take the exam. However I have no hope of passing it.

I wrote to Mary Hay [11] accepting her invitation. And certainly am glad she asked me. I am going down tomorrow to let the photographer have another try at me. I certainly am anxious to get home, I always liked B[loomington]. in June better than any other time, regardless of the weather.

. . . Use the car all you can, it is good for it.

---

[9] Kenneth S. Davis wrote: "He did approximately twice as well as he'd done the year before, passing a few of the ten to fifteen different tests. . . . In the autumn his examination record helped determine his courses for this second Choate year." *A Prophet in His Own Country*, pp. 91–92.

[10] Frank Charles Wheeler, who taught Greek and Latin at Choate, 1916–1952.

[11] Daughter of the Logan Hays, Springfield, Illinois.

I have decided to [room] as I explained to you.[12] I really think it will be better and I think you will think so too, when I explain it. Was awfully sorry to hear that you had been indisposed. It was probably due to the weather. Hope you will feel better soon.

Love
ADLAI

To Mrs. Lewis G. Stevenson

Sunday [June 21, 1917]

Dearest Mother:

Well in four more days I will be travelling toward the best home in all the world. About half the school, that is the fellows who don't have to take Board exams have left already. We can do just about what we want to around here now, because the school year is over.

I am pretty nervous about my exams; every one is. I ought to pass Geometry as I got 85 in the final school exam, one of the best mark[s], however fellows have flunked in better condition that I am in. I got 63 in my final exam in English which was not bad as there were only 2 passes in my class. That would have passed the board, but I had the grammar almost all wrong. However if my themes are good enough on the board I will pass. I have to take 3 latin exams. I am bound to flunk the composition exam. Mr. Wheeler figures that I have a fighting chance to pass the Cicero as I know the speeches that we have had pretty well and am just about passing on sight translation. He says I ought to get the history question altogether correct. This is about the most important exam. Personally I doubt if I can pass it. He says I ought to pass Caesar, however I am also very doubtful about that also.

My first exam is geometry and comes tomorrow at 2 P.M. English comes Tuesday and all 3 latins Wednesday. I have already packed the box I am going to leave here and am going to start on my trunk soon.

Love,
AD.

Buffie and Adlai, accompanied by Nora Caroe, Buffie's French teacher at Miss Wright's School, spent the summer of 1917 at the HF Bar Ranch near Buffalo, Wyoming.

[12] He meant that the next year he would room with Henry P. (Harry) Stearns and James (Jim) Millholland, although his mother preferred he room alone.

To Mrs. Lewis G. Stevenson

Thursday

Dearest Mum:

Well we have arrived at our destination at last. It certainly is a beautiful place. Buffie & Nora have a little cottage together and I have one all to myself. I expected that there would probably be another man in with me, there are 2 or 3 in all the other cottages. Buffie's cottage is in or rather on the edge of a little grove of cottenwoods which border a very pretty and fast flowing mountain stream. Almost directly back of us the ground rises into the first range of the Big Horns, beautiful mountains. It is certainly a wonderful location. We arrived in Clairemont about an hour and a half late. Clairemont consists of a water station and about 3 or 4 stores. We waited there about an hour for the train to leave for Buffalo. The ride from Clairemont to Buffalo on the little 2 car train was lots of fun and the scenery beautiful. Buffalo is a very pretty little town with paved streets and lots of autos. When we arrived they were having a 4th of July celebration with broncho busting, racing etc. The ride out here (18 miles) in the motor car was really very beautiful, it was an almost steady ascent.

The people out here are awfully nice. Mr. Horton is a dandy. The ranch is almost full. It only accomadates 100 and there are about 95 here all ready. There is a very nice woman, Mrs. Goodwin from Cleveland here with her husband son and daughter.[13]

She took me out to the corral and told me all about the place, (she has been her[e] 4 years). Her son is a very nice fellow (17) and goes to Thathcher if that's the way you spell it. There is also a girl here named Edith Layman from St. Louis whom I met in Charlevoix last summer. I have not spoken to her yet, but will soon. Our trunk did not come from Chicago on the same train with us, however I suppose it will be here tonight. There [is] only 1 train a day from Clairmont to Buffalo. I think we will have a fine time out here. The horses are not very good, in fact quite rotten so tell father he does not need to worry about any accidents from bucking bronchos etc.

I haven't asked Mr. Horton about the typewriter yet, but will today. I think all the clothes I need is a pair of riding breeches in order not to wear my army trousers out. Buffie did a very fine job of packing the

[13] Frank Horton owned the dude ranch. Ralph Goodwin and Adlai dreamed that summer of ranching in the West after college.

grip. She put in about a dozen shirts for me and only 1 collar, so I am washing that. Also only 1 necktie which will be worn out very soon.

Love
AD.

To Mrs. Lewis G. Stevenson

Thursday

Dearest Mum:

It's been a long time since I've written for you see when Buff arrived I turned that responsibility over to her.

I rode for 10 hours on a roundup yesterday on the "Big Five" cattle rangle. Ralph [Goodwin] and I left at 6 A.M. with the cow boys and it was a wonderful experience. It took until noon to get the cattle out of the hills and the herd rounded-up. Another man and I had to clear an entire cañon that was filled with very dense brush and it took three of the hardest hours of riding that I ever expect to do. The afternoon was employed in roping and branding calves. I "rode herd," that is kept riding around the herd with about 8 other men to keep the herd together. Every few minutes I would have to go tearing over the plains for a runa-way steer. However, it was lots of fun and a great experience. In the evening Ralph and I and 4 of the "hands" went into Buffalo to see a wrestling match. It was very good but needless to say I was pretty tired by the time we got home. We slept all morning.

What had I better do about going East. The Goodwin's are really anxious to have me stay until Sept. 1st and then go home with them. However, I think I had better leave about the 23, go to Bloom[ington] get the car and drive to Charle-[Charlevoix]. I should arrive there about the 1st of Sept and could spend a couple of weeks before I started East. Let me know what you think I had better do immediately so I can make arrangements.

Buff is fine and I am having the best time of my life.

Love
AD.

P.S. Give the enclosure to Father and tell him to please act accordingly.[14]

To Mrs. Lewis G. Stevenson

Sunday [September 30, 1917]

Dearest Mum:

Well school has started. There are almost 200 fellows here this year

---

14 This was not saved.

and 68 new ones. I, as one of the old fellows had charge of some new ones when they came. We have the best room in School, it certainly is a dandy. Stearns came Wed. night and we are all through fixing it up. It looks fine. Millholland came last Sunday night, the same time I did. He was on the train that I got on in New Haven.[15] Friday morning Harry Stearns and I drove down to New Haven in his car and spent the day getting ads.[16] I have entire charge of the permission for tailors, haberdashers etc. to show in school and, as a result, I am pretty busy getting dates straightened out etc.

I was in N.H. yesterday afternoon and did not get back until dinner was about over. I have about $600 worth of advertising now, and hope to get some more. We are going to try to get the first edition of the News out about the 11th or 12th and I will send you a copy. The new fellows are a fine looking bunch. I have found 4 or 5 especially that I like awfully well. I have got quite a bunch to go out for the News and the competition ought to be an awfully good one. We are going to call a meeting of the prospective heelers this afternoon. . . . There seems to be some pretty good material for football among the new fellows and we are likely to have a pretty good team after all. Tell Buff I will send her a schedule as soon as they come out.

I find that I can get into Princeton without taking Physics, Solid Geom. and Trigonometry by substituting 2 years of Spanish or German insted. I expect to do this as it makes it much easier and Spanish is a coming language. Have you heard from my fall exams yet. Please send me the report immediately because it will make some difference with my course. I am feeling fine and like school far better than I did last year. The room is fine and I am never going to room alone again.

Love
Aᴅ.

To Mrs. Lewis G. Stevenson

Thursday night [October 4, 1917]

Dearest Mum:

As I have all my work for tomorrow I am writing you in study hall.

---

[15] The second year at Choate he roomed with Henry P. (Harry) Stearns and James (Jim) Millholland.

[16] He was business manager of the *Choate News* and Stearns was editor. Mr. Stearns wrote on September 5, 1952, his "Recollections of Adlai Stevenson at Choate." He stated among other things: "I recall Steve as a hard worker. *The*

I received Buff's letter today containing the exam report. All in all I think I should be satisfied with passing french. I was surprised that I got such a rotten mark in English. I guess they marked very hard as the exam was pretty easy. I though[t] it was anyway. That was really the least important of them all, because I can take it any time. I did a good deal better in Latin than I had expected. I decided to take Cicero again this year instead of Virgil because it will make me sure of passing it, the comp, and the Caesar exam in the Spring, which if I took Virgil I would get no practice in grammer and the chances are I would not be able to pass the comp Caesar & Cicero exams again. Furthermore it will make the Virgil much easier and also make my freshman latin much easier. I was certainly glad I passed that French. 9 months work in 2 weeks [17] More luck than brains. I am taking french III now. It is a pretty hard course but I think I can do it. Only 3 fellows passed the French III exam last spring; it certainly was a hard exam. An easy one is due to come this spring. I certainly hope it comes.

We beat Stamford High yesterday in our first game. I was official time keeper for Choate. We are going to try to get the first edition of the News out on the 12th. I have about $700 worth of advertising now and hope to get some more. $800 will cover, or very nearly cover the printing expenses . . . and if I possibly can I want to cover the printing expenses by the advertising, then everything we make from then on, through subscriptions, will be clear profits. I am pretty busy keeping the dates for tailors, haberdashers, etc. to show at school [word illegible]. I get a bunch of letters every day. Our room is fine. It and the one like it are undoubtedly the best rooms in School. Everyone says so at least. I am feeling very well. I think I told you in my last letter why I am taking Spanish. By taking 2 years of it I avoid taking Physics, Solid & Trig. It makes it much easier. Do you know where my gold watch chain with the knife & pencil on it is? It was not in the jewel box. If you find it please send it. Am feeling fine. Weather fair. Hope you all are well.

Love

AD

News, the *Literary Magazine* and studies kept him busy most of the time. . . . Steve was, of course, an ardent Democrat, and we had many arguments on politics, sometimes long into the night. His sense of humor was always present, and the arguments never became bitter. . . . Of the various boys with whom I roomed in school and college Steve was the most congenial. . . . He has always been thoughtful and sincere." The Choate School Archives.

[17] He apparently is referring to a "cram course" just before he returned to Choate.

To Mrs. Lewis G. Stevenson

Sunday [October 7, 1917]

Dearest Mum:

Evidently you don't, yet, quite understand about my substituting Spanish. By taking Spanish now I won't avoid taking Physics, Solid, and Trig. because I will have to take them in my freshman year at college and won't have to take another modern language. It really is the best way to enter Princeton and Solid and Trig are worthless subjects anyway. Physics is very good but I will get plenty of that in college.

I am getting along fine. Last night we had a very select feed up in our room. Mr. Temple and Mr. Moulton [18] were there. We had a lot of fun. This morning Harry Stearns and I led the whole school to church. You see he is vice president of the sixth form and, as we always walk together, I led the line. After church I walked with Mr. & Mrs. Stearns and Harry over to the place where they have been staying recently. They are awfully nice. Last night, Mr. Seymour,[19] Mrs. St. John's brother, gave us a very interesting talk on the Kaiser.

We beat Bridgeport High yesterday 18–0. I was timekeeper and also helped call the roll on the bleachers. You see we make everyone come to the games & if they don't they get sat on. It certainly is nice to be one "in authority," and believe me I exercise my authority.

The News is coming along pretty well, except that Mr. Shortleidge [20] made Harry write all his editorials over again. I have about $700 worth of advertising. I have been given a topic to speak on in St. Andrews in several weeks. I am afraid I'll make a fool of myself trying to tell the School about religion. They seldom give a meeting to anyone except old, ie, the oldest fellows in School.

Tell Buff I did not get to N.H. [New Haven] this week. . . .

Love
AD

To Mrs. Lewis G. Stevenson

Sunday [October 14, 1917]

Dearest Madre: (Notice the Spanish).

Yesterday and today have been wonderful days. Yesterday afternoon

[18] Paul Russell Temple taught German and Guy Edwin Moulton taught Latin and French.
[19] Professor Charles Seymour of Yale University.
[20] Raphael Johnson (Rafe) Shortlidge taught mathematics.

we played Pomfret. They have not been beaten in football in three years, needless to say we went down to defeat. However the score was only 12–0, which is certainly far from bad. I met their star half back. He is a friend of Harry [Stearns]'s and an awfully nice fellow. Last night we had movies, Joanne the Woman with Geraldine Farrar. It was a wonderful picture but I had seen it. It was the picture I went to see last Spring with Mrs. Stewart and her son & daughter in Lakewood. After lights the 9th floor Hall had a very select feed in [Richard Robertson] Higgins' room. One of the fellows had received a box. We had chicken, meat loaf, crackers, jam, peanut butter, all sorts of candy and many other indigestable luxuries. Mr. Temple was there and we had a great time. We went to bed about 12. I got room grades this week and expect to enjoy them thoroughly. But the greatest joy of the year thus far was the coming out of the News, the first issue of the season, which occurred last night. It is undoubtedly the best first issue the News has ever had. All the masters say so. I am sending you one. I hope you will look it over and read some of the stuff, also look at the amount of advertising I got. I am quite proud of it. I am enclosing a football schedule. We only have four more games scheduled but they are all good ones. We are going to have a dance after the Taft game next Saturday and Har[r]y is going to have a girl up from Hartford for me.

We are only going to have Thanksgiving day this year for a holiday. . . .[21]

On December 22, 1917, Lewis G. Stevenson was appointed Chief Special Investigator of the U.S. Navy by Secretary of the Navy Josephus Daniels. He, his wife, and Buffie moved immediately to Washington, D.C., and Adlai joined them for the holiday season. Ellen Bruce Lee, the daughter of the Stevensons' friends Mr. and Mrs. Arthur Lee, arranged to "float" Adlai in Washington society. Buffie's diary reads that he "dances like a prince now" — but years later Mrs. Ives wrote: "I think he spent most of his time just standing self-consciously in the stag line" [22]

To Mrs. Lewis G. Stevenson

Sunday [probably January, 1918]

Dearest Mum:

Well things are going on just as usual here nothing exciting ever

[21] There is a page missing from this letter. It ends here, with no signature.
[22] *My Brother Adlai*, pp. 109–110.

happens. Fellows are beginning to talk about the dance and the festivities a good deal, and some of them have even started to fill out their programs. A good many of the fellows have engaged their rooms already. Do you know definately if you and Buff are coming? The Dramatic Club has first choice of rooms and I can always get rooms for you but it would be good to know definately as far in advance as possible.

I will write to Dougie Hay [23] next week asking her to come. I wish I knew if there was going to be a dance at Rosemary this winter, because I woul[d]'nt ask her unless I thought she would ask me up there.

The News competition is going to end pretty soon and believe me the heelers are certainly working. I don't believe it will hurt them though.

One of the new fellows is a Russian. He has only been in this country a few weeks and he certainly is interesting. He talks English very poorly but can speak French and German excellently.

Tell Buff to write me often and give me all the dope on Washington Society. I certainly had a wonderful vacation and it is awfully hard to start work again. I went out skating this morning but the ice was not much good, as we had a big rain storm here the other night, and the ice was covered with an air crust.

Well as usual I have not[h]ing to say and so adieu.

AD.

P.S. Tell Pa not to over investigate.

To Mrs. Lewis G. Stevenson

Sunday, January 27, 1918

Dearest Mum:

I just finished an epistle to Dougie Hay expressing the extent of my grievance at her not being able to come to the dance. By the way I wish you would let me know pretty soon if you are coming or not as I have had a programe filled for a couple of weeks and if you don't come I'll have to let the fellows know. It is probably to late for them to get rid of the dances as it is. Furthermore, I doubt if I can get rooms so you had better let me know in a hurry. Please come if you possibly can work it for it will be a good opportunity to see this joint.

We had quite a little snow here last night and it is pretty cold here today. I played hockey or rather tried to yesterday. We have movies, by way of amusement, last night and they were pretty good. The main

---

[23] Daughter of Mr. and Mrs. Logan Hay of Springfield, Illinois.

reel was Douglas Fairbanks in Wild & Wooly. It was an awfully good picture but of course I had seen it before. A certain Doctor Fitch [24] from New Haven preaches the sermon this afternoon. He was here last year, however, I don't remember wheather he was especially good or not. Later: Well he just finished speaking and he certainly was good. Mr. St. John asked the Fifth & Sixth forms to come down to his house this afternoon and hear Dr. Fitch talk about the war. He has been over in Belgium and France for quite a while.

I am on a committee of 3 from the Fifth form to select our class pins. The News competition ends next Saturday night when we have our elections. Trigonometry classes start Tuesday. It comes 4 hours a week and if I drop Bible & War History I will have 22 hours a week. However I think I can handle it alright.

Love
ADLAI.

To Mrs. Lewis G. Stevenson

Sunday [February 10, 1918]

Dearest Mum:

I certainly have been busy this week. Besides my lessons which are taking quite a little time and my News work and an occasional few minutes devoted to the persual of literature, I have had all the Dramatic Club publicity to handle and believe me it was some job. Yesterday the Dramatic Club shoved another sweet job off on me, namely to have charge of decerating the Dramatic Club room for the dance. I also have been pretty busy writing to different firms about pins for the fifth form.

I have engaged a room for you. It isen't much good however, it is the best I can do and I guess you will be able to live in it for a couple of days. We had a very interesting lecture last night by Prof. Clark [25] of Yale on the Italian part in the war. He had the most beautiful moving pictures I have ever seen. They showed fighting in the Tyrol alps and were really very beautiful. Tomorrow the Hockey team plays Kent and a very exciting game is expected. Kent has won every game thus far this season. I hea[r]d from Dave [Merwin] the other day and he is coming down to the festivities. An Alumni from Harvard has been down here this week and he says Dave has the Lampoon cinched. We certainly hope he makes it. I heard from Le Roy Whitmore [26] this morning

---

24 Dr. Albert Parker Fitch. *Choate News*, February 2, 1918, wrote: "one of best sermons ever heard."
25 Charles Upton Clark, who lectured on "Italy in the War."
26 A friend from Bloomington.

and he says to tell Buff that "he is very glad to hear that she is doing well." He says he may enlist in the Navy.

Tell father I was mighty glad to get his birthday letter and that he is a brick to give me the watch. Tell him not to worry about my health etc.

Love to all
AD.

To Mrs. Lewis G. Stevenson

Sunday [March 3, 1918]

Dearest Mum:

I spent yesterday afternoon down in New Haven. It certainly was a treat to get away from this place for a few hours. I had to go down and see the man who prints the News on business and took [Jim] Millholland and [Lewis] Morrow along with me. We went down right after school, got lunch in N.H. [New Haven] . . . and then I went and attended to my business. After that was finished, which was in about half an hour, we went up to the college and made a bunch of calls. Then came the principal feature of the afternoon, namely a regular dinner at the Taft grill. And believe me it certainly was good to have a variety in ones food.

"Nothing But The Truth" is going to be in New Haven next Sat. and a bunch of us are intending to take Mr. Temple. You see we'll only have to chip in about 50¢ apeice and he will take us down in his car. Pretty good scheme eh?

The spring vacation begins March 29th (I think I can get away by the 28) and lasts until the 9th I believe. Do you know where you will be? In Wash. or Hot Springs? It really makes no difference to me where you are. I might have to stay here untill the 30th however, I don't believe so.

Dean Brown [27] of Yale had the services today and was awfully good. The reason for the numerous mistakes in this letter is the presence of a great and boisterous mob of fellow convicts.

As usual I have nothing further to say that will interest you except that I am feeling unusually well and chiper. Tell father that as yet I have not had a quiet moment in which I might pen him an epistle. Tell Buff that numerous fellows have been asking about her, chiefly R. Stephenson and Henry Plate [28] (the fellow that played the fiddle).

Lots of love
AD.

[27] C. R. Brown, dean of the Divinity School, Yale University.
[28] Roger Stephenson, Choate 1920; Henry W. Plate, Choate 1918.

To Mrs. Lewis G. Stevenson

Friday evening [29]

Dearest Mum:

Your very encouraging and delightful letter of Wednesday night just received. It is a very great relief to know that my visit did your soul good. Certainly my ten days with you all this Spring were the happiest of my life and it is certainly a great gratification to think that you enjoyed them. I do wish I was still there with you but life cannot be all play and after all one should be able to enjoy school altho it is no eazy thing to do. It was most kind of you and father to let me have the Ford and I am sure it was a great saving for us all. I do hope and feel sure that you will improve steadily now and soon be able to go to Bloo[mington]. where I will meet you in a couple of months.[30]

AD

To Mrs. Lewis G. Stevenson

Monday evening [31]

Dearest Mum:

I had a very good intentions of writing you a nice long letter today but put it off until it was too late. The weather today and yesterday has been gorgeous. It really makes it almost impossible to study and stay indoors. I'm afraid I haven't yet recovered from my wonderful vacation. I do hope the weather there is as glorious as it is here and, if so, I'm sure you will soon be feeling fine. Only 9 more weeks of school and for old Bloomington. It will be great to go back there again and loaf around for awhile.

AD.

To Mrs. Lewis G. Stevenson

Sunday [April 21, 1918]

Dearest Mum:

This is a rotten day, but I suppose we should not kick about one bad day after the good weather we have had recently. The weather last week, except for one day, was very good and I played tennis most every afternoon. I am playing 5th man on the team and hope to raise

29 This postcard is postmarked April 12, 1918.
30 His mother was at Hot Springs, Virginia.
31 This postcard is postmarked April 16, 1918.

to fourth. Yesterday afternoon we opened our baseball season by a 15–0 victory over Canterbury school. From the looks of things we will probably have a corking good ball team this season. I am enclosing a schedule which may interest you. We also race Middlesex in crew next Saturday and I think John Keays [32] will be with them. We beat them last year and I certainly hope we do this.

Did I tell you about my experience on the way to the team from the Benedict? I don't remember wheather I did or not so I will tell you again to make sure. Father ordered the taxi at 7 to come immediately. I waited in great anxiety, after finishing my breakfast, until 7:40 when a Ford drew up. As you remember it was a very windy and rainy morning and the driver's hat blew off after we had gone a couple of blocks. After wasting some five minutes backing up for it we started out again and went for a couple of blocks when the dinged thing ran out of gasoline. It was then about 10 of 8 and after waiting of about 10 minutes waiting for the driver I got out and went to a nearby hotel to try and get another, but they said it was impossible and so I stood out in the middle of the street madly hailing every passing machine and finally [persuaded?] a good natured driver to take me down. Needless to say I did not have a lot of time to waste at the station. Jim [Mill-holland] and Lee [33] were on the train of course and Louie Morrow was also on. By the way I don't believe I told you about seeing a girl on the train that I knew. Well it was this way; a girl got on at Wilming-ton who some way or other looked very familiar but I couldn't place her and therefore didnot speak. However, after a few minutes she turned around and asked me if I wasen't Adlai Stevenson. I then realized that it was Eleanor Stuart, a girl I used to know in Blooming-ton. She is a Junior at Smith. Buff probably remembers her, she is Roland Graham's sister and had been visiting her older brother at Wilmington. We had a lot of fun talking about Bloomington etc. She hasn't been there for a couple of years and consequently was very anxious to hear all the news. . . .

If you notice any obvious incongruities in this epistle, attribute it to the howling mass of fellow prisoners that are infesting the room.

I have been working pretty hard since I got back and certainly hope I can pass off some of my exams. I certainly hope I can get into college next fall but really don't think I should try to do it if it will be necessary to work all summer.

Have you decided just what you are going to do this summer yet and when are you going home? Also please tell father to send me $50 to pay

[32] A student at Middlesex School.
[33] F. Lee Hardesty, Choate 1918.

for the Liberty Bond I bought last fall. I will pay him back or some of it back next summer when I receive the money I hope to make out of the "News."

Well I will write soon again and give you all the dope I have over looked. I am feeling fine and certainly hope you are improving.

Love to all
AD.

To Mrs. Lewis G. Stevenson

Friday [34]

Dearest Mum:

Your delightful letter of Thursday just arrived. Was very sorry to hear the weather had been bad and that Buff had a cold. The weather has been wonderful here the past week and I have played tennis every afternoon. I hope to get in the match with the Yale Freshmen Thursday. The tennis training table has started and I am sitting at it. We play Pawling in B.B. [baseball] tomorrow and row Middlesex in crew. The M. crew is coming tonight. I hear [John] Keays is off the crew on account of studies. Will write Sunday. love to all.

AD.

To Mrs. Lewis G. Stevenson

May 12, 1918

Dearest Mom:

I was extremely surprised and sorry to hear of Louis'es death.[35] I suppose I will get the particulars in the Pantagraph, however, if I don't I will write you and you can send them to me. It really does not seem possible that he has gone and I feel as though I should come home to the funeral, but then I don't suppose I could do much and it would break into my work. What will his wife do? I suppose it was quite a shock for Uncle Bert [Louis's father] and the whole family in fact. However, it is a great consolation to know that he died in the service and after all some have got to loose their lives over here as well as over there; their share of glory may not appear as great at first but eventually their services will be recognized and their memories will receive the admiration and respect of all that knew them.

I think that this is only a forerunner of what we are all going to

[34] This postcard is postmarked April 27, 1918.
[35] Louis E. Davis, son of Mr. and Mrs. H. O. Davis, was killed in an airplane accident in Texas while he was in pilot training for World War I.

suffer before the war is over. It is the first time that the seriousness of the situation has struck home so closely and seems unfair that we have to loose one so dear to us but after all it may prove a blessing in disguise and it will add another cog to the wheel which is going to be our country's only salvation.

Please don't worry about his death as he generously sacrificed his life for a cause that should inspire in us all the spirit of sacrifice which alone can unite us in a general endeavour to maintain our countrys standards, which have so many times in the past proved so high. And then we may all rest satisfied and comfortable in the knowledge that his work on this world is completed, and that God has seen fit to take him from our midst and give him everlasting peace.

We have lost seven of our alumni now and have 136 in service, which I think is a very good showing. In fact it is one of the best prep school records in the country when the number of alumni that the various schools have is considered.

The past week has been a very happy one for me. As one of our alumni has recently received the Croix de Guerre and two others received commissions we decided that it was high time we had a vacation. Consequently, last Tuesday morning, before school we all gathered on the front steps and after a very great deal of cheering and marching around in mob form, we managed to convince [Mr. St.] John that a holiday was appropriate. He finally acquies[c]ed. Mr. Temple asked Morrow, Millholland, Olmstead [36] and I if we would like to go riding with him in his machine. Needless to say we accepted. It was a wonderful day and he took us all the way up to Saybrook on the sound. We had lunch there at "Ye Olde Saybrooke Inn" and came back by way of New Haven. It was a glorious day and one long to be remembered. But the crowning feature of the week is that I have made my debut on the Choate tennis team. I played doubles in the match with Bridgeport High Wednesday. Much to my disgust we lost our match but evidently the coach thought I had a little ability as he coached me personally one whole afternoon and the next day told me to dress for the match with New Haven High. Much to my surprise he had me play in both the singles and doubles. In my first singles set my opponent beat me 6–1 but then I got started and took the next two sets 6–3, 6–4 much to the surprise of the gallery. The coach was really quite overjoyed and fell all over my neck. However, the day was not destined to be all victory for me as I lost my doubles match. If I can keep playing the way I am now I think I can hold fourth place on the team and will get on the Pomfret and Taft trips. I am going to do my best anyway. . . .

[36] Chauncey L. Olmstead, Choate 1918.

Yesterday the baseball team got beat up at Pomfret 3–2 in a 12 inning game. From what the fellows said that went up there I guess it was quite a game. After dinner we had movies, Douglas Fairbanks in the Man from Painted Past. Needless to say it was awfully good. After the movies the Fifth and Sixth forms met in the Grill Room for the long expected "feed" which your little sonny staged. From various remarks that Sixth formers said to me and to others I guess it was quite a success.

Once more I beg you not to grieve over Louis'es death. In war one must not grieve but rejoice that a man can give his life for such a noble cause and pray for a speedy termination of the war.

Please add my sympathies to ours and if its possible for me to do anything for Uncle Bert or anyone, let me know.

Love to all
ADLAI

P.S. I heard from Bruce [37] the other day and she asked me to come down to her commencement on June 3rd, which of course I can't do. I also got a letter from Miriam [Buckley] [38] asking me to come down to Brynn Mawr for some entertainment they had last night. Tell father that it will be impossible for me to go up to Rosemary to see Dougie Hay as I am dreadfully busy now. I was elected Editor-in-Chief of the News for next year today.[39]

I have been thinking the matter of college over and have decided that the thing to do is get in if possible. One of the best fellows that is going down there from here next fall has asked me to room with him. He is Elridge [Eldredge] Snyder from Summit, N.J. and a corking fellow. We will talk about my going in more fully when I get home.

Please write often and I will whenever I have time.

AD.

To Mrs. Lewis G. Stevenson

Tuesday night [May 21, 1918]

Dearest Mum:

I really could not find a minute in which to write you Sunday. You see I am getting out my first issue of the News as Editor-in-Chief this

---

37 Ellen Bruce Lee, a friend from Washington, D.C.

38 A friend studying at Bryn Mawr.

39 He not only became editor in chief of the *Choate News* that spring, but he was elected vice president of the senior class (Sixth Form), captain of the tennis team, secretary of the Athletic Association, and president of St. Andrews for the next year. "Quite an accomplishment after just two years at Choate!" Mrs. B. F. Sylvester, Jr., archivist at Choate, wrote to the headmaster, Seymour St. John, November 16, 1966.

week and as it is going to be an exceptionally good one, I have been unusually busy and will be all week.

Last Saturday was about the most victorious day we ever had around here. The crew beat the 2nd Yale Freshmen by a length and a half, the ball team beat Trinity 13–0, the second team beat Wallingford High and above all Lewis Morrow won the Yale Interscholastic tennis title and Millholland won the consolation prize. It is really quite a feather in the School's cap to win that and needless to say we are very proud of it and especially of Lewis. Of course we had a big celebration in the evening and managed to keep the town awake most of the night. Yesterday afternoon we (the tennis team) played Hopkins School from New Haven and beat them 6–0. I played 3rd man and won both my singles and doubles. I guess my place on the tennis team is assured now.

Did I tell you that I am in a special Spanish class with one other fellow and that the master says we may be able to take the two year Spanish exam next month. I have barely a fighting chance of passing it but I think its worth trying. Things are going on about the same as usual except that we are beginning to do a little more work, if that is possible, in preparation for the Exams next month.

I was very much interested and grieved at the account of Louis's death. He certainly died like a soldier and I shall always be proud of his remembrance.

Love to all
AD.

To Mrs. Lewis G. Stevenson

Sunday night [May 26, 1918]

Dearest Mum:

Yesterday afternoon the baseball team went up to Simsbury to play Wes[t]minister. About half the school went up to see the game which we won 6–0. I didnot go as we played New Briten [New Britain High School] in tennis. I am playing regular third man on the team now. Pretty good rise from 6th at the begining of the season n'est pas? We played Loomis Wednesday and beat them 4–2. I played third and beat my man 6–1, 6–3, much to the elation of the coach. Tomorrow we go up to Taft for the big match of the season. We are going up in machines and I am contemplating a most enjoyable day. I'm afraid we'll get beat but we will give them a good hard fight anyway. The team plays Kent tomorrow. This is one of, in fact the biggest game of the season, and I certainly hope we can beat them. They are coming tonight in order to rest up for the game.

I had to work pretty hard last week getting out my first News as

Editor-in-Chief. However my efforts have been well rewarded because the general opinion is that it is about the best issue of the season. When you receive it look at the picture on the right side of the front page and see if it resembles anyone you ever saw befor[e]. Also read the article about the 1918 board as [I] wrote most of it. Also read the editorial which is another product of my pen.[40] Furthermore notice my name in the headlines on the Loomis Tennis match.

Last night we had a bonfire all built for the celebration for the Westminster victory but of course it had to rain and crab the act. By way of entertainment last night we had the Tuskeegee singers and as usual they were very good. I got room grades this week regardless of all I had to do. I am think seriously of going to Blairstown after college exams. That is the prep. schools religious conference and an awfully good thing. I will write you more fully about it later.

AD

To Mrs. Lewis G. Stevenson

Saturday night [June 1, 1918]

Dearest Mum:

Well the festivities are over and we have once more settled down to work. We did not go up to Taft Monday as it was raining most of the day. We beat Kent 4–3 in one of the best and closest games I have ever seen. We had a big bonfire and pajama parade in the evening, livened with many firecrackers. We (the tennis team) left Wednesday at about eleven o'clock in two machines for Taft. . . . It was an awfully good ride and we had lots of fun. The Taft manager met us and showed us all around until time for lunch. Personally I was not at all impressed with Taft and the fellows and am thoroughly convinced that I made no mistake in not going there. We started playing about 2:30. I played 3rd man for us and played their captain. He beat me 7–5, 6–1. I was rotten and should have beaten him but was a little nervous I guess. I also lost my doubles 6–3, 6–4. None of us were playing well and they won all the matches. Coming back we stopped in Waterbury and got some fruit to eat on the way. We got back about 7, in time to get all dolled up for the Alumni Banquet. Needless to say there was much shaking of hands with the old fellows and shooting the bull. The Alumni banquet was a lot of fun. All the old masters made speeches

[40] Articles and editorials in the *Choate News* were unsigned at this time. Unfortunately the collection of the *Choate News* at the Choate School is incomplete. This particular issue is missing. The school has the issue of May 11, 1918, the issue just before this one.

and we had some real food. The dining room was decorated with allied flags etc. and everything was very patriotic.

To Mrs. Lewis G. Stevenson

Thursday after [41]

Dearest Mum:

I am still finding it difficult to find time to write you a nice long letter as things a[re] pretty lively during exam period. I have some good news for you, the best yet, *I* think. I was elected president of St. Andrews [42] for next year providing I come back. You did not know your son was a young evangelist, did you? The Blairstown conference that I told you about is very interesting and quite a bunch of fellows are going.

Love,

AD

Sunday, June 10 [1918]

Well now that I have a few minutes I will continue this letter that I started about 2 weeks ago. I won't go to the trouble to explain the festivities and commencement exercises, you can read about them in the News. The dance was the best I have ever seen here and I had by far the best time I ever had. Last Monday we went up to Pomfret. Mr. Temple took some of us in his car. It is about 80 miles up there and we had a great time. Frankly, I liked Pomfret very much; the fellows were mighty nice to us and showed us all over the place. It is certainly a nice school and, in my opinion, has it all over Taft. We won the match and started back about 5:30. We stopped in Hartford and had a big blowout at the Bond as an end to the season. Friday night we had the tennis banquet; a mighty good one too. I was elected captain for next year.

Last night there was an Athletic Association meeting to elect officers for next year. The A.A. is the governing body of all the School's athletic questions and the officers are the big athletes of the School. However, by some freak that I can't understand I was elected Secretary. It strikes me as very amusing when the other two office[r]s are the two bigest athlet[e]s in School. I was also elected vice-president of the Sixth form, which is the most important of them all. If I come back next year it looks as though I'd be a pretty big duke.

Final exams ended Friday I passed all my exams for the first time. I

[41] Postmarked June 7, 1918.
[42] The school's religious society for all denominations.

[53]

got the second highest mark in Trig: 88% and Mr. [Raymond R.] Mc-Ormand wrote *Splendid* on my book. I got 82 in Spanish, did I tell you that I am going to take the 2 year Spanish exam. I don't believe I've a prayer of passing it but I'll do my durndest. My other marks were 78 in French, 74 in Algebra and 69 in Latin. I certainly hope I can pass all my college exams, if I do I'll go to college next fall.

I was very much interested to hear of Johnny's and Lu's [43] wed-[d]ing; I had rather expected it some time soon. I certainly wish I was with you all now, sitting on the balcony porch looking out across the pasture & Country Club. Doubtless things are very beautiful there now, they are here too. I took a little walk into the woods with my Spanish master [44] yesterday and enjoyed it immensely. Well it won't be long now till I get there and we'll take some great old rides out into the country.

I havent had an opportunity to tell you about the Blairstown conference. It is a religeous conference held by the prep. schools each year at Blair Academy, Blairstown, N.J. Each school sends a delegation to talk over prep. school government. The greatest speakers in the country . . . are there. The mornings are given up to bible clases and lectures which are invariably most interesting and instructive. The afternoons are entirely devoted to sports. There's an inter school track meet, tennis tournament, base ball games etc. In the evening after dinner the various delegations gather on the campus and sing their songs, give their cheers to other schools etc. I have been requested to go very earnestly and think I will enjoy it very much. We are going to have a good delegation this year and should show up well in the athletics etc. It lasts from the end of college exam period, June 22nd to June 29th, and then I'll come right home.

Well I've run out of dope and will have to stop. I do hope you all are feeling well and are enjoying life in general.

Love to all

AD.

P.S. I got a letter last week from Uncle Martin Hardin [45] saying he had seen St. Andrews card etc. It was very nice. Tell father that the 10 iron men [dollars] came in most conveniently as financially I was beginning to totter.

AD.

[43] Mr. and Mrs. John Brokaw of Bloomington, Illinois.
[44] Norman L. Willey.
[45] The Reverend Martin D. Hardin was a Presbyterian clergyman. He conducted the funeral services when Lewis G. Stevenson died in 1929.

Adlai spent the summer of 1918 with his family. If he could pass the Navy physical examination and the college entrance examinations, he would enlist in the U.S. Navy as an apprentice seaman stationed at Princeton University. He returned late in August to the Choate School to study for these examinations.

To Mrs. Lewis G. Stevenson

Friday, August 31, 1918

Dearest Mum:

I received your most welcome letter of Tuesday today. Was overjoyed to hear that you were feeling so much better. You must keep on feeling good now and don't overdo. Tell Pa he had better get in good condition while he can because I'm seriously contemplating taking a couple of falls out of him the next time we meet. Alas! You are all wrong about my making such great progress. I am making pretty good progress but the Virgil is a huge task for 3 weeks and I am afraid I haven't a prayer of passing it. Don't worry I won't be through befor[e] time for exams.

Love to all,
Ad.

To Mrs. Lewis G. Stevenson

Sunday [46]

Dearest Mum:

Was very glad to hear from your letter of Wed. that you had reached Chi[cago]. alright and were feeling well. Don't overdo. I think they are going to have us live in barracks at P[rinceton]. and if so I will send my pictures etc. home. Don't send me anything until I let you you know. . . . We start a week from tomorrow. I will leave here next Sunday morning with [Eldredge] Snyder. He has invited me to stay with him until College opens. Please don't worry so much about my going into the service. I am awfully anxious and enter automatically at entering Princeton. I think I will take the artillery course but haven't decided. Feeling fine.

Love,
Ad.

[46] Postmarked September 9, 1918.

To Mrs. Lewis G. Stevenson

Tuesday, 9:30 P.M. [early September, 1918]

Dearest Mum:

I think I shall take a few minutes off from my never finished studies to write you, although I have not had the inestimable pleasure of a letter from you all for some time. Howeve[r], I trust you are very busy and consequently have not had time to write.

I am each day gaining in erudition and sincerely believe that you will not recognize me in my present intellectual disguise when next we meet. I really am working pretty hard this week, in fact everyone is, as the exams come next week. I am going to leave here Sunday morning and go directly to P[rinceton]. We have engaged a room at the Nassau Inn for the period of exams and so do not have to worry about accomodations. I think, if the Gods are with me, that I may pass my exams. The Virgil is, I find, an enormous task for so short a time but, as I said before, if the Gods are with me, very close by, I may pass. The gov[ernment]., as yet, has apparently not completed its arrangements for college students but there is nothing to do and so I shall go on until I get some definate information. I think I will pack the stuff I left here last Spring in two different boxes. One that I may want and one that I probably will not want. I shall leave them here and request the office to send them when I find it advisable. In the meantime I will drift around with my trunk and suitcase. I shall probably spend the time between the exams and opening of college with [Eldredge] Snyder, providing there is any time to spend.

I registered Saturday and sent my card to the board there, that Fred wrote me about.[47] I expect my certificate tomorrow or the next day. Am feeling very well and taking good care of myself. I have been trying to collect my "news" money here and have had fare success. If everything turns out right I ought to make altogether over $550 of which I get about 26% or about $130. Not so bad, eh? Don't overdo and take good care of yourself for, in spite of the war, we'll have a great old time this winter. Tell Buff to be VERY careful of the car and that I expect to see it in as good condition as when I left. Also thank father for the $10 he sent me. It came in handy to pay my board bill for that week. Well I must close and seek a few hours repose.

Love
Ad.

[47] He registered with the Selective Service Board in Bloomington. Fred Robinson was Lewis Stevenson's secretary.

Part Three

Princeton
1918–1922

When Adlai E. Stevenson entered Princeton University in the autumn of 1918 his freshman class numbered a little over five hundred students. During the next four years although he never became a scholar he absorbed much from lectures and books. There was about him "nothing of the 'yokel' or 'hayseed' then ridiculed by city people," Herbert J. Muller observed. "At the same time he was free from snobbishness, for he had no reason to feel acutely class-conscious or in the least uneasy about his social status." [1]

Stuart Gerry Brown remarked that during the revival of interest in the career of F. Scott Fitzgerald in the 1950's, he and Adlai E. Stevenson were frequently linked in discussion of Stevenson's college days. Stevenson led an active, happy social life at Princeton. He shared the gaiety of the early twenties, he liked to write, and he loved Princeton "with a passion. But the parallel ends there," Brown wrote. "Stevenson met Fitzgerald only casually and never moved in the older man's circle. Nor was he given to the kind of frenetic search for values and meaning in life which ended, for Fitzgerald, in tragic futility. Stevenson's liberal religious outlook, his habit of disciplining himself to moderation, and his ideals of progress for mankind and the social obligation of the individual were well-formed. The cynicism of the 'Lost Generation' rubbed against him but did not rub off on him." [2]

Adlai E. Stevenson's classmate William E. Stevenson recalled that during their Princeton days, "Adlai was known for his good nature. His sense of humor and friendly interest in people made him a delightful companion. . . . In later years I was surprised that his wit was criticized by political opponents, because his humor was in no

[1] *Adlai Stevenson: A Study in Values* (New York: Harper & Row, 1967), p. 23.
[2] *Adlai E. Stevenson: A Short Biography, The Conscience of the Country* (Woodbury, N.Y.: Barron's Woodbury Press, 1965), pp. 19–20. Fitzgerald was in the Class of 1917 and thus was not in college when Stevenson was at Princeton.

way an affectation but rather an inherent part of his very nature." [3]

Another classmate, T. S. Matthews, wrote: "He was a slight, dark, nervously lively boy with a quick, lemony laugh; his ready mockery had a tentative air and was never wounding because it somehow included himself." Matthews also observed that while at Princeton Adlai was shy and apprehensive, he "kept his eyes about him" and "learned so much so fast." [4]

Adlai's three and a half years of working for the Daily Princetonian *gave him, perhaps, the most solid satisfaction of his undergraduate years. News stories and editorials were unsigned, however, and there is no way to determine those that he wrote. In addition to the newspaper, he enjoyed his classmates, sports, and girls. Moreover, he — not his mother — was "running the show." At Princeton, he recollected years later, he had better things to do than become a scholar.*

"I didn't like mathematics or the physical sciences," he wrote on January 28, 1957, to his biographer, Kenneth S. Davis. "But I enjoyed geology so much — and not because it was easy! — that I well remember regretting that I had not had more of the natural sciences. But certainly my tastes were largely humanist and I loved the history and English and literature courses — all history and all literature."

His academic record is given on the pages following.

[3] "Two Stevensons of Princeton" in *As We Knew Adlai: The Stevenson Story by Twenty-two Friends,* edited and with preface by Edward P. Doyle, foreword by Adlai E. Stevenson III (New York: Harper & Row, 1966), pp. 18–19.

[4] "Portrait, with Scratches: Adlai Stevenson," *Vogue,* May, 1966, p. 192. Years later Matthews visited Governor Stevenson in Springfield, Illinois, and afterward wrote: "What I could hardly fail to notice . . . was the rate and extent of his development since our college days; in comparison the majority of our classmates seemed to have stood still." Letter to Walter Johnson, November 8, 1966.

	NO.	HRS WK		
FIRST YEAR	WKS	Lab	Rec	GROUP *

First Term   Dec. 1918

† Advanced French
† Spanish 1
† Chemistry 1
† American History
† Naval Discip. & Adminis.

Second Term   March 1919

Latin	12		3	4
Mathematics I (Elements of				
Pl. & Sph. Trig.)	12		3	4
English	12		2	4
French 106	12		3	4
Chemistry I	12	3	3	5
Physical Education	12		3	p

Average for term   4.27
Group for term   5

Third Term   June 1919

Latin	12		3	4
Mathematics I (Elements of				
Pl. & Sph. Trig.)	12		3	5
English 102	12		2	3
French, Adv.	12		3	5
Chemistry I	12	3	3	5
Physical Education	12		3	f sub p

Average for term   4.53
Average for year   4.40
Group for year   5

* Explanation of Plan of Grouping:
  1 = Highest standing   4 = Low standing   7 = Bad failure
  2 = High standing   5 = Passing
  3 = Fair standing   6 = Failure
† Course being pursued while enrolled in Naval Unit.

SECOND YEAR	NO. WKS	HRS WK Lab	HRS WK Rec	GROUP *
First Term Feb. 1920				
Philosophy 201	18		3	3
Geology 201	18		3	3
History 201	18		3	3
French 201	18		3	5
English 201	18		3	3
Average for term 3.40				
Group for term 4				
Second Term June 1920				
Philosophy 202	18		3	4
Geology 202	18		3	3
History 202	18		3	5
French 202	18		3	5
English 202	18		3	3
Average for term 4.00				
Average for year 3.70				
Group for year 4				

THIRD YEAR	NO. WKS	HRS WK Lab	HRS WK Rec	GROUP *
First Term Feb. 1921				
History 301	18		3	4
Politics 305	18		3	2
Economics 301	18		3	2
English 301	18		3	2
Astronomy 301	18		3	4
Average for term 2.80				
Group for term 3				
Second Term June 1921				
History 302	18		3	4
Politics 306	18		3	4
Ancient Oriental Lit. 330	18		3	3
Economics 302	18		3	3
English 302	18		3	2
Average for term 3.20				
Average for year 3.00				
Group for year 3				

* Explanation of Plan of Grouping:
1 = Highest standing   4 = Low standing   7 = Bad failure
2 = High standing   5 = Passing
3 = Fair standing   6 = Failure

FOURTH YEAR	NO. WKS	HRS WK		GROUP *
		Lab	Rec	
First Term Feb. 1922				
Geology 305	18		3	2
History 409	18		3	2
English 401	18		3	3
Politics 307	18		3	4
Economics 403	18		3	3
Average for term 2.80				
Group for term 3				
Second Term June 1922				
Geology 306	18		3	3
History 410	18		3	2
English 412	18		3	2
History 310	18		3	3
Politics 308	18		3	3
Average for term 2.60				
Average for year 2.70				
Group for year 3				

* Explanation of Plan of Grouping:
  1 = Highest standing   4 = Low standing   7 = Bad failure
  2 = High standing   5 = Passing
  3 = Fair standing   6 = Failure

When Adlai E. Stevenson addressed the senior class banquet at Princeton University, March 22, 1954, he reminded the students:

" 'University' is a proud, a noble and ancient word. Around it clus-
ter all of the values and the traditions which civilized people have
for centuries prized more highly. The idea which underlies this
university — any university — is greater than any of its physical
manifestations; its classrooms, its laboratories, its clubs, its athletic
plant, even the particular groups of faculty and students who make
up its human element as of any given time. What is this idea? It is
that the highest condition of man in this mysterious universe is the
freedom of the spirit. And it is only truth that can set the spirit free.

The function of a university is, then, the search for truth and its
communication to succeeding generations. Only as that function is
performed steadfastly, conscientiously, and without interference,
does the university realize its underlying purpose. Only so does the
university keep faith with the great humanist tradition of which it
is a part. Only so does it merit the honorable name that it bears.

[63]

When you depart, think occasionally upon your university's inherent ideas and purposes, as its outward trappings recede. Don't forget that Princeton is a university, as well as *your* university; and that it has obligations to the whole of mankind not just to you — obligations which it can neither ignore nor shirk, and which cannot, consistently with its honorable name and its place in the community of scholarship, be sacrificed to passing passions and prejudices.

The right to the serene pursuit of truth did not descend like manna from heaven; it was won by hard fighting, and the fight goes on and on to the end of time — even as the struggle between good and evil. In this continuing battle for freedom, Princeton and her sister universities are at the farthest front, and so should you be who are Princeton's children. As the archive of the Western mind, as the keeper of Western culture, the university has an obligation to transmit from one generation to the next the heritage of freedom — for freedom is the foundation of Western culture. As graduates of this university, as individuals who have made in it an investment of the golden, irretrievable years of your lives, you have an obligation to oppose the efforts of anyone, for whatever reason or in the service of whatever interest, to divert Princeton or any sister institution from her classic objective. If you are to be true to your democratic traditions and realize your own best selves you cannot, I suggest, do less.

And I hope you will carry away with you some of the wise serenity of the timeless courage, the unhurried objectivity which is the atmosphere of Princeton and which represents the collective imprint of its founders, students, and teachers who have gone before you.[5]

The handwritten letters that are included in Part Three, except for those identified as being deposited elsewhere, are in the Elizabeth Stevenson Ives collection at the Illinois State Historical Library. Adlai E. Stevenson's original spellings of certain words are presented as he wrote them — no "sic" has been added. We included all the letters we could locate for these years.

Sometimes he dated his letters or the postmarked envelopes were saved. When he just wrote the day of the week on the letter and the envelope was not kept, we have tried to ascertain the date through internal evidence in the letter. In such cases, we have placed the date within brackets. William M. Leary, Jr., of The Papers of Woodrow Wilson, kindly checked the Daily Princetonian and other sources to locate the dates of many of the letters. In addition, Stevenson's classmate Edmund S. De Long helped identify names and explained references that were unclear.

[5] Published in Adlai E. Stevenson, *What I Think* (New York: Harper, 1956), p. 179–180.

To Mrs. Lewis G. Stevenson

September 23, 1918
Monday night

Dearest Mum:

This has been a very successful day. In the first place I was on the list of those admitted to the Univ. Evidently I passed my exams or some of them this fall. I then enrolled in the Univ. and went to take my medical exam for the Navy. They had regular Gov. Naval doctors and I had to fill out the regular N.R.F. enlistment blank. I passed the medical exam alright much to my surprise. It was a pretty stiff exam and a lot failed, chiefly because of eyes. My chest expansion was 4″ and I weigh 131 stripped. Height 5′9″. Father is already a good friend of the Lieut. Commander here and the latter has asked father to go and see the Gov. of N.J. for him tomorrow to arrange about the draft transfers to the fellows that enroll here.[6]

Love,
AD.

To Mrs. Lewis G. Stevenson

Friday, September 27, 1918

Dearest Mother,

As you perceive I am writing my first letter on Princeton stationery. I can't say that the sensation is particularly unique, but it certainly is a satisfaction to know that I am a regularly admitted student and consequently a Princeton man.[7]

I have not written you for some time so I will endeavour to give you some idea of the many occurences of the past week. Monday the list of the students that had been accepted by regular admission, that is by examination, was posted on the Bulletin board and much to my surprise and satisfaction my name was on the list. After that I went to the Gym and was examined for the Navy. I was one of the first ones examined as they took the fellows from the West first. They didnot finish the examinations until yesterday so you can have some idea of the number of fellows that applied and the time it took to examine them. Thanks to your unceasing care I passed the physical exam pretty high. A good many failed, chiefly on account of eyes. It was very funny

[6] Lewis G. Stevenson, who was visiting Adlai at Princeton, was Chief Special Investigator of the U.S. Navy.
[7] Some of those who were in military training at Princeton were not students in the university. They were not, therefore, members of the Class of 1922.

to see some of the fellows that were color blind. That was one of the most important parts of the exam.

Following this, about which I assure [you?] I was very nervous at first. I had a room assigned to me: 64 Little Hall. It is, I think, a fairly nice room. There is a large study and two small adjoining rooms. There are supposed to be four fellows in each double room, however, only one of my roommates has arrived yet. He is a very nice fellow named [James Hendrick] Terry from New York and he went to Exeter. Father has talked to him and likes him very much. He knows Helen Clark and the Thayers, and I think I'll like him alright. I don't know who else will be assigned to this room with us.[8] I forgot to tell you that [Eldredge] Snyder decided to join the army and consequently we cannot room together. Practically all rooming arrangements have been cancelled anyway. If nobody else is assigned to the room I think I'll try to get [Lewis] Morrow in with us as he is in my company.

Tuesday we didnot do much except get our room in order or partial order. We are only allowed a bureau, desk, bed and chair and no room decorations.

Wednesday we drilled and got our room furniture and signed a lot of documents, etc. Thursday we went thru the regular enlistment process and had our finger prints etc. taken. We are sworn in on October 1st. That was Wednesday I mean. Yesterday we drilled most all day and started to get our courses arranged in the afternoon. I think my courses will be something like this: Naval instruction, advanced French, Law, history and chemestry. I'll probably have to work pretty hard but I won't be the only one.

We get up at 5.55, have breakfast at 6.15, lunch at 12.15 and supper at 6.15. We have to march to and from all meals in fact will have to march to classes when they get started next week. This is certainly a great life but it will do me a lot of good. I'll probably stay here all year and then if I'm lucky I'll get sent to an officers material school, next summer. It's pretty hard to get an Ensign's commission I find.

John Harlan is Lieut. Commander.[9] I have not spoken to him yet but father did and I will soon. Dave Grey is here in the Naval unit. All the fellows in the naval unit live in the same dormitory. There are quite a few fellows around here that I have seen or met before. Bill

[8] He ended up with four roommates — James Hendrick Terry of New York, William E. Hale of California, Ralph Goodwin, whom he had met at the HF Bar Ranch in Wyoming in the summer of 1917, and Lewis B. (Louie) Morrow of Memphis, Tennessee, and Charlevoix, Michigan. Helen Clark was the daughter of Edward H. Clark, a close friend of Lewis Stevenson. Lewis Stevenson first met Mr. and Mrs. Benjamin B. Thayer in California and they became lifelong friends.

[9] John Marshall Harlan was a member of the Class of 1920. After graduation he went to Oxford University as a Rhodes scholar. He became a successful lawyer and in the 1950's was appointed an associate justice of the Supreme Court.

McIlvaine [from Chicago] and Louie [Morrow] are in here now raving about Charlevoix [Michigan] and filling the room with smoke. I like Bill very much. Well I'll write again soon as the real work does not start until Monday, although I think I've been working pretty hard already.

Love,
AD.

To Clara Louise Calhoun [10]

September 28, 1918

Dear Miss Calhoun:

Will you please have any mail addressed to me, or to the Choate News, forwarded to me at 64 Little Hall, Princeton, N.J.

I have enrolled in Naval Training Unit that the Navy Department has organized here and, thus far, like it very much, although we have to work rather hard, in fact, very hard I think.

I suppose that by this time the fellows have all come back and school is getting started. I regret very much not being able to come back this fall but hope to get down there sometime soon. We are all awfully anxious to see everyone again and are planning, providing we can get leave, to come down some week-end to a football game.

Kindly remember me to Mr. St. John and Mr. Temple.

Very sincerely
ADLAI E. STEVENSON

To Mrs. Lewis G. Stevenson

Sunday, September 29, 1918

Dearest Mum:

A few days have elapsed since I wrote you last in which time we have done a good deal of drilling and walking about, but have had no classes yet. They start tomorrow. I don't know definately just what my course will be yet but *do* know that they, combined with drill, will give me plenty to do. Don't worry about my loafing too much.

[James Hendrick] Terry has gone to the infirmary with a bad cold. There are several cases of influenza in the Army here and a few in the Navy, however, I don't think Terry has it. I was very fortunate in being able to get Ralph Goodwin and Louis Morrow in our room. They are going to move up here tomorrow.

John Harlan, whom you remember I told you was in charge of

[10] Secretary to the headmaster of the Choate School. This handwritten letter is in the archives of the Choate School.

the battalion here, came to see me this afternoon. Needless to say I felt very much honored. He is certainly a fine fellow and I like him very much. He is in Naval aviation and says he will probably get sent to Boston Tech. in a couple of weeks. I wish he was going to stay here. You can't get in Naval aviation until you are 19 and 6 months so I guess I'll go out for the line, although I am awfully anxious to get into aviation. The Navy has without a doubt got it all over the Army here.

We marched to Chapel this morning and heard President [John Grier] Hibben speak. I don't think he is an especially forceful speaker but his ideas etc. are fine. Harlan inquired very particularly for you and Buff. When you were coming etc.

Altogether I like everything around here very much but fear that I will soon have very little time to enjoy myself.

Love
Ad.

To Mrs. Lewis G. Stevenson

Friday night [October 18, 1918]

Dearest Mum:

I am beginning to worry why my induction papers don't come from the draft board there. You see when we signed our induction papers here they were sent to our local boards and they (the boards) were supposed to return our releases (from draft) immediately. Mine has not come yet and if it does not get here by Monday I might not get in. I telegraphed father tonight. Things go on the same as usual. The informal football team plays the paymaster's team tomorrow in the Stadium. It will be the first game that I have witnessed in the Stadium. I am certainly glad I came in on exams and got in this fall. It makes a lot of difference when you are a regularly admitted candidate. I am beginning to work a little harder now. Coat came today.

Ad.

To Mrs. Lewis G. Stevenson

Tuesday evening [October 22, 1918]

Dearest Mum:

Well I have taken the oath of allegiance for 4 years service anywhere in the world and am now a real "gob" in the U.S. Navy. Believe me I am certainly one hot looking little "Jack" and you will just about split when you see me. I have bought a good uniform to wear on liberty. Most all the fellows got one as the gov. stuff is not very good. It cost $35.00. Please let me know just how Dave [Merwin] got into Marine Aviation. I have been thinking of that myself but didnot know you could get in under 20. Let me know just how he worked it. Working hard.

Love,
AD.

P.S. Papers arrived O.K.

To Mrs. Lewis G. Stevenson

Sunday, October 27, 1918

Dearest Mum:

Yesterday was quite a gala day here for the freshmen. But before explaining it all you must remember that all the fellows who are here in the freshman class are not freshmen, but only those that entered by examinations, as I did. In other words all the fellows that came in on certificate etc. to join the military organizations are not ranked as Princeton men and are not included in the class of 1922. I certainly am glad that I came in by exams and am a real Princeton man. Although it is very difficult to maintain all the old college customs etc. the difference between the regular Princeton men and the others is very obvious. For instance whenever "Old Nassau" or any of the P[rinceton]. songs are sung the non-regular men are not allowed to sing and have to stand at attention.

Well to go on with the events of Saturday. At 3:00 all the regular freshmen assembled in front of Witherspoon hall for the annual freshman P-rade. We P-raded around the campus singing Princeton songs and cheers led by John Harlan, who by the way, is the high duke here and a wonderful fellow. We then went to the steps of Whig Hall for the freshman picture. The fellows in the Navy Unit formed a huge "P" on the steps and the Army and non-military fellows filled in. I havenot seen the picture yet of course but I think it ought to be very good. When this was over and it took a long time to get it done we did some more P-rading and went to the big assembly room in McCosh hall to elect officers for the 1st term.

The election of officers was a matter of great interest to me. It is all done by the various big prep schools. Each one nominates a fellow for certain of the offices, and some of the schools like Hill have a man up for all 3 offices, and the school with the most representatives or the one that can induce the most "non-prep," (fellows that didnot go to some big prep school and don't know who to vote for), fellows to vote for their man wins. It is all graft but very interesting. Of course after the first term when the fellows get to know each other they don't vote that way but for the best man. I voted for Hill's man for Pres. but he was not elected. [Everett] Case from Hotchkiss got it. The fresh. class is about ¼ Hotchkiss fellows. A fellow named [Kenneth] Drummond from St. Pauls got V-Pres. And then when it came to electing a Sec.-Tres. much to my surprise and inquietude, I was nominated and then, with the other 5 or 6 nominees, had to get up and stand befor[e] the whole assembly and then walk into an adjoining room during the balloting. Of course I felt like a fool coming from such a small prep school and knowing so few fellows. However, I afterwards learned that I got a good many more votes than I had expected. A Hill fellow named [Philip] Strong was elected and then we went out and did some more P-rading and cheering etc.

After mess, we had a big smoker to which a bunch of Army fellows were invited. The various musical organizations put on some very good musical numbers and then each company put on a stunt. It was a lot of fun and lasted until about 10 o'clock. John Harlan was in charge of it all and certainly is wonderful at putting thru anything he undertakes.

Altogether it was a very pleasant day. At the other smoker we had, Admiral Goodrich told us a lot of yarns but unfortunately he was not well last night and could [not] come to the smoker.[11] I think I told you before that he is one of the ranking officers in point of length of service in the country and needless to say he is intensely interesting and has had innumerable exciting experiences in different parts of the world. I had a Spanish exam yesterday which I "killed." I am rather doubtful about my chances to pass the chemistry and History exams tomorrow. They will be awfully hard.

[11] Rear Admiral Caspar F. Goodrich was the commandant of the naval unit at Princeton. He had known Vice President Stevenson. Adlai's mother replied to this letter: "I hope I can show you the futility of getting the tobacco habit. . . . In the matter of health alone, it should never be considered by you, for your throat is your most delicate organ. . . . Then your eyes and above all your nerves . . . but they are, of course, secondary to the moral side. What is your desire after all in life? Wouldn't you have me believe that you had but one big object in life and that is to lead it as decently, uprightly as is possible, and be an example of every moral virtue to your fellow men? . . . Please remember you had two grandfathers who never found it necessary to smoke and they were held in the highest esteem. . . . I must leave you to decide all things for yourself but I shall pray that you be led into light in this matter. God help you." Elizabeth Stevenson Ives and Hildegarde Dolson, *My Brother Adlai* (New York: Morrow, 1956), pp. 123–124. Mrs. Ives wrote: "Manlike, Adlai seems to have blandly ignored the subject from then on, in his letters home."

How is father getting along?? He must have had a terrible time and I feel sure that the "flu" is not half as bad here as there. Have you decided when you are going to come? Let me know beforehand so I can notify the Peacock Inn.

I am going calling this afternoon on a Prof. Phillips [12] who is one of the big ducks in the faculty. Ralph [Goodwin] knows him.

Love to all
AD.

P.S. [James Hendrick] Terry's mother and father were here just now. They are very nice people

AD.

After the Armistice, November 11, 1918, the role of apprentice seaman no longer dominated the lives of college men. Navy discipline was relaxed and Adlai received his formal discharge in January, 1919.

To Mrs. Lewis G. Stevenson

Sunday [January 12, 1919]

Dearest Mum:

Friday night I, along with the other freshmen, who went in Whig Hall was initiated. It was some initiation and it took about 2 hours to go thru it. They put black bags over our heads and we had to go thru the whole thing crawling on our stomachs. They certainly did paddle us and we had to crawl thru a long winding passage under the foundations of the hall. After the initiation was over we were led upstairs and the blindfolds were removed. Pres. [John Grier] Hibben, who is a member of Whig made a speech and told us all about the Society. Pres. [Woodrow] Wilson and Pres. [James] Madison were members of it. The society meets every Friday and listens to a debate etc. There are also fireside talks every so often when prominent members of the faculty give talks on various topics of interest. You can be either an active or an inactive member. I have to be an active member as I am taking Hall English which is a course you can take in place of regular Freshman English. It is mostly the science of oratory, argument etc.[13] I think it will prove very worth while. I am going to have

---

[12] Alexander Hamilton Phillips, Professor of Mineralogy.

[13] Apparently Stevenson did not consider his experience in the Whig Society to have been important to his later development as an orator. "He thinks that perhaps the major reason why he did not debate at Princeton was not that he lacked interest, but that in his time (1918–1922) there was little debate and speaking among under-

to work pretty hard with Latin (we are reading Pliny) Chemistry and Math. (coordinate Geometry). I have the same Prof. in French as last term and I have a big drag with him, so that won't be so hard.

Last night was the Philadelphian Society meeting for the freshmen and a number of excellent speeches were given by prominent seniors. I enjoyed it a lot.

I don't understand why the battery for the car should be "no good." It is the one that was in it when it was bought and I can't understand why it is not alright. Tell father to inquire if there is any guarantee on it and if so to see what can be done about it. Are you going to drive up to Phila.? I could come down most any afternoon and drive up with you.[14]

Love

AD

I saw John H[arlan]. the other day and he inquired for Buff.

To Lewis G. Stevenson

Saturday [January 18, 1919]

Dear Father:

I have a little good news for you. Last night the Choate Club of Princeton was organized and I was elected Sec. & Treasurer. All of the larger prep. schools have clubs at the colleges to further interest in that college at their respective schools. The rub regarding the officers is that the president and vice-president must be from the upper classes and the Sec. from the freshman class. In other words I got elected, by some miracle, over the other freshmen.

Last night the basketball team played and beat Rutgers. It was a very good game and the first one I have seen in the gym.

When you send the other stuff please send me my *blue Choate memory book* and all the unframed pictures that are in it. We have our room fixed up pretty well now but I think I can use those pictures. Tell Fred [15] that I received the stuff he sent me and thank him for me.

Love

AD.

---

graduates." Russel Windes, Jr., and James A. Robinson, "Public Address in the Career of Adlai E. Stevenson," *Quarterly Journal of Speech*, Vol. XLII, No. 3, October, 1956.

[14] His mother and Buffie were in Washington with his father at this point.

[15] Fred Robinson, Lewis G. Stevenson's secretary.

To Mrs. Lewis G. Stevenson

Sunday night [January 19, 1919]

Dearest Mum:

Having studyed hard most of the afternoon I have decided to rest a few minutes and give you all the dope I have acquired recently.

In the first place, a meeting was held Friday night by the Undergraduate Schools Committee to organize the Choate Club of Princeton. All the larger prep. schools have clubs at the various colleges whose purpose is to arouse interest in that particular college at their respective schools. This is the first year that we have had one at Princeton and in connection with its organization I have some good news for you. The president and the vice-president are, according to custom, always elected from the upper classes and the secretary from the freshman class. Charlie Haines and Pete Kennedy were elected president and vice president and I was elected secretary.

I am getting my work fairly well under way now and, although I won't have to work especially hard, I will have to work more than last term. I talked over dropping a subject with father and we came to the conclusion that it would be rather foolish to drop Chemistry as I would only have to take it next year and, furthermore, I am passying it thus far. I am getting plenty of exercise swimming most every afternoon and occasionally going skating. I enjoy Bill [Hale] a lot and Ralph [Goodwin], Jim [Eldredge Snyder], [Edward Sydenham] Page and [Webster B.] Todd are all nearby so that we are pretty well fixed. Our room has not been at all cold yet and we have laid in a large supply of wood in anticipation of some cold weather, however, now that we have the wood, it probably won't come. Our room is really quite comfortable and I am well satisfied.

Do let me know how you are getting along down in the sunny South and tell Buff not to let any shark nip her toes when she is struggling thru the foam.

Love
Ad.

To Mrs. Lewis G. Stevenson

Friday [January 24, 1919]

Dearest Mum:

"Chic" Hardwick that you mentioned in your letter is one of Harvard's most famous athletes and Russ Ayres, the master at school that coached me in tennis, used to room with him. — I was asked to receive at the Freshman reception at the Pres. house next week. Needless to say I didnot refuse. I guess my duties as a receiver will consist in introducing the freshman to the Pres. etc. There is also going to be a tea dance. I am heeling the Princetonian and believe me it is some work. I only started yesterday but have been chasing around all day looking for stories. Think I will go to N.Y. this week.

Love

A<small>D</small>.

To Mrs. Lewis G. Stevenson

Tuesday [January 28, 1919]

Dearest Mum:

I went to N Y this past week-end with Ralph [Goodwin] and Louie [Louis Jones]. We had an awfully good time and the two girls (besides Lucy who was chaperone) were very nice. One of them was Roberta Lewis from Chicago and the other was Dorothy Mason from Evanston. We had a great time and got back Sunday night. Thusfar I have written 2 stories for the "Prince" and both were printed. It is awfully hard work but quite worth while and interesting. I was ta[l]king to Jim Douglas the other day and he urged me to stay out for it.[16] I have to write a story a day from now on.

Love.

A<small>D</small>

To Mrs. Lewis G. Stevenson

Saturday evening [February 1, 1919]

Dearest Mum:

I have just returned from the movies (a pleasure which I have had to forego to a great extent since I went out for the "Prince") and thought I would write you tonight instead of waiting until tomorrow. The reception at Prospect [at the President's house] came off this afternoon and was a great success. The duties of a receiver were rather uncertain but I introduced fellows to some of the girls and made myself generally useful. Of course the house (it is a beautiful house) was awfully crowded as almost the entire class, over 400, a lot of girls and a great many of the faculty were there. It was a the-

---

16 James Douglas, Jr., of Chicago was an upperclassman. He later became Assistant Secretary of the Treasury in March, 1932, Secretary of the Air Force, 1957–1959, and Deputy Secretary of Defense, 1959–1961.

dansant and I had a great time. The girls were awfully nice but I liked two in particular. One of them lives in New York and goes to Miss Halls [School] at Pittsfield. She was awfully nice and knew Hester [Merwin] very well. The other lives in Morristown and is the sister of a fellow I knew at Taft. She went to Westover [School] and knew a lot of girls I know there. I also met Paula Van Dyck. She is the daughter of the professor [17] and a corking dancer. Altogether I had an awfully good time and wish they would have a reception every week.

The basketball team played Columbia Friday night and beat them 27–15. It was an easy game but the Gym. was crowded and there was much noise. I have been working awfully hard on the "Prince" but am afraid I haven't a chance of making it. Only 13 men out of 37 have been retained in the competition and I am one of them, but only two men are going to be taken on the board from this competition and several fellows are way ahead of me so I fear my chances are rather small.[18] John [Harlan] and Jim [Douglas] have both urged me to stay out but it takes so much time I fear it will interfere with my studies, however, I think I will stay out for a while longer as I hate to be a quit[t]er. John asked me if Buff was going to be up here at the time of the Junior Prom (March 15). I think he is going to ask her and I think it advisable that she be here as he will probably lead the Prom., if he is reelected Pres. of the class. Well I haven't any more dope except that the freshman uniform tests start next Sat. and I will have to work like a fool.

Love
AD.

To Mrs. Lewis G. Stevenson

Friday [February 7, 1919]

Dearest Mum:

Thanks muchly for the $2.[19] Along with the nice fat check that father left me I now feel financially very stable. Father spent several days with me and we had a great time together. He did a lot of awfully good work for me for the "Prince" and, providing I stay in the competition, it will be of great assistance. The freshman uniform tests begin tomorrow and if I fail any of them I think I will drop the "Prince" as it

[17] Mrs. Ives wrote: "It shows what a green new Freshman he was, to refer to the famous Henry Van Dyke in such anonymous terms." *My Brother Adlai*, p. 127.

[18] Throughout his lifetime he was always extremely self-critical, and he seldom was satisfied that he had done as well as he should have.

[19] The corner of the card is torn so the correct amount does not show.

takes a great deal of time and I haven't much chance of making it this competition anyway. I saw George Funk [20] the other day and we had a long talk. He has a moustache. John H[arlan]. was reelected pres. of 1920.

AD.

To Mrs. Lewis G. Stevenson

Sunday [May 25, 1919]

Dearest Mum:

I have decided to take a few minutes off from work (Prince work) to let you know I am still thriving and that we lost most of the games this week-end. In the return ball game with Harvard (we won the first one) at Cambridge Saturday, they won in a very close game. The track team was also beaten by Harvard. We won from the Harvard Freshman ball team down here and the Golf team defeated them also so that helped to even things up. But after all it was pretty bad to lose the ball game and track meet. Furthermore the Varsity tennis team lost to Yale and both Varsity and Fresh. crews were beaten by Cornell so it wasn't exactly a successful weekend.

I have been averaging about 7–8 hours a day on the "Prince" the last couple of weeks. The competition ends this week and I want to finish up strong although I'm afraid I haven't much chance of being taken on.

It is certainly interesting work and I like it a lot but I'll enjoy a rest when the competition is over. John Harlan makes an excellent chairman and he works awfully hard on it himself.[21] He was elected to next year's Senior Council the other day and will probably be chairman of it next year. Jim Douglas and John Fennelly are thinking of going out to Horton's this summer.[22] I'm going to do my best to get them to.

Final exams start in about 10 days and I am going to have to do some tall studying the next few days. How is everything around Bloomington? I am getting more and more anxious daily to get back and look the town over. Dale Warren just asked me today when Buff was coming down. When is she?

Love
AD.

[20] A Bloomington friend and Princeton upperclassman.
[21] Harlan was chairman of the *Daily Princetonian* board. Adlai won the competition to be a member of the board a few days after this letter was written.
[22] Fennelly was a Princeton upperclassman. Adlai refers to Frank Horton's HF Bar ranch in Wyoming.

To H. O. Davis

Monday [23]

My dear Uncle Bert:

I received today a clipping from the Pantagraph and a note from mother in regard to William's death.[24] I feel sure that you feel the same about dear old Bill as mother and I do; that he is far better off now than he could ever have been here with all the suffering he must have endured. However, it is a very sorrowful moment for us all and I hasten to ad[d] my sympathy. Some way or other, since I first remember William at the old Chestnut St. house, I have always had a peculiar liking for him and, on his occasional trips to Bloomington in the last few years, mother and I have taken a genuine joy in his visits to the house.

I doubt if anything has ever made a greater impression on me or will remain in my memory longer than the story mother told me, a long time ago, of William's life and the heroic and clean fight he had cheerfully made against his very hard lot from the time he was a little boy. Certainly he had the makings of a real man and, had not some better judgment than ours deemed it wiser, he would undoubtedly, with such a winning personality, have accomplished great things. I think that to have fought a losing fight with the cheerful obstinacy that was his for so many years is an eloquent example of that silent heroism that one so often reads about but seldom sees portrayed in real life.

College is great, and although I think you are right about it not being a necessity for success, it certainly is a big help and a lot of fun while it lasts. I hope to get home about the middle of June and am very anxious to see you all again as it seems a long time since the happy day I had with you at Mt. Clemins last summer.

Give my love to Aunt Florence and my best to you Uncle Bert.

ADLAI.

Adlai spent the summer of 1919 at Frank Horton's HF Bar ranch in Wyoming. His mother decided to rent a house in Princeton for his sophomore year. Mrs. Ives wrote: "My brother thought that was really too much. He did his tactful best to discourage our coming, but he was too tactful — or probably Mother was too determined. I remember

---

[23] Probably late May, 1919.

[24] William O. Davis, son of Mr. and Mrs. H. O. Davis, died on May 22, 1919, at the age of twenty-nine. He had suffered from epilepsy since childhood.

his saying he'd be too busy to see us often, but I was so charmed at the prospect of spending eight months in Princeton I was blind to his qualms. It wasn't until recently that he told me how apprehensive he'd been. He said, 'I thought it was the cruelest thing a parent could do — coming to live at a son's school.' He admitted it hadn't been nearly as bad as he'd expected." [25]

Mrs. Ives recalled that her brother used the family Hudson to drive the family or his dates around the countryside. Adlai usually came to the house for Sunday dinner accompanied by such friends as William Hale, H. Hamilton ("Monk") Hackney, Charles Denby, Winchester Jones, and Douglas Ward. Mrs. Ives remembered that her brother usually carried a briefcase loaded with books and work for the Daily Princetonian.

During the Christmas holiday, their father joined them in Princeton. Buffie wrote in her diary: "December 25th — one of the happiest days I've ever spent. First, not a family row." She added later: "Father was so delighted to see us again he must have been angelically good-tempered. My clearest recollection of my brother is sitting on his spine at blissful ease, before the fire, while Mother and I read aloud." [26]

Buffie learned that some of her brother's roommates had nicknamed him "Rabbit." He explained to her that it was because of his taste for raw carrots and salad. Several classmates told her, however, "they called him Rabbit because he moved so fast — and he still does." [27] *Classmate T. S. Matthews wrote: "This was obviously not respectful, but like many nicknames it was based on something singular: He did have a nervous habit of wrinkling his nose, and he did have a kind of rabbit-like wariness."* [28]

Mrs. Ives wrote: "It's always interested me to watch how eagerly Adlai enters into things and absorbs new experiences, with a quickness and direct concentration, and an intense curiosity. I think I realized this all the more sharply at Princeton because I was uncertain about what I wanted to do." [29]

At the end of his sophomore year, Adlai sailed for Europe with a number of his classmates including T. S. Matthews, William Tucker, H. Hamilton Hackney, John Wainwright, and Jake Waxter.

[25] *My Brother Adlai*, p. 127.
[26] Ibid., p. 131.
[27] Ibid., p. 128.
[28] "Portrait, with Scratches," p. 238.
[29] *My Brother Adlai*, pp. 128–129.

To Mrs. Lewis G. Stevenson

On S.S. *New York,*
8th day out
(Tuesday) [June 29, 1920]

Dear Mother:

I have at last determined that it is about time for me to begin to wade thru the enormous lot (ie. it seems like an enormous lot) of letters I've got to write before this sturdy ship makes some port or other.

Incidentally, before I begin to recount the incidents of the voyage, I might say that the present concensus of opinion is that we will reach Southhampton sometime Friday — Hoo-ray! Until then we'll all continue to brace ourselves for the next roll — Whoop — there it is. I am writing this illegible epistle perched up in a bunk listening to Harry [Colt] and Tom [Matthews] compose poetry on some — of the many — queer passangers on the boat. There is certainly sufficient material to inspire some remarkably satirical poetry.

However, I better tell you about the trip and not dwell at too great length on the peculiarities of some of my fellow passengers. On getting on the boat at N.Y. I was not surprised to find that our cabin was down somewhere in the depths of the ship at the end of a very complicated system of passageways, stairs etc. But it appeared perfectly comfortable and really quite clean so Bill [Tucker] and I decided that as an economical measure it had really been a very good one and we were quite satisfied. Everything was delightful that first day out. We discovered that there were in all some 15 Princeton men aboard — three of them, including Bob Campbell and Jake Waxter were, and still are stoking. There are also two Harvard boys aboard and they are mighty good chaps. One of the[m], Harry Colt by name lives in Paris and was in the same class at St. Paul's as Bill [Tucker] & Tom [Matthews] and the rest. He is really an awfully good scout and I have gotten to know him very well. He is president of his class at Harvard and was on the track team and football squad. . . . There are also quite a lot of Yale fellows and three or four of them are stewards in the steerage. We hear some wonderful stories when the stokers and stewards etc. are off duty. In fact we're getting quite intimate with the entire crew and needless to say there are some very interesting characters. One in particular — a Jugo Slav — is most entertaining. He has been all over the globe which is not strange as most of the crew have, however, the remarkable thing about him is that he has a really beautiful baritone voice and can sing off hand any selection from any opera in the correct language.

Well, as I said, the first day was fine. We all got chairs together on deck and Harry, Tom, Bill, Rummie Marvin, and I eat together with Bishop Matthews [30] and two other clerical celebrities — the Bishop of California and the Bishop of Ohio. There are about a dozen Bishops on the boat all going to the Lambeth conference and they are, for the most part, quite a venerable looking body of men. . . . The first couple of meals were rather a disappointment but we have since discovered that the food is really exceptionally good and one just lives from meal to meal — that is, of course, providing you are not suffering from that horrible malady — mal de mer — and, strange to say, thus far I have not had a qualm. (In fact I think that I must be becoming a very good sailor.[)] Tom hasn't been sick either, but he says there is something wrong and is beginning to get suspicious.

But to get back to the subject — the first 4 or 5 days were extremely calm, almost calmer in fact than I thought the ocean could get. It was very pleasant on deck and astonishingly warm — too warm for vests in fact. But alas, the fair weather on deck made it unbearable in the cabin and it was practically impossible to sleep so we determined to sleep on deck. It was really one of the most amusing things imaginable to wander from place to place looking for a place to sleep and finding everything filled with with slumbering passengers. We finally found a cool corner of the dining saloon that was not occupied and passed a very pleasant night there. It was so beastly hot that for 2 or 3 nights I don't believe more than a third of the passengers slept in their cabins.

We passed the days reading and playing shuffle board, deck tennis etc. Harry Colt and I are the undefeated champions at deck tennis. But the quietness of the passage was to be short lived and a couple of days ago the wind freshened up and the boat has been pitching unmercifully ever since. Last night it was so bad that the racks for the dishes in the galley broke loose and $500 worth of crockery was broken. Yet the seamen say that the boat has not really begun to roll yet. Its lots of fun to lie in your bunk and hear bottles etc. go crashing to the floor in the cabin around you — hear women scream etc. But in spite of it all I remain undaunted and eat ravenously. It is, however, extremely difficult to write as you have probably observed so I'll continue later.

Love,
ADLAI

[30] Tom Matthews's father.

To Mrs. Lewis G. Stevenson

Sunday, July 4, 1920

Dearest Mother:

This is almost the first moment I've had to write you a card since we arrived in London Friday. In the space of this card it is naturally impossible to tell you what a wonderful time we're having and how intensely interesting everything is, however, I hope to write you fully this evening and shall tell you all about everything.[31] Everything is much cheaper here than in N.Y. and they say Paris is *very much* cheaper than London. Feeling fine.

ADLAI

To Mrs. Lewis G. Stevenson

July 21, 1920

Dearest Mother,

We are back in London now and, although I enjoyed the country and the various places of interest that we saw, it is rather good to get back to the metropolis again. Last night we took a walk and went out to Buckingham Palace and saw the guests arrive for some sort of big dinner. Had the final fitting of my suits this morning and they pleased me very much. We leave for gay Paris tomorrow. Got yours & Buff's letters this morning.

Love
ADLAI

To Mrs. Lewis G. Stevenson [32]

July 26, 1920

Dearest Mother:

I do indeed feel guilty for not having written you for so long, but — well seeing Paris somehow does not give one very much spare time and since we arrived Thursday and I haven't been able to come down to

[31] T. S. Matthews wrote that when all the Princeton group gathered at the Regent Palace Hotel in London "we held a meeting to decide what to do first. Adlai was all for going to the British Museum. I was against it, on the grounds that it was sight-seeing, which was not what we had come for — anyway, not what *I* had come for. Adlai won." "Portrait, with Scratches," p. 193.

[32] On this letter and several others written by Adlai on this European trip someone crossed out words and wrote in words where his were difficult to read. This was done in different ink from the original. We tried to follow the original faithfully, but it was difficult.

realities for Paris in some way or other has a charm & beauty that is absolutely unique and I can't seem to get tired of it or bored even for a few minutes in which to write a letter. However, I shall now try to make up for lost time and tell you all we've been doing since I last wrote.

We left Oxford on Friday the 16th and started out on foot (leaving all our luggage at Oxford) for Banbury.[33] Jake Waxter and I started out ahead of the other three and walked about five miles when my feet — I had on those black shoes, as my new ones which I had made in Oxford were not ready, and heavy woolen knickerbocker stockings which made a pretty tight fit — started to hurt, so we sat ourselves down on the roadside, under a great and ancient tree, while I fixed my feet up and then started on. The country around Oxford is really beautiful and in fact all the country we passed thru was quite different from anything in America and the thached cottages of the farmers lent it a peculiar quaintness. Jake and I walked a few miles further — it was a beautiful day and everything was glorious (except my feet) — when the others caught up with us. We journeyed on a little farther, Bill [Tucker] and I gradually dropping farther and farther behind, and at last came to a little town. Tom [Matthews], in a more or less prostrated condition, was waiting for us. We stumbled into a little tavern and had some ale and Tom informed us that he could not keep up with the pace that Jake and Jack [Wainwright] were setting. We agreed with him and determined to set our own pace — ie, as slowly as possible. We stumbled on to the next town — Deddington — which was a very typical old English town. Here we met the others and created a good deal of excitement walking thru the town. We managed to secure some lunch consisting of bread and cheese & cider and then bought some cakes and wandered out the road toward Banbury way. We didn't get very far before we all unanimously decided that a rest was needed so we lay down under some more wonderful trees and ate our cakes. After awhile we got under way again and, with only a short stop at Adderborough — a very ancient village — we at last reached Banbury at about 7:30. After stopping several places we at last located the best hotel and, after a sumptuous dinner, hit the hay. Jake & Jack got up early the next morning and started out for Leamington à pied, however, Bill, Tom and I decided that all the walking we were going to do on that trip was included in the 24 agonizing miles of the pre-

---

33 Adlai, T. S. Matthews, and four other classmates rented a house in Oxford for a week. Matthews wrote: "Adlai, who really did like sight-seeing or thought he ought to, 'did' all the colleges, or as many as he could." "Portrait, with Scratches," p. 193. At the end of the week they set out on a walking tour.

vious day. Consequently we took a train for Leamington and got there about lunch time. After lunch we took a bus out to Kenilworth to see the castle.[34] That famous ruin lived up to my fondest expectations and it was indeed impressive to sit there and look at those massive walls and towers — the last relics of what was once the most magnificent and powerful castle in all England. We staid there quite a while and I read the history of the castle which was indeed most interesting. In the late afternoon we returned to Leamington and got rooms at the Y.M.C.A. for 4/– including breakfast. Jake & Jack blew in in the ev[en]ing pretty well tired out but still cheerful. The next day was Sunday and we heard that services & a parade etc. we[re] going to be held in the court of Warwick Castle so, of course, we looped over to Warwick. That afternoon spent at Warwick Castle and in that very ancient village was one of the most delightful of my life. The castle — as you probably remember — is quite remarkable and is probably the best remaining example of a real fortified Norman castle in England. It is remarkable kept up and the state apartments, where many kings etc. have staid, are very magnificent although we could not see them on Sunday. The entire town attended the service which was quite impressive although I enjoyed watching the people far more than listening to the sermon. After the service the gates to the gardens were opened and we went out and looked them over. The gardens seemed to extend for miles so, of course, it was impossible to see but a small part of them. They were most beautiful and the grass everywhere was about on a par with the greens of a good golf course. We decided to go on to Stratford that night and, after supping in Warwick, we caught a bus and had a most delightful ride thru Shakespeare's own country to Stratford. After securing rooms we went out and looked the town over. Parts of it are very quaint but, on the whole, I didn't like it as well as some of the other towns we went thru. In the morning we went to Shakespear's house and the church where he is buried etc.

Perhaps you have heard of the annual summer Festival that is held at Stratford in honor of Shakespeare. All his plays are produced by an excellent company under the direction of Forbes-Robertson. Well anyway the festival was beginning that day and Cymbelaine was to be given at the Memorial Theatre that evening. So we secured tickets and had lunch. In the afternoon we walked out into the country and reclined on the banks of the Avon and read. It was really most delightful and it was quite an inspiring atmosfere. I read the Lay of the last Minstrel by Scott & Bill read Cymbaline and consequently was able to refresh our memories as regarded the play. We stayed out there un-

[34] Adlai was a devotee of Sir Walter Scott.

til almost time for the play to begin and then hastened back. The theatre was well filled and I was surprised to see how many Americans thei[there] were. I enjoyed the play immensely and it was quite a novel experience to see one of Shakespeare's tragedies produced by English actors at Stratford in a theatre erected in memory of Shake. The next morning (Tuesday) we said farewell to Stratford and took the train back to Oxford where we changed our clothes and got washed and shaved — a very delightful process after five days on the road. We went on to London in the afternoon and put up at Moseley's hotel that night. In the evening we took a long walk out around Buckingham Palace & back thru the Mall. The next morning we went to the tailors and had the final fitting on our suits. That night we went to the opening of a new comedy — I'll Leave It To You — It was awfully clever but apparently a first night isn't a very important event to London theatre-goers.

The next morning Bill and I left for Paris by AIRPLANE! Tom had to go to the country with his father and hasn't arrived yet. Jake had to wait for some money from home and Jack waited for him. The airplane passage cost us $42 — about 2½ times as much as it would have cost on the train. It sounds pretty extravagant but it was, I think, altogether worth it for the experience was wonderful and the trip across the channel is beastly and an awful lot of trouble with customs etc.

The plan was to leave from the [illegible] wood flying field of the Handl[e]y-Page Co. at 12 noon and at 11 a car met us at the Victory Hotel to take us to the field. It was, of course, most exciting and the others were there to see us off. An old friend of mine from Choate happened to get in the same motor that we did and I had a long talk with him on the way to the field. He flew in a different plane than we did though. At the field it was quite thrilling for there were a large number of the enormous Handley-Page planes already to leave and their motors were running to warm up. We showed our passports in the office and a customs man asked us if we had any dutiable goods and thats all there was to it. We then proceeded to enter the plane, which carries 10 people and is fitted up with windows, wicker chairs etc. There was even a lavatory in it. We happened to be the only two passengers in the cabin as the one other passenger was out in front with the pilot. As it was my first time up everything was, of course, most interesting. We had an excellent view of London while flying over and could see the whole course of the Thames etc. After about 45 minutes flying we reached Faulkstone [Folkestone] and landed there to deliver some freight. We stayed for about 15 minutes and had time to see the great airdrome & hangers which are located there and were used during the war by the R.A.F. While crossing the channel we could see a large number of boats which looked like little toys floating around in a river. The flying over France was most interesting for you could observe most clearly the different methods of cultivation employed by the French and how they differed from the English. The ground in France looked like a vast puzzel composed of pieces of wood set in straight geometrical figures and painted all shades of browns & greens. I've run out of paper & will have to finish this letter later.

Love
AD.

To Mrs. Lewis G. Stevenson

Friday, July [30], 1920

Dearest Mother:

You may be surprised to be getting a letter from me from Coblenz, but don't worry for we are having a wonderful time [and] are not getting into trouble. On the other hand, the Germans are most effusively polite to all Americans, especially here where one might say that the Americans were "on top."

Frank Murray, Bill Tucker and I got military passes into the occupied territory from a colonel that Frank knew at the American Military legation in Paris and here we are at Coblenz on our way to *Berlin*. We left Paris last night at 9 and arrived here, via Chateau Thierry, Epernay, Challons-sur-Marne etc., at noon today. An American Captain met us at the train in a Cadillac limousine and brought us to this Hotel where he had billeted us. Not bad, eh?

We went out to Ehrenbreitstein this afternoon and have been looking the town over since. It is indeed very pretty but we haven't much time to spend on this trip as we all want to get back to Paris by the 7th — I especially, to meet Buff and Father, so we are leaving for Weisbaden at 5:30 where we will spend the night. Then back here by boat tomorrow morning — for the Rhine between Coblenz & Wiesbaden is, they say, the most beautiful part. From here we will go on to Cologne arriving there tomorrow night or afternoon. At Cologne George Piper [35] is going to meet us and then to Berlin Sunday. We will spend Sunday night and Monday in Berlin, coming back to Paris by way of Verdun, Rheims, Chemin des Dames etc.

Altogether it sounds like a pretty good trip and if we enjoy it all as much as we have this first part it will certainly be an immense success. Last night while riding on the train just out of Chateau Thierry

[35] A Princeton student.

[85]

I saw a sight that is indeed hard to describe. You will remember that last night, the 29th was the sixth anniversary of the first declaration of war between Servia & Austria and that the moon was full and — here anyway — very brilliant. Well anyway when a couple of miles out of Chateau Thierry I could [see] the ruins of walls and houses on the surrounding hills standing out against the sky and bathed in the brilliant white of the moon. A little further down the track we passed a great field of neat little white crosses arranged in symmetrical rows and stretching away over the hills — the final resting place of some 30,000 American soldiers and marines. It also occurred to me that it was almost exactly 2 years and 1 week ago that the Chateau Thierry offensive was begun, which lended a kind of subconsciously romantic air to the scene. All this, augmented by the brilliant moon, the ruins sillouetted against the sky, the desolation of the landscape and the fact that it was the 6th anniversary of the war gave a most effective atmosphere of tragedy and at the same time hilarity to the night. In the next compartment to me a girl started to play a violin — this was the middle of the night as we were following the Marne — and before long the whole car had assembled to hear[,] and how she could play. Some man who had heard her before said that she was rapidly becoming the most prominent violinist in France. A memorable night.

Love,
ADLAI

P.S. My address is now — Morgan, Harjes & Co. Paris, France.

To Mrs. Lewis G. Stevenson

Sunday, August 1, 1920

Dearest Mum:

Here we are in Berlin! And needless to say its quite an experience to be looking over the German capital. There are very few Americans here or other foreigners and the Germans don't seem to be too anxious to have foreigners around. However, although Americans are about as popular here as the proverbial snake at a lawn party, they treat us, nevertheless with considerable respect and we are having a wonderful time.

We left Paris Thursday night and arrived in Coblenz the next afternoon. We left Coblenz that evening and went to Weisbaden. The trip down or rather up the Rhine to Weisbaden was beautiful and we saw many remains of ancient castles etc. The Rhine country is indeed beautiful and I wished we could have staid there longer, however, we discovered that the best way to go to Berlin was from Frankfort which is further up the Rhine from Weisbaden so we could not take our trip down on the boat.

We got an excellent room at Weisbaden and then went out to another place for dinner. It was, I believe, called the Kurhaus and we had one of the best dinners I've ever had. It cost us about 45 marks apiece or almost $1.25 as the mark is worth about 2¾ cents. After dinner we went to a famous cafe & dance hall that an American officer had told us about at Coblenz. Unfortunately the place was pretty dead and so we didn't have a very wild party. I am afraid that this hasn't been a very good season at the German watering places for Weisbaden appeared to be almost dead and the hotels nearly deserted.

We went back to the hotel about 12 o'clock and then bickered with the porter in German for about an hour (or rather Bill [Tucker] bickered for Frank [Murray] and I aren't too hot on that extremely ugly language). At last we discovered that the best way to get to Berlin was to leave Weisbaden for Frankfort at 5 A.M. and get a train from there at 7:30 which gets to Berlin at 8 P.M.

It was about 1:00 by the time we got to bed and we had to get up at 4 so, needless to say we didn't get much sleep that night. We got up in the wee hours and just got the train in time, in fact we hopped on as it was moving out. We met an extremely nice young fellow, and a very well educated one, on the train. He lived in Metz and told us that Lorraine, contrary to several stories we had heard, preferred to belong to France. Alsace, however, he said wanted and should belong to Germany. One hears many conflicting stories here about those provinces, but from what this man said, and he considered himself a Frenchman, I think the above disposition would have been the best.

We had breakfast at a hotel near the station, which by the way is the second biggest in Germany and a beauty, at Frankfort and had a long talk with the head waiter who spoke English as most of the head-waiters do throughout Europe. He was extremely nice and said the same thing that all Germans say, namely, that Germany would have won the war had not America entered and again like all Germans he could not understand why America entered against Germany. He seemed to think that the U. S. played the Germans a dirty trick by entering the war at all and he told us that the general opinion throughout all Germany was that America was Germany's best friend and that she (Amer) would never fight against Germany. He said that it was a great surprise and shock to all Germany when America entered the war against her.

The trip to Berlin which we had determined to take during the day in order to see the country was frightful and the train was horribly crowded. There was, however, in our compartment a young German about 22 years old who informed us that he was a comedian and was just returning from an engagement at Baden. He fulfilled all the requirements of a comedian and kept us in an uproar all the way to Berlin. We arrived last night and got rooms here. It [the Excelsior] is an excellent hotel and, were it not that there is a 50% tax on all Americans in all the Berlin hotels, would be very cheap. As it is we are paying about $1.50 a day for a luxurious room and breakfast. We had a delightful sleep last night and got up about noon today. We had an enormous breakfast in our room and then determined to go out and see the horse races which started today. We hired a car for about $2.00 each to take us out to the track and back. On the way out he he took us all over the city and around the principle buildings. The city is indeed a beautiful one and I was especially surprised to see how happy ever[y] one appeared to be and how the entire city apparently turned out for the races.

The track, which is quite a long ways from the center of the city, was huge and very beautifully laid out. It was all turf and covered with jumps etc. More like a steeplechase than a race course. All the races, there were seven of them, started from different places and wound around over the course, according to the distance, finishing at the same place. We had seats in the grandstand and, making little pools of our own, managed to get quite excited over the races. There was an enormous crowd of people there and it offered an excellent opportunity to study the German people and their characteristics. In the first place, the language, in my opinion, is a very disagreeable one to hear. As for the people my general opinion, gathered from seeing a great number of them together is unfavorable, however, individual ones that I have met have, as a rule, impressed me very favorably, in fact I like them very much. The women to me are quite unattractive and dress abominally, but that, I suppose is due to the exorbitant prices of clothes etc. in Germany.

After the races we once more entered our cab and returned to Berlin riding like plutocrats. There are surprisingly few automobiles in Germany and even very few taxis. The price of gasoline and oil makes their use by Germans impossible I suppose and consequently only the most wealthy can afford to have them. We had dinner at a restaurant on Potsdamer Platz and then came back here to write letters. And now you know what your wandering son has been doing since he hit Germany. We are leaving Tuesday for Brussels where we will meet

George Piper and go to Rheims, Verdun and some of the other battle-fields. We should get back to Paris on about the 6th or 7th, where I will meet father & Buffie and bum around with them.

I had a wonderful time in Paris as there were quite a lot of Princeton fellows there and we all bummed around together seeing sights both night and day. I went to the opera with Frank the night before we left and saw Thais. It was very beautiful and there were some wonderful voices in the cast. The opera is certainly a marvellous sight. Paris is the most fascinating city I have ever been in and I almost believe I should like to live there. As for the French people, I wasn't particularly attracted by the men but the women are, for the most part, very good looking and awfully well dressed.

Of course I saw all the regulation sights like the Louvre etc. and also a great exhibition of German guns, airplanes etc. out at the Invalides. We had a very nice room at the Hotel Metropolitain on Rue Cambon just off the Rue de Rivoli and Rue St. Honoré, for 15 francs a day each or about $1.25 including breakfast.

> Best love
> ADLAI

To Mrs. Lewis G. Stevenson [36]

Wednesday, August 17, 1920

Dear Mother:

Needless to say I am extremely apologetic for not having written long before but it seems that I have been suffering from a temporary aversion to all forms of communication and then I thought that Buffie's profuse epistolary effusions might possibly serve for both of us. However, she has informed me that that is by no means the case and, having had the wherewithalls thrust upon me, I have begun at last.

My last letter was, I believe, from Berlin and I shall attempt to recount my various adventures from then up until the present. I believe I told you about the 2 very attractive and interesting Germans that we met in Berlin and also about the delightful dinner party we had with them. Talking with them and getting the viewpoints of the highest class of Germans was indeed an interesting and valuable experi-

---

[36] This letter was written from Zermatt, Switzerland. His father and Buffie had met him in Paris. When their father went to Berlin on a business trip, Buffie and Adlai revisited Switzerland. Buffie wrote her mother on August 17, 1920: "Darling: After great effort, Ad has gotten a letter written to you — he simply *works* when he writes! He would say much more than he does if it weren't such an effort." Quoted in *My Brother Adlai,* p. 133.

ence and I enjoyed it immensely and have also acquired a much ameliorated and less prejudiced view as regards Germany and the Germans.

We left Berlin Tuesday evening for Cologne after having spent a most delightful day driving around the beautiful town of Potsdam and inspecting the palaces. The gardens of Fred. the Great's palace were beautiful and I really enjoyed them more than the very formal and magnificent ones at Versailles. After going thru these gardens — the gardens of the old palace — as it is called, we went over to the new palace or the palace of the Kaisers. That building easily surpasses anything I have seen this summer in its beauty and the priceless magnificence and ostentatiousness of the interior decoration. We were conducted thru it by a guide and we marched for some hour & a half from room to room, each one apparently surpassing the previous one in grandeur.

The palace is surrounded by enormous gardens & extensive parks and we should have liked to have spent several hours looking around, but unfortunately, by the time we had finished going thru the palace it was almost time for the train back to Berlin and we had to hurry down to the station. We had dinner in Berlin and then got on the train for Cöln. As usual we had to sit up all night, however, by this time we are getting rather used to it. In fact this summer has, if nothing else, taught me how to adapt myself to circumstances or, in other words, how to sleep in any posture whatever.

We arrived in Cöln the next morning about 9 o'clock and, on inquiring at the station, discovered that we were going to have a very difficult time getting to Rheims. However we secured tickets for as far as the Belgian border and then went out to see the town. The cathedral was of course first and I enjoyed it very much. We then mounted a sight seeing car and toured all over that very quaint and interesting old town.

We left in the afternoon on the first leg of our journey to Rheims and at 12 o'clock we had to get out at a small town on the border. Here we had to go thru the douane etc and also stay until 5:30 when we could get a train which would take us thru Belgium to a town on the French border. Frank [Murray] and I had a very novel walk thru the devastated remains of the town in the middle of the night and then at last we lay down on a grave stone & tried to go to sleep, however, that proved anything but comfortable and sleep was quite impossible so we walked back to the station and at last managed to get a few winks on the station platform. It was a dizzy night in every sense of the word and we were quite well satisfied when our train at last arrived.

I shan't attempt to recount the viscissitudes of our trip to Rheims — suffice it to say that it was an astonishingly hard place to reach and that we changed trains exactly 8 times in all. We spent several hours in Soissons on the way and hired a car to take us over the "Chemin des Dames" battlefield. It was over the possession of this road that we rode along that the severest fighting of the entire war occurred. It was intensely interesting and the complete devistation and destruction of the countryside and the little villages surpasses all the powers of description. I was told by a very delightful Frenchman, whom I met later, that the country surrounding Soissons was the best agricultural country in France and he also added that, in his opinion, the region would never be repopulated again for the constant shelling had left the land so rough and uneven that it would be impossible to cultivate it.

We visited a number of other completely demolished towns all of which had changed hands dozens of times during the war. The train from Laon, — where the German gun that shelled Paris was placed — to Rheims ran on a newly constructed bed thru a an almost totally bare country with trenches & barbed wire stretching away on both sides of the track.

We arrived in Rheims in the evening, secured rooms and had a very acceptable cleaning up as you may imagine after 2 days & nights in those dirty trains. As we were having dinner who should arrive but 5 other Princeton fellows on bicycles. We all had a big party together and then walked around the town for a while. They went on to Paris in the morning by train and we got a car and went out to inspect the battlefields around Rheims. We spent several hours walking thru the remains of Fort [illegible] and the very well preserved trenches that surround it. The ground was practically paved with iron and, although it has been thoroughly cleaned up, I found lots of unexploded shells, hand grenades etc. I also found a French bayonet which I am bringing home and many other souvenirs which are a little to bulky to carry about. It was all extremely interesting. I should have liked to have spent many more hours wandering about. We looked the cathedral over very carefully and I was really astonished that it was not more demolished than it is. If the Germans had really wanted to demolish it it is obvious that they could have done so very easily. I was interested to learn that, although the Germans penetrated to within 2 miles of Rheims, they never took it, and that it underwent a constant

[91]

bombardment night and day for 4 years. I also was told that in 1914 there were 16,000 houses in Rheims and that on Nov. 11, 1920 [1918] there were exactly 14 that remained intact. From this you can roughly estimate what the town looks like. However they are rebuilding it very rapidly.

We got to Paris that evening and Frank, Bill [Tucker] & I got a room together at the Oxford & Cambridge Hotel. That night we all, about 12 of us, had a big party together and in the course of the evening we found ourselves at the Folie[s] Bergère. Imagine my astonishment to see Father walk in all of a sudden. Of course he said he was just looking for me but it certainly looked as though he had started out on a little party of his own and that I had accidentally interrupted it. I met father & Buff the next day for lunch and hung around with them most of the time for the next few days until we started for Switzerland.[37]

Bill and Tom [Matthews] decided to go down to Lugano and Frank waited in Paris for Bill Moore to show up and then they were to go to the Olympic games together. Father was going to Berlin and I equipped him with a letter of introduction to my German friends.

Buff & I set sail for Geneva and had to spend the night on the train sitting up. At Belgarde — on the Swiss frontier we had to go thru the usual harrowing process of the douane and again when we arrived at Geneva. We stayed at the Beau Rivage and I found it rather expensive as compared to France. In the afternoon we took a boat and went over to see Aunt May De Lapalud.[38] They have a very pretty little chalet and we had lots of fun talking to them. The next morning Buff dragged me around to all the shops in Geneva and went out to Aunt May's again for dinner.[39] The following day we took a boat for Lausanne — having decided to come here until father got back from Berlin. We spent the night at the Beau Rivage and got under way again the next morning for Zermatt. The ride up here was beautiful and took the greater part of the day. We had to change trains at Visp — down at the foot of the valley — and while we were having lunch who should walk in but Harry Hart.[40] He had fallen off of some rocks and hurt his ankle, and consequently had left his companions in the mountains and

---

[37] Mrs. Ives wrote: "Father chose the Café de la Paix for our first dinner, but later Adlai introduced us to all his favorite little restaurants in Montmartre. He knew that section like a book. In fact, I think he'd explored, on foot, almost every inch of Paris." *My Brother Adlai*, p. 142.

[38] A family friend.

[39] Buffie wrote her mother on August 12, 1920: "Today I am shopping, Adlai following me reluctantly. He is a wonderful companion, and is so amusing in shops. He really has excellent taste!"

[40] A Princeton student.

was going to meet them at Zermatt — they were to come across the mountains.

He staid a couple of days with us here and then the others came and we all took a couple of trips together. Day befor[e] yesterday we went up to a cabin that is situated above the great glacier that comes down the side of the Matterhorn. On the way up we left Buffie and I told her to go home. Imagine our great astonishment when — about 4 hours later — we were finishing our lunch up at the cabin, to see Buff plodding up the mountainside. We were all very much dumfounded and *I* certainly never thought she could walk so far. Harry & I went out and inspected a glacier and before we got back Buff & the other boy started down. We caught up with them on the way and got back in time for dinner. All in all it was quite some walk and I'll have to hand it to Buff. Harry and the others left yesterday morning and in the meantime Buff & I are resting from our exertions.

Well I believe that's all the dope, but I shall really write again soon.

Love

AD.

Buffie wrote her mother on August 20, 1920: "Adlai is the easiest, most delightful companion. We will never have a happier time together." She wrote to her mother in another letter that Adlai was thinking of attending law school for a year, studying a year at Oxford, working a year on a London newspaper, and then joining the diplomatic service. Buffie asked her mother, "Would Father be very mad?"

Years later Mrs. Ives wrote: "The only time I can remember his being cross was the day a batch of copies of the Bloomington Pantagraph *arrived, in which some of Adlai's travel letters were published — a parental 'surprise' that nearly gave him a fit. He was very angry and said the letters were abominably done, and that if he had known they were going to be published, he'd have at least tried to write well!"* [41]

To Mrs. Lewis G. Stevenson

September 5, 1920

Dear Mother:

For some reason, and I guess its a quite obvious one, I always feel rather sad and dejected when I head a letter "Sept" — the abbreviation of that month, delightfully climatically, but — well, rather depressing in that it always marks the beginning of the winters work. But, strange

[41] *My Brother Adlai,* p. 144.

enough, even after a summer as delightful as the past, "Sept" doesn't have the same dire effect it used to and I feel almost anxious to get back to college again.

Father has secured me a passage on the Mauretania sailing from Cherbourg on the 18th which will get me back just in time for the grand and fatal day — I had rather hoped that we would have a few days together first, in which I could recount the all absorbing events of the summer. However, we were very fortunate to get that and after all we should let well enough alone.

It does seem hardly possible that the summer is almost over — fading into my life's history as it were — when it seems but yesterday that we were all talking it over, and not without conflicting opinions, at Library Place. Yet I think you can remain assured that your consent — given a little hastily according to father — has been thoroughly justified for the summer has proved most advantageous in every respect.[42]

Buff and I had a delightful, if quiet, stay at Zermatt. However, I think it would have been far more interesting had we gone to Berlin with father and I regret that we didn't for, from all his accounts, he must have had an intensely interesting & valuable time — hobnobbing with Germanys capitalists etc. Frank Murray & another Princeton fellow came up and stayed a couple of days with us and then Frank was coming back with Bill Moore — President of the Class of '17 & twice captain of the track team — and we were going to climb the Matterhorn. But they didnot have time to come back before their boat sailed so that fell through. I did, however, get a good taste of real climbing before I left in doing the Breithorn. It is quite close to the Matterhorn & just a little lower. We — the other people in the party & guides — left Zermatt one morning at ten o'clock on the Gornergrat funicular, which was up to the Gornergrat hotel from where, incidentally, you get what is considered the best view in Switzerland including 53 glaciers, dozens of mountains etc. But to resume the account of my maiden effort as a mountain climber — we got off at the second station and started on the first leg of our journey to the summit, namely to the "cabane" from which the parties start for the ascent. This "first leg" consisted of a climb down the precipitious side of a mountain and a three hours walk across the Gorner Glacer — second

---

[42] Kenneth S. Davis wrote: "With the sharpening and enlargement of his critical faculties, that summer of 1920, came a marked improvement in his abilities as a writer. The letter in which he described his climb up the Breithorn, for example, contained an unprecedented lyricism." *A Prophet in His Own Country: The Triumphs and Defeats of Adlai E. Stevenson* (Garden City: Doubleday, 1957), p. 129.

largest in Switzerland — and then another two hours across the Théo-dule Glacier, which runs under or rather around the base of the Breithorn. After crossing these glaciers we saw our destination, the "cabane," perched up on a great rock about 500 ft. directly above the surface of the glacier. Someone asked in a voice of astonishment how we were expected to get up there and the guide informed him that there was a path. General consternation as to how there could be a path up the almost perpendicular side of a rock. However, although the path was hard to distinguish the as[c]ent to the cabane was not so awfully hard after all. But I must return for a few moments to the glaciers.

Although the surfaces are very hard, in fact if you fall on them you are sure to cut your hand in a dozen places, it is nevertheless quite difficult walking for they are all up an[d] down and seamed with dozens of crevasses and looking when you are on it for all the world like a frozen sea — frozen in very tough weather. The large crevasses are very dangerous and to fall in them is certain death for they are often many hundreds of feet deep. To make matters worse the guides entertained us with stories of people who had fallen in crevasses and issued from the foot of the glacier as much as 30 years later — their bodies perfectly preserved. I couldn't help but think what an efficient preservative cold storage was.

Despite the harrowing details I found the glacier most interesting and the ice formations were intensely beautiful. While we were cross-ing the second glacier in the afternoon I saw something sticking out of the ice that looked rather peculiar and discovered that it was the pick of an alpine stalk. We finally chopped it and also a hat and pair of snow goggles. As these things had obviously been in the glacier sometime, the guides concluded that they probably belonged to a party that had been lost on the Théodule during a snow storm last fall. I am bringing the ax home and shall keep it for further trips to Switzerland as a reminder of the dangers of the mountains. We reached the cabane in the late afternoon, had supper and, after witnessing a glorious sun-set, went to bed for those of us that were going on up had to get up at 4.

I shall never forget that night. It was intensely cold, the moon full and brilliant and not a cloud in the sky. I found it quite impossible to sleep and actually sat or rather lied spellbound looking out of the window until time to get up. My window faced the Matterhorn which rose like a jagged column of granite out of a sea of sparkling white. Down below me, glittering in the moonlight, lay a vast glacier which occasionally uttered a reverberating groan as the ice cracked or moved slightly. In every direction great jagged peaks shot up and stood out black against the unearthly blue of the sky and over all was a choking and almost maddening silence. The intense cold and clearness of the atmosphere made the stars unbelievably brilliant and everything seemed magnified and brought closer while the real vastness of the scene was unconceivable. It was a sight that I shall never forget and I know hardly whether to call it beautiful or horrible for there was something about it that was awe inspiring and at the same time fascinating, frightful and supernatural. I could not determine whether it was nature — whether I should thank God or Satan and in fact I feel sure there was more of the latter in it — an awful grandeur that was really not beautiful but rather magnetic and fear-inspiring. Anyway I lay their enthralled and at last got up and went out to look some more — it fascinated me and I stood there stiff from [cold?] and unable to realize that this was merely a "clear night in the Alps."

After breakfast, and it was before the sun had risen, we all started off, roped to our respective guide. As we climbed higher & higher across the snow I could see the ultramarine of the sky between the mountains toward the east begin to fade. However, the sun didn't rise for a long while — not until all the stars had disappeared and the clouds beneath us in the valley looked like the burning crater of a volcano did it at last jump up over the top of one of the mountains. And then we had to put on our snow goggles for the endless snow in an instant became dazzling brilliant and sparkled like a floor of diamonds. The guide kept me moving steadily and I was convinced that I should die several times before reaching the top, but tant m[i]eux for me for if we had even stopped to rest I doubt I would have ever gotten under way again.

We reached the summit long before the others and the guide said we had made the ascent in as fast time as he ever believed it had been done. Some consolation anyway. I can't attempt to describe the view — suffice it to say that we could see into 4 countries and had an excellent view of Monte Viso which is within 10 miles of Marseilles on the Mediterranean.

The descent was accomplished in an hour and a quarter which the guide said was the best time he had ever heard of. But my record was made at a price as I had a very sore foot when we reached the cabane and consequently could not do the Matterhorn which I had intended to do on the following day. About 2 hours later the rest of the party came in and we started down to Zermatt, getting back in time for dinner.

It was a great experience and I enjoyed it immensely but was rather disappointed in not being able to do the Matterhorn. We left Zermatt the following day and met father down here and since then life of a criminal luxury in this beautiful hotel. Mrs. Stanley McCormick of Chicago, Washington, New York etc. is here and most attractive. We see a great deal of her and are going out in her car soon.

Best love
ADLAI

The letters that Adlai wrote during the fall of his junior year have been lost. He was one of the organizers of Princeton's Cox-Roosevelt Club and a member of the committee that brought Governor James M. Cox to Princeton to speak during the presidential campaign of 1920. The central issue of the campaign, as Adlai saw it, was the necessity of the United States joining Woodrow Wilson's League of Nations. Thirty-four years later, Adlai E. Stevenson recalled the mood of 1920 when the Wilsonian dream was not yet wholly dissolved: "A terrible war to make the world safe for democracy had just ended victoriously. A noble concept, the League of Nations, had emerged from the chaotic aftermath of that elemental struggle. It was the twilight of kings, the dawn of world-wide democracy. Optimism was boundless and people proclaimed that we were on the threshold of the new era of universal and perpetual peace and prosperity." [43]

To Mrs. Lewis G. Stevenson

Sunday [December 4, 1920]

Dear Mother:

This is the most beautiful winter day I've witnessed — with the first snow of the season, the winter has been ushered in most gloriously. I wish you could have see[n] McCosh walk and the trees around Prospect embedded in snow — about 2 inches on the smallest twig.

I am looking forward to coming home for vacation and can leave here on the 17th. However, you haven't let me know what the plans are yet so I have made no reservations yet.

Went to dinner at Mayor McClellan's [44] the other night and had a perfectly delightful time. Sat on Mrs. McClellan's right and had for a dinner partner Princess Ruspigliosi (something like that). She was

---

[43] Address at the Senior Class Banquet, Princeton University, March 22, 1954. Published in Stevenson, *What I Think*, p. 173.

[44] George B. McClellan, Princeton 1886, LL.D. 1905, mayor of New York 1903–1909, professor of economic history at Princeton.

[97]

nice and simple, and awfully interesting. Her mother is an American and they are living on Long Island until things settle down in Italy. . . .

Work, scholastic, is piling up and my anticipated leisure after the football season has failed to materialize.

Best love to all

ADLAI

On February 1, 1921, Adlai was elected managing editor of the Daily Princetonian. *His father immediately released the story to the* Bloomington Pantagraph *and the Chicago* Tribune, *but inaccurately. The* Tribune *wrote, "The position . . . is the highest on the paper and the most sought after honor in Princeton literary life."*

To Lewis G. Stevenson

Wednesday [45]

Dear Father:

Once more my [may] I protest (as usual in vain I suppose) against your assumption of the duties of my publicity manager. As in the past, when I have strenuously objected, you have nevertheless gone ahead and, with the apparent intent of pleasing a mere child, put things in papers which were altogether wrong in point of fact & most embarrasing to me. And now again; assailed from all sides with clippings from the Chi. Trib. to the effect that I am head of the Princetonian & as a matter of fact am only second. Consequently many stories about how it got in, can't understand it, etc. Please desist & do me a real favor.

ADLAI

To Mrs. Lewis G. Stevenson

April 12th, 1921

Dear Mother:

It occurred to me the other day that I have neglected to put a five cent stamp on the last letter I wrote, ergo I suppose you haven't heard from me for some time.

Your letters from Montreux were delightful and vividly recalled the happy weeks Buff, Father, and I spent there last summer. It is indeed a beautiful place and must be especially so in the early spring. However, in my estimation Princeton is almost supreme at this particu-

[45] This postcard is postmarked February, 1921.

lar time of year and it is difficult for me to conceive of anything more beautiful than the view out toward the Junction in the early morning while the grass is still damp and a mist envelopes everything.

Things around here are very much the same. I play tennis on the club courts every afternoon and am enjoying myself thoroughly. At present I am working on a committee which is drawing up, with a member of the Faculty, the constitution for a new organization which is to have entire control over all matters pertaining to the clubs; administration, methods of election, etc. The Prince manages to get out every day and continues to interest me. Tom McEachin was elected President of the club for next year and I was elected Secretary of the Board of Trustees.[46] I didn't want the Presidency and wasn't too keen for the other job. However, it doesn't take very much time and gives me a vote in all the Trustees' meetings etc.

You probably wonder why I never have any news but for some reason or other there never seems to be anything happening worthy of comment around here. The Stillman case is still on but no longer occupies headline positions on the front pages of all the New York papers.[47] There was a little article in the Pantagraph the other day saying that Ann Stillman had been finally located at Elkhart where she was visiting a school friend — Elizabeth Keyes. Ambrose Chambers, Dave's [Davis Merwin's] roommate, married a girl named Billard in Boston the other day. I got an invitation to the wedding but of course didnot go.

I suppose by this time you are in Italy and I do hope you haven't found it necessary to walk to get there due to the numerous strikes which seem to infest that unhappy land. In my next letter I hope I'll have something of real interest for you.

Best love to all,
Adlai

To Mrs. Lewis G. Stevenson

Thursday, April 21, 1921

Dear Mother:

If you can find a copy of May Vanity Fair I wish you would read the story about "Some of My Best Friends are Yale Men" By Heyward Broun; in which he suggests that the best way to improve the feeling between Harvard and Yale would be for the two to get together once

---

[46] He was a member of Quadrangle Club.

[47] The divorce case of Mr. and Mrs. James A. Stillman. See the New York *Times,* April 2, 4, 5, 11, 12, 15, 1921, for mention of the case.

a year in Madis[o]n Square Garden and sing in unison "To Hell With Princeton." The enclosed clipping from the Lamp[oon] was written by Bob Sherman '20, who is at the Harvard Law School this year, in way of a reply and I feel sure you will appreciate it.

The baseball team looks awfully good and we have [won] six successive games. Yale was beaten by Holy Cross 14–1, all of which looks rather good for us. The crew also looks very promising and what with Yale already defeated by Penn it appears as though we might repeat last year's performance with victories over Harvard and Yale. The house parties come on the 14th of May and I am seriously considering having Harriet Cowles down. Bill [Hale] will probably have a girl from Vassar also and so we will have them stay together. Mrs. Hale is in the East now and was down here for a few days to see Bill. I had dinner with her at the club one night and she inquired very particularly for you. I have found Miss Green and have weekly treatments from her.[48] She has a very nice room at a house on Bank Street and I think I will continue going to her for the rest of the spring in order to get my hair in good shape for the summer.

Louie Jones is rowing on the Varsity crew and will probably get his letter. The general concensus of opinion, not only in Quad[rangle Club] but on the Street in general seems to be that we undoubtedly have the second best section and needless to say it makes Cap [and Gown] pretty sore. I believe we did slip one over and I think we are in a fair way to resume our old prestige next to Ivy.

The weather is beautiful and the trees are in full blosom. However, I suppose the beauty of Montreux in the spring beggars anything else.

Best love to all,[49]

To Mrs. Lewis G. Stevenson [50]

May 3, 1921

Dearest Mother:

The enclosed clipping from yesterday's Prince may interest you. Needless to say it was a great surprise to me to be one of the first 12 men nominated by the present Senior Council. The Council ordinarily nominates the 12 most prominent men in the coming Senior Class and that I could be considered in that category was quite unexpected. Only five men out of this ten, making a total of 15 which composes the

---

[48] His mother was fearful that he would lose his hair and she urged him to have scalp treatments from a woman she had gone to when she lived in Princeton.
[49] This letter is typewritten and not signed.
[50] This letter is typewritten.

Senior Council and is equivalent to the number elected to Skull and Bones at Yale, are elected next fall. Of course I will not be elected among the five taken on this spring but now I at least have hopes of making it next year.[51]

You will perhaps recognize some of the other men nominated among the first 12 of the class. The five that will be elected are I think; Bill Stevenson, President of our class and captain of next year's track team, Don Lourie, the football player, Ridge Trimble, Tom McEachin and [Everett] Case or [J. Russell] Forgan. Of the 12 men nominated four were Ivy men, 2 Cap, 2 Quad, 2 Tiger Inn, and 2 Cottage. Looks rather well for Quad doesn't it? especially as Chas Denby will probably get on some time next year.

I think I told you that I am going to Europe with Bob Brooke, Eve Case, and Ogden West of Chicago. We have secured passage on the "Finland" sailing from New York on June 25, which will give us just a few days here after commencement. The Princetonian is to play the Yale News in baseball on June 18th and the event promises to be most amusing. The Prince played the Tiger yesterday and we were victorious 5 to 4. I played short stop and, of course, was a stellar performer in the position.

On Friday and Saturday of this week I have to go to a convention on the Eastern Intercollegiate Newspaper Assoc. at Columbia, as the representative of the Princetonian. I am not looking forward to it very much, especially as I may have to miss the Cottage house party. However, it ought to be very interesting as there will be several promine[n]t journalists who will speak at the banquet and we are to be taken thru all the offices and press rooms of the "Times."

Was interested to hear all about Ed Hackney, Jim Douglas etc. I have been thinking about joining Ed, John [Harlan], and Monk [Hackney] on their trip to Spain, but don't say anything to them about it.

Best love to all,
ADLAI

To Mrs. Lewis G. and Elizabeth Stevenson [52]

May 13, 1921

Dearest Mother and Buff:

I fear that more than a week has intervened since my last letter but I have really been more than usually busy during the past week.

[51] He was right. He was not elected that spring.
[52] This letter is typewritten.

What with a prolonged trip to New York, numerous tests and un-
avoidable duties, I really have not had much time. The trip to New
York consisted of a convention of the Eastern Intercollegiate Newspaper Association at which I was representing the PRINCE.[53]

As seems always to be the case in such matters, it was a frightful
bore and, as a representative of one of the larger colleges and better
papers, I had to sit by the hour and answer the questions of an endless
number of befogged but hopeful journalists from the smaller colleges.
On Friday evening they had a banquet at the Astor but the man who
was running the convention told me on the side that most of the excellent speakers had fallen through and so I was among those not
present. Instead I met Chuck Carpenter, a Quad[rangle] boy whom
Buffie will remember and who is now the intercollegiate heavyweight
wrestling champion. He recently wrestled an exhibition bout of 20
minutes with "Strangler" Lewis, the world's champion, at the Hotel
Commodore and had been given some complimentary tickets to bout
to be held that night at Madison Square Gardens for the world's
championship. Of course this was more attractive than the banquet
and so I joined Chuck and it was a very exciting evening.

I spent the night at a Columbia fraternity house and it was certainly
a dizzy bunch of men. Before the convention adjourned on Saturday I
was elected Vice-President of the Association for next year, with the
provision, however, that I would not have to do any work.

Everything around here is very much the same and the we[a]ther,
except for an occasional rainy day, is very good. The house parties
start to-night and I am having Harriet Cowles. I was not taken on the
Senior council this spring but still have a chance of making it next fall.
I cant understand how they happened to nominate me among the first
10 of the class. The Stillman case continues to be fought out in the
courts with many questionable revelations.

Best love to all,

*Adlai sailed to Europe on June 25 with his Princeton friends Everett
Case, Robert Brooke, and Ogden West. In July he and H. Hamilton
(Monk) Hackney went to Spain where Edgar Hackney and John M.
Harlan were studying at the University of Madrid. After the visit to
Spain, Adlai joined his mother and sister in Lausanne. Then he re-
turned to Princeton for his senior year.*

[53] He was elected vice president of the association for the coming year.

To Mrs. Lewis G. Stevenson

Thursday, July 28, 1921

Dear Mother:

We arrived here from our southern trip yesterday morning after four most interesting days in which we saw thoroughly the wonders of Seville, Granada and Cordova.

After cleaning up, we sat up all night on the train, yesterday morning, J.M.H[arlan]. Ed Hackney & and another Princeton boy who is staying here with them came down to the hotel and we went out to see the Royal Palace. Monk [Hackney] & I spent this morning in the Prado museum & saw the pictures of Velasquez, Murillo & the other great Spanish painters.

To-night John [Harlan], Monk & the other Princeton boy & I are going to a bull fight and tomorrow Monk & I are going to Toledo. We leave Sunday morning for Paris & arrive there, if all goes well Monday noon. I shall expect to find word at Morgan Harjes where you are & where I am to meet you. Was awfully sorry that Etretat was such a washout. I hope you will enjoy Switzerland better.

Although I am not enthusiastic over Modern Spain as a nation, the trip down here has been well worth while & I enjoyed the sights in the Southern cities immensely. John starts in a week to spend some time in the South with Dave McAlpin who is going to join him here soon. He then goes to Austria, Czechoslovakia & Germany. I may go to Austria with him providing he gets up from here in time.

Have written long letter to father and will write to Uncle Bert [Davis].

Best love
ADLAI

To Mrs. Lewis G. Stevenson

Sunday [October 2, 1921]

Dear Mother:

You have probably seen that we won from Swarthmore yesterday in the opening game of the season. I was surprised to have Clayton Blair come up to me during the game. He had dinner with me and we went to the movies together. This is his last year at Swarthmore and doesn't know what he is going to do next year. We had a delightful visit and was a real pleasure to see him again.

[103]

Work on the "Prince" has been pretty hard but is letting up now that college is under way and things are getting organized. It may interest you to know that I am taking Constitutional Interpretation — the hardest course in College.[54]

The dope about Het's [Harriet Cowles's] inheriting the money seems to have been invented by [Louis] Jones and [William] Hale to get a rise out of me — I guess they were successful. Various faculty people ask about you from time to time — Prof. Hall, Howe, Mrs. Phillips [55] etc. Seward Collins has been here over the week-end. He is studying medicine at Columbia. Schulyer Jackson, Tom Matthews, Sewie and I had a big bicker last night — a battle of gigantic wits to which I was largely a bystander.

Am feeling fine and enjoying myself immensely. Hope you and father have enjoyed the rest at Battle Creek. Is Buff arriving on the 17th? I have not heard from her but must make arrangements to meet her in New York.

Best love
ADLAI

To Mrs. Lewis G. Stevenson

Wednesday [October 12, 1921]

Dear Mother:

It may interest you to hear that I was elected to the Senior Council by the class yesterday.[56] It was certainly a surprise to me for there were some 23 men nominated only 3 of which were to be elected and I didnot think I had a chance. However, it seems that I got the largest vote of the bunch. I am very glad that I was not one of the 5 taken on by the 1921 Council last Spring because it means a great deal more to be elected in a general class election. There are now a total of 13 men on the Council and we expect 2 more tomorrow night which completes the total of 15 — the same number that make Skull & Bones at Yale.

No news in particular except that Don Lourie and Hank Garrity

54 This was taught by Professor E. S. Corwin. Adlai also had courses in history, economics, English, and geology.

55 Walter Phelps Hall, assistant professor of history; Sheldon J. Howe, instructor in history and politics; Mrs. Alexander Hamilton Phillips.

56 His father had "leaked" this news to the Bloomington *Pantagraph*, "to Adlai's discomfiture, as usual," Mrs. Ives wrote. *My Brother Adlai*, p. 161.

are both out of the Navy game which comes Saturday due to injuries. Am feeling fine & working hard.

Love to father et al.

ADLAI

p.s. Are you getting the "Prince" regularly?

To Mr. & Mrs. Lewis G. and Elizabeth Stevenson

Sunday [November 6, 1921]

Dear Mother, Father & Buff:

Yesterday was indeed a glorious day for Princeton! You have no doubt read the accounts in the papers, but I do wish you could have been here to see it for it most thoroughly avenged the tie last year and the one of the year before which you saw.

I will proceed to recount the events of the week-end. Friday was an exciting day with the arrival of many old friends from Harvard and Yale, Ralph [Goodwin] and [illegible]. Winch[ester] Jones girl arrived and that night he had a dinner party for her at the club . . . and we all had a delightful time. The Senior Prom came that night and I enjoyed it thoroughly although it wasn't as good as some other proms. Saturday morning the crowds started to pour in and Princeton's academic slumber was mercilessly disturbed. Susan Scott came down for the game — arriving about 12:30. We had lunch at the club with Bee [Norman P.] Davis and then joined the seething mass to the Stadium. The game needs no enlargement except that the spectators on both sides were exhausted when it was all over.[57] There were 54,000 people here, a record for the Stadium. Susan had to go right back after the game. In the evening we had a dance at Quad[rangle] and it was a marvellous party. Don Lourie & all the heroes of the game were there and it was a veritable riot of joy.

Today things are beginning to quiet down and everyone is absorbed in the newspaper accounts of the games sandwiched with long and detailed individual opinions. Tell father that a Mr. Elisha Camp called on me the other day. He seems to be a very good friend of all the Ewings and has a son in the Freshman Class. I also had a talk with Mrs. Lyle Funk[58] the other night. She [is] sailing soon for Europe to join Eleanor who is studying there.

Best love

ADLAI

[57] Princeton defeated Harvard 10 to 3.
[58] She was from Bloomington. Eleanor was her daughter.

Adlai's mother decided that she and her daughter would live in Princeton a second time. Adlai delayed finding a house for them. He remarked in 1963 that he still felt that it was a dreadful thing to do to a son.

To Lewis G. Stevenson

Monday [November 14, 1921]

Dear Father:

Received your special this morning. I don't believe you would have been so peremptory in your demands about looking for houses if you fully appreciated the exacting demands for time on an active senior in the "two big game weeks" of his senior year.

I had intended to do all I could as soon as the opportunity presented itself & have done so this morning. Mr. Galt, of Murray & Galt, said that he had delayed answering mother's letter until *he* found time after the Yale game. You will therefore hear from him soon. As for the Wheaton house, Mr. Howe — the other real estate agent, informs me that it is no longer on the market. The address is Hodge Road.

The other eligible houses are Prof. [R. M.] McElroy's on the corner of Stockton Ave. & Edgehill Rd. The latter is the next block beyond Library Pl, opposite the Armour's. I think it a good location and it is furnished, but they are not leaving until the latter part of January. In my opinion quite time enough to come. The price is $225 per month.

Mr. Howe also mentioned the Kemmerer[59] house on Fitz Randolph Dr. — the street that Admiral Goodrich lives on. Not as good a location as the other end of town.

In regard to Mrs. Edmonds house, I do not think it would be very satisfactory — a little out of the way; below the end of Library Place. Mr. Howe is writing you at once about all these houses & some others.

Personally I can see no reason for coming to Princeton — if you want to come at all — until after Christmas — about the first of February.[60] There is nothing doing here now & I thought perhaps the family would like to go south somewhere for Christmas — Pinehurst, Southern Pines, [illegible] or some other place where mother would enjoy the weather.

I would have Buff examined & see if she is subject to an attack of appendicitis. [illegible] Mildred [Bromwell] seemed to think she had an attack in Paris.

[59] Professor and Mrs. E. W. Kemmerer.

[60] His mother and sister rented a house in Princeton from February, 1922, to June, 1922. This is the last extant letter from Princeton.

I am getting along splendidly, enjoying myself & wasting *no* time. Wish I had some to waste. I got the highest mark in the entire course in the first test in Constitutional Interpretation. It is extremely hard but I rather like it.

Best love to all,
ADLAI

P.S. Am going to room with Chas. Denby & Norman Davis at Harvard Law School.

Mrs. Ives, in recalling Adlai's last months at Princeton, wrote: "I remembered thinking that college had matured my brother, and hadn't given him what I was glibly calling 'complexes.'" My Brother Adlai, *p. 163.*

In the spring, Adlai was appointed to two commencement committees. In the voting by his classmates, he received 8 votes for "biggest politician" and placed third. The winner had 124 votes. He received 28 votes for the man "who thinks he is the biggest politician" and placed second. The winner had 41 votes. He received 2 votes as "the man most likely to succeed," placing eighteenth on that list. He was ninth on a nine-man list for "best all-around man outside athletics." Twenty of his classmates received votes as "wittiest" but he did not receive any of them.

Part Four

Harvard Law School
1922–1924

*A*dlai E. Stevenson was a reluctant law student. If the Daily Panta-graph had been Stevenson property, he might well have returned to Bloomington to begin a career in journalism. But the paper was not controlled by the Stevensons and moreover it was staunchly Republican. Lewis G. Stevenson insisted that his son attend law school. Jesse Fell and Grandfather Adlai E. Stevenson had been lawyers, and Lewis had regretted his own lack of legal training. Anyway, his father explained, a good knowledge of the law would be useful "no matter what you do later."

As a result, during his senior year at Princeton Adlai had applied and had been admitted to the Harvard Law School. In the summer of 1922 he and Ralph Goodwin went to Wyoming to work on a ranch. During the summer they decided to try ranching together. When Adlai asked his father for financial assistance, Lewis exploded. He warned his son if he were not back in time for law school, he would go to Wyoming and bring him back. (Near the end of his life Governor Stevenson wondered what his life would have been like if he had lived it his own way. He commented that he felt that he had been pushed into things and asked: "What if I had become a rancher, for instance?")

While young Stevenson had enjoyed his four years at Princeton, he was not happy at the Harvard Law School. He did not fail, but at the end of his second year his standing had fallen below the level of his class. His happiest memories of life at Harvard were the various activities he participated in with old and new friends. He particularly enjoyed the opportunity of skiing in the New England countryside.

At the Harvard Law School during his first year he roomed at Claverly Hall with two Princeton classmates, Charles Denby and William B. McIlvaine, Jr., and a Choate friend, Norman P. Davis, a Harvard senior, known as B. The second year the four added Francis T. P.

Plimpton, a law school classmate of Adlai's from Amherst College, and rented the top floor of a ramshackle yellow frame house at 35 Bow Street.

The handwritten letters that he wrote home are in the Elizabeth Stevenson Ives collection, the Illinois State Historical Library. His original spellings of certain words are printed as he wrote them — no "sic" has been added. We included all the letters we could locate for these years. Sometimes he dated his letters or the postmarked envelopes were saved. When he just wrote the day of the week on the letter and the envelope was not kept, we have tried to ascertain the date through internal evidence in the letter. In such cases we have placed the date within brackets. Helen E. Land of the Department of History, Harvard University, assisted us in locating a number of dates through checking a variety of sources.

To Mrs. Lewis G. Stevenson

Tuesday night, September 26, 1922

Dearest Mother:

We have just finished abstracting some cases in property! Doesn't that sound formidable? And maybe its not! This Harvard Law School is the most feverish place Ive ever seen — everyone works ALL the time and still about 25–35% get dropped every year. All we've heard since we arrived were gruesome tales of disaster from our friends and staggering stories of astonishing hours of work when the big reviews begin in March. Until then it is a comparative loaf. Just do your work from day to day — and it can be done easily in about 8 hrs. Oh the news is certainly encouraging and I'm looking forward to a very delightful winter. Everyone around here insists that the Harvard Law School is the hardest graduate school of any kind in America. It certainly is a charming prospect and attendance at a total of 4 classes so far substantiates the worst I've heard.

Chas. [Denby] Bill [McIlvaine] & I were the first ones taken into Lincoln's Inn — the best of the Law School eating clubs and we were over there for brunch and dinner today and will eat there regularly from now on. Its a very nice house, the men seem like a splendid bunch and the food is very good. Dick Cleveland, Dave McAlpin, Jim Douglas, Bob Sherman and some other Princeton men are in it. Edgar Hackney flunked out last spring and is trying to get in Penn now. Corney [Cornelius] Trowbridge has given up law and gone into the ministry! Dick [Cleveland] walked back with Bill & I and bickered with us here in the room for a while after dinner. Dave McAlpin flunked one course last spring. Bill and I began to tremble when we arrived and are shaking now.

B. [Davis] will not graduate [from Harvard] until February and then will have to stay out until next fall when he will enter the law school. Our rooms are very comfortable, large, sunny, etc. As yet we are a little disorganized but are rapidly getting order out of chaos. It was certainly a pleasant surprise to find the rooms furnished. Chas & I got the best bedrooms, being the first here, Bill got the next one & B, being last, did not score to heavily.

I don't like Boston or Cambridge but it doesn't make much difference because we apparently are not going to have time for an enjoying of the urban communities. Have met a lot of old acquaintances and am quite happy but we all will have to get adjusted to an entirely different standard of work and life in fact. The law school is sort of like being in business, not college. We have so many enormous books & notebooks to carry that we have to carry them back & forth to class in satchels. More bad news later.

Best love
ADLAI

To Mrs. Lewis G. Stevenson

Sunday night [1]

Dear Mother:

No new developments. One day is very much as another, with a perpetual anticipation of the week-end as a slight respite from the monotonous drudgery of the week. Yesterday we attended the football game as is our wont on Saturday afternoons. In the evening we went into Boston for dinner and then to a movie — a very good one too at which D. W. Griffith appeared in person and addressed the audience with a few well chosen, if not startling, words.

This morning we slept late, absorbed the papers, discussed the football situation at length and loafed luxuriously. This afternoon B [Davis] borrowed a Ford and we drove out to Milton to see his attractive young sister who is in school there. We had tea in the demure and chaste confines of the young ladies seminary and came back along the river at sundown. It was delightful to get out into the country and see the trees in their blazing autumn garb. To discover that there really were trees and grass after all was a pleasant revelation to me after being cooped up in this God-forsaken city for 3 weeks.

[1] Mrs. Ives thinks this letter was written in October, 1922, when she was visiting Louise Thoron in New York City. Letter to Walter Johnson, November 26, 1967.

Uncle Bert [H. O. Davis] called me up from N.Y. Friday and said there were no recent important developments and that I need not come down to see him unless I wanted to. I had a nice long talk with him and he seemed very cheerful and well; and exceedingly kind and well disposed toward us all. Dave [Merwin] seems to be working conscientiously and had assured him that he could work and get along with me if he could do so with anyone.[2]

Tell Buff not to worry about coming to Boston to see me. She wouldn't enjoy it here a bit and I'd much rather go down to N.Y. sometime to see her. It would be a splendid excuse and I'd enjoy it more than having her here. Did you know that old John P. Wilson[3] had died?

I'm feeling splendidly, getting lots of exercise and am in top form generally. Do hope you all are well and things are serene.

Best love

ADLAI

To Mrs. Lewis G. Stevenson

Sunday, October 8, 1922

Dear Mother —

Another week has crept by. I'm becoming more immune to the terrors of the law school and am rapidly adjusting myself to the monstrous routine — the law is indeed a jealous mistress and thus far not a particularly attractive one. But parts of it are quite interesting and I may learn to enjoy it.

There are a lot of nice men around here. Saw Jerry Beard[4] yesterday — he is involved in the Business school and as much at sea as the rest of us. We all went to the football game yesterday and, in spite of the rather inclement weather, enjoyed it tremendously. Last night Chas [Denby], B [Davis], Bill [McIlvaine] and I went to the theatre in Boston with most of the rest of the law school. There are no movies here so on Saturday night everyone goes to the theatre for a little concentrated recreation. Everything is concentrated; work, play and exercise. I've been playing squash every afternoon and enjoy it tremendously. Its splendid exercise and doesn't take long.

Chas, Bill, Irv. Harris, Princeton '20, a Harvard boy named Bob

---

[2] H. O. Davis was in poor health. Davis Merwin was now working for the *Daily Pantagraph*. The Merwins and the Stevensons, who would inherit the paper on the death of H. O. Davis, were discussing the possibility of Adlai's working for the paper.

[3] A Chicago lawyer and a summer resident at Charlevoix, Michigan.

[4] Adlai had first met him at Horton's ranch in Wyoming.

Finley, and myself study together most every night. Talking over cases is about the best way to study so we're going to make a practice of doing it as much as possible.

I still find it hard to reconcile myself to Cambridge. To my mind its a most unattractive place. As for the University the thing that impresses me particularly is that nobody seems to know or care to know *anyone* else. And then the freshmen can't be distinguished from anyone else. Its entirely different atmosphere from Princeton — a city club rather than a country club.

Had a long letter from Hite. Her plans seem rather indefinite but she is still expecting to go abroad in December. Dale Warren told me over the phone that Noel Symonds was now in Spokane, had been seeing a lot of her and apparently had fallen most completely.[5] Hurray for the competition, bring 'em on; the more the merrier!

The entire Princeton delegation in the graduate schools here — about 50, are going down to the Yale game. We're looking forward to it already.

> Best love
> ADLAI

P.S. Feeling fine etc etc.

To Mrs. Lewis G. Stevenson

Thursday, October 12, 1922

Dear Mother:

Today is Columbus Day — just what it is and what it signifies — I don't know and thusfar have been unable to ascertain. However, its a holiday and that's what counts.

Last night Chas [Denby], Bill [McIlvaine] & I went out to dinner in Newtonville with some Princeton grads that are working in Boston and living out there, including Dale Warren. There were about 15 of us in all but we were the only ones from the Law School. The avowed purpose of the party was to organize a Princeton smoker before the Harvard game. Anyway it served as a splendid excuse and we had a very merry evening.

Today was spent in concentrated loafing but to-night the work starts again. As yet my opinions of Cambridge have not been mellowed — I thoroughly dislike the atmosphere and the whole place as much as ever. I've met, thru "B," [Davis] a lot of very nice Harvard men

---

[5] Hite was Harriet Cowles, Adlai's "love" from his Princeton days. Noel Symonds was a Princeton man and a good friend of Dale Warren.

and find life among a small section of the undergraduate body quite agreeable.

Called on Rob't Richardson [6] yesterday but he was not in. I'll make another attempt tonight.

Find little moral foundation in the law but a great deal that is interesting if a bit obscure at times. I have to argue a law club case on Nov. 7th and am getting worried about it already.[7] Haven't seen a blade of grass, except a few square ft. on the campus, since I've been here but I'm still searching.

Best love
ADLAI

To Mrs. Lewis G. Stevenson

Wednesday [October 25, 1922]

Dear Mother:

I didn't write Sunday because there was nothing to say — nothing new to say. To-morrows are much like to-days here and were it not for for the ever present tomes the monotony would be deadly.

The Center game was great to watch and we all enjoyed it tremendously and were needless to say loyal supporters of the invaders.[8] Harvard has a splendid team and I'm afraid we'll have a hard time beating them this year but there's always hope and we are always at our best against them.

I have almost finished my law club brief but will have to do some more work polishing it up before the actual argument takes place in Nov. Its hard but interesting work preparing them and gives you some idea of what a practicing lawyer has to do when he has a case before a superior court that involves a nice distinction or problem in law.

Buff seems to be quite gay in Bloomington and I'm delighted that she is having such a nice time and being so congenial with everyone. Its really not such a bad place afterall.

If you have a little rug somewhere around the house you might

---

[6] Robert Dale Richardson, a cousin on the Fell side of the family. He became a Unitarian minister.

[7] His mother wrote him: "Dearest Laddie: As the time draws near for your argument, I wonder if you are in doubt about your success? Success as regards your equanimity? I hope you will let this be an opportunity to prove to yourself that if you have done all that was necessary in preparation, nothing is worth getting nervous over. . . . Be perfectly sincere, serious and natural. Show that you are doing the best you can and everybody respects that." Quoted in Elizabeth Stevenson Ives and Hildegarde Dolson, *My Brother Adlai* (New York: Morrow, 1956), p. 166.

[8] The Harvard–Centre College game was played on Saturday, October 21, 1922. Harvard won 24 to 10.

send it for my bedroom. It's nice to have something to step on instead of the cold floor in the mornings. If you haven't one don't worry because I can get a bath rug here for a couple of dollars.

Feeling splendidly getting lots of exercise etc. so don't worry.

Best love
ADLAI

To Mrs. Lewis G. Stevenson

Sunday [October 29, 1922]

Dear Mother:

I've just come in from squash at B [Davis]'s club. Its a beautiful day and I think will go out for a little walk.

Father left last night after a very pleasant visit. He arrived early Friday morning, B. showed him around for awhile and then he attended one of my classes and seemed very much impressed with the display of erudition not to mention the thirsty intellects of the semitic element. In the afternoon he had a business talk with Scott [9] and then we went out for a walk. I sent him down to Boston early intending to study hard. As a matter of fact we did study for awhile until a visitor informed us that there was a big Harvard-Dartmouth dance down town. So we at once shifted our scenes and departed for the scene of festivity & make our initial bow into Boston society. When we arrived we found a drunken, seething mob besieging the doors and the good news that all the tickets were sold. However, by a little diplomatic handling of a ticket secured from an ejected drunk and pass out checks we all managed to drift in at illegally reduced prices. Although the party was more of a fight than a dance and not much good it was nevertheless a lot of fun.

Up early the next morning and to class where father also arrived fascinated with the intricacies of the law as presented by the smartest collection of men in the world — the faculty. In the afternoon father went to the game with us and enjoyed it all tremendously. After the [Harvard-Dartmouth] game we all sat around the room awhile and then loquaciously celebrated the news of Princeton's unexpected victory. Bill [McIlvaine] & Chas. [Denby] had other things they had to do, so father took Scott [Bromwell], B & I to dinner and the theatre; and left us afterward to take the train to N.Y. to meet Buff.

I was intensely disappointed that you did not let me know you

[9] Scott Bromwell, son of Mrs. Charles (Letty) Bromwell. Mrs. Bromwell was the sister of Mrs. Carl (Julia) Vrooman, of Bloomington. Scott Bromwell and Stevenson were second cousins.

wanted to see the [Harvard-] Chicago game. If you would always just warn me sufficiently in advance I could arrange it.

Love
ADLAI

To Mrs. Lewis G. Stevenson

Friday [November 3, 1922]

Dear Mother:

Anticipating celebrations for the Harvard-Princeton encounter start a week from today and everyone is engrossed in exchange of advance dope on the game and its accessories — parties etc. So the intervening days should pass rapidly and with less monotony than is the general wont of the law school.

I saw Robt. Richardson again the other day. In fact he came up to see me and we had a very elevating few moments — if not enlivening. I am still busy with my case which I must argue Tuesday night. They are an awful bore and require rather more time than the experience is worth I think. Just as soon as its over I'll have to start preparation for another one. This second one is a "double," that is there are two men for counsel on both sides.

Had a letter from Buff asking for Hallie Davis' [10] address which I sent her. Don't know definitely yet whether she is coming or not. I wish you had gone up to the [Harvard-] Chicago game for it will be a famous one and well worth seeing and having seen. Furthermore none of the big Eastern teams will ever play out there again because of the "Big Three" agreement to discontinue intersectional games away from home.

Still don't find Harvard particularly to my liking and we all continue to go to bed with a tacit cheer for Princeton and wake up with a groan for Harvard and the daily routine in general.

Best love,
ADLAI

To Mrs. Lewis G. Stevenson

Sunday [November 12, 1922]

Dear Mother:

Well the week-end is over and it has been a glorious one indeed. Buff arrived early Saturday morning and ever-faithful Dale [Warren]

10 A Washington, D.C., debutante who married George Percy.

met her at the station, took her to some relative's of his for breakfast & to dispose of her baggage for she was staying there overnight.

Friday night I went to the Princeton smoker and we had a great time seeing a lot of the boys again and also getting the dope for our class notes in the Alumni Weekly. After the smoker we migrated to the Copley [Plaza] for a big party. And it certainly was a big party literally speaking — I've never seen such a frightful crowd in my life. All in all there were about four or five girls there I knew including Jeanette Harlan and Abby Rockefeller.[11] However it was pretty good fun just the same. Got up late Saturday morning and greeted all the new Princeton arrivals and went down for Buff about 12. The people she was staying with live on Commonwealth Avenue in an old and genteel mansion and are typical "beans" — flat footed and everything. We went out to Hallie Davis' for lunch in Cambridge and from there to the game. As for the latter, words fail me. The Princeton team — all green and without experience — simply beat Harvard by spirit and fight alone.[12] It was a glorious day for us and after having lived in this Harvard atmosphere for a couple of months I would rather have beaten them than Yale a dozen times. After the game Buff & I went over to a tea dance at the Hasty Pudding Club which was also a polite battle. Buff went to dinner with Dale [Warren] & Mr. Horton [13] and this morning I met her and we had lunch together at the Copley and then to the train and farewell. She's going down to the Benson's [14] this week-end for the Yale game and I'm trying to get a couple of tickets so we can sit together.

The Harvards are accusing us in no disguised terms of dirty foot-ball. It makes us all so sore we can't see. I guess about the only thing Harvard & P. can play together to their satisfaction is marbles. I hope Yale beats them about 20 to 0 to see if they accuse Yale of dirty foot-ball also. If they win they won't say anything but loose and at once then a terrible to do. I'm afraid they're fundamentally poor losers. Now to work for another week.

Love

ADLAI

P.S. I won $25 from Scott [Bromwell] which did my heart good.

---

[11] Miss Harlan was John M. Harlan's sister. Miss Rockefeller was the daughter of John D. Rockefeller, Jr.

[12] Princeton won 10 to 3.

[13] Lydiard Horton, a family friend who had lived for a time in Bloomington.

[14] Buffie frequently stayed with Mr. and Mrs. Lawrence Benson when she visited Princeton.

To Lewis G. Stevenson

Sunday [November 12, 1922]

Dear Father:

Enclosed please find the first of the "bad news." [15] However, it only happens twice a year so don't think its going to be a regular occurrence.

Buff & I had a great time together. She seems very well and is app[a]rently having an exceedingly gay time in New York. She enjoyed her visit up here tremendously and got almost as excited at the game as I did. She seems to thoroughly detest Harvard already — after a two day visit which is quite proper and as it should be from my standpoint, with which you are familiar. Harvard certainly displayed the worst sportsmanship yesterday I've ever seen — and certainly didn't expect to see here. Of course they accused Princeton of dirty football — we expected that but we didn't expect them to cheer our penalties etc. I think the secret of it all is that Harvard has so long been in the habit of having her own way about anything that they simply can't have a proper reaction to a fare and square trimming.

The game was a beauty. Wish you could have seen it. George Owen wasn't as good against us as he was in the Dartmouth game and you remember he didn't cover himself with glory in that game. But the astonishing thing was that Princeton — a green and unusually inexperienced team — played absolutely faultless football while Harvard with all their stars and finished coaching made error after error which we immediately seized and turned to our advantage. The result was that we didn't need to use much of our open football and trick plays so that we can save them all for Yale this Saturday. The score could have been larger than it was and all in all it was an easy victory for us. I won $25 from Scott [Bromwell] which seemed perfectly right and just.

Love
ADLAI

To Mrs. Lewis G. Stevenson

Friday [probably early December, 1922]

Dear Mother:

Have been working hard since you left and have my brief finished at last. I'm leaving here on the Wolverine on Wednesday December 20

[15] Adlai apparently enclosed his account from the Harvard Law School.

and will get home the following evening; got my ticket yesterday and am all set!

My cold is practically all well and the cough has stopped completely.

Mrs. [Marian Monk] Chase called me up yesterday and I'm going to dinner with them Sunday at a Mrs. Monks, a relative of hers. Mr. [Lydiard] Horton sent me a note saying that he had ordered one of the evaporators which he told me about and which I'll install on arrival.

Went to dinner the other night with Mac Veagh [16] and found him quite pleasant and amusing but a bit affected and "bumptious."

We had a dinner here in Cambridge Tuesday night for Professor Conklin [17] who is giving the Lowell Lectures in Boston this year. It was good fun seeing a lot of the medical students again and very interesting discussing all about things at Princeton.

The galosh period has arrived again what with a busy snow during the last couple of days so we are now veritable "flappers."

There being no additional news, I can proceed no further. Please don't forget about the Christmas cards — providing its not very expensive to have them made up — very simple ones.

Love
ADLAI

To Mrs. Lewis G. Stevenson

Thursday [December 14, 1922]

Dear Mother:

I won my second case last night by the decisive point score of 25–15. Being relieved of that anxiety I can work peacefully until Wednesday and then for home and the parental hearth.

Tomorrow night the annual Christmas dinner takes place at the Inn. It is customary for most of the professors to attend and partake of the brimming bowl with the struggling students. President [A. Lawrence] Lowell has signified his intention of attending but the general impression seems to be that his august presence will not seriously affect the tenor of the evenings entertainment.

What would you think of my going up to Lake Placid about the 28th? You see we have to be back here on the 3rd of Jan. anyway and I thought it would be a good way to get in some good out door exercise before coming back here for the long winter grind. There

---

[16] Ewen MacVeagh, son of Ambassador Charles MacVeagh.
[17] Edward Grant Conklin, professor of biology, Princeton University.

are a lot of people going to be there I know not to mention the Princeton Hockey team and besides being an invigorating few days would be good fun. I could get in the [illegible] with Irv. Harris for about $8 a day, which wouldn't be bad for only 4 or 5 days. However, we'll talk it over when I get back.

Best love
ADLAI

Adlai spent Christmas at home in Bloomington. His sister remembers that he and his father had a lively time discussing legal problems. Adlai went to Lake Placid just before the New Year.

To Mrs. Lewis G. Stevenson

Sunday [December 31, 1922]

Dear Mother:

If there is a heaven on earth I've found it at last. We arrived last night only an hour late. They held the train at Utica for us or we would have been all night getting here. Jim Douglas, John Fennelly, Teddy Donnelly [18] and others were on the train.

It is now noon & we're waiting to go into lunch. Skiing is the most delightful sport I've ever indulged in. There are about 800 people here including many acquaintances so I'm having a wonderful time. We have to leave Tuesday morning.

Best love
ADLAI

To Mrs. Lewis G. Stevenson

Wednesday [January 3, 1923]

Dear Mother:

Well we're all back at work again just as though nothing had happened to interfere with the routine. We left Placid yesterday morning at 11 and after changing at Lake Clear, Utica and Albany finally arrived in this jolly old hall early this morning. We met some friends in Albany who are working there now[,] managed to while away the hours without much difficulty.

Lake Placid was delightful and it did me a world of good beside the fact that I never had more fun or enjoyed anything more thoroughly. I regretted intensely that I was only there such a short time for there is such a lot to do and so many nice people to play with. I didn't ar-

[18] Friends from Chicago.

rive until Saturday morning and so really only had two full days but managed to cram in a lot of activity in that time. Sunday morning I made my initial effort and [on] skis and found it wonderful sport. In the afternoon we got a sleigh and some girls and went for a ride taking our skis along. The evening was spent in having a good time generally with our gang all assembled and perhaps sho[c]king the elderly inmates who were engaged in their New Year's eve and Sunday devotions combined. Monday morning it was rainy so we played bridge — faut de mieux. In the afternoon Darwin Kingsley, "Max" Schniewind (one of the best of the ex-debs of N.Y.'s 400) and I went for a long walk overland to John Brown's place where we ate pan cakes & had a merry time generally. Coming back it got dark & we got lost which made it all the more fun. In the evening Darwin, Irv Harris & 3 girls and I went for a sleigh ride to another place for hot cakes. Finally to bed & off in the morning & my happy story is told.

Best love
ADLAI

P.S. Send Aunt Julia's [19] address so I can thank her.

To Mrs. Lewis G. Stevenson

Sunday [January, 1923]

Dear Mother —

Its been snowing constantly ever since we returned and now even Cambridge is quite beautiful in its white mantel. We are planning a week-end trip up to Jaffrey [New Hampshire] some time in the near future, but are not sure just when, for at present I'm involved in another case. This time an inter Club argument; the Chief Justice on which is a professor. So the preparation must be even a little more exhaustive than the others. However the welcome check will be employed for its intended purposes so have no fears about misappropriation and many thanks. Father too has sent me one so for the time being I'm quite wealthy.

The Ewings & Merwins [20] were exceedingly nice to me at Lake Placid altho to be sure I was there such a short while and so busy that I didn't see much of any of them. I had a nice talk with Uncle Lou — he seemed in excellent spirits and pathetically friendly and loquacious. Cousin Spencer loaned me his skis to use for, due to the number of guests, there was a decided dearth. Dave seemed well & happy and happy and

[19] Mrs. Martin D. Hardin.

[20] Mr. and Mrs. Spencer Ewing and Mr. and Mrs. L. B. Merwin (Uncle Lou and Aunt Jessie) of Bloomington. Dave was their son. Eleanor Bumpstead was a niece of Mrs. Ewing.

was with Eleanor Bumpstead constantly, thereby causing I[rving]. Harris some discontent as regards the anticipated progress of his affaire de coeur among the enchanting environments of Lake Placid in winter.

If the weather continues the status quo, the suggested quilt might not be superfluous equipment. Tell Buff that Bob Spier [21] was at L.P. and asked for her, as well as the family in general, very particularly. He was on sort of a house party with not very attractive people and seemed, altho not confessedly, to be having a non-too exciting time. Tell Buff I've just read the review of "Literary Studies" — Sir Arthur Quiller-Couches new selection of essays and lectures including the famous Byron lecture. A splendid book to read and keep, I should imagine.

The enclosed, tell father, is a proof sheet from the Law Review containing the citation & some notes on the case we were discussing.

Best love

ADLAI

To Mrs. Lewis G. Stevenson

Sunday [late January, 1923]

Dear Mother & Buff —

I was delighted to hear that you are comfortably installed and that the rejuvenation under salubrious southern skies had already commenced. That you are both becoming interested in golf is good news indeed and I'm sure that a lot of exercise for Buff, at something she *enjoys* doing, will be the panacea of the evils of aenemia.

For me the last week has been an epochal one, with two visits to the Chicago Opera the distinguishing incidents. Wednesday night Bill [McIlvaine] & I donned dress coats and went in to be enchanted by Tosca with Claudia Muzio, Crimi & Fanichi. The following event extravagance again lured us and we heard Walkuere; this time with Cyrena Van Gordon, Grace Halst, Barklanoff and Forrest Lamont. I enjoyed them both tremendously but, being totally different, I can't determine which "weaves the more potent spell."

Picture my pleasant surprise to receive as my share of the Princetonian dividends a check for $792.80. As you know I have invested $100 of it in some stock which we expect to sell next week at a gain of perhaps $40. After a few such minor speculations I'm going to buy a bond of some reliable variety and enter the capitalist class therewith.

---

[21] Robert Spier had been John M. Harlan's roommate at Princeton and one of Buffie's "beaux."

With the exception of the above observations the to-morrows proceed as the yesterdays; with me working perhaps a little harder and enjoying the work more. As for knowing what it's all about I'm not particularly confident but, with the increasing application, the reward of effort may be more light.

I'm going to Poland Springs' Maine for Washington's birthday. We have a vacation Thursday & so we're leaving Wednesday night & returning Sun., cutting Fri. & Sat. in the interest of the great outdoors.

Best love
ADLAI

To Mrs. Lewis G. Stevenson

Sunday [February 11, 1923]

Dear Mother:

The initial week of my 23rd year was an auspicious one if conscientiousness is any criterion for the future. All of which proves that between Monday morning and Sat. night I put in 60 hours of work. The realization that more sustained application is necessary than heretofore has suddenly possessed me and I expect to apply myself very diligently henceforth.

Buff will be interested in hearing that Dick Cleveland's engagement to Bishop Golar's daughter [22] has been announced. That is, not formally announced, but it leaked into the papers a little previously. She called on us with Dick at Princeton last spring, as you probably remember.

As for the news, there is none. I had a very sweet letter from Mrs. St. John [23] on my birthday including a personal invitation to come and stay with them at the "Festivities" on Washington's Birthday. They are arranging a section reunion at the Club for Washington's birthday also but I've decided to go up into the country somewhere instead. Bill [McIlvaine] Chas [Denby], Dave McAlpin, Darwin Kingsley and I are going together. Since we can't get into Poland Springs we will probably go to Jaffr[e]y or Conway N.H.

I'm delighted that you & Buff are so well pleased with Southern Pines and particularly that golf has begun to weave its subtle spell on your heretofore impervious minds. I'm sure it will do you a lot of good & Buff particularly. Ben Thoron dropped in the other night & delayed my work for an hour of fruitless bicker and also to hear that he had not

[22] Ellen Douglas Gailor, daughter of Thomas F. Gailor, Episcopal Bishop of Maryland.
[23] Wife of the headmaster of Choate.

been favored with a letter from our fair charmer any more recently than I.

Did I tell you that Ralph [Goodwin] had been operated on for appendicitis & was now recuperating in the Ojai Valley, Calif. His ranching future seems somewhat shaken. Tell Buff her letter about the Burts [24] was a masterpiece of analytical observation but that there is no such word as "amalgoration."

Best love
ADLAI

To Mrs. Lewis G. Stevenson

Sunday [February 18, 1923]

Dear Mother:

Another week of 50 hours work has passed. We are working on a regular schedule now — from 9 to 1 in the morning, from 2 to 5 in the afternoon, and from 7:30 to 10:30 at night. Of course all the time cannot be counted as actually used in work because there are bound to be occasional interruptions, so we are really only working about 8 or 9 hours a day, but as far as I can see you can't get in any more than that — the day is too short.

I have stopped smoking entirely for lent, at least and feel exceedingly virtuous. There seems to have been reformatory wave around here for everyone is swearing off something.

Friday night, after much persuasion, I did society for the first time in many weeks, and went into the last of the Junior Supper dances at the Copley [Plaza]. According to Boston standards it was a great party, but I didn't get much of a thrill out of it and withdrew, with others, at a discreet hour.

Cousins Richardson, Harriet & Emmet, have been here over the week end seeing Robert. I called on them after dinner Friday evening and had a long and quite pleasant talk about things in general. They have rescently heard from Aunt Fannie — her tidings as to Uncle Bert were not happy.[25] It seems the accident aggravated the asthma and he's having a hard time of it.

We have finally secured accomadations at Poland Springs thru the intervention of an influential Bostonian with whom Darwin Kingsley is acquainted. He told them to fix us up and apparently that's all there was to it. So Bill [McIlvaine], Chas [Denby], Dave McAlpin, Darwin

---

24 Mr. and Mrs. Struthers Burt.
25 H. O. Davis — Uncle Bert — had asthma and spent a good deal of time in California. Aunt Fannie Fell, daughter of Jesse W. Fell, was living in California.

et all, et moi depart for the North Wednesday night with the idea of coming back Sunday full of health and renewed vigor. The spring vacation comes on Sat. April 14 to Monday April 23. If you are expecting to remain in the East that long, I'll go wherever you say. If not I'll go down to Princeton — to loaf and play golf. B [Davis] has asked us to spend a couple of days with him in N.Y. with golf at Tuxedo. However, thats a long time off and I won't make any plans until I hear from you and what you contemplate doing.

I was delighted to hear that Buff had undertaken to elevate the movies.[26] As for suggestions from me I regret that at present I have none and little time to ponder it. But I should like, at some future time, to collaborate and contribute my quota of imaginative extravagances.

My health continues as always good and the anti-Cantabrigian feeling less virulent.

> Best love
> ADLAI

Adlai and his friends James Douglas, William Tucker, Darwin Kingsley, Charles Denby, William B. McIlvaine, Jr., David McAlpin, and Francis T. P. Plimpton went to Poland Springs, Maine, over Washington's Birthday. Mr. and Mrs. Loring Underwood and their daughters Lorna and Nina joined them. After this weekend Adlai was a frequent Sunday visitor to the Underwoods' home in Belmont, Massachusetts.

To Mrs. Lewis G. Stevenson

> Monday night [February 26, 1923]

Dear Mother —

Probably the best week-end I ever had! Douglas, Tucker and Kingsley went up Wednesday night and Chas, Bill, McAlpin, Plimpton and I left after classes Thursday noon. All the girls . . . and Mr. & Mrs. Underwood went up early Thursday morning.

We arrived just in time to clean up for dinner and then to join the rest for a great gorging contest. After dinner and a few hands of bridge we put on our snow clothes and all went out to the toboggan slide. It was a clear night and the moon just full — a gorgeous sight. We had a very merry time of it and then crept back exhausted to bed.

The following day was a riot of exercise. The morning consisted of a long cross country ski run ending in time for another tremendous meal.

---

[26] Mrs. Ives thinks she was trying to write a "scenario" at that point. Letter to Walter Johnson, November 26, 1967.

In the afternoon we all dispersed following our various inclinations & ended up with a hockey game. After dinner we started off on a sleigh ride which was accompanied with much good cheer and rough housing. The fancy dress ball was in progress when we got back and so we did a bit of dancing and called it a day.

Saturday consisted of more exercise of the same variety — tobogganing, skiing and skating — with large and hilarious meals thrown in — all 14 of us ate at one table so the conversation was fast and furious. More exercise Sunday morning and we departed early in the afternoon to board a car reserved *exclusively* for us. There ensued a riotous 5 hour ride back to Boston and of course the breaking up in the North Station was a sad and depressing affair. The girls were a great bunch — not an unattractive one among them, in fact all knockouts. — [Charles] Denby was working overtime with his lady love, Max Schniewind, but how much time he made I can't say. I'm afraid he has a long way to go before she surrenders.

Its impossible to do justice to our outing in words for it was simply a succession of amusing little incidents and we were all absolutely weak with laughter from beginning to end. I can't wait until we all go back again next year.[27] Incidentally the whole thing, Ry fare and all, cost only $32 for 4 whole days.

I returned to find a note from Rob't Richardson to the effect that his mother & father were here. So I called on them at his room this morning and had dinner with them tonight and later brought them up to my room for a visit since Robt had to study and we had no place to go. The latest developments are that Robt will go to Oxford to study theology next year providing he can get in some good college. We didn't discuss the Pantagraph at all. They didn't suggest it so I didn't bring it up for after all there wasn't anything I wanted to talk with them about. They are to be here several days more so I'll see them again.

The enclosed arrived from father who is now in New York & writes that he will manage Sprague pro[v]iding Clark's matter "which means cash" doesn't demand immediate attention.

Love

ADLAI

---

[27] His mother replied to this letter: "It was good for you to get a change and from the tone of your letter it must have been a success. I shall now expect you to go to Jaffrey [his mother apparently was misled by Adlai's letter of February 11 that they could not get reservations at Poland Springs and might go to Jaffrey] for several weekends for rest & recreation. Please do so. . . . Father writes glowingly of your health, spirits and poise [he had just visited Adlai at Harvard]. Glad indeed to know you are well and enjoying a rare opportunity — that of really *learning*. As much as possible, seek the association of wise people. . . . Don't waste much time

To Mrs. Lewis G. Stevenson

Sunday [early March, 1923?]

Dear Mother:

Last Sunday Bill [McIlvaine], Chas [Denby], [David] McAlpin, [Darwin] Kingsley & I went out to Belmont, a suburb of Boston, and spent the afternoon and greater part of the evening with the Underwoods. Another girl who was up in Poland [Springs] with us was also there and we had a very jolly day of it.

The Underwoods have a very nice house; apparently not tremendously wealthy, but very aristocratic, refined and cultured. Mr. Underwood's is, I believe, by profession a landscape architect or something like that. At least he has a hobby for ornamental gardening and goes around giving illustrated lectures on European gardens etc.

The daughters a[re] very attractive — one came out 2 or 3 years ago & the other last year I believe. We arrived early in the afternoon and all (8) set out for a tramp across the slushy countryside. It turned into a most raucous and amusing "walk" when we left the roads and started to struggle thru bottomless snow for the remainder of the afternoon. Most of the time was spent submerged to the waste and struggling valiantly against the snow and debilitating hysterics. However, we all got back about tea time none the worse for it. After tea, we sat around & amused ourselves until supper, at which Mr. Underwood presided and constructed a Welsh rabbit of rare delicacy. Then followed a session of bridge and conversational jesting. Came a late hour and we piled on McAlpin's 2 passenger Ford and returned to the "diggins" after a most pleasant day among the snows and ladies. Incidentally we are figuring and hoping for some invigorating week-ends down at the Underwoods place on the Cape during the spring!

Last night some loyal Princetonians assembled at a banquet at the Lenox where I encountered Dale [Warren] for the first time in many weeks. He was or seemed as healthy & gushing as usual but informed me that he had been ill & away for some time. He informed me that he was convinced that Buff was married or engaged & he wanted to know all about it. The tone of a letter of her's to him seems to have been that a great "something" had taken place in her life and he assumed that love had flown in. However I assured him his fears were unfounded & he seemed much relieved.

on mediocres. Better be alone, thinking for yourself. And have some fun out of it — encourage and nourish your sense of humor. Life is dull, even stupid, without it." Quoted in Ives and Dolson, *My Brother Adlai,* p. 169.

Ben [28] called this morning, in fact he's been here all morning & has just withdrawn. It seems that Hite [Harriet Cowles] has likewise informed him of her impending arrival in N.Y. and he is quite thrilled over the prospect of seeing her. But she informed neither of us as to the date of her arrival or when she was going to sail. The Lamberts' address in New York, where she is going to stay, I'm not sure of but tell Buff I'll let her know as soon as I find out. I don't believe she's sailing right away for she told Ben she was going out to Manchester, Conn. for a visit. If I can spare the time & she isn't engaged by Ben's previous arrival, or some such contingent circumstance, I may go down to N.Y. next week-end.

The enclosed from Uncle Bert's secretary arrived the other day. I was delighted to hear that he had improved.

As for coming to Bloomington at Easter, I'll be glad to do it if you think best but we might wait and see what happens before making any definite plans.

Best love

ADLAI

To Mrs. Lewis G. Stevenson

Sunday night [March, 1923?]

Dear Mother —

If this letter isn't very coherent you can attribute it to my state of mental vacuity — the result of a long and arduous day.

Last night Francis [Plimpton], Chas [Denby] and I staged a novel party. Our companions were Lorna Underwood, Cornelia Hallowell and Pauline Ames [29] — the ne plus ultra of all New England lineage and an inhabitant of the largest residence on Commonwealth Ave. Lorna as usual had the original idea — we wandered down into the foreign quarter of Boston below Scoll[a]y Square. It was quite an experience and gave us a glimpse of the old world. The open air market which stretches for blocks along a narrow and crooked old street. Saturday night is the big night when all the poor people do their marketing and the street echoed with the vendors shouts, snatches of laughter and song. It was a warm, balmy evening with a promise of spring in the air — the lurid gas flares and the hurdy gurdys lent a very South European atmosphere to the whole enchanting scene. And then we boldly entered an old and villanous oyster bar and ate a tremendous sea food dinner in little al-

---

28 Benjamin W. Thoron, a student friend.
29 Miss Ames married Mr. Plimpton.

coves on hard and narrow benches. Then followed the usual visit to the Brunswick for dancing. It was a most entertaining evening and the girls got a tremendous kick out of it.

This morning we had our usual ride — three hours of bright sunshine but oh what a lot of mud — there were 8 of us, seven men and Lorna — and of course we came in spattered from head to foot. Vignale has some new horses — I rode one of them, a hunter from G. B. McLeans farm out of Washington. To-night, I've just returned, I went to Marcien Jencke's house for supper with a happy company of "young people." But I must say I don't get much kick out of the parlor games — consequences and the like, which seem to be such a prevalent form of entertainment in Boston society. I have received the scarf & ties — they're fine. You have excellent taste even in men's apparel.

love

ADLAI

To Mrs. Lewis G. Stevenson

Sunday [March 25, 1923]

Dear Maw —

Is Buff going abroad & if so when? Hite [Harriet Cowles] is sailing Saturday, Mar. 31, this Saturday. Buff said something sometime ago about sailing that day too. Hite is sailing on the "Reliance," United Amer. Line — it was the only boat she could get passage on. I will probably go down for the week-end and if Buff is going the same day I can see them both off & thereby make the proverbial double killing.

The week has been uneventful except for the august and welcome entrance of spring on the seasonal stage which in this latitude portrays such a lively scene of ever changing action. To be sure Bill [McIlvaine] & I did see the two national championship hockey games which were played here this week on Wednesday & Saturday between the Boston A.A. team and St. Paul A.A. They were, of course, marvellous games as the players are all really professional altho they play disguised as amateurs. The B.A.A. team will go, as a result of this series, to the Olympics in Paris next year as the American representative.

I am feeling splendidly, exercising regularly and enjoying myself in spite of the mountains of work that must be scaled. So have no fears as to my physical welfare.

Hester Petersen has called me up extending an invitation for tea this afternoon. Her mother is here. I had forgotten Hester's first name but Bill remembered it and thereby saved me some embarrasment. I accepted the invitation with alacrity and will betake me, appropriately garbed, to their hostelry at the "correct" hour this afternoon and balance cups with them for awhile.

I have of late had many letters from erstwhile colle[a]gues.[30] Bill Hale writes that he has been basking in Egyptian sunshine for some months — he portrays the amenities of life as a gentleman vagabond with unaccustomed fervor. Of course he was in at the [illegible] out at Tut's tomb and managed to talk he [his] way into the inner tomb.

Bill Tucker, strange & wonderful! has taken a job with a construction Co. in Palermo, Sicily. It is a 9 year undertaking and he apparently has slid peacefully into the ways [of] the Italians.

Bill Stevenson sends a glowing account of his legal soundings at the training ship of Eng. barristers. His work seems to interest him tremendously and he enthusiastically defends the Oxford system against Harvard. However, work doesn't seem to interfere seriously with his athletic conquests.

Monk Hackney, following in the footsteps of brother Edgar, seems to have enfolded Eng[land]. & the Eng[lish]. in his ape like embrace. Jesus Coll[ege]. "bumped" its way to the head of the river in the annual bumping races on the "historic Cam," so Monk is rejoicing vociferously.

Ralph Goodwin is out in Ojai, Calif., with his family still recuperating from the loss of his appendix. His plans for the future are viscous to say the least, but ranching seems to have been deserted for the immediate present.

Frank Peach is no longer selling lumps of sugar to the negro grocers in Baltimore's wrong side, but is now bending his colossal energy & talent to the advertising business. His heart strings remain as sensitive & responsive as ever!

Ken Drummond has given up manufacturing something or other and is using his glib tongue & politic ways in the fine art of selling bonds.

Thus far my recent news extends and no farther. I may add that Bill Steve[nson] said that he was convinced J[ohn]. M. H[arlan]. was destined to be a very successful lawyer which will no doubt accord with Buff's views on the subject. Dale [Warren] has not been seen recently. Dick C[leveland]. is little in evidence except at lunch at the Inn & then he comes & goes quietly.

Best love
ADLAI

P.S. How about vacation? Have been asked to Balto. [Baltimore] & was thinking of going to Prin[ceton]. for a few days. But if you want

---

[30] Some of his Princeton friends.

me to come home I can do so altho it would only leave me 5 days there.

p.s.s. Quad[rangle] got excellent section. Took 5 of Cap [and Gown]'s men and only lost 1 to them.

To Mrs. Lewis G. Stevenson

Sunday [April 1, 1923]

Dear Mother:

The Easter parade on Commonwealth Ave. is over and I have returned to the lodgings to write the customary Sunday letters. Bill [McIlvaine] & another fellow & I went to church at Emmanuel Episcopal. Saw all the 'beans' in their Easter outfits, heard some excellent music & a meaningless sermon. The subsequent parade was excellent exercise and gave us an opportunity to [see?] the aristocrats of Back Bay on exhibition. And we saw some quaint sights too.

Yesterday afternoon I went riding in the country with Irv Harris and Dave McAlpin. We had a jumping lesson at the paddock before we started and it was great fun. The horses are all thoroughbred trained hunters and we certainly had some thrills at the jumps. I managed to keep my saddle pretty well but lost my stirrups a couple of times and didnot display exactly finished form. I expect to go out there once a week on Saturday afternoon or Sunday morning from now on. You can ride as long as you please for $3 and the horses are splendid, so its really an excellent opportunity to learn the fine points of riding an English saddle in addition to a lot of fresh air and good exercise.

I am going out to Winchester to have dinner with Dick Higgins tonight. Mr. Temple [31] is to be there and I look forward to seeing him again.

I have arranged to go to N.Y. Friday noon, arriving there at 6. So if Buff wants to do anything that night I'll be at her disposal. I didnot go down to see Hite [Harriet Cowles] off because the only time I could get away was Friday and she had already made plans for that evening — with one of my competitors no doubt. I sent some flowers to the boat and telegraphed bon voyage etc.

The annual [Quadrangle] club dinner comes Saturday night at Delmonico's so it will work in very well with seeing Buff off — I should have a very pleasant week-end were it not for the haunting feeling of time lost that one always feels here when not actually at work.

We had a terrific blow some time ago when we were informed that we would be unable to keep these rooms next year, if we wanted them. It seems that, in the interests of "more college life" for the undergraduates,

[31] A master at the Choate School.

the Univ. has passed a rule that no graduate can live in University dormitories. So we are ejected and have spent odd moments during the last two weeks in a frantic search for quarters. But we signed a lease the other day for what promises to be quite as good as this. The location is about the same — just a block down Mt. Auburn St. There are 8 rooms, 2 baths and a sleeping porch for early fall and late spring. In all it accomodates 6 men, which, if we all come back, includes the four of us here now, B. Davis and Francis Plimpton. The latter is a boy from Amherst and a very good chap. He lives here and in New York — also in Bermuda. His father is President of Ginn & Co. the publishers. His other qualifications are that he keeps a car.[32]

If you want me to come home for Easter [vacation], which I can do perfectly well, please let me know so I can get a reservation. If I come I'll leave Friday, arriving in Bloom. Sat. night, the 14th.

Darwin Kingsley has asked me to go to South America with him this summer. Its pleasant to think about but quite out of the question, I imagine. Tell father I don't need a[ny] money and will write him when I do need some.

Best love
ADLAI

p.s. The cost of the rooms for next year is $250 — quite a bit less than these.

To Mrs. Lewis G. Stevenson

Sunday [April 8, 1923]

Dear Mother:

Came down to New York Friday afternoon and had dinner with Buff & Aunt Letitia [Stevenson] at her hotel. Buff seemed very well & happy. We had a long talk & she seemed to think that you were anxious for me to come home for vacation so I will do so.

I spent the night with Hunt Dickinson and was up early the next morning, so that we would have plenty of time to get to the boat. Dale [Warren] came down to see Buff off and so all four of us went down to the dock together after stocking up with milk en route.

Buff has a very nice cabin; I got he[r] a desk [deck] chair so I think

---

[32] This was the beginning of a lifelong friendship, and Francis T. P. Plimpton served as deputy to Ambassador Stevenson on the U.S. delegation to the United Nations, 1961–1965. See his chapter, "They Sent You Our Best," in *As We Knew Adlai,* edited and with preface by Edward P. Doyle, foreword by Adlai E. Stevenson III (New York: Harper & Row, 1966), pp. 254–267.

she was quite comfortable.[33] It was a beautiful day and they anticipated a pleasant crossing so I'm sure everything will be lovely. After the ship sailed I called on some of my "business" friends around town and then joined Doug & Dick [34] for lunch at the Yale Club. Went to the matinee in the afternoon with Aunt Letitia and had a really delightful time with her. After the theatre I met some more of "the boys" and we discussed our respective futures and then adjourned to Delmonicos for the [Quadrangle] Club dinner. It was an elaborate affair and great fun to see everyone again. The new section is great — best bunch I've ever seen in the Club. Spent the night at Dick's & took the 10:10 train down here [Princeton] this morning. At present I'm sitting here in Cap [and Gown] &, as you see, improving each hour. We're motoring up to New York after dinner in time for me to catch the midnight back to Boston & the books. I'll plan to leave Friday [for Bloomington] if I can get a reservation.

Best love

ADLAI

To Mrs. Lewis G. Stevenson

Sunday [late April or early May, 1923?]

Dear Mother:

Another week has gone and spring has come, with a flood of soft sunshine and crisp air! It is a glorious day and already I begin to feel the disconcerting effects that come with the mellifluous aroma of waking life. But the ravages of winter's percipitant retreat have left the streets a sea of mud, so all is not yet joy. After the rigours of a New England winter one takes sort of a personal pride in the approach of spring — one looks with an air of complacency and greeting an acquaintance perhaps raises the eyebrows with a feeling of self satisfaction; much as to say "I told you so — there was bound to be an end of winter sometime."

Chas [Denby] has had a slight touch of grippe and has been in the infirmary a few days but will be amongst us again tomorrow. Last night Bill [McIlvaine] & I & 2 Eli law students went to dinner in an Italian dive down in the Latin or Neapolitan district of Boston. It was quite an adventure & the first I've [d]one of really old Boston. Bill & I were expected to join our lady friends & "some of the boys" at the Brunswick

---

[33] His sister was sailing to England to visit her cousin Millie Bromwell, who had married Sidney Bailey, the British naval attaché in Washington, the summer before in Charlevoix, Michigan.

[34] Unable to identify Doug. Dick is Hunt Dickinson.

Hotel to dance so we had to hasten back to Cambridge to don the uniforms and then managed to arrive an hour late — i.e. not until after 11. After it was over — at 12 — the other men took the girls home and Bill & I went out to Moorhead [Morehead] Patterson's house here in Cambridge. He is a law student — married and very wealthy. In addition to his wife there were 3 other girls there and some other men. We sat around, danced, drank Pat's expensive champagne and finally bowed out about 2:30, after quite an eventful evening. Bill & I are going out to Belmont to the Underwood's this afternoon to stay for supper. You'll no doubt think me getting awfully gay but it is confined entirely to the week-ends and makes the week's work a little more palatable after a little change.

Love
ADLAI

To Mrs. Lewis G. Stevenson

Monday night [late April or early May, 1923?]

Dear Mother —

I didn't have an opportunity to write you yesterday — I was out all day and, taking your advice, forebore from writing the customary letter when I returned.

We rode all morning — a soft warm spring day; it was too good! I'm afraid the lure of the saddle & the open country has found an easy and willing victim in me. Another extravagant inclination to overcome! But I can say with becoming modesty that I am beginning to cut a not unpleasant figure on a horse and find myself able to keep at the front of the field over hedges and brooks with seldom the loss of a stirrup and thusfar not a fall this year. What bravado! I'm knocking loudly on my 'chamber door.'

I went to the Underwoods for dinner & a mighty fine dinner it was. Mr. Underwood had gone to the cape [Cape Cod] for the weekend to try out the new & famous Eastward Ho golf course. So Dave [McAlpin] presided over the roast beaming benignly on Nina [Underwood] who has but lately returned from California. As always in the bosom of that most natural of families we had a riotous time. After lunch we spread rugs on the terrace and drank our coffee and bathed in the sun. Thus went the whole afternoon; a few neighbors dropped in and as tea time approached the usual delegation came out from Cambridge to pay homage. Dick Cleveland was among them — he doesn't look very well and is quite nervous but most affable and apparently cheerful. [Norman] Davis, [Charles] Denby and Denny Holden stayed for supper and we came in together in time to follow the fire engines amid great excitement to a false alarm fire in Harvard Yard. Thence to bed for the sweet sleep of the comfortably weary and up betimes for a protracted struggle with the books. Thanks for your most excellent letter.

ADLAI

To Mrs. Lewis G. Stevenson

Sunday [35]

Dear Mother:

Chas. [Denby] Bill [McIlvaine] & I came out here for the week-end with Francis Plimpton, a fellow law student, the boy who is going to room with us next year. This is his ancestral manor and an exceedingly interesting place — filled with pre-revolutionary family relics, autographs of George Washington and other celebrities ad infinitum. The family spend most of their time in New York & Bermuda but were up here overnight to arrange things for the summer. The farm comprises some 800 acres, principally of woodland and is primarily a dairy farm on the order of Larry Bensons except on a much larger scale.

Mr. Plimpton is an interesting straight laced old Puritan with many hobbys, of which the farm is one. He is chairman of the Board of Trustees of Amherst College, President of Ginn & Co. the publishers and quite a well know[n] gent. He and Mrs. Plimpton the second returned to New York this morning leaving us in complete control of the manor.

Yesterday we played golf at the Norfolk Country Club and are going riding this afternoon. The schedule ends up with work tonight and back to Cambridge — about 20 miles — in time for classes to-morrow.

I called on the Chases [36] last Sunday but found that they had gone to Europe sometime ago so I dropped my card in the letter slot and my conscience was placid once more.[37] The native & imported wonders in this old house have left me simply spell bound and I've had a delightful

---

[35] This letter is headed "Lewis Farm, Walpole, Massachusetts." It probably was written in early May, 1923.

[36] Mrs. Chase and her daughter Margaret.

[37] His sister wrote that their mother "didn't hesitate to mix in homilies and reprimands when she thought they were needed." This sentence in the letter may be the result of one of his mother's reprimands: "By the way, I have had it in mind to scold you about the small courtesies of life. Never neglect to acknowledge a favor, promptly and adequately. Never let any debt of honor from a postage stamp to a fortune go without proper, prompt acknowledgement and courtesy. It is easy and unpardonable to neglect, forget and evade, and so form the habit now of not so doing." Quoted in Ives and Dolson, *My Brother Adlai*, pp. 177–178.

& enlightening time examining them all. The dining room table is from the house Washington lived in at Germantown etc. etc.

As to the approaching exams my lack of confidence increases daily but it doesn't seem to have a dampening effect on my spirits in general.

Love

ADLAI

To Lewis G. Stevenson

Sunday [late May, 1923?]

Dear Father:

Things are going fine with the beautiful weather making it progressively harder to keep to the books and their appalling contents of undigested knowledge. Its only about 3 week[s] now until the first exam and I certainly have some few things to learn.

I was very sorry to hear about Aunt Jule. It was a great surprise. She seemed so strong & vivacious when we called that I thought she would probably last out the summer anyway. I wired cousin Julia according to your instructions.[38] I thought the remarks, editorial & obituary, in the Panta[graph] were done in excellent taste and thoroughly proper.

Beech Nut has been suffering along with the rest of the market during the present depression but its keeping more stable than most and unless something unforseen happens I think I'll hang on until it gets back up to my purchase price of 74 again anyway.

I wish you would send me 2 o[r] 3 hundred dollars for I'm getting pretty short what with 300 tied up there for the time being. Also I had to pay, or rather paid it than forwarding it to you, my Univ. bill for the 4th quarter in tuition & second half in rent which was $215. So a little "reparations" would go big just now with your profligate offspring.

My best to the office — i.e. Fred.[39]

ADLAI

To Mrs. Lewis G. Stevenson

Monday morning [probably late September, 1923]

Dear Mother:

Have just returned from a delightful week-end at Plimpton's venerable country estate. Jack Gifford, Bob Finley, Plimpton & myself left in

[38] Aunt Jule (Mrs. Matthew Scott), the sister of Grandmother Stevenson, had recently died. It was her large farm properties that Lewis G. Stevenson managed. Cousin Julia was Mrs. Scott's daughter, Mrs. Carl Vrooman.

[39] Fred Robinson, Lewis G. Stevenson's secretary.

Mrs. Lewis G. Stevenson, Adlai's mother

The home in Bloomington, Illinois, of Vice President Adlai E. Stevenson

Adlai with his grandfather

Adlai at one year
COURTESY OF MRS. ERNEST L. IVES

Three-year-old Adlai poses at Charlevoix, Michigan, with his sister Elizabeth ("Buffie")
COURTESY OF MRS. ERNEST L. IVES

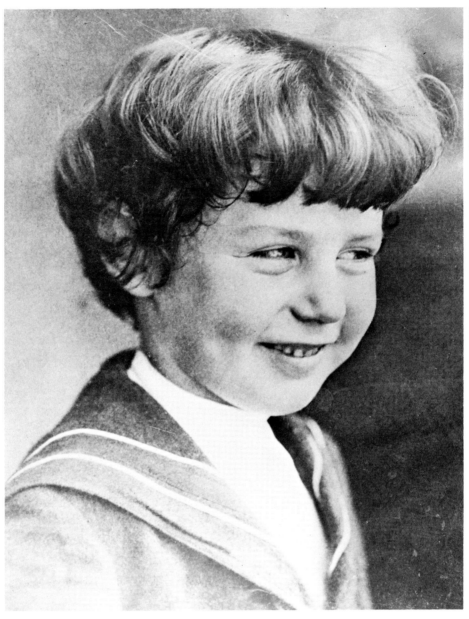

A childhood portrait taken in Los Angeles

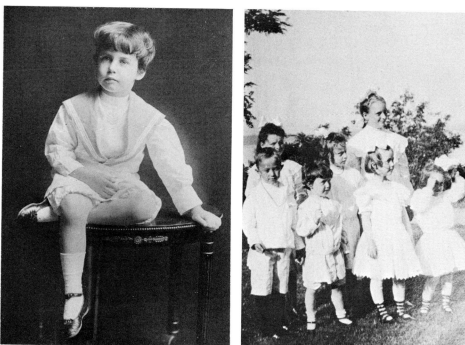

A childhood portrait
taken in Los Angeles

A summer birthday party
for Buffie at Charlevoix

Buffie, Adlai, and Dr. Grace, a friend of the family,
at the beach in Charlevoix

Adlai and Buffie with their father,
Lewis G. Stevenson

COURTESY OF MRS. ERNEST L. IVES

Buffie and Adlai at Grandfather
W. O. Davis's cottage, Charlevoix

COURTESY OF MRS. ERNEST L. IVES

Adlai flying a kite with friends at Charlevoix in 1904
From left to right: Mary Funk, Dr. Grace, Dorothy
Whitney, Adlai and Buffie

The first letter handwritten by the future governor of Illinois to his father, 1907

New Orleans La,
7014 St. Charles,
Jan. 2, 1911.,

Dear Grandfather
          I received your
fine Christmas present and
I thank you a thousand
times !! . I am going to put
it in the bank and save it
          I hope you had a merry
Christmas and a happy
New Year.
          I have been too busy
playing to ~~right~~ write sooner, I
hope you will pardon me.
          With love to grandmother
and you — Adlai

A well-intentioned letter at the age of ten

Adlai at thirteen

Choate School portrait, 1916

Adlai E. Stevenson on the far left in a school play at Choate, 1917

At Princeton University, probably 1920

Adlai with friends Alice Eno, Ridgeway Trimble, and Marie Thayer in 1920 at the Princeton house rented by his mother

William A. Tucker, Frank Murray, and Adlai in Berlin, summer, 1920

Adlai at Montreux, Switzerland,
September, 1920

Adlai in the back yard
of the family home,
Bloomington, Illinois, 1924

Adlai on a camping trip in Canada, 1925

*Henry Capen, Paul Jefferson, and Adlai en route
to the Kentucky Derby, May 1925*

*Claire Birge and Adlai Stevenson, August, 1925,
in Bloomington, Illinois.*

Adlai with his mother, father, and nephew Timothy R. Ives, Bloomington, Illinois, 1928

A.E.S. in Washington, D.C., 1933

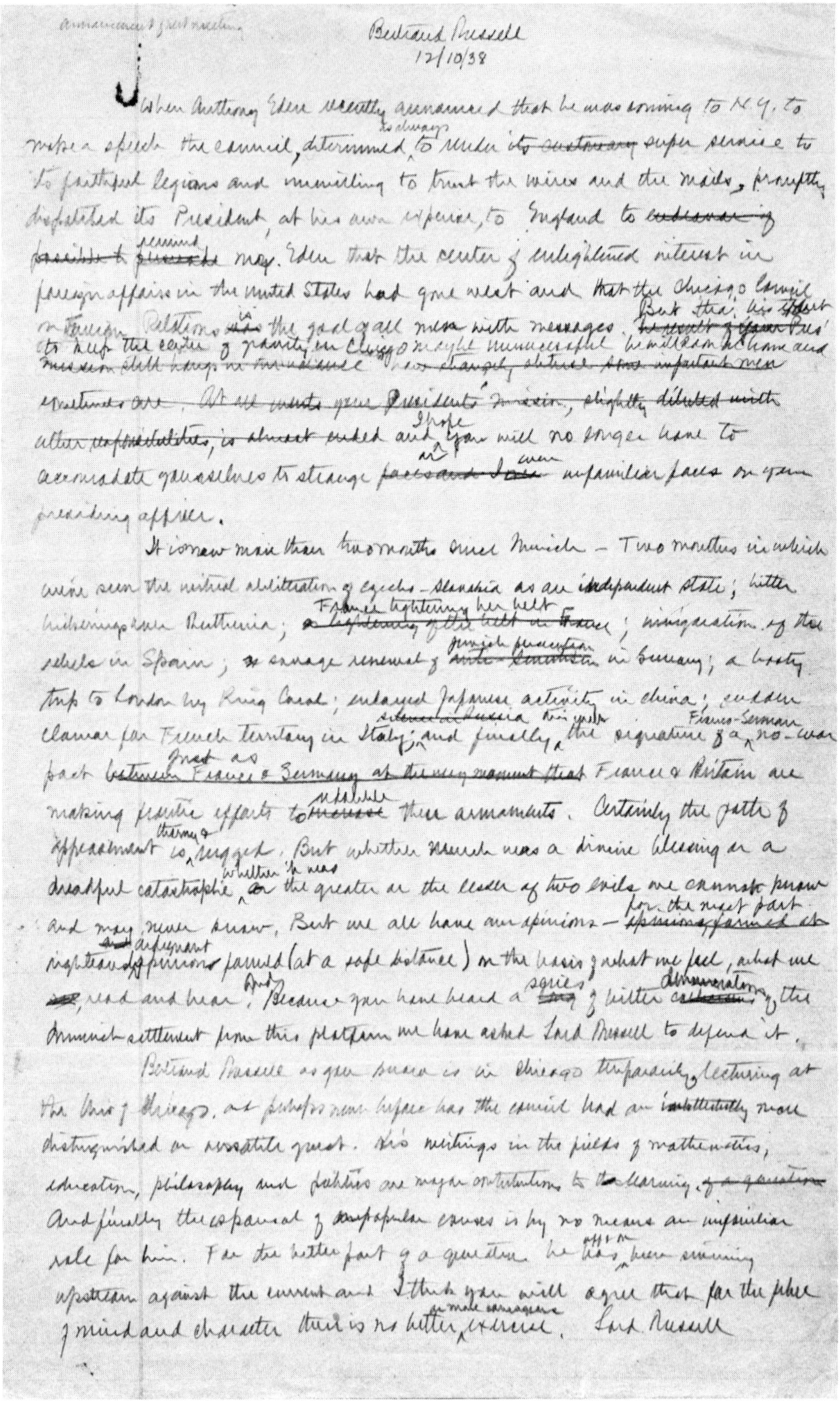

Bertrand Russell
12/10/38

[handwritten manuscript draft, largely illegible]

Manuscript of an introduction of Bertrand Russell to the
Chicago Council on Foreign Relations, December 10, 1938

the latter's car after lunch on Saturday, went to the Brookline Country Club and engaged in a splendid round of golf on that famous course. Afterward we motored out to the "Lewis Farm" — the Plimpton place — arriving just in time to get dressed for dinner. After dinner Mr. Plimpton entertained us with some accounts of the glories of his ancestors and stories about some of the ancient colonial relics that fill the house.

We had a refreshing sleep on frigid sleeping porch but well armed with water bags and "puffs" — large and luxurious comforters. We were up early the next morning for a typical N. England breakfast with fish as the crowning dish. Soon were all off to church at Walpole, where we worshipped in the same old meeting house that the Plimpton's have attended for over 100 years. Back to the farm for dinner and an afternoon of tennis. Then followed supper, an evening around the open fire and bed.

It was wonderful to get out doors again & I've come back feeling like a king. The air is crisp and cold — autumn is very much here. Tell father to send me money — the initial expenditures are always large.

Best love
A<small>D</small>

P.S. If you find anywhere a letter containing application blanks to Prin[ceton]. football games, please forward it.

To Mrs. Lewis G. Stevenson

Sunday [October 7, 1923]

Dear Mother:

The eager anticipation of this week-end already fills me with an ill surpressed excitement. What with having a 100% family reunion in Buff's apartment in New York, a trip to Princeton and the football game, the week-end indeed looks like an epic one.

Last night Chas [Denby], Bill [McIlvaine] & I went to see Pavlowa and her company workout at the Opera House. After witnessing a performance by a public favorite of many years standing it would seem that the elegant thing to do is to sigh a few discreet and well calculated remarks relative to that persons artistic decline. But this being my first encounter with Pavlowa I can't accurately estimate her 1923 form. To me, however, it was very wonderful, but I even responded more enthusiastically to the dancing of Novakoff (I believe) the man who supported her.

Bill & Chas. & I went out and stayed out on our respective mounts for 3 hours today and then ended up with a good lunch at the Lenox. I can't but anticipate the most ghastly weather this winter for New England has been blessed with most glorious days this fall, and this Sunday was like the rest.

Having nothing of interest to impart I may as well conclude and reiterate that you may expect me for dinner at "the apartment" Thursday evening. My train arrives about 6:15 and I will come directly over.

Best love

ADLAI

To Mrs. Lewis G. Stevenson

Monday morning [October 15, 1923]

Dear Mother:

Am just back from a most delightful week-end in New York. Friday, Columbus Day, is a legal holiday thruout New England and since we only have one class on Saturday Bill [McIlvaine], B. [Davis] and I left at noon on Thursday for a good extended week end. We stayed at the Davis house and there was also staying there a girl and her mother from Cuba — old friends of the Davis'. The girl was very attractive and what with Irene [Morrow] & Marie [Thayer] from Memphis & Martha Davis who came down from Vassar for the week-end we were well supplied with attractive girls.[40]

On Saturday we motored to Princeton for the game. Marie had made an engagement to go to New Haven for the Yale game so Martha went with us. We had a late lunch at Quadrangle (incidentally the club look[s] beautiful, new furniture, flowers etc) and were thru just in time for the game. Afterward we had tea at Ivy & then started home only to have the car break down. We finally got it repaired & after an hilarious & maudlin ride arrived back in New York about 10. I sat up & listened to Mr. Davis talk about democracy etc until about 12:30 — as you can imagine he is quite fascinating & has a tremenduous fund of information.[41] Sunday afternoon he gave us a box to the World's Series ball game — it was a great experience.

Am feeling fine & very happy —

AD

40 Adlai knew Irene Morrow from summers in Charlevoix. Martha Davis was a sister of Norman P. Davis. Marie Thayer was the daughter of B. B. Thayer of New York, an old friend of Lewis G. Stevenson.

41 Norman H. Davis was an adviser to Woodrow Wilson at the Paris Peace Conference and Undersecretary of State, 1920–1921.

To Mrs. Lewis G. Stevenson

Monday [early December, 1923?]

Dear Mother:

My failure to write yesterday was due to an absence from town & time occupied with social activities which allowed no time for my epistolary duties. I went out to Lancaster, Mass. Saturday afternoon with Haven Parker — a Harvard student of the better class & a fellow law student. His father, former Atty General of Mass. is a very distinguished old member of this august Commonwealth. The family was delightful — there are in all six children — two girls in Bryn Mawr, two older unmarried ones and an older brother who roomed with Norman Armour [42] in law school and is now commissioner of the Mass. State Police. Saturday night we played Mah Jong and, it being one of my initial attempts, I was of course invincible.

Another incident of the evening which I must not neglect to mention was the fact of many succulent pheseants at dinner. Apparently they are quite plentiful in the woods thereabouts. The entire day Sunday was spent at the ancient country place of the Fuller's [43] who reside in that locality. The theory of the celebration was the formal announcement of the engagement of Miss Anna Fuller to Mr. C. J. Hubbard, captain of the Harvard footballers during the past season. There was a large crowd of select Boston damsels and Harvard students and during the greater part of the day we indulged collectively in sundry wholesome outdoor sports — tag football, baseball and field hockey. There were occasional intermissions for punch and luncheon. With the arrival of tea time physical exercise closed and the jolly and exhausted army moved into the house to sound the subtlety of each other's tea line. It wasn't long before everyone in the [vicinage?] had turned out for the reception which was now in progress. We stayed a while and then returned to the Parker's for another tremendous dinner accompanied with much jollity and wit. After a general bicker fest which touched a wide range of subjects, B [Davis] & I made our adieux & together with Haven & the 2 girls who were catching the train for Bryn Mawr, motored into Cambridge arriving in due season and in time for a long night's sleep.

I haven't heard from you for a long time. I do hope you are not ill now as a result of your exertions in N.Y. I shall probably get home Sunday or Monday before Christmas which I understand comes on Tuesday.

[42] The American diplomat.
[43] Unable to identify.

We don't get out until Saturday but I'll probably leave a day early & go to N.Y. & leave for home from there.

Best love

ADLAI

P.S. I don't want to bring a trunk but haven't room in my fitted suit-case. Have you one you can send me?

To Mrs. Lewis G. Stevenson

Sunday [January, 1924?]

Dear Mother:

I went in to Letty [Bromwell]'s to dinner to-day. Letty was away — in Washington seeing about selling her house. She has been offered about $135,000 but expects to get more — hence the negotiations. Peggy Pierce [44] was there and we had a great time. Conversationally it was quite stimulating; she is equipped with an eloquent and unretiring tongue, not to mention a quite unusual fund of information — derived from observation and analysis, not education. She is up here for a rest cure and is staying with Letty.

To our intense disappointment there was some confusion about our reservation for horses and therefore we were deprived of the usual Sunday ride this morning.

I had a letter from my "Junior amour" — Claire [45] — to the effect that the crowning feature of her holidays had been to meet Buffy in New York. Her dissertation on the "adorable" Buffy and the "fascinating" Mr. Armour [46] was most amusing. I'm afraid Buff has quite alienated her affections.

How goes the rest cure? [47] I haven't heard from you or father for several days & so am conjecturing that you are still at Battle Creek. I hope & feel sure it will do you a lot of good but nothing but *mental* peace will ever make your physical condition what it should be. Of this I feel sure & its all in accord with your theories anyway so I hope you are trying to look at things as dispassionately as possible.

---

[44] Mrs. Vinton Pierce was a widow. She was a close Washington friend of Mrs. Bromwell.

[45] Claire Birge of Greenwich, Connecticut. Her grandfather, Julius Birge, had a cottage at Charlevoix. See Part Six, "Letters to Claire Birge."

[46] Alison Armour was Buffie's "beau."

[47] Adlai's mother was at the Battle Creek, Michigan, Sanitarium for a rest cure. There was a dispute between the Merwin and Stevenson families over control of the stock of the *Daily Pantagraph*. This is discussed in Part Five.

[*142*]

I received the box of clothes and the candy. Generously thankful therefore!

Best love
ADLAI

To Mrs. Lewis G. Stevenson

Monday morning [48]

Dear Mother —

Yesterday was so full I neglected to write you so I'm getting it in this morning before the lectures begin. Its horribly cold here now and its hard to keep any place warm so I live in my fur coat.

The crumbling of the air castles is about over now. It did leave me a little bewildered for a couple of days and then unconsciously I found myself unconsciously forgetting all about it and quite as merry as usual — a little mortifying to myself in my self imposed role of the martyred lover! [49] In calm, collected and dispassioned retrospect I feel quite sure that she suddenly made up her mind to marry this long suffering swain just this winter — she's always known him — he lives out there and also roomed with her brother at Yale and has been pressing his suit for many years. So when she arrived back in Santa Barbara after most a year away in Europe and just recovered from another breakdown she probably felt like changing the old order and hence signed up this omnipresent suitor. But from my angle it does go to show the manifest absurdity of this "distance lends enchantment" & absence stuff.

Saturday night Bill [McIlvaine] & I went in to see the hockey game at the Arena. It was a double header & both games were mighty good so we had a well worth while evening of it. Sunday Bill & I went into Letty [Bromwell]'s for lunch but imagine our surprise & horror when we arrived — Scott & Peggy [Pierce] came out for us — to hear that Margaret Harding [50] had just died and Letty was emotionally indisposed. We stayed for lunch but the big tea party which had been planned for the afternoon and for which we had furnished the cocktails had, of course, to be called off.

In the evening, Chas [Denby], Bill, [Francis] Plimpton & I went into

---

[48] Although the envelope is postmarked May 19, 1924, it seems likely that this letter was filed by someone in the wrong envelope. From the references to the cold and to watching a hockey game, it probably was written sometime in the winter of 1924.

[49] Adlai had recently received the news that his "love," Harriet Cowles, had just been married.

[50] A Washington, D.C., friend of Mrs. Bromwell and her daughter Mildred.

the Bazeley's for Sunday night supper. There were in all four "beaus" and six men and what sort of a time we had playing "Consequences" & brain test games you can readily imagine. Am enclosing check for $400 — thanks loads for the $60.

Love
ADLAI

To Mrs. Lewis G. Stevenson

Thursday [late winter, 1924?]

Dearest Mother —

I went down to N.Y. on the 'one o'clock' on Saturday and was in the apartment with Buff in time for dinner. We had a jolly time together discussing a little of all things. I had a sore throat and was feeling sort of bum so it wasn't hard to keep me in bed all Sunday morning. Mary [51] cooked us a famous luncheon and by that time my cure was complete.

In the afternoon the *exceedingly* interesting Mr. [Isaac] Marcasson of Saturday Evening Post fame came and, loquacious like most of his race, he gave us a very pleasant and enlightening hour or so. Miss Mitchell [52] an attractive and super intellectually sophisticated person also arrived. Also a recent and admiring acquisition — one Mr. Noble [53] — who made a very nice genuine and wholesome impression. In the evening Doug Ward, [Morrison] Ulman and Dave Robbins [54] came in to see me and we had a jolly old bicker. All in all a good day — the *restful* qualities whereof would have warmed your heart.

Monday morning I went to Dr. Watson and I was delighted to learn that the most he could prescribe in the way of dental ministration was a cleaning; which was forthwith administered. Aunt Letitia [Stevenson] met us for lunch and we all had a few hearty laughs. Aunt Letitia's great and I like her a lot. Apparently she has derived the greatest kick in years out of living a few days with Buff and seeing the "men." Then followed a trip to Brooks for some shirts, to Sutton's where I purchased a very excellent 18th century book on riding. We Jewed them down from $35 to $25 — which I grant you is a munificent gift but it will in some measure help to discharge my colossal obligations to the Underwoods. Buff took me to the studio of a Mr. Bryant Baker, an English sculptor of no insignificant merit and reputation — at least so I gathered from his impressive display of work. He gave Buff a photograph of

[51] Buffie's servant.
[52] Valentine Mitchell, a New York friend of Buffie's.
[53] Mrs. Ives is unable to recall his full name. Letter to Walter Johnson, November 26, 1967.
[54] Friends from Princeton.

his bust of [Woodrow] Wilson and autographed it. It will make an excellent addition to our art gallery.

At this juncture in the day's activities I removed from Buff's wing to the Princeton club — there to consort for a short while with some of the boys — and thence to Dickinsons where I partook of a large and sumptuous dinner with Mr. & Mrs. Dickinson.[55] A couple of hours of pleasant converse passed rapidly and I was back in the apartment by ten, there to find Bob Spier entertaining Buff. She promptly kicked him out & we went to bed. I went downtown Tuesday for luncheon with some of the younger financiers. Was glad to see Bill Tucker again. He is working in N.Y. now after living two years all over Europe. Miss Mitchell and Lyle Barber came to dinner and then we all separated for the theatre — Buff & Lyle to see Rachel Carruthers latest and the girl and I to Outward Bound — It was great and I've never enjoyed anything more.[56]

I hated to leave Buff but, being anxious to get out here in the country for some work and exercise, made my ultimatum and left on the midnight — arriving here yesterday in time for lunch. Played golf yesterday afternoon and after dinner drove over to Belmont & spent the night at the Underwoods. Lorna [Underwood] & I played 18 holes at Weston this morning — had a tremendous luncheon at the club house, dropped Lorna at home, and was back here by 3:30. And now for 3 days of work with an occasional ride on the Plimpton horses.

Best love,
ADLAI

P.S. The enclosed [photograph] was taken sometime ago on the front porch at the Underwood[s]. From L to R — Lorna, moi, Nina, Dave [McAlpin?]. Save it please.

To Mrs. Lewis G. Stevenson

Wednesday Night [57]

Dear Mother:

Buff has written me about the outcome of the A.A. affair.[58] Its doubtless been an ordeal for her but I'm sure she'll be better off for it — she's done a lot for him and she'll be rewarded with interest for her

---

[55] Parents of his Princeton classmate Hunt Dickinson.

[56] His sister had provided a date and two tickets to Owen Davis's *Outward Bound*. She and Mr. Barber, of Bloomington, went to see the new play *Expressing Willie* by Bloomington's Rachel Crothers.

[57] This letter probably was written late in February or during March. Adlai had spent Washington's Birthday at Poland Springs, Maine. Lorna Underwood Sagendorph to Walter Johnson, letter, January 15, 1968.

[58] Alison Armour and Adlai's sister had just broken up.

present suffering. I have just written her a letter with hopes that it may have a cheering effect.

I'm taking tomorrow afternoon off to go thru the Boston Museum of Fine Arts — Lorna Underwood who is quite artistic — paints & models — has offered to take me there. So I'm meeting her in town for lunch and then for an elevating afternoon.

The enclosed is a photo of part of our party at Poland [Springs, Maine]. Reading from left to right there is Jim Douglas, Cornelia Hallowell, Francis Plimpton, Eleanor Jackson (now in Bermuda), May Bremer, Darwin Kingsley, Alice Candee from Wilmington and your adoring son.

As for plans about Easter vacation, which comes from the 12 to 21 of April, I have been considering going to White Sulphur. 'B' [Davis] has written them and they will give 8 of us a cottage for a week at $35–$40 board and lod[g]ing, apiece. Of course its only tentative and since it would probably cost quite a bit when you figure in the Ry fare we probably won't do it. If not and you have nothing you want me to do I'll probably go to Princeton & play golf for a few days and then spend a few days with Darwin Kingsley in town with expeditions to surrounding country clubs.

Best love

ADLAI

To Mrs. Lewis G. Stevenson

Sunday [spring, 1924?]

Dear Mother —

. . . I went to a dinner party at Cornelia Hallowell's Friday night before the Bremer's dance at the Brookline C.C. [Country Club] The dinner was great fun and the dance probably the best that Boston's had for some years. It was a rustic fancy dress and we were all very rustic and comfortable. Yesterday May Bremer, Max Schniewind, Chas. [Denby] & I motored out to one of the Bremer's country places (they have 3) for lunch. It was an interesting old house near Scieutate [Scituate] on the Cape and was built in 1780. Mrs. Bremer just got it a year or so ago & has redecorated and furnished it in its exact period. We hoped to play golf in the afternoon but a cold drizzle developed so we just loafed around the country side and sat on the cliffs overlooking the sea. Then came tea before a big open fire and much funny conversation. We had dinner at a refined road house outside of Boston, danced awhile and called it a good day.

I slept all morning and am working this afternoon & evening.

Love

ADLAI

P.S. The letter before the last was beautiful — I consider the best you've ever written me. By "guilty" I mean selfish; in being so happy when I don't believe you & father and Buff are as happy as I am.[59]

To Mrs. Lewis G. Stevenson

Sunday afternoon [May 18, 1924]

Dear Mother —

The last week is upon us and the fear of God is strong within me! I always seem to get worried before exams and wonder how I can possibly get thru. I don't know that there is any more reason for nervousness this year than ever before but when I consider the appalling amount of law which we are presumed to have absorbed this year it hardly seems probable that I've learned even half of it or enough to get thru. However, here's to lady luck, bribed with one last mighty week of work!

We had a great ride this morning — the fruit trees are all in blossom and the country is like fairy land. A stiff breeze was blowing & it was great to drink it and feel it in your hair.

Yesterday the "greatest Princeton ball team in a decade" came up here and was soundly trounced by a bum Harvard team.[60] Princeton baseball has certainly reached a climax & rumors are current that there is to be an entirely new coaching staff, advisory board & what not. May their efforts be to some avail!

Tell Buff to be sure & send me that suitcase & enclose my straw hat in it. Also you might discontinue the Panta[graph] pretty soon, as I won't have much time to read it from now on.

Best love,

ADLAI

[59] In a letter that is not extant, Adlai had apparently expressed a feeling of "guilt" because he was enjoying his weekends so much. His mother wrote him: "Your optimism and faith are contagious and have given me a boost. . . . Now, my dear, you must not feel guilty unless there is a reason and the only reason for guilt is wrong-doing. I do not believe we can have too much happiness unless it interferes with the happiness of others. Then it is selfishness. I believe God wants His children to be happy. . . . You say, 'Laddie is getting his eyes open.' They can't see too much or too far. 'Know thyself.' Know the world, know values, know what

To Mrs. Lewis G. Stevenson

Friday morning [May 23, 1924?]

Dear Mother —

Four exams are behind me now with only two remaining — and those at the end of next week. So for the nonce we are having a little respite. I think I passed these last two so that there still remains only one in doubt — and a very grave doubt it is!

I played golf yesterday afternoon after the exam and am playing again this afternoon with Bill [Hale?],[61] May Bremer and Cornelia Hallowell — and then to work again.

Great excitement! Harriet Field and a girl named [Janet] Hubbard from Lake Forest just drove up. They are on their way to the Hubbard's summer place at Annisquam and have invited Bill & me out there for Sunday. We will probably go!

Had a letter from Julia Buchland [62] inviting me to stay with them until the races at New London. Guess I'll laugh that off. The plan of motoring home with Bill has fallen thru — he doesn't want to wait around New York until the convention is over.

Chas Denby has come down with the measles and is in the infirmary. Isn't it tough luck? However he may be able to take the two remaining exams if his eyes are alright.

Please tell father to send me $150 — I'll have some bills to pay & expenses before I get off.

Best love
AD.

To Mrs. Lewis G. Stevenson

Sunday [May 25, 1924]

Dear Mother —

The hardest week on record is over! Its now 2:30 and with the exception of yesterday evening I've worked steadily between 10 & 12 hours a day since Monday morning. And the coming week will be worse with an exam on Tuesday and Thursday. In short the immediate present

you want — above all, know God, universal Good. Stand for that, whatever befalls." Quoted in Ives and Dolson, *My Brother Adlai,* pp. 176–177.

[60] Harvard won 17 to 0.

[61] William B. McIlvaine in a letter to Walter Johnson, January 19, 1968, writes that he is almost certain he is not the Bill referred to in this letter since he never played golf with Adlai Stevenson or the two girls and never planned to drive to Chicago with Adlai. William Hale is dead.

[62] Unable to identify.

is not equivalent to playing the role of the prone philosopher on a bed of roses. Thus far I'm keeping my spirits and physical well being intact and if I can continue to do so for three more weeks all will be well. I do hope *I can* keep my mind functioning for I've learned a great deal this last week but still have a lot more to absorb before my success in the exams is assured.

Its a glorious day and we've decided to go riding this afternoon to insure the old health for awhile longer.

Had a letter from Claire [Birge] the other day to the effect that the "women folk" were going abroad for the summer, sailing June 17. My plans are to leave here about the 16th — our last exam is on the 14th — and probably spend a day with them in Greenwich (if I'm invited) and then join some boys for the races in New London on Friday and Saturday. Then to motor up to New York & stay with [Francis] Plimpton during the [1924 Democratic] convention. The motor trip back to Chicago with bill [Bill Hale?] will probably not develop for he won't want to hang around in the East for the convention week. Received the money from you and mucho gracias!

Love

ADLAI

Lewis G. Stevenson had been working for months to obtain the Democratic presidential nomination for David F. Houston, Secretary of Agriculture in Woodrow Wilson's cabinet. Adlai's father placed Houston's name in nomination at the convention in New York City. The convention deadlocked over the candidacies of Alfred E. Smith of New York and William McAdoo of California. Finally, after 103 ballots, John W. Davis received the nomination on July 9.

Lewis G. Stevenson arranged for Francis Plimpton, Norman P. Davis, Robert Finley and his son to be assistant sergeants at arms at the convention. Adlai not only served as a messenger on the floor of the convention but he attended the strategy conferences planning the Houston campaign.

When the platform committee recommended an equivocal endorsement of the League of Nations, Woodrow Wilson's Secretary of War, Newton D. Baker, presented a minority report and pleaded eloquently for an unqualified endorsement of the ideals of Woodrow Wilson. Years later Adlai E. Stevenson recalled: "It was the most moving speech I think I have ever heard." [63]

[63] Russel Windes, Jr., and James A. Robinson, "Public Address in the Career of Adlai E. Stevenson," *Quarterly Journal of Speech*, Vol. XLII, No. 3, October, 1956.

To Mrs. Lewis G. Stevenson

[June 23, 1924]

Dear Mother —

The convention opens tomorrow and things are buzzing. Of course father is frightfully busy but, as you may have observed from the papers, he is making great progress and has a mighty good but very dark horse in Houston. Frankly I don't think he has much chance of getting the nomination and it looks more & more as John W. Davis was the man. If Houston should get it by any chance father will certainly deserve a lot of credit for Houston was the darkest of all horses when father arrived here and had a lot of political enemies due to the fact of his unfamiliarity and lack of sympathy with political methods while in the Cabinet. B. Davis & I are to be assistant Sergeants at Arms & father has also fixed it up for Bob Finley and Francis Plimpton.

I went down to New London to the races on Thursday [June 20] & had the time of my life. Thursday night there was a big dance at the Griswald where I saw many old friends of both gendres. Francis & I spent the entire day Friday on the "Alida" — the Bertron [Bertrand] Borden's yacht and the third biggest among the several hundred at the races. Lorna Underwood was staying on it with Elizabeth Meeker and they asked Francis and I out for lunch. Of course we accepted and then Mrs. Borden asked us to come back for dinner, which we also could not decline. We thought that about enough[;] for the two men who were cruising with the girls looked a little bored with us but no not at all, Mr. Borden insisted that we come back for supper after the dance — which we also did. And then he put his beautiful lau[n]ch with a crew of two at our disposal to take us way up the harbor to our hotel. Well all in all it was the best & most luxurious day of my life and I'll probably talk to you about it at length.

Plimpton & I motored up on Saturday and last night I had supper at the Davis' with Finis J. Garrett, democratic whip in the House, Senator [Key] Pittman et al. This afternoon we played golf out at Ardsley on the Hudson — a beautiful course & club and stayed out there for dinner — on an open verandah overlooking the Hudson at sunset — gorgeous! Am staying with Plimpton at 61 Park Ave. — and am writing this surrounded by the greatest collection of mathematica rara in the *world!*

Part Five

The Daily Pantagraph
1924–1926

H. O. Davis — Uncle Bert — had been in bad health for many years and spent a great deal of time in California.[1] The Daily Pantagraph, as a result, lacked leadership and its afternoon competitor, the Bulletin, was beginning to make inroads on the Pantagraph's circulation. In 1922, Davis Merwin, Adlai Stevenson's cousin, went to work on the Pantagraph and by 1924 was publisher and general manager.[2]

By this time there had been heated disputes between the Merwins and the Stevensons over the control of the Daily Pantagraph. The will of Grandfather W. O. Davis lacked legal precision. It provided that the shares in the paper be held in life estate by W. O. Davis's three children, H. O. Davis, Jessie Merwin, and Helen Stevenson, then passed to their children. There were, however, by 1924 five grandchildren of W. O. Davis — three Merwins and two Stevensons. (H. O. Davis's two sons died before he did.) The Stevenson family believed that the remaining shares of stock — less ten shares that had been given to a longtime employee of the paper — should be equally divided between W. O. Davis's two surviving children, Helen Stevenson and Jessie Merwin. The Merwins believed that the stock should be divided between the two families in proportion to the number of grandchildren in each family — thus the Merwins would receive 60 per cent of the stock.

After heated family disputes, it was decided to institute a lawsuit to interpret the will. While the case was in the courts, the families agreed that Adlai E. Stevenson would join the Daily Pantagraph as managing editor.

After he returned to Bloomington from the Democratic convention in New York in July, 1924, he started to work on the paper. His sister wrote: "My brother deplored the family feud, but he enjoyed the chance

[1] He died on July 16, 1925, in California.
[2] He was the publisher until 1935 when his brother Loring C. Merwin succeeded him.

to do some writing and reporting again. His loved friend Lloyd Lewis, the author, editor and humorist, once told me before his untimely death that Adlai was 'the best natural-born reporter he'd ever known.'" [3]

In the district court the Stevensons lost the lawsuit. But on appeal to the appellate court, the decision of the lower court was reversed. The Merwins appealed this decision to the Illinois Supreme Court on a writ of certiorari.

The Supreme Court refused the writ, thus sustaining the appellate court's decision that the remaining stock of the Daily Pantagraph *was to be divided equally between the two families. While the case was on appeal, however, the Merwins had acquired the ten shares of stock that W. O. Davis had given to an old employee years before. As a result, despite the higher court decision, the Merwins had voting control of the* Pantagraph *company.*[4]

During the months the case was in the courts, Lewis G. Stevenson urged his son to complete his law degree. As a result, in the autumn of 1925 Adlai entered the Northwestern University Law School in Chicago. He spent weekdays at the Law School and weekends in Bloomington working on the Daily Pantagraph. *The dean of the Law School, John Henry Wigmore, stimulated Adlai's interest in the law. In addition, Stevenson told Kenneth S. Davis that a visit to Washington to be an usher at classmate Charles Denby's wedding strongly influenced him. Denby was serving as a secretary to Supreme Court Justice Oliver Wendell Holmes. Adlai later recounted the unforgettable afternoon he spent with Mr. Justice Holmes and how the talk ranged from the law and legal education to the Civil War.*[5]

In June, 1926, Northwestern University awarded Adlai E. Stevenson his J.D. In his course work he had received 5 A's and 9 B's, doing his best work in such courses as International Law, Professional Ethics, Constitutional Law, and Labor Law. Shortly after graduation he passed his examination for admission to the Illinois Bar.

While working on the Daily Pantagraph, *Adlai not only supervised the makeup of the paper but also did some reporting. On March 18,*

[3] Elizabeth Stevenson Ives and Hildegarde Dolson, *My Brother Adlai* (New York: Morrow, 1956), p. 181.

[4] Many years later Adlai E. Stevenson in a letter to Loring C. Merwin, publisher of the *Daily Pantagraph*, referred to the "anxiety" of the Merwins "to get control of the paper by any means" and noted that this had made Stevenson's relationship to the paper "uncomfortable" thereafter. December 20, 1945. Mr. Merwin wrote: "Adlai and Dave had radically different temperaments. They never could have worked together successfully." Letter to Walter Johnson, December 14, 1967. Mr. Merwin and Mrs. Ethel Sinclair of the *Daily Pantagraph* were most cooperative in checking material in the *Daily Pantagraph* for us.

[5] Kenneth S. Davis, *A Prophet in His Own Country: The Triumphs and Defeats of Adlai E. Stevenson* (New York: Doubleday, 1957), p. 152.

1925, a tornado swept through southern Illinois, killing over eight hundred people and injuring three thousand. Adlai went to Carbondale and Murphysboro to write eyewitness stories.

Adlai's childhood friend Joseph Bohrer accompanied him to the scene of the tornado. Years later he wrote: "Adlai wrote several very moving stories for the paper. It was really the first time I knew Ad had such talent and power in expressing himself." [6]

SCENES ON PANAMA LIMITED SPEEDING IN STORM CENTER [7]
(By Staff Correspondent.)

On Board the Panama Limited, Centralia, Ill., March 19. — An atmosphere of catastrophe and havoc pervades all trains enroute to the storm stricken area of southern Illinois. This train is carrying three cars of volunteer nurses and doctors, many of whom saw service on the muddy fields of Flanders and know, without being told, something of what awaits them. There is an air of calmness and passengers speak in tones of suppressed anxiety.

There is a young bride aboard. She sits erect with hands grasping a paper, which she clutches spasmodically. "We were married a month ago," she told her fellow passengers, "and live in a small house next to the Methodist church in Carbondale." Her voice at this juncture trembled and broke, her slender form seemed shaken with fear and misgivings, as a trembling finger indicated a line in the newspaper story stating that the church had been blown down. A few seats from the young bride, sits a mother, down whose anxious face tears are coursing. A fellow traveler is endeavoring to comfort her, but all to no avail, for what are words in the face of dire distress and fearful misgivings. Only a few days ago her small son was a happy, rosy-cheeked, carefree schoolboy at Murphysboro. All night long the mother had waited and worried in a distant city as the telegraph and the radio flashed across the nation the news of the storm disaster and the horrifying story that the school which the young son attended, had collapsed under meteoric speed and fury of the storm and that the lives of many small children had been crushed out.

What pain of relief and anguish of despair await these travelers when we reach Carbondale and the worst or best is known?

[6] "Boys in Bloomington," in *As We Knew Adlai: The Stevenson Story by Twenty-two Friends,* edited and with preface by Edward P. Doyle, foreword by Adlai E. Stevenson III (New York: Harper & Row, 1966), p. 5.
[7] *Daily Pantagraph,* March 20, 1925.

GRIEF AND DESPAIR HOLDS UNDISPUTED
SWAY IN EGYPT [8]
(By Staff Correspondent.)

Carbondale, March 20. — Carbondale is whispering quiet tonight. Streets are lined with cars and the sidewalks with groups of men, but the crowds which have inundated this little town are not happy fair time crowds.

Rather are they sombre and suppressed. Groups are talking in undertones but their discussion is not punctuated with jests and bursts of laughter, but with long and eloquent silences. Among the many refugees steadily coming in from surrounding towns, where death has marched triumphant, there is an atmosphere of dazed bewilderment. Suffering and agony is still in a blind and speechless state. It will be many hours before losses are all known and pent-up grief bursts forth in all its volume. Relief headquarters has been established in Elks hall but there is not enough room and cots have overflowed the porches onto the lawn.

An endless caravan of nurses and doctors is passing out on the roads for the stricken towns. Doors of morgues here are besieged with parents, wives, sweethearts, hoping against hope that their loved ones are not within. On many of the store windows are lists of dead, mute witnesses of sorrow that is Egypt's. Military lines have been thrown around West Frankfort and Murphysboro. Latest estimates tonight are that dead in Murphysboro may exceed 500. The entire town west of the tracks is literally flat. Ambulances pass thru in a grim and endless procession. Bodies are still being extracted from the ruins and hurried burials have commenced. All trains passing thru Murphysboro are being stopped and passengers solicited for funds. A pall of dry-eyed, inarticulate depression has settled over sunny Egypt. In a few weeks the peach orchards will be in blossom but it will not be the happy, joyous time of yesteryear for these simple, honest country folks.

STOICISM AND HEROIC SPIRIT
PERVADES THE STORM STRICKEN AREA [9]
(By Staff Correspondent.)

Carbondale, Ill., March 20. — "Hello Tom, how's your folks." "Folks is all going to live, but the old hut is gone." That is what one hears on

[8] Ibid., March 21, 1925.
[9] Ibid.

every side in Murphysboro, except that frequently the folks are not all going to live.

The stoicism and heroic spirit of the citizens of Murphysboro in the midst of appalling life and property loss will never be forgotten by the myriads of relief workers that have poured thru there in the last two days. The storm spared part of the town. Already the industrious house-holders have begun to replace shingles and patch up houses that are still standing.

There are now more than 180 dead and 250 seriously injured in Mur-physboro alone and it will always remain a miracle that there was not ten times that many. More than 75 square blocks presents a more com-pletely devastated area than the Chemin Des Dames did after five years of constant bombardment, and in Murphysboro it all happened in less than five minutes. Fire swept over a large area. The wreckage still smokes and in some places burns brightly. Fire apparatus charges thruout the streets incessantly. Many and strange are the freaks of the tornado. One sees mattresses and clothing in trees. Automobiles are on front porches, pianos and clocks standing quite unharmed and uncon-cerned amidst wreckage that no longer even faintly resembles a dwell-ing. Trees are rarely broken, most of them have been torn up by the roots. The streets thruout the whole north part of the town are im-passable and it is virtually impossible to distinguish one house from the next.

The Gods might have sown a field of kindling and bricks over the face of a bleeding and smoking world.

There is nothing more pathetic than the dry eyed, haggard people that one sees everywhere, stumbling over the wrecks of ruined houses, wistfully surveying the mass of bricks, wood, china, books and clothing that once was a happy home.

A little girl sits quietly weeping on a pile of rubbish, hugging a shattered doll. A cow wanders aimlessly and hungrily among the smouldering ruins. An old lady was sitting with her aged husband. She was unharmed, of him there remained to her two limbs and a watch with the crystal intact. A diamond was torn from the finger of a woman.

Tom Chamberlain's wife was nursing her baby. She is unscathed and the baby was found three hundred yards away, half buried in the mud. A plank was driven six inches deep into a tree.

Floyd Collins' rescuers could not have worked with more inspired fury than did the men who today tore thru the ruins of Logan school in search of seven missing children.[10]

---

[10] Floyd Collins had been trapped in a cave. The attempt to rescue him was a front-page story for days. See F. L. Allen, *Only Yesterday* (New York: Harper, 1931), pp. 193–194.

The relief work is everywhere being conducted with admirable dispatch and efficiency but among the townspeople all is confusion. A steady stream of curiously garbed and bandaged people passes thru headquarters at the Elks in search of missing or injured friends and relatives. Many of the doctors have not taken off their aprons in 36 hours but the situation is well in hand now. The few available hearses in Murphysboro are racing back and forth to the cemetery, carrying two caskets at a time, many of them small ones. Of formal funerals there are none, but of heroic fortitude there is much.

TRAIL OF SCATTERED AND TWISTED WRECKAGE LEFT BY THE "FOUR HORSEMEN" [11]
(By Staff Correspondent.)

Murphysboro, March 22 — Four days have elapsed now since the Four Horsemen of the Apocalypse disappeared over the Indiana line on their mad, devastating race, leaving behind them a wake of horror and destruction that beggars description. The catastrophic fury of the elements has never been more fearfully demonstrated and it will be many years if Egypt, that erstwhile land of milk and honey, ever effaces the ghastly vestiges of a moment's elemental wrath.

From the eminence on which stands the rubbish heap that once was Logan school, the tomb of some 30 little children, one looks out across the north and west quarters of the city. Viewing this broad expanse of scattered, twisted smouldering wreckage one cannot but reflect on the futility of life and the insignificance of man. Truly our destinies are cradled in the laps of the Gods. Atropos has clipped a bundle of threads and behold what horror remains as the mute but eloquent witness of her disfavor! Off to the north one sees an occasional gaunt and ragged wall silhouetted against the sunset sky, all that remains of the Mobile and Ohio shops, the mill and the wholesale house. But it is the wreckage of the small and humble homes that thrusts the iron of pathos deepest. Reflect that each board, each rag of clothing, each battered pan represents loving work and pennies saved. In a dreadful moment all is gone and perhaps not even a foundation remains to attest the saving of a life of honest toil, struggle and frugality. And then consider that many of the loved ones who made toil a pleasure have gone forever. To see on every side the human spirit triumphant over cruelty that has removed all that makes life worthwhile is an exhibition of heroism and

[11] *Daily Pantagraph*, March 23, 1925.

abiding faith in the essential rightness of things that surpasses all understanding. Indeed, the tornado disaster presents no greater moral lesson and no greater manifestation of magnificent stoicism than this steadfast endurance in the face of monumental adversity.

It scratches the very heart of one to think that hundreds of families have lost their all just as life was unfolding its rewards. It is horrible to think that a thousand dead are being buried in a dozen towns simultaneously. It stirs the wells of sympathy to know that tents and charity will have to provide for many thousands for a long while. But have we thought that it will be a generation before the crippled, the disfigured, the bed-ridden, the blind, the insane have ceased to bear constant and touching witness in their life-long innocent suffering to the horrors of that fatal March Wednesday. We all know that there are thousands of injured but only those that have walked thru the hospitals, seen the suffering, seen the amputations, smelled the anasthesia laden air, know how desperately injured many of the victims are.

I saw a farmer dressed in his best blue suit, pale but dry-eyed and composed, push his way thru a crowd in front of a morgue and emerge a moment later carrying a tiny white casket not three feet long. The crowd gave way in reverent awe and closed behind him intent on its own business. He placed the casket tenderly beside him in his Ford and drove away. That was Mary, aged 2. Baby Jane is still inside; he will come back for her. A big strapping, fine looking miner opens a cheap watch and gazes with tear-dimmed eyes at the photo of a girl inside. Wistfully he inquires of the guard at the morgue door, "that's my Ruth; is she inside?" "No," and away he goes on his fruitless search.

A mother hen accompanied by her new hatched brood, scurries about clucking frantically. I wonder if she too is looking for a lost one? In a field not far from town stands a cow; she has been standing there four days. The wind deposited her with such force that all four legs are sunk in the mud above the knees and were she alive she could not move. The animals suffered too!

The mad confusion and traffic congestion that prevailed here Thursday and Friday has largely subsided. Everyone is working and with duties systematically assigned, order has come out of chaos and there is no longer unnecessary duplication and confusion from too many over zealous volunteers. The one danger now is the spread of tetanus. Some of it was inevitable when one stops to consider that it was not until four hours after the storm that Murphysboro got in touch with Carbondale, and during that period there was much hasty and unsterile first aid administered. A plentiful supply of antitoxin has arrived and the crisis seems to be over. The water conditions are still very bad and the town is plastered with notices warning the people to boil their water before using it.

A doctor in Murphysboro thought it was more important to patch up his house than to help with the injured and dying. He has irrevocably lost his practice. Slacking next to looting is the greatest sin thruout the stricken area. The Boy Scouts are doing valiant work in a quiet, obedient way. What with tents and Pullman cars furnished by the Mobile and Ohio, there is no longer any serious exposure problem. Clothing, with the exception of men's shoes, is plentiful here. Everyone has given every extra thing they possess and shipments are coming in from outside.

The brick walls of a wholesale house fell on all four sides but the charred cans have remained standing piled up a story high in regular rows. Such are the vagaries that one sees on all sides.

In March, 1925, George Washington Butler, clerk of the Round Lick Association of Primitive Baptists, persuaded the Tennessee legislature, of which he was a member, to make it illegal "for any teacher in any of the universities, normal, and all other public schools of the state, to teach any theory that denies the story of the divine creation of man as taught in the Bible and to teach instead that man has descended from a lower order of animals."

A young high school biology teacher in the mountain town of Dayton, Tennessee, discussed the Butler law with a friend who was chairman of the county schoolbook committee. They disapproved of it and decided to challenge it. The next day John T. Scopes lectured on evolution and his friend complained to the authorities. Scopes was bound over to a grand jury.

Clarence Darrow, the most famous defense lawyer in the country and an agnostic, Arthur Garfield Hays, a lawyer for the American Civil Liberties Union, and Dudley Field Malone, who had campaigned with William Jennings Bryan for the Democratic party, came to Scopes's defense. Meanwhile Bryan was retained by the World's Christian Fundamental Association to assist the prosecution.

When Darrow led Bryan through a series of devastating questions, the Great Commoner revealed his dense ignorance of science. He also made a fatal admission. He agreed that when the Bible said the world was created in six days, it did not necessarily mean that a day was twenty-four hours; it might be many years. As a result, Bryan, whose position was that the Bible must be read literally, had himself interpreted the Bible. During the last minutes of Darrow's cross-examination there was an outburst of derisive laughter from Bryan's own followers. Soon after the trial Bryan was dead.[12]

Adlai E. Stevenson wrote the following editorials in Bloomington. He read the news dispatches and various articles about the trial.[13] *He was in sympathy with Scopes. He thus was opposed to Bryan, his grandfather's friend and running mate ih 1900 and one of the idols of his own youth.*

THE BIG CASE IS ON [14]

Actual work in the court at Dayton, Tenn., was begun yesterday morning in the hearing of the famous case of the people of Tennessee against John T. Scopes on an indictment charging him with having violated the law against teaching the theory of evolution in the schools.

No parallel to this kind of a trial is known in the recent history of the United States, and naturally the interest of the people is widespread and intense. However, the natural interest of citizens has been played upon and accelerated by modern publicity methods and by the prominence of the lawyers concerned in the prosecution and the defense. It has been charged that such men as William Jennings Bryan and Clarence Darrow are taking part in the case because of the personal prestige they enjoy as the limelight of publicity beats upon their bald heads. Both these men should be old enough, and enough experienced in the ways of the world, to resist any desire for cheap notoriety, and they can be given the benefit of a doubt when such charges are made.

The trial is going far afield, from present indications, aside from the constitutional questions involved in the right of a teacher to instruct in whatever theories of science he believes to be true, the scope of the testimony is to bring in a wide range of "expert" evidence as to the truth or falsity of the theory of evolution and the truth or otherwise of the literal language of the Biblical story of creation. Undoubtedly the vast mass of the people will receive instruction along these lines, if they read the evidence carefully, in a manner they have never before enjoyed.

Whatever may be thought of the case in the form in which it is developed, there are certain considerations which make it more palatable to the taste of the public than have been made other notable court trials

[12] Lawrence Levine, *Bryan: Defender of the Faith, 1915–1925* (New York: Oxford University Press, 1965), pp. 324–357, is a thoughtful account of the trial.

[13] Mrs. Ethel Sinclair, librarian, the *Daily Pantagraph*, letter to Carol Evans, January 5, 1953.

[14] *Daily Pantagraph*, July 11, 1925.

of recent years. Take the Harry Thaw case, for instance, or the trial of Loeb and Leopold in Chicago.

In the Dayton trial the public can at least know that no questions of gross immoral conduct is involved. The public will be gratified that if conviction is secured there will be no hanging or death in an electric chair. Neither will there be talk afterward of "justice being cheated", and the usual aftermath of noted criminal trials. The worst that could happen to John T. Scopes if the court and jury finds him guilty would be imposing of a fine of $100 to $500 in the discretion of the court, if such a fine were actually assessed, being a poor school teacher John might not be able to pay it. But in the present state of public sentiment, he could pass the hat and raise ten times the maximum amount of his fine within a few hours.

But in any event, the case is likely to be appealed to higher courts, and eventually reach the United States supreme court. If Tennessee's law is sustained, other states may take the cue and pass similar ones. An epidemic of such laws would prove a detriment to both the educational system and public morals.

As far as Dayton's refreshment stands and hot-dog booths are concerned, we predict they will do a thriving business for a few days. But let the trial drag along into the second or third week, and we believe the crowd of court house fans will dwindle to a point that concessionaires will be ready to pull up stakes and start on the old county fair route.

GENESIS VS. EVOLUTION [15]

A great Englishman once said that "the ignorance of the so-called educated classes is stupendous." But quite apart from the medieval aspect of the great battle between today and yesterday, Genesis vs. Evolution, Tenn., 1925, there is a fundamental aspect of this trial which is equally humiliating.

The law prohibits the teaching of any theory that denies the divine creation of man as taught in the Bible. It was passed by the general assembly of the state of Tennessee, composed presumably of conscientious Americans of better than average intelligence. The character of this measure is precautionary. The good people of Tennessee feel that the tenets of science are iniquitous and apt to vitiate the minds and morals of their vigorous intelligent young men and women. The conclusion is then that the solons of Tennessee feel that anything but the literal acceptance of the Bible and the traditional tenets of faith is subversive of the moral and spiritual public welfare.

[15] Ibid., July 20, 1925.

This was exactly the state of mind which gave an impulse to the Inquisition in Europe, particularly in Spain. But that was 500 years ago. The Bible is an historical and literary monument. But it has been the unchallenged "best seller" of the ages, not because of its historical and literary value, but because it has revealed the word of God and pointed out the clear, unequivocal road to happiness thru the life of Christ. If the children of Tennessee find the Bible any less puissant as a guide to a better and more fulsome life because they have evolved from the amoeba rather than from ready made men created by God it is a sad commentary on our spiritual and intellectual independence.

And incidentally, if our mental processes as a nation have become so devitalized that we must be blindfolded and led by the hand, then it is high time that those champions of democracy, who seize each patriotic occasion to reaffirm their belief in the infallibility of the great public mind, view with alarm our latter-day degradation. Truly, if men and women can not distinguish between right and wrong and profit from the Bible unless they know whether Genesis or evolution is right, then we have reached a sad state of incompetence.

MAN AND BEAST [16]

St. Paul said, "The truth shall make you free." The most recent religious atavism is drawing to a close. This will probably be the last day of the humiliating trial in Dayton. It is probable that the jury will find the Tennessee statute constitutional. Assuming that it does, what has this trial proved for us? Has it proved that the theory of evolution is fallacious? Has it found for us a great truth which in the words of St. Paul will make us free?

Of course not. The answer is manifest. This whole commotion is simply another indication of the tenacity of the human mind in clinging to inherited ideas, in holding on to convictions acquired by association. It was this same attitude of mind that resisted the Copernician theory, which threw Galileo into prison, which has treated the greatest philosophers with contempt, and sent renowned inventors to their graves in penury.

We only wish that the legislature of Tennessee had paused to inquire whether the evolution theory is inconsistent with what is supposed to be essential to religious belief. Dr. James McCosh, the eminent Presbyterian divine, sometime professor of metaphysics and logic in Queens college, Belfast, and later president of Princeton, said in his farewell address at the latter institution:

[16] Ibid., July 21, 1925.

"When a scientific theory is brought before us, our first inquiry is not whether it is consistent with religion, but whether it is true. If it is found to be true on the principle of the induction of Bacon, it will be found to be consistent with religion on the principle of the unity of knowledge."

Perhaps if these sentient words of the old Scotch divine had been brought to the attention of the Tennessee legislature they would never have fallen into error and we would have been saved this mortifying recurrence of mediaevalism.

One can't help but speculate as to what the position of Mr. Bryan would be if at some future time scientists should prove the accuracy of the evolutionary hypothesis, just as they have proved that the earth is round and revolves about the sun. According to Mr. Bryan, the issue is clear, the Christian religion cannot survive if the theory of evolution is true. What if the scientists are right, what if the anthropologists know more about the history of man than the theologians? If evolution is right, must Christianity go into the discard? To pit the faith of millions against the universal opinion of scientific men exposes the millions to the conclusion that if science is right then their whole religion is wrong. So Mr. Bryan has quite unconsciously balanced the whole of Christianity against a scientific theory.

But this unconscious refinement of the foundation of Christianity is not to be viewed with apprehension, for thruout the ages Christianity has been a living, progressive revelation of faith built on much firmer foundations than even the fundamentalists believe. Its enduring usefulness and inspiration did not depend on whether the earth was round and does not now depend on whether man evolved or was created.

In the words of Thomas H. Huxley:

"Thoughtful men, once escaped from the blinding influence of traditional prejudice, will find in the lowly stock whence man has sprung the best evidence of the splendor of his capacities, and will discern in his long progress thru the past a reasonable ground of faith in his attainment of a nobler future."

$100 FINE [17]

Twelve reasonable men have found John Thomas Scopes guilty of violation of the intellectual obscurity law down in Tennessee and he has accordingly been fined $100. Thus endeth the first chapter in a comedy both amusing and humiliating.

And now that Mr. Bryan, than whom there is no more conscientious

[17] Ibid., July 22, 1925.

and sincere man alive, has won his smashing victory for the "old time religion" and Tennessee is purged of malignant plotters against our traditional theology, we stop to wonder what the consequenc[e]s will be. Is this trial down in the little court room in Dayton going to have the great transcendent spiritual effect with which we were beguiled in the anticipatory stages? Will an irresistible tide of spiritual exultation sweep across the country accompanied by loud hosannas from the faithful and repentant?

No, of course not. The case will doubtless be reviewed by an appellate court and may perhaps reach the supreme court on the constitutionality question. But the public mind is migratory, it will soon move to something else and Dayton will become but a memory even as the flood in the other Dayton [Ohio] has become but a memory.

Darrow and Malone and Hays all did the best they could and tho they lost the verdict, they have scored a great intangible victory for their cause. Indeed theirs is the only result of any widespread significance and importance.

Certain laws of human psychology are almost inflexible. Forbidden fruit is always the sweetest and particularly so is it to young people. What young people are affirmatively refused is generally what they most eagerly want. The whole purpose of education should be to stimulate intellectual curiosity and the garish light of publicity has done this for the theory of evolution in a way which would make the most inspired apostle of truth green with envy. Tho the students of Tennessee may not hear academic lectures on evolution, we venture to say that the tenets of that vicious and prohibited faith will be quite as familiar to Tennesseeans as they are elsewhere. But the more widespread understanding of evolution will not be confined to Tennessee. We merely have that state to thank for the unconscious intellectual impetus.

So the intolerance act has presented a rare opportunity for popularizing, in the best sense, scientific truths. Scientists can now unfold the truths and theories discovered by scientific inquiry to a tremendously enlarged, enlightened and receptive audience. Thus the ultimate result of Tennessee's fanaticism will be an enlarged audience for the fascinating scientific story of our Neanderthal and Cro-Magnon ancestors.

EVOLUTION IN THE FEDERAL COURTS [18]

The clear and single issue at Dayton has been settled. Teacher Scopes was guilty of violating a statute prohibiting the teaching of any other than the Bible theory of creation. Nothing remains now except for the

[18] Ibid., July 24, 1925.

appellate courts to determine whether the state or federal federal constitution was violated in enacting the law.[19]

Of course the popular issue, evolution against the Bible, never entered the trial at Dayton. So neither the fundamentalists nor modernists can derive much satisfaction from a trial that did not judicially settle the question of whether the theory of evolution can be reconciled with the Biblical story of the creation. But now word comes from Washington that a convenient phrase in the 1925 District of Columbia appropriation bill is the vehicle for an injunction proceedings against the auditor and disbursing officer of the district. This bill provides that "no part of this sum (for the public schools) shall be available for the salary of any superintendent who permits the teaching of, or any teacher who teaches disrespect for the Holy Bible."

Under this clause it would seem that injunction proceedings against the disbursing officer would force the courts to define "disrespect for the Holy Bible" in order to determine whether the teaching of evolution is disrespectful. If the evolutionary hypothesis cannot be reconciled with the Bible it must contradict the Bible and is therefore "disrespectful." So it follows that to pass on the question of disrespect the court will have first to resolve the problem of possible reconciliation and to do so the court will have to take expert testimony. Thus at last the evidence of scientists, religious liberals, fundamentalists, clergymen and educational leaders, all of which was ruled out in Tennessee, will have to be admitted.

Where Dayton failed, it would seem that Washington has won and a court, after all, will find itself no doubt an unwilling arbiter in this controversy between the literal and scientific interpretation of the Bible. But whatever the outcome of the whole thing will be, time will show its utter futility, for the cause of religion can never be harmed, nor can the human mind ever be legislated out of its curiosity and constant inquiry after new truths.

But there is a public moral and precept of great importance which should, and in all probability will come out of this controversy. We must ask ourselves dispassionately and without prejudice whether it is wise for a legislature to attempt to do the sort of thing the Tennessee legislature did. After all, should not education be the province of educators, who certainly have the moral and spiritual public welfare as much at

[19] The Tennessee Supreme Court later threw out the fine on a technicality, thereby blocking Scopes's attorneys from testing the constitutionality of the law. Mr. Scopes received a scholarship to the University of Chicago where he studied geology.

heart as our legislators? Should not scholars in every field of research be the best judges as to what should be taught in that field?

In June, 1926, after passing the examination to practice law in Illinois, Adlai E. Stevenson decided to take what he called "one last fling" at journalism. At a bachelor dinner, Adlai, George Norton, and Robert Page discussed their desire to visit the Soviet Union and observe the Communist experiment at first hand. The only way to gain admission to the Soviet Union was as foreign correspondents. The object would be, Stevenson explained, to interview the Soviet Foreign Minister, Georgi Vasilievich Chicherin. The Foreign Minister had refused to see any of the American correspondents stationed in Moscow. Anyone who could obtain an interview would have an important news scoop.

"But why should Chicherin see you, when he won't see the experienced correspondents who are already there?" Adlai was asked.

He replied: "He might see me precisely because I'm young and naïve. He might think I'd be more sympathetic to new ideas than older and more sophisticated men. At least, it's worth a try." [20]

Adlai's father helped him obtain credentials as a foreign correspondent for the Chicago Herald-American and Hearst's International News Service. George Norton received credentials from the Louisville Courier-Journal, and Robert Page decided to accompany them even though he had no credentials.

On July 24, 1926, Adlai sailed with his mother and sister on the Conte Biancamano for Italy. On arrival, he took a brief trip in Italy with his family. His sister wrote that while on a train, she had tucked her feet under her on the seat, trying to sleep. "A Fascist guard came in and screamed that I was under arrest — for defiling the upholstery. Adlai was so furious he got white, but he kept his head and got me unarrested. The more changes we saw in our beloved Italy, the more my brother despised the new regime." [21]

Adlai left his mother and sister in Italy and joined Norton and Page in Vienna. The visas they had applied for in New York were not waiting for them in Vienna. Page gave up and the other two went to Budapest in hopes the visas would be waiting for them there. When they were unable to obtain visas there, Norton decided to join a group of religious leaders who were planning to enter the Soviet Union through Poland. (They were turned back at the border.) Adlai, meanwhile, journeyed to

[20] Quoted in Davis, A Prophet in His Own Country, pp. 153–154.
[21] Ives and Dolson, My Brother Adlai, p. 188.

Belgrade, to Bucharest, to Sofia, and finally to Istanbul. After two days of waiting in the office of the Soviet consulate, he gave up temporarily and went sightseeing. When he returned to the consulate two days later, the consul reprimanded him for not having returned sooner since the visa had been authorized.

The Soviet authorities, however, had no suggestions as to how he was to travel from Istanbul to Russia. Adlai had himself rowed to an Italian freighter, and he persuaded the captain to take him aboard. Five days later the ship docked at Batum in the Caucasus. Soviet authorities confiscated his French-Russian dictionary, a copy of Sir Bernard Pares's History of Russia, *and all of his other papers.*

Alone, without a dictionary, and among Russians who spoke no English, he managed to travel to Tiflis, capital of Georgia, and then to Baku on the Caspian. There he boarded a train for Moscow. For five days he shared a compartment with a man who never spoke. Years later he would recall that he had never felt more "utterly isolated, nor more miserable physically." [22] *His first sight in Moscow when he stepped out of the railroad station was a group of "wolf children" — homeless orphans of the civil war — crouched on the cobblestones eating a jar of jam someone had dropped.*[23]

In Moscow Adlai stayed at a house run by the Friends Service Committee. There he met Walter Duranty of the New York Times, *William Henry Chamberlin of the* Christian Science Monitor, *and H. R. Knickerbocker of the International News Service. He heard from them of the struggle between Stalin and Trotsky for control of the government since the death of Lenin two years before.*

Years later Stevenson told Kenneth S. Davis: "The atmosphere of fear was palpable, as palpable as the abject poverty of the masses. I never knew whether or not I was being followed, but I did know that people were afraid to be seen talking to me. One of the Russians I talked to was Karl Radek, the old Bolshevik theoretician, who was later killed in the Purge." [24]

During his first day in Moscow, Stevenson talked to Chicherin's press secretary and presented his ideas about the settlement of the outstanding problems between the two countries and explained that an interview

[22] Davis, *A Prophet in His Own Country*, p. 157.

[23] *A Speaker's Book of Facts — 1952* (Washington: CIO Political Action Committee) stated that Stevenson wrote a story about the plight of Russia's homeless children. If so, we have been unable to locate it. This is the only mention of such a story. Mrs. Ives did not remember it and it did not appear in the *Daily Pantagraph*. Stevenson never mentioned any such article to Professor Robert Tucker, who accompanied him on a trip to the Soviet Union in 1958.

[24] Quoted in *A Prophet in His Own Country*, p. 158.

with the Foreign Minister would be of immense value to "both our countries."

The press secretary advised him to return the next day. He did for a month but with no success. He then left Moscow for a two-week visit to Leningrad and then traveled to Sweden and returned to Bloomington in October, 1926. He wrote two stories for the Daily Pantagraph.

ITALIAN OBSERVATIONS [25]
By Adlai E. Stevenson

Italy is old as a race, but young as a nation. It was less than seventy years ago that Italy ceased to be what Metternich had termed "a mere geographical expression." There came that superb moment which saw the birth of Italian unity; the Bourbon kingdom of the two Sicilies, the Hapsburg provinces of Lombardy and Ven[e]zia, Papal Rome and the duchies of Tuscany, Parma and Modena became one. Garibaldi and Cavour laid down the bellows and a new nation arose ph[o]enix-like from the fire that Mazzini had lighted.

Victor Emanuel II found himself king of a united Italy and the Pope in protest sentenced himself to voluntary confinement in the Vatican. This new kingdom in the land of the Caesars continued to be a tourist mecca — its enchanting beauty and priceless heritage of art were fixtures. But the world was in the throes of capitalism and Italy, wanting in resources, dropped behind in the international race for development. Indeed it is only within the last 30 years that industrialization has moved on apace.

Humiliation of Italy

So that critical day in May, 1915, dawned to find Italy a first class power only by courtesy and a second class power in fact. Again she faced a crisis but emerged to plunge with fierce determination into the war. Then came the "dark night after the disaster of Caporetto," but, as by a miracle, Italian resistence held firm along the Piave.

In Milan Benito Mussolini, editor of the socialist paper, Popolo, tho still suffering from a recent wound, set himself to battle the influences which he felt arising and to prepare for the storm which he foresaw with his extraordinary gift of anticipation. There was grumbling in the army and sinister whisperings among the socialists behind the front. "Great words have crossed the frontier" — the Italian socialist move-

---

[25] *Daily Pantagraph,* November 27, 1926. These articles were transcribed from photocopies of Stevenson's typescript furnished to the editors by the *Daily Pantagraph.*

ment was hypnotized by Moscow and turned suddenly toward the extreme ideas of Lenin. Mussolini, the socialist, said on Oct. 17, 1917; "We must abandon the great phrase of 'Liberty.' There is another which in this third winter of the war ought to be on the lips of the cabinet when they address the Italian people and it is discipline!"

"Our dilemma offers us only two alternatives, either discipline today in order to achieve victory tomorrow, or collapse following on defeat." In these words was embodied the germ of Fascism, an idea destined to gather such force that in exactly five years it was to make the ex-socialist editor the greatest autocrat the world has known since the abdication of Nicholas II.

Treatment in Peace Meet[ing]

With the reorganization of the army and the victory of the Piave, enthusiasm and morale returned and at last came the official report; "The soldiers of what was once one of the most formidable armies in the world have retreated in disorder down the valleys. . . ." The Italian arms had triumphed and the Austrians were in flight. Then followed the momentous days at the peace conference when proud kingdoms were divided as the spoils. Italy clamored for colonies for her increasing population. But her demands were unavailing and she was awarded only Triest[e] and the "lost provinces" in the Trentino. Even the Dalmation territory, promised in solemn treaties, was denied her.

The blame for Italy's poor bargain at Versailles lay with herself. The cause was her traditional and fatal weakness — disunion. Mussolini writing in the Popolo two months after the armistice spoke of the "profound humiliation" and the "miserable spectacle" of the country, "torn by political quarrels" while England and France, "united and strong" gave an immense impression of solidarity and determination. The failure at the peace conference was but an echo of the devastating weakness, futility and vacillation of the government. Things went from bad to worse. The lira dropped in value day by day. Thousands were thrown out of work with the closing of war industries. The government had made no preparations for demobilization and the streets were filled with distressed and disillusioned veterans.

Within four months after the armistice the first manifestations of bolshevism occurred in Milan, and a month later 45 persons gathered together for the first meeting of the "Fasci," (derived from the Latin word "fa[s]ces," or bundle of rods carried by the lictors of ancient Rome as a symbol of authority.) Followers of the new faith multiplied miraculously, but with equal rapidity disorder and radical socialism were paralyzing the country. The revolutionary propaganda had taken effect and the populace became impudent and insulting to the bourgeoisie. Strikes were perpetual. For championing the activities of d'Annunzio at Fiume, Mussolini was imprisoned within two days after he had been overwhelmingly defeated at the polls.[26] A storm of protest, however, caused his almost immediate release.

Rise of Fascismo.

During the ensuing interval Mussolini continued to "live dangerously," following the precept of Nietzsche. Communism gathered momentum and had there been a strong leader it might easily have seized the reins of power. In September 1920, the socialists seized the factories in many places and attempted the "dictatorship of the proletariat" on a large scale. Military revolt was imminent in the army. The government did nothing. In Turin the Soviet which had set itself up as a tribunal of justice found two men guilty of "fascismo" and condemned them to death. They were to have been thrown alive into the great furnaces of the metal works, but the furnaces without the technicians to keep them up had gone out, so they were shot. Bombings and outrages were frequent.

With an impotent government at Rome the growing and well disciplined Fascisti were the only counter force to bolshevism. Violence and bloodshed were incessant thruout the land. But such was the growing force of Fascism, that in the elections of May, 1921, Mussolini found himself the leader of a parliamentary group that had sprung from nothing to 33 [35] members.

Here was the first conquest of the new spirit of Italy and the first great manifestation of the new feeling of hope and accomplishment that has radiated from Italy thru all Europe — the restless spirit of youth which is everywhere supplanting the old order with its faith and its passion.

Thenceforth Fascism was no longer simply a movement of reaction against bolshevism; new and greater roles suggested themselves to its tireless leader. "Revolution," he said, "is a discipline which substitutes itself for another discipline, it is an order, a hierarchy, which takes the place of another order." Soon after appeared his new review "Gerarchia" (Hierarchy.) "A hierarchy ought to terminate in a pin-point." So with Il Duce as the "pin-point" the bellicose, anti-government precepts of Fascism spread across the country like wild fire. His program was one of opposition to the government because it was senile. "There are

[26] The poet Gabriele D'Annunzio, with a band of volunteer "legionnaires," seized the Adriatic port of Fiume in September, 1919. Italy and Yugoslavia were in negotiations over Fiume at this point. D'Annunzio ruled over Fiume for months until the Italian government ousted him. In November, 1919, Mussolini was defeated for a seat in the Chamber of Deputies.

now," he wrote, "two states within the state, two governments, two leaders. I am the Mustapha Kemal of a Milanese Angora, swift, irregular and victorious, in opposition to a Roman Constantinople, feeble and paralyzed, the eternal Byzantium." The conclusion of the congress of Rome was logical; "For the country's sake it is necessary to subdue this state within the state, to subdue the revolutionary force by the conservative force. There cannot be two states within the state." But the movement was too vital to die by command. When at last in October, 1922, revolution seemed imminent Mussolini was offered a post in the ministry with the hope that he could check it. But the offer was rejected. With rapidity and precision his plans were executed. On the morning of October 28 the Fascist call to arms was placarded all over Italy and at dawn on October 30 the first black-shirted legions marched into Rome. The prime minister, [Luigi] Facta, suggested armed resistence but the king wisely refused to sign the decree and Mussolini took over the government with the words, "And now let us get down to work." [27]

"BENEFICENT TYRANNY"
RULE OF ITALY TODAY [28]
By Adlai E. Stevenson

Italy did get down to work and has been at work ever since. Italians have always preferred to follow personalities rather than principles. This is the primary reason why the rank and file of Italians are working with a spirit that is altogether new. For its dynamic, dramatic qualities, Mussolini's character has few historical counterparts. Italy presents a cleaner, a more vigorous and enthusiastic atmosphere than ever before, tho it is reassuring to observe that the old picturesqueness still remains; the indolent count still courts the heiress, street singers still stop under your window and the gondolas of Venice are not yet equipped with motors.

That Italy's industries are expanding with unprecedented rapidity, that her enlarging foreign trade and aggressive maritime movement have caused no little surprise around the world, that predatory poverty no longer infests the streets and that she is united by a race conscious-

[27] In August, 1922, Italian trade unions called a general strike. Mussolini's Fascists had grown to hundreds of thousands by now and his "Black Shirts" smashed the strike. On October 24, at a Fascist rally in Naples, forty thousand passed in review, shouting, "On to Rome." Mussolini sent an ultimatum to Prime Minister Facta: "Either the government will be given to us or we shall seize it by marching on Rome." The King refused Facta's request for a declaration of martial law to deal with the Fascists and instead called Mussolini to Rome (from Milan, where he had safely retired during the "March") to form a new government.
[28] *Daily Pantagraph*, November 29, 1926.

ness and a spirit of proud nationalism for the first time since the Caesars; all these can be attributed to the fact that Mussolini has kept promise "to supply Italy with a government." Likewise there have been important reforms of taxation, in the judiciary system and education. Mussolini has capitalized and exploited Italy's only great natural resource, man power, as never before. There is no coal and there is no oil but of water power there is an abundance. So great generating plants are supplying the new and growing industries, thus preventing the dangerous infection of unemployment. Innumerable measures have been adopted to accelerate the economic development. Except on pressing business Italians cannot leave the country. Mussolini has ordered everyone to stay at home so their money must be spent at home. The lira is rising and Italy is today the best advertised and greatest "go-getter" in the world.

It is evident that order has come out of chaos and that Italy has witnessed the sunrise of a day of prosperity. But the "beneficent tyrant" who prefers "five thousand rifles to fifty thousand votes" has conferred these benefits by locking the lazy quarrelsome boy in a straight-jacket, stuffing a handkerchief in his mouth and then hypnotizing him with juggling feats performed with sticks of dynamite.

Those incidents and measures in his career which to us as Americans, bred in the democratic tradition, are hardest to condone have all been eloquently if not altogether convincingly explained by Fascists whom the writer has interviewed. In his handling of the Corfu incident in 1923 Mussolini snapped his fingers at the whole world in a not indecisive manner.[29] Many of us have asked if this dangerous impudence was necessary. The Fascisti reply in Mussolini's own words: "One can understand how thousands and thousands of Italians who in the past 20 years have wandered all over the world, know from bitter experience what it means to belong to a nation which is weak in a military sense and without prestige." Hence Corfu was a well directed if unscrupulous thrust at the Italian inferiority complex and a virile gesture of nationalism.

The relentless prosecution of and ultimate suppression of the Masonic order is justified on the ground that freemasonry in Italy is purely a political organization and does not partake of the same social character as in this country.

As the Fascist government has become more firmly intrenched and

[29] In August, 1923, an international commission that was drawing a boundary between Greece and Albania was attacked on Greek soil allegedly by bandits. Several Italian members of the commission were killed and Mussolini demanded an indemnity of 50 million lire. When Greece refused, Mussolini ordered the Italian fleet to shell the Greek island of Corfu and then to occupy it. The League of Nations investigated and recommended that Greece pay the indemnity. When the Greeks agreed, the Italians evacuated Corfu.

the personal authority of the chief has more closely approximated that of the Czar, the right of free speech has proportionat[e]ly been denied. The process has finally culminated, since the last attempt on his life, in the total abolition of the opposition press. This combined with other repressive measures, such as the dissolution of all opposition parties and organizations has created a situation which finds a counterpart only in Russia.

One cannot but be surprised to find such apparent inconsistencies in the expressed opinions of a man so eminently decisive, collected and forceful as Mussolini. In 1921 he said; "The nation turned to us when our movement appeared as a liberator from tyranny; the nation will turn against us if our movement takes on the guise of a fresh tyranny." Yet he has consistently denied the existence of "liberty" in the Fascist vocabulary and has substituted "order" and "discipline." Writing in 1923 he said; "Be it known then, once and for all that Fascism knows no idols, worships no fetishes. It has already stepped, and if need be, will quietly turn around to step once more over the more or less putrid body of the Goddess Liberty." One wonders just how much liberty you can take away before you begin to tyrannize.

The object of all these repressive measures, of course, is to eliminate any vestige of opposition to the Fascist regime. Imagine being liable to imprisonment for the mere expression of an antipathetic point of view no matter how sincere! And this same Mussolini in 1914 used three words before a court which was trying him for a published criticism of a government act: "What we stand in need of are dissensions, clashes of view, strife. Unanimity, uniformity, spell brainlessness and death. Gentlemen of the jury, render homage to the ancient philosopher, Heraclitus, who declared, 'Strife is the origin of all things.' Well, then, allow us to go on with our strife, give us freedom for this, and you will render homage to a great philosopher and to a very great principle — the principle of Freedom!"

It is evident that to insure its position and the safety of its chief Fascism has adopted the same tactics that communism has in Russia, tho under considerably different circumstances. Historically suppression leads to violence. Taking away free speech is taking away the safety valve.

What the future of Italy is no one can say. It shares the danger of collapse and chaos with all dictatorships. Another Mussolini to carry on will not be found. But already it is being whispered that the son is father to the man and the party is bigger than the chief. In other words that Fascism is a wholly new political philosophy that can never be drowned in blood. One thing is clear, that Fascismo has done great things for Italy; shaken her out of an industrial and commercial lethargy and restored her national prestige while at the same time causing no little misapprehension as to imperialistic ambitions. Mussolini ranks with Lenin as one of the great national idols of all time, but Italy must have peace and tranquillity if the vigorous tree that he has planted is to bear all its potential fruit. He has a profound and first hand knowledge of the Italian temperament and psychology and it is possible that if he can survive the assassins bullets a few more years he will succeed in demonstrating the utilitarian benefits of his regime. With the success of the experiment insured real tranquility may supplant the present dangerously charged atmosphere.

Part Six

Letters to Claire Birge
1923–1928

During the summer of 1923, while Adlai E. Stevenson was vacationing at Charlevoix, Michigan, he met Claire Birge of Greenwich, Connecticut. Miss Birge was visiting her St. Louis grandparents, who were summering at Charlevoix.

The acquaintanceship between the twenty-three-year-old Stevenson and the seventeen-year-old Miss Birge developed into a tender friendship. Over the next five years they corresponded regularly and saw each other on occasion. Stevenson asked her to marry him in December, 1925.

Miss Birge — now Mrs. Richard H. Bassett of Milton, Massachusetts — saved eighty of Stevenson's handwritten letters, postcards, and telegrams, and graciously permitted the editors to see them. They were not discovered by the editors of The Papers of Adlai E. Stevenson until Volume I was in page proof. As a result it was necessary to include a selection of them as a separate section rather than to intersperse them in the volume with other letters already in type. Regardless of necessity, these love letters do naturally belong together in a separate section.

The letters Claire Birge wrote to Stevenson apparently were not saved, except for the one she wrote him after receiving his letter on September 5, 1928, that he was soon to marry Ellen Borden.

When Stevenson returned to Bloomington, Illinois, after the vacation at Charlevoix, he wrote his first letter to Claire.

Thursday [September 6, 1923] [1]

Dear Claire,

It was dear of you to send me the book! From my point of view not so much because I am anxious to read it, as I am, but because it furnishes me a legitimate opportunity to write you, permission for which was deprived me by the rude and altogether thoughtless management of the Pere Marquette Ry. on a soft moonlight night not long ago. I was having such a delightful time and hoped for more but the shifting of cars and the hour effectually interrupted my "idle wanderings in the sweet fields of your presence."

To meet and have some hours with you after all these years in which we've both grown up has contributed in no insignificant degree to make warm and colorful what was a very drab and stupid summer for me.

As for the business tangle [2] which will determine whether I remain here or go back again this year, Alas! I can still say nothing. However, it appears as though I would probably be wisest to stay here. Hence I shall in all probability be unable to see you in Greenwich before you return to school. But I can assure you that the prospect of doing so is hardly resistible and makes my decision to stay here a hard one indeed. I am nevertheless hoping in the way of some self consolation that I shall find it necessary to make some "business trips" to New York during the winter and that perhaps I will be fortunate enough to see you then.

Once more at home I suppose you are having a gay and happy time. No doubt recollections of dances at the Casino and aimless meanderings by motor form an unfavorable contrast; but for me they arouse a host of enchanting memories.

If the opportunity presents itself and the inclination is not artificial, I hope I may hear from you sometime.

Yours,
ADLAI

Adlai returned to Harvard Law School for the year and Claire attended Miss Porter's School in Farmington, Connecticut. Although Claire was unable to leave school, Adlai visited Claire's parents at Greenwich in November and met Claire's brother Walter and sister Grace. En route to Bloomington for Christmas, Adlai met Claire in Greenwich and she

[1] The envelope is postmarked September 7, 1923.

[2] For a discussion of the controversy concerning ownership of the *Daily Pantagraph*, see pp. 153–154 above.

visited with him in New York City, where his sister Buffie had an apartment.

December 29 [1923] [3]

Dear Claire —

It was good to see you again — *awfully* good! But best of all it served very pleasantly to dispel any uncertain illusions as to whether the eloquent impression you left with me this summer was at all due to environment — Charlevoix and all the romantic childhood associations it has for me and always will have. But no it wasn't Charlevoix, it wasn't that last of sweet sad memories. Indeed if anything, I found you even more attractive, fresh, and invigorating in Greenwich. And the allusion to Greenwich, by parity of thought, leads me to New York with you and I must hasten to express my concern as to whether you were too dreadfully late to your bridge party. I do hope you weren't and that that perhaps you can again sometime be persuaded to lunch with me in Buff's apartment when we're not in quite such a rush.

And what with "rush" here I am on the holidays. Phoenix like, tranquil and phlegmatic Bloomington has been reborn and the unaccustomed activity has completely bewildered me. In fact there was even a "society" wedding to-day (peculiar time for weddings to be sure) but gracious what *momentous* events! Not that we're constitutionally unable to cope with the situation but for more plausible reasons, the family had decided to migrate to Chicago to-morrow. On Monday comes the Princeton Triangle show with attendant festivities; hence I look forward to quite a convivial time of it.

The prospect of going back to Cambridge is a distressing one so I have decided to stay over until next Saturday, thereby contracting for ominous mountains of additional work to make up. Indeed its self-alarming to see how my disrespect for responsibility increases with the years. This text presents a splendid opportunity for a germane little moral lesson which, however, I don't believe you need and therefore will spare you it.

You must be having a great time and when next I see Walter I shall ask for a detailed account of Master Hugh's attention and an estimate of his position in your regard.

Don't forget to give a lot of love to Grace and to dispatch one of

[3] The envelope is postmarked December 31, 1923.

those priceless epistles when the opportunity presents itself. I suppose this is the season for good *wishes* for the New Year but for Claire there will be *prophecies* from

ADLAI

P.S. Met a former Rosemary girl the other day who remembered you but of course have forgotten her name.

Adlai and Claire corresponded regularly during the remainder of the school year and during the summer of 1924, which she spent in Europe with her family. On her return, Adlai visited with her and then returned to Bloomington where he was working on the family newspaper, the Pantagraph.

Thursday, September 25, 1924

Dear Claire —

Here I am back once more in the pra[i]rie garden and still thinking how good it was to see you again and how much you had improved, were that remotely possible, after the most eventful and illuminating summer abroad. What with more school, constantly increasing social experience and more travel, it would seem that the education of Claire is to be a very thorough affair. But I hope she refrains from the only too natural tendency and eagerness of girls of her age to gain worldly experience. For super-sophistication is dangerous and though sometimes they don't have quite as good a time (judging by accepted but fictitious standards) it is the simple, honest and naturel girls that make the finest women and are most admired by men in the long run.

All of which sounds very paternal and is a bit foolish in that you know it already. However, I feel that you will condone the offenses of a doting admirer and fellow in this everlasting search for truth and the really worthwhile things in this vale of tears, which were we all at peace within ourselves, would be rather a vale of smiles instead.

The country out here is quite lovely now — the usual endless monotony is now one of increasing colorfulness. Indeed the pace in the Corn Belt is altogether liveable but I fear the winter is going to be tedious in the extreme. However, in spirit, I shall attend your school plays and German and thus gain enchanting relief. . . .

Don't neglect me Claire. You are constructing a very excellent and detailed autobiography by the way.

Best love
ADLAI

Sunday [November 23, 1924] [4]

My dear Claire —

Among the more recently discovered amenities of life in a small town is performing in amateur shows. So conjure up, if you, can, the absurd spectacle of your devoted scribe singing and dancing his way to inglorious public acclaim in a pretentious forthcoming musical show. However, my ignominy is somewhat relieved for the cause is charitable. And after all what figurative crimes are committed in the name of charity! And then in self defense and with pardonable pride I must say that the general run of my fellow performers have not a much more auspicious future in the musical comedy world than myself. The rehearsals have not been altogether monotonous though and I must say that I've found the 20 odd female members of the cast vastly amusing. They seem to be largely recruited from the ranks of the "typewriter chauffeurs," are never without a large mouthful of well masticated gum and the natural position of the body is hand on hips, lower jaw distinctly drooping and expression otherwise slightly defiant and bewildered. The manner of speech is highly entertaining. To be sure the accent has sometimes been scathingly characterized as 'nasal' and 'Middle Western.' But then after all it is a highly developed lingual peculiarity and I have come to regard it with a great deal of admiration; as a feature distinctly peculiar to this part of the country and therefore an important contribution to the composite America. Strange and wonderful as may be the voice culture of the local "Tiller Girls" their remarks, independance and self assurance are even more refreshing. To be sure my ideas of the refined and unrefined have necessarily undergone a temporary transformation to conform to the exigencies of the present situation. And then there is the question of the rolled stocking and short skirt which gives rise to a shocking or stimulating display of bare knees at all times. However, it seems to the custom of the country, and who am I to object! So all in all I'm having quite an amusing time of it at present!

Thus far I've missed the football games and the happy collegiate gatherings more than anything else. But as far as the football itself is concerned the games over at the University of Illinois have not been a bad substitute. I wonder if you went to the Yale-Harvard game. Of course I suppose you did and how I envy you! I recall a very delightful day in your house after the Y-P game last year — but of course you were not there — and Grace was awfully shy.

4 The envelope is postmarked November 24, 1924.

Eleanor Bum[p]stead was here for a few weeks and helped keep the fall quite gay. We rode some and disported ourselves generally in healthy and becoming fashion — though it was somewhat of an effort for me to keep her lady like!

I suppose your life continues idyllic and active as ever and I have most eloquent visions of you in Arabian costume on your knees praising Allah.

Yours
ADLAI

Sunday, February 15 [1925] [5]

Dear Claire —

I'm sure it has been at least a year since I last wrote you or heard from you. And for me its been in large measure an uneventful year. However, I still manage to find important business engagements in Chicago when the week ends come round — and the 'business' generally presents an agreeable respite from the week's monotonies (or is it ys). I saw Margaret Willing not long ago — I believe she served a term at your present residence. Fortunately quite a few of my former classmates have assembled in Chicago so it makes it quite pleasant to go up for an evening of 'sweet converse.'

The journalist's lot becomes constantly more engaging and I've about decided to become a 'knight of the quill' — at least for the time being. Along with some other people, I'm thinking of buying the evening paper here and assuming the rôle of editor and publisher, if you please! Needless to say for one of my verdant years and experience to assume such a responsibility is just a little absurd, but then I've always been a bit of an egotist. At present my duties are numerous but somewhat indefinite. Yet I do find time to indulge my penchant for editorials and book reviews; in fact may do some of the latter for the New York Evening Post — Aren't you impressed! Was in Springfield the other day to hear Sr. John Finley [6] of Manhattan address the Lincoln Centennial Association. He made a splendid speech on Lincoln's education pointing out the absurdity of the modern view that 16 years of preparation and finally a degree make an education. Self education, the constant and inexorable habit of self cultivation, make the only education worthy of the name and formal, academic education is of no consequence unless it stimulates and imbues one with a life long insatiable curiosity to know the truth.

[5] The envelope is postmarked February 15, 1925.
[6] John Huston Finley, editor of the New York *Times*.

And now having discussed my egocentric self at great length, I will relieve your anxiety and desist. Your attitude relative to 'coming out' seems to me eminently sensible. Personally I should imagine it was an awful ordeal — consciously trying to be popular! But that disagreeable aspect won't apply to you and you'll doubtless have a lot of fun — and then perhaps be glad that it's over. How much better to approach it as an interesting experience and important adjunct to one's social education rather than as an organized man hunt! And its the girls that obviously are not trying to "go big" — if I may relapse to the vernacular — that always have the best time. So you'll have to deal very judiciously with the bombardment of proposals that awaits you.

Did you know that Davis Merwin married Miss Underwood [7] not long ago? Well he did quite suddenly and the 'happy young couple' leave soon for the customary adaptation period. Hope she finds it easy! (Illustrating my feline tendencies)

Will the candle sputters so station AES will 'sign off' with the customary protestations of abiding devotion —

ADLAI

Thursday, March 26 [1925] [8]

My dear Claire —

What a nice letter! One of your most enchanting characteristics to me is your complete acceptance of, satisfaction with, and everlasting faith in life. At best it seems to me that your letters always breath[e] a refreshing contentment with things as they are — a complacent joy in your daily life — whatever it may be. It is a wonderful and blessed thing for one so young to recognize the inevitability of all things and accept them with such abounding good faith and tranquil honesty. All of which probably means nothing to you, but I sometimes marvel at the consistent good nature and cheerfulness that permeates all your letters.

But I was so sorry to hear you had been ill and "relegated" to the "pest house" — as we used to call it. However, German measles doesn't disturb even such devoted interest as mine. In other words German measles can't be rated very high in the sympathy market. But, tho I've heard of it being done, I won't accuse you and and your "fellow sufferers" of practicing a fraud in order to enjoy the mild pleasures of the infirmary for a few days!

At last something has come to relieve the monotony of the winter.

---

[7] Josephine Underwood of Evanston, Ill.
[8] The envelope is postmarked March 27, 1925.

I was afraid it was to be devoid of those enduring experiences which are the comfort of life's twilight and collectively serve to build up one's philosophy of living and standards of human values. But there I go, almost forgetting to tell you about it.

Last week I was sent down to Southern Illinois to "cover" the tornado disaster and arrived about 24 hours after the storm. Everything was in the most appal[l]ing confusion, the destruction in Murphysboro beggar[e]d description, the pathos and suffering everywhere fairly hurt your heart. For some reason which I can't explain (for I don't look particularly formidable with a shovel) I was put in charge of a gang of 25 grave diggers. What a delightful and appropriate occupation you no doubt will say. Well any way it afforded me a few tranquil moments in a chaotic sea; so I perched on a tombstone and contemplated the futility of all things mundane and the utter insignificance of man in the face of natural forces. I can't say it fortified my belief in divinity; for such innocent suffering and divine justice triumphant would be paradoxical. But it did fortify my belief that natural, if not spiritual, destiny is not always man made.

And there amidst all that death was repeated proof of the value of a human life and one could not but feel that the great soul of the world was kind and just. I saw workmen excavate a school house, in the vain hope of finding some children still alive, with an impassioned fury that surpasses belief: I saw doctors operate successively for 24 hours without taking off their aprons. The scenes at the morgues with parents, lovers, children, identifying their dead, dry-eyed and stoic in their savage grief, was a marvel of human fortitude and heroism. But enough of panegyrics!

I am coming to New York around the 20th of April for the Associated Press meeting. Of course I suppose it would be too much to hope that you might be in Greenwich then. But it will be pleasant to hope and after all there's no harm in hoping, is there?

Affectionately
ADLAI

Sunday, May 31 [1925] [9]

Dear Claire —

I've come to an obvious conclusion — All extremes of temperature are beastly. I come to this same conclusion every hot day in the summer and every cold day in the winter. But thusfar have been able to do nothing about it. But I suppose that, along with many other natural

[9] The envelope is postmarked June 1, 1925.

facts, simply demonstrates the superiority of man as an evolutionary product. For man has so eagerly propagated and distributed his race that only in the exceptional instances is he perfectly adapted to the climatic environment. And since the other natural creations, birds, trees, plants, animals, fish etc either adapt themselves or else refuse to survive they don't suffer in any marked degree from weather. Therefore it follows that man must be somewhat inferior for practically nowhere is there a climate which is always agreeable to mankind and adaptation in general is only the result of varying degrees of discomfort.

Truly the above is a distinct departure from what I had intended in this letter and as a piece of logical reasoning would not bear any close inspection. I suppose it was inspired by the miserable frame of mind in which I found myself when I suddenly resolved to write you. Anyway is it an awful day — one of those dull, lifeless ones when your "wrists get damp" — as Kipling or someone said.

Yes I agree that an observing girl can get quite a little lesson in sophistication at the house parties. Also occasionally even the wise undergraduates can learn something. But I'm glad you had a good time even if the kick was a little vicarious — the spectator rather than the participant. College parties should be a fact of every girls social education. They can teach much besides being lots of fun. But unfortunately in a great many instances the lessons learned are the wrong ones and *forced* excitement and thrill takes the place of real wholesome fun. But that's beginning to sound just a bit didactic and ministerial!

I went down to Louisville a couple of weeks ago to the Derby and stayed with Watson McFerran.[10] It turned into three riotous three days and reawoke my memories of Memphis and the firm conviction that life in the south most closely approximates the perfect. (Except for the heat) On Sunday we motored down to Lexington thru the blue grass country. It is very beautiful along the Kentucky river — far more lovely than I had imagined. Seems strange that one doesn't hear of it more often.

At present I am largely concerned with the anticipation of going east for reunion. I hope to get to Princeton the 12th and will probably be around for a week so unless you are rushing off somewhere I may see you long enough to shake hands and say something like 'My how you've grown! ['] or something equally appropriate.

I was sorry indeed to hear that poison Ivy had attacked you. It would seem that you have had your share of misfortunes this year. I suppose by this time, dressed in spotless white and with majestic tread you

10 Unable to identify.

have marched up and been presented with a diplomma — thereby automatically taking your place among the *educated* women of America. Therefore let me add my heartfelt felicitations and the admonition that learning only begins when *others* stop teaching.

Fare thee well and best love

ADLAI

In June Stevenson attended his class reunion at Princeton, visited with Claire in Greenwich, and traveled to Washington to investigate the possibility of a career in the diplomatic service.

June 26 [1925] [11]

Claire dear —

I am home again but my spirit still wanders — wanders disobediently but joyfully back to Greenwich and some lyric, never to be forgotten hours in soft, leafy colorful twilight and then again in bright sunlight close to the warm sweet earth with all the world stretched lazily out around us. But that was all just a setting — nature's ephemeral, unreal background for a lovely reality that has possessed my mind and inward eye everlastingly.

They seem but a minute now — those few short hours and I can think of so much that I should like to have talked with you about. And then as I reflect it seems, (to my mortification) that I must have done most all the talking when it was you that I wanted to hear — you whom I have known so well and so long in the imagination and those strange mystical currents of the spirit, and in reality known so little. To know a person in the literal sense of the word is by no means easy and perhaps you've forgotten that this was the first real, searching talk we have had since those far away happy days when our paths crossed in Charlevoix two years ago. You have matured and become a woman in those two short yet long years and I was pleased, my ego flattered, to find you much as I had pictured you — honest, clean sincere, seeking the best in life and giving the best. I hope and know you will always be the same — seeing only the beautiful and the good, oblivious of the paltry, sordid hypocrisy and artificiality of this workaday world that makes distorted fools and slaves of so many of us.

My philosophy and mental meanderings have finally emerged at this clear, precise and unoriginal conclusion: man's greatest aspiration should

[11] The envelope is postmarked June 27, 1925.

be to be his *own best self.* I am convinced that welfare and uplift of others is impatient and futile and that the most efficacious manner of improving all mankind is to let his uplift and welfare complex extrovert itself on himself. Intolerance in all things is the most poisonous and insidious of all vices and perhaps by far the most prevalent. Therefore the cultivation of absolute, unqualified charity and tolerance is the most important single factor toward the realization of one's best. You know as well as I that nothing soothes the vanity of a small man so much as his consciously felt sense of moral or ethical superiority — and no single thing distinguishes the man truly great in spirit like tolerance toward others and realization of his own shortcomings.

I don't know just why I should be telling all this to you other than that it is about the only definite concrete conclusion that I have reached after years of too much mental turmoil. So don't be shocked, Claire, if men get drunk, if they try to kiss you. But gently and firmly resist all the seemingly in[n]ocuous things that combine to cheapen you. Remember that the women all men most admire are the women that they *think* (at least) their mothers were.

I was down in Madison until Sunday night and had a pretty good time — as good a time as you could have playing around with a lot of people you never saw or heard of before. Sunday night I motored up to New York with another fellow. We passed thru Greenwich in the wee hours and my heart fluttered just a little as the memories came surging back to my sleepy head.

Monday afternoon I went down to Baltimore and on Wednesday went over to Washington with Anthony Carey [12] to investigate the diplomatic service. It was a profitable and interesting day before I boarded the train for home and fireside.

I was relieved to observe in my fleeting glimpse of you at the races that there were no apparent manifestations of poison ivy. And now good night my blessed Claire

ADLAI

P.S. Won't you please, please stop off here if only for a few minutes en route West. Or let me know when you come thru Chicago and how long you'll be there between trains and if possible I'll come up "on business." XX

Claire spent the summer with her family at the Elkhorn Ranch at Bozeman, Montana.

[12] Unable to identify.

Friday, July 17, 1925

Claire m'dear —

What a splendid, carefully thought out and well written letter that was! One of the nicest I've had and I'm so grateful for it. I like to think of you being able to express your self so articulately, but even more that you have such vigorous, wholesome, sensible ideas. Of course its perfectly absurd to worry your lovely head about 'mankind' — that traditionally sick beast. Worry about anything is a most destructive and futile state of mind and fortunate indeed is the person who has such nervous and emotional self-possession that they can always think and feel constructively. I think you have that quality to a great extent and it augurs well for the happy, worthwhile life that we all are searching for and that you are going to have. I fear you thought me a dreadful cynic and doubter — perhaps something of a lost soul. Perhaps I am, but its only because I've always been restless and never quite content with myself. But, mayhap, when the 'great calm' comes I too may be sunny and fine like you.

And now may I beseech you from the bottom of my heart never to consciously lose your candid, cheerful air. Its probably your most attractive characteristic — and after all "God *is* in his heaven and all's well with the world." It distressed me to have you say that perhaps after you had been out of school for a couple of years you would be able to see things in "their true relations." St. Paul said, "the truth shall make you free." But he who sees always the best sees the real truth for the evil is only the man made half truth. 'Thus endeth the *n*th lesson' — *learned from you*[.]

Yes, I've read "Where the Blue Begins." Its a charming book and a right lucid mirror of life for many of us. So you remember how Gissing in the darkness "heard chiming voices, wheedling and tantalizing." I hear them too and thats' what makes me so everlastingly restless. I am enclosing a review of a book I read this week. Of course its mostly nonsense but we all like a little nonsense.

I was dreadfully sorry not to see you in Chicago. But inasmuch as I had already planned to go up that week end I hardly felt I could justify going up Wednesday too — only to see you for a moment. Of course I shall always think you every sort of wretch for not coming down here. Alas, I fear my love is unrequited! But you will stop on the way back, won't you? [13] Please, please, please, as I'll administer a resounding spank-

[13] En route home in August, she visited the Stevensons in Bloomington.

ing when next we meet. But I've still a better idea. I had a letter from Buff today and she is anxious for me to meet her in San Francisco, August 5 and go out to Honolulu, arriving back Aug. 26. How about coming along. Buff and I together might make adequate chaperonage. If I'm not able to go I'll probably be coming out to the Big Horns for a camping trip of a couple of weeks around the first of August. When will you be coming thru here en route home? For I must not miss you and as a charitable, christian child you can't refuse to stop for a little missionary work en route.

I'll bet you're having a glorious time out there and promising yourself to go back every year. Let me know when you are ready to stay for good and I'll come out and join you.

Best love always
ADLAI

P.S. Tell Walter I enjoyed his letter very much — and not to ride with a burr under his saddle.

Saturday night, September 19, 1925

Claire dear —

Thanks for the postal. But I may say that the impact thereof completely eludes me. I gather that not content with a month of campfires in the Yellowstone you are now bent on penetrating the wild fastnesses of New York state. Anyway, thru the clouds of my bewilderment, I can't but feel impressed and pleased that the nature instinct has possessed you so completely. I wish I could have been with you and hope your moments under the stars gave you the same peace and release that mine did.

I have just finished a week of most intense and exacting work. Hence you may lay any abnormal vagaries in this note to my devitalized mental condition. The telegraph editor was taken suddenly ill and I had to go in his place with only the most indistinct knowledge of the duties thereof. As a result I've labored diligently and hectically every day this week from 1 in the afternoon " 'till three o'clock in the morning," with a minute and a half off for dinner. I recount these horrors only to impress you with the fact that my business apathy and indifference while you were here is, unfortunately, not the even tenor of my ways.

Having "gone native" or rather being one of those abominable people given to using the first person I will have to continue in this vein for a moment, begging forgiveness.

After a few moments painful deliberation I have resolved to forego

[191]

the simple and pleasant physical amenities of life in gallant Blooming-ton. Having tasted, without marked exhileration, the stale cup of life here, I have determined to go to Chicago and take my last year of law at Northwestern. The phlegmatic complacence of life in a small town where everything is made so easy, in contrast to 10 years away from home, has slightly innoculated me with languor and apathy. Lest the insidious germ take complete possession of my spirit, I am indulging my ebbing restlessness and am not motivated by any great and absorbing love for the law. For to be sure I like newspaper work infinitely better. So thats that, and I am resolutely returning once more to the unlovely realm of apartments and indifferent restaurants.

I hope you have some vague and sympathetic understanding of my Ishmaelite tendencies. But there I go again! Sympathy seeking is the weakest characteristic of mankind! I don't want your sympathy. I want your respect and how I ever hope to get it with this disordered, pur-poseless life of mine I don't know. But then "hope springs eternal in the human breast" — and I'm much too human, or rather earthy.

The crickets are chirping merrily. The bludgeoning dark has beaten down the merciless sun and a rare east wind is fanning the pra[i]ries. The stars have come out to gossip and wink. Its a soft, fragrant, lovely night and I wish you were here. No I don't, why *must* I be always wishing! I'm glad you're where you are and I hope and know you are wholly happy — as becomes you.

Love to all the family and to you my heart —

ADLAI

Adlai and his parents spent the Christmas holidays in New York City. Claire was now living there. During the visit Adlai asked her to marry him. The following letter was written on the train to Chicago where Adlai returned to resume his studies at the Northwestern University Law School.

Thursday evening [December 31, 1925] [14]

Claire —

Here its Thursday afternoon. Mercilessly the train stabs into the sink-ing sun and drags me reluctantly along. I feel as tho I was deliberately running away from all things worth while — into an uninviting chasm of unlovely, small, finite things. But I'm all torn asunder now — part of me lingered behind — it can stay there tho and be happy in its small silent

[14] The envelope is postmarked December 31, 1925.

way. I wish I could stop thinking about Tuesday afternoon — its very poignant now, just six o'clock. Its sweet to think about, but sort of frightens me — perhaps its a mistake to look down the flower bordered, beckoning avenues of the mind's imaginings only to be turned rudely aside on to the stony streets of reality! Forgive me, Claire, if I caused you a moments pain or distress — I'm thoughtless and selfish I know — but remember whatever may happen to us I shall always love you exultantly and reverently. I wanted to come over and hold your hand for an instant longer Wednesday morning — but I was afraid the ubiquitous maid would not understand if I walked into your room and knelt by the bedside.

Rode down on the train with Mrs. Woodrow Wilson and found her a very amiable and pleasant woman. Went to an elaborate but somewhat boring dinner in Wash last night and afterward to a dance at Mrs. Joseph Leiter's [15] house which was rather good fun despite the throngs of liveried footmen. This morning I went to see the "greatest living American" — Justice Holmes — among other things the sage said "A sense of responsibility is often a confession of intellectual weakness" — i.e. to be conscious of the responsibility in a situation means that your intellectual faculties are not fixed unqualifiedly on the pure problem of reason.

May 1926 find you meeting more of life as successfully as you have met the rest — and particularly the competition of jealous debutantes.

Good night blessed Claire

AD

Friday [February 12, 1926] [16]

Claire dear —

This protracted silence is most unbecoming. Here its been six weeks since I saw you and in all that veritable aeon only one letter! Truly you're being very cruel and I can't see that such harsh treatment is merited. But then perhaps the fairy prince has at last come into your life sweeping old friends and old faces into an ecstasy of oblivion. Who might it be? I left you withstanding such a multitude that I can't think which ingenious soul might have discovered the key to the hidden places of your heart.

Not content with the foregoing, I have another cause for active distress. To wit, months, indeed years ago, you promised me a photograph.

[15] Wife of the capitalist.
[16] The envelope is postmarked February 12, 1926.

I didn't ask for a grand one — just any one, no matter how old or how bad or how simple. In fact I would rather prefer one of those — it would seem more intimate and familiar. At present my art gallery includes two clippings — one from the N.Y. Times and one from Town and Country. So you can see it needs some bona fide augmentation.

I went to a movie party last night — first movie in months and the greatest and most perfectly done I've ever seen. 'The Big Parade' — see it by all means, but perhaps you have already. Anyway its a good argument for the League of Nations —

Love
Ad

Sunday, April 25 [1926] [17]

Claire dearest —

Twenty! My, what a multitude of years. Its marvelous the way you keep your youth and vitality. I suppose they're just hosts of gray hairs, but I trust the hearing and sight are still good!

And it seems but yesterday "when you were seventeen" and we sat on a little grassy knoll above the ravine (leaning against a barbed wire fence) reading the "Life of Christ." And I thought you such a sweet, wistful, contemplat[iv]e girl. I remember at the time I couldn't determine whether you were a little sad & aloof or whether you were in the adolescent, frantic, groping stage — searching for some clue, some magic touchstone, to restore order and quiet out of the chaos and tumult in your mind.

Did you once stop and think what a truly remarkable and elastic thing the human mind is? We hear a lot about the extraordinary resiliency of our physical bodies — how much punishment and mistreatment they can endure. But at least we can to some degree measure and control the degree of that abuse. And even among the most ignorant there is some intuitive sense or understanding of physical capacity.

Mind on the other hand is practically uncontrollable. From the time a new born baby becomes conscious mentally and begins to register impressions just think what a tumult pours into his mind, conscious & sub-conscious. And the clamoring eagerness with which the hosts attack the four walls of his mind increases in geometric proportion as he grows & the walls enlarge. Finally the assault reaches a triumphant climax of ferocity at or around the adolescent stage, just when interior alterations are going on too and since life is growing more complex each year the

[17] The envelope is postmarked April 26, 1926.

volume that has to be absorbed is constantly increasing. I believe the average laborer in the street today has had more passive intellectual exercise than the average nobleman of 500 years ago. And its an eloquent commentary on the mechanical efficiency of our minds that there isn't far more insanity than there is.

Just what the thesis of this long digression is I don't know. But anyway I do know that these last three years have been critically important ones in your life, Claire, and you've achieved them gallantly and gracefully. Physical growth is about over for you and your lov[e]liness is a testimonial to God, good inheritance and your own life. But most of all I think you've really succeeded in restoring mental and spiritual tranquility without sacrificing your curiosity and acquisitiveness. Thats' a remarkable thing, Claire. For people that have any mind at all it generally takes a long, long time & many never achieve it.

And now that you have your "house" more or less in order an enchanting prospect should lie before you. A whole lifetime of calm, intelligent growth — a whole lifetime to build stone by stone a perfect edifice on those splendid foundations; in short a perfect woman on those foundations of character, mind & body. And it is only now that you are beginning to learn the really important lessons — to distinguish wheat from chaff, to recognize and appreciate true values. As somebody said "When the half-gods go, the gods appear." I think more & more that that is about the most important thing in life — to keep rooting all the time for the worth while things. But to know the worth while things — thats the hard part.

Gracious, I've talked in this paternal vein quite long enough. So you're back in Greenwich now! I suppose its pretty dull after the gayeties in town. But when spring gets under way (unless we have to perform a Caesarian operation to get it) it must be very beautiful out there and I think you'll be glad you're not in town.

Dined at the McFaddens [18] last night and saw the Moscow Art theatre do Lysistrata. I regretted intensely that my Russian is so weak. It must be very vulgar & very funny. A Russian girl was sitting near me — at one moment she was crimson and at the next rolling with mirth.

Tonight I must go to a fancy dress at Mrs. Alden Carpenter's.[19] Seems funny, a real party on Sunday night. But I suppose that means some stage folk, so it ought to be fun. Had a most amusing wire from [Francis T. P.] Plimpton some time ago. I hope to get down for his

[18] Mrs. Parmalee McFadden, of Chicago, and her daughters, Eleanor, Frances, and Marian.
[19] Rue Winterbotham Carpenter, first wife of John Alden Carpenter, the composer.

wedding in June & perhaps you could give me half an hour some afternoon if I apply now. Yes?

Devotedly

AD

Late in July Adlai sailed with his mother and sister to Italy. In Vienna he joined two friends for their proposed trip to the Soviet Union. Delays in receiving visas led his friends to abandon the visit, but Adlai persevered until he obtained his visa.

Saturday, September 11 [1926] [20]

Claire dear —

I don't suppose you'll be able to read a word of this. I'm writing it on a very unseaworthy train "somewhere in Russia." I'm forced to write in pencil for I've loaned my pen to an American woman socialist and pacifist whom, God be praised, & to my great consternation I discovered on this train. Travelling alone in this very "furin" land is not so pleasant &, knowing a little Russian, she descended like the proverbial guardian angel.

I left [Robert] Page and [George] Norton, my two travelling companions, in Buda-Pest & flew to Bucharest by way of Belgrade. In Bucharest I remained three days, and had a bit of a glimpse into life in the Anglo-American colony there, thanks to some people I knew there. From Bucharest to Constantinople again by air, over the Balkans at 7000 feet & me in nothing but a fedora hat & a light raincoat. I was just begginning to resign my self to death by freezing when we suddenly hopped down over the sea of Marmara & there was Constan, the Golden Horn, Bosporus & all of it. To my great confusion I discovered that an Italian freighter was going up the Black Sea the following day & there wasn't another for ten days. So I saw Constan in one night & there followed a day long skirmish with passport and customs officials, commissionair[e]s & boatmen. Finally I got aboard the good ship 'Diana,' a little smaller than a minute, & was pleasantly surprised to discover an elderly American mining engineer as one of the other 3 passengers.

For 5 days we skirted along the asiatic coast of the Black Sea stopping at the little Turkish ports of Samsun & Trebizonda[?] to unload cargo into picturesque & venerable galleys manned by the weirdest looking

[20] The envelope is postmarked September 12, 1926.

Turkish stevedores garbed in the most approved Eastern piratical rags.

At last we dropped Anchor in Batum[i] & I had my first glimpse of Soviet Russia. Batum[i] you remember was Jason's destination on the quest for the Golden Fleece. After a thorough & even bodily search by the officials we at last got ashore. After a few hours looking over the half deserted port & marvelling at the mixed naked bathing I said farewell to my American friend, with something of the sensation of a man about to jump off a bridge tied to a cannonball, and took the train for ancient Tiflis in Caucasus on the old caravan route where East really does meet west. The night was a little terrible — besides myself in the compartment were 2 men one woman & two children. Tiflis was a really new experience — Tartars, Kurds, Armenians, Georgians, Persians & Russians of all kinds mixed up in a melange of costuming that leaves you fairly dizzy. As a child I used to get exasperated at a 3 ring circus because I couldn't see everything at once. So it was at Tiflis only there were a dozen rings.

The next day started the long hop to Moscow — four days by express train. The first day we crawled south east across the blazing hot desert-like plateau on the south side of the Caucassus — an endless semi-arid country peopled by Kurd shepards & their flocks of wooly black & brown sheep. Occasionally I saw herds of camels grazing and frequently bullock caravans bo[u]nd for Tiflis. At midnight we reached Baku, the oil city, & then turned north around the east end of the Caucassus and skirted the Caspian Sea until the next afternoon when the road turns more to the west & at last yesterday we came out on the great green, smiling valley of the Don dotted with heards of cattle & in the distances the sun shining on the green domes of Orthodox churches marking the location of clusters of whitewashed tha[t]ched huts — communities of the long suffering Russian pe[a]sants. All night & morning we've been passing over a corner of the great & fertile Ukraine — the granary of Europe. Tonight we will reach Moscow, God willing, & at last I will be in the heart of new Russia. From there I'll go to Leningrad, Helsingfors & home by Copenhagen or Stockholm where I'll probably arrive about as soon as this letter.

I never felt quite as "deep in the bush" — no up to date outside news for more than two weeks. But I trust America hasn't dropped under the sea & that you're still there — your own dear self. I'll call you up when I reach N.Y. about the middle of October & give you all the 'low down' on the corners of Europe.

Love

AD

October 27, 1926

Dearest —

Its a cold, cheerless forbidding autumn day. The leaden sky has neutralized the frosty warmth of the foliage. This morning mother & Buff & I motored 90 miles to another town where I had to see a lawyer relative to my admission to the bar. I got home too late to do it in the usual way and now I must wait until December.

I was in Chicago for a few days last week and found your sweet letter and the little Russian stories. A couple I had read before but the others were new to me. Isn't it wonderful how that strange people living away off there by themselves in semi isolation have developed to a supreme degree that greatest quality of all art — simplicity?

I am planning to move back to Chicago next week to commence my belated career as a lawyer. I must confess, heretical and un-American as it may seem, that I view the prospect without the least eagerness. Its not laziness altogether either, but I know perfectly well that if I am to make a "success," sooner or later I must "sell out" — I mean chuck most of my ideas and my acute sympathy for the less fortunates. A stony and obedient loyalty to class and vested interests seems to be the necessary adjunct of a life time of hard and imagination-less work. . . .

Car, sais-tu chaque jour je t'aime d'avantage. Plus qu'hier, et bien moins que demain.

AD

January 4 [1927] [21]

Dearest Claire —

Its been months if not years since I wrote you last! I would be a faithless soul indeed if my thoughts of you were measured by my recent vigorous correspondence. But, thanks to the agility of imagination and memory, I've been with you much this winter. Did you ever notice what a satisfaction, if only momentary, there is in hallucination? Frequently this winter I've stood in stag lines more asleep than awake and watched you dance by only to shake myself and wander out to cut in on some inadequate substitute. But its been fun even to imagine that you were there, how you looked, how you were dressed and what you said — perhaps it was, "Well, I know *you* well enough to suggest sitting out and

[21] The envelope is postmarked January 5, 1927.

picking up the threads where we left off." I've visualized the god[d]ess dancing around all the ballrooms in New York just a little dissatisfied with the great shifting panorama that makes it so hard to really get acquainted with people.

You were a darling to send me the lovely lighter. What thoroughly practical ideas you have! And, mirabile dictu, its one of those rare ones that works every time. Needless to say I'm like a child with a new toy. But most of all I like it because its such an omnipresent, tangible reminder. It and your photo are right in front of me now — the former, by the way, being one of the principal adornments of my new little apartment. I do wish you could see it — about as big as a minute but I've got it quite decently fixed up with some Italian antiques, brocades, old prints etc. Never have I felt so foolishly domestic — moving things around, falling off chairs, shopping for wastebaskets and picture hangers. There's even a kitchenette and a "dinette" (just guess what a commodious apartment that is) but thus far we haven't tried to have any meals served. Its taken just a month to get partially installed and my respect for housewives has increased a thousand fold!

I'm working in a law office [Cutting, Moore and Sidley] and a very good one which I was exceedingly fortunate to get in at this time of year. By 'working' I mean from 8:45 to 6 and often in the evenings. So please observe that your adoring but indolent Adlai has taken to it with a 'fierce joy.' And strange to relate I've not minded it at all yet. But that doesn't mean that I in any sense approve of the system which makes a man intellectually and morally subservient to his natural interests in direct proportion to his degree of "success." So you see I'm still theoretically a revolutionary but practical enough to realize that there's little I can do about it — hence conform.

I've lots more to say but its getting very late & I must be 'bright eyes' early in the morning. Please write at once if not sooner & tell me all about yourself.

The same love carries over from '26
Ad

p.s. Enclosing an article I wrote at time of Mussolini's new measures. There's not much in it — so don't be surprized.

In March Claire sailed to Europe for a six months' visit. She and Adlai corresponded regularly.

May 17 [1927] [22]

Claire dearest —

I've just reread your last three letters. Or rather I read them some little while ago and have just emerged from an enchanting reverie — for I too have just been in Spain. Your letters reawaked the past and "I sailed away in fancy" to view again those unforgotten scenes that we both love now — scenes at once exalting, exasperating and bewitching.

I'm glad you enjoyed and appreciated it so fully and I've even concluded that at heart you too are an abandoned romanticist. Its only the romanticist that can see and feel all the hidden corners and suggestions of beauty that make the passionate whole that isn't in the guidebook!

You've been so sweet to write me so regularly and fully — and such good letters too, you're so observant and faithful in portrayal! and then I feel a new warmth and reality about these letters, more ease and facility, as tho there was some blood in the pen! Quite a contrast to those treasured, stiff, laborious little compositions of your school days — accurate grammatical works that vaguely reminded me of a little girl, uncomfortable in pigtails and starched organdie (or is it 'y' and does it starch?)

I do hope you are quite well and that the malady was soon bested. I must say it sounds as tho you had been frantically active thus far. But I suppose you're taking things easily in Paris. But of course that's impossible and all you'll succeed in doing is to gasp out a new resolution for the morrow as you tumble into bed exhausted each night. . . .

Devotedly
AD.

January 19, 1928

Dearest Claire —

As always I seize the pen and write the above a little shame-facedly (is there such a word?) for my delinquency. But then you mustn't lose patience with me — for every one that's written twenty and much better ones are composed but suffer an abortive death in the pressure of things.

I have a confession to make! You could never guess what I've just been doing — cooking my own dinner in my kitchenette! Its a secret passion in which I occasionally indulge and always look forward to with the wildest anticipation. But candidness forces me to confess that by the time the two or three dishes and utensils necessary to these intricate

[22] The envelope is postmarked May 18, 1927.

feasts are washed & put away I'm quite fed up on it for another couple of weeks — and then again the irresistible impulse seizes me and I rush home to burn my fingers and make a frightful mess once more.

In regard to my alleged social desirability, I call it deliberate mendacity on the part of your informer. Tho to be sure I have had an excellent good time here. But its insidiously easy [to] lose one's sense of values and become simply a reliable stuffed shirt in a place like this where anyone that's white, washed and reasonably mild mannered can trot around like a circus pony night after night and mislead himself into thinking that its all worth while. And then the dread ennui is inevitable when you feel yourself making a grim and conscious effort to be gay when your mind is somewhere else. Tho I don't for a moment mean to disparage Chicago or its people for all places and all peoples are much the same when you really get to know them, I've concluded — as has everyone else I suppose.

I was delighted to observe in your last letters that you seemed so happy, contented and were having such a good time. I hope you've mastered the restless feeling that seems so prevalent among girls — that if they're not going out every night they're miserable — much better the antithesis. It can indicate nothing except a total lack of resources. How nice you are taking dramatic lessons! Or have you given them up for something else by this time? . . .

Best love —

AD

Adlai wrote Claire on March 1, 1928, that his sister Buffie had returned from Turkey, where her husband, Ernest L. Ives, was a member of the staff of the embassy, to have her baby in Chicago. Adlai also wrote: "And speaking of the law, I feel myself wandering with growing assurance in its bewildering maze — tho I can't say my salary reflects marked capacity as value to my employers! I can't either say that I love it with a fierce passion — indeed as a profession its rather disappointing, since its not a profession at all, but rather a business service station and repair shop. Lots of it is rather fun, tho, and its satisfying to find that, in Chicago at least, the brightest, most entertaining and companionable of my contemporaries are generally lawyers." On April 19, Adlai described his young nephew Timothy Ives, born on April 9. He wrote of his own life: "I've become one of the standardized earnest young men whom I used to dispise so wholesomely. In short, I've given up trying to solve the mystery of life and I'm enjoying it fully without asking too

*many disturbing questions! So there — tho honesty compels me to con-
fess that I have perpetual symptoms of poisoning from a malignant little
germ of doubt and revolt which seems to decline to respond to treatment by large doses of 'ambition' and those other popular misleaders of
thought."*

June 1 [1928] [23]

Dearest Claire —

Most a month has gone by since the little photos came. It was sweet
of you to send them, for, after all, they're all I've seen of you for a long
time! I thought them surprisingly good likenesses and was profoundly
reassured to find that I could still recognize you — indeed to find you as
lovely and patrician as ever. It was pleasing to see that the flight of a
year and more hadn't made marked changes in your face & expression, tho,
to be sure, it does seem a little more mature and definite. Paternally I
might say you do seem grown up at last! Are you? I hope not — but
whether you have or not you'll always seem a big little girl to me — so
there!

I don't quite understand why you should be worrying about what to
do next winter already. I do believe you're trying to make a problem of
life — trying to organize it. Its hard to do Claire and forcing things generally only gets us mixed up. As you said, you really don't know just
what you want, so don't try to give birth to a plan prematurely. As Sir
William Osler or someone said, "We must live in day-tight compart-
ments." There I am preaching again!

I'm in the country again for the summer, living with the same group
of boisterous young men and in rather cramped quarters [24] which, of
course, makes letter writing to a young lady rather an awkward activity.
But I'm resolutely disregarding all their facetious remarks! My brother
in law sails tomorrow & Buffy has gone east to see him off. She's coming
back to Bloomington to stay a month before going herself, but the separation was only achieved after days of weeping, wailing and gnashing of
teeth. She hasn't recovered as rapidly as might be since the baby and so,
after numerous family scenes, she was finally pe[r]suaded to let him go
by himself and stay here until she was quite well again. The complica-
tions have been endless, but now it seems to have been decided to leave
the baby here until they are shifted from Constantinople. Which means
that Mother has to look after the young man and then probably take
him over to them in the fall — to Berlin they hope. Constantinople is

[23] The envelope is postmarked June 2, 1928.
[24] Adlai and a group of friends had rented a house in Lake Forest for the summer.

alleged to be "impossible" for very young babies. Its all a little mysterious to me for after all babies have been born and raised there for a good many hundreds of years. But somehow the logic and force of that argument didn't seem to be very pe[r]suasive!

My nephew Timothy Reed Ives, Esq., is a most beguiling young man and, while waking up, achieves in rapid succession the most extraordinary expressions and facial contortions you've ever seen. He seems to be perpetually hungry and, candidness forces me to observe, but without derision, "all wet." There seems to be unanimous and thankful opinion on only one point — he *doesn't* look like me.

My trip to New York doesn't seem to grow any less remote and I've developed the hitherto unknow[n] and, I daresay, proletarian anticipation of "a holiday" as a "trip" or anything which gets me out of chains. Otherwise life is pleasant and full — much too full in fact & I'm beginning to know first hand why culturally American businessmen come off second best — there isn't time enough to keep up. . . .

Love
A<small>D</small>

September 3, 1928

Claire dearest —

I felt mortified that you had to prompt me with a post card, when in reality I've been writing you volumes for weeks, tho, to be sure, the volumes somehow never got on paper. I'm in Bloomington for the first time in months to spend Labor Day with the family. Life among the senior Stevensons, now that Tim has been removed from their midst, affords drowsy moments for contemplation — moments that are elusive and hard to capture in the city. So I'm improving this one with a letter to you and incidentally giving the writing hand some exercise which it hasn't had much of for a long time.

Life has been very full for me this summer, as it seems to have been for you to[o]. I've concluded that destiny is inevitable and can't be forced — for all of a sudden I find me, the cynic, the happy victim of one of life's most commonplace tricks. The news I have to impart will probably be little more surprising to you than it was to me. By aloof, playful indifference I had come to think that I could never genuinely fall in love again, and now behold the worldly young man become an earnest, breathless moon calf again — given to fits of exultation and bitter despondency — all of the symptoms of adolescent heart trouble! It really seems a little ridiculous, but don't laugh at me Claire. Indeed that respectable and long popular custom of marriage will probably claim another votary about the end of November. The engagement won't be announced until about the first of October so please exercise discretion unusual in the female. Somehow I never thought I would be passing such news on to *you*, and, if I did, that certainly it wouldn't be by letter. But my long anticipated trip East somehow doesn't materialize — I had so much wanted to have a good reunion, talk it over à deux and get the blessing of my best loved friend. Except I hate that horrid word 'friend' — ours must be something more than friendship — I can't explain it, but you'll know what I mean!

In looking back I observe that with unbecoming ego I've entirely overlooked introducing my victim: Enter Ellen Borden,[25] a poet (see Sept. Poetry Mag.), a musician, a linguist, an athlete and not quite 21. (Please don't say anything about cradles!) And in spite of these impressive talents quite normal and, need *I* say, most attractive. I'm sure you'll like her loads and I only hope it won't be long before we can have a good three cornered gathering without any preliminary self-consciousness. I shan't try to tell you any more about her — you may judge for yourself, but be sure to judge correctly!

You sound as tho you'd been having a very gay and active summer and I daresay Dark Harbor [Maine] was a welcome rest after a month of 'one night stands.' Of course I was a little distressed to find you, a good New Yorker, disloyal to Al Smith. But I firmly expect you back in the fold by November. I wish we could have a good violent political discussion or indeed any kind of a discussion — in short I'd like to see [you] most dreadfully — Its been almost 2 years since we've had any kind of a visit and there's lots to catch up on. Do tell me all about yourself.

Love always

AD

After Claire replied to the letter of September 3, Adlai wrote on October 25 that the wedding would be on December 1. The last letter in this collection follows:

November 25, 1928

Claire dear —

Your very sweet note has come and the suggestion is an enticing one. However, I'm afraid it can't be arranged very conveniently; but I have a counter-proposition to suggest!

[25] For a fuller account of Adlai's engagement to Ellen Borden, see Part Seven.

We sail at or about midnight, Tuesday, December fourth, on the Samaria, Cunard line pier at 14th St., I believe. I propose that we conduct an informal reception in our quarters prior to sailing time. There *I* can be inspected for sea worthiness and *Ellen* for appropriate blushes!

So please come aboard *that* boat *that* evening accompanied by anyone you care to enlist and we'll have an evening of wild whoopee until they shout "visitors ashore."

I'm so sorry none of the beloved Birges are to be here for the wedding. You were too good to send the lovely red horses and the antique china is among our 'chefs d'oeuvres.'

Things get increasingly hectic and I'm momentarily anticipating a touch of gibbering idiocy — but Ellen, fortunately, remains disconcertingly calm and collected.

Please keep the boat in mind — it will be splendid seeing you again —

Best love
ADLAI

Part Seven

Young Lawyer in Chicago
1927–1933

*I*n 1927 Adlai E. Stevenson joined the conservative and distinguished Chicago law firm of Cutting, Moore and Sidley as a law clerk. He obtained the job with the help of his Princeton friend M. Ogden West, who had a brother-in-law in the firm. Among the other clerks who became lifelong friends were Edward D. McDougal, Jr., and James F. Oates, Jr.

Mrs. Ernest L. Ives wrote that their father "with the spirit of a born promoter plus the instincts of a very proud parent, was eager to fix things up . . . but my brother insisted he wanted to get a job entirely on his own." After Adlai got his job, she added, "Father must have been a little startled to discover that they were all Republicans." [1]

Adlai E. Stevenson worked conscientiously and cheerfully, drawing a salary of $125 a month. The firm was engaged in corporate and general practice. In the two years before the stock market crash in 1929, the firm was often busy preparing new issues of corporate securities. The young law clerk also handled a good deal of probate work for the firm.

After the crash, and as the depression grew more and more severe, the firm was busy, along with a reduced load of ordinary legal work, in assisting clients whose businesses had been shattered to recover what could be salvaged from the wreckage.

His fellow law clerk, later his law partner, and close friend, Edward D. McDougal, Jr., recalled that Adlai was assigned the task of repossessing articles sold by clients on the installment plan to customers who had defaulted in their payments. One day Adlai and a court bailiff went to a theater to repossess the projector. The matinee performance was about to begin and the proprietor begged for a delay until after the performance. He then produced two tickets and Adlai and the bailiff slipped into the darkened auditorium. On his return to the office late

[1] Elizabeth Stevenson Ives and Hildegarde Dolson, *My Brother Adlai* (New York: Morrow, 1956), p. 164.

that afternoon with the projector, he said, "I remembered the Biblical passage in the book of Micah: 'to do justly and love mercy'; also Portia's plea in The Merchant of Venice: 'to let mercy temper justice,' and concluded that mercy should temper justice in this case — for two hours. 'Besides,' he added, 'Jean Harlow was on the screen!'" [2]

Although legal work absorbed the great bulk of his waking hours and energy, Adlai E. Stevenson both before and after his marriage in 1928 led an extremely active social life. As one writer noted, however, "He was only mildly interested in the gay goings on of the younger set in the roaring '20s. He liked a friendly drink, but a wild round of speak-easies seemed a terrible waste of time. He attended the debutante parties, was always correct and rather formal, but he could never understand — and still can't understand — why anyone would be interested in an aimless social life." [3]

Mrs. John Paul Welling, an extremely close friend of Stevenson's from the 1920's until his death, wrote that his charm for women "later so famous" must have been "there" in the late 1920's: "For I remember giving a debutante lunch at the old Casino Club for the daughters of some of my family's friends, where the girls (drinking only sherry but smoking incessantly) argued hotly as to who was first with Adlai." [4]

Among the young ladies in Stevenson's social set who would be extremely close to him for a lifetime were Jane Warner (Mrs. Edison Dick) and Alicia Patterson (Mrs. Harry Guggenheim).

In addition to a busy social life, he was active in the Chicago Council on Foreign Relations, an organization designed to stimulate interest in world affairs and in American foreign policy.

By 1930 Stevenson was a member of the executive committee and the board of directors of the council which included, among other influential individuals in Chicago, William Pratt Sidley, head of Stevenson's law firm, Harriet Welling, Clay Judson, Graham Aldis, John P. Kellogg, Silas H. Strawn, and Professor Quincy Wright.

Although he personally was not affected particularly by the great depression, he learned something of the problems of the unemployed and others on the verge of economic disaster by working at the Lower North Side Community Council and at Hull House.

---

[2] Address at the Adlai E. Stevenson Memorial Ceremony, the Auditorium, Chicago, October 24, 1965. The original is in Mr. McDougal's possession.

[3] Joe Alex Morris, "Rebel in Illinois," *Saturday Evening Post*, April 2, 1949, p. 113.

[4] "Friend of the Family," in *As We Knew Adlai: The Stevenson Story by Twenty-two Friends*, edited and with preface by Edward P. Doyle, foreword by Adlai E. Stevenson III (New York: Harper & Row, 1966), p. 43.

In the summer of 1926, while the twenty-six-year-old Stevenson was en route to the Soviet Union, his sister met Ernest L. Ives, First Secretary at the American Embassy in Turkey.[5] Three days after they met they were engaged. Buffie's mother, however, persuaded them to postpone marriage for a few months, and she and Buffie returned to Bloomington. According to Buffie, her father "simply exploded. There I was, planning to marry a stranger he hadn't even seen." Her mother and brother, she later wrote, "backed me up all the way."

Her father decided to accompany her to Naples where she was to be married — "to 'give me away' — or snatch me back; I wasn't sure which," Mrs. Ives wrote. ". . . Adlai not only talked to Father but, as I found out later, wrote him a long letter which must have been very persuasive indeed, judging by Father's sudden shift from roaring lion to lamb."

When she sailed from New York City the telegram that meant the most to her was from her brother:

THERE IS NO PARTING. BON VOYAGE. BEST LOVE TO YOU BOTH.

Aboard ship she wrote him: "You can't imagine what an effect your splendid letter had on Father. . . . Your letter (to me) was wonderful, and it is so good that we can express the nearness we feel. . . . You should hear OLD PAPA tell me he thinks you have a 'master mind, and altho' a boy, one of the great men he has ever known.' He has utter awe of you, as I have love and confidence."[6]

Not many letters written between 1927 and 1933 were saved. We publish almost all of them in this volume. There are a number of letters about the business affairs of the Pantagraph, *of which Stevenson was vice president and a member of the board of directors. Only samples of these are included. The Stevenson letters to his mother and sister were handwritten and are in the Elizabeth Stevenson Ives collection at the Illinois State Historical Library. The other letters included in Part Seven were typewritten. The carbon copies of most of these letters are in the Stevenson collection, Princeton University Library. They are identified as A.E.S., P.U.L. We are grateful to Robert Rosenthal, Director of Manuscripts, the University of Chicago Library, for making Stevenson's correspondence with Robert M. Hutchins available to us. Stevenson's idio-*

[5] Joseph C. Grew, *Turbulent Era: A Diplomatic Record of Forty Years, 1904–1945,* edited by Walter Johnson (Boston: Houghton Mifflin, 1952), Vol. II, Part IV, contains numerous references by his chief to Mr. Ives's work in Turkey.

[6] *My Brother Adlai,* pp. 194–195. The letters mentioned were not saved.

syncrasies of style and spelling are retained as he wrote them — no "sic" has been added.

To Davis Merwin

April 13, 1928

Dear Dave:

I was delighted with the March statement.[7] At last it looks as though the tide has begun to turn.

I enclose clipping, and suggest that names of individual attorneys and physicians, etc. be used as little as possible, except where the news is sensational. It makes the others jealous.

My nephew is a robust and very ugly young man though to be sure he has more hair than I have.[8]

Yours,

By the spring of 1928 Adlai and Ellen Borden had decided to be married. Her mother, Ellen Waller Borden, was from an old Chicago family. Adlai's prospective father-in-law, John Borden, inherited a fortune from his father, William Borden, and had greatly increased his wealth as an associate of John Hertz in the Yellow Cab Company and through investments in oil. In 1925 John Borden and his wife were divorced. There were two daughters from the marriage — Ellen and Betty. Ellen in 1928 was eighteen.

Before being presented to Chicago society in December, 1926, Ellen had attended St. Timothy's exclusive preparatory school at Catonsville, Maryland, and had spent one year studying in Florence, Italy.

The future Mrs. Stevenson was very pretty and very rich. She was also witty, gay, and intensely interested in literature, particularly poetry. When one of her poems was published in the Chicago Tribune, *Adlai sent a copy to Bloomington to be placed in the family album.[9]*

---

[7] Mr. Merwin wrote him on April 10, 1928, that advertising in the *Pantagraph* had increased over the year before. This letter is in the Adlai E. Stevenson collection, Princeton University Library (A.E.S., P.U.L.).

[8] Mr. and Mrs. Ernest L. Ives returned to the United States for the birth of their son Timothy Read Ives on April 9, 1928.

[9] Kenneth S. Davis, *A Prophet in His Own Country: The Triumphs and Defeats of Adlai E. Stevenson* (New York: Doubleday, 1957), p. 172, reprinted the poem. Davis wrote: "He was obviously devoted to her as a *person* and not just as the leading deb, or as an heiress. She enjoyed his sparkling conversation, his good dancing, his charming manners; and life with him, she decided, would never be

To Mrs. Lewis G. Stevenson

Monday [10]

Dearest Maw —

We motored out to L.F. [Lake Forest] after lunch Saturday — played tennis & then motored up to Lake Geneva to the Fairbanks in time for dinner.[11] Nice house party. Fine golf with Mr. Northrup, headmaster of Latin school Sunday A.M. Ellen played hockey on Lake Geneva girls team & so distinguished herself that Mr. Fairbank advised me never to have a stick in the house. We left at 5:30 arriving at chateau in time for elaborate supper party, Turkey etc. etc. given for "Mr. & Mrs. Stevenson" — Stuart girls were there etc.[12] Didn't see Sunday's paper about Ellen. Wish you would send such things to me. Ira Nelson Morris wants to arrange trip to Morroco for us.

Love
AD.

To Mrs. Lewis G. Stevenson

Sat. A.M.[13]

Dearest Maw —

You[r] wire just this minute received & I was so relieved & happy to hear that Buff had departed without untoward incident.[14] The more I see of your masterful handling of details and arrangements the more impressed I am with your extraordinary executive capacity — Why didn't you give me some of it? I go out to Lake Geneva this afternoon to visit the wife & in-laws. Looking forward to your return & a good uninterrupted "bicker."

Love
AD.

---

boring. These things she would say to interviewers in later years. She would deny, in these later years, that she had ever really loved him."

[10] This postcard is postmarked July 30, 1928.

[11] Mr. and Mrs. Kellogg Fairbank had a country home at Lake Geneva, Wisconsin. Mrs. Fairbank — Janet Ayer Fairbank — was a novelist.

[12] During the summers of 1927 and 1928 Adlai and several others rented a house they called "The Chateau" in fashionable Lake Forest. The Stuart girls were the daughters of John Stuart of the Quaker Oats Company.

[13] This postcard is postmarked July 28, 1928.

[14] Mrs. Ives and her son had just sailed for Europe. Adlai's mother was now at Stockbridge, Massachusetts.

To Mrs. Lewis G. Stevenson

Monday [15]

Dearest Maw —

Letter from Pa from Onawa Iowa says he has been feeling badly but is better now. Usual grief from the farms.[16] Your splendid letter came today & was delighted to hear that Buff and her troop got off without any major casualties. You certainly do get things done, & now I hope you really have a *rest* & can suspend worry for awhile. Had beautiful week end with the Bs [17] — Mrs. B expects you & father whenever you can come & wants you to understand you won't be "visiting" — just "staying." I never was happier or felt better & I'll get lots of sleep this week! Don't stay away too long but don't hasten back until you're really rested.

Love
AD.

To Mrs. Lewis G. Stevenson

Tuesday [18]

Dearest —

Another lovely letter breathing peace and tranquility! I'm so delighted that you've found a place "far from the madding throng's ignoble strife." And Buff too is getting rest & quiet & little Tim is commencing his international life in the most restful way I know — the sea. Last night . . . I had two good sets of tennis before dinner & I was asleep before 10. Ellen's quiet reassuring way, which I so long thought dreamy indecision even is resolving itself into an ordered calmness and is exceedingly good for an intense "planner" like we are. My happiness & certainty envelop me & I feel already her calming effect.

Love
AD.

[15] This postcard is postmarked July 30, 1928.

[16] Many segments of the agricultural community were in a serious economic depression long before 1929. Lewis G. Stevenson had worked closely with George N. Peek and Hugh S. Johnson of the Moline Plow Company to seek relief for agriculture through the McNary-Haugen bill, which called for federal subsidies to farm goods sold abroad at prices lower than in the United States. President Calvin Coolidge vetoed the bill.

[17] Ellen, her mother, and sister, Betty.

[18] This postcard is postmarked July 31, 1928.

To Mrs. Lewis G. Stevenson

Thursday [19]

Dearest Maw —

Last night went out to Lake Geneva. Ellen, Mrs. B[orden] & I had great fun. I'm feeling more & more like a son in law with the latter & feel sure we're going to get along famously. Today was epic! At 11 I called on Mr. B [John Borden] at his office — we talked an hour & what I rather dreaded turned out most pleasantly. He's really a very pleasant man if a little arrogant & determined. He gave me lots of advice — but not as advice. Says Ellen will have about a million exclusive of what she inherits from her mother, whom he says is worth probably a million. He wants E. to live on my income — tho she should be able to use some of her own income for dresses etc. Thinks we should live in Lake F[orest]. instead of the city, etc. etc. Father in Bloom[ington].

AD

To Mrs. Lewis G. Stevenson

Thurs — PM [20]

Maw!

Mr. McPherson [21] just solemnly summoned me to his room — With quaking knees I responded, but, wonder of wonders instead of firing me he raised my salary beginning Aug 1 to $200 per mo! On top of that I broke down & told him I was engaged & wanted a month to six weeks vacation. To the month he acquies[c]ed eagerly — to the 6 weeks he hesitated on the ground of example to the other young men but said he would take it up with his partners. Hereafter Aug. 2 will always be my lucky day.

AD.

To Mrs. Lewis G. Stevenson [22]

Dearest Maw:

Thanks for your sweet letter. I *do* need the "mother visits" but as you say its hard just now to get any consecutive time together — My days of bachelorhood with the boys in L.F. [Lake Forest] are few — hence I like to spend as much time out there as I can — the number of things

---

[19] This postcard is postmarked August 2, 1928.
[20] This postcard is postmarked August 2, 1928.
[21] Donald F. McPherson, a senior partner of Cutting, Moore and Sidley.
[22] This postcard is postmarked October 8, 1928.

I have to do, quite outside my office is literally appalling — (I'm trying to shake some of it off as best I can) — naturally I want to be with Ellen as much as possible — we've so much to decide and do. So you can see that until we get back in Jan. there is [not] much time for any really good visits. Hope you noticed that Zenith is up to 135. My profits on that alone now $8000.

Love
AD.

P.S. Please bring wedding list. Will have to get started soon. Ellen liked the frame so *much!* But not the picture.

On December 1, 1928, in the chapel of Chicago's fashionable Fourth Presbyterian Church, Ellen Borden became the bride of Adlai Ewing Stevenson.[23] After the wedding the Stevensons left on a six-week honeymoon for the Mediterranean where they motored through Tunisia, Algeria, and Morocco. On their return in mid-January, 1929, they moved into an apartment at 76 East Walton Place.

To Mrs. Lewis G. Stevenson

January 17 [24]

Dearest Maw:

In accordance with your suggestion I have cabled Buff as follows — "You must decide. Have written." My feeling about you going over in the spring, spending the summer and coming back in the fall with Buff & Ernest was that if Buff comes over now, at time of transfer she will want to stay several months which will delay their settlement in Copenhagen. And I'm not sure its altogether fair to Ernest to charge him with the responsibility of moving the goods & chattels from the south end of Europe to the north end. Also if Buff comes over now with Tim & nurse & you go back with her & then they come back to U.S. a year from now it will be a large aggregate expense. And if they don't come back E[rnest]. will not get a visit in America which I think would be good for him & them. Hence it seemed to me if you went over in May, after they were settled, & spent the summer — a beautiful season on the Baltic

---

[23] Hermon Dunlap Smith, who first knew Adlai when as boys they played together at Charlevoix, Michigan, wrote: "I believe I was first aware of his extraordinary charm and wit at his bachelor dinner. . . . This could easily have been a dismal affair, but it was enlivened throughout by the original and sparkling humor of the groom." "Politics and R & R," in *As We Knew Adlai,* p. 34.

[24] No year on the letter. Ernest L. Ives was transferred from Istanbul to Copenhagen in 1929. This letter was written before the transfer and therefore must be January 17, 1929.

— and you & Buff came back in the fall E. could come over again later alone for a few weeks & Buff & he could go back together. Of course this plan would be subject to the objection that their house or apt. would have to stand idle while they were both in U.S.

. . . Copenhagen I suppose is a fairly desirable post — certainly more important commercially than Vienna. Its a quaint old city — tho a little dull I fear — but that won't hurt them. And its close to Stockholm, Berlin, etc. You can sail to Copenhagen direct from N.Y. on good boats — Danish-Amerika line & Swedish-American line. Or one can go to England & take a splendid overnight service from Hull. Or you can fly!

. . . All well happy & thanks for the household hints for E[llen].

Love in haste

AD

p.s. New maid Mary Dean — a jewel! Believe it or not! Can't find enough to do — very quiet & refined — good cook, cleanly, middle aged etc etc.

p.s.s. Have forwarded your letter to Aunt Jessie [Merwin]. I thought it was splendid — you certainly are a "writin fool." . . .

To Mrs. Lewis G. Stevenson

February 1, 1929

Dearest Maw —

I am stealing a moment from my employers to thank you and Buffy for your splendid & eagerly awaited letters. The tome *"alone"* I of course couldn't resist reading to the frau — whereupon, so impressed was she with mature wisdom & advice, that she put it away for further reading later.

I feel very guilty for not having written in detail long ago but we've been suffering from a severe attack of society — wedding, engagement parties & then just parties. But it's all over this week & we look forward to some earnest housekeeping. The apt. is really exceptionally attractive & comfortable & I'm sure you'll approve of everything we've done. As an economy etc. Ellen has decided to have a slip cover made for the sofa instead of having it upholstered. But I haven't time to tell you all about the apt. & from the way Ellen is dashing around all day long it doesn't look as tho she was going to have much either — at least for awhile. Nig Bowen is engaged to Kay Thorne [25] — I distinguished myself with a speech on the homelife of the Stevensons at the announcement dinner! We are contemplating a house in Lake F[orest]. for the

[25] Clymer S. Bowen, who shared the bachelor house with Stevenson, and Katherine Thorne of Lake Forest.

summer & have been out once to look them over. Found one fairly nice tiny little one for $200 — but Ellen didn't like the "Sears Roebuck" furniture!

Dave [Merwin] was in yesterday with statements books etc in great abundance. We showed a net profit for 1929 after all deductions — taxes, carrying charges on Bulletin [26] etc of $113,000 + or an actual net income of $171,000. He seems satisfied with the situation & optimistic for the future.

Mrs. B[orden]. probably won't leave for Europe until April or late March. She leaves next week to visit in Cambridge and Florida for 3 week[s] and then back here for March. Betty [Borden] *most attractive and still heart whole, tho under perpetual seige!* We are getting beautiful set of antique flat silver from the Lemon collection in Louisville — Monnie [27] giving it to us, though he "thinks plated just as good." Went to the Opera with Mrs. Rock. [Edith Rockefeller] the other night — asked all about Buff & Ernest. Mrs. B[orden] has had dinner with us twice & Uncle Monnie once. That's the extent of our entertaining — no teas for 150 yet — or ever I hope!

I wish I could see that fat little angel.[28] We will send a wedding picture of Ellen — but the one of both of us isn't good of her.

Best love to all —

Ad

On March 26, 1929, Lewis G. Stevenson had a severe heart attack. (He died on April 5.) One day when Adlai visited him alone in the hospital at Bloomington his father gasped to him that "politics is a hazardous life, full of ingratitudes." Then his father added some earnest words about "duty to serve," "need to serve," "an obligation."

According to an interview that Kenneth S. Davis had with Adlai Stevenson years later, his father had never suggested a political career to him. But his memories of this last talk with his father convinced Adlai that his father had always had undisclosed ambitions for him.[29]

In 1928 Jane Warner's father suggested that Stevenson run for the state legislature but after a brief consideration of the suggestion Adlai decided not to do it. But in 1930 he gave the idea serious consideration, although nothing finally came of it.

[26] In 1927 the *Pantagraph* purchased the Bloomington *Daily Bulletin* and merged the two papers. *Editor and Publisher*, October 1, 1927.

[27] James B. Waller, Mrs. Borden's brother.

[28] Mr. and Mrs. Lewis G. Stevenson were visiting Mr. and Mrs. Ives and their son Tim in Istanbul.

[29] Kenneth S. Davis, *The Politics of Honor: A Biography of Adlai E. Stevenson* (New York: Putnam, 1967), p. 106.

To Mrs. Lewis G. Stevenson [30]

Dearest Maw —

Last night we went to the Opera with Col. & Mrs. Sprague.[31] It appears that the gods have been busy weaving plans over my innocent head. I broached the subject of the legislature to him only to discover that he has talked to all the Democratic "big shots" & has been to see Mr. [William P.] Sidley — who has eagerly consented. He has talked with the ward boss, [Edmund L.] Mulcahy (not French!) who is at outs with [Lawrence C.] O'Brien, the present representative [to the legislature], & Mulcahy is at present finding out what the chance is of giving me the organization support instead of O'Brien. Unless he can assure me of that Sprague says he wasn't even going to speak to me about it —

AD.

To Mrs. Lewis G. Stevenson [32]

Dearest Maw —

My delay in writing for three days has been due to the fact that I have been trying a very difficult jury case — didn't have lunch for 2 days! It was the hardest birthday I ever put in & ever will I hope. At six thirty last night the jury brought in a verdict against me! I[t] was very disappointing but I have the satisfaction of knowing that the case couldn't have been tried much better. Even the judge told me that. What news from Buff. — Brock,[33] as your [you] surmised, has done little or nothing — excuses about 50% good. All well with E[llen] & me & maid still very satisfactory. Thanks loads for lovely birthday letter — made me very happy. Couldn't read Disraeli quotation.

AD.

To Mrs. Lewis G. Stevenson

Sat. A.M.[34]

Dearest Maw —

We are having lots of quiet evenings now — good reading and bitter chess & checker contests! Mrs. B[orden]. leaves today for 10 days with

[30] This postcard is postmarked January 23, 1930.
[31] Colonel Albert A. Sprague was influential in Chicago Democratic party politics.
[32] This postcard is postmarked February 6, 1930.
[33] A tenant on a Stevenson farm.
[34] This postcard is postmarked February 15, 1930.

the Kingsley Porters in Cambridge, Mass. No developments on the house sale yet — am waiting to see how things turn out with the Fortnightly [Club]. Its bitterly cold here again — everyone has left town — it looks as tho the winter sports expedition was going to fall thru this winter much to my disappointment. Am playing squash regularly & am going to sign up with a physical culture instructor for 3 sessions per week. Betty [Ellen's sister]'s letters few & say little — in Egypt now —

AD.

To Mrs. Lewis G. Stevenson [35]

Dearest Maw —

. . . had a long talk with J. Ham Lewis [36] re politics, one with Col. [Albert A.] Sprague in the morning & in the afternoon had a back room conf. with Alderman [Dorsey] Crowe and Committeeman [William J.] Connors! The latter eloquent Irishmen tried e[a]rnestly to persuade me to run for the State Senate with extravagant assurances of success. But I told them I didn't "choose to run."

Note what the sage Alverta [37] says re March weather — perhaps you better stay a little longer!

Love
AD

P.S. Please indorse the enclosed dividend check for $1.00 & return.

To Mrs. Lewis G. Stevenson

Mon.[38]

Dearest Maw —

My work has piled up so voluminously since I made my departure for the hospital last Thursday that I've no time for a good letter.[39] Family matters are progressing satisfactorily — the young man is losing some of his enchanting birthday appearance — in short he's getting to look more human tho he still has some distance to go. He's become a great hospital attraction! Ellen seems to be doing well — is very cheerful &

---

[35] Although this letter is undated, it probably was written in January or February, 1930. The part that has been deleted mentioned possible sculptors of a bust of W. O. Davis. He was elected to the Hall of Fame of the Illinois Press Association, October, 1929. The bust was unveiled November 21, 1930, at the University of Illinois.

[36] J. Hamilton Lewis, U. S. senator from Illinois.

[37] Alverta Duff was for many years housekeeper in the Stevenson home in Bloomington.

[38] This postcard is postmarked October 13, 1930.

[39] On October 10, 1930, the Stevensons' first child was born. They named him Adlai Ewing Stevenson III.

happy, but terribly weak. I hope it won't be long before you can run up for a look see! Uncle Lou [Louis Merwin] called up today to congratulate. Saw no announcement in Panta[graph]. Send me one.

In the late spring of 1931, Adlai and Ellen sailed to Europe to visit his sister and brother-in-law in Copenhagen. (Mr. Ives was about to be transferred to Pretoria, South Africa.) Adlai III — "Big Boy" or "Goliath" as his father nicknamed him — was left with Alverta Duff in the Stevenson home in Bloomington. The following letters were written to Mr. and Mrs. Ives and his mother (who was visiting the Iveses at this time) after Adlai and Ellen had seen them in Copenhagen. Three of them are undated but range from late May to June 20, 1931.

To Mrs. and Mrs. Ernest L. Ives and Mrs. Lewis G. Stevenson

Wednesday [40]

Dear Buff, Ernest & Maw —

All is well — in fact very well! This is the first available moment we have had since we left Copenhagen — such is life in Stockholm!

Kalmar [Sweden] we reached after an endless journey thru endless forests at 11:30 & shipped in a tiny spick & span boat for Visby. The crossing was rough but we came thru intact while the Swedes sprayed the deck profusely. We docked in ancient Visby at 8:30 & spent the morning looking over the enchanting old town. Ellen did not less than 15 miles on foot in the course of [the] day & was still smiling when we set sail at 10 in the evening — in broad daylight! Visby was, if anything, even better than we had anticipated. The 14th century walls are almost intact and the numerous church ruins incredibly beautiful. In the afternoon we went up the coast aways to a bathing resort & had a dip in the icy Baltic & a delicious sun bath on the mighty wooded cliffs under a cloudless sky & read the history of old Visby. Dinner at the lovely hotel overlooking the sea & back to town to make a complete circuit around the old walls in the everlasting twilight.

At Nynäshamn we disembarked (at 5:30 A.M.!) & caught the train for Stockholm arriving at 8:30. I called on Crocker [41] at the Legation & he at once asked us for tea in the afternoon. I had a pleasant chat with Mr. Moorehead,[42] an obviously very able man, & then we took to our feet for sightseeing & shopping. At the hotel at 4 o'clock we found a telephone message from Mrs. Moorehead asking us to dinner the same

[40] Written from Stockholm.
[41] Edward Crocker, secretary of the American legation.
[42] John Motley Moorehead, American Minister to Sweden.

night. At tea with the Crockers we hooked up with Lieut. [Hugh] Waddell a U.S. Army officer in the Swedish Calvary school. He took us to the Mooreheads magnificent house to a most elegant dinner — one Swedish woman, the Czech-Slovak minister & his wife, Col. Pierson the U.S. military attaché & wife, Lieut. Waddell, Mr. & Mrs. Moorehead & ourselves. We had a gay time & finally ended up at the Czech minister's legation drinking highballs & dancing at 2 A.M. It was an amusing evening for a couple of corn fed provincials!

Today is has rained & we have been sightseeing industriously using Lieut. Waddell for transportation. . . . Tomorrow the chivalrous cavalryman is taking us to [illegible] in the afternoon & we dine with the Crockers. Friday we will go to Upsala & Friday night to Oslo.

Ellen has bought some Swedish glass which we will take back with us to avoid the duty — the shops here all seem very expensive. Mr. Moorehead has told me horrible news about the current condition of the stock market, but even that hasn't crushed our spirit. I suppose I've been sold out but this trip has been worth 5 years of drudgery. Ellen & I are still babbling about Copenhagen and all our adventures. Indeed we're already planning to descend on you in So. Africa or wherever you may be two years hence. In the meanwhile we'll live in the memory of the epic experiences you gave us. Tach sa muche & then some!

Ellen says for Buff to remember her to the King of England *and* Prince Eric! Many thanks Maw for the B 21[?] & your letter. Please don't over do because there will be plenty to do when you get back home — don't forget Big Boy & the back yard!

Love to all

AD.

P.S. Excuse this scrawl — I am prone on the bed while Ellen dashes off postcards at the desk. Crocker tells us glowing things he has heard about So. Africa & the Czech's we met knew Ernest in Egypt & the Masaryks very well.[43] Francis [44] is getting divorced. Cutting Moore & Sidley seems charmingly remote now & I haven't worn glasses for 2 weeks!

To Mrs. Lewis G. Stevenson

Sat. night

Dear Maw —

The end of a perfect day in Oslo — but day never ends here. Oslo has been far more pleasant and interesting than we anticipated. E[llen]. bought some little enamel trinkets as presents and a lovely eiderdown

---

[43] Mr. and Mrs. Jan Masaryk. He later was foreign minister of Czechoslovakia.
[44] Daughter of Charles R. Crane of Chicago and wife of Jan Masaryk.

coat & cap for Big Boy — it will probably be large for him for a couple of years. Its a pretty smallish city with splendid views from the high hills surrounding the city. We climbed one & had lunch at the top.

. . . Do take care of yourself as well as everyone else! We are still talking about Copenhagen tho the new adventures are crowding in. Had tea at Alice Eno's & she & husband were at the Crockers for dinner & took us home.[45]

Best to Ernest & a big hug for Tim.

Love
Ad

To Mrs. Lewis G. Stevenson and Mrs. Ernest L. Ives

Dear Mother & Buff —

This is inscribed en route from Oslo to Goteburg Sweden. I have just read Ellen's effort manifestly composed under the influence of mild intoxication & hasten to contradict anything disparaging to my own exemplary conduct.

The trip thru Norway has been comfortable and liesurely — the the itinerary sounds as tho we were holding our hats on all the time! We had no untoward experiences except that E. started things off by leaving her silver fox in the hotel in Oslo & miscellaneous minor articles were contributed to hotels along the route. I hasten to add that the fur was found pursuant to our telegram & awaited our return to Oslo. I might also add in justice that I lost the precious itinerary at an early stage & had to reconstruct it from memory & with the aid of hotel proprietors. We left all our luggage except my big suitcase & E's bottle bag in Oslo — jumping back & forth from boat to auto thru the fiords we would never have been able to handle it all. The scenery was majestic & in places spectacular — most every day we walked & climbed for miles & miles — E's dogs are blistered beyond recognition & taped up like a Napoleonic trooper — mine are flat, but we are burned brown & simply spurting with health & happiness. Norway was a fortunate selection & two weeks there would be a tonic for anyone. I am distressed that B[uffy] & Ernest didn't have an opportunity to see it before they left Scandinavia.

We received your telegram at lovely Sandane & the letter from Theresa [46] at Balholm — it was a great comfort to E. & she has been examining the photos of Big Boy furtively at odd moments ever since.

---

[45] Alice Eno Hopkinson had lived next door to the house Mrs. Lewis G. Stevenson had rented in Princeton while Adlai was an undergraduate. She had married a British diplomat who was now stationed in Stockholm.

[46] Adlai III's nurse.

Of course we don't understand the meeting in Brussels but will probably have a letter at Goteborg explaining all your plans.

I am afraid E's taste of Continental society at Copenhagen & Stockholm has spoiled her for Chicago & we are working on a diary of our stay in Denmark while the memory lingers on. I never realized before how much is lost to the conventional tourist. Buff & E[rnest] can take warning that we set our course direct for them every vacation henceforth! I feel that South A[frica]. is going to be their biggest experience to date & I trust Buffy realizes now that it really is an opportunity & a great adventure.

Love,
Ad

P.S. Please advise when you can just when B & E are sailing — addresses etc. Its hard to think of them so far away — but all the same I wish it was us! A big hug for Tim. Am asking E[rnest]. to forward these letters.

To Mrs. Lewis G. Stevenson and Mrs. Ernest L. Ives

June 20 — afternoon [47]

Dearest Maw & Buff —

Your deluge of mail has just reached us & I am a little bewildered as to your precise address. The earlier letters I mailed this morning care Ernest before yours were delivered.

We sail in an hour after a bright sunny day in this surprisingly charming city — a felicitous conclusion for our splendid trip. We were much interested in the news of Buffs eventful four days in London — that girl can certainly get more done in less time — it would have taken Ellen or me 4 days to get organized. E. has passed on the news about the presentation & the divorce to her mother already. The latters address is Bankers Trust Co., Paris. We have written a hasty inadequate note of thanks & farewell to Ernest.

I will forward the $500 at once upon my return — but where to? But perhaps that ques. will be answered on a more careful scrutiny of all these letters. I suppose you saw the pictures of the bairn [Adlai III] in Theresa's letter — E[llen]. has been walking around in a daze of joy ever since. Please don't be concerned about our health — this has been the most healthy trip I ever had & Ellen has gained pounds on Norwegian fish & cheese & looks better (really) than at any time since she

---

[47] Written from Goteborg, Sweden.

took me for better or for worse. My appetite continues good also —
thank you!

I didn't find Alverta [Duff]'s letter & feel sure it was among all those
papers we gave you. Sp[a]. sounds like a good place & we both wish
we were with you — I'm not a bit ready to go home but Big Boy makes
our farewell much easier & E's almost joyous. Please don't overdo,
Mother! My turn at admonitions! Did you see or hear anything of the
Spears [48] in London — I think E. would be interested in any dope from
that quarter. So glad you saw Mrs. Baur [49] — can't do any harm & who
knows what good.

But we must dash for the boat — all love & please keep us advised of
your plans & addresses.

Love

Ad

*On August 27, 1931, Davis Merwin, president and general manager of
the* Daily Pantagraph, *wrote Adlai Stevenson that on July 29 the* Daily
Pantagraph *had reported the filing of a praecipe of a $5,000 trespass suit
against a Bloomington constable. There was an error in the story and
when this was discovered the paper published an apology. On August 26
the constable filed a $25,000 suit against the* Pantagraph *for damages.*

To Davis Merwin [50]

August 29, 1931

Dear Dave: —

I have your letter of August 27th and enclosures. After an examination
of the clippings and the declaration, I can make the following observations:

1. The plaintiff has a substantially good case as far as the actual
   words published are concerned. — They probably amount even
   to a libel per se, under the Illinois decisions regarding libels on
   a man in connection with his business or activities.
2. There is no privilege by virtue of the fact that the praecipe had
   been filed. The privilege applicable to the publication of judicial
   decisions, records, and actions cannot be invoked here.
3. The retraction and apology will not constitute a justification or

---

[48] Ellen Borden Stevenson's aunt, Mary Borden, married General Edward Louis
Spears in 1918. He later was made a Knight of the British Empire.
[49] Mrs. Jacob Baur, Chicago civic leader.
[50] This letter is in A.E.S., P.U.L.

bar to the action, but will mitigate damages and will help to disprove malice.

4. The plaintiff has complied with the several technicalities of pleading in libel actions so as to give no basis for a demurrer on technical grounds.

5. I believe the best theory of defense is that the newspaper article merely repeated what a third party had said, and it named the third party. While this is not a defense in itself, it is probably sufficient to change the usual rule as to malice. The latter rule is that actual malice is not necessary to sustain an action for libel, as the malice will be presumed from the lack of justification. The defense suggested above would alter this rule and compel the plaintiff to prove that the defendant had actual malice. In such case the retraction and apology, and the fact that the article was a quotation from a third party, and was repeated as being a part of anticipated litigation, would be helpful as tending to indicate the want of actual malice.

6. The retraction has eliminated the possibility of exemplary damages, and accordingly plaintiff's recovery, if any, would be limited to actual damages.

My feeling is that, at worst, the defendant could collect only actual damages, and from the character of his employment I feel that he will probably not be able to prove very substantial damages, probably less than $1000.00. It also seems not improbable in the malice theory above suggested, that the plaintiff's case might fail altogether. At all events, I do not think it would be worth while to settle the case for more than $200.00. If you wish me to go into the matter further, we could, of course, prepare a memorandum of law, and consider more thoroughly the procedure in asserting the suggested defense, providing you conclude not to effect a settlement and it becomes necessary for the Pantagraph to file its plea. . . .

Yours very truly,

Robert M. Hutchins and Adlai E. Stevenson became close friends soon after Hutchins left the deanship of the Yale University Law School to become president of the University of Chicago. Hutchins wrote years later: "It was in 1929 that I first met Adlai Stevenson in Chicago at a party given by the daughter of the founder of the University of Chicago, John D. Rockefeller. This was the only time in my life I ever saw solid gold plates in actual use. I remember that — and Adlai Stevenson." [51]

[51] "What Kind of World?" Los Angeles *Times,* August 30, 1965.

To Robert M. Hutchins [52]

October 7, 1931

Dear Hutchins:

Having been advised by Insull, Hord et al that you have little to occupy your time and talents these days other than some meagre duties at the University, I have generously concluded to come forward with a proposition.[53] Please do not misunderstand "proposition," I mean an offer; and by "generously," a gratuitous opportunity to sell your stuff from the pulpit to the yokelry down in the Bible Belt. Again may I urge you not to misconstrue "sell" — the *quid pro quo* will be largely psychic. It seems probable to me that as your true character becomes better known in this latitude, your opportunities to declaim under spiritual auspices will be increasingly infrequent. Accordingly this invitation will doubtless be irresistable. Incidentally and sordidly, I must also point out that Bloomington has been grossly neglected by the University of Chicago evangelists.

In case the foregoing does not make everything quite clear, I enclose some correspondence which you may return, together with your well considered acceptance or rejection, at your convenience, — or sooner. In a vein even more serious, I do hope you will find it convenient to shed light in dark places and point out to the beleaguered farmers the many causes for giving thanks.

Yours,

P.S. I sincerely hope that we will have occasion to exchange personal profanities soon. In the meanwhile my distinguished sentiments to your wife.

AES.

To Davis Merwin

June 4, 1932

Dear Dave:

After our conversation the other day, it occurred to me that in your absence it might be well for our families to be very discreet conversationally about the Pantagraph and its policies locally and politically, and

---

[52] This letter is in the University of Chicago Library.

[53] Robert M. Hutchins wrote to Walter Johnson, December 12, 1967, that Samuel Insull, Jr., Stephen Y. Hord, Adlai, and he, "since we were all about the same age, used to exchange satirical comments on one another and on our betters." Hutchins did not accept the invitation to speak in Bloomington.

I have so cautioned mother.[54] Of course, what I have in mind is to forestall any opinion locally that the parents are running the show again. Any questions from the public demanding owner consideration that cannot be conveniently handled or dismissed by the staff can be referred to me, which, because I am in Chicago, may eliminate some of them easily. Perhaps it would be well for you to say something to Jake [55] about this.

. . . I have no misgivings about your absence whatever and I earnestly hope you will try to dismiss business from your mind altogether. If you will relax utterly, I am confident you will come back quite restored — and that things will look better all around. Don't forget that the old antidote is for snake bites only.

Best regards and luck.

Yours,

The Democratic candidate for governor of Illinois in 1932 was Henry Horner, judge of the Probate Court of Cook County. (He was elected in November.) Adlai E. Stevenson did a great deal of probate work for his law firm and thus knew Horner professionally. In addition they became good personal friends. Horner was an avid collector of Lincolniana. He and Stevenson frequently discussed Lincoln, Jesse Fell, and Illinois history.

When the campaign train of Franklin D. Roosevelt came to Chicago that autumn, Judge Horner took Adlai E. Stevenson to meet the Democratic candidate. As soon as Horner introduced him, Roosevelt recalled that his father and Vice President Stevenson had been friends and that he himself had worked with Adlai's father in the Department of the Navy during the war.

Mrs. Ives wrote years later: "F.D.R.'s grace and warmth at that first hurried meeting left Adlai stammering, surprised and devoted." [56]

---

[54] Mr. Merwin was planning an extended vacation because of his health. In response to this letter, he wrote on June 6 that he agreed "heartily that during my absence it will be most important to leave the impression that affairs are running just as usual, and making it clear whenever necessary that none of the parents are in any way actively involved. I shall caution mother to that effect, and shall, as you suggest, instruct the staff to refer to you such questions as may need to be answered by an officer or stockholder." These two letters are in A.E.S., P.U.L.

[55] Jacob L. Hasbrouck, an editor of the *Pantagraph*.

[56] *My Brother Adlai*, p. 113.

To Henry Horner [57]

August 15, 1932

Dear Judge:

I have your letter of August 10th from Vandalia. The excerpts from the Pantagraph I had seen and I have written the editor to caution our so-called humorous [humorist]. The editorial was frivolous, but I am confident in no way intended to indicate any change or changing heart of the Pantagraph.

In the present circumstances, I am utterly unable to understand how any independent honest newspaper proprietor could think twice before making his decision, and you may rest assured that toward the end of the campaign your candidacy will receive vigorous support in the Pantagraph.

I have heard encouraging reports of the progress of your acquaintance campaign down State. I wish you could have some one write a series of articles about your non-political activities, largely Lincoln and the Probate Court. To be saturated with Lincoln is to be saturated with Illinois, and I am confident that the story of your intimate acquaintance with the historical panorama of the whole State would help in a large measure to dispel the mistrust of a Chicago candidate. I feel sure that the down State papers supporting you would welcome something like this and I am going to speak to Colonel [Albert A.] Sprague about it.

Faithfully yours,

To Jacob L. Hasbrouck [58]

August 15, 1932

Dear Jake:

I enclose some clippings. I wish you would ask Bish [59] to refrain from derisive comments of this kind, as it puts us in an equivocal position. The editorial I am sure was not critically intended, but there should be no equivocation as to our position. As you will doubtless agree, the State is confronted with a serious political crisis and support of Judge Horner must be forthright and vigorous when the time comes. We cannot afford to leave any shadow of doubt where we stand in a matter which leaves independent newspapers with a clear duty to perform.

Yours,

[57] This letter is in A.E.S., P.U.L.
[58] This letter is in A.E.S., P.U.L.
[59] Stanley Bishop, a *Pantagraph* reporter.

To Louis FitzHenry [60]

September 14, 1932

Dear Judge FitzHenry:

I have just received from the Pantagraph a copy of your award in our recent arbitration hearing with the I.T.U. [International Typographical Union] Local, and I take this opportunity of thanking you for your courtesy and kindness in undertaking and disposing of this controversy.

I sincerely hope our past harmonious relations with the I.T.U. will be resumed and that we both will not soon again find it necessary to impose upon your public spirit and distinguished reputation for judicial fairness.

Doubtless you share my elation and growing confidence about the campaign. I only hope that Judge Horner can conquer the "towers of darkness" down State. If from time to time you have any comments or suggestions on the Pantagraph's treatment of the State campaign, I hope you will pass them on to me. Also, if you come across good editorials in down State papers on the Horner campaign, I wish you would send them to me.

Faithfully yours,

To Henry Horner [61]

December 3, 1932

Dear Judge:

For some reason, I have recently received various requests from people who aspire to State positions, asking my help through you.

Accordingly, I am enclosing a letter and memorandum from Frank H. Funk, who was a friend of my father's and who has long been prominent in central Illinois.

James Clark, a popular and respected Bloomington citizen, has also asked me to say a word in his behalf. He has been on the Commerce Commission for eleven years, serving successfully as Assistant Commissioner and in later years as Supervisor of Orders. My associates in this office, who represent our utility clients before the Commission, tell me that he is capable, accom[m]odating and his long experience and familiarity with the whole State make him an especially useful servant.

That these men should ask my help is flattering but puts me in an embarrassing position. I have assured them that my family and I could and would ask for no favors and that I would merely pass the applica-

[60] This letter is in A.E.S., P.U.L.
[61] This letter is in A.E.S., P.U.L.

tions along for you to consider on their merit alone. I hope you will take me at my word and any disposition you make of the matters will be agreeable with me.

Faithfully yours,

To Mrs. Lewis G. Stevenson [62]

Dear Maw —

Have just forwarded a jolly cable from Buff. How was the trip — I hope not too hard and that you have surrendered without a struggle to the langurous breezes & sunshine of the Southland. We must all be in good shape for Buff & Tim so as to give her as little concern as possible[.] Am sending her an Xmas cable today.

Love

AD.

To Mrs. Lewis G. Stevenson

December 27 [63]

Dear Maw —

Christmas eve Mrs. B[orden]. came out & had dinner with us & we talked & listened to the Radio — Grace & Jimmie [64] came to deliver presents & early to bed. Sunday was a warm spring day & Mrs. B drove in town with us about noon with the car piled with our offerings. Mrs. B., Betty & Bob,[65] Harold Wallace & we comprised the Christmas dinner which John [66] helped to serve with great dignity & efficiency. You were missed & Mrs. B. spoke so kindly of you. . . . Big Boy [Adlai III] had to stay at home with a slight cold. . . . Ellen was much pleased with her luncheon set and used it yesterday. Big Boy took the canary to his heart as nothing else — and there was enough else to provide an orphan asylum. The 5 iron & I fitted perfectly — so you can consider your work well done. I also drew a needed umbrella, leather travelling toilet case fitted, socks, beautiful monagramed dress muffler & a street muffler. So I will have to do very little exchanging this time. All in all it was a very happy Christmas tho the attendance for the last one in

---

[62] This postcard is postmarked December 22, 1932.

[63] No year on the letter but probably 1932.

[64] James H. Douglas, Jr., had been a friend of Adlai's even before they attended Princeton together. His wife was a close friend of Ellen's.

[65] Mr. and Mrs. Robert Pirie.

[66] John Duff worked as chauffeur and houseman for Mrs. Lewis G. Stevenson. When she was away from Bloomington he worked sometimes for her son and daughter-in-law.

the old house was disappointing. In the afternoon we made up enormous baskets of food, clothing & toys for a poor family which eased the conscience.

I am happy to hear that you are mending & I think we must learn that you can't take any chances with this crazy climate. Today again it is as warm as spring & the last vestige of winter has disappeared even in the Northland — Our trip is off, to my intense regret & of course Ellen had declined all sorts of engaging New Years festivities, so she is crushed two ways. But something will turn up — it always does.

The photos were very disappointing — the group ones utterly impossible. We sent you one of the best ones of Ellen & the two children. There was only one other of the three of them that was any good & only one of the two children.[67] We will try it again later on sometime. The individual ones of me were awful & nowhere near as good as the ones Moffett took last winter which you didn't like & I didn't order. Keep me advised about Buff & Ernest —

Love
ADLAI

P.S. A package has just come from Durban [South Africa] on which I have paid $4.25 duty marked underwear. I am send[ing] it on to you.

By 1932 Adlai E. Stevenson was secretary of the Chicago Council on Foreign Relations. In that role he wrote the following article about the council. There are two drafts of the article with some slight differences between them. We have used the one that has corrections in his handwriting. Years after this article was written he wrote on one copy, "Written by AES for some local magazine — 1935." His memory must have been faulty since in the article he mentions that this was the tenth anniversary of the council. That would mean the article was written in 1932. Furthermore, Graham Aldis is described as president in the article. His term was from 1931 to 1933. The two copies are in A.E.S., P.U.L.

CHICAGO LOOKS AT THE WORLD
by Adlai E. Stevenson

The war introduced international politics to interior America. It revealed problems, names and places which few people west of the State Department had ever suspected. But the war was just a prelude. When

---

[67] The Stevensons' second son, Borden, was born on July 7, 1932. This is the first extant letter that mentions him.

the thunder of guns ceased, the rattle of voices commenced. Out of the clamorous meeting of the international creditors in Paris emerged the Versaille[s] Treaty and a host of problems and perplexities which made many intelligent people cease wondering what the war was really all about — so engaging were the contents of this new Pandora's box. Our comfortable frontier isolation was irrevocably shattered once we began imbibing international politics with our morning coffee, and speaking familiarly, if not always affectionately, of mandates, minorities, and protocols.

With the end of the war a happy alliance took place: the lecture bureaus felt the political growing pains; the experts heard about the dollars and promptly enlisted to assuage the pains. Before long, Foreign Policy Associations in Boston and New York were packing them in to hear discussions of the new world and its complexities. The distinguished importations of the lecture bureaus brought stirring messages from harassed, confused Europe, and it was not long before the social and intellectual merits of the luncheon lecture penetrated Chicago, thanks to the mature conviction of a small group that in the post-war world La Salle Street, Downing Street and the Bund were vitally concerned with one another. Thus in 1922 the Chicago Council on Foreign Relations came into being "To promote Public Discussion of the Foreign Relations of the United States." Such was the expressed motive of its organizers, and such is its primary motive today, although it has inevitably evolved into a forum for the impartial discussion of the affairs of all nations whether directly affecting the United States or not. Because the war-born world consciousness had many votaries and few shrines, the Council was a healthy baby, is still thriving, in spite of the present alarming prevalence of anaemia among publicly supported organizations, and gives abundant promise of great longevity.

From October until June, a series of weekly luncheon meetings are held, usually on Saturdays, at which experts speak on outstanding topics of international affairs. Questions and discussion follow the address. The Council is non-partisan and aspires to preserve absolute impartiality on all controversial subjects. As many addresses must be partisan, occasionally two speakers are selected to present opposing views at the same meeting, and colorful have been the fire-works from some of the more inflammatory quarters of the globe. But more often a partisan presentation is balanced by an opposing view at a subsequent meeting.

On March 18, 1922, George W. Wickersham opened the first meeting of the Council with a discussion of the Treaties which had just been negotiated at the Washington Conference. In the ten years following, many distinguished men and women have addressed the Council, among them such unforgettable figures as Georges Clemenceau, whom Chicago remembers not so much as the Tiger of France as her shrewd and distinguished statesman; the stooped, hawk-like Lord Robert Cecil, co-founder of the League of Nations, and one of the great Englishmen of his time; Fridtjof Nansen, intrepid explorer of the North Pole and the New Internationalism; and Sir Norman Angell, the brilliant and witty English economist, whose repeated appearances before the Council are high spots in the year's program. But the Council does not always go so far afield for its authorities. Occasionally, it finds equally good ones in its own front yard. Frank O. Lowden, Melvin Traylor, Silas Strawn, Charles S. Dewey, Samuel Harper, and Quincy Wright have served not only as directors of the Council for many years, but as some of its most distinguished speakers.

The Council is controlled by its President, Graham Aldis, and three other officers; an Executive Committee; and a Director and Assistant Director who maintain the Council office at 140 South Dearborn Street. Among the present directors are the former presidents: Victor Elting, William B. Hale, William C. Boyden, Silas Strawn, William P. Sidley, Clay Judson and George A. Richardson. From the little group of twenty who founded the Council ten years ago, the membership has grown into an organization of several thousand.

In addition to its meetings, the Council publishes a fortnightly news Review, "Foreign Notes," edited by the Director, Clifton Utley, and sent to all members as well as to an increasing circle of subscribers throughout the United States and Canada. The Review provides a brief, accurate survey of developments in international affairs, and a special article by some expert on the outstanding international problem of each fortnight. A series of books on American Foreign Policies has also been published during the last three years.

The world is too much with us — very possibly. Those golden days when we never heard the dawn coming up like thunder out of China 'cross the sea are gone forever. We can no longer escape the fact that Europe is not five thousand miles, but only a stone's throw away from us. (And since we have of late taken to living in glass houses, not even that.) The intelligent thing for us to do now is to inform ourselves as accurately as possible on the great international questions which are of increasing concern to Congress, and consequently to the public opinion behind Congress. The purpose of the Chicago Council on Foreign Relations is not only to stimulate interest in these questions, but to provide reliable information, and the opportunity for unprejudiced discussion and consideration of them. After all is not knowledge of our neighbors' problems, and the tolerant understanding bred of knowledge, the greatest insurance of peace in the world?

To Mrs. Lewis G. Stevenson

January 3, 1933

Dear Maw —

New Years eve was a big night in Lake Forest but we finally did get to bed & slept until noon on Sunday. Had 6 to lunch & a very merrie time thanks to the fact that Anna [68] had her *worst* hangover from her own New Year's eve celebration & the lunch reflected her bewilderment. The turkey came in upside down etc! John [Duff] served & if it hadn't been for him there would have been no lunch. We are going to have to give poor old Anna our ultimatum tho she did afford us more fun than I've ever had before. Last night we went to a very elegant and vinous dinner at the Casino [Club] given by Mrs. [Kingsley] Porter. . . . We have 3 days of peace now — then one more party & I think we'll be about thru for the season.

The pajamas are splendid & the gloves fit like gloves! I didn't get the tricycle — thought we'd wait until the spring when he can use it on the sidewalks more & will be a little larger. His size now is so small I'm afraid he'll outgrow it very soon. . . .

Love
AD.

P.S. We went thru a couple of houses yesterday. Ellen is very keen about the large one I told you about — it is in good condition but will require a lot of decorating. Wish you could see it.

To Mrs. Lewis G. Stevenson

[January, 1933]

Dear Maw —

Am glad to hear that you have started the northward migration — from all I've hear[d] Winter Park must be a good all around place. Mrs. Borden is leaving here next Tuesday & I think they plan to be married on Sat. the 28th — if this is changed I'll let you know.[69] She will be staying with Mr. & Mrs. Kingsley Porter, Cambridge, Mass. I think thats sufficient address. And thats where the wedding will take place. Ellen will probably go down for the wedding — doesn't want to, expense etc. But I think its the thing to do. Betty [70] will go too.

Many thanks for the c[hec]ks — the car has been all checked over at

---

[68] The Stevensons' maid.
[69] Ellen's mother married the composer John Alden Carpenter.
[70] Ellen's sister.

the Cadillac — $26 worth, which I will repay out of the cks. John [B. Duff] is ready to leave on short notice & all is well. I am very busy at the office & it looks as tho the vacation might not come off — at least until March. We hope to go to the inauguration if we can afford it & can meet up with Buff & Ernest perhaps. We are giving a large party at 1020 [Lake Shore Drive] on Feb. 3 — I wrote the invitations in the form of a newspaper story & had them printed at the Panta[graph] — will send you one. — about 40 for dinner (56 asked!) and about 80 asked afterwards. Had lunch with Mrs. [illegible] today — there are opportunities in Wash[ington] for the younger men of independent means etc etc. But I don't believe I'll press for anything now — unless it is offered & they never are! There will be plenty of opportunities & with things as uncertain here I think it would be best to stand by for the present.

Please send me Buff's recent letters after you have digested them. We enjoyed the letter from Patterson [71] — also the prayer —

Love
AD

Big Boy is incredible — he gets better every day — always smiling & gay and vigorous. He & little Squeak [Borden] are devoted — the baby laughs whenever he comes near. You haven't told me how the new nurse is working out.

To Mrs. Lewis G. Stevenson

February 9, 1933

Dear Maw —

Enclosed are the latest from Buff. I have wired her at the dock to telephone us when she arrives which should be today sometime. — I can't get the exact time from the Company yet.[72] It has been 20° below for 2 days & the road impassable so John hasn't been able to start.[73] It is much warmer today & the motor club says you can get thru to Indianapolis — so he will start at dawn tomorrow (Saturday) & should reach Wash[ington], unless weather & roads are bad, Sunday night. You will note in Buff's letter she plans to go to Mayflower [Hotel] so I am changing my directions to John — unless our telephone conversation brings forth another plan.

We are planning to stay with the Douglas' [74] over the inauguration &

[71] Jefferson Patterson, Foreign Service officer, who had served in Turkey with Mr. Ives.

[72] Mr. Ives had just been assigned to the Department of State, Washington, D.C.

[73] John Duff was to drive to Washington to meet Mr. and Mrs. Ives and drive them to Florida.

[74] Mr. and Mrs. James H. Douglas, Jr.

will probably come South for a week after. I have written J. Ham [75] for seats to the V-P. inauguration as you so wisely suggested. Grace D[ouglas]. says she will get us seats for the pres. inauguration, ball etc. Buff & E[rnest]. can doubtless fix themselves up when they are down there. Very busy at office —

Love

AD

Confusion and despair were the keynotes of the closing weeks of the Hoover Administration. Unemployment reached well over twelve million, farm prices continued to decline, and the nation's banking system was collapsing. By March 4, 1933, thirty-eight states had ordered their banks closed and in the remainder the banks operated under restrictions. At 4 A.M. of inauguration day, Governor Herbert Lehman of New York and Governor Henry Horner of Illinois, upon urgent entreaties from Washington, closed the banks in their states.

"This is a day of national consecration," the new President told a hundred thousand somber spectators. "This is preeminently the time to speak the truth, the whole truth, frankly and boldly," Franklin D. Roosevelt continued. "Nor need we shrink from honestly facing conditions in our country today. This great Nation will endure as it has endured, will revive and will prosper. So, first of all, let me assert my firm belief that the only thing we have to fear is fear itself — nameless, unreasoning, unjustified terror which paralyzes needed efforts to convert retreat into advance."

He was prepared, he told the audience, "to recommend the measures that a stricken Nation in the midst of a stricken world may require." As he concluded his speech, he said: "We face the arduous days that lie before us in the warm courage of national unity; with the clear consciousness of seeking old and precious moral values; with the clean satisfaction that comes from the stern performance of duty by old and young alike. . . . We do not distrust the future of essential democracy." "The people of the United States have not failed." They ask for "direct, vigorous leadership," for "discipline and direction under leadership. They have made me the present instrument of their wishes. In the spirit of the gift I take it."

Since Adlai E. Stevenson had an ear infection, he did not attend the inaugural ceremony. Instead, he, like millions of Americans, listened to the speech over the radio.

There was excitement in the air. Young men were flocking to Washington to work for an administration that promised a New Deal for the

[75] Senator J. Hamilton Lewis.

American people. The thirty-three-year-old Stevenson called on his father's old friend Harold L. Ickes, Roosevelt's new Secretary of the Interior, and suggested that he might like to be part of the New Deal.

To Mrs. Lewis G. Stevenson

April 4, 1933

Dear Maw —

Her[e] I am back in the traces and already feeling as tho I had never been away — except in the matter of vitality. We had a nice trip home & I stopped at Dr. Franks Sat. morning on the way up from the station. He blew air thru my ears & said they looked fine — will blow them out a few more times & then I'll be discharged. We had a nice dinner with the Douglas' & I had a very pleasant interview with Mr. [Harold] Ickes who seemed much interested in my vague suggestion that I might be interested in government employment!

The first quarter earnings make it apparent that we will have to cut our dividend at least 25% commencing with May — Dave [Merwin] wants to make the cut this month.[76] Please keep this [in] mind & plan to adjust your expenditures accordingly. We may & probably will have to make further reductions later.

I have sent the c[hec]k. for $100 to the Peoples bank as I think you will probably need it. Please sign the enclosed return where indicated (H D S) and return in the enclosed envelope. I am paying the balance due on the tax of $271.55 & also the first installment of your Bloomington taxes of 159.14. At your convenience you can reimburse me.

Hasty love!

AD.

To Mrs. Lewis G. Stevenson

April 6, 1933

Dear Maw —

I enjoyed your letter and the sage advice . . .

The routine of life here quickly dispels holiday memories & by this time I hardly feel I've been away — except for the children who surprise me every night. I wish I could tell you about big boy [Adlai III] — but of course it would take a book & one has to be with him a long while to get the whole picture. If laughter is a tonic I'm perpetually tight —

[76] Davis Merwin had written on March 18, 1933, that wages and dividends would have to be cut in view of declining revenue from advertising in the *Daily Pantagraph.*

[238]

he's the funniest one man show in the world. He has now taken to throwing imaginary snow balls at his mother which he makes under the table. If you ask him to do anything uncongenial, correct him etc he takes on an injured, pained expression & says "Addie got a cold"! Squeak [Borden] has become very large & handsome, says Da Da & laughs out loud at his brother all the time.

I am advised that yesterday the nominating committee of the Chicago Council on Foreign Relations nominated me for President. I am presiding this Sat. but won't be elected Pres. until the annual meeting in May.

Davis [Merwin] reports that the cut has been accepted as well as can be expected. Our first quarter will show very small earnings and dividends are really being paid out of surplus — of which we have some fortunately. But of course we can't go on that way & will have to make a cut of 25% commencing with the May payment.

Had a most pleasant time in D.C. Saw Mr. & Mrs. Rainey, Gillespie, Doc Matthews, Patterson, Ickes, Monk Dunn (who happened to be in town, saw in the paper we were there & looked us up) Ben Thoron and went to the Douglas' for dinner.[77] I missed Ham Lewis who was in committee hearings all the while and [Congressman] Martin Brennan but left cards on them.

We have found our home! An old brick farm house, barn etc on 13 acres just 4 miles from L.F. [Lake Forest] station on the highest spot in Lake County with a lovely view in all directions — price about $15,000.[78] Anxious to have you see it. Do try to get stronger & quieter & we'll have some fun. Mrs. Rainey said she had some things to say to you but didn't get a chance! I can't believe it because she's the greatest long distance talker I've ever seen. Frank blew out my ears yesterday & says in one more treatment I'll be dismissed. Am anxious to hear the news from Ernest [Ives] — but I suppose there has been none. I wrote him from Washington that I thought, as did Pat [Jefferson Patterson] & [H. Freeman] Matthews, that he would hear nothing until he reported on Ap[ril] 15 & then only if he got a clearance from the doctor.[79] In that case he will be appointed Consel Gen. somewhere.

Love
AD.

---

[77] Henry T. Rainey, congressman from Illinois and Speaker of the House of Representatives; Congressman Frank Gillespie from Bloomington; H. Freeman (Doc) Matthews, a Princeton friend, now in the State Department; Jefferson Patterson; Monk Dunn, a Princeton friend; Benjamin W. Thoron, an old Washington friend of the Stevensons.

[78] They finally did not buy it.

[79] Mr. Ives had contracted malaria in Pretoria, Union of South Africa, his most recent post.

To Mrs. Lewis G. Stevenson [80]

Dear Maw —

The news from Buff & E[rnest]. is great. I am so glad they will have a good touch of [Washington] D.C. & I would have B. there as much of the time as possible. She can come out to Bloom[ington]. later & will help E. there by making acquaintances etc. I don't know what to think about Algiers — Ellen & I were there a couple of days & thought it a lovely interesting city but it must be hot in the summer. Of course its a perfect winter climate — a great resort for English people — & you're just a days motor trip from the desert & real warmth in winter. But from a career standpoint it doesn't sound as important as Lima.

All well — Love

AD.

In July, 1933, Adlai E. Stevenson became a special attorney and assistant to Jerome Frank, general counsel of the Agricultural Adjustment Administration in Washington.

George Peek, who had worked closely with Lewis G. Stevenson on farm problems in the 1920's, was the head of the AAA under Secretary of Agriculture Henry A. Wallace. Wayne Chatfield-Taylor of Chicago, who was working with Peek, mentioned Stevenson's name to Peek. "Why, that is Louie Stevenson's boy — and he ought to be well backgrounded in farm problems, all right. Let's get him if we can." [81]

Edward D. McDougal, Jr., who was in the firm of Cutting, Moore and Sidley at the same time as Stevenson, prepared a skit describing what occurred when Adlai asked senior partner William P. Sidley for a leave of absence.[82]

---

[80] This postcard is postmarked April, 1933, but the day is canceled out.

[81] Davis, *A Prophet in His Own Country*, pp. 192–193.

[82] Adlai E. Stevenson was honored at the Third Annual Eleanor Roosevelt Memorial Award Dinner, April 12, 1965. Mrs. Danny Kaye produced a show based on the television program *This Is Your Life*. A number of people took part, all of whom were concealed behind a curtain and who first spoke without appearing on the stage. Adlai was asked by the master of ceremonies, Steve Allen, to identify the voices. Mr. McDougal prepared the skit, of which this is the first portion, about Stevenson's requests in 1933, 1941, and 1947 for leaves of absence from the law firm. Steve Allen took the part of Adlai and McDougal the part of Mr. Sidley. "I must confess that a great deal of the material in my skit is apocryphal," Mr. McDougal wrote, "but the interviews actually took place and the attitude of the head of the firm was about as outlined." Letter to Walter Johnson, November 15, 1967.

Adlai, do you remember . . . . ?

Time: 1933
Place: Chicago. Offices of a leading law firm. In the sanctum sanctorum, the head of the firm sits at his desk. Enter a law clerk in the bloom of youth, on the run, pursuant to appointment.

HEAD OF THE FIRM: "Good morning, Adlai."

ADLAI: "Good morning, sir. I greatly appreciate your taking time to consider my problem. I respectfully request a leave of absence. Mr. George Peek, head of the Agricultural Adjustment Administration, has asked me to go to Washington as its special counsel. I will gain valuable experience which, on my return, will enable me to represent with greater competence the firm's distinguished clients who pursue farming.

HEAD OF THE FIRM: "My boy, a rolling stone gathers no moss. You have been with us only six years. You are still on trial. You appear to have some difficulty as yet in distinguishing a tort from a trust. Your court pleadings verge on the overextended. Take those bills of complaint in the replevin suits for Electrical Research Products and Timken Oil Burner. They were as interminable as Gibbon's *Decline and Fall*. And another thing: John Harmon of the telephone company reports that in the last coinbox robbery case your cross examination of the defense was positively philosophical. Let me remind you that the object in those cases is to convict, not to lead the accused into admitting that virtue is its own reward. My point is, to qualify for partnership requires a long apprenticeship, unremitting application and unswerving purpose. You run a serious risk in breaking the continuity of your service. There can be no assurance of an opening here on your return."

ADLAI: "Thank you sir. Your remarks are to the point, but I feel I must go."

Part Eight

The New Deal
1933–1934

*F*ollowing his inaugural address, President Roosevelt called Congress into special session and proclaimed a bank holiday. On March 9 he sent an emergency banking bill to Congress. It was adopted that day. On March 10, the President asked Congress to reduce government expenses and cut veterans' benefits. This was passed five days later. On March 13, the President asked Congress to modify the Volstead Act to legalize the sale of beer and light wines. It passed this bill three days later.

By March 19, Anne O'Hare McCormick wrote in the New York Times: "The yearning of America is for action, almost any kind of action. Roosevelt makes a flying start by satisfying that long-balked appetite. . . . Two weeks of Roosevelt have changed the atmosphere of the capital, have raised the morale of the country. . . . No President in so short a time has inspired so much hope."

On March 16 Roosevelt sent to Congress the Agricultural Adjustment Act to increase farm prices and pay benefits to farmers in exchange for reduction of acreage. Next the President asked Congress to create the Civilian Conservation Corps and authorize federal grants to the states for direct relief to the unemployed. On March 29, he asked Congress to establish federal supervision of the stock market. On April 10, Roosevelt asked Congress to create the Tennessee Valley Authority. Three days later he asked Congress for legislation to save small homeowners from mortgage foreclosures. On April 20, the President took the nation off the gold standard. On May 17, he asked Congress to pass the National Industrial Recovery Act designed "to obtain wide re-employment, to shorten the working week and to prevent unfair competition and disastrous overproduction."

When Congress passed the NIRA on June 16, the first hundred days of the New Deal were over. Rallying public support to a degree unique in American history, Roosevelt had launched an experimental program designed to achieve a more democratic economic and social system. Hope and triumph had replaced the cynicism and despair of 1932.

[245]

"The air was yeasty and rarefied," George W. Ball, who first met Adlai E. Stevenson in 1933 Washington, recalled. "It seemed to offer little resistance to forward motion, and we were, all of us — to a greater or lesser extent — guided by two operational principles. We were convinced that our predecessors had made a mess of it and that nothing done up to that point in history was much good. And we had the satisfying feeling that there was nothing we could not do." [1]

The Agricultural Adjustment Administration, when Adlai E. Stevenson joined it in July, 1933, was sharply divided over policy. George Peek and his supporters wanted to raise farm prices and nothing else. He favored letting the farmers grow all that they wanted and have marketing agreements to control the flow of farm goods into the home market. In addition, he wanted a government-supervised export program to sell surplus farm products abroad at any price.

Secretary of Agriculture Henry A. Wallace, Assistant Secretary Rexford G. Tugwell, and others disagreed. Dumping the surplus overseas was not realistic. They insisted that production had to be reduced. Moreover, Tugwell, Jerome Frank, the general counsel of the AAA, and others wanted not only to improve farm income but advocated reorganizing the system of agricultural production and distribution and pushing through reforms to relieve the poverty of sharecroppers, tenant farmers, and farm laborers. They also favored control over packers, millers, and big milk distributors to make sure that increased farm prices came out of middlemen and not the consumers. The differences between these positions and the clash of personalities led President Roosevelt to remove Peek from the AAA on December 11, 1933, and make him a special adviser on foreign trade.[2]

The handwritten letters that Stevenson wrote to his wife and mother are in the Elizabeth Stevenson Ives collection, the Illinois State Historical Library. Carbon copies of all other letters are in the Adlai E. Stevenson collection, Princeton University Library. They will be designated as in A.E.S., P.U.L. Not many personal letters from this period were saved. We have used all that we could locate. Stevenson's idiosyncrasies of style and spelling have been retained as written.

After Stevenson returned to Chicago in October, 1934, he delivered a speech on his Washington experiences. This speech is the last item in this part of Volume One.

[1] "With AES in War and Politics," in As We Knew Adlai: The Stevenson Story by Twenty-two Friends, edited and with preface by Edward P. Doyle, foreword by Adlai E. Stevenson III (New York: Harper & Row, 1966), p. 138.

[2] Gilbert Fite, George N. Peek and the Fight for Farm Parity (Norman: University of Oklahoma Press, 1954), pp. 251–262. See also Bernard Sternsher, Rexford Tugwell and the New Deal (New Brunswick: Rutgers University Press, 1964).

To James Hamilton Lewis [3]

July 17, 1933

Dear Senator Lewis:

When in Washington two weeks ago I made an effort to reach you, but was unsuccessful. I wanted to discuss with you an appointment which had been offered to me in the legal department of the Agricultural Adjustment Administration. It seemed to be a promising opportunity to get some experience with this new administrative law which should prove useful after my return to private practice.

At that time I was told by Mr. [George] Peek that political sponsorship was unnecessary. Upon my arrival today, however, I am advised that proper letters must be procured before the appointment can be confirmed.

Accordingly, I will appreciate it very much if you will send a letter to me at Room 504–A, Department of Agriculture, addressed to Jerome N. Frank, General Counsel, Agricultural Adjustment Administration, recommending my appointment to the Legal Division of the Agricultural Adjustment Administration.

I called at your office today and was disappointed to miss you. I hope it will not be long before I have an opportunity to make a personal report on my activities.

With kindest regards to you and Mrs. Lewis and many thanks for your courtesy, I am,

Cordially yours,

To Henry Horner [4]

July 17, 1933

Dear Governor:

I have just arrived in Washington to assist the General Counsel to the Agricultural Adjustment Administration. At the time I agreed to undertake this work a few weeks ago Mr. [George] Peek, the administrator, informed me that political sponsorship was unnecessary. On my arrival today I am advised, however, that due to some patronage difficulties, formal letters recommending appointment in this Department are now necessary for confirmation.

Accordingly, I will appreciate it very much if you will send a letter to

[3] This letter is in the Adlai E. Stevenson collection, Princeton University Library (A.E.S., P.U.L.).
[4] This letter is in A.E.S., P.U.L.

[247]

me at Room 504–A, Department of Agriculture, Washington, D.C., addressed to Jerome N. Frank, General Counsel, Agricultural Adjustment Administration, recommending my appointment to the legal division of the Agricultural Adjustment Administration.

I concluded to do this work for a while with the thought that the experience might prove useful when I returned to private practice in Chicago. I am sorry to bother you with this troublesome detail, but I suppose such things are necessary in the Federal Service.

With kindest regards and many thanks for your courtesy, I am,

Cordially yours,

Mrs. Stevenson and the two boys remained in the Lake Forest house that Adlai and Ellen had rented before they knew he was to go to Washington. When Adlai arrived in Washington in July, he stayed with Ernest L. Ives and John Kennedy — husband of Stevenson's old friend Ellen Bruce Lee — in the Kennedy home at 2121 Bancroft Place. Mrs. Ives and son Tim were at Charlevoix, Michigan, with Helen Stevenson.

To Ellen Stevenson

Wednesday P.M. [late July, 1933]

Lambkin!

Think of it — I left the office at 7 P.M. — I think that's the earliest yet and I feel now as tho I had only done a half days work! Imagine my surprise this morning to find that John S. Miller of Chicago had arrived to do a month's work in our legal dept. He's a partner of Orville Taylor & Frank Busch & should be a pleasant if temporary addition — God knows we need additions as the volume of work is mounting steadily & we can't handle it properly as it is. Tho we don't actually have any titles — we're all assistants to the General Councel we do have formal titles on the Government book and mine is Special Attorney, Agricultural Adjustment Administration. Yesterday I received notice of my formal confirmation, took the oath of office etc. Imagine my surprise and delight to find my salary listed on the appointment as $6500. Tho my pay for the first two weeks is waiting for me at the disbursement office I actually haven't had time to call for it. I suppose there will be 15% deducted under the economy act — which would leave about $5600 net. I have nothing to do with [Donald] Richberg — he is Gen. Counsel in the Industrial Recovery Administration [NRA]. Our Gen. Counsel is a Jew named Jerome N. Frank [5] — who is as smart and able as he can be.

[5] Jerome N. Frank had been a successful corporation lawyer in Chicago in the 1920's. In 1930 he moved to an even more successful practice in New York. He be-

There is a little feeling that the Jews are getting too prominent — as you know many of them are autocratic and the effect on the public — the industries that crowd our rooms all day — is bad. Don't mention this to anyone — I've noticed it from the start and my cell mate Mr. Woodward,[6] an older man a very able rate lawyer, agrees with me. Frank has none of the racial characteristics and has done a dreadfully difficult job as well as could be hoped for — he's indefatigable & literally works most all night every night but he's brought several other Jews down who, tho individually smart and able, are more racial. Woodward tells me that Frank was handed to Peek without the latter's having anything to say about it & there's been some friction since the start. Apparently Felix Frankfurter [7] who has the Pres. confidence persuaded him to appoint Frank at the same time he appointed Peek and even then Frank's confirmation was held up two months! This is all confidential & I'd treat it with discretion because stories of disharmony are popular & grow with great rapidity.

The work is complicated but interesting and vastly important — in essence we're really creating gigantic trusts in all the food industries to raise prices and eliminate unfair competition thereby increasing returns to the farmers ultimately. Every one from flour millers to mayonnaise manufacturers are here and each day I hear all about the troubles of a different industry in the conferences and spend the night drafting a re-marketing agreement to correct them. Then the objections begin to flow in from all over the country. Finally we hold public hearings and at last the Sec'y of Ag. signs & approves the agreement etc. etc. The procedure is complicated — too complicated and I would like to tell you all about it but it would take forever. Furthermore it is changed almost daily! If anything my complaint would be that there is too much drafting done by the legal division and too little administering but I hope that situation

---

came general counsel of the AAA at the age of forty-four. He searched the law schools and leading law firms to build up his staff. Among others he hired Thurman Arnold and Abe Fortas from the Yale Law School and Alger Hiss, Lee Pressman, John Abt, and Nathan Witt, graduates of the Harvard Law School. Arthur M. Schlesinger, Jr., wrote: "He provided exciting leadership, fascinating his aides with his speed and lucidity, shaming them with his memory, resourcefulness, and limitless energy. The young men, dazzled by his example, worked twenty hours a day, slept on couches in their offices and hastily briefed themselves on the agricultural life." *The Coming of the New Deal* (Boston: Houghton Mifflin, 1959), pp. 50–51. Schlesinger adds that the old agricultural specialists resented these strange urban types. "There were too many Ivy League men, too many intellectuals, too many radicals, too many Jews."

[6] Thomas Woodward shared an office with Stevenson. He was a Princeton graduate, too, but older than Adlai. Mr. Woodward has recalled that in 1933 Stevenson was well read in the English classics and the King James version of the Bible. Mr. Woodward was impressed with Stevenson's ability offhand to quote phrases and sentences from his previous reading. Interview with Walter Johnson, April 11, 1967.

[7] Professor of Law at Harvard University.

will be corrected when we get a better background of experience. Later I may have to go out into the "field" to conduct public hearings.[8]

To Mrs. Lewis G. Stevenson

[August, 1933]

Dear Maw —

I hope Ellen has forwarded my letters to her as I have had little time to write. I enclose dividend c[hec]k for your A T & T — you should sign and send to the Co. the enclosed change of address.

I should like to tell you all about everything but I haven't time now — suffice it to say that affairs of state manage to keep me & everyone else busy all day & most of the night. Thus far my efforts have been confined to the Calif. fruit trade but I don't know what it will be next week. I hope to be able to get into the packers problems. It is very interesting and important work but very exacting — because everything is an emergency.

I have enjoyed your letters so much — continue to write me at 2121 Bancroft Place — I will stay there until E. [Ernest Ives] goes & maybe afterward. Some people in the R.F.C. [Reconstruction Finance Corporation] — one of whom was in law school have asked me to come in with them and I may do so — a letter from [Francis T. P.] Plimpton today recommends it. He was staying with them until he left. Three of them have a large & elegant house and want a fourth.

I havent seen anyone or made a telephone call — I ran into Mrs. Bass [from Bloomington] at the hotel & she asked me for lunch tomorrow. I hope to be able to go. And now back to the fruit business!

Love,

AD.

P.S. Will you please be sure to send Robert Richardson [9] a wedding present from me or us — a nice one.

Friday — Children's hour

To Mrs. Lewis G. Stevenson

Tuesday night [10]

Dear Maw —

Enclosed find signature card for your brokerage account which you

---

[8] The remainder of the letter was not saved.

[9] A cousin.

[10] This letter is undated. Since Ellen and the two boys came to Washington in September, 1933, it could have been written in August or early in September.

should sign in both places indicated by a check & mail . . . in the enclosed envelope. Also find enclosed statement for Sept. premium on the Fidelity Insurance and receipts for Aug. & July payments.

I had a glorious rest & romp with the bairn [Adlai III] & have come back to my tasks much refreshed and [in] body & mind — and with a good wholesome sunburn. Perhaps it would be well for you to go up to see the kids etc before Ellen is in the last minute throes of closing the house.[11] You could have Geo. to help & to drive the car down, leaving the day before she does. I wrote Mrs. Warner's agent a letter asking her to reduce our rent to $100 per month. Ellen may be able to rent the house furnished for 75 — but I'm afraid its unlikely. Had lunch with Wayne [Chatfield-Taylor] and [George] Peek[']s two personal attys today — they want me to take up some new work — reviewing the agreements before signature by Peek. I will probably do it — tho the plans are all very tentative now. Of course it is very responsible work & would be hard & interesting — but I would have little personal contact with the industries any longer — tho more contact with the Administrator etc.[12]

Sent Buff a wire [13] & Ellen sent a lot of assorted magazines which make a nice host present. Hope you got to Bloom[ington] O.K. & are taking it easy now against the next big reunion!

Love
Ad.

To Mrs. Lewis G. Stevenson

Tuesday Night [September, 1933]

Dear Maw —

I'm afraid I've neglected you again — but there just doesn't seem to be time to do half the things. Ellen & the babes arrive tomorrow morning & am I happy! The servants arrived safe & sound in the car Sat. evening — Annie was there to meet them & I went to Baltimore to spend the week end, and had a very good one by the way with riding, golf & old friends.

---

[11] His mother was now in Bloomington.

[12] When George Peek read a story in the Chicago *Herald-Examiner*, March 18, 1935, that Adlai E. Stevenson might run for political office, he wrote to prominent Chicago Democrat Walter J. Cummings of the Continental Illinois National Bank and Trust Company, on March 20, 1935: "Adlai Stevenson was on the legal staff of the AAA when I was trying to administer that Act, and was one of the few outstanding loyal members of that staff. I have the highest regard for him in every way. . . . The party or anyone else, in fact, will be fortunate if they can annex him." Letter in A.E.S., P.U.L.

[13] Mrs. Ives had left to join her husband, who had recently been appointed consul general in Algiers.

I unpacked my trunk and put all my things away last night. Everything is in order & the servants have finished the cleaning which, of course, had not been properly done. The house is really too large & we may rattle a bit — tho I guess it will fill up a little when the gang arrives.

This letter from the bank was sent to me to forward to you. Buffs total income for 3 years will be about 12000 — perhaps a little more — but of course the curve has been a declining one & her income for this year will be less than 4000. I am also enclosing two oil checks. I found a black silk tuxedo vest at 2121 [Bancroft Place] which I think must be Ernest's & will send it if Buff mentions it when you hear from her. Work continues feverish at the AAA & the farmers continue to cry help! help! & so do we! I hope Buff's first reactions to Algiers are better than they were in S.A. [South Africa]. How are you getting along with your tonsils and when will the ordeal be over? When you come down we'll take some nice motor trips down to Va & see all the ancestral spots. Keep me posted on the Bloom[ington] news — if any.

Aunt Letitia writes that Adlai H. is engaged & I have written him. Enclosed is a letter from Aunt Julia [14] which I am answering tonight. Was so glad to hear your long lost silver was also found — at least thats some consolation. I have had no report from the woman who took over the management of that house (Frank Jones) we looked at which the note holders bought in foreclosure. She should make periodical reports to the other owners & when you see Fred Capen [15] you might ask him to suggest it to her. I'm not concerned as there can't have been any net income by this time.

Love

AD

The Eighteenth Amendment was repealed in 1933 and the Federal Alcohol Control Administration was created to help reestablish the alcohol industry and regulate its activities. The FACA was a subsidiary agency of the AAA. Adlai E. Stevenson was asked to go into the legal division. In January, 1934, he became chief attorney in the new agency with a salary of $7,500. He wrote codes for pricing and regulations for distribution of alcoholic beverages.

[14] Aunt Julia was Mrs. Martin D. Hardin and Aunt Letitia Miss Letitia Stevenson, sisters of Lewis Green Stevenson; Adlai H. was Adlai S. Hardin, Aunt Julia's son.
[15] An old family friend in Bloomington.

To Mrs. Lewis G. Stevenson

[January, 1934]

Dear Maw —

I've been in a frenzy for days trying to get rid of my old job and get into my new one. I think the worst is over and that I'll now be able to get to work at:

FACA
Transportation Bldg.
Wash D C
(new address)

In a way I hated to leave the AAA — had made many good friends there — but this new work looks promising & if it doesn't please me I can leave any time on a week's notice. I wish I could take time to write you a really good letter — but the days just aren't long enough. Tonight we're going to Capt. Smith's [16] for a party for Mrs. Eckels married daughter & her husband! I don't know why Ellen accepted but I'll retreat very soon after dinner. Ellen will probably go to Yorktown for the week end with the Taylors [17] & I'll go if I can get off in time. Had a jolly evening with Mr. & Mrs. [George] Peek. Glad to hear your buddy Mrs. Allison [18] has turned up — don't overdo, remember the boys will be rougher than ever when you get back.

Love
AD.

To Mrs. Lewis G. Stevenson [19]

Dear Madam —

The Chief Attorney of the FACA presents his compliments & advises you that he has a hell of a job! Ten or 12 hours a day will just about handle the mail — with 5 assistants — without giving me any time for the important work. But its a lot of fun & a lot of "experience." We are going to N.Y. Friday night. [Francis] Plimpton is putting on a stag party of all my old law school friends Sat. night & the wives will foregather for Ellen. We will stay with B. [Norman P.] Davis & it sounds like a pleasant respite. Had a very nice letter from Chester

[16] Horace Smith, a White House aide.
[17] Mr. and Mrs. Wayne Chatfield-Taylor.
[18] A friend from Charlevoix.
[19] This postcard is postmarked February 13, 1934.

Davis [20] which I will send you — also nice letters from the Bloomington people who were here — also a letter from Buff to Ellen full of good sage advice. Adlai Hardin is being married on the 22nd & asked us to come up, but we won't be able to do. We will send him a present — from us & perhaps you should send one too? Feeling fine — [illegible] clean & nose clear!

Love
AD.

To Mrs. Lewis G. Stevenson [21]

Dear Maw —

Its hot & I have a sunburn! You would love it & I tremble with fore-boding for the future. I think you better spread your sails & move north, you've been there in the tropics long enough & the cherries will be in blossom in a day or so. We had tea at the Hennings Sunday — yester-day — with Daisy & Frances Pillsbury! — just back from Fla. & bound for home.[22] They'll come to us Wed. for tea — but of course I won't be there. Working like h—— See what your cards did for me!

Love
AD.

To Mrs. Lewis G. Stevenson

Tues. A.M. [23]

Dear Maw —

Another beautiful warm spring day — both bears [the two boys] & the pup and Nanny come down to work with me in the car. Thats the perfect way to start a day — a ten hour day!

I think Buff is quite right about long separations from Ernest & with her happiness as your ultimate goal I think you better realize that and do your level best to making them both happy with you.

I wonder whats happened to B [Mrs. Ives]'s Christian Science — she never seems to mention it any more & in Africa he[r] letters were full of it. I never suspected that it was a very deep & abiding faith — but I guess it won't hurt her to have passed thru it!

Love
AD

---

[20] Successor to George Peek as Administrator of the AAA.

[21] This postcard is postmarked April 2, 1934.

[22] His mother had spent the winter in Florida. Arthur Sears Henning, Chicago *Tribune* correspondent in Washington, was an old friend of Lewis G. Stevenson. The Pillsburys were a Bloomington family.

[23] This letter is postmarked April 3, 1934.

On April 7, Davis Merwin wrote Stevenson that the joint federal-local project to complete the Bloomington airport was endangered for lack of funds. Stevenson and Martin Brennan, congressman at large from Illinois, immediately called on Harry Hopkins, Administrator of the Federal Emergency Relief Administration and the Civil Works Administration. Merwin also described in this letter the increase in advertising revenue in the Daily Pantagraph, *continued interest in the "Family Circle" feature stories, and plans for a group insurance program for* Pantagraph *employees.*

To Davis Merwin [24]

April 12, 1934

Dear Dave:

Martin Brennan and I had a very satisfactory conference with Harry Hopkins this morning and I was very happy to be equipped with your letter as it furnished us the only factual information we had. In our presence he telephoned Major Lord of the F. E. R. A. [Federal Emergency Relief Administration] in Chicago and the conversation sounded very promising. I suspect you will receive assurances in the early future that the project will be completed. Hopkins suggested that the smart ones knew not later than February 28th that C. W. A. [Civil Works Administration] would be demobilized and that no materials could be bought after April 1st. Accordingly, he suggested that the matter had been mismanaged there for failure to exhaust all the material allocation before April 1st.

The lineage gain for the year to date is very encouraging and I would like to see the audit for 1933 at your convenience. I read with great interest the "Family Circle" and it seems evident that the employee interest in the contest is still very keen. When it begins to wane definitely, I would terminate the contest without delay so as to avoid satiation and prejudice to future competitions of this kind.

The group insurance plan interested me very much and I am heartily in favor of something of this kind though I believe it may be some little time before it becomes compulsory by legislation. If the employees disclose a very preponderant approval, I would go ahead with the Sun Life Company contract. Do I understand that the minimum retirement annuity at twenty-five dollars monthly is payable for life, regardless of length of service or salary received. If after retirement age an employee continues on the payroll, is his salary included in the payroll on which the premium payable by the Pantagraph is based. Perhaps this would

[24] This letter is in A.E.S., P.U.L.

make very little difference but it seems not unlikely that there will be a number of those cases. I take it that in the event of an employee's death before retirement, the Pantagraph's contributions are not returned, though I find it hard to distinguish this situation from resignation or discharge before retirement.

Yours,

On April 23, 1934, Congressman Frank Gillespie of Bloomington wrote Mrs. Lewis G. Stevenson stating that the Daily Pantagraph *had made a "vicious fight" against him in the primaries, published inaccurate stories, and used fictitious names on letters to the editors. He also mentioned that he and Mrs. Gillespie had recently had tea with Adlai and Ellen. "We are all much impressed with your wonderful son."*

To Frank Gillespie [25]

May 1, 1934

Dear Congressman:

Mother has been ill for several months in the sanitarium and I am acknowledging your letter of April 23rd with regard to the Pantagraph's attitude in the Primaries.

Having, as you know, democratic sympathies which are hard to conceal and with which the community and the office are familiar, my family must of necessity avoid interference with the Pantagraph politically, or its independent character which we have been trying for years to build up would be lost. I regret the misrepresentations to which you refer and that the paper saw fit to oppose you in the Primaries. Correspondents are not always accurate, but, as you know, it is difficult to confirm spot news stories. You are quite mistaken, however, about the use of the Letter Column for fictitious letters.

I am taking the liberty of sending your letter to the office as I think the abuses to which you refer should be brought to their attention.

Faithfully yours,

On May 4, 1934, Davis Merwin wrote Stevenson a two-page letter denying the charges of Congressman Gillespie. Mr. Merwin also wrote that federal funds still had not been issued for completing the airport project and he enclosed a business report on the Daily Pantagraph.

[25] This letter is in A.E.S., P.U.L.

To Davis Merwin [26]

May 16, 1934

Dear Dave:

Thank you for your recent letters. I sent you the Gillespie letter only for your information and had not intended that you go to the trouble to reply so fully. I think it best to leave the matter just where it is.

I note the delay in the airport project. My recollection is that [Harry] Hopkins agreed to the general appropriation but made no specific promises to any irregular appropriations, and I believe he intended to leave this entirely within the discretion of the Chicago office.

My acquaintance with the State Farm Life Company is so meager that I am not in a position to have any thoughts on the subject. If we reject the Sun Life, I can see little justification for taking on a Company as small and young as this one.

The operating statement is encouraging and I will return the audit . . . as soon as I have had a moment to look through it.

Very truly yours,

To Mrs. Lewis G. Stevenson [27]

Dear Maw —

Summer with all its savage fury has come to Wash — & of course I'm having a fine time! So glad to hear you've found the road back — don't wander — and we'll have a big time this summer. Don't worry about Buff — or if you must think about what might have befallen her! The bears [the two boys] are surviving the heat easily & I think Ellen will go north about the 4th of July —

Love
Ad.

To Mrs. Lewis G. Stevenson [28]

Dear Maw —

I have a vacation until Thursday so we are all off tonight on the train for Boston after a couple of days of frenzied work getting ready. I'll have three full cool days there — and the Carpenters [29] won't arrive

---

[26] This letter is in A.E.S., P.U.L.
[27] This postcard is postmarked June 22, 1934.
[28] This postcard is postmarked July 1, 1934.
[29] Mr. and Mrs. John Alden Carpenter, Ellen's mother and stepfather.

[257]

until after I've left — probably the sixth or seventh. I hope to have an opportunity to look the housing situation for you over. We're going out to the Acheson's [30] for lunch in about a minute. All well —

Love

AD

To Mrs. Lewis G. Stevenson

Friday night [early July, 1934]

Dear Maw —

Your two letters which arrived today suggest that the old lady is making good progress in spite of the heat — I hope she isn't fooling me. I had three glorious days in Mass[achusetts] with Ellen & the babes & hosts of servants.[31] The days were hot, the water cold and the nights cool. I can't but believe that, with the exception of occasional foggy days, you would find the climate warm enough & the cool nights invigorating. The house situation seems good — some nice roomy well furnished ones, of course not on the sea, for $300 for the season up. Tim and Buff [Ives] I know would flourish — she would soon find many friends & if Tim takes to the beach the way the bears do he should be in a transport of delight most of the time. At the last minute we took the dog too!

I had dinner last night with Mr. [George] Peek & lunch with him today. I've resisted his blandishments and definitely decided to go back to Chicago now while the goings good & the omens auspicious — tho I feel sure I'll come back here again sometime to do some more government work. Peeks proposition was very tempting but the thing for one to do is not to get diverted but to go back to Chicago & finish what I started — make my place etc. Ellen concurs & its a comfort to get it settled. I notified McPherson & Burgess [32] today & suggested coming

[30] Mr. and Mrs. Dean G. Acheson. Mrs. Acheson had been a summer playmate at Charlevoix, Michigan.

[31] Ellen and the two boys spent the summer at Manchester, Massachusetts.

[32] Kenneth F. Burgess, of Stevenson's old law firm of Cutting, Moore and Sidley, wrote him on July 12, 1934, "As you know, I have greatly feared that if you stayed too long in Washington you might unfit yourself for a more routine existence such as is called for in the practice of law. You have a fine personality, many friends, ability and industry. It seems to me that you can make out of yourself what you will, and that your future lies largely in your own hands. I am glad that you are coming back." Donald F. McPherson wrote on July 10, 1934, "We are all delighted that you have decided to return here. . . . Do not come back with the impression that your work will be confined to routine tax matters. We have no such thought in mind. It will be our desire to have you take full advantage of your recent experiences in administrative law and to do other important work." Both letters are in A.E.S., P.U.L.

[258]

back Oct 1 which will give me a chance to wind up gracefully here & get a good vacation.

Wayne [Chatfield-Taylor] has moved in, Alley [33] comes next week & perhaps a fourth. All is well on the Potomac! And I'm going to spend the week end on it on a yacht Wayne & some other men have chartered. So glad to hear all the good news from Buff. I've sent the amazing bath letter to Ellen — she'll return it to you. I suppose the thing to do is for Buff to go up to Mass from the boat, pick out a house, get settled & then you come along with Alverta [Duff]. If she's bringing a maid you won't need anyone else — unless you bring the car which would probably be a great convenience —

Love
AD.

To Mrs. Lewis G. Stevenson [34]

Dear Maw:

Don't worry any more about my vacation — I'm going to get a good one this summer in Mass[achusetts]. or Canada — or perhaps Mexico. Three more weeks on the tonsils won't get you to Mass. much before Aug. 1. By that time Buff should be well settled & I expect to get there shortly after Aug 1. Had the most heavenly week end. Set off with 3 men at noon on Sat. on their yacht and cruised 140 miles down the river & up Chesapeake bay — jumping overboard for a swim occasionally and doing a lot of fishing with indifferent results. Returned early this A.M. & feel like a million — to find the heat broken!

Love
AD.

To Mrs. Lewis G. Stevenson [35]

Dear Maw —

A couple of days before Buff lands I'll radio her to go right to Boston on arrival & will arrange for Mrs. C's [36] car to meet her & take her to a hotel nearby or to Ellen's house if she has taken one by that time. Buff can then spend a few days canvassing the countryside, select a "villa" & wait for you! Is that a satisfactory program? I doubt if I can take off a day just to meet her unless necessary — plus expense etc. Ellen writes,

[33] James Alley of the Reconstruction Finance Corporation.
[34] This postcard is postmarked July 9, 1934.
[35] This postcard is postmarked July 11, 1934.
[36] Mrs. John Alden Carpenter.

as I suspected, that the children are a little hard on Mr. C's nurse & that she'll have to get a house — I hope befor[e] Buff arrives —

AD

To Mrs. Lewis G. Stevenson and Mrs. Ernest L. Ives

July 30, 1934

Dear Maw & Buff —

Ellen reports that all is well on the Mass[achusetts]. front. And have you noticed the temperatures you escaped? [37] Dave [Merwin] writes that it was 103–8 for 8 consecutive days in Bloomington – and of course Chicago has broken all weather bureau records. That's the beauty of Wash[ington] — you don't expect anything else!

Had a quiet, pleasant week end over at Hackneys [38] farm — drove back early this morning. Friends have given me letters to two people in Hawaii & the Administration instructs me to call on the Governor first etc. My plans are mostly made & I expect to get off Friday afternoon & meet Ellen in Chicago the following morning. We will have 4½ days in San F[rancisco]. — all work for me. But in Hawaii I can't see much more than 2 or 3 full days of work out of the 9 & the prospects for some real vacation are very good. I hope to get back here on Labor day & up there before the 10th for some vigorous loafing with you all. I have had no report from you since I was there & I hope all is well & that the old lady is pushing ahead with conviction.

. . . everything but corn destroyed by drouth on all farms & the bugs are enjoying the corn enormously. But who cares!

Best to Alverta [Duff] —

Aloha!
AD.

Tell Tim [Ives] I'm going to spend the night in the tree house with him.

Enclosed is an old letter from Buff I find in my desk —

To Davis Merwin [39]

July 31, 1934

Dear Dave:

I am leaving Washington Friday for San Francisco to do a last job

[37] Mrs. Ives and her son Tim had returned from abroad and were sharing a summer house with Mrs. Stevenson in Manchester, Massachusetts.
[38] Princeton classmate H. Hamilton Hackney.
[39] This letter is in A.E.S., P.U.L.

for the government. I will be at the St. Francis Hotel for four or five days meeting with various groups of the liquor industries and am sailing on the eleventh for Hawaii to organize the industries out there. I will have a large hearing on the Wine Industry in California on my way back but hope to leave for Washington early in September.

After about a week here cleaning up, I will be at Cooli[d]ge Point, Manchester, Massachusetts until October first when I will resume with Cutting, Moore and Sidley.

Hastily,

To Mrs. Lewis G. Stevenson and Mrs. Ernest L. Ives

Friday P.M. [early August, 1934]

Dear Maw & Buff —

I'm off in a couple of hours after frenzied preparations — last minute conferences etc. I could not find your book of music — but Ellen may have put it away somewhere. I've lots of letters of introduction to people in the islands — and 9 days to do my work in! So I'm sure we'll have most a week of idleness. I'm taking a trunk of clothes back to Chicago with me & will bring it back empty on the return trip for refilling.

I hope everything goes well there and that you will keep a daily eye on the bairn and Dandie [the dog]. In Sept. we'll have a couple of week[s] en famille before Buff goes back! The heat here has abated somewhat and I do hope you haven't suffered up there — or perhaps its been too cool! We will have a full day in Chicago — at the Fair,[40] I hope. I'm going to avoid the office — I'll see enough of that only too soon! We will leave Chicago Sat. night at 9:35 on the Overland Limited — C. & N.W.[41] — and reach San F. Tuesday A.M. Our address there will be the St. Francis Hotel until Sat. — we sail at noon on the S.S. Lurline, Matson line, arriving Honolulu Aug 16. While there I think we will be at the Royal Hawaiian Hotel, but I could be reached c/o Alcohol Tax Unit, Bureau of Internal Revenue, Federal Bldg. We will return on S. S. Malalo sailing Aug 25 & reach San Fran. on the 30th. I may have to stay there a couple of days for some hearings, but hope to get back here shortly after Labor day & up there a few days later.

Relax! Love! Aloha!

AD

[40] The Century of Progress Exposition.
[41] Chicago and North Western Railway.

[261]

To Mrs. Lewis G. Stevenson

Wednesday, August 15, 1934

Dear Maw —

Our voyage ends tomorrow morning after 4½ days of calm sunlit seas and uninterrupted idleness and rest. I should have been a sailor — the sea and its detachment are tonic for the soul. We don't know whats in store for our 9 days in Hawaii but I'm sure its all good [42] — San F. was an awful beating! We hope [you] and the young are all flourishing — as we are. Aloha — as they say in these parts —

A.D.

To Davis Merwin

September 8, 1934

Dear Dave:

I have been back here [Washington] a couple of days laboring under an accumulated mass of work. I have read your letters of September 1st and August 31st and am delighted to note the marked improvement in the quality of the engraving.

I think you were wise to get the Bloomington architects into the picture but I would certainly proceed with the experienced newspaper plant architect.[43]

Without very careful consideration, my present reaction is that we should attempt to finance the project our [out] of the investment account and accumulated funds without borrowing. We can, of course, discuss this more in detail after I get back. Of course you will have to announce the building program sometime but I would hold it until you are ready to start.

I hope to get away from here by the middle of next week. My trip to Hawaii was a pleasant and interesting experience but except for the boat ride, there was no vacation in it. Accordingly, I am anxious to have a rest until I resume at Cutting, Moore and Sidley on October 1st. After next week you can reach me at Cooli[d]ge, Point, Manchester, Massachusetts.

I will plan to come to Bloomington for a week-end with you shortly

[42] The Honolulu *Star-Bulletin*, August 24, 1934, reported that Stevenson organized the wholesale liquor dealers association and the regional board which was to administer the national code for the liquor industry.

[43] Plans were being drawn for a new building for the *Daily Pantagraph*. Mr. Merwin had retained an architect who had designed a number of newspaper plants to work with local Bloomington architects.

after my return. I am anxious to hear about everything in detail and am also curious to know if there have been any developments in your personal plans.

Yours,

To Mrs. Lewis G. Stevenson

Monday night [mid-September, 1934]

Dear Maw —

So happy and reassured with your telegram. I was distressed that I mishandled the departure so badly.[44] I'm sitting in our cozy living room with a big fire, snug & contented — like a fat turnip! Are you? We've had a wonderful rainy day! Tim [Ives] came early & I spent the morning with Dr. Horton; lunch, a long nap & then to Gloucester with Ellen & all 3 boys. I bought a couple of live lobsters & such screaming & shrieking in the back seat as you've never heard. Adlai was afraid at first but before long he was holding one in each hand and waving them at a very frightened Dandy [their dog]! We ended up at 6 with a lobster race on the front porch at your house.

If the weather is fine tomorrow we will have our fishing expedition which I'm sure excites me even more than the boys —

Love — don't press — just unlax!

AD

P.S. If you wish I will forward these checks to the bank in Bloom-[ington]. for deposit hereafter — if they will take them without your endorsement.

66 — its a magic combination & I believe it signifies the start of a new & happy life. Incidentally the figure "66" is used to advertise the *high power* Phillips gasoline!

To Mrs. Lewis G. Stevenson

Sunday A.M. [late September, 1934]

Dear Maw —

Rain again! But we've had several days of warm sunshine. Yesterday we all had lunch with the Carpenters and afterward Big Ellen [Mrs. Carpenter] joined us and we went to see Mrs. Chase's lovely pictures and then out to inspect the magnificent Crane estate at Ipswich — the

[44] Adlai had now joined his wife and two boys for a vacation at Manchester, Massachusetts. His mother, who had spent part of the summer there, had returned to Bloomington.

most magnificent country place I've seen in this country. We had planned to drive in this morning & see them off on the boat but they've just telephoned to say that the boat is delayed by fog & won't sail until this afternoon — in the meanwhile Robert [45] & Alverta [Duff] had already started in your car with the luggage. But I guess they can take care of themselves for a few hours. We are going to Mrs. Kingsley Porters to lunch and then we will go to the boat.

Buffy seems much better and quieter — I had a good long talk with her alone last night and except for her concern about you everything seems to be well. She & E[rnest]. are undoubtedly more harmonious and happy than they have been for a long time and you shouldn't waste any worry on them that will retard the turnip's development! Even their financial condition appears to be sound and in spite of diminished income they seem to be getting along well.

Our young are flourishing — at the moment resisting violently an attempt to put on sweaters — and Ellen & I have found a perfect tennis court on an adjoining estate which has been deserted for the summer. So all is well! And will be better as you are better — so sprout tubers & not violets!

Love
AD.

To Mrs. Lewis G. Stevenson

Sunday night [late September, 1934]

Dear Maw —

What a day! After all our complicated and intricate plans were carefully made around a noon departure for the Ives the ship was delayed by fog and only now have they started for town — 9 P.M.[46] But the getaway was orderly tho somewhat marred with anti climax!

Robert starts early tomorrow and should reach Bloomington Wednesday night. I have told him to spend the balance of the week on the place unless he gets other instructions from you. He has specific directions on the yard, garden, car etc that will take the balance of the week & by that time you can let him know —

Robert Enochs
602 S. Madison St.

Alverta [Duff] is moving over here tomorrow A.M. to stay until we leave next week end. They are taking her into Boston to see the ship

[45] Robert Enochs worked for Adlai's mother.
[46] Mr. and Mrs. Ives and their son Tim sailed from Boston for Algiers where Mr. Ives was consul general.

tonight & she has been in a tizzy of excitement all day. Timmie & the Bears [Adlai III and Borden] spent a last day of raucous play which ended in the construction of a "train" on our front porch consisting of *all* the furniture except the beds. I still have hopes that the walls of this house will be standing when we retreat!

Love
AD.

P.S. As per your directions Robert started west with $45 out of the check you gave Alverta and $15 salary which I gave him today.

P.S.S. Don't be disturbed about your heart or about anything — all is snug and well among the vegetables! And try to discuss "symptoms" as little as possible — just "unlax" & be happy that things are not worse — in fact quite good, indeed *very* good! [47]

To Mrs. Lewis G. Stevenson

Friday [late September, 1934]

Dear Maw —

Our motor trip was a great success and very educational. We stopped at all the historical spots, read signs, wandered thru graveyards and never lost the road! Both days were sunny and warm except for the night which we spent in Provincetown in a warm dripping fog lulled to sleep by the music of far away bell buoys. We had the top down and I came back with a nice coating of sunburn. Yesterday was another clear beautiful day and we had lunch at Myopia with the Langhornes [48] & played tennis with Mr. [John Alden] Carpenter in the afternoon. Today its beautiful & bright again and my faith in the climate is returning — suspiciously!

We will probably leave the middle of next week — Ellen, Big Boy [Adlai III] and I by motor; Lizette, Alverta [Duff] and Squeak [Borden] (and Dandy) by train. We can get back in a leisurely 3 days by motor, taking the boat from Buffalo to Detroit. The other "troops" will leave by train a day later. We will stay at 1020 [49] until we decide about a house. Alverta (who has enjoyed herself here immensely, I think) will, of course, go right to Bloomington. I suspect we'll decide to live in town and take a 3 year lease to get really settled at last. The country in the autumn and spring is very seductive and in many respects I hate

[47] His mother was unwell and mentally depressed. Soon after her son returned to Chicago to resume his law practice, she moved to the Churchill Hotel, a block from where he lived.

[48] Colonel and Mrs. George Langhorne of Chicago, friends of Mr. and Mrs. John Alden Carpenter.

[49] The Lake Shore Drive house of Mr. and Mrs. Carpenter.

to give it up. But in the long run I think the city is probably best — and sometime we may get our farm!

How's it going? I find carefree repose a most pleasurable state and would like to go on for another month.

Best love

AD

After Adlai E. Stevenson had decided to leave government service to resume the practice of law, Arthur Krock, head of the Washington bureau of the New York Times, *wrote him:*

> I heartily congratulate you, although I feel that the government is losing a damned good man. It encourages me about the country whenever any one from another city can give up Washington on his own notion and go back to his own community. As I have frequently said to you, Chicago, in my opinion, is so great a city that to participate actively in its throbbing life is very unlikely to be monotonous and is certain to be constructive in a national sense.
>
> I shall miss you, and, if she will permit me to say so, I shall miss the occasional sight of the lovely Ellen.[50]

In February, 1935, Stevenson delivered a speech to the Legal Club of Chicago recounting his experiences in Washington. One member of the audience wrote him: "The paper which you read before the Legal Club last Monday night was the most enjoyable one which I have listened to during my ten years of membership in that organization." [51]

AGRICULTURE, ALCOHOL AND ADMINISTRATION

I am loath to remind you of the venerable remark — that it is better to keep still and be thought a fool than to speak and remove all doubt; and I suspect the only justification for my present exposed position tonight is that as an ex-New Dealer I am virtually immune to scorn and ridicule, if not minor venality and petty corruption.

From a confusion of suggestions for my subject I have abstracted some comments on Agriculture, Alcohol and Administration generally — for the reason that I went to Washington to solve the farm problem and ended up in alcohol — and in so doing I attended the agonizing nativity of two large, important and I believe enduring administrations.

I approached the Washington scene contemplatively. Visions of a

[50] September 12, 1934. This letter is in A.E.S., P.U.L.
[51] Edward E. Barthell, Jr., February 14, 1935. This letter is in A.E.S., P.U.L.

tranquil and philosophical study of government at close range beguiled me. But my dream cloister was abruptly shattered. I arrived in the middle of July, 1933, and left work my first day at two in the morning of my second day. But I got use[d] to that very soon. The singular prevalance of almost irresponsible working hours among the small as well as the great was a constant source of wonder to me. Perhaps it was due to emotional reaction to the feverish environment and the comparatively astronomical importance of everything. At all events, it is a phenomenon which many have noted.

Those of you who knew Washington in her stately complacency would hardly recognize her now. For madhouses, I am sure the A.A.A. in its early days has had few equals. Although the crop year was far advanced, we were deluged with angry delegations demanding help of some kind, before any adequate administrative machinery had been provided. My first job was a marketing agreement for the fresh California deciduous tree fruit industry. The delegation from California was only a little upset when I asked what "deciduous" meant! That agreement was the second control program put into effect by the A.A.A. and we learned about the intricacies of the economics of perishable commodities, working night and day against the rapidly maturing crop — and highly perishable crops can't wait to go to market. At last, an elaborate agreement was ready, but our rejoicing was interrupted by a wire from California — "a few days of intense heat has decimated the pear crop and no control of shipments will be necessary this year."

I hesitate to tell this learned society about the economic philosophy of the A.A.A. In 1933 we had enormous surpluses of wheat, cotton, tobacco and hog products, which had accumulated as a result of wartime expansion, economic nationalism, strangled foreign trade and reduced domestic consumption. Farm prices had fallen far below costs of production. Merely to avert farm ruin, and incidentally ruin to most of us, it was imperative to eliminate the surpluses. As matters then stood production control seemed to be synonymous with crop reduction. But, the fulminations of certain editors notwithstanding, it was never contemplated that reduction, once started, should be continued indefinitely.

Adjusting production to meet falling demand is nothing new. Manufacturers always check or cease production when they can no longer sell their goods, but agriculture is less flexible. Disused farms suffer more than disused factories. While factory production can be adjusted almost from day to day, planting and live stock breeding are annual matters, and incidents of successful voluntary cooperative control among farmers are rare. When prices fall the inevitable reaction of farmers is to make up their loss by increasing the total units produced and prices decline further, or if a crop shows a profit farmers always over-produce it in the hope of making some money. The principle is simple and is illustrated by an anecdote that G. W. Hill of the American Tobacco Company told at a tobacco hearing about his former patron, James B. Duke, who confessed that the secret of his great wealth was very simple — he always bet against the farmer and never lost. When cotton was high, he planted tobacco and when tobacco was high he planted cotton.

Cooperative planning under Federal guidance can and has in part overcome these difficulties. It provides a mechanism through which farmers can work together for a control of production — can do in part what industry can do for itself. The history of our freely competitive agriculture has been a succession of mass swings creating recurring cycles of over and under production. After the emergency adjustments of the last two seasons, the natural sequel is the continued use of the adjustment principle to shorten the swing and preserve the balance. Because I believed in this principle, I went to Washington (to insure its success) and, though mistakes and false starts are inevitable, I will risk my distinguished reputation as an agronomist that the principle of co-operative adjustment in agriculture will survive legislatively when this emergency is forgotten and the New Deal has joined its predecessors.[52]

But farm economy depends vitally on consumer buying power and that means industrial recovery. To restore fair exchange value to farm products enables farmers to buy industrial goods. Whatever increases purchasing power increases the manufacturers' market. Consumers gain nothing in the long run by getting farm products at less than cost. During the five years since 1929, industry has maintained an average price level of 84% and an average production of 57%, while agriculture's price level has been only 60% and its production level 87%. And keep in mind that this production level includes the year of the worst drought [1934] in our history. In short, the only real "scarcity economics" has been the tendency of industrialists to reduce production, maintain prices and force consumers out of the market. Paradoxically these same interests are now the critics of the farmers' moderate retreat from the peak production of 1929. How well the adjustment program

[52] After the Supreme Court declared the processing tax of the AAA unconstitutional in January, 1936, the Roosevelt Administration got Congress to approve the Soil Conservation and Domestic Allotment Act. This law offered farmers bounties for not planting soil-depleting commercial crops and for planting soil-enriching grasses and legumes including soybeans. In February, 1938, Congress created the second Agricultural Adjustment Administration. The new law established soil conservation as a permanent program, authorized crop loans and crop insurance for wheat, and empowered the Secretary of Agriculture to assign national acreage allotments and subsidies to staple farmers.

has already succeeded is evidenced by the fact that the exchange value of all farm products is now more than 80% of the pre-war level as compared to 55% two years ago this month. And the price raising effects of the N.R.A.[53] have made the farm problem a lot harder. But in the long run the solution of the farm problem must probably be found in the alternatives of a restoration of our foreign markets by reciprocal trade agreements and general tariff reduction, or in withdrawal of millions of acres from cultivation, with attendant severe dislocation of population, or both.

There is a lot more to the A.A.A. than wheat, corn, hogs and cotton. During the six months I was there, I negotiated with producers, processors or handlers of everything from Atlantic oysters to California oranges, and from Oregon apples to Florida strawberries. Walnut and asparagus growers from California, rice millers from Louisiana, lettuce shippers from Arizona, shade grown tobacco handlers from Connecticut, potato merchants from Maine, candy manufacturers from Pennsylvania, chicken hatchers from everywhere, date and grape shippers and olive canners from California, pea canners from Wisconsin, peanut processors from Virginia and the Carolinas; — all these and dozens more came to confess their sins and beg for help. We laughed a little when the wintergreen trust appeared, and more at the pimento magnates who wanted an embargo on Spanish pimentos. The mayonnaise people won an endurance contest with the cotton seed crushers with three continuous months on the doorstep, and the Boston mackeral fishermen arrived in the Potomac in a Gloucester schooner. But the big laugh came the morning a Georgia delegation led by a senator and a couple of congressmen arrived and calmly announced that the Pa[c]kaged Bees Industry was going to hell! . . .

Of course, few of the proposals got beyond the stage of perfunctory consideration — most of them wanted to fix prices or guarantee the cost of production, and none of them at first had anything that resembled an intelligible proposal when they arrived. Law, economics and hotel bills usually wore them out and after one last round of highballs on the bed at the Mayflower [Hotel], they would fade out and make room for the next one. I remember an old farmer from Arkansas. After the baffling third degree on economics and law, he solemnly announced to the meeting that he would be satisfied with railroad fare home. We were spending too much time with these hapless projects, so the inevitable committee was appointed to sift them out. This committee, one lawyer and

[53] The National Recovery Administration brought industry under codes to shorten hours of work, increase wages, and stop price-cutting. In May, 1935, the Supreme Court found the NRA unconstitutional.

one economist, achieved no little fearsome notoriety and was known far and wide as the "delousing division" — their technic was so swift and effective that our visitors, including Congressmen, generally found it possible to catch the afternoon train. One of the members of this committee, Jack Dalton, is now czar of the sugar industry and tells me that this time the louse is bigger than he is!

At first the legal division was only ten or fifteen men — but we had no enforcement problems then and were only academically concerned with constitutionality — I think it has now more than 150. (The pressure was terrific, — hearings, and conferences by day and drafting by night.) The hearings and industry conferences were a liberal education, different types of people with different motives from different parts of the country, the appalling variety of common abuses and of the problems presented by different cultural and marketing methods. Sometimes there were refreshing incidents of candor — I remember once I asked the pontifical elderly president of a large company the purpose of an obscure provision in the proposed code. He said: "I've known every one of these men, my competitors, for years — Individually they are my trusted friends — but as chocolate manufacturers they drink blood, preferably mine! Every one of them has a joker in this code and that section's mine." The counterparts of this confession and the jokers were numerous and I am confident that industry in distress washing its wretched linen in the goldfish bowl before an umpire has been a very wholesome minor byproduct of all this government interference. . . .

In many smaller crops, and there are more than 125 raised commercially in California alone, the economic situation was similar and always dreadful. In a number of instances shipments from remote producing areas to the consuming markets did not return enough to pay the costs and the farmer received a net bill for the excess — in short, the farmer had to pay for the privilege of giving his products away. Because our distribution and marketing system is inflexible, costs fell but little as retail prices declined and most of the burden of reduced consumer buying power was passed back to the farmer. In short, relatively rigid intervening costs prevented reduction of retail prices in line with reduction of farm prices, with the result that the declining prices did not cause a compensating stimulation of consumption. With most commodities which are not materially affected by export demand, it is generally true that within limits the grower's return is in inverse ratio to the quantity marketed. In short, he will get more for 75% of his crop than for all of it, with little increase in consumer price. By diverting low grades, controlling auction markets and by elaborate systems of regulating the total shipments in interstate commerce, there have been seen some surprising results. Marketing agreements were designed to provide orderly marketing of the regulated quantities and the Secretary of Agriculture's report for 1934 states that thirteen of these agreements increased returns to growers for the last season more than thirty million dollars. That money went immediately to pay interest on the mortgage, paint the barn and buy shoes — perhaps it paid judgments and attorneys' fees — so I take some pride in the fact that of those thirteen agreement[s] I wrote ten.

As legislation sometimes repeals the lawyer's wisdom, the dismissals in the A.A.A. last week have repealed some of my speech, and I'll have to talk about Jerome Frank, the former General Counsel, nunc pro tunc.[54] Many of you know him. I have never encountered a more agile, rapacious mind. What with Ezekiel, Tugwell and a dozen less familiar names,[55] the intellectual atmosphere was pretty well conditioned around the A.A.A. and if I didn't have the least idea what they were talking about most of the time, I could always be pretty sure I had considerable company. Incidentally, there seems to be a prevalent misconception about Ezekiel — he wasn't a New Deal importation and has been in the Bureau of Agricultural Economics for ten or twelve years. I have found it hard to describe Jerome Frank. I can't easily characterize him as "radical" — in fact, I don't even know what radical means anymore.[56] But perhaps he was — certainly he was often indiscreet in speech and it wasn't hard to get the impression sometimes that mingled with his fervent interest in recovery was a not inactive interest in reform. He talked about making distribution of milk a public utility, (but there's good conservative support for that,) and he expressed concern over

[54] As cotton acreage was reduced under the AAA, landlords cast sharecroppers off their farms. Alger Hiss, representing the legal division of the AAA, wrote an opinion that declared that every individual tenant farmer had the right to continue in his place during the life of the cotton contract. Jerome Frank persuaded the Acting Administrator of the AAA to issue the directive early in 1935 while Chester Davis, Administrator of the AAA, was on a trip. When Davis returned he demanded that Wallace fire Frank and several others in the legal division for administrative insubordination and for making the AAA too reformist. Early in February, 1935, Frank and several others were fired. President Roosevelt, who admired Frank, appointed him to the Reconstruction Finance Corporation.

[55] Mordecai Ezekiel was the Secretary of Agriculture's economic adviser. He called the AAA "the greatest single experiment in economic planning under capitalist conditions ever attempted by a democracy in times of peace." Schlesinger, *The Coming of the New Deal*, p. 46. Rexford G. Tugwell was Assistant Secretary of Agriculture and an original member of President Roosevelt's Brain Trust.

[56] Arthur M. Schlesinger, Jr., wrote: "Tugwell and Frank and their adherents had two things in common—a city background, which disposed them to think in terms not just of the farmers but of the impact of farm policies on consumers and the entire economy; and a passionate liberalism, which disposed them to think in terms not just of filling the farmer's purse but of reorganizing the system of agricultural production and distribution." *The Coming of the New Deal*, p. 51.

the depression profits of various processors and handlers who some-how neglected to pass much of the reduced farmer's price on to the con-sumer. He precipitated a lot of controversy by insisting on the right of the Secretary to examine the books of parties to marketing agreements to see if they were complying, and somehow business doesn't seem to be exactly eager to disclose its books!

He was always very fair with his men. Once during the controversy in December a year ago, which ended in George Peek's resignation, a letter fell into Jerome's hands from a prominent man in California reporting that I had said in Los Angeles that Peek was giving the radicals just enough rope to hang themselves. Jerome called me in, read the letter and as I got up to catch the first train for Chicago, he laughed heartily and remarked that perhaps the institution of agriculture would survive in spite of his misdeeds and then asked me to take on the legal direction of one of the brain trust's pet projects! Frank was an indefatigable worker and used to schedule appointments from eight in the morning until eleven at night. One night in the early days, when the slaughter of the innocent pigs was under consideration, he fell asleep when we were working together. Awaking suddenly, he announced that "the only way to solve the pig problem was to amend the Hebraic law and let all orthodox Jews eat pork." [57] He liked to illustrate the economies of the farmer by the story of the young Jewish couple that got married so they could cut down living expenses by sharing the same bed, and then had twins!

I cannot begin to tell you about the variety of legal problems (that) we ran into — the obvious constitutional questions — whether the par-ticular license was in fact a regulation of interstate commerce, price fixing and the due process clause, whether the processing taxes are for public purposes and the separation of powers concept — (although invalid delegation of legislative authority did not worry us much in those days). Then there were questions of statutory construction — whether a dairy that furnished a milk warmer to a house where a baby had been born was granting a rebate; whether moss for reindeer food and reindeer meat were agricultural products within the meaning of the act, and, more seriously, whether a license can be issued without a market-ing agreement; whether producers can be paid for increasing produc-tions rather than decreasing, and the meaning of various phrases

[57] Hogs were threatening to flood the market in 1933. The AAA bought six mil-lion pigs. Some pork was processed and distributed by relief agencies. But about 85 per cent of the pigs slaughtered were converted into inedible products. It was the most unpopular action ever undertaken by the AAA.

throughout the statute. The administration of the act raised another host of perplexing questions too long to enumerate.

When you stop to consider that these problems were multiplied by each of the government agencies in Washington, you can begin to appreciate the vast importance of the lawyer in the New Deal. Hence the hordes of young law review editors that are overrunning Washington and variously known as "Anthony Advocates," "Frankfurters" and "Hot Dogs." [58] The A.A.A. legal division attracted some exceptionally able men. Jerome Frank tried desperately to get men from all over the country, but he had to get good men and get them quick. There seemed to be an abundance of available material in New York passionately eager to serve the cause of recovery or reform and I suspect in part unemployed or unsatisfactorily employed. Some of these men were remarkable workmen and fairly spurted economics and liberal wisdom, though I'm sure they couldn't distinguish a cow from a heifer and I don't believe they looked so good to some of the rugged plainsmen from the west. . . .

Of the many men I encountered in Washington, I respect none more than George Peek, who was Administrator of the A.A.A. during most of my service. Mr. Peek talks slowly, directly and uses the simple, homely metaphor of the farmer. His sincere, forthright approach and embarrassing capacity for distinguishing reform from recovery caused some unfortunate misunderstandings. This friction, together with the rapid and disorganized growth of the A.A.A. in time created a situation which required each document for the Secretary's approval to carry initials and memoranda of numberless prima donnas. As the red tape tightened and the process slowed down, the industries became restive and finally an administrative technician was loaned by the Army to untangle the thing. He labored diligently and in about three weeks produced a chart showing the course of a marketing agreement or Code from its inception to the Secretary's approval. I was fortunate enough to see one of the few copies that was ever exposed to the less privileged. It never got in the newspapers. It looked like a chart of the movements of the ball in a football game; after exactly 50 downs (and frequent penalties and losses), if the document was not worn out or lost, it got to the Secretary's desk.

But with the advent of Chester Davis that administrative absurdity was abruptly ended. Mr. Peek brought Chester Davis to Washington as his chief assistant and left behind him, as his successor, perhaps the

[58] Many of these lawyers had studied with Professor Felix Frankfurter of the Harvard Law School.

best qualified and ablest administrator in Washington. Davis has spent all his adult life with the farm problem and has the qualifications rarely found in combination of authentic knowledge in his field, the confidence and respect of farmers and food industries alike, diplomacy and just congenital administrative talent.

And then *I* took on alcohol! A year ago this week I forsook the A.A.A. to become Chief Counsel of F.A.C.A., which you will at once identify as the Federal Alcohol Control Administration. Well, I traded a headache for dementia praecox.

. . . The FACA is Exhibit 1 in the museum of current extra legal activities and getting away with it to most every one's satisfaction. I doubt if a more ominous situation ever developed with the rapidity of repeal.[59] Late in 1933, it abruptly became evident that repeal was im[m]inent and that the gigantic industry was about to throw off its shackles before Congress convened and before any regulatory legislation could be enacted to deal with this dangerous social problem. Although we had adequate revenue statutes of the prohibition period, there was no machinery to keep the former bootleggers from swallowing the legal industry or to regulate the vicious practices which had caused its legal death fifteen years ago. In October [1933] an interdepartmental committee was appointed to consider the whole problem and make recommendations. Various plans were suggested. The Brain Trust recommended a government monopoly based on the Secretary of Agriculture's licensing powers, and there is a lot to be said for it. But a business of that magnitude could not be planned and established in three weeks and should not be without express Congressional sanction.

So six Codes of Fair Competition under the Industrial Recovery Act [The NRA] were thrown together in a few frantic days after some perfunctory hearings. By an executive order their administration was turned over to a new administration and the FACA came into being with Joseph H. Choate, Jr. as Chairman but without furniture, office or personnel. By the usual practice of raiding other government bureaus, a skeleton organization was assembled in a few hours to control importing, distilling, rectifying, brewing, wine making and wholesale distribution. By some more departmental drafting and beating the bushes a little in Baltimore and New York, a so-called legal division was manned and when I arrived I found I had a couple of able men from the Prohibition and Industrial Alcohol Bureaus, one boy just out of law school, several more with an average of two years' experience answering court calls, an expert on aviation law, and a famous gentleman jockey!

[59] The repeal of the Eighteenth Amendment became effective on December 5, 1933.

Aside from the not inconsiderable task of handling volumes of confused inquiries, writing regulations on everything and organizing all six huge industries for self-administration and policing purposes, we were bedeviled for several months with a quota system of imports. The idea was to capitalize the demand for imported liquor by trading some of our commodities. Monthly import periods were established and a figure of several million gallons was pulled out of a hat. Some amateur magicians parceled the total around among the exporting countries and then by remarkable legerdemain divided it up (on a scientific basis!) in various quantities of various beverages among some 1700 importers. The results, surprising enough, were not wholly satisfactory. First came the ambassadors of the countries we had overlooked, then the ambassadors of the countries we had mistreated, [illegible] all other countries — and then the angry throng from New York — each with an English speaking lawyer or Congressman, which in New York is just another form of liquor lawyer. It was great fun and I saw every nationality from Greece to Latvia pass through all the emotional stages from imperious insistence to humble bribery. Some even offered an option — Napoleon Brandy or Mum[m]s 1911, and one even offered both. (I can't remember if his quota was increased!)

Social welfare is the first consideration of the alcohol codes and they are only secondarily designed to promote industry welfare, in contrast to the NRA codes. Pursuant to the fair trade practice sections for consumer protection, elaborate and meticulous regulations have been carefully prepared to cover labeling, standard bottles, standards of identity (and incidentally it took nine months to define whiskey!), false advertising, etc. In time these regulations will afford the consumer a protection he never enjoyed before and it is hoped that ultimately the several States will wholly withdraw from these fields of legislation and the Federal standards will become the sole and uniform requirements. Conflicting State requirements have been very vexatious both to the States and to the conscientious who are trying to comply. The liquor industry affords a good illustration of those fields in which the public welfare can be served with maximum efficiency by exclusive Federal control. There are, of course, provisions to protect the States from interstate violation and provisions to prevent old abuses — bulk sales, the use of prizes and premiums to induce sales and the old tied house. The former abuse of retail outlets controlled by manufacturers or wholesalers, presents an unanticipated modern counterpart. We now find large retail chains controlling wholesalers and pretty soon I suspect they will be in the distilling business.

But the most interesting thing about this system of alcohol regulation is the permit system. Originally the distilling, rectifying and importing codes prohibited any one from engaging in these industries except pursuant to a permit issued by the FACA. The purpose was to help keep the bootleggers, crooks, racketeers and irresponsibles out of the industry and to discourage the early tendency to create excess productive capacity, with the ultimate loss of a lot of invested capital. These permits can, of course, be revoked or suspended for violation of the Code or regulations after administrative hearings before the Code Authority and the FACA. Scores of permits have been revoked — at first with some misgiving because there is no legal basis or at least a very insecure basis for the permit system under the Industrial Recovery Act. But instead of this arbitrary and probably illegal power to put a man out of business provoking the protest and attack that was anticipated, a singular thing happened — two of the three industries that were originally exempted voluntarily requested that the system be instituted in their industries! — and I am informed that the last, the brewing industry (which has always seen the light a little late, if at all) is expected to follow soon. The explanation, of course, is that the more enlightened and reputable industry members, and strange to say there are many, realize that proper control is the only insurance of the success of repeal and therefore their best safeguard and protection. The permit affords a very effective method of enforcement and only one abortive effort was ever made to test its legality — by a Porto Rican importer, and we arranged a successful compromise with him! In short, the liquor codes are being enforced and Congress will probably be asked for some permanent legislation this winter to support the permit system as a regulation of interstate commerce.[60]

The supreme advantage of the present system is its flexibility. The codes can be readily amended to meet the changing conditions and rapid developments in these new industries. An act of the last Congress would, in many respects, have been obsolete or inadequate in a few weeks.

. . . And now if you will bear with me a few minutes longer I want to add my voice to the dissonant discussion of a subject of first importance to every one and of particular concern to us as lawyers — Administration!

Since Rome, government has been the special concern of lawyers and the profession has been more than a craft — it has been the creator and the conduit of social and governmental principles. Here in our land government was formerly largely recruited from a profession strongly imbued with the seventeenth and eighteenth century political concept

[60] Congress enacted the Federal Alcohol Act in 1935.

of individual liberty. The succeeding era of economic freedom modified our concepts of political liberty and, with the swift advent of the Industrial Revolution, the discussions of the forum remained political but the center of interest passed to the market place. Gradually the sheer mechanics of living made political equality of far less significance than economic equality.

"There ought to be a law," we say, and when we get it, we don't concern ourselves about its administration until we become conscious of its personal impact — and I suspect that Rochefoucauld was right when he said that "Our love of justice is simply our fear of suffering injustice." But today we are emerging from an era when people thought the way to cure all social ills was by political methods, and yet at the same time remained contemputuous toward everything political. The pressure of an increasingly complex society and impatience with the stately processes of the law have created a widespread and constant demand for an ever increasing measure of administration. Finally farmers, bankers, business men, the railroads, the unemployed and most every one else threw themselves on the government when the depression reached its apex two years ago, and the field of governmental administration expanded so rapidly and set up such a variety of instruments functioning in such wide areas of individual activity that we are now confronted with the problem of how we can supply adequate safeguards.

It seems to me futile for the legal profession to waste its energy in inherited protest; in echoing insistence that law be applied only by litigation. For a profession already suffering growing criticism for its anachronisms and ancestor worship, it seems incongruous solemnly to condemn the spread of the administrative system; for whatever its defects or its virtues, it is the inescapable medium through which government must work if it is to answer the demands of our society. We may as well recognize that we are in a period of accelerated administrative expansion which may last a generation. Edward Corwin in a recent book had called the breakdown of the concept of the separation of powers and the present rapid growth of administrative law the "Twilight of the Supreme Court." [61] It had its day of power under Marshall, the Congress under Taft and now the Executive branch is in the ascendancy.

Government is no longer as Aristotle and Livy said, an empire of laws. Government is ultimately a government of men and the alchemy

[61] Edward S. Corwin was professor of jurisprudence at Princeton University and author of many books including *The President: Office and Powers* (New York: New York University Press, 1941).

of administration converts the abstraction of the state into the concrete. Law is interested in regularity and protection of private rights — it works by redress, while administration is law in action and is interested in getting something done. As Dean Pound [62] says, it "achieves public security by preventive methods * * *. It is personal. Hence, it is often arbitrary and is subject to the abuses incident to personal as contrasted with impersonal or law-regulated action. But, well exercised, it is extremely efficient; always more efficient than the rival agency can be!"

It has been pointed out that the development of an administrative law is "no more radical than what took place when the Court of Chancery developed the principles of equity to mitigate the harshness and severity of mediaeval common law," and, after the living example of France with her Roman tradition of administrative law, "there seems to be no reason why the administrative law of the future should not be regularized and developed as part of the ordinary legal system of the land."

At all events, the baby elephant is growing in the very garden of our profession and growing rapidly. Shall we watch and mumble, figuring that if necessary we can always cage him with constitutional limitations? Or shall we train him to be a socially useful animal? If we choose the latter, our first concern must be the quality of administration, which, I suspect, at present is not very good. But I believe a start has been made and that a residue of the many able younger lawyers who have been recently attracted to Washington will remain as career men. But more and more must be recruited to a service which heretofore has offered but little of honor and less of monetary reward. I can look forward mistily to the time when government service will be one of the highest aspirations of educated men, as it is already in older lands. To say cynically that a general improvement of our administrative personnel under the spoils system is hopeless, is fashionable, particularly among lawyers who have been educated backward and, of course, find it difficult to face forward. However, these administrative agencies are the media through which the modern state can best call to its service that expert and specialized knowledge which becomes so necessary as government enters the economic field, and I have detected a growing consciousness in statecraft that bad government is bad politics and that good government means good men. If you agree with some that the future of our complex civilization is a race between education and disaster, you will agree that not only will government be all the better for the highly educated man, but with its increasing administrative scope it cannot go on without him.

[62] Roscoe Pound, dean of the Harvard Law School.

I will conclude with the words of Brandeis and Stone (Oklahoma Ice Case) upholding the right of state and nation, "to remold, through experimentation, our economic practices and institutions to meet changing social and economic needs." [63] Our economic life is being rapidly remolded and what is called the "New Deal" in essence is little more than the use of the power of government to preserve private enterprise by regulating its abuses and balancing its deficiencies. But the machinery is personal, arbitrary and dangerous and the lawyer, the craftsman of social principle, which we call justice, must contribute his skill and experience to that remolding or the bar will have signally failed society in a great opportunity.

[63] *New State Ice Co.* v. *Liebmann*, 76 L. ed. 747, 1932.

Part Nine

Lawyer and Chicago Civic Leader

1934-1940

Arthur Krock of the New York Times once remarked that Adlai E. Stevenson had already developed an inquiring, incisive mind by the time he arrived in Washington in 1933. But, Mr. Krock added, Stevenson did not as yet have the style — both written and oral — that he had acquired by the time he returned to government service in 1941.[1]

Stevenson became president of the Chicago Council on Foreign Relations in 1935. Over the next years, he developed a reputation for informed, pellucid, and eloquent speech. He once commented: "I was scared to death when I spoke. I still am for that matter." But as he looked back on his experiences at the council, he felt that he had improved as a public speaker through "hard work and deliberate and diligent discipline." [2]

George W. Ball, who in 1939 joined the law firm of which Stevenson was a junior partner, recalled:

> The Council was a vital place in Chicago during that period of great national debate. It was an oasis of discontent in a complacent society brainwashed each morning by Colonel McCormick's insistent xenophobia. We watched with growing delight as leading citizens came in droves to overflow luncheons of the Council, to expose themselves to views that were not confined to the admonitory passages of Washington's "Farewell Address." The attraction for many — the more cynical of us suspected — was hardly the wisdom of the speakers so much as Adlai's wise and scintillating introductions.[3]

Members of the council took Stevenson's introductions of visiting speakers as spontaneous, when in fact his remarks had been written and

[1] Interview with Walter Johnson, November 20, 1966.
[2] Russel Windes, Jr., and James A. Robinson, "Public Address in the Career of Adlai E. Stevenson," *Quarterly Journal of Speech*, Vol. XLII, No. 3, October, 1956.
[3] "Flaming Arrows to the Sky: A Memoir of Adlai Stevenson," *Atlantic*, May, 1966, p. 41.

rewritten until every word and sentence satisfied his increasingly exacting standards of style.[4] (*Many of his handwritten introductions are reprinted in the following pages.*)

Upon his return to Chicago, Stevenson was appointed government member of the code authority of the National Recovery Administration and as government member of the code authority for the wine industry by the Federal Alcohol Control Administration. Early in 1935 he was made a partner in the firm of Cutting, Moore and Sidley.

Edward D. McDougal, Jr., his law partner and close friend, said that as a lawyer Stevenson was "hard-working and conscientious and highly intelligent on the job." Otherwise, he would never have been made a partner in the firm.[5]

But the fact remained that he was frequently bored by the practice of law. Robert M. Hutchins wrote:

> Once long ago when he told me, as he often did, how much he disliked the practice of law and I replied, as I always did, by proposing he join the University of Chicago, he said: "I'll tell you what I'm going to do: I'm going to stay in this infernal law firm until I make $25,000. Then I'm going to the chairman of the Democratic National Committee and say, 'Here's $25,000; I want to be an ambassador.'"

Mr. Hutchins has added: "The remark was a joke, but it reflected a deep desire." [6]

Stevenson wrote biographer Kenneth S. Davis on March 19, 1957:

> My fascination with public affairs — at home and abroad — must date from infancy, or almost! And in a curious inverted sort of way, have never found my own affairs quite as absorbing. Law, business, profit, *making* money, have never interested me as much as impersonal public affairs.[7]

He was active not only in the Chicago Council on Foreign Relations between 1934 and 1940, but he was on the board of directors of Hull House, the Immigrants' Protective League, the Illinois Children's

[4] Harriet Welling, "Friend of the Family," in *As We Knew Adlai: The Stevenson Story by Twenty-two Friends*, edited and with preface by Edward P. Doyle, foreword by Adlai E. Stevenson III (New York: Harper & Row, 1966), pp. 43–44, discusses Stevenson's introductions.

[5] Quoted by Kenneth S. Davis, *A Prophet in His Own Country: The Triumphs and Defeats of Adlai E. Stevenson* (New York: Doubleday, 1957), p. 199.

[6] Robert M. Hutchins, "What Kind of World?" Los Angeles *Times*, August 29, 1965.

[7] This handwritten letter is in the possession of Kenneth S. Davis.

Home and Aid Society, and the Library of International Relations. In 1937 he became president of the Legislative Voters' League, which watched the Illinois legislature carefully and graded the performance of the legislators. The Chicago Daily News wrote in November, 1937: "Mr. Stevenson accepted leadership under the compelling conviction that the opportunity for a necessary service constituted a civic obligation."[8]

He also during these years deepened his friendship with writers and newspapermen like Lloyd Lewis and Carroll Binder of the Chicago Daily News and with teachers at the University of Chicago, including Samuel Harper, professor of Russian history; Bernadotte E. Schmitt, professor of modern history; Quincy Wright, professor of international relations; and Jacob Viner, professor of economics.

Stevenson's old friend Jane Warner Dick recalled:

> He absorbed from life and people what most people absorb from books. Though he was not reluctant to answer questions, he would rather ask them, as many a well-informed newspaper reporter discovered to his dismay. And his remarkably sensitive and perceptive antennae were accurately attuned not only to people but to places and situations.[9]

The Stevenson papers included in this part of Volume I are in the Stevenson collection at the Princeton University Library unless otherwise indicated. We have used almost all of the personal letters written during these years, but have been more selective in publishing his introductions of speakers before the Chicago Council on Foreign Relations. Stevenson's idiosyncrasies of spelling and style are printed as he wrote them.

To John Borden

October 10, 1934

Dear Mr. Borden: —

We have just returned and I am again behind the familiar desk after my wanderings. The Bookkeepers have referred to me a memorandum of services rendered to you in 1931 by Mr. [Edward D.] McDougal and myself in connection with a contract with S. R. Morgan, relative to a gas pipe line in Michigan.[10] My recollection is that we undertook this

---

[8] Quoted in Davis, *A Prophet in His Own Country*, p. 201.

[9] "Forty Years of Friendship," in *As We Knew Adlai*, p. 281.

[10] During the years of the depression, Adlai E. Stevenson undertook to salvage some of the investments of Ellen Stevenson's father, John Borden.

work on the understanding that, if the project developed, our services would be compensated in stock and that you would not be called upon to make any cash payment.

If this is the case, please let me know so that I can have the item written off the books, as it recurs for billing automatically every few months.

We have about decided to live in town and are in the throes of trying to find a house and get settled. I hope it won't be long before we will have a glimpse of you . . . and can catch up on the past year.

Yours,

To Joseph H. Choate, Jr.[11]

October 10, 1934

Dear Mr. Choate: —

I have just returned to my familiar desk and find your excellent photograph awaiting me. It was more than kind of you to send it, and the inscription makes me a little homesick for the "tough job" and the gentle boss. I am going to hang you in my cubicle, and I hope that it will not be long before you can inspect the execution.

My sincerest thanks for the picture and your many kindnesses. Ellen joins me in best regards to you and Mrs. Choate.

Faithfully yours,

Robert M. Hutchins, president of the University of Chicago, had recently visited the White House and it was rumored that he would be appointed to a high government position.

To Robert M. Hutchins [12]

October 13, 1934

Dear Bob:

I have just returned after my tour of duty in the Capitol. I suspect what I hear is true and I hope to have a glimpse of you before you leave for the "front."

Perhaps on one of your aimless walks through the loop, you will let me buy you a lunch.

Yours,

---

[11] Chairman of the Federal Alcohol Control Administration.
[12] This letter is in the Hutchins collection, the University of Chicago Library.

On October 28, 1934, portraits of Vice President Adlai E. Stevenson and Governor Joseph W. Fifer were unveiled in the circuit courtroom of McLean County, Illinois. Governor Fifer and other members of the McLean County Bar Association spoke. After Governor Fifer had eulogized the Vice President, Stevenson said: "I am exceedingly affected by these recitals of virtue these men have chosen to say. You knew Mr. Stevenson better than I." He declared that he would always cherish the memory of this occasion and added:

> To be sure, the circumstances of Adlai E. Stevenson's life called him aside from the bar but, like anybody enjoying political circumstances, he returned to the bar, and he died a colleague of you gentlemen of the McLean County Bar who have gathered here today.
>
> I wish he could be here and, as Mr. Fifer states, he probably is here in spirit.
>
> I wish very much that we all may look forward to the time when these walls will be adorned with the portraits, not only of these two gentlemen who have added lustre to this bar, but with the portraits of David Davis, Judge Louis FitzHenry and many other members of this bar who have achieved recognition by the public.
>
> I think that such a time will come and I think that when it does come, this bar of McLean county will perhaps be the foremost in the United States among bars comparable with it in size, in the number of great men who have passed before this bench, foremost in the heritage of wealth and glamour that it has derived from such distinguished men as are portrayed here today, the honorable Joseph W. Fifer and the honorable Adlai E. Stevenson.[13]

To Robert M. Hutchins [14]

November 15, 1934

Dear Bob:

Enclosed is a clipping [15] just sent me from Washington. It is amazing the way you continue to fool all of the people all of the time!

Yours,

[13] *Daily Pantagraph*, October 28, 1934. Stevenson's boyhood friend Joseph F. Bohrer, who attended the ceremony, wrote: "I had known that Ad could write well from his earlier story on the Murphysboro tornado, but this was the first time I realized his superior talent with the spoken word." "Boys in Bloomington," in *As We Knew Adlai*, p. 13.

[14] This letter is in the Hutchins collection, the University of Chicago Library.

[15] The clipping, from the St. Louis *Star-Times*, November 6, 1934, described the opposition within the New Deal to an appointment for Hutchins. The reporter stated: "When Hutchins gets in anywhere, you simply can't see anyone else for his dust. He is brilliant, but arrogant; dynamic but irritating; the kind of go-getter who brings home the bacon and the rest of the butcher shop with it."

Mrs. Helen Stevenson's health had deteriorated seriously by 1934. Dr. Edward Stevenson of Bloomington was convinced that her physical ills were in part the result of her being extremely depressed over separation from her son and daughter. At Adlai's urging she moved to the Churchill Hotel in Chicago near his home, and for a time her health seemed to improve. In 1935, after going on a trip, she stopped in Milwaukee to see her cousin Harriet Richardson. There she became ill and went to a hospital, where in November, 1935, after a brief illness, she died.

When Mrs. Stevenson moved to Chicago her correspondence with her son ceased. This seems to be the last letter Adlai wrote his mother that was saved.[16]

To Mrs. Lewis G. Stevenson [17]

[no date]

Dear Maw —

Please sign this application for a renewal of the Kansas insurance where indicated and return.

I went down to Bloomington yesterday for Jim McMurray's funeral [18] — performed staggeringly as a pallbearer and saw all the boys. Everyone enquired for you.

I wish you could be persuaded to come to Chicago and come at once. The reasons are obvious. It would do you good to see me and the children and Dr. Irons.[19] You could be quite comfortable in an apartment in the Whitehall with Viola [Van Valey] and a nurse, and we could deliberately work out the future plans. You could see a psychologist here a few times and perhaps get some good ideas! Viola could go to Bloomington at any time & get the necessary things for the trip South — unless, by chance, you decide to take hold of the problem now and go to Riggs! [20] Dr. Favill or someone here can doubtless find us a suitable nurse if and when necessary — and Dr. Irons knows a lot of places in the Southwest that might be good.

But most of all I think you owe it to yourself to get together and have

16 For a fuller account of Mrs. Stevenson's last years, see Kenneth S. Davis, *The Politics of Honor*, pp. 118–119.

17 This handwritten letter is in the Elizabeth Stevenson Ives Collection, Illinois State Historical Library (E.S.I., I.S.H.L.).

18 The funeral of James M. McMurry, business manager of the *Daily Pantagraph*, was on November 7, 1934.

19 Dr. Ernest Irons, general practitioner and diagnostician.

20 Dr. Austen Riggs ran a sanitarium for nervous disorders at Stockbridge, Massachusetts. Viola Van Valey was Mrs. Stevenson's maid for a short time.

some fun — Even Ellen wants you to come here to see the children &
discuss the house, farm etc! We can have your car brought up and get
any number of chauffeurs by the hour, day or week to drive you around
— also wheel chairs to the lake and short walks etc, etc!

I feel as tho I was writing a prospectus but I really feel that you
should come over here and be yourself for awhile — and then we'll
plan the future. Going to Bloomington wouldn't be difficult but I doubt
if it would be as beneficial after you got there — but perhaps I'm
flattering myself as a tonic!

At all events Dr. Irons doesn't think your proving anything by staying
there. Don't let *fear* interfere — courage ma brave — you are in the
image of God & he knows no fear! . . .

Love
AD.

P.S. At last we'll be in our new home this week end.

*On January 9, 1935, Janet A. Fairbank suggested to Stevenson that he
should write Mayor Edward J. Kelly thanking him for personally intervening and ordering garbage collection on their street.*

To Edward J. Kelly

January 11, 1935

Dear Mr. Mayor:

My neighbor, Mrs. Kellogg Fairbank, has sent me your letters of
December 27th and January 8th with regard to our garbage problem
on North State Street.

Your prompt and effective response was very gratifying. To a good
Democrat, it is cumulative evidence of the fine service your administration is rendering in even the smallest details. Your aggressive action and
the prompt results seem to have impressed the long-suffering residents
of "our street" not a little!

Faithfully yours,

*Victor Rotnem of the Agricultural Adjustment Administration wrote
Stevenson on February 25, 1935, asking if he could obtain a letter of
political endorsement from Senator J. Hamilton Lewis for lawyer John
Abt, who desired to transfer from the Agricultural Adjustment Administration to the Department of Justice.*

To Victor Rotnem

March 6, 1935

Dear Vic:

I was in Washington recently but just long enough to get snarled up with the National Labor Relations Board and the Department of Justice. . . .

I remember John Abt at least by name, and his cousin, Dr. Abt, Jr., is our pedi[a]trician. I would like to do what you suggest except that I have had some unsatisfactory experiences in similar situations with Senator [J. Hamilton] Lewis — mostly indirectly. As you know, he has become very sensitive on patronage and while in the FACA [Federal Alcohol Control Administration] I was informed that he would not recommend any lawyer from Illinois except upon approval by his friend William L. O'Connell here in Chicago. Furthermore, I think Abt would make a mistake by trying to get his endorsement unless he had been to Senator Lewis personally, identified himself and asked his blessing. Then, with O'Connell's approval, Lewis would probably do the necessary. Because of some other circumstances, too complex to recount, I am reluctant to write a letter direct without some foundation.

I would like to suggest that a new District Attorney will probably be appointed in Chicago before long and that Abt might like to consider coming back here as an Assistant District Attorney. If he is interested, and I should think it might be more attractive than Justice from many angles, he should not waste his fire on Lewis yet. If he *is* interested in the latter situation, tell him to sit tight for awhile and I will advise you if there are any promising developments.

Best regards.

Sincerely yours,

To Howard R. Tolley [21]

March 11, 1935

Dear Dr. Tolley:

This will introduce to you my very good friend, John P. Kellogg of Chicago, who is interested in a large live stock enterprise in the southwestern part of Virginia.

I have taken the liberty of telling him that you are the fountain of all

[21] Director of the Giannini Foundation and professor of agricultural economics at the University of California; later Administrator of the Agricultural Adjustment Administration, 1936–1938.

wisdom on the future development of land utilization — or that you can refer him to some one who knows the section of the country in which he is interested. I will appreciate any advice and counsel you can give him.

I miss our frenzied discussions of the economics of California crops, but in the last few days I have had a pleasant reminder of the past with Burke Critchfield and Gerald Pearce, whom I have been helping as itinerant representatives of the California Wine Industry.

Kindest regards and apologies for my imposition!

Faithfully yours,

On March 18, 1935, the Chicago Herald-Examiner *headlined a story,* "Dwight Green Post May Go to A. E. Stevenson." *Political reporter Charles N. Wheeler explained that Walter J. Cummings, chairman of the board of the Continental Illinois National Bank and Trust Company and treasurer of the Democratic National Committee, had recommended Stevenson for the post of U.S. District Attorney to replace Republican Dwight H. Green.*

To James Hamilton Lewis

March 18, 1935

Dear Senator Lewis:

I am enclosing a clipping from today's Herald & Examiner, which I thought might interest you. I suspect that it was as much of a surprise to Mr. Cummings as it was to me.[22]

Faithfully yours,

To George N. Peek [23]

March 18, 1935

Dear Mr. Peek:

I thought you and Wayne [Chatfield-Taylor] might be interested in this — or at least amused! I wish I could believe in fairy tales, but I don't even know Mr. Cummings.

Although I have no allusions about the probability of political miracles, if you could drop a note to Walter [Cummings] or [Attorney

[22] Senator Lewis replied on March 21, 1935, "I beg to assure you that there is nothing that indicates that you have been presented for any office and therefore there will be no record that you were defeated or denied anything for which you have applied or as to which you are being mentioned."

[23] Special Adviser to the President on Foreign Trade.

General] Homer Cummings, or Senator Lewis — (without severe loss of self respect!) — I would appreciate it immensely.[24]

Our affectionate regards to Mrs. Peek and yourself.

Faithfully yours,

To Stanley F. Reed

March 19, 1935

Dear Mr. Reed:

Although I cannot express surprise, I can express my delight that you have received an active lawyer's highest reward, and I want to add my felicitations to the chorus.[25]

I am enclosing a clipping from one of yesterday's Chicago papers, which induced a pleasantly high fever until I discovered that Mr. Cummings was even more surprised by the article than I!

Our kindest regards to Mrs. Reed.

Cordially yours,

To Louis FitzHenry

March 19, 1935

Dear Judge:

I am enclosing a clipping from yesterday's Herald & Examiner, which I thought might interest you. It was as much of a surprise to Mr. Cummings as it was to me. I am sure that neither he nor any one else has any interest in promoting me and I am not nursing any illusions about the likelihood of my appointment.

But if you have any advice for me or would care to write the Attorney General, whom I do not know, I would, of course, appreciate it immensely.

Best regards.

Faithfully yours,

To Harold L. Ickes

March 19, 1935

Dear Mr. Ickes:

I enclose a clipping from yesterday's Herald & Examiner, which I

[24] Mr. Peek wrote Walter Cummings on March 20, 1935, praising Stevenson's work on the legal staff. He added: "The party or anyone else, in fact, will be fortunate if they can annex him."

[25] Mr. Reed had recently been appointed Solicitor General.

thought might interest you. I suspect it was as much of a surprise to Mr. Cummings as it was to me. Of course, I would be delighted to have this appointment, but I doubt if any one is actively interested in promoting me and I have few illusions about the likelihood of my appointment.

I will appreciate immensely any advice you can give me and if you could consistently speak to the Attorney General, I am sure it would be helpful, as I have never met him. Please disregard this letter, if for any reason whatever it would cause you the slightest embarrassment, and accept my renewed thanks for your many past courtesies.

Please give Mrs. Ickes our kindest regards.

Faithfully yours,

Judge FitzHenry wrote on March 20, 1935, that the position of U.S. District Attorney was purely senatorial patronage, and if Stevenson wanted the post he would have to persuade Senator Lewis. The judge mentioned that Michael Igoe of Chicago was being considered for the post.

To Louis FitzHenry

March 22, 1935

Dear Judge:

Thanks immensely for your informative and helpful letter. As I told you, I had no illusions about getting this appointment and from the news reports Igoe's appointment seems apparent. I talked to Senator Lewis in Washington last week after I heard that inquiries had been made about me locally. He seemed surprised and noncommittal, but of course very cordial.

We are living in town now and I hope when you return to Chicago you will find time to have dinner with us some night. Please have your secretary let me know when it will be convenient.

Faithfully yours,

Edward J. Kelly had been elected mayor by the Chicago City Council to complete the unexpired term of Anton Cermak, who had been killed in February, 1933, while riding with Franklin D. Roosevelt, by an unsuccessful assassin of the President-elect. In 1935 Mayor Kelly ran for the office and was elected.

[293]

To Edward J. Kelly

March 28, 1935

Dear Mr. Mayor:

This is the first political endorsement I have ever written. It would be reassuring to know that there would be other opportunities to express respect for a public official with equal sincerity and satisfaction.

Under most trying circumstances, you have somehow managed to restore Chicago's safety, self-respect and solvency. A man in distress does not reject his best friend and Chicago will not reject you!

As a citizen, I am happy to acknowledge my debt for what you have already done and my confidence that your usefulness to Chicago has only begun.

Cordially yours,

The Secretary of the Interior wrote Stevenson on March 25, 1935, that no one would be appointed who did not have the approval of Senator Lewis. Ickes observed that he doubted that the Senator was pleased to learn of recommendations through newspaper accounts. Moreover, the appointment already had been decided upon, according to his information.

To Harold L. Ickes

March 28, 1935

Dear Mr. Secretary:

It was more than kind of you to write me at such length. After I had written to you, I learned that the appointment had been virtually agreed upon but that there had apparently been some investigation and consideration of me, probably without Senator Lewis' knowledge. I presume therefore that the newspaper story which I sent you was merely the culmination of these rumors.

With renewed thanks and kindest regards, I am

Faithfully yours,

James B. Alley, general counsel for the Reconstruction Finance Corporation, wrote Stevenson on March 28, 1935, saying that from time to time he would like to appoint him as a special counsel to act for the RFC. But before it could be done, Stevenson needed approval from Senator J. Hamilton Lewis and Senator William H. Dieterich.

To James B. Alley

March 30, 1935

Dear Jim:

Thank you very much for your good letter and your most flattering suggestion. Of course I can go on the "Approved List" and unless I hear from you to the contrary in the very near future, I will ask the Illinois senators to write appropriate letters to you. I have little doubt that Senator Lewis will respond, but I do not know Senator Diet[e]rich as well.

Naturally I would be delighted to handle any work of this kind which you could assign me. Specifically, your suggestion about railroads is of particular interest in view of the fact that I am associated with two very experienced railroad lawyers. Douglas F. Smith was formerly Assistant Commerce and Valuation Counsel of the Union Pacific for many years and is very familiar with regulatory procedure. Kenneth F. Burgess was formerly General Counsel of the Burlington. Cas[s]ius Clay [26] knows him well and I believe is thoroughly acquainted with his very formidable background in railroad work.

I only tell you the foregoing in the event that you have any misgivings about my competence in matters of this kind. Even though I handle them in my own name, I would, of course, have the assistance of these men, which of course would be reassuring to you.

Normal succession of events would seem to indicate that in about a year or so James B. Alley will be Solicitor General of the United States, and I am warning you now that when he is, I will be the first applicant.

Yours,

To James Hamilton Lewis

April 2, 1935

Dear Senator:

I am advised that the Reconstruction Finance Corporation has a matter pending, which it may wish to refer to me for attention here in Chicago. However, I am not included in its approved list of attorneys in various cities. I would like to handle this work but in order to be eligible I must have letters from you and Senator Dieterich.

If you can do so, I wish you would write a note to the General Counsel of the Reconstruction Finance Corporation, James B. Alley, "approving me." I do not know Senator Dieterich at all well, but I am

[26] Counsel for the Reconstruction Finance Corporation.

writing him as per the enclosed copy. If you can say anything to him, I am sure it would be helpful.

I am sorry indeed to be bothering you again so soon and please forgive me.

Faithfully yours,

To William H. Dieterich

April 2, 1935

Dear Senator:

I am imposing on a very inadequate acquaintance to ask a favor. The Reconstruction Finance Corporation has a list of attorneys in various cities approved by the Senators. The Corporation has in contemplation a matter in which they might want me to help here in Chicago.

Accordingly I am taking the liberty of asking you and Senator Lewis to write notes to James B. Alley, General Counsel, Reconstruction Finance Corporation "approving me." I am sure Senator Lewis can give you any information which you may desire.

I apologize for bothering you and will appreciate anything that you may be able to do in this connection.

Cordially yours,

Senator Dieterich immediately wrote a letter of approval to Mr. Alley. Senator Lewis explained to Stevenson that he would have to clear his request through William L. O'Connell and John Hopkins of the Chicago Democratic organization.

To William L. O'Connell

April 9, 1935

Dear Mr. O'Connell:

Thank you very much indeed for your courtesy this morning. I have called Mr. Hopkins and find that he may be out of town for several days. I will, of course, see him as soon as he returns.

If in the meanwhile you could write a letter direct to Mr. James B. Alley, General Counsel, Reconstruction Finance Corporation, Washington, D. C., I suspect it would serve the latter's purpose and avoid any awkward delay until I can see Mr. Hopkins.

I hope to have a further opportunity to renew my acquaintance with you and incidentally to learn something about local politics, in which I hope to take a more active part — thanks to an irresistable, congenital urge!

Cordially yours,

On April 15, 1935, Senator Lewis explained that he had wanted Stevenson to go through the usual procedure lest he be charged with having gone over the head of the Chicago Democrats. Stevenson was approved and he undertook his first assignment of a railroad bankruptcy for the RFC in Chicago in May, 1935.

To James B. Alley

April 18, 1935

Dear Jim:

I am enclosing for your personal information a letter just received from Senator Lewis, which perhaps explains his attitude, — but his complex machinery doesn't operate very smoothly!

I have not had the "green light" from Mr. Walker but I will be ready to go when I hear from him.

Yours,

To J. Hamilton Lewis

April 18, 1935

Dear Senator:

I have your letter of April 15th and wish to thank you for your kindness. I understand the situation and apologize for causing you all this inconvenience.

Ellen joins me in kindest regards to you and Mrs. Lewis.

Faithfully yours,

To Robert B. Watts [27]

April 18, 1935

Dear Mr. Watts:

A man named Fred T. Gibbs, 1970 East 72nd Place, Chicago, Illinois, called on me the other day with regard to a position with the local Regional Labor Board. He stated that Dr. B. M. Squires (I believe

[27] Special counsel with the National Labor Relations Board.

formerly Chairman of this Board) recommended him favorably to Washington last fall, but that he has heard nothing since. He is anxious to find out what, if anything, he can or should do in these circumstances to further his appointment.

He seemed intelligent, vigorous and apparently has had some considerable experience in railway labor matters. I told him I knew nothing about these situations, had no connections, etc., but that I would write you a letter to be passed on, if you saw fit.

I have no personal interest in this matter whatever and hope you will forgive my imposition — and do anything or nothing as you see fit.

With kindest personal regards, I am

Very truly yours,

To Francis T. P. Plimpton

May 3, 1935

Dear Francis:

A woman resident of Brooklyn has an estate of about $500,000, consisting solely of personal property — chattels and securities. The will leaves the entire estate in equal shares to a son and daughter, designating them as co-Executors. They reside respectively in Chicago and California. The son, a client of mine, is working on some plans for gifts to reduce probable inheritance taxes and is anxious to know what the cost of administration of the estate would be were his mother to die now. It may be assumed that she will die without debts, other than the usual current, last illness and funeral expenses.

Can you give me an estimate of probable fees which gougers like yourself would exact for administering such an estate, and also an estimate of the maximum executors' fees which the court might allow. I do not need an elaborate discussion of statutory maximums but merely the "usual and customary" in such cases.

Of course, I realize that details of routine significance like this are offensive to you, but perhaps "one of the younger men" — Stevenson or Debevoise [28] — has some appropriate experience which would be available to me.

At all events, my thanks, apologies and sentiments to you and your associates!

Yours,

[28] William E. Stevenson and Eli Whitney Debevoise were lawyers in the Plimpton firm. William E. Stevenson was a close friend and Princeton classmate.

To James B. Alley

May 23, 1935

Dear Jim:

My sincerest felicitations to you and your bride — which I hope to amplify in person before long.

This letter will be delivered to you in person by Donald F. McPherson, a senior member of this firm and a long and fine friend of mine. You may recall my speaking of him. I hope you will be in Washington when he calls and be able to spare a moment to meet him personally, as he is anxious to know you and explain the embarrassing dilemma in which I find myself.

Last week Mr. [Cassius] Clay, on your kind suggestion, referred to me the Reconstruction Finance Corporation's problem in the reorganization of the Chicago & Great Western Railway Company. Regretfully I have today advised him that circumstances compel me to decline the job. We are not in any way involved in that case, but one of the partners in my firm has recently engaged in work which might possibly some time cause us and you embarrassment if I intervened on your behalf in the Great Western case. Though the possibility may be remote, I believe you will agree that your interests demand the very strictest unity of purpose in this whole field of railroad financing. I am disappointed that the thing has turned out this way and I doubt if this peculiar situation would be duplicated again.

I am going through various procedural maneuvers in the Insull Utility Investment cases,[29] but nothing of consequence affecting your interests is likely to happen until fall.

Best regards and many thanks for this flattering demonstration of confidence.

Yours,

Thomas Woodward, vice president of the U.S. Shipping Board, who had shared an office with Stevenson at the Agricultural Adjustment Administration, wrote on May 23, 1935, and expressed the hope that Stevenson would return to Washington. He added: "We need more of your humor."

[29] During the depression the utility empire of Samuel Insull collapsed. It was in receivership.

To Thomas M. Woodward

May 25, 1935

Dear Tom:

I enjoyed your letter, but I wish you had delivered the message in person! I miss those chaotic days — and the leaven of your active yeast — more than I can tell you.

My rare visits to the Capital this winter have been between trains, but if I have another opportunity I'll get that lunch!

I was happy to have a reassuring report on the health conditions among the young Woodwards from Ellen. I suppose they will be off for the summer before long and you'll be at large again.

Yours,

To James B. Alley

June 18, 1935

Dear Jim:

I acknowledge receipt of your telegram of June 17th, advising me that the Corporation had instructed Chicago Title and Trust Company to institute proceedings to enforce collection of the indebtedness of William and Bertha Robertson and had approved my employment as attorney therein.

I have not received any information with regard to this matter from the Chicago Title and Trust Company, but I presume they will communicate with me shortly.

In the meanwhile, I hasten to express my thanks for your kindness in this regard and I accept the employment under my existing contract with Reconstruction Finance Corporation.

Sincerely yours,

In May, 1935, Stevenson was elected president of the Chicago Council on Foreign Relations. His phrase "depending, of course, on developments in the next few weeks" may refer to the Italian invasion of Ethiopia, September, 1935.

To Wilbur J. Carr [30]

September 17, 1935

Dear Mr. Carr: —

I am taking the liberty of enlisting your help in the following regard. The Chicago Council on Foreign Relations is an old established organization of very considerable standing here in Chicago. It corresponds to the Foreign Policy Association in New York. Last year Secretary [Cordell] Hull indicated some disposition to address the Council when time permitted and the circumstances seemed propitious.

In view of the fact that he has made some addresses lately and present conditions suggest the timeliness of public statements on several subjects, we are earnestly hoping to induce him to come out here this Fall and address a luncheon meeting. He will have a large and enlightened audience and, of course, can choose his own subject matter.

I feel strongly that it would be desirable for a number of reasons to make a speech in the middle west and, from a very superficial view to be sure, the time seems ripe — depending, of course, on developments in the next few weeks.

Dr. Walter Lichtenstein, the Foreign Expert of the First National Bank of Chicago, will probably call on Secretary Hull in this connection before long. I hope you will find it possible to say something to him in advance so that he may have it in mind.

If Secretary Hull cannot come, we would, of course, be delighted to have someone else from the department.

With kindest personal regards, I am

Faithfully yours,

Stevenson introduced Leland Stowe to the Chicago Council on Foreign Relations in September, 1935.

Today the Council commences its 14th season and as your President, it seems fitting to pause a moment to congratulate ourselves and survey the future. After 13 years our membership has grown from a handful

---

[30] Chairman of the Board of Appeals and Review of the Department of State and chairman of the Board of Foreign Service Personnel of the Board of Examiners and chairman of the Foreign Service School Board.

to more than 1600 and I think I can safely say that we have become an institution in this community. That our job has been done well is evidenced by the fact not only that we have survived at all, but that our vitality has grown with the years and that today the Council is the only organization in Chicago devoted exclusively to the discussion of Foreign Affairs.

For these things I congratulate you and they make it somewhat easier for me publicly to confess our shameful poverty! As many of you know our bi weekly Bulletin, Foreign Notes, has achieved a deserved reputation, but as many of you don't know, it has been financed largely by a few private contributions. In addition our general budgetary difficulties are incessant — a vigorous animal needs food & how we preserve our extraordinary vitality in a state of chronic malnutrition is something of a mystery.

At our last meeting I enlisted you[r] aid in increasing our revenue from memberships and I can report this morning with thanks that your efforts have resulted in 199 members in the last 10 days. I hope you will continue your helpful activity by extending the radius of the Councils educational influence and you will find at your places cards for suggesting names of people who might be interested in the Council. If you will leave these at the table or send them in to the council they will be checked to avoid duplication and followed with literature. Further in this connection I am distressed to have to report an alarming increase in domestic conflict among our membership. A careful investigation discloses that in many instances only one member of a family is a member of the Council with the result that he or she frequently neglects to communicate notices of meetings or pass on Foreign Notes. The unhappy consequences of such omission are obvious. But happily a simple remedy is available guaranteed to preserve domestic tranquility — Each member of the family should join the council!

For the last 10 mo[nth]s we have watched the orderly evolution of a war and since this meeting was announced that war has become an actuality. None can foresee the ultimate implications of what has and is taking place. But we do know that an important chapter in history is being written rapidly and while we approach a dramatic test of the age old ambition to subject to the reign of law not alone men but states. Leland Stowe, a Pul[itzer] Prize winner for [illegible] for 9 yrs Paris Cores [correspondent] of the N Y H – Trib [New York *Herald Tribune*] returned to America a few days ago after attending the meetings in Paris & Geneva and studying the Italian attitude at first hand in Rome. I suspect we have never had a better qualified speaker or a more timely address. The Council again welcomes Leland Stowe.

To Newton Jenkins

October 10, 1935

Dear Mr. Jenkins:

Thank you for your letter of October 5th. I am sorry that you did not see fit to become a member of the Chicago Council on Foreign Relations, and I note with interest your statement:

"It is my conviction that your organization (the Chicago Council on Foreign Relations) is a training school for treason to our country."

I am going to take the liberty of asking you the following three questions:

1. Have you ever attended a meeting of the Council?

2. If so, what did you hear that convinced you that the Council was a training school for treason to the United States?

3. If you have not attended a meeting, on what evidence do you base your quoted conviction?

I hope you will see fit to answer these questions and will not misconstrue the sincere curiosity which prompts this letter.

Sincerely yours,

Stevenson introduced Ernest B. Price to the Chicago Council on Foreign Relations on October 25, 1935.

On next Friday November 1 Count Kabayama will address the Council on "The Internal Situation In Japan." Count Kabayama is coming to Chicago with the Japanese Ambassador who will decorate Dr. John H. Wigmore. He is a very important industrialist in Japan and a member of the House of Peers. His address will be frankly partisan and should be exceedingly interesting as an authoritative exposition of Japanese attitudes.

I am happy to report a gain of 236 members since our last meeting on October 8 or a total gain since the season commenced less than a month ago of 435 members against a loss of only 36. Accordingly our total membership today is 2005 — an all time high. This is highly gratifying but please do not feel that the success of your efforts to enlarge the field of our influence is embarrassing — the staff can still handle the mail without inconvenience!

This week you have received membership cards together with a long and engaging letter of explanation. I apologize for this nuisance — it will cause some confusion at the door; many of you forgot to bring them today and some will always forget them (including my wife). The only justification is that they ARE necessary, and I bespeak your cooperation and strict adherence to the membership rules — besides as the attendance gets larger and angrier the cards should prove useful to identify the dead and wounded around the portals of our forum!

Its appropriate that we return to the orient and Red Lacquer [room in the Palmer House] simultaneously. This is our evidence of managerial delicacy to which I feel constrained to call attention. In another sense we're at home today for this is one of these too infrequent occasions when we find the best man among our fellow townsmen. Ernest B. Price was called from Johns Hopkins last winter to direct International House at the Univ. of Chicago, with which you are all familiar or should be. Because of his long residence in China in the American Foreign Service and as Pres. of China Airways Mr. Price is eminently qualified to evaluate recent developments in Manchukuo.[31] We have not been acutely aware of ominous rumblings in the Far East because of the African War. But external relations of Manchukuo are strained and Japan appears to be threatening penetration into Outer Mongolia at Russia's expense. Wider conflict in Europe might afford Japan an opportunity to consum[m]ate her expansion program.

Its an honor to welcome Dr Price as a student of Far Eastern Affairs and as the distinguished director of our cultural cousin — International House. Dr Price.

Stevenson introduced Professor Harley F. MacNair to the Chicago Council on Foreign Relations on November 22, 1935.

Because the recent general election in England proved a fulsome endorsement of the government's foreign policy and indicates its continuation with undiminished vigor, we feel that the Council should have a clear exposition of that policy and of the British point of view. To this end we have invited C. Douglas Booth, member of the Royal Institute of International Affairs, to address us. He is in this country for a short visit and will speak before the council on next Wednesday, the day before Thanksgiving, on "England's Foreign Policy after the Elections."

A few weeks ago Ernest Price delivered from this platform an exceptionally thorough and enlightening discussion of Japan & Manchukuo. Since then China proper has abandoned the silver standard &

[31] Japan seized Manchuria in 1931. In 1937 the Japanese invaded North China.

the agitation for the autonomy of North China has grown in volume & mystery. And again we find at hand a speaker qualified to evaluate the current phases of China's internal problem. Dr. Harley McNair took his PhD at the Univ. of Cal[ifornia]. and for 15 years was professor of history and government at St. Johns College in Shanghai. In 1927 he went to the University of Washington as Professor of Far Eastern Government and Diplomacy and in 1928 came to the Univ. of Chicago as Professor of Far Eastern Institutions and History. His writings on China are voluminous and authoritative — some 10 books and numerous contributions to periodicals, the Encyclopedia Britannica and the Encyclopedia of Social Sciences. Mr. McNair went back to the Orient in 1934 and returned to Chicago only this summer. We welcome him as a distinguished Chinese scholar and as the husband of the former Florence Ayscough whose several volumes of translations of Chinese poetry are well known and well loved. Dr. McNair's subject is China in 1935 — an eyewitness account — and we congratulate ourselves again for matching the headlines in punctuality.

Stevenson introduced C. Douglas Booth to the Chicago Council on Foreign Relations on November 29, 1935.

Dr Gustav Stalper speak[s] on next Thursday, Dec. 5, on "Economic Aspects of the Present European Crisis." If this title, "Economic Aspects of the Present European Crisis" seems a little too spacious it is not an attempt to puff the speaker, because Dr. Stalper is an outstanding economist and, until the advent of the Hitler government, was a member of the Reichstag, a member of the Budget Committee and Editor and Publisher of Germany's foremost economic publication — "The German Economist." With Italy at war, Germanys economy controlled by severe restrictions and budgetary and currency problems threatening the downfall of the Laval government in France, we believe you will welcome this opportunity to hear the views of a celebrated European economist.

"I see this aged England, with the possessions, honors and trophies, and also with the infirmities of 1000 years gathering around her — I see her not dispirited, not weak, but well remembering that she has seen dark days before; indeed with a kind of instinct that she sees a little better on a cloudy day, and that in storm of battle and calamity she has a secret vigor, and a pulse like cannon."

These words were spoken 90 years ago this month by Ralph Waldo

Emerson. Tho "aged England" is almost a century older they seem as pertinent today as they were in Manchester in 1845 and we have recently seen the English people overwhelmingly endorse a very firm and consistant foreign policy. We have heard from this platform and elsewhere various motives attributed to England, but not yet have we had a forthright presentation of the English viewpoint. Major C. Douglas Booth is by birth and education a Canadian. After the war he was identified with the Liberal Party and later travelled extensively in Europe and America as political correspondent of the London Sunday Times. Through long residence in England he understands clearly the English viewpoint and his Canadian background and experience in this country enable him to be objective about British policy, tho sympathetic to it. He will speak on British policy after the elections.

Stevenson introduced William R. Castle to the Chicago Council on Foreign Relations on December 18, 1935.

The Charter of the CCFR recites as the first object of its formation "The promotion of public interest in the Foreign Policy of the United States." The meeting today, and for the first time this year, is devoted to a discussion of American Foreign Policy and probably not since the Council was incorporated 13 days [years] ago this week, has the scrutiny of our Foreign Policy been more timely or important.

To remind you that since the inauguration of President Roosevelt there has been an economic Conference in London, a bloody revolution in Cuba, a Pan American conference in Montevideo, another disarmament conference, a silver purchase Act with oriental repurcussions, recognition of Russia after 14 years, the Jones-Costigan Sugar Control law[,] Reciprocal Trade Agreements Act and treaties with 6 [or] 8 nations, and Phillipine Freedom is to mention only some of the incidents of the past three years which have received only brief public attention in our absorption with domestic problems. But now a momentous hour has arrived and in the shadow of world war the government is rapidly and drastically revising our historic neutrality policy and abandoning the doctrine of the Freedom of the Seas for which we have fought for 150 years — in search of a formula which will promote peace abroad and insure it at home.[32]

Mr William R. Castle has generously come to Chicago to discuss some aspects of these policies. We are honored to have Mr. Castle — he

[32] The Neutrality Act, August 31, 1935, among other things, imposed an arms embargo on both sides in a war and forbade American ships to enter war zones.

has himself played important parts in the formulation of American Foreign Policy in other critical times. From 1927 to 1930 he was an Assistant Secretary of State; during the London Naval Conference of 1930 he served as an Ambassador to Japan, and from 1931 to 1933 was Undersecretary of State. In addition to many other distinctions he is an Overseer of Harvard University and I hasten to remind the Yale and Princeton men here present that this fact must not diminish respect for Mr Castle as I am reliably informed that the Overseers of Harvard are more concerned with education than football. Its a privilege to welcome Mr Castle to the Council.

Mr. Castle's speech created a furor among council members. Among other things it attacked Secretary of the Interior Harold L. Ickes for urging a restriction on oil exports to Italy during the Italo-Ethiopian War and thereby encroaching upon the authority of the Secretary of State to control foreign affairs. Ickes wrote Castle on December 31, 1935, charging that his speech was "a deliberate slur upon your government."

To Harold L. Ickes

December 19, 1935

Dear Mr. Ickes:

I am taking the liberty of enclosing copy of a letter to Secretary Hull and copy of the speech therein referred to.

Familiar as you are with the Chicago situation and with the objectives of this organization, you can readily appreciate the unfortunate situation and embarrassment both to the Council and to me personally which this speech has caused.

I am hoping that if you feel as many of us do that the speech demands an answer from a qualified speaker, you will, at the first opportunity, emphasize my request to Secretary Hull.

With cordial regards, I am

Respectfully yours,

To Cordell Hull

December 19, 1935

Dear Mr. Secretary:

I am reluctant to again urge you to consider speaking in Chicago — or to suggest some one else who might properly represent the Administration, either officially or unofficially.

Yesterday Mr. William R. Castle bitterly attacked the Administration's foreign policies. His speech has been widely quoted in the Chicago papers and has caused much conflicting comment. It was grossly partisan and has embarrassed the Council, which has succeeded in preserving a scrupulous non-partisanship for many years. You can appreciate therefore my anxiety to get a properly qualified presentation of the other side, together with a correction of some of the factual errors and misplacements of emphasis. We do not want a partisan political controversy, but, to maintain our integrity, this speech must be answered and I bespeak your help in securing a competent dignified presentation of the Government's policies.

Of course, it would be both an honor and great satisfaction to have you here at any time, but if this is still inconvenient, I hope you will be able to suggest some one else.

For your information, I am enclosing a copy of Mr. Castle's speech and some newspaper clippings.

With sincerest regards and best wishes, I am

Respectfully yours,

To Cordell Hull

December 20, 1935

Dear Mr. Secretary:

In connection with my letter to you of yesterday, I am enclosing for your information editorial clippings from the Chicago Daily News of yesterday, December 19th, and from the Chicago Tribune of today.

Mr. Castle's speech has, at least locally, opened for the first time a new field of attack on the President and the Administration. Many informed people here feel the speech was wholly unwarranted and a dangerous political expedient.

I hardly need to add that I personally, as well as President of this organization, share this aggravation, and I reiterate my hope that you will see fit to come out here some time or suggest some one who might be available.

Faithfully yours,

To Loring C. Merwin

December 31, 1935

Dear Bud:

. . . I note that in the current issue of the Illinois State Historical Society magazine there is reprinted an old letter describing Bloomington ninety-eight years ago, which was originally published in the Pantagraph in 1909.[33] I thought possibly that in view of its present publication in the Historical Society magazine, it might be worth while to reprint it in the Pantagraph as a feature story some time. It might even be possible to trace some of the present descendants of the author of the letter, etc.

Hastily yours,

Stevenson introduced Professor Bernadotte E. Schmitt to the Chicago Council on Foreign Relations on January 11, 1936.

I am told that some members of the Council are under the impression that our season [ends] around March 1. Tho I sometimes wish this were true our luncheon addresses will of course, as in the past, continue to the end of May and I remind you that a membership is good for one year from the date of issuance — not merely to the end of the season or to the end of the calendar year.

A foreigner confidently advised me not long ago that there were only three important things about Chicago — The University, the Stockyards and the weather! I believe you will agree that the statement is correct, at least in part, and that the University is certainly one of the most important things about Chicago — and incidentally the solace of presidents of the Chicago Council on Foreign Relations. Today we have again tapped the inexhaustable resources of this great collection of scholars and Prof. Bernadotte Schmitt has gen[er]ously consented to give us his most timely observations on American Foreign Policy as seen from abroad.

Foreign Policy, like any other policy is designed to work and has to be tested by results. So it is not enough merely to discuss it abstractly here at home — To measure its usefullness it must constantly be reexamined at the point of impact abroad. Our opportunities for a comprehensive survey of external effect of policies are of course very rare. However we have such an opportunity today for Dr. Schmitt returned only very recently from a 7 months trip thru the Far East and Europe and has carefully checked foreign opinions of our policies along his route.

Dr. Schmitt is well known to most of you. Briefly I can remind you that for the last 5 years he has been Chairman of the Department of History at the University of Chicago, the author of numerous books and

[33] *Journal* of the Illinois State Historical Society, October, 1935.

articles on history and international affairs including "The Coming of War — 1914" which won for him the Pulitzer prize in 1931. The Council again welcomes our distinguished fellow townsman — Dr. Schmitt.

Stevenson wrote Colonel A. A. Sprague, an influential Chicago Democrat, seeking his assistance in persuading Secretary of State Hull to speak before the Chicago Council on Foreign Relations. Sprague replied that it would be unwise for Hull to answer William R. Castle's speech. Undersecretary of State William Phillips appeared before the council on February 15.

To Albert A. Sprague

January 14, 1936

Dear Colonel:

Thank you for your letter returning Secretary Ickes' letter to Mr. Castle.

I quite agree with you that the last thing in the world I want to let the Council in for would be a controversial debate on our foreign policy in which the Administration participated officially. What I do want, however, is some one who can give a constructive recitation of various aspects of our policy, wholly unrelated to anything Mr. Castle may have said. In other words, it should not be an "answer."

In short, it would be in accordance with the charter purposes of the Council if we could have some time this winter or spring a speech reviewing the foreign policy of the United States during the period of the last few years by a competent spokesman, who could interpret the Administration's motives constructively and dispassionately.

Faithfully yours,

Stevenson introduced Ernest Gruening to the Chicago Council on Foreign Relations on January 25, 1936.

The last two meetings of the Council have been concerned with American Foreign Policy and today Mr. Gruening is to discuss another aspect of our external policy. Next week — Saturday — promises to be one of the most important meetings of the year and will also be devoted to a discussion of American Policy — Neutrality — and the legislative proposals to solve this vitally important and intricate problem. Prof.

Philip C. Jessup of Columbia Univ. Law School — a distinguished authority on the International Law of Neutrality — will describe the bills pending in Congress, one which he drafted in large measure, and will I am sure make an important contribution to the clarification of the issues and conflicts involved in this delicate question of which we are destined to hear so much in the immediate future.

And now I have a surprising confession to make — my painstaking research in the Councils a[r]chives discloses that in 13 years of cultural missionary work we have explored virtually every spot in the world — except our own colonies! How it happens that we have been so interested in other empires and so neglectful of our own I'm sure I don't know. But our sins of omission are to be expiated forthwith for Mr. Ernest Gruening has come to Chicago to speak on our colonial policy — and its gratifying to be able to cure our past deficiencies in the person of the Director of the Division of Territories & Foreign Possessions of the Dept. of Interior. Before his appointment to this responsible post 2 yrs ago, Mr. Gruening was widely known as one of this country's most enlightened, liberal editors. For many years he was the editor & publisher of Maine's largest paper — the Portland News. For several years he was an editor of the Nation and the N. Y. Eve. Post. Because of his intimate familiarity with Latin-American affairs Pres. Roos[evelt]. appointed him adviser to our delegation to the Montevideo Pan American Congress. Thereafter followed his appointment to his present post and he comes to us fresh from a survey trip to Porto Rico and other insular possessions. He has chosen as the subject for his authoritative discussion of our colonial responsibilities — Toward an American Colonial Policy. Mr. Gruening.

Stevenson introduced Philip C. Jessup to the Chicago Council on Foreign Relations on February 1, 1936.

The recent discussions of American Foreign Policy which commenced with an address in December by William R. Castle, former Under-Secretary of State, critisising the conduct of our Foreign Policies since the advent of the present administration, will be continued at our next meeting on Saturday Feb 15. And I am pleased to announce that the Honorable William Phillips, Undersecretary of State will be the speaker. Mr. Phillips has just returned to the United States from the London Naval Disarmament Conference and we have not yet been advised of the subject of his address. His acceptance of our invitation is a gratifying recognition of the counsel and affords Chicago the unusual privilege of hearing not only the second ranking office of the State Dept. but also one [of] our country's most distinguished and experienced diplomats. I trust this address will command an attention befitting the speaker's distinction.

On the last day of this month the temporary neutrality act hastily adopted last summer expires. In this brief interval Congress will debate and adopt legislation designed to solve the bewildering and perilous problem of American Neutrality. Standing in the ominous shadow of war in Europe we seem to be nationally united in our anxiety to avoid war — and its comforting to find us united even on that — but we are all in bitter disagreement as to how neutrality is to be insured and many people even insist that it can't be done! (Some advocate strict, mandatory legislation, others would give the President limited discretion and still a third school believes that any legislation would be dangerous.)

Because of the intricacy of the problem we have asked Philip C. Jessup, prof. of international law at Columbia, to discuss our policy and the issues presented by the pending legislative proposals. We enlisted Prof. Jessup because of his eminence as an authority on the subject. He was associated with Elihu Root in the formulation of the Root Protocol on adherence to the world court in 1929. Last year he published "United States and Stabilization of Peace" and only very recently there has appeared the first of four volumes on "Neutrality, its History, Economics and Law" of which he is the co author. He has played an important part in the drafting of various neutrality bills and served as a member of the Committee on Neutrality appointed by the Peace Council of which our fellow member Quincy Wright of the University of Chicago was also a member. Its a privilege to welcome Mr. Jessup as our guest today.

To Loring C. Merwin

February 5, 1936

Dear Bud:

I have your letter of January 31st, enclosing the December and annual operating statements, which I have examined with great interest and satisfaction.

At your leisure, I wish you would let me know the relative country and city circulation, the cash condition and the most recent figures on the investment fund valuation, together with an estimate of the balances payable on the building.

I presume that the year-end audit will be completed in due course and that you will let me have a copy temporarily to look over.

Ellen is in the hospital and we hope for deflation in the very near future.[34] Please tell Marjorie [Mrs. Merwin] that "Foreign News" is my modest contribution to intellectual pre-natal influence.[35]

Yours,

On February 7, 1936, James W. Morris, Assistant Attorney General, Department of Justice, wrote Stevenson that the Attorney General had mentioned to him that Stevenson desired a position in the department. Morris suggested that Stevenson visit him the next time that he was in Washington.

To James W. Morris

February 10, 1936

Dear Mr. Morris:

I acknowledge with sincere thanks receipt of your letter of February 7th. I am afraid there has been some misunderstanding, as I did not have in contemplation joining the Department of Justice. Perhaps the confusion arose from the fact that I was apparently considered, without my knowledge, for appointment as United States District Attorney here in Chicago last spring, and it is probable at that time some one spoke to the Attorney General about me. I appreciate very much your courtesy in writing me and the Attorney General's interest.

I am going to take the liberty of suggesting, however, that there is a man in Washington whom I know intimately and who was for many years associated with my firm here in Chicago. He is exceedingly anxious to get into the Department of Justice and to that end has already had some conversations with the Solicitor General and John Dickinson, I believe. John Paul[d]ing Brown is a man about forty years old, a graduate of Harvard University and Harvard Law School and has had a very considerable experience in private practice for some fifteen years. He went to Washington about a year ago to work in the Legal Division of what is now the Federal Alcohol Administration. He is very anxious to resume more active legal work than that Division affords and would, I am confident, be a very valuable man to the Department of Justice. He is an accomplished trial lawyer and can secure the highest recom-

[34] John Fell Stevenson was born on February 7, 1936.
[35] The Chicago Council on Foreign Relations published *Foreign Notes* for its membership.

mendations. If there is any possibility of your finding a suitable place for him, I should like very much for you to so advise me and I will ask him to call on you without delay.

Let me thank you again for your courteous letter.

With best wishes, I am

Sincerely yours,

To Wayne Chatfield-Taylor

February 13, 1936

Dear Wayne:

This is great news and I hope to heaven it is more than one of these rumors.[36]

Would [you] like me to ask Ned Brown and Harold Amberg of The First National [Bank] to write letters to Morganthau? [37]

Ellen presented us with a third fat son last week and is flourishing. Our love to Adele [Mrs. Taylor].

Sincerely yours,

Stevenson introduced William Phillips to the Chicago Council on Foreign Relations on February 15, 1936.

Because a scrutiny of our Foreign Affairs has seldom been more timely or important we have devoted four consecutive meetings to a consideration of our Foreign Relations — and today we conclude this interval of self examination.

The meeting today is noteworthy in the history of our council. In the past 13 years we have been addressed by many men distinguished in politics, scholarship and leadership. Clemenceau, Nansen, Lord Robert Cecil, Von Kuhlman, Karensky and many other men of world renown have spoken before us, but never before have we succeeded in entrapping a ranking incumbent officer of our own State Department. Indeed I believe that this is the first time in a long while that anyone enjoying or suffering the delicate responsibilities of Mr. Phillips office has publicly diagnosed the condition of our Foreign Affairs and his acceptance of our invitation out of the many is an honor and affords us an unusual privilege.

The severe patience with which you endure my ponderous prelimi-

[36] Mr. Taylor was appointed Assistant Secretary of the Treasury.
[37] Henry Morgenthau, Secretary of the Treasury.

naries always embarrasses me and today I have resolved to reward you with exceptional brevity. So I will only remind you that as Undersecretary of State for the last 3 years Mr Phillips has participated in the formulation of our policy in a most critical period. Japanese aggression, Revolution in Cuba, Recognition of Russia, rearmament of Germany, the Montevideo Conference, the naval conference, Reciprocal trade agreements, war and neutrality are only some of the more perplexing developments of these troubled years. (The lot of responsible men in government in a period of affirmative action is always hard and Mr Phillips' lot must have been exceptionally hard in these recent years; but I suspect they have been rich in memoir material!)

But Mr. Phillips has not always been Undersecretary of State. Starting in 1903 as private secretary, in the idiom of a modern magazine, to the late great Ambassador to Great Britain, Joseph H. Choate, he has served our country for more than 30 years in many administrations and in numberless places and positions at home and abroad. He has been minister to the Netherlands, minister to Canada and Ambassador to Belgium. As the Council we are honored by his visit to us and as citizens we are gratified that thru its distinguished Undersecretary the State Dept. is making a public accounting of its stewardship of our Foreign Affairs for the last 3 years.

Before we proceed with the questions I want to announce that on Monday February 24 Joseph Israels will address the Council. Mr. Israels has been in Ethiopia for 6 mos. as war correspondent for the N. Y. Times. He will illustrate his remarks with moving pictures taken in the war zones in November and December. This will be the first showing of these pictures in the Middle West.

To Thomas Hewes [38]

February 17, 1936

Dear Tom:

I have received the announcment of the formation of Hewes Prettyman and Awalt, and I want to add my felicitations. It is certainly a most formidable gathering of brilliance and versatility and I foresee great honor and prosperity.

Wayne Taylor's appointment was the best news I have had from the front for a long while.

Sincerely yours,

[38] Mr. Hewes had recently formed a new law firm in Hartford, Connecticut. He and Stevenson had known each other in Washington, D.C., in 1933 and 1934.

To James W. Morris

February 17, 1936

Dear Mr. Morris:

Thank you very much for your kind letter of February 13th. I am delighted to know that you are interested in Mr. [John P.] Brown and I am taking the liberty of asking him to call on you some time at your convenience.

I want to repeat that I think he could be an exceptionally useful man in brief writing, court and technical law work.

I need not tell you how sympathetic I am with your problems and with some government experience myself, I can in a measure understand the constantly vexing problem of personnel.

With kindest regards and renewed thanks for your interest in me, I am

Sincerely yours,

To William Phillips

February 17, 1936

Dear Mr. Phillips:

The enclosed newspaper clippings do not include the article in the Chicago Daily News which I gave you Saturday afternoon. Although the press treatment was very unsatisfactory, it was actually better than I anticipated in view of the local dista[s]te for anything creditable to the Administration.

The audience's response to your speech was very gratifying and many partisan folk have said to me that they "did not know there were men like that in the Administration." I have written the Secretary as per the enclosed copy.

Thank you again for coming and I earnestly hope that we will have further opportunities to see and hear you out here.

Sincerely yours,

To Cordell Hull

February 17, 1936

Dear Mr. Secretary:

Personally and on behalf of the Executive Committee of the Chicago Council on Foreign Relations, I want to thank you most cordially for your part in Mr. Phillips' address on Saturday.

The speech was a fine, dignified and forthright review of your administration of the State Department and made a wholesome impression
on the audience. The press of course was apathetic, which, as you know,
is always the case in Chicago when the subject matter is creditable to
the Administration.

With sincerest respect, I am

> Faithfully yours,

*On February 17, 1936, R. J. Dunham, commissioner of the Chicago
Park District and close friend of Mayor Edward J. Kelly, wrote Alderman Mathias "Paddy" Bauler, powerful Democratic boss of Chicago's
43rd Ward, and urged him to consider Adlai E. Stevenson as an alternate delegate to the Democratic Convention. Dunham pointed out that
Stevenson lived in the east end of the ward (1246 North State Street in
Chicago's Gold Coast) where the Democrats were weak. Dunham remarked that Stevenson could help build up the strength of the Democratic party in that part of the ward. "He is young and active and a very
good speaker," Dunham added. Bauler responded that the young man
"was not registered and has apparently just moved into the ward. Of
course, we want to help all the young men that we can, but you can
readily appreciate that in these times, the supply by far exceeds the
demand." Bauler pointed out that after great effort his organization had
succeeded in registering eighty-one voters in the Ambassador Hotel but
only ten bothered to vote. "This [is] typical of east end politics as it
affects our ward," he commented. He added that the president of the
43rd Ward Organization would be the alternate delegate, but that he
was sending Stevenson a card "requesting that he come to our meetings."*

*When Dunham sent Stevenson a copy of Bauler's letter, Stevenson
wrote the following letter in pencil. It is possible that the letter was
typed from the handwritten draft but there is no carbon in the Stevenson papers, only the pencil copy.*

To Robert Dunham

> February [no date], 1936

Dear Mr. Dunham — Thank you very much indeed for sending me
copies of your very flattering letter to Bauler and his reply. You more
than did your part and I appreciate it. Bauler's reply is, I presuyme, a
characteristic commentary on our current municipal politics. While, in-
sofar as it affects me personally, I am disappointed at his complete in-

difference, I am far more concerned with the implication of thoughtless disregard of long range party welfare.

The attitude of to hell with him & the east end of the ward is a brief and eloquent answer to the familiar question as to why more men like yourself don't take an active part in our municipal politics. And, as you know, in spite of its apparent popular strength the Dem party locally & nationally never needed active sympathy "on the east side" as much as it does today[.]

My missionary work among the heathen, a familiar role in my family for several generations, can never be very useful unless the party leaders occasionally recognize and thus enlist some of these younger men in the active Dem party[.] Of course our salvation is that that the Republicans have likewise always likewise overlooked this potential advantage in enlisting some of the "other half[.]"

Cordially

When Stevenson wrote Senator Lewis for information in order to introduce him to the Chicago Council on Foreign Relations, the Senator furnished the information but wrote, "However, as the folks at home know me enough to dislike me quite cordially or feel kindly generosity, it would be quite sufficient to call attention that 'this is Lewis.'" Stevenson introduced the senator to the council on March 2, 1936.

On Saturday of this week Count de Roussy de Sales will speak on the Political and Economic situation in France. Count de Sales is special correspondent of two important Paris newspapers and has just returned from an extended visit to France. The formation of the new Flandin government and the perennial problems of French internal economy foretell an interesting address by an exceptionally competant and well informed speaker.

For me to introduce to a Chicago audience Senator James Hamilton Lewis seems presumptuous and the significance of his topic, International Finance as an Obstruction to American Neutrality, is so apparent that it also needs no amplification by a wholly unnecessary presiding officer.

But before I surrender my present advantage I do want to remind you of some things one is apt to forget about Senator Lewis. As whip of the Senate and a member of the Foreign Affairs Committee he has played an important part in the formulation of our current neutrality legislation which the Congress will reconsider next year. I also remind you that during the war he was whip of the Senate, which was constantly confronted with the problem of neutrality. He represented the

United States at the Safety at Sea Conference in London and was charged by Pres. Wilson & the Secretary of War with various confidential missions to the Allies. He served our citizens on missions to Jerusalem and Rome and has been decorated by the King of Belgium and the Greek Government and has been honored in England with membership in the Knights of the Round Table.

Latterly he has been to Berlin in the interests of American creditors and while on a similar mission to Russia last summer you will recall that he fell ill & had a narrow escape. Perhaps he concluded that death was better than life in Moscow. This brief summary will suffice to indicate that Senator Lewis, as one of the Elder statesmen, has had an almost unequalled continuity of experience with our Foreign relations and the complex problem of American neutrality which he will discuss today. It is a privilege to introduce to you your distinguished Senior Senator, fellow townsman and fellow member of the Council — Senator Lewis.

Mayor Edward J. Kelly and Patrick Nash, the two bosses of the Cook County Democratic party, broke with Governor Henry Horner and ran Dr. Herman Bundesen against him in the Democratic primary. Horner won handily in a bitter campaign.

To Henry Horner

March 11, 1936

Dear Governor:

Mr. O'Brien communicated to me your flattering invitation to serve as Treasurer of your Primary Campaign. I indicated to him some reasons why I thought it best to decline. A reason I did not mention, because my plans were still indefinite, is that I have now decided to take my wife south soon for a few weeks vacation. She had a baby in February and it is now important for her to get a complete rest, which she cannot get at home.

I appreciate very much this evidence of your confidence and I regret that I cannot serve you, but you may be assured that I will be doing whatever I can.

Cordially yours,

On March 12, 1936, Harvard Law School classmate Francis T. P. Plimpton invited Stevenson to attend an "orgy of the Kent Club Marching and Chowder Association" in New York City. Stevenson wrote in longhand on the bottom of Plimpton's letter. It is possible that this was typed but there is no carbon in the Stevenson papers, only the hand-written reply.

To Francis T. P. Plimpton

[no date]

Dear Francis —

Altho not a member of the K [C] M & C A or even the [illegible] Inside Straight and Pleasure Club, I appreciate immensely the suggestion that I foregather with this group of once promising young men. That I cannot do so on the indicated dates is accounted for not by any timidity about matching wits with city slickers — indeed I'm eager to have at you — but because I have an early engagement with St. Christopher and 3 weeks of tranquil travel and [illegible] relaxation in Mexico.

My dove presented me with a third fat son early in February & for that and many other reasons we will be arriving in the mtroplis on Friday Mar 20 and sailing that afternoon at 4 P M on the S S Yucatan for Vera Cruze. I[t] would be a pleasure to me and a piece of very good fortune for you, if we were to find you & Pauline on board that vessel prepared for a couple of weeks of intensive rest in Cuernava[ca] and Acapulco. I appreciate that people of your stripe would sacrifice much for an evening or so at the green tables, but I suggest that you make a last attempt to conquer your cupidity and do brief homage to the latent tastes of a once eager mind by putting aside "things" for a moment and joining us in this lyric Mexican venture!

On March 14, 1936, Loring C. Merwin wrote to Stevenson about an open house for the new Pantagraph *building and added a postscript that "unexpectedly" that morning he had become the father of Amanda Fell Merwin. Mr. Merwin added that she "shows promise of being a staccato virtuoso."*

To Loring C. Merwin

March 17, 1936

Dear Bud:

Really I am astonished that any kin of mine could father such a forward young lady. My recollection is that she was invited for April 1st and here she is muscling in two weeks ahead of time!

However, I am relieved to hear that in other respects she is conventional and that she has such a promising voice. John Fell salutes and says that he will be glad to meet Amanda Fell in a vocal due[t] any time — quantity and not quality to count.

Of course, I can imagine that your condition is precarious and you have my profoundest sympathy, in which Ellen does not join. Give our love to Marjorie. — We are off on Thursday for three weeks and will hope for a glimpse of her work soon after we get back. I am disappointed to miss the opening, but it looks like now or never for the vacation.

In connection with the primary campaign, I feel that we should vigorously endorse Horner in the Democratic primary as against Bundesen — and not simply as a protest against "boss" domination of the party from Cook County but *constructively* on the basis of his record and his personal integrity and courage. Much can be said for what he has done and what he has tried to do and prevented others from doing.

In the Republican primary, I haven't any very definite views, — except that [C. Wayland] Brooks, with whom I went to school, is probably the least qualified of the lot, though doubtless he has the strongest support. It is a sad state of affairs when the [Chicago] Tribune owns the leading candidates, Bundeson and Brooks, of both parties.

Yours,

To Henry Horner

April 15, 1936

Dear Governor:

I returned to Chicago yesterday in time to vote and found your kind letter of March 18th awaiting me.[39]

I do not want to be the last to offer my sincere congratulations. I was familiar with the general downstate situation and the results there did not surprise me, but your showing in Cook County against manifold obstacles seemed to me a remarkable tribute to you and a wholesome protest.

As a Democrat with downstate background, I hope that this stinging rebuke to Cook County leadership will serve a useful purpose and that some intelligent and tolerant appreciation of the downstate attitude and the importance of statewide party unity will result.

With your leadership, I look forward to the fall with confidence and trust you will command me at any time.

Faithfully yours,

[39] Governor Horner had written that he understood why Stevenson could not be the treasurer of his campaign but that he had wanted him to do so "for I desired a name with the integrity of which the whole [Cook] county would be impressed."

Stevenson introduced Walter Millis to the Chicago Council on Foreign Relations on April 15, 1936.

In 1935 Germany admitted deliberate violation of the armament limitations of the Versailles Treaty and it has now been almost 6 weeks since she occupied the Rhineland & repudiated the Locarno treaties by the same very effective accomplished fact method. During that interval I have had the enviable pleasure of spending 3 weeks out of the United States & beyond the orbit of newspapers, or at least of newspapers I could read. The experience was a comforting one; and abstract contemplation in a remote & sunny vacuum resulted in the confident & profound conclusion that a new war in Europe growing out of the unfinished business of the last war was preposterous — and that peace at last was man's hard won destiny — except in politics.

But when I returned to Chicago yesterday I found awaiting me the announcement of today's topic — Europe — New Roads to War! Such an abrupt encounter with reality is a little disquieting and suggests that my vacation vacuum was more actual than figurative. Perhaps if the chancellories of Europe could be briefly transported to a tranquil Mexican village it would have a sedative and possibly a pacific effect on the discordant frightened voices.

Walter Millis' books, "The Martial Spirit" and "The Road to War" are well known to you and it is a privilege to be able to hear him discuss a subject in which his research is profound and his analysis arresting. Apparently his interest in war & its causes is congenital because he is the son of an American Army officer. Since his graduation from Yale Mr Millis has been engaged in editorial writing — for the last 10 yrs on the staff of the N. Y. Herald-Tribune. He will discuss the recent political history of Europe and the excellent progress that has been made on the road to the next war.

Norman H. Davis had been the chief United States delegate to the World Disarmament Conference that met during 1933 and 1934 and to the London Naval Conference, 1936. Japan walked out of the conference. France, Great Britain, and the United States agreed to abandon tonnage quotas set under the Five Power Treaty of 1922. The signatories, however, did agree to some limitations on the armament of warships.

To Norman H. Davis

April 17, 1936

Dear Mr. Davis:

I want to renew the invitation of the Chicago Council on Foreign Relations to address a luncheon meeting this spring. We hope very much that you will find it convenient to accept and to discuss the London Conference and its results — or for that matter anything you wish.

I need not add that it would be a great honor to have you here and that you would have a large and intelligent audience. I do want to point out, however, that the middle west gets little opportunity for personal contact with the figures in world affairs and, with a wholly inadequate press, it is small wonder that public opinion out here is somewhat eccentric. William Phillips spoke before the Council some time ago and I believe was impressed with the importance of more direct and accurate information on foreign affairs in the middle west.

We can, of course, arrange a meeting on a few days notice at any time to suit your convenience. I hope it will be possible for you to come.

With kindest regards, I am

Faithfully yours,

To Wayne Chatfield-Taylor

April 22, 1936

Dear Wayne:

We have recently returned from a vacation in Mexico — most successful! I find that in my absence I have in some mysterious manner been booked to address the Junior Chamber of Commerce on The United States and Foreign Trade, — about which I know somewhat less than I know about the arrangement of the scales on the cobra grande!

Won't you, will you, won't you comfort my troubled spirit with some references to speeches, articles:

1. Stating the principles involved in the Hull-Peek controversy.
2. Analysing the results of the reciprocal trade agreements to date.
3. Analysing comparatively our foreign trade position over the last few years.

I appreciate that these are no longer matters of daily concern to you and that I am imposing on a very busy man — in short, that I am something of a louse generally; because, of course, the transparent motive for this letter is my anxiety to avoid any work and investigation myself.

Anyway, help, help!

Yours,

To Mrs. Carl Vrooman

April 27, 1936

Dear Cousin Julia:

Many thanks for your good letter of April 24th. John Fell Stevenson will probably resent it bitterly if you do not make a cribside obeisance before long. The children may go out to Lake Forest the end of this week, but I hope you will have a chance to look in before you leave for Europe.

I was much interested in what you had to say about Mildred Fitz-Henry's application for a position with the Council.[40] I know that she possesses most all of the qualifications for our job and I sincerely hope that she will get it. However, as you can understand, I am somewhat embarrassed in this matter because of my personal interest in the welfare of Judge FitzHenry's family. There have also been one or two other applications filed by personal friends of mine, with the result that I have concluded that the proper way is to appoint a committee to make a selection from the most eligible applicants, of whom Mildred is one. In short, I am going to have to avoid personal intervention so far as possible.

The Boston party sounded very attractive to Ellen, but I am afraid she spent all of her spare money in Mexico on our vacation and will not be able to go.

Affectionately,

To Wayne Chatfield-Taylor

April 29, 1936

Dear Wayne:

I am off for Boston in a few minutes on business and hastily acknowledge receipt of the ponderous envelope full of indigestable information. I am deeply grateful and mortified for putting you to this trouble.

Your kind remarks anent my admission to this firm are deeply appreciated. Of course the delay to which you refer is due to the fact that they were naturally reluctant to make any public confession before they had to.[41]

I saw my wife the other day and she confirmed your suspicion that we were again going to enjoy the baronial surroundings of 620 Lake

[40] The assistant directorship of the Chicago Council on Foreign Relations was open. Miss FitzHenry was the daughter of Judge FitzHenry of Bloomington.

[41] Mr. Taylor on April 27, 1936, had congratulated him on his being made a partner in the law firm of Cutting, Moore and Sidley but he asked Stevenson why he and the firm had to keep this information "from me so long."

Avenue [Lake Forest] during May — which will again impair my hard earned taste for prunes.

Can I assume that you are going to spend some time out here this summer? I look forward to seeing you immoderately.

Yours,

On May 15, 1936, Clay Judson, who had been president of the Chicago Council on Foreign Relations from 1927 to 1929, wrote Stevenson: "Have I told you recently what a splendid job I think you do as a presiding officer? I am more and more impressed every meeting I attend. It should be on your conscience that you are not serving your country by going into politics. You would be a great success. With your background and ability you ought to be able to accomplish some real good."

THE PRESIDENT'S REPORT TO THE ANNUAL MEETING OF THE CHICAGO COUNCIL ON FOREIGN RELATIONS, MAY 12, 1936

1. Annual meeting
2. Review the year — membership, speakers, meetings
3. Mary's retirement
4. Treasurer's report
5. Nominating Com report
6. Speaker — "Germany from within."

For the last couple of days I have searched in vain for some way of relieving the monotony of this annual meeting. Even stockholders annual meetings are sometimes enlivened with questions about the Presidents salary etc & I thought of reversing the tables this time and asking you for a salary for your overworked President — but I dismissed that once hastily with the certain knowledge that you would probably rise indignantly & say the question is not "why a salary" but "why a President." The potency of this reasoning so dispirited me that I abandoned further efforts to improve the formula for this meeting & so, with your indulgence, I will proceed with a brief review of the year & the dispatch of the business required by our charter & by laws — which contrary to the general impression are not a myth and really exist — tho copies are extremely rare & not without interest to collectors like Mr. Hale, Mr. Elting, Mr. Rosenthal.[42]

---

[42] William B. Hale was president of the council, 1924–1925; Victor Elting was president of the council, 1923–1924; Lessing Rosenthal was a member of the board of directors, 1925–1926. Kenneth T. Jackson, *Chicago Council on Foreign Relations: A Record of Forty Years* (Chicago: the Council, 1963), pp. 63–65.

I've observed that most all presidents have been reporting successful years lately & I'm happy to say that the council is no exception — Like the armament industry the Council thrives on trouble and thanks in some measure to a troubled world our net paid membership has increased in the last year from 1606 to 2050 as the corporation tycoons say or a wholesome increase & a gratifying evidence of the fine cooperation the management has received thruout the year. During the past season we have had 20 luncheon meetings including an address by the Undersec. of State — the highest ranking officer of our own state dept. that has ever spoken before us. The average attendance was 650. The program has been designed to give some continuity of treatment to various aspects of world events & to shed as much authoritative light from as many points of view as possible. If subject matter has been omitted it has been due usually to inability to secure a genuinely recognized and able commentator & if some of the speakers have not measured up to the high standard we attempt to maintain & always improve it has been due to the occasional necessity of making blind dates in some emergencies and not from want of diligence on the part of your executive staff.

Speaking of the Ex. staff I remind you that thruout the season Mr. [Clifton] Utley has been broadcasting on Monday nights & that the exceptional quality of these broadcasts by the Director of the Council have enhanced our prestige not a little. Under his Editorship Foreign Notes continues to en[j]oy an ever enlarging field of very creditable influence. Mr. Utleys rapidly growing prominence in the field of Foreign Affairs is well known to all of you and you will be happy to hear that he is going abroad this summer again & will return in the fall to open our season again as Director of the Council.

And now, tho I am loath to approach the subject, I have come to the bad news. After 4 years of spirited & resourceful devotion to the Council and its welfare Mary de C[oningh], the assistant Director, is deserting us, for no better reason than marriage. For several years it has been possible to reason with her, but of late insidious & unfair influences have been secretly at work with the devestating & unreasonable result that I have indicated; leaving us no choice but to surrender her or move the Council to her new home Princeton N.J. And after careful consideration we have concluded that the latter is impractical. But perhaps she will address [us] soon on Foreign Affairs as vocational training for marriage.

But I suspect some of you may have come to hear Mr. [Wallace] Deuel & without further comment on this irreperable loss I will ask Mr. [Stuart] Otis to read the treasure[r]'s report:

I wish I could squander some more of your precious time telling you not merely that we need money — because your generosity somehow always enables us to get what we need for the publication fund, but to tell you how much better we could do our job and improve our services if we had a little more money than we actually need or as somebody said you can work better on a cushion than a board!

The Nominating Committee is required by the by laws to report its slate of officers and members of the Executive Coun. to the annual meeting and further provides that nominations may be made from the floor. The Committee consists of Mr Will. B Hale, chairman, Mr Geo. Richardson [43] & Mr Carroll Binder.[44] Mr Hale I understand is out of town and I will ask Mr Richardson to read the report.

I admit that I appointed this nominating com & you wouldn't believe me if I professed surprise at what they've done — because of course I've known it a week — but you will agree that my predicament is embarrassing & I am going to ask Mr R[ichardson]. to see this thing thru as presiding officer while I tremble in my chair.

Its always gratifying to witness the democratic process — to see the sovereign people exercise their considered will after a fair & vigorous contest!

I cannot pass on without reminding you the eight retiring members of the Ex Com — Mr. [William B.] Hale, Mr George R[ichardson], Mr [Lessing] Rosen[thal], Mr [Silas] Strawn and Mr [Victor] Elting, Mrs [William G.] Hibbard, Mr [Quincy] Wright are all original members of the council & 4 of them have served as President. For 15 years they have given generously of their time, money advice & council. I am reconciled to their leaving the Ex Com only because I know that their interest in this their child will continue undiminished.

I appreciate the honor which you have again bestowed upon me & assure you that if you permit me to survive for another year in this exposed position I will get off this platform forever. The manner of my selection should make the transition from democracy to Nazi Germany almost imperceptible. If Mr D[euel]. will come back again I'll promise him a proper introduction. But now I will only remind you that he has been in Germany continuously for the last two years as a distinguished member of the Foreign Service of the Chi D[aily]. News — he has returned to the U.S. only within the last fortnight & will give us an authentic eyewitness account from behind the scenes in the worlds most important theatre of interest. Mr. Deuel.

---

[43] A Chicago businessman who worked for Mr. Marshall Field.
[44] Foreign news editor of the Chicago *Daily News*.

To Mrs. Jacob Baur

May 14, 1936

Dear Mrs. Baur:

As a member of the [Chicago] Council [on Foreign Relations], you are doubtless familiar with Foreign Notes which is designed to keep our members currently informed on significant developments abroad. The publication now has a wide circulation throughout the Middle West and has become one of the most valuable activities of the Council.

The revenue from Council memberships does not yet fully cover the additional cost of publishing Foreign Notes. For 1936 this expense will be about $2400, part of which has already been raised. In an effort to insure publication of Foreign Notes through 1936, we are asking some former contributors, who believe in the educational value of our work, to renew their contributions to the Publication Fund.

If you wish, your contribution may be entered in whole or in part as gift memberships in the Council on Foreign Relations at $5 each. I suggest this because many members wish to provide gift memberships for one year for friends who have not yet joined the Council. In this way your contribution to the Publication Fund will serve a doubly useful purpose. The names you suggest on the enclosed card will be carefully checked in the Council office to avoid duplication with the present membership.

Whatever contribution you can make toward this Fund will be deeply appreciated.

Sincerely yours,

To Sydnor Walker [45]

May 21, 1936

Dear Miss Walker:

On behalf of the Chicago Council on Foreign Relations I am happy to endorse the request of the Library of International Relations for assistance from the Rockefeller Foundation.

The Chicago Council on Foreign Relations is one of the several cooperating organizations supporting in a very modest way the work of the Library. We have found the Library of value in our own work and hope that it may receive the funds necessary to insure its perpetuation and growth.

[45] Miss Walker was on the staff of the Rockefeller Foundation.

The easy access which the Library affords to current periodical information on current international affairs is useful in the preparation of "Foreign Notes," the bi-weekly publication of the Council. We frequently receive requests for information concerning current international affairs and the availability of the Library, equipped as it is, relieves us of this burden.

The purpose of the Chicago Council on Foreign Relations is primarily educational, through lectures, broadcasts and publications. A well equipped and accessible Library in downtown Chicago is an important supplement in our educational work.

The Council believes that a Library, providing current information and also able to assemble materials for more extensive research provides a natural center for work in adult education in the international field. Numerous organizations in Chicago can avail themselves of the Library and supplement their work by its use, thus gradually developing a greater knowledge of international affairs in this important area.

Sincerely yours,

To Conrad L. Wirth [46]

June 19, 1936

Dear Mr. Wirth:

I am presuming to write you about my friend Ralph W. Pierson, who has been doing publicity work in the Department for the last year. As I may have been in some degree responsible for his obtaining this appointment, I have of course been interested in his progress in the Park Service, which has been the principal interest of this talented young man for many years.

The excellent radio program "Treasure Trails" seemed to me exceptionally good publicity and I was gratified to hear from Pierson that he had written the script. I hope and trust that he is earning a place for himself in the Service and that his work will merit recognition and advancement.

Sincerely yours,

To Ralph W. Pierson

June 19, 1936

Dear Ralph:

I have been out of town for some time and have not had an earlier opportunity to acknowledge your letter of the 8th. I have written Mr.

[46] Assistant director of the National Park Service, Department of the Interior.

Wirth as per the enclosed copy and I hope it will prove of some service to you.

From my own observation and a similar experience of a close friend of mine who got into government service through me, I am impressed with the importance of maintaining tactful harmony with superior officers — particularly officers of inferior capacity who are always self conscious. I hope you can improve your relations with the woman you mentioned and, of course, although I do not know your precise circumstances, I would never complain to higher ups. It may take longer to get recognition for good work — but it is far surer and safer to "take the rap" like a good soldier.

My kindest regards to your mother and congratulations on your new offspring.

Sincerely yours,

On July 27, 1936, a St. Louis lawyer, Sterling E. Edmonds, wrote Stevenson saying that he and former Democratic Senator James A. Reed were inviting a group of Constitutional Democrats "who are opposed to the present alien control of our party's name and machinery" to a conference to discuss what to do in the campaign between President Franklin D. Roosevelt and Governor Alf M. Landon. "We are agreed," Edmonds stated, "as are all who have any knowledge of Constitutional history, that the reelection of President Roosevelt and his perseverance in his collectivist policies . . . presents one of the gravest problems which has ever confronted the free American citizen." Edmonds closed by saying that he had been informed that Stevenson was a Democrat who could not accept Roosevelt's policies.

To Sterling E. Edmonds

July 31, 1936

Dear Mr. Edmunds:

Thank you for your letter of July 27th inviting me to attend the meeting of "Constitutional Democrats" in Detroit to discuss what we can and should do in the present campaign.

I suspect you have been misinformed about me. At all events, I do not share your concern about the sinister consequences of President Roosevelt's reelection, and I do not believe that his reelection "presents one of the gravest problems that has ever confronted the free American citizen." On the contrary, I believe that President Roosevelt's contributions to the welfare of free American citizens entitle him not only to re-election but also to their profound gratitude. As a Democrat I have observed with no little satisfaction that even the Republican leadership seems to recognize these contributions by the sincere flattery of imitation.[47]

I do not mean to imply for a moment that I approve of everything that this Administration has done or the manner in which it has been done. But the balance of achievements and failures, the balance of good and bad, leave me in no uncertainty as to what I "should do in the present campaign." I shall vote for President Roosevelt thankfully and with pride in a Democratic Administration which has again in an emergency served the country well.

With sincerest regards, I am

Faithfully yours,

James Farley, chairman of the Democratic National Committee, Frank Walker, and W. Forbes Morgan wired Stevenson on August 31, 1936, asking him to serve on the Chicago branch of the finance committee of the Democratic National Committee.

To W. Forbes Morgan

September 8, 1936

Dear Mr. Morgan:

I apologize for my failure to reply to your telegram of August 31st, which arrived during my absence in Canada on a brief vacation.

. . . I will, of course, be glad to be of such help as my time and circumstances permit, and please do not hesitate to call upon me.

Sincerely yours,

Stevenson was inaugurating his second year as president of the Chicago Council on Foreign Relations. Clifton M. Utley served as executive director of the council from 1931 to 1942. Stevenson introduced Mr. Utley, who spoke to the council on September 25, 1936.

I want to preface my remarks today and for the ensuing season by

[47] This probably refers to the 1936 Republican national platform, which endorsed a number of New Deal measures.

assuring you that I share you[r] disappointment at not seeing a new face on the platform. Your patience last year earned something better. In my role of an essential nuisance — like an in-a-door bed — I promise to make my appearances as brief as the dignity of our speakers and my own conceit will permit.

Today the Council inaugurates its 15th season with the world in such delicate health that we are assured of perhaps the most interesting season since the Council was founded in the year 1922, when armaments were to be progressively abolished and the machinery of collective security was going to insure peace on earth and good will among men. In these brief intervening years we have witnessed the disheartening and rapid rout of world idealism before the impact of economic nationalism. But here in the midlands we have also witnessed an accompanying wholesome growth of intelligent interest in foreign affairs. To promote and satisfy that interest has been our educational function in this community, and that we have succeeded in some measure is attested by the gathering you see here today and by the fact that our membership has increased from a handful to almost 2200. Perhaps in time *all* of the Chicago newspapers will even realize that the council is not a club but an important Chicago institution — an active adult educational institution.

Tho our recent growth has been most gratifying there is no truth in the rumor that we may soon be obliged to hold our meetings in Grant Park or the even the stadium. On the contrary, tho vigorous and proud, we are still poor — indeed I must confess that we are still on relief! Last year we came closer to balancing our budget of about $15000 than ever before, but we were again obliged to come to you for help. However a condition of honest self support is within sight and to that desirable end I again bespeak your cooperation. In addition to bringing guests and coercing people into joi[ni]ng I remind you that many people have made gifts of memberships in the Council — its only $5 per year.

Miss [Ellen] Bartel who has succeeded Miss de [Coningh] as assistant to the Director tells me that the grief of these huge luncheons would be materially assuaged if you all tried very hard not to change your reservations later than 2 P.M. of the preceding day — Also that guests at todays meeting may become members by the payment of only $4.50 at the new membership desk near the door and finally I must ask you to please remember to bring your membership cards for identification at the door — one of the penalties of our luxuriant growth is that it is no longer possible to recognize everyone — or to save the metaphor ever[y] flower in our garden!

As an earnest of our intention to treat you to only the best in the season ahead I proudly announce that Edgar Ansell Mowrer, just back from Spain and his post in Paris, will address the Council one week from today on War by Proxy in Spain as a symptom of Collective Insecurity. I sometimes think that next to Edgar Mowrer about the best informed man on Europe today is [our] own director — Clifton Utley. As you know Mr Utley has spent the summer abroad — largely in Germany and will again commence our season by portraying the further evaluation of a dynamic state — Germany in 1936.

To Mrs. Elizabeth C. Johnson [48]

October 2, 1936

Dear Mrs. Johnson:

I have your letter and note your apprehension that the communist activity is injuring our country. I do not share your misgivings and I find no cause for alarm — unless another period of suffering and want overtakes the people before we have fully recovered from the last one. As you know, communism like fascism is a manifestation of social unrest and hunger always precedes violence and revolution.

From the dark days of 1932 we have made a remarkable recovery, and though the expense has been great, the distressed have been cared for and many of the old abuses and economic injustices have been cured. These things have been done by the affirmative action of the government and for the present at least private property and capitalism have been preserved in our country and democracy is working.

The best protection against the influences you fear is not suppression but elimination of the causes. Our present government has recognized this and I am going to vote for President Roosevelt.

Sincerely yours,

The Chicago Council on Foreign Relations always faced the difficult problem of persuading Chicago newspapers to give adequate space to its speakers in the news columns. Instead the council usually was relegated to the society page where the attendance of prominent society women invariably was mentioned.

[48] Mrs. Johnson, of El Monte, California, wrote Stevenson protesting Communist activity in the country.

To Mary Welsh [49]

October 2, 1936

Dear Miss Welsh:

Thank you for your letter. I enjoyed it and appreciate your taking the trouble to write me. Furthermore, I agree with everything you say. By suggesting my hope that in time the newspapers will recognize the importance of the Council as an educational institution and give us more news coverage, I did not mean to imply that the social coverage (particularly yours) has not been adequate or that I am unappreciative of the help that it has given us.

You see there are many men in Chicago who have been skeptical of the Council because of a suspected social flavor. Gradually I hope they will come to realize that we have something to offer. If the newspapers treat us as serious news as well as social news, we may in time be able to attract more of these people, who, as you know, need us badly!

By aspiring to the news pages, I do not mean to disparage the society pages — or bite the hand that feeds us.

Sincerely yours,

Stevenson introduced Edgar Ansel Mowrer to the Chicago Council on Foreign Relations on October 2, 1936.

Because citizens as good as we all need no reminder I merely state the irrelevant fact that Tuesday is the last day to register for the November election.

Before introducing to you a speaker whom you already know I must publicly deny the ominous rumor that we may soon be obliged to hold our meetings in Grant Park or at least the Chicago Stadium. To be sure we have added 335 members in the last two weeks (and if the loyalists can hold out a little longer we should get a lot more) but I can assure you that we are in no immediate [danger] of outgrowing the loop, and I urge you to use the cards on the tables to suggest possible members. You can leave them on the table or at the door and they will be carefully checked to avoid duplication.

Last year at this time we were occupied with war in Ethiopia — this year it is war in Spain [50] — what it may be next year no one can

[49] An editor at the Chicago *Daily News.*

[50] In July, 1936, General Francisco Franco launched a revolt against the Spanish government.

for[e]tell. Last year we witnessed a disheartening rebuff to the age old ambition to subject to the reign of law not only men but states. Today we are witnessing something even more sinister — a bloody conflict between brothers which many people suggest is but a ghastly prelude to the more ghastly drama to follow. Because we are destined to hear much of the conflict between fa[s]cism and socialism we are devoting two consecutive meetings to Spain. Next week Maxwell Stuart [Stewart], an authority on Spain from which he has just returned will speak on the immediate situation in Spain and the long and intricate historical background of the Civil War.

Today Edgar Ansell Mowrer will tell us something of his recent experiences and observations in Spain and using S. as a point of departure will discuss of the larger European rivalries [in] which he sees them mirrored. Mr. Mowrer is the younger member of the famous team of Mowrers which has has contributed so much to the quality [of] foreign correspondence in American journalism. That he was born in the distinguished city of Bloomington, Illinois is not his only distinction. For more than 20 years he has lived abroad while his reputation has been growing at home. He has written a number of books and in 1932 was awarded the Pulitzer Prize for the best Foreign correspondence of the year. That year he published his famous book Germany turns the clock Back — which was apparently read without audible applause by Adolph Hitler. Since then he has been writing for the Daily News from Paris. Mr. Mowrer.

Stevenson introduced Maxwell Stewart to the Chicago Council on Foreign Relations on October 9, 1936.

Last week someone said to me, a little indelicately I thought, that he wasn't quite as much interested in our membership figures as he was in finishing his des[s]ert in tranquility. So I hesitate to belabor you with a further recitation of our achievements, but I feel that you share in some measure my satisfaction in the wholesome growth of this educational project and that you believe that the widespread, discriminating interest of the electorate in public affairs, both foreign and domestic, is in the long run the best insurance of survival of a democratic system of government. So, at the risk of further offense I report with gratification that our membership is now 2400 a net increase of 325 since the season commenced. But please donot feel that the success of your efforts is embarrassing — the staff can still handle the mail without inconvenience.

We have asked Dr. Gustav Stalper to come to Chicago next Tuesday to discuss the recent currency stabilization agreement and the problems incident to devaluation in France, Italy, Holland and Switzerland. Those of you who recall Dr. Stalper's speech before the Council last year will anticipate a stimulating and enlightening discussion of this all important and promising development & because of the brief interval before this meeting you can make reservation[s] at the door.

Last week Edgar Mowrer used Spain as a point of departure to paint with arresting realism a sombre picture of the future of Europe. Today Maxwell Stewart will describe in detail the genesis and meaning of the vicious conflict in Spain which I remind you in a few years has passed thru monarchy and dictatorship to democracy and in which those conflicting philosophies now seem to be locked in a death struggle. Mr. Stewart for many years has been the FPA's [51] specialist in international economics and has just returned to the U.S. after witnessing the grim spectacle in Spain from the beginning. We are fortunate to have a speaker so eminently qualified to clarify the confusing military and political panorama and to comment on the familiar statement that in the Spanish civil war the government can lose but the Rebels can never win.

Stevenson introduced Gustav Stalper to the Chicago Council on Foreign Relations on October 13, 1936.

Commencing with the Japanese invasion of Manchuria in 1932 [52] defiance of the League of Nations and repudiation of treaty obligations has become not the exception but the order of conduct among the so called dynamic states. With the League ostensibly moribund one now hears much of plans to recreate and revitalize the League and recently the smaller powers, aided by Russia, administered a severe rebuke to the great powers and defeated their attempt to unseat the Italian delegation. Because the League may again emerge as a factor in world politics we are contemplating for the first time in a long while an appraisal of the League's position and prospects. We also have in mind a meeting on Holland which as a small state with a great colonial empire presents an interesting problem of neutrality in a divided world. We hope to be able to announce this meeting and a meeting on the League soon.

[51] The Foreign Policy Association of New York.
[52] Actually 1931.

Five years ago last month Britain cut the pound loose from gold and was promptly followed by the other countries known as the sterling bloc. The subsequent history of the failure of the economic conference in the summer of 1933, devaluation by the U. S. and the progressive strangulation of international trade by the manifold restrictions dictated by nationalist philosophy are familiar to all of you. And now in a very dark hour a portentious event has occurred. We have joined Britain and France in an informal agreement to stabilize our currencies and France has at last taken the preliminary steps to effect the long delayed devaluation of the franc. Other so called gold countries, Holland, Switzerland and Italy have followed the lead and already in some places tariff barriers have been lowered and trade restrictions relaxed.

If international commerce and the gradual restoration of economic health is the best insurance of peace on earth these recent developments may be the happiest event of recent years. But there are serious implications in devaluation and stabilization which few laymen are able to analyse and evaluate. Hence like cautious patients we have sought the assistance of one of the foremost diagnosticians — Dr Gustav Stalper — who as you know was a member of the Budget Commission of the Reichstag and editor & publisher of the famous *German Economist* until the advent of Hitler. We welcome Dr. Stalper again and also Madam Stalper whose reputation as an economist I am told compares favorably with that of her distinguished husband.

Mrs. Ernest L. Ives recalled that her brother told her that he never worked harder on a speech than the one he delivered at Carleton College, October 23, 1936. He explained to her that he worked out a "balanced, reasoned presentation of the case of Democrats versus Republicans, from which one could only conclude that the Democratic case was overwhelming." The audience was attentive and her brother was satisfied as he finished that he "had struck a solid, sober blow for Roosevelt." After the speech he heard two students agree it was the best political speech they had ever heard. One of them added in a puzzled tone, however: "But could you figure out which side he was for?" [53]

I want to preface my remarks by assuring you that this is not intended as a political speech. I say that for several reasons: In the first place, it

[53] Elizabeth Stevenson Ives and Hildegarde Dolson, *My Brother Adlai* (New York: Morrow, 1956), pp. 113–114.

will effectively prevent you from saying it is the worst political speech you have ever heard; secondly, I have never made a political speech and I confess, without shame, that it is all I can do to listen to most of them, let alone make one; and, finally, were I to attempt one it would not be before an intelligent academic audience without any single dominant interest which I could seize upon for my excursion into the familiar wonderland of irrational praise and intemperate damnation.

But for this very reason I welcomed your distinguished President's very bad judgment in inviting me here this morning, because in this atmosphere, we can, perhaps, step aside from the sound and fury and reason together quietly and tolerantly. I believe that you and I by education have a great responsibility to democracy — a responsibility which is happily epitomized by the educational ideal of Carleton College, which Mat[t]hew Arnold expressed in the familiar words: "To see life steadily, and see it whole." Whether you vote for Governor Landon or President Roosevelt is not so important, but that you pay your debt to democracy soberly and intelligently is important; for you, the discriminating and enlightened electorate of tomorrow, are the burden bearers of democracy and the continuing insurance of the survival of our system of things at a time when political and economic freedom is everywhere being challenged and engulfed. So I ask you to accept as a political text the ideal of your College: "To see life steadily, and see it whole;" reject prejudice, emotion and partisanship — scrutinize the parts, but see the whole. I appreciate that this is hard to do in the confused clamor of a campaign. I appreciate that it is difficult to separate the light from the heat. But if you cannot retain your perspective, no one can.

In this spirit of dispassionate analysis, I am going to attempt to trace aloud briefly the process of thought by which I have reached my decision in the present campaign.

My anxiety is not so much to convince you that my decision is right. — My anxiety is to convince you that the method is right; that we must apply to political decisions the same process of intelligent selection and rejection which you have come here to learn; the same quality of thoughtful analysis which distinguishes the educated from the uneducated. I feel strongly about this because I know historically that the dynamic minority that knows what it wants — the special interest, if you please — is the constant menace of democracy and government truly representative of all the people.

It may be purely philosophical and it certainly is not important, but it appears that in national elections independents usually vote negatively, not affirmatively. That is, they vote against some one rather than for some one. In short, I do not think one votes for Governor Landon so much as he votes against President Roosevelt in the present situation. So let us examine the reasons for voting against Roosevelt.

In the first place, responsible Republicans no longer charge Mr. Roosevelt with an attempt to be a dictator after the style of Stalin and Hitler, and even the wild assertions that he intends to tear up the constitution and destroy the Supreme Court are heard no more. Also, we now don't hear that Governor Landon is a creature of [William Randolph] Hearst. Fortunately most of this political mummery has been eliminated from the campaign.

But there are other good reasons for voting against President Roosevelt:

He has not kept faith with the Democratic platform of 1932. — This familiar statement always recalls the classic remark of the negro pullman porter to the two congressman loitering on the car platform: — "I remind you gentlemen that platforms is to step in on, not to stand on."

He has permitted Congress to abdicate.

He has extended federal control over business, industry, banking and agriculture.

He has challenged American traditions.

He has invaded legislative fields reserved to the States.

His budget is unbalanced.

He has spent vast sums of money.

He has increased our taxes!

Now these individually are formidable and collectively would seem to constitute reason enough to vote against President Roosevelt. Nor is it sufficient to say that he meant well, and that his intentions were good. Hell, I am told, is paved with good intentions and I know the bankruptcy courts are. At this point you see I am almost convinced that I should vote against Mr. Roosevelt — he has made too many mistakes; he has experimented with me too much and the vision of a tortured guinea pig haunts my sleep. But I remind you that we are in an academic atmosphere, imbued with the scientific spirit, searching objectively for the whole truth and not content until all the evidence is in. Our text is to see the thing steadily, and see it whole.

And what is the whole? The whole is the good with the bad, the right with the wrong, the successes with the failures. We must balance the evidence and see where we come out. I will spare you a tiresome recitation of the balance sheet for the answer is apparent — success outweighs failure. The intervention of an aggressive government in three years has restored our national health. If this were a political speech, it would be appropriate at this juncture to pause a moment and rhapsodize on this amazing achievement — to remind you of the prophets of the new era, of banished poverty, of the chicken in every pot — and then of bread lines, muttering masses, burning corn and smokeless chimneys. But this is not the place for dramatics, and I will call my next witness to justify what the government has done.

"Government is the residuary legatee of all the successes and all the failures of all of us. Government must keep itself going and keep the people going too.

"Government must intervene to relieve the sufferings of the people. It is intolerable in the modern world, with its elaborate mechanism of trade and finance, its highly industrialized and mechanized economy, that our people should be left to starve or to endure privation almost worse than starvation. It is intolerable that the monetary mechanism evolved for the sole purpose of achieving stability and human welfare should be permitted ever again to run amuck as it did from 1929 to 1933. It is an archaic superstition that money is stable if its value remains fixed in gold only, while prices collapse more or less generally to the point of bankruptcy, as they did in that tragic period. During the last three years government policy put an end to deflation, brought about some measure of recovery, achieved monetary stabilization and provided necessary relief. Let us not be unmindful of the depth of economic despair from which in three years we have emerged, nor the vital necessity of government action along these lines, however critical we may be of the extent and manner in which public expenditures have been made, or of this and that."

My witness, strange to say, is not [Rexford G.] Tugwell or [Felix] Frankfurter, or any of those familiar demons of the newspapers, but Russell Leffingwell, a senior partner of J. P. Morgan & Company, one of the great Wall Street bankers whom the Democrats so love to vilify. But I suspect that quite as important as material recovery and the accompanying reforms is the fact that essential democracy seems to have emerged unscathed in spite of the dire prophecies, and my supporting evidence is that I am here today and that you and I and 40,000,000 other voters are trying to decide, in accordance with our best traditions, whether to thank or to spank President Roosevelt.

At this point in the analysis the balance of the evidence suggests that the New Deal, though by no means all it ought to be, has worked surprisingly well in a material way and with little sacrifice of precious principles. In short, it has been in tune with the times, and has brought us through without serious misadventure. So I am about to conclude that President Roosevelt is entitled to my vote after all. But the story is not finished and you can properly say: This is all well enough; we admit that incredible things have been accomplished and we are deeply appreciative, but where do we go from here? Have not we paid too dearly for this rapid recovery? Is not inflation ahead from which few can escape, and hasn't he encouraged radicalism and sold our birthright — the American system?

Now, at last, we approach the fundamental issues of this campaign — the things that many years from now may have historical significance (and I suspect that America will be here many years from now whoever is elected).

With respect to inflation, I can only offer an uneducated guess. Granted that neither party or candidate favors currency inflation, what we are talking about is credit inflation. Simply stated the controls on too rapid credit expansion are the reserves required of member banks of The Federal Reserve System and taxation. As to the former, we must trust whoever is president, that a highly competent non-political Reserve Board will continue to handle the situation with the caution it has already displayed; (and on this score I will charitably refrain from recalling the political auspices for the great credit orgy of the late twenties and its consequence, which I believe is commonly known as the "crash.") With respect to the inflationary restraint of taxation, I believe you know the answer. As prosperity grows government income will increase and government expense decline. Ultimately, there will be a surplus and when there is, which party and what president would be most likely to resist the inevitable and terrific pressure from business and finance to reduce taxes? Here again I am reluctant to invoke the record of the past.

And now what of the future of our system of things? Isn't Landon the man to look a second time at what has been done, to discard the bad and keep the good and to consolidate the gains which Roosevelt has made and which Landon has quietly embraced in large measure? Perhaps, but I don't think so. And I believe that in a fundamental way President Roosevelt's reelection may provide insurance against the sort of thing America has most to fear. President Roosevelt has had the vision and courage to adapt our economic structure to the changing circumstances of the modern world, and for the still critical period that lies just ahead it would seem wise to conserve the confidence which he enjoys among the distressed masses, who were the worst victims of the depression. They feel and with reason that he has tried to restore hope and equalize opportunity. If he were defeated, it is not hard to envision a union of the more radical elements behind irresponsible leadership, which he has hitherto checked and counterbalanced. And there will be no shortage of radical leadership for a long time to come.

Though often wrong and often raw, the effectiveness of the social and economic measures of this Administration is the best insurance against radicalism of the right or the left, and there is little choice between them. Reforms should be administered by those who vigorously and successfully proposed them and should not be placed in other hands at the behest of those who have evolved and supported much of what lies at the roots of the malady. To be sure, there is urgent need for conservative restraint in the administration of reform. I think this is insured in the years just ahead for two reasons: In the first place, the Democratic membership in Congress is bound to be reduced in the next Congress, and even more important is the clear evidence that President Roosevelt is a keen judge of public opinion and is well aware that with the restoration of normal processes the tide is running conservatively and there is little enthusiasm for more reform.

But before I conclude I must advert to one reason why I would feel obliged to vote against Mr. Landon, even if the evidence for Mr. Roosevelt, which I have clumsily reviewed, were less convincing. I am afraid the Republican party has learned little and has again fallen victim to an ancient error; an error acutely distressing to many Republican sympathizers. They are advocating a policy of aloofness, isolation and narrow nationalism. They would abrogate the reciprocal trade agreements; they would make tariffs more prohibitive of foreign trade than ever before. It was the loss of our foreign markets for agricultural surpluses that occasioned the demand for crop control and a planned economy for agriculture. It is the loss of foreign markets for industry that is responsible in large measure for persisting unemployment. But if we don't buy we can't sell, and the best antidote for regimentation and discontent is wholesome international commerce. The reciprocal trade agreements sponsored by President Roosevelt are the first thaw in a frozen world. That way lies hope and peace. The other leads to another economic suicide behind a Smoot-Hawley tariff wall.[54]

In conclusion, let me remind you that conservatives in critical moments are sometimes politically short sighted. In France they fought a pacific German republic, and got Hitler. In Russia they fought Kerensky and got Lenin. In a world of violence and conflict between extremists, it is not easy to see life steadily and see it whole. But there is a middle road and we are on it. I hope we stay there!

[54] The high protective tariff bill passed by Congress in 1930.

To W. R. Joslyn

October 29, 1936

Dear Mr. Joslyn:

I enclose herewith, in accordance with my telephone conversation, check payable to your order for $200, which I understand you will hold together with a check for $100 awaiting the outcome of the election.

If President Roosevelt receives a majority of the electoral votes, you will return my check together with the check for $100. If Governor Landon receives a majority of the electoral votes, you will deliver my check to your customer.

Please acknowledge the enclosure on the above terms on the enclosed copy of this letter.

Very truly yours,

Stevenson introduced Edward C. Carter to the Chicago Council on Foreign Relations on November 6, 1936.

In view of the recent plethora of speeches incident to the settlement of our quadriennial national dispute I was afraid you would be in no mood for further speaking today. Tuesday's pleasantness or unpleasantness (according to your point of view) was a comforting reminder that our democratic system of peaceful settlement of political controversy has survived the challenge of our times with no apparent diminution of vitality. But it also reminded me that the great experiment of subjecting states as well as men to a reign of law and to the peaceful adjustment of disputes has not succeeded so well and the future of the League of Nations has become a matter of first interest and concern. So we have asked Walter Laves, Director of the Mid-West office of the League of Nations Association, to discuss the future of the League. Mr Laves has just returned from Geneva and will speak on next Friday the 13th. Those of you who have met Mr Laves know that he speaks with disinterested objectivity, in spite of his official connection, and I for one can look forward even to Friday the 13th with eager anticipation.

Not only have you been engulfed in speeches lately but events in the Far East have recently been obscured by Europe, so I count your attendance today a tribute to our distinguished guest — Edward C. Carter. I need not recall Mr Carter's important services in the war or the fact that he has been in and out of the orient for many years. His intimate knowledge of the East and his constant familiarity with the latest developments in China and Japan in his work as Director of the Institute of Pacific Relations enable him to discuss as few occidentals can the mystifying succession of crises in Sino-Japanese relations — which for regularity match the crisis in Illinois relief administration. If any of you don't know, which is unthinkable, or overlooked Carroll Binder's excellent reports [in the Chicago *Daily News*] of the meeting at Yosemite this summer of the Institute of Pacific Relations, I hasten to advise you that Pacific is spelled with a capital P, is a noun not an adverb, and refers to an ocean not to peace — and we welcome with pleasure Edward C Carter, the director of a great world organization specializing in the political and economic affairs of the nations bordering the Pacific.

Stevenson introduced Emil Ludwig to the Chicago Council on Foreign Relations on November 25, 1936.

Six weeks ago I made a solemn resolution not to challenge your patience with further statistical information about the Council membership. But, enfeebled by the commercial influences attendant on the approaching Christmas season, I find myself no longer able to resist the temptation to advertise the fact that our membership is now 2485 — and to remind you that memberships in the Council make exceptionally useful, unique and convenient gifts.

We have in immediate prospect a meeting on Belgium, whose peculiar position in Europe invites careful attention in the perhaps historic moment in which we are living. Also we have not overlooked the forthcoming Pan American conference at Buenos Aires which is the occasion for the first visit of a President of the United States to a foreign country in 17 or 18 years. We hope to announce these addresses soon, subject to sudden change and substitution in the event of untoward developments in the European love nest.

I want also to remind you that a not unimportant result of the most recent readjustment of our clocks was to advance the hour of Mr. Utley's regular Monday night broadcasts on Station W. G. N. from 8 to 8:30.

Today's meeting is not only an opportunity to hear a man we all know but have never seen, but it is also something of a departure from the orthodox discussion of the political and economic aspects and implications of events. For today we are going to discuss *men;* because the chronicle of these times is in large measure the record of the purposes of some living makers of history. The historian of tomorrow may look back upon this post war period as a singular interval because the destinies of millions have been directed by a handful of men — not kings — who for the parts they have played must take their places with some of the historical characters which Emil Ludwig has described so brilliantly and explained with such penetrating psychological insight. Mr Ludwig was born in Breslau in 1881. Before the war he was much in England and during the war was employed by the German government as a journalist in the principal political centers of German speaking Europe. He has come to this country from the Argentine which has commissioned him to write a biography of the Liberator — Simon Bolivar. The Council welcomes a great international biographer and the creator of a new school of biographical writing — Emil Ludwig.

To William H. Dieterich

December 17, 1936

Dear Senator Dieterich:

I am taking the liberty of recommending for your favorable consideration John R. Duff, formerly of Normal, Illinois, which you will recall adjoins Bloomington. John Duff is a young man of fine appearance and mentality, and comes from a family of exceedingly self-respecting and high class negroes, who have lived in Normal since the Civil War. Various members of the family have been employed by my family for four generations. John was my mother's houseman and chauffeur for a number of years and went to Washington with me when I went there to live several years ago. When I returned to Chicago, he secured a position and remained in Washington.

I can testify from long personal experience with John that he is loyal, intelligent, well mannered and scrupulously honest. It is a pleasure to me to be of this small service to him.

With sincere personal regards, I am

Faithfully yours,

To Mrs. Ernest L. Ives [55]

December 31, 1936

Dear Buff —

Thanks for your letters — I hope you were well rested when you disembarked in Algiers — but I'll bet you're whipped by this time and

[55] This handwritten letter is in E.S.I., I.S.H.L.

it must have been a cruel blow to have to leave the mimosa & bougain-vill[e]a for the frozen north at this time of year.[56] The time to transfer from Algiers to St[oc]kholm is July!

This is the last day of the year and the last day of one of America's best known law firms. Cutting Moore & Sidley is no more & you can do a sköl (?) to Sidley, McPherson, Austin & Burgess. Sounds like a trunk falling downstairs doesn't it?

Congratulate Ernest on his splendid savings in 1936, but don't congratulate him on his election bets — what's more, being illegal, I can't collect them for him! If you feel a little filthy with money — as you no doubt do — let me know what you can spare and I'll get you some securities. Your Gulf Oil has gone up 10 points.

Happy New Year you Swedes!

Love —

AD.

Stevenson introduced Professor Samuel N. Harper to the Chicago Council on Foreign Relations on January 8, 1937.

Today you are to be addressed by about the most popular speaker that has ever appeared before the Council and, not content with that, next week we have arranged for you to hear another one of the most successful speaker[s] we have ever had, for today is Prof. Harper's 5th appearance and next week will be Salvador de Madariaga's 3rd. This remarkable man, novelist, critic, professor, statesman, lecturer, linguist and diplomat last summer resigned his most recent post as Spain's permanent delegate to the League of Nations after 5 years of unsolicited service to the Spanish republic as ambas[sador] at Washington and in various capacities. I donot know his attitude toward the present conflict in Spain — he has apparently broken off relations with the government, and has never espoused the rebels — but wherever his sympathies you can be sure of as stimulating and valuable an hour as the season will afford.

Commencing the new year with Samuel Harper and de Madariaga the Council is, to borrow a phrase with which this austere audience is quite unfamiliar, "shooting the works." But I'm told much is expected of 1937 so the management is merely setting the pace and we trust you will be able to keep up with us.

---

[56] Mr. Ives was being transferred to Stockholm in January, 1937, to be the U.S. consul general. Adlai's sister had visited in the U.S. during the fall of 1936.

I've never felt my humble function in these meetings as superfluous as today & I asked Sam Harper if he wouldn't introduce me instead — but he declined coldly and demanded all the formalities accorded strange[r]s — which I have no intention of giving our fellow member and long time benefactor. For the benefit of the new members and guests, however, I deem it appropriate to point out that the speaker is prof. of Russian Language and Institutions at the Univ of Chicago — from whence so many of our blessings flow — that he is the son of William Rainey Harper, the great first Pres of of the Univ of Chicago, that he has been travelling to and from Russia almost continuously for 33 years and that he returned from his last visit of 5 months like Santa Claus on Christmas morning and today will continue a series of biennial reports on Soviet Russia which commenced just 10 years ago and like the visits of a biennial Santa Clause have become landmarks in the evolution of this organization.

To Mr. and Mrs. Ernest L. Ives [57]

January 9, 1937

Dear B & E

How's it going? At the moment you must be approaching your new domicile & we hope it will be all you anticipate — tho I suspect the trek across Europe was even more!

Glad you had an encounter with Bullitt [58] — he must be a good guy, tho Sam Harper, my Russian expert, is not very flattering about his work there.

I'm frantically busy with office work — on the day & night shift again — and on top of it all I've been commanded to act as general Chairman of the President's Birthday ball for Chicago — ain't that hell!

I don't believe I ever thanked Ernest for the dates — there elegant and we are still munching & the children filching. John Fell thrives — tho I havent been home in time to see him since last Saturday.

So glad you gave Unc. Lou Merwin a good time. The Richardsons [59] write that they are thinking of coming to Sweden to see you next summer. Better drop 'em a note — and how about the Allen Browns! [60]

Ernest certainly looked resplendent in his monkey suit at the airport

---

[57] This handwritten letter is in E.S.I., I.S.H.L.

[58] Ambassador William Bullitt had made an official visit to Algiers. Mrs. Ives enclosed a photograph of Mr. Ives meeting the Ambassador at the airport. Bullitt was the first U.S. ambassador to the Soviet Union after recognition in 1933.

[59] Their cousins Emmet and Harriet Richardson.

[60] A distant cousin of the Stevensons.

— I think there's a place for him in Hollywood when he wants it! Ho hum its Sat. night & I'm still at the d—— office.

Love
AD.

Stevenson introduced Salvador de Madariaga to the Chicago Council on Foreign Relations on January 16, 1937.

Introductory to some very flattering remarks on the Chicago C of FR the Christian Science Monitor of Jan 7 says —— quote [61] —— As middle Westerners you will doubtless be most gratified to hear, from Boston, that you are the spear head of this attack on the [illegible] of provincialism. Furthermore it appears that this conquest of the hosts of darkness is another triumph of feminine leadership, for the Monitor goes on to say —— quote [62] —— So our shameful secret is out & all the world knows that Middlewestern men are unwilling recruits in this great crusade. So I am impelled to suggest that it is up to the ladies to save the fair name of the midlands by increasing masculine attendance at our meetings. Doubtless some of you have influence with the benighted men of your acquaintance & all of you have the effective feminine weapon of relentless reminder!

For some time we have been searching for a speaker on the probable course of Bri[ti]sh policy which will play such an important part in directing the destiny of Europe in the year ahead. Will she bluff again, will she temporize & compromise or will she stand firm. What are the English people thinking. We think that George Slocombe will be able to answer these and many other questions next Saturday. Mr Slocombe is a familiar author, Chief Foreign Corres of the London Herald & Foreign Editor of the London Evening Standard.

As I told you last week this is Salvador de Madariaga's 3rd appearance before the Council. We wish we could induce him to make us a habit, for no more scholarly experienced and accomplished European has appeared before us. As an author he has written much on Spanish and English literature and poetry and on international affairs. As a scholar he was professor of Spanish literature at Oxford and is now director of Spanish studies at Oxford. He has served the League [of Nations] & the world in many capacities since he assumed the position of Chief of the disarmament section in 1922. More recently, in the

[61] Not in the manuscript.
[62] Not in the manuscript.

summer of 1935 he was chairman of the League Committee of 5 to deal with the Ethiopian situation. He has rendered great & unsolicited services to the Spanish Republic for 5 yrs as Ambassador to the U.S. & France & only last summer resigned as Spain's permanent delegate to the League of Nations. Perhaps no living Spaniard is better known thruout the world & commands more universal respect than Salvador de Madariaga.

& now I have a sad announcement to make. Our distinguished friend Salvador de Madariaga has suddenly fallen victim to the current plague and is in the hospital. This unhappy event is not without its compensations however for, by dint of some very heroic maneuvering yesterday afternoon Valentine Williams graciously consented to take a midnight airplane from N. Y. and is present in the flesh, refreshed after about 2 hrs sleep. You know Mr Williams best as the writer of popular crime & mystery stories. But he is also a famous journalist and was the first accredited war corres[pondent] to either the French or British fronts in the world war & his reports of the early engagements electrified England. He then joined the Irish Guards and was twice severely wounded before being finally, as he puts it, blown into fiction. His career as a fiction writer has, however, been interrupted by periodical relapses into journalism and whether it was such a relapse as his interest in crime that led him to Spain I don't know. But he is just back from Spain where he interviewed Gen Franco and attended the nobility of the insurgent gov. Mr. Williams subject is Spain now.

Stevenson introduced Carroll Binder to the Chicago Council on Foreign Relations on January 18, 1937.

Because the affairs of China and Japan are somewhat interrelated we have arranged to cover both countries in this and the following meeting with a view to presenting an integrated picture of the situation in the Far East. Western comprehension of whats going on in China was hardly simplified by the incredible kidnapping of Ch[i]ang Kai Shek and the fantastic sequel of kidnapper and captive walking hand in hand into the police stateion. And now the Kuomintang, the Nationa[l]ist party is in convention in Nanking & perhaps something is about to be revealed of all this and future policy of the central government toward the Chinese communists and the Japanese.

To solve this Chinese puzzle we have enlisted a man you havent heard before who appears to have glamorous qualifications for this task.

For the present I'll only tell you that he took up residence on the Indian Frontier of Tibet at the mature age of 4 and he is now Foreign Adviser to the Grand Lama of Tibet. Ill tell you more about the adventurous career of Gordon Enders when you come to hear him talk on China at the next meeting on Sat. February 27.

Tho I enjoy occasional speculation in speakers, a sure thing is very comforting. Hence I am not a little pleased that we were able to induce Carroll Binder, our fellow member, to speak on Japan Today. We are indebted to Mr Binder not only because of four addresses before the Council during the past 10 years, but also because he has for many years given us valuable assistance in the formulation of our program and the selection of speakers as a member of the Executive Committee of the Council. I remind you that for 18 years Mr Binder has been a reporter, special writer and foreign correspondent for the [Chicago] Daily News and is now in charge of its Foreign page with which you are all thankfully familiar.

Mr Binder has travelled extensively in the Far East and has studied intensively the problems and politics of Japan. It is gratifying to find once more in our own family a man so peculiarly qualified to discuss the significance of the recent cabinet crisis and the growing conflict between Big Business and the Army for the political mastery of Japan — a conflict which bears importantly on the future in the Far East.

To Mrs. Ernest L. Ives [63]

February 3, 1937

Dear Buff:

I was delighted with your rapturous letter on arrival at Stk. [Stockholm] & I hope your joint enthusiasm is still undiminished & don't fail to charm your chief and his wife! I wish I had time for a decent letter — but I haven't & whats more I have no sensations to report anyway — except that I've been in the dog house again working most every night for the last three weeks. Mr. Borden's [64] damn oil refinery came within an ace of the wringer & I had to jump in & do some heavy negotiating on that last week in the middle of everything else. But I think we've pulled it out for the moment — by sacrificing most of his stock interest and his job which was the only income he had left. Its all pretty tragic as his present (third) wife had a baby just before Christmas.

We are well, thank heavens, & aside from the pressure of work all is well — particularly John Fell whom I see once a week, on Sunday, & find most fetching.

[63] This handwritten letter is in E.S.I., I.S.H.L.
[64] Ellen Stevenson's father.

The real purpose of this letter was to ask you to sign and return the enclosed division orders. I have closed the estate [65] at last & will get at your income tax return as soon as I can get a few nights off. I wrote you awhile ago about investing some of your money — I was going to buy you a few more shares of First National Bank but in the meanwhile it has gone up from 293 to 345 a share.

. . . We didn't get to the Inauguration but it rained incessantly & I don't believe we missed much.

We were delighted with E's [Mr. Ives's] biographical sketch in the Foreign Service Journal. At least in Algiers the life of a Consul seems to have improved markedly! I thought it a really excellent job & I hope he can dig up something in Sweden — and how about you! Or aren't wives permitted to contribute? We talk about war in Europe constantly — Do you?

Love   Ad.

To Mrs. Ernest L. Ives [66]

February 20, 1937

Dear Buff —

Too good letters to you leave me a little baffled. I am delighted that you find Stk. [Stockholm] so much to your liking, but I was distressed to hear that you were laid up with bronchitis and Tim "raving with fever." It hardly sounds like a good start & I hope Ernest has escaped. I'm afraid you overdid — and I thought you were going to lean over backwards to keep fit. No parties — nothing — is worth the feeling of being only half well. Whereupon I add that I've been low for 10 days with a cold or something resembling the grippe, and so far I've only missed a half day at the office tho we had to abandon a plan to go up to northern Wisconsin over this week end (Wash. birthday) for skiing. I'm glad to hear that you are taking an interest in that sport — there is nothing better & I envy your facilities there. Last winter here was the coldest on record and as usual in this intemperate climate, this has been the warmest — no snow & little ice so far.

You sound pretty swank with a new Packard & a 12 room apartment. I hope prosperity is not going to your head. . . . I was pleased to note that you were promptly hooked for a speech & if you write anything out I hope you will send it to me. Ellen & I both remarked that Swedish photographers do you greater justice than we have noted before. The newspaper photographs were excellent & the charity ball certainly looked regal. I will put them away for you.

[65] Their mother had died in November, 1935.
[66] This handwritten letter is in E.S.I., I.S.H.L.

Aunt Lizzie [67] & Cousin Charley [68] passed away within a week & I wasn't able to get down to either funeral. I have written Helen Culbertson (I believe she was named for Mother) and also Cousin Alice Brown. Our family is vanishing rapidly & it gives me a wistful, lonely feeling — but I suppose it happens to everyone & that we must realize that we've suddenly become the older generation now. I sent nice flowers from "Buffy & Adlai" to both funerals.

Things are shaping up nicely in the country & the furniture is all in use. We are going to start on the garage pretty soon and by the time you get back next fall I think we'll have something pretty nice to show you — which only cost about twice what I anticipated! [69]

Because your income will be quite large this year I think you will save money jointly if you take the exemption and the dependant deduction. I will plan to do this unless I hear from you to the contrary. I suspect you will be sending some money along for the tax & for investment before long. You know you can always sell securities if you need money all of a sudden. Your 1st National Bank is now up to 390 — too bad we didn't get some more! The boys are fine & John Fell's walking a little!

Love   ADLAI

To Dr. E. M. Stevenson [70]

March 4, 1937

Dear Ed:

I have your letter of March 2nd. . . . I only wish it were possible to contribute some of grandfather's library or works but there are few available and none that I care to part with. The story is a long one and I suspect you are not familiar with it. The disposition of grandfather's library twenty-five years ago has always been something of a mystery. Parts of it are at the McLean County Historical Society and there [are] a few miscellaneous things scattered among the family. What Aunt Letitia [Stevenson] did with the balance I do not know, but I suspect most of it was given or thrown away — inconceivable as it may now seem.

Grandfather's book "Something of Men I Have Known" has become

[67] Lizzie Lawton, sister of W. O. Davis.
[68] Charles Brown, a distant cousin.
[69] Adlai and Ellen had recently completed building their country home near Libertyville on the Des Plaines River. Family heirlooms of the Fells, the Osbornes, the Ewings, and the Stevensons were moved from Bloomington to the new home. The house cost $24,976.01 to build.
[70] A relative in Bloomington, Illinois.

very rare and we have actually only two copies. I am trying constantly to acquire additional ones for my children, but have so far been unsuccessful. If you run into any of them, I should count it a great favor if you would let me know as I am eager to get some more and so is Buffy. I have one bound volume of manuscript speeches, which, of course, I would not care to surrender, and miscellaneous printed pamphlet speeches, but no extra copies. If, as I sort these things out from time to time, any extra copies turn up, I shall be glad to send them on to you for this library.

I am sorry that the news is bad, but I think you can appreciate the circumstances. We are still hoping that you and Sally [Mrs. Stevenson] will have a free evening in Chicago some time as our trips to Bloomington are infrequent and getting more so.

Yours,

To Mrs. Ernest L. Ives [71]

March 27, 1937

Dear Buff:

You sound busy as a one armed paper hanger and I hope the worst is over for you — it seems to always work that way — emergencies have an affinity for one another. There doesn't seem to be anything but emergencies in my life any more & tho I'm fed up with this unremitting pressure I don't seem to be able to do anything about it. Of course I was delighted to hear about the success of your speech — tell Ernest he better start asking honorariums for your services! The apt. sounds splendid and spacious & I haven't any sympathy with your complaints about views — you're spoiled; come back here & see how you enjoy looking into chimney pots spouting bituminous smoke!

You sound as tho you were running amock with your money & I can't understand why women seem to think everything has to be perfect. Tim seems to be having a lot of bad luck — flu, bronchitis & now measles — the Bears [72] have a much better system — just one long cold! Do I understand that you imported a butler into that country? I suppose you'll now have to hire an interpreter for him. Tomorrow's Easter & you'll be in Norway in the snow — well we'll be in Libertyville in the clay! — its only a foot deep now & autos get stuck in our nice new driveway. Ho-Hum — I'd like to change places with you — for awhile.

I enclose a pencilled copy of your income tax return. You will note that I claimed a deduction of $1050 for your trip home last fall on the

[71] This handwritten letter is in E.S.I., I.S.H.L.
[72] His sons, Adlai III, Borden, and John Fell.

theory that it was a business trip. I have little home [hope?] of getting away with this & you will doubtless have to pay an additional tax of a couple of hundred dollars — but I thought it was worth taking a chance & you should send me a nice well prepared list of expenses — passage, railroad, living etc aggregating this sum. Don't include anything for Tim & date the letter in January. It need not be carefully itemized — just general classifications of expense — so I can have something to put up a scrap with the government auditors. Your account on the 5000 is as follows:

By cash		$5000
Income tax	$2309.90	
Subscription right to 10 shares Industrial Rayon @ 30–	300	
100 Marshall Field, common	2677.50	5287.40

Bal due from you to me $287.40 — you can send me a check for this or I will pay it out of our joint account — whichever you prefer.

You will note from the enclosed clipping that we are contemplating a vacation in Ireland — quick & cheap & motivated at this time by the possibility that Aunt Lucy Porter may sell Glenveigh Castle & it will be too late next year. It probably won't work — all my partners will quietly slip away leaving me on the hot seat! [73]

I'll send you a photo of John Fell soon — he's superb! I wish I could think of something important to say, but by this time in the week I'm so licked I [can't?] write, let alone think. The house is most finished now & all Ellen has to do next week is move out of our present house to another one on Astor street & take the extras & summer stuff to the country — fortunately I'll be out of town on a job! If you can get ahold of a February Harper's there read the article on the reorganization of the State Department by Hubert Herring.[74] I can't find a copy just at the moment.

Love — Ad.

Stevenson introduced Jacques Kayser to the Chicago Council on Foreign Relations on March 27, 1937.

Thanks to the cooperation of our cultural ally, The Library of Inter-

[73] The pressure of work forced the cancellation of this visit to Mrs. Stevenson's great-aunt, Mrs. Kingsley Porter.
[74] "Department of State," *Harper's*, Vol. 174, February, 1937, pp. 225–238.

national Relations we are today inaugurating a new service which we trust is going to answer an inaudible demand. Recognizing that many of you are bedeviled with an insatiable thirst for more wisdom and that the interval of a week or more between our meetings is an interlude of painful, empty suspense for most of you our good friends at the Library have graciously proffered their aid and henceforth you will find posted outside the door a list of suggested reading in the general field of the speaker's topic — and thus may our program of adult education be further advanced while satisfying your ungovernable appetite for learning with a minimum of independent effort.

We have asked Hubert C. Herring to speak before the Council on Friday, April 9, on Reorganization of the State Department. His recent article in Harper's on this subject has attracted widespread attention and has precipitated animated discussion in Washington.

Several weeks ago Count Roussy de Sales spoke most interestingly on France under the government of Leon Blum. Meanwhile some new and important events have transpired. In the foreign field abrupt and decisive action has apparently averted a threat of German occupation of Spanish Morocco; and now there is evidence that French patience with Italian intervention in Spain has reached the breaking point. It seems probable that some very belligerent gesturing will follow the Easter homage to peace. At home the government has been surprisingly successful in restoring the shaken confidence of capital. The first law was hastily subscribed and the popular Front appears to be intact. But there are mutterings on the left and formidable demands from the Communist wing. As the demands of his supporters grow will not Mr Blum be obliged to yield and in so doing will not capital again take fright and flight? If so how can the rearmament and social reforms be financed — and is the upshot a further swing to the left and communism?

This sequence of events has been suggested and Jacques Kayser who has just arrived in the U. S. can tell us much of what's ahead for France. He is a member of the French Bar, a professor at the School of Advanced International Studies and has lectured in Germany, Hungary, Czechoslovakia, Holland, at Oxford and the Royal Institute in London. He is the author of a biography of LaFayette, The Dre[y]fus Affair, Peace in Peril, Europe and the New Turkey and he writes constantly for the Daily press and the Reviews. Finally this remarkable young man is a practical politician and V-P. of the Radi[c]al Socialist party. As one of that party's experts on Foreign Affairs he represents a point of view quite different from the extreme nationalism we usually associate with French politics. Mr. Kayser

To James Hamilton Lewis

April 3, 1937

Dear Senator:

Upon my return to the city after a few days absence, I find your letter of March 24th regarding a position for Mr. Wysocki with the Illinois Bell Telephone Company.

As Mr. [William P.] Sidley has already advised, it is almost impossible to secure employment at the Telephone Company at present. I have personally confirmed the situation again today and in spite of our cordial relations with that Company, with which you are familiar, it will be impossible for the present to find Mr. Wysocki any sort of work which would be attractive to him.[75]

I strongly recommend that you ask him to come in to see us, as it is not at all unlikely that something could be arranged at the Western Electric Company. I need hardly assure you that both Mr. Sidley and myself would be more than glad to be of any service to you in this connection.

I have for some time been wanting to congratulate you on your speech at the recent Victory dinner here in Chicago. Because of the crowd and confusion, I was unable to see you that night, but I did want to tell you how much I admired it. Independently of the merits or demerits of the President's proposal,[76] I agree that the cynical assumptions of the opposition as to the quality of the men whom he would appoint is grossly unfair — assumptions which even his bitterest critics would have to concede could hardly be justified by the record to date.

My sincere regards to Mrs. Lewis.

Faithfully yours,

Stevenson introduced Hubert Herring to the Chicago Council on Foreign Relations on April 9, 1937.

Because our season is advancing and I may not have many more opportunities to address you on the state of the Council, I trust you

[75] A little later a job was found for Mr. Wysocki. Senator Lewis wrote Stevenson, November 22, 1937: "I must thank you and beg you to thank the Telephone Company in my name. . . . I have received letters from his people and . . : the head of the Church, gratefully expressing the pleasure of having what he termed 'the one promise made politically to him fulfilled.'"
[76] In February, 1937, President Roosevelt asked Congress to empower him to appoint a new justice in any federal court when an incumbent failed to retire at the age of seventy. In the case of the Supreme Court, six justices were over seventy.

will indulge my passion for gratifying disclosures and let me report or rather prophesy that the Council has at last earned the reward of industry, virtue and self respect — we are self supporting! As this is the season of the year when we usually pass the hat to make up the deficit you should be elated to hear that after being on relief for 15 years the Council is no longer a mendicant!

However, that malevolent Executive Committee with which I am obliged to consort is not content with this happy state of affairs — has doomed your elation to short life, and has contrived another scheme by which to plague and impoverish you. In short you are now asked to contribute even larger sums to a Development and Reserve fund to insure the permanency of this institution and to insulate it against adversity. We believe that the providence of this program will appeal to those of you who are anxious to maintain the quality and integrity of this forum and see the council established as a permanent fixture in the civic life of Chicago and the Middle West. We hope to initiate the fund this year with the sum of $2000 and we will await your largess confident that now we are off the dole you won't forsake us.

Hubert Herring has for many years been a distinguished figure in the field of Foreign Affairs as a writer and as founder and director of the Committee on Cultural Relations with Latin America whose annual seminars in Mexico City have for 12 years attracted scholars from all over the U. S. Similar ventures in Central and South America and the Caribean and a life of indefatigable travelling have established his prominent position as an interpreter of Latin America. More recently he has made social and economic studies in Spain, Germany & Sweden & still more recently he has focussed the nation's attention on an important department of our government whose stately traditions have not been ruffled even by the whirlwind of the New Deal.

Mr Herring's recent article on the State Dept. in Harper's magazine has provoked such widespread discussion that we felt you would like to hear him discuss that department of our government which he knows so intimately and which inspires and directs so many of the policies which we study here. Mr Herring

On April 26, 1937 Professor Grace Abbott of the School of Social Service Administration of the University of Chicago wrote Mrs. Frances Perkins, Secretary of Labor, urging her to appoint Adlai E. Stevenson to the post of Commissioner of Immigration and Naturalization and saying, among other things, "Mr. Stevenson is a gentleman always and very pleasant to deal with." [77] After an appointment with Mrs. Perkins, Stevenson wrote the following letter.

[77] This letter is in the Grace Abbott collection, the University of Chicago Library.

To Frances Perkins

May 4, 1937

Dear Madam Secretary:

I have given careful thought to your very flattering suggestion regarding the possibility of my appointment as Commissioner of Naturalization and Immigration. I have also discussed the matter at length with my partners and my family.

For a variety of reasons, some of which I suggested to you, I do not feel that I can interrupt my work here to accept this appointment. I am not unmindful of the honor you have done me, nor am I indifferent to the important and inviting character of this service. But, frankly, I am not sufficiently interested in it to be able to dismiss with confidence the manifold reasons why I should remain here for the present.

I have little doubt that if and when something comes along that interests me particularly, my excellent resolutions, which you have already enfeebled, will evaporate! In the meanwhile, if I can be of any temporary service to you or the Administration, I hope you will call upon me.

Thank you for your kindness and cordial reception. It was a pleasure and experience which I shall not soon forget.

Faithfully yours,

To Mrs. Ernest L. Ives [78]

May 15, 1937

Dear Buff —

I've been delayed in writing you by a variety of things. Two weeks ago we went to Wash[ington]. on a call from Secretary Perkins. She offered me a job as Commissioner General of Naturalization & Immigration. It was flattering but I wasn't interested & turned it down. We then borrowed an auto from the Taylors [79] & spent a couple of beautiful days motoring around Virginia in the lovely Charlottesville district — back to Chi[cago] on Sunday. The country was glorious — fruit trees in blossom — woods spattered with white dogwood and purple Judas trees! And as we rolled along a road a few miles beyond Monticello we passed an historical sign saying that the house was the oldest in Albemarle county and was built by Gen. Joshua Fry! [80] We stopped &

[78] This handwritten letter is in E.S.I., I.S.H.L.
[79] Mr. and Mrs. Wayne Chatfield-Taylor.
[80] An ancestor of the Stevensons.

walked in across the blood red fields & there stood an ancient frame house of spacious proportions — but not "grand" — weather beaten & neglected these many, many years. It is occupied by a poor tenant farmer now who showed us around — the old oft painted wooden wainscoating, the ancient locks on the doors from England, the heavy blacksmith made nails. Its all dreadfully run down, but the property — 300 acres — is beautiful and the location perfect. Just 9 miles from Charlottesville on the main road south, with fine views, a stream, woods — and of course worn out soil! There are chimney ruins of old slave bldgs etc & the place could undoubtedly be reconditioned — tho at considerable expense. We made inquiry when we got back to town & were told that it could be bought for about $6000! It looks to me like a great possibility & when you come back this fall you better run down there & look it over. Good hunting & horse country — but I forget — you're a skier now!

After we got back from our brief vacation Ellen threw herself into our next move & over this last week end we got installed in our mechanical house in the country. No sooner moved, or almost moved, than we greeted a new nurse for the children . . . we have engaged a wizened little old Austrian woman. She speaks excellent French, is intelligent & gentle & we hope will have a cultivating effect on our roughnecks — if she lives! I have some doubts as to whether she will be able to handle the monster John Fell! Our garage & stable bldg. is well under way & should be finished by July 1. If you've never seen a 'moderne' stable you've something in store.

We are planning to go to Ireland on July 9 arriving back here in just a month. The trip will allow us 2 weeks there and we will spend 1 week visiting Ellen's great aunt — Mrs. Kingsley Porter at Glenveagh castle in Donegal and a week motoring around in southern Ireland. I will also escape the severe heat of July which is usually the worst month here. Ellen is talking about staying here and working on the development of the place, saving money etc. But I think we'll go — she needs a change as much as I do.

I ran into Harriet Richardson [81] the other day on the street and she reported a new baby had arrived at Bob's.[82] She was keen to hear all about you & Stockholm etc. You must plan to see her when you come back. I had lunch with Bob Hutchins the other day. He & Maude are going bicycling in Denmark for their vacation. Any letters you could give him — sending them to me — would be most welcome I'm sure. They don't go in for society etc much on these vacations, but if you

[81] Granddaughter of Jesse Fell.
[82] Her son Robert Richardson.

knew someone in the legation or consulate who could help them get organized it would be useful. Also he said that if you had an[y] ideas as to the best part of the country to concentrate on for bicycling they would like to have them.

I have no news of consequence from Bloom[ington]. All is well at the Panta[graph] with minor problems coming up from time to time. After the decimation of the winter everyone seems to be keeping alive. I hope to go down for a week end before long to look things over. Of course the trouble is we are so darn busy out on the place & I have only the week ends to help out.

I have authorized the expenditure of $1000 on the McLean farm to replace & repair the tile & to build a couple of concrete dams to stop the erosion. The conservation corps have also planted a lot of trees in one useless corner at no cost to us. This is a necessary expenditure to preserve the value of the farm & I have delayed it already for several years. It will seriously diminish our farm revenue this year but will prove a profitable investment I'm sure. Also I have made a joint contribution of $50 to the Unitarian Church from us in Mother's name. I hope you don't mind.

. . . I certainly envy you that trip to Norway & it must have been fun to see Pat [83] again.* The [John Alden] Carpenters get back tomorrow. I don't know what their future plans are, but I guess you'll see them during the summer. I enclose the most recent letters from Alverta [Duff] — I don't believe they have any news. I am still struggling with Mr. [John] Borden's unhappy business affairs in which the girls are heavily involved.

Love in haste!
AD

* You must be an intrepid aviator. But only fly if you're not in a hurry or don't have to?

Stevenson presented the president's report to the annual meeting of the Chicago Council on Foreign Relations on June 3, 1937, and introduced Sir Josiah Stamp to the council.

With today's meeting we conclude our season and surrender you to your own devices for 4 months — a matter of little regret to an indolent

[83] Jefferson Patterson, foreign service officer, who had been on the embassy staff in Turkey with Mr. Ives.

President, tho I am not insensible to the acute distress which this vacuum will occasion among so many eager students of the higher terrestrial learning. But this interruption is ordained by ancient custom & I have no doubt that you will spend the time well in further research in our field & be back in the autum[n] each with a new convert to the great American pastime of lunch and learn.

Unfortunately custom has also decreed that this shall be the annual business meeting of the Council which means reports and elections. I shall forego the temptation to deliver an excellent address I have prepared on the Council — its care and feeding — with some reflections on the forum movement in America — whence it came and where its going. But perhaps you will indulge me a moment while I proudly report a few significant figures: 1st — we end the year with a net paid membership of 2371 — a gain over last year of 300 and a gain in the last two years of 800. As of June 1 we have a dues delinquency of only .2%. We have had 26 meetings this season; a total attendance of almost 18000 and an average attendance of 700 as against an average attendance last year of 650.

Furthermore there is evidence that these gratifying developments are not wholly attributable to a troubled world. Tho there is no doubt that catastrophe, not culture, is still our best ally. In commenting on our allies I cannot fail to thank on your behalf the Council staff & Mr. [Clifton] Utley & Miss Bartell [Ellen Bartel]. Mr Utley's Monday night broadcasts have now become a radio fixture and his mail would be respectable even in Hollywood!

In the absence of the Treasurer, Mr [Stuart] Otis, I am going to ask Mr. [Paul] Russell a member of the Finance Com[mittee] to give the Treasurers report. You will note that we operated within our normal revenues for the first time & have demonstrated that an organization of this kind with nominal dues can be self supporting. Altho most gratifying we cannot look forward to this situation in perpetuity nor can we even meet much increase in our cost of doing business, let alone develop. Hence the reserve & development fund which Mr R[ussell] mentioned for which we bespeak your generosity to the end that we can insure the maintenance of the quality of our work and perhaps enlarge its scope and influence.

Mr [Clay] Judson as chairman of the nominating committee will present its report on officers and members of the Ex[ecutive] Com-[mittee] for next yr. The by-laws provide that nom[inations] may be made from the floor. Hrg. [hearing] none do I hear a mo[tion] to approve the report & to instruct the Sec'y to cast a unanimous ballot for the nominees?

I am always impressed by the splendid docility with which good Chicagoans permit the bosses to exercise their sovereign will. And I am gratified that our distinguished guest has had this opportunity to witness the vigorous democracy of the Middle West in action.

And now it is my duty to surrender this platform which you have patiently permitted me to occupy for so long to my successor — Mr [Laird] Bell — who is in Calif. so, tho you are entitled to immediate relief, you will have to bear with me a little longer.

Sir J[osiah] Stamps gracious acceptance of our invitation or rather importunity — his distinction & high esteem both here and abroad permit us to conclude this season at the very peak. As you know he is director of the B[ank] of E[ngland], chairman of the London Midland & Scottish Ry & chairman of the London School of Economics. It would be educational to you to hear a recital of some of his numerous positions, achievements and distinctions, and his many publications on economics, education and public affairs, but it will be even more educational to hear him — if I've left him any time. His subject is Foreign Affairs from the British standpoint — a title prepared by us of course to permit him to talk about anything he likes. Sir Josiah Stamp

To Mrs. Ernest L. Ives [84]

June 16, 1937

Dear Buff —

I've been on "heavy duty" again lately & I'm afraid I havent written you for a long while. Your letter enclosing the newspaper picture with the mound in the background just arrived but I find it a little difficult to read the text of the article. I wish you had sent along a translation. I'm happy that you are feeling better about life again & that Tim has fully recovered & of course the excavation sounds very exciting but you haven't told me anything about it — where it is, what you expect to do etc.[85] I think an interest of this kind in the country must be not only very gratifying to you but would promote the best of good feeling among the natives — & hence the Dept. [of State]

J. Ham [86] has been after me to be appointed Assistant Atty General which would mean moving back to Wash[ington]. But I'm getting lazy & I like our country place so much that I find it easy to resist — so I wonder if perhaps the time isn't approaching when I might say "no thanks" but how about a ministry for Ernest. Of course the trouble is

[84] This handwritten letter is in E.S.I., I.S.H.L.

[85] Mr. Ives was digging at a Viking mound on the outskirts of Stockholm with the permission of the Swedish government.

[86] Senator J. Hamilton Lewis.

that E's from Va. & it might be a little more trouble than Ham would care to take on. We can talk it over this fall.

The [John Alden] Carpenter's got off yesterday & are looking forward to Sweden. We met for a brief moment the Englishman whose house they took & his Swedish friend the other day. Of course they spoke very nicely of you etc. We spent a very pleasant evening with Mrs. Flack's daughter & her Scotch soldier husband at the [Edison] Dicks.[87] She said how much her mother had enjoyed you etc. We liked them *very* much & he will grow on you I think — tho he certainly doesn't look much like a British Indian Army officer.

Tonight I leave for my 15th reunion at Princeton. Its ha[r]d to believe it all happened so long ago. Do you remember that heavenly spring in the mousetrap when mother was so happy — at least I thought she was — and you were having your usual beaux trouble! I am going to Pittsburgh to spend tomorrow at the Rolling Rock Club as Dick Mellon's guest — along with some 20 others invited from all over the country. I suspect it will be a monumental affair & probably the reunion will be something of an anti climax.

The house is all settled now & the stable almost finished. Everything looks very smart & it is really a great success. I went down to Bloom[ington] a couple of weeks ago — Decoration Day — & decorated the graves with flowers — bushels of them — from our own garden! The house is all in order. . . . We've done about $700 worth of tiling at the Heyworth farm and I tramped all over it.[88] In time it will I am sure largely increase its productivity and value. I hope to be able to get out to Iowa during the summer tho everything appears to be in good shape there for a change! We had the usual severe floods on the Wabash & the corn was put in very late so I'm not very hopeful for that place this year.

I deposited $3327.18 — extra & regular Panta[graph] div. — to your account today & 1109.06 — regular div — on May 15. The market has all gone to pieces here in the last few weeks what with the labor troubles everywhere & rumors about lowering the price of gold — but everyone expects an upswing again toward fall, so if you have any spare change I would invest it while they are down. That motor boat sounds pretty swell & all in all it seems to me you are rather well fixed.

The boys are all fine & Ellen's busy as ever

Love
Ad.

---

[87] Pauline Bancroft Flack lived in Stockholm. She was born in New York and had married a Swedish naval officer. Unable to identify others.

[88] Adlai and his sister had inherited a number of income-producing farms from their family.

p.s. Tell Ernest I was most interested in his letter & its comforting to hear that all is not tranquil on the labor front even in Sweden. The Pitney Bowes Postage Meter stock [is] rated as a fairly good investment stock — with little speculative attraction!

p.s.s. I enclose a letter about the [Joshua] Fry house — you will note that my first report about the price was entirely wrong — tho I suspect it could be had for considerably less than the asking price.

On June 17, 1937, James B. Alley, general counsel for the Reconstruction Finance Corporation, wrote Stevenson that he was resigning to practice law in New York City. He thanked Stevenson for the legal work that he had done in Chicago for the RFC.

To James B. Alley

June 22, 1937

Dear Jim:

Your letter reporting that you had finally managed to disentangle yourself reminds me that it has been just about four years since you made the first threat of this kind. But I take it that it is final this time and even Jesse Jones [89] can't hold you any longer.

Although I am sorry to see you leave the government that you have served so well, I am sure you are doing the right thing and furthermore I have no doubt that you will go back to Washington some time for another tour of duty. I hope the association in New York is just what you want, and, of course, you have my sincerest good wishes — not to mention my thanks for all you have done and tried to do for me in the RFC.

Please give my best regards to your charming wife and do not fail to inspect our summer villa in the country if you pass this way again.

Sincerely yours,

p.s. I find the RFC is the holder of some $50,000 debentures of the Vicksburg Bridge & Terminal Company as pledgee of the Canal Bank of New Orleans. Representing bondholders — the issue is $5,000,000 — we have been trying to organize this property under 77B for a long while. The plan contemplates payment of twenty cents on the dollar to debenture holders, which we believe is more than fair in view of the value of the property. For some reason the RFC has joined some other

[89] Chairman of the Reconstruction Finance Corporation.

debenture holders and is now attacking the plan and also the validity of the mortgage securing the bonds. We feel that the RFC must have been misled and that there is little chance for the objectors to do much but spoil the reorganization and force foreclosure, which would certainly wipe out the debentures entirely. I don't suppose you know anything about this, but if you think it worth while I would be glad to talk with some one in the organization or the loan agency in New Orleans, as I feel quite confident that the Corporation has nothing to gain by resisting the reorganization.

To Mrs. Ernest L. Ives [90]

July 10, 1937

Dear Buff—

I have been in such a frensy of work lately I havent had an opportunity to write — In the evenings there is always a lot of consultation about work around the place & then by the time I go over the papers I bring home from the office with me I'm usually so tired I can't face a letter. We had reservations & were all set to sail for Ireland today & then at the last minute duty intervened & I was obliged to advance our sailing two weeks & I'm not sure yet whether I'll be able to get off then or whether Lucy [91] can take us in at that time.

Its been over 90° all week & humid as hell — but our house is very successful in spite of the flat roof. The air conditioning apparatus is a great help & its a relief to know that we're not going to be cooked after this first major test. The garage-stable bldg is all but finished now & very grand! I expect to move my horse over next week — when its too hot to ride and just as we go away.

The boys have both had pink eye, but not seriously. We think they got it in a swimming pool. They are alright now & John Fell gets huskier every day. He is walking & chattering and very entertaining. I wish Ellen could have taken the older boys away somewhere for a few weeks — the change would do them good, but we can't do everything & I really need my vacation more this time than ever before.

I have been trying to trace the wagon & bicycle shipment which Alverta [Duff] reports you haven't received. Have Ernest call Akt W. Larka, 10 Skippsbron 10 & tell him it was shipped on the SS Scanmail from N.Y. on May 8. They don't seem to be able to do anything from this end but write letters. I hope Tim is getting in shape & I can't under-

[90] This handwritten letter is in E.S.I., I.S.H.L.
[91] Mrs. Kingsley Porter.

stand why he should have such bad luck there. Sorry to hear Mrs. [George] Langhorne was not satisfied with her house & I hope it will work out OK. Tell Mrs C[arpenter] that Ellen is fine, very busy and keeping out of trouble — tho she did stay at the Villa Venice last Saturday night until 3:30 A.M. . . . while I was at home in bed!

I'm keen to hear more about the excavation work and I hope you find the new minister attractive — give them the benefit of the doubts. We never take any photos, but that [is] no reason why you shouldn't! No important news from Bloom[ington] — except that John Morrissey is dying from sclerosis & the effects of alcoholism. The Panta[graph] is doing fine & Alverta reports that Bob is keeping the grounds is [in] good shape.

I am struggling desperately to salvage something out of the Old Dutch Refinery for the girls large investment — tho there is little hope to get anything for Mr Borden. Its been a terrific lot of work & taken a great deal of time — 3 days this week — from my office work & of course wholly without compensation even for expenses — let alone my time. It will have to stop somewhere as it isn't fair to the firm.

I hope you are all happy and well — you ought to be

Love — Ad

On July 23, 1937, Governor Horner asked Stevenson if he would accept an appointment to a commission to celebrate the one hundred and fiftieth anniversary of the adoption of the Northwest Ordinance of 1787.

To Henry Horner

July 26, 1937

Dear Governor:

I appreciate very much the honor you have done me, and, of course, I will be glad to be of any possible service as a member of the Northwest Territory Celebration Commission of Illinois.

With kindest regards and best wishes, I am

Faithfully yours,

J. L. Houghteling, a Chicago friend and member of the Chicago banking firm of Peabody and Houghteling, replied to the following letter from Stevenson: "Your letter about my job is most welcome. As the real leader of Young Democracy in Chicago, your support and approval means a lot to me."

To J. L. Houghteling

July 24, 1937

Dear Lawrence:

I read with great interest and satisfaction the report in the paper the other day of your nomination as Commissioner General of Immigration. I take profound satisfaction in this appointment, not only because of the honor to you, but because I know something of the work of this office and its great importance, and I know what you will bring to this post in intelligent and humane administration. It is a comforting prospect!

Of course, the thought of you and Laura leaving Chicago is disquieting and you place me in a little more exposed position in our front line trench! But what I lose here is a gain there, and will help to subdue grumblings of our local adversaries.

Sincerely yours,

Stevenson, at the request of Professor Sophinisba P. Breckenridge of the School of Social Service Administration of the University of Chicago, wired Senator J. Hamilton Lewis urging an appointment in the Social Security Administration. Lewis wired back on August 8, 1937: "The candidate was never presented to the Senators, Congressmen or Committee at Chicago or anywhere. . . . I have wired Miss Breckenridge that of course if she is recommended by such people as yourself and Miss Breckenridge I will not allow the lady to be rejected. I am sorry those supporting her did not recognize that some little recognition to the officials who represent the State of Illinois would have avoided the present complication. Best wishes."

To James Hamilton Lewis

August 6, 1937

Dear Senator:

I appreciate very much indeed your kind telegram regarding Miss Van Driel. I am very much surprised that she had not long since made herself known to you. For that reason, I think your action all the more charitable because I thoroughly appreciate the acute embarrassment which nominations of unknown persons purporting to be from Illinois must cause you.

I do not know Miss Van Driel personally, but I am told by competent judges, including Miss Breckenridge, that she is exceptionally qualified for the position. I wired you merely because I thought her confirmation might have escaped your attention and that the government might be losing a good servant by oversight. I might have known better, and please forgive my intrusion and believe me to be

Most faithfully yours,

To Sophinisba P. Breckenridge

August 6, 1937

Dear Miss Breckenridge:

I enclose a copy of a telegram from Senator Lewis and copy of my reply regarding Miss Van Driel.

I am surprised that she had not long ago introduced herself to the Senator, as his peculiar sensitiveness in regard to Illinois patronage is a matter of common knowledge. I hope Miss Van Driel will make proper amends promptly, as I do not like to find myself in the position of endorsing candidates, as I have before, who have not performed the usual courtesies which he insists upon.

With best wishes, I am

Sincerely yours,

To Mrs. Ernest L. Ives [92]

August 11, 1937

Dear Buff —

I've had bad luck this summer. First we were going to Ireland for a vacation on July 9. Work forced me to postpone departure to July 23 & then more work made it impossible to get off on that date, & finally Aunt Lucy Porter cabled saying she had rented her castle commencing Aug. 5 — so there ceased to be any good reason for going to Ireland at all.

At last I've got my work under control and now we are planning to leave N.Y. on the Monarch of Bermuda on August 24 for a couple of [weeks?] down there — returning Sept. 11. Meanwhile we have had Borden's & Bear [Adlai III]'s tonsils and adenoids out & tho still a little wan they are recovering rapidly. Bear's were enormous, tho we had assumed Borden's were worse because he keeps his mouth open. Are Tim's bad? You might give some thought to this as it is much easier when they are young.

The "farm" is developing rapidly & expensively. The garage-stable is

[92] This handwritten letter is in E.S.I., I.S.H.L.

all finished if not paid for. I get up every morning at 6 & ride before breakfast! Its delightful and the rural life is definitely congenial to me. Ellen has now taken on a job doing some experimental decoration for the Stevens Hotel & what with new servants, the farm, the children etc is busy as a bird dog. The forthcoming vacation & change of scene will do us both good — in fact its essential tho I am jealous of every minute at the farm & spend the week ends working like a beaver.

Mary Marquand from Princeton spent the week end here with the Fennelley's [93] & came to our house to dinner. She seemed very patrician & it was good to see her again. She said Helen Benson had set the town by its ears by having her lady's maid ride her horses in the horse show & hunt! What a woman — and what a maid! I am enclosing a poem of Eugene Field's written about grandfather during the Worlds Fair. Dutch [Hermon Dunlap] Smith found it in a Field biography.

I haven't heard from you for quite awhile nor has Ellen heard from her mother recently. The last letter implied that Mr. [John Alden] Carpenter wasn't very well. I hope everything is going well and that you are having a good time with the motor boat. Did you receive the shoes & did the bicycle & wagon arrive O.K? Everyone seems to be talking Sweden & I suppose you're having lots of visitors. Please keep fit & don't try to do everything. Happiness seems to bear a direct relation to nervous equilibrium with us & that means the rested feeling, tho I don't think it has so much to do with physical rest as nervous relaxation.

John Fell is wonderful — big & rough — waddling & squirming & chattering all the time. The boys dote on him & they're very engaging together, tho he can be very stern with them. We have a new nurse after a brief experiment with a French governess. She's a quiet, godly Scotch woman and we think her very good — modest demure, soft spoken but firm. She reads well & seems genuinely fond of the children.

I saw in the paper that a vice counsel from Barcelona had been transferred to Stockholm so I guess you'll be hearing some gruesome stories before long. Pierrepont Moffett [94] having done his term in the sticks seems to be back at the home base again. All appears to be well in Bloomington — Marjorie M[erwin]. is having another baby this fall & Alverta [Duff] is still at work between fits of asthma — I'm afraid she's getting worse — at least she doesn't seem to be growing out of it as some cases do. Best love and what[s] the news with you?

AD.

---

[93] Mr. and Mrs. John Fennelley of Lake Forest, Illinois.
[94] A foreign service officer. See Nancy Harvison Hooker, ed., *The Moffat Papers: Selections from the Diplomatic Journals of Jay Pierrepont Moffat, 1919–1943* (Cambridge: Harvard University Press, 1956).

To James Hamilton Lewis

August 13, 1937

My dear Senator:

Thank you for your wire of August 8th advising me of Miss Van Driel's confirmation. From what I hear about this woman and her qualifications, I am confident that she will bring to her work in the Social Security Administration experience and competance of a high order, and I feel confident that you will not regret her sponsorship.

Your comments about the Attorney General's office are, of course, very interesting and your consideration of me is very flattering. I shall be glad to discuss the matter at any time after my return the middle of September.

I trust that the heat and the prolonged session have not seriously fatigued you.

Cordially yours,

To Mrs. Wayne Chatfield-Taylor

October 11, 1937

Dear Adele:

Ellen has finally disgorged your sweet letter and I am sending it on to Buffy today. Your researches anent Viewmont [95] are provocative and I suspect you will see Buffy down there before long, if not all of us!

I have just had alarming news that Ernest [Ives] has been transferred to Belfast after only nine months in Stockholm. Of course, it has upset them dreadfully and it is difficult to determine what to do at this distance. — Never having had any political influence, he is sensitive about attempting to use any. After a week of hesitation and consultation, I have asked Wayne to find out if he can discreetly and without any embarrassment to him what the reason for the transfer is.

We are all well and still living out in the country while Mr. [John] Borden and his new brood are temporarily occupying our house in town. Jack and Louise [96] are spaciously and happily settled in your beautiful house and all is well in this quarter.

Ellen sends her best love and says she is going to write to you soon (which, as you know, means some time).

Affectionately,

[95] The Virginia house of the Stevensons' distinguished colonial ancestor Joshua Fry.
[96] Mr. and Mrs. John Kellogg.

Mr. Taylor advised Stevenson on October 14, 1937, that Mr. Ernest L. Ives was expected in Washington shortly to discuss his transfer from Stockholm. As a result, Mr. Taylor suggested that it might be ill-advised for Stevenson to attempt to intervene in the case at this point.

To Wayne Chatfield-Taylor

October 18, 1937

Dear Wayne:

Thanks very much for your letter. I suspect your advice is good and I am awaiting Ernest's return. The trouble is that the transfer will then be an accomplished fact, that is, his successor at Stockholm will arrive before he leaves. So I presume nothing can be done about the transfer and that they will have to move again. But perhaps he can at least find out why he was transferred so soon and what it implies, if anything.

Many, many thanks for your help and I will take the liberty of discussing the matter with you again or asking Ernest to do so when he gets to Washington, if he needs help.

Sincerely yours,

To Porter King

November 2, 1937

Dear Mr. King:

I have your letter of November 1st and the enclosure, which I have never seen before. Old souvenirs of this kind are very precious to us, as my grandfather's collection was destroyed many years ago. Incidentally, the menu is an eloquent reminder of times that are past and I dare say the speaking that night was pretty elaborate too!

You were more than kind to send this to me and I very much hope that when you are in Chicago we may meet and perhaps have lunch.

I am writing your mother.

Very sincerely yours,

To Mrs. J. H. King

November 2, 1937

Dear Mrs. King:

Your son has sent me the menu of the banquet in Anniston in 1892 in honor of my grandfather, at which your husband was toastmaster. It was indeed kind and thoughtful of you to send me this and I appreciate it immensely. It will be a precious addition to our little collection of souvenirs of my grandfather. As I told your son, I suspect the speaking that night was a fair match for the succulent menu!

With sincerest gratitude, I am

Cordially yours,

Although Adlai E. Stevenson's term as president of the Chicago Council on Foreign Relations ended in June, 1937, he frequently was called upon thereafter to introduce speakers to the council. On November 15, 1937, he introduced George Slocombe.

Last spring I made a solemn covenant with you to step off this platform for good and I assure you that my perfidy today is wholly involuntary and that I am an unwilling pinch-hitter for your president who has, metaphorically, been benched by business. So please restrain your righteous indignation while I make short work of a few announcements and my friend George Slocombe.

On Friday, December 3, Mr Takaishi, editor of the famous Tokio paper, Nichi Nichi, and of another great paper at Osaka will speak on "the case for Japan." Tho in this country on his own initiative he is in a position to reflect the official and the popular points of view in Japan, and for those of us that didnot know there was a case for Japan this should prove a very instructive address.

I must confess that my faithless appearance today is not quite as uncongenial as I have intimated because I have been trying to introduce George Slocombe to this audience for almost a year. Last winter he eluded us on 12 hrs notice and, tho we dispatched an airplane for him at 4 o'clock in the morning, it couldn't get thru, and he spent several days on a spongy island in the great inland sea of Kentucky in philosophical contemplation of man's eternal struggle with the elements and with a quickening admiration of Noah as a boat builder. Knowing his remarkable gift for being at the scene of any trouble I had little expectation of seeing him today and his presence suggests that either America is a tranquil place just now, or that something dreadful is about to happen in Chicago! At all events if you respect his mentality and wide experience in the world as much as I do you will be immoderately pleased to have him here, even tho he is just 10 months late in arriving! But I seem to recall that I was instructed to introduce him and not reflect on floods and their incidental inconvenience to presiding officers, so I suppose I should add that he has been everywhere, seen everything, knew Mussolini before he was a Duce and Hitler before he was a fuehrer and even Paul Mowrer before he was an editor; [97] that he has been foreign editor for 3 great London papers, has written many books, the most recent of which "The Dangerous Sea" is not about Kentucky — in the flood of 1937 but the Mediterranean which he will discuss today. Mr. Slocombe.

To Louis Brownlow [98]

November 27, 1937

Dear Dr. Brownlow:

At [Professor] Sam Harper's house the other night you suggested that you might be feeling well enough to speak publicly after the first of the year. I hope very much that you can be persuaded to address a luncheon meeting of the Commonwealth Club some time between January 3rd and 18th on the plan for the reorganization of the federal government. This is a good Club comprised largely of active middle-aged business and professional men, and it is in a position to pay whatever fee you think proper.

I think a discussion of the motives and purposes underlying the plan of reorganization would be of great interest and educational value to this group, which has considerable resonance in Chicago.

I hope personally very much to have this opportunity to meet and hear you again.

Sincerely yours,

To Louis Brownlow

December 13, 1937

Dear Dr. Brownlow:

I was delighted to have your letter of December 9th. The date you suggest, Wednesday, January 12th, for your talk to the Chicago Commonwealth Club is entirely satisfactory and unless I hear from you to the contrary, I will tell them to announce the topic as "Administrative Reorganization of the Federal Government."

The Club meets at the University Club at 12:30 and the average attendance is upwards of sixty. They are mostly middle-aged men and a very representative cross-section of business, industry and professional men in Chicago, with the usual conservative flavor — and probably

[97] Of the Chicago *Daily News*.

[98] Director of the Public Administration Clearing House in Chicago. With Charles E. Merriam and Luther Gulick, he had drafted the plan for reorganization of the federal government which President Roosevelt submitted to Congress.

largely ignorant of the fundamental problems and purposes of the reorganization plan. At these meetings the speaker usually commences about 1:15 and concludes about 2:00.

You did not mention your fee and I will assume it is the usual $50, unless you think it should be more; in such event, do not hesitate to say so as the Club is by no means impoverished.

Many, many thanks and kindest regards.

Sincerely yours,

Louis Watermulder, of the Northern Trust Company of Chicago, was chairman of the board of the Lawson Young Men's Christian Association. He invited Stevenson to be a member of the board.

To Louis Watermulder

December 14, 1937

Dear Lou:

Since the meeting yesterday afternoon I have been giving some thought to the Lawson Y.M.C.A. I am impressed with the enormity of your responsibility there and the desirability from your point of view of an active, cooperative Board. It appears to me that there is a lot of work to do, which to do well will require something more than good intentions and occasional attendance at meetings. I am confident that a good, active Board could make some real contribution to the usefulness of that wonderful plant.

As I explained to you, I do not think I am prepared to devote the time which the job requires and I do not think the requirements will diminish much as time goes on. Hence, I think you had better leave me out, much as I regret it.

Incidentally, I want to congratulate you — it is a large undertaking and I appreciate the sacrifice you are making. On the other hand, these so-called "sacrifices" are some times our greatest pleasures and this certainly must be a satisfaction to you.

Sincerely yours,

On November 22, 1937 Senator James Hamilton Lewis wrote Stevenson that he had written Attorney General Homer Cummings about a position for him. Mr. Cummings had replied: "I have a very high opinion of him and would be glad to talk to you about the matter." Lewis added in his letter: "It is a very serious question for you as to whether you would feel justified in giving up your present secure relation and promise for the future to return to official life here, unless you and your attractive wife, prefer to make the Capital and the pursuit of public affairs your existence."

Stevenson replied that he thought he would prefer an appointment in the Department of State that would lead to an appointment overseas. Lewis replied on December 9, 1937, "Let me have exactly your wishes. I will take the subject up at once leaving the matter of the Attorney General out."

To James Hamilton Lewis

December 16, 1937

Dear Senator:

Thank you for your further letter. I am afraid I did not make myself altogether clear. Of course, I do not know what the Attorney General or the State Department might have in mind for me and it is difficult to decline appointments that have not been offered, but I do not feel that I want to or can afford to go back to Washington now and interrupt the very satisfactory progress I am making here both professionally and in the community.[99]

Accordingly, though I hesitate to say that I am not interested, I suspect it is quite unlikely that anything is available which would warrant my leaving Chicago permanently at this time.

I appreciate your interest more than I can tell you and I hope it won't be long before I have an opportunity here or in Washington to discuss these things with you personally.

Ellen joins me in sincerest good wishes to you and Mrs. Lewis, and please remember that I am yours to command if I can ever be of any service.

Faithfully yours,

P.S. I thought the enclosed clipping from the Daily News last week might be of interest to you.

A.E.S.

As a result of his prominent role in the Chicago Council on Foreign Relations, Adlai E. Stevenson received many invitations to speak about world events. The following speech was handwritten and delivered early in 1938. It was transcribed in 1959. The original text is missing.

---

[99] In a letter on December 4, 1937, to his old friend John Paulding Brown, Stevenson wrote: "I don't think I want to go back just now even if the title should be attractive, etc. — and Mr. Sidley [senior partner of his law firm] is dead against it."

I see by your program that my subject is "A *Reveal* of Foreign Affairs in 1937." I am only moderately well prepared to *review* the principal developments in foreign affairs this year, but I certainly have no revelations for you — like the humble negro preacher, I must confess that I am not a prophet let alone a revealator." In fact, I am only a simple lawyer with an amateur taste for international politics — an avocation, which by the way, I can recommend to you highly, because the field is never exhausted, you stand as good a chance as the next man of being right, any miscalculation is quickly forgotten if you immediately engage your adversaries in fresh speculation, which is quite free. It's sort of like dermatology. I'm told it's a popular field of medicine because you are never disturbed at night, your patients never die and they never get well!

The past year has been a good one — a good one for foreign correspondents and amateur investigators like me and a dreadfully disquieting one for everyone else (another good reason for embracing my hobby — you flourish on disaster). In fact it's been the best year in a long while for there are now two full-sized major wars in progress where we have only had one at a time in recent years. And that of course makes the future very bright because two fires in a small town where there are not many firemen divide their efforts and if a third breaks out they are apt to be entirely ineffectual — until it comes to picking up the salvage when the whole town has burned.

But the parable isn't a very good one and perhaps if I don't get down to business your chairman won't feel so badly about not paying me my customary large hon[or]arium for coming all the way out here from distant Chicago at my own expense to tell you things you already know or at least won't miss if you don't know!

I am not going to review all the incidental developments of the year tho some of them are vastly diverting — the house cleaning in Russia for example and the Pan Islamic movement which has set the British by the ears in Palestine and is rapidly spreading throughout the Arab world as my friend Mr. [Ernest] Ives who has lived long in Algeria can testify, and the creation the other day of a full blown fascist state in Brazil the greatest republic of South America and the sensational terrorist plot disclosed in Paris recently. Rather in view of the limited time available, and to simplify the job for myself, I think I'll concentrate on the three principal theatres of activity during the year — the Mediterranean, Europe and the far east — which is really no division at all because the world is so small that about the same parties and the same motives and neutrals are involved everywhere.

First in the Mediterranean: During the year Basque resistance has been liquidated on the west coast of Spain with the fall of Bilbao and Santander after prolonged siege, and the Moors and landlords and Italians and Germans have made a thrust toward the sea to drive a wedge between Valencia and Barcelona but have now withdrawn apparently to the south coast where the weather is warmer. The lines are no closer to Madrid and this most amazing civil war of modern times is still a stand-off with the outcome still largely dependent on external events. The incredible travesty of non intervention,[100] however, has been exposed and Mussolini is no longer blandly denying the presence of Italian troops in Spain. In fact we find him this year publicly congratulating General Franco and applauding the idea of Italian troops after the fall of Bilbao — indicating, I suppose, their terrible rout at Guadelhara [Guadalajara] just a year ago. (Incidentally the scorn of the German press was an enlightening commentary on Italian-German unity for the Germans insisted that all credit was due their aviation and without it the Italians could never have dislodged the starving Basques and their airplanes). But of course all this bickering at the two heads of the Rome-Berlin axis was bad medicine as the rest of the world might think that it wasn't a civil war after all, so when Santander fell Franco got a break and his own Spanish troops were permitted to march into the city amid resounding applause from Rome and Berlin.

But piracy broke out and neutral ships were attacked in the Mediterranean and there followed the Lyon conference and some plain talking to Mussolini; whereupon the piracy stopped in the face of a French threat to open the Spanish-French frontier to men and munitions and Mussolini then came clean to the extent of admitting he had a few boys in Spain and if the powers would grant Franco belligerent rights so that he could blockade the loyalist ports — (having all the Spanish navy) — and the French would continue their non-intervention he, Mussolini, would be willing generously, to withdraw an Italian for every alien withdrawn from the Loyalist ranks. As the figures then were approximately 100,000 to 15,000 this magnanimous gesture was rejected — so after several weeks delay while things were rearranged in Spain and several ship-loads of Italians went home for the winter, M. suggested a commission go to Spain to investigate, but that he must reserve the right to reject their findings. Meanwhile the French patiently keep the border closed and Russia is rapidly liquidating her support because of various preoccupations at home and M. has got everything well stacked to give Franco another try. It looks as tho the offensive might start up the south coast toward Almeria any day. The fact is that M.'s diplomatic

[100] Britain, France, Italy, and Germany had agreed not to intervene in the Spanish Civil War.

accomplishments in Spain are if anything greater than his military ones. Simply stated, he has kept the other powers from intervening for a year and a half while he has all but conquered Spain — really a greater feat than the conquest of Eth[i]opia. The technique simply stated is to cause an incident — prolong the agony of settlement as long as you can and then just as everyone reaches the breaking point cause another one quickly and start to work to settle that one — so that you keep the rowdy customers in the side shows while the circus goes on in the main tent undisturbed.

So this horrible sanguinary fratricidal war goes into its 18th month. Civil war in U.S. — 1,000,000 casualities in 4 years — Spain almost 2,000,000 in 18 months. What's going to happen I don't know — but the stakes are high and the Italian investment in a Fascist Spain is substantial not only in money but in Fascist prestige. My own guess is that it looks bad for the government and fatal if England and France or rather if England's paralysis is long extended. You see, E[ngland]. has not been able to make up her mind how she feels about Spain. English gentlemen travellers and officers garrisoned at Gibralter and investors in the great English mining properties in Spain don't like disorder or radicalism and the Spanish Rep[ublic]. was certainly disorderly and talked radical tho it never got around to doing anything very radical. So tho the masses in England, I am told, have from the start been sympathetic to the Sp[anish]. government and its fine plans for liquidating medievalism, social injustice and illiteracy in Spain, the ruling classes, with of course many noteworthy exceptions, have rather favored Franco and the prospect of an orderly conservative government and have dismissed the frantic warnings of France and the liberals, confident in the belief that by standing aloof when it was all over they would be invited to come in and finance the reconstruction and thus could buy Italy out of her hard won foothold and mould the future to fit England's own purposes. This has and is the controlling British view — hence the prolonged travesty of the non intervention committee and all the fantastic gesturing and ventriloquism of the last year. But there is a growing feeling of uncertainty in England about the validity of this argument and the presence of German artillery on the coast of Spain behind Gibralter and across the straits at Ceuta and rumors of Italian fortifications and air bases in the Balearic islands are very disquieting, and Germany is taking more coal and iron and copper from Rio Tuito than the English like and the possible emergence of a real fascist state below the Pyrenees on France's last undefended border is no more pleasing prospect to the English than the French.

Bear in mind that for more than a hundred years England has controlled the straits of Gibralter and has seen to it that the Spanish government behind the rock is always friendly and feeble and at the other end of the great lake there was Egypt under English military occupation and the Suez Canal was controlled by an international company owned largely by Britain and France, B[ritain] having hastily purchased the shares of the old Kludine [Khedive?] of Egypt tho years ago for 15,000,000 to clean up some more or . . . unclean debts he had contracted in the casinos and other places in Paris. And then in the middle of the lake was Malta, the great naval base and along the shores were France, a friend, and Italy a winter resort and vineyard. So the life line of the empire was well insulated.

But in recent years everything has changed with astonishing rapidity culminating in Britain's hasty withdrawal from the Med[iterranean]. two years ago in the face of Italian threats and now at the year's end Malta is acknowledged as indefensible to air, Alexandria likewise, Italy has cut out an empire in Africa on the Egyptian frontier and on the shores of the Red Sea and could destroy and close the Suez Canal in a jiffy. Palestine is in turmoil, a vast army is garrisoned in Libya on the other border of Egypt, Germany has a foothold in No. Africa in Spanish Morroco and menaces France's manpower supply in Algeria and Morroco and now Italy is in the Balearics directly athwart the French–N. African line of communications which is more important to the defense of Paris than the Alps. Finally, Italian soldiers, German guns and German planes are in possession of almost everything in the Spanish peninsula but the rock of Gibralter.

It's a remarkable and horrifying transformation to the Havre!

And now a word about the Far East before we end this tour somewhere in Europe. I suppose you are all familiar with the peculiar contest that has been going on in Japan for 5 years or more — the contest between the military and big business. It's a long complicated story of political intrigue and even assassination. It couldn't happen here or most anywhere else because in the West the armed forces of a country are the servant of the state and not a political part of the state — not a policy forming arm of government. In Japan the converse is true and in recent years the military has for the most part been in the ascendency. That there has been provocation from the Chinese can't be denied. The reawakened Chinese unity and nationalism that Sun Yat Sen fished out of the ashes of the corrupt old empire in 1910 was bound to manifest itself as the program of unification advanced with the march of Chiang [Kai-shek] from Canton to Nanking in 1927 and the subsequent gradual consolidation of the country and the elimination of the old Feudal war lords that the Japanese had used so well. With growing self confidence the anti-Japanese propaganda increased in volume. The surgical removal of Manchuria in 1932 and 1933 and the destruction of Chopai was further provocation and anti Japanism became the preoccupation of the students, the intellectuals, the patriots. Chiang Kai Shek counseled caution, deliberation — like a great oriental he compromised, kept his face at home and kept the Japanese guessing, all the while building and building but he could never control the anti-Japanism and in the last two years more than 50 Japanese residents in China were murdered. Just a year ago he was kidnapped by Chang the younger, the narcotic son of old Chang Tso Lin, the Japs best friend, and told that if he didn't fight the Japs he would die — that the Communists' armies which he had been fighting for years would support him — he extricated himself from that predicament in exchange for a pardon for his kidnapper and still held off.

And finally last spring when Prince Konoye, a great aristocrat but a political unknown became premier, it looked as tho big business and the conservative moderates had won out in Japan, and then in July the incident of the Marco Polo bridge happened [101] and it soon became apparent that the militarists had again taken things in their own hands, were determined to force the Chinese to love them at the point of the bayonet. (Tell story).[102] What happened in Tokyo of course I don't know, but the government couldn't very well back out, and furthermore it probably looked like a pretty good opportunity to bite off No. China in view of the preoccupation of a Europe paralyzed with the antics of the dictators who were all taking what they wanted. Also it was quite apparent that the Chinese were getting stronger and stronger and there was also the ever menacing spectre of Russia all around Manchukuo and outer Mongolia against which Japan seems to have designs. So far there are some other reasons the government jumped in with a will and the great conquest of North China commenced. Then the Japanese sailor was shot in Shanghai and that invasion commenced only to meet resistence which the Japanese had never contemplated. For two months the Chinese fought the Japs to a standstill around S[hanghai]. and also retarded the advance in N. China. But that you know all about and the only significance in the Japanese miscalculations of Chinese resistence is history. From what I have been told the punishment of China has been very considerably more expensive than the J's contemplated, which may make them more disposed to discuss peace even while they are on the crest of victory. A long war for Japan would be a defeat — gold depletion, standard of living — capital for reconstruction in China.

[101] Japan invaded China.
[102] Not included in the handwritten manuscript.

If I may indulge myself in some guess work I would guess that C. K. Shek is and has been quite prepared to talk peace — that the war was never to his liking — that like all students of Chinese history he knows his greatest ally is time and that in spite of all the heroics about just beginning to fight, etc. he will be ready to talk peace after Nanking falls and some of the more belligerent generals have had a tummy full. In short, there seems to be every reason to both belligerents why the war should stop — and, if anything, Japan's interest in peace would be greater, what the peace terms will be I don't know — certainly autonomy for N. China — economic cooperation — of settlement in Shai [Shanghai] — perhaps Chinese adherence to the anti-Communism treaty.[103]

. . . then the future of the Old World is probably once more in the hands of the warrior castes and the civilized era which begun with the Renaissance is concluded.

Whether the democracies of the Old World are disintegrating beneath our eyes, I don't know. France has always been realistic — the memory of 1870 and 1914 can never be effaced, but she knows she can't go it alone, flanked by fascism on two sides and maybe three — and never wholly confident how her Soviet alliance will work with Japan sitting on the Eastern frontiers of Russia like a cat before a rat trap. So France must go with England and wait for England to figure it all out, and perhaps work it out, before it's too late.

And England is sadly perplexed about it all as I indicated awhile ago. She is badly extended for close-in fighting — she's exposed everywhere. Also, she isn't homogen[e]ous like France. There's the Scotchman, etc. etc. And there is the Times [of London] and a large segment of great influence that may be pro Nazi or just anti-French and that are counselling tolerance and appeasement — anything within reason to avoid the war. A distinguished Englishman whose name is familiar to all of you said to a friend of mine this summer in London — (quote).[104] Then there are the business men of the city of London — keep the peace and prosperity — and all the people on this side of the table argue cogently that given enough time the Italians and the Germans will lose their taste for berries — will get restive under the severe sacrifices of self-sufficiency, may again like butter better than cannon and will throw out the dictators as they bring home fewer and fewer scraps from their forays in the democratic land. And then on the other side of the table there are those who are saying today in London — our empire is disintegrating, we must be firm, we must defend our historical position

[103] Pages 7 and 8 of the handwritten manuscript were missing.
[104] Not included in the handwritten manuscript.

before it is too late; dictators — great dictators — don't get overthrown so early — they know the temper of their people and they'll play the last card — war — before they quit — why wait, it will only get harder and harder. And on this side of the table also sit the great English moralists and I will conclude this desultory address by quoting as an illustration of Britain's conflict of emotions — a letter from the Hon. Josiah C. Wedgemarad [Wedgwood?] to the Editor of the Sunday Times: (quote) [105]

And finally Britain's gigantic rearmament program moves ahead with frenzied intensity and there are those who say — wait just a little longer, perhaps a year, maybe two, and when we are quite ready, if it can't be avoided, we will save the 19th century and the era of liberty and justice!

Thank you.

The Stevensons moved into Chicago for the winter of 1937–1938. One evening in January, 1938, their home on St. Mary's Road near Libertyville caught on fire. A dispute between local fire companies as to which had jurisdiction and confusion between the engine crews when they did arrive ended any hope of saving the new home. By the time Adlai and Ellen Stevenson had driven forty miles from Chicago flames were bursting through the windows and the roof. As a neighbor expressed his sympathy to Stevenson, some burning debris floated through the air and landed at Adlai's feet. He picked it up, lit a cigarette, and said, "Oh well, as you can see, we are still using the house." [106]

To John P. Brown

January 20, 1938

Dear John:

Thanks for your good note. It was a dreadful catastrophe and there is nothing left and practically nothing saved, though the Degas was in town and a few other things of importance, but, of course, most of the old records, mementos, etc. were lost.

The fire happened in the middle of the night and the horse jumped the paddock fence and two intervening wire fences and knocked for admittance at Stuart Otis' stable, where he spent a comfortable night eating good hay!

[105] Not included in the handwritten manuscript.
[106] Noel Busch, *Adlai E. Stevenson of Illinois* (New York: Farrar, Straus & Young, 1952), p. 4.

We appreciate your note more than I can tell you and perhaps some time we will have another house to exhibit, though it won't be as nice a one.

Yours,

To Stanley Reed

January 22, 1938

Dear Mr. Justice:

I merely want to add my voice to the chorus of congratulations and tell you how happy I am that your splendid service and fine career have been so amply rewarded.[107]

I take great personal satisfaction in the unanimity of approval of my Republican associates and countless acquaintances, who, you know, find little to commend.

With sincerest good wishes and kindest regards to you and Mrs. Reed, I am

Faithfully yours,

On February 15, 1938, Stevenson spoke to the Wayfarers Club of Chicago.

When your Secretary, evidently laboring in the utmost distress and already armed with courteous rejections from most of the members of this Club, asked me to present an entertainment this evening he suggested that I tell a lot of funny stories about early Illinois and my ancestors downstate. It occurred to me that though probably I couldn't do anything better, I certainly couldn't do anything worse! But if I had any doubts about the solution of my predicament they were shortly resolved for me by the burning of my modern steel fire-resisting house a short time ago with the destruction of all my source material on early Illinois and my antecedents. However, that lamentable event served two purposes — it abruptly restored to me a lively interest in material things which caused me acute distress at the prospect of approaching liability for income taxes after suffering a large non-deductible loss. And that in turn caused me to conclude that as income tax time approached you would probably *all* be muttering protests and secretly plotting revolution. The process of thought from my fire to your income tax I confess is a little complex.

---

[107] While serving as Solicitor General of the United States, Mr. Reed had just been appointed to the Supreme Court.

. . . At all events the current inflammation [illegible] at least suggests the interesting possibility that revolution in our country may now be more likely on March 15th than May 1st! So it seemed to me that if any of you are contemplating a revolution it might be timely and perhaps instructive to see one, in the tranquil security of the Chicago Club.

The picture [108] you are going to *see* interested me immensely, perhaps because I travelled across Soviet Russia from the Caucasus to Finland a few years after the revolution, before outsiders were invited or even wanted there, and heard and saw much that aroused an insatiable curiousity about that amazing social and political upheaval that was commenced, transformed and practically completed in nine short months. And I think the picture will interest you too, not only as the first comprehensive historical document of the kind, but also because of the immense possibilities for good and evil which are implied in pictorial history. The use of moving pictures in education is growing rapidly and, as you know, the University of Chicago has made some important experiments with them in the natural and physical sciences. But the possibility of *history* in pictures is both stimulating and disconcerting; the overpowering sense of being an eye witness of great events; thousands of school children with diverse backgrounds watching exciting men enacting thrilling events — not make believe, but the real people and the real events. Written history reaches only the comparatively few but let it flow in pictures and not only is its power of deception multiplied, but it becomes an instrument to arouse profound popular emotion. And if the editor of the film or the narrator distorts the emphasis, omits a little something or even alters the sequence, we have the subtlest, most penetrating propaganda respected by thousands, perhaps millions, as history!

This picture illustrates the point in a curious way. It was first shown publicly in this country at an "arty" theatre in New York and, though it is clearly partial to the Revolution, it was promptly boycotted and the theatre picketed by Communists! Why; because Max Eastman edited the film and makes the running commentary and Max Eastman is a Trotskyite and there is too much of Trotsky for the stomachs of good Stalinites! There was quite a commotion and the picture was proscribed and has not since, I believe, been exhibited in public theatres in this country.

A man named Herman Axelbank spent thirteen years assembling these fragments of film. Some of them were taken by the Czar himself, some by his photographer, some were used for propaganda for the White armies, others for the Red; some are the work of contemporary

[108] The film that he introduced in this speech was *From Czar to Lenin*.

adventurers; many were found in the archives of the French, English, German and Japanese armies of occupation and in private film libraries in Europe and America. That a record as complete as this could be assembled is the more remarkable when one realizes how rare the motion picture camera was twenty years ago. The film starts in 1913 with pictures of the Czar, the royal family, the impressive Grand Duke Nicholas and from that time on you have a look at almost every familiar figure to the collapse of the last intervention; Kropotkin Rodzianko, Miliukov, Kerensky, Kornilov, Kolchak, Yudenitch, Kalinin, Kamenev, Klara Zetkin, Vera Figuer [?], Krupskaya, Sokolnikov, Zenoviev, Bucharin, Radek, Stalin, and of course Trotsky. You even get a glimpse of John Reed and Big Bill Hayward; and then it ends with a remarkable intimate study of Lenin in the animation of earnest speech that gives one some visual comprehension of the magnetic energy that must have inspired and awed his followers.

To refresh your recollection and clarify the movie a little, I am going to remind you of the chronology of events in the Russian revolution:

In 1914 the land hunger of the Russian peasants had not been satisfied by the reforms commenced by Stolypin; the factory proletariat had been influenced by growing Bolshevism and labor troubles could be foreseen, and the program of Russification was resented by the Ukrainian and other minorities. But in spite of all forebodings the people responded to the first shock of war with great and enthusiastic demonstrations of patriotism and the mobilization was carried out in good order.

The first mistake was the failure of the cabinet to take prompt measures to mobilize industry for war and though the army and navy were in good condition their munition supplies were inadequate and soon exhausted, and very shortly had to be imported from Japan and the United States through Vladavostok.

The supreme command of the armies in the field was given to Grand Duke Nicholas, an honest, loyal officer and a commanding figure. A very able officer, Gen. Alexiev was appointed chief of staff. Almost at once the military advisers of France and Great Britain began interfering. The Russians had planned an invasion of Austria but because the allies were crumbling before the German attack on the western front, the Russians were persuaded to divert three ill-equipped and ill-prepared armies into East Prussia and, though this strategy relieved the pressure at the Marne, it cost the Russians the dreadful Tannenburg. The constant fighting throughout the winter of 1914–15 exhausted Russian munitions and there followed the disastrous retreat before Von Mackensen during the summer of 1915.

The country was profoundly stirred but the Czar would not accede to the Duma's request for a shake up of the cabinet. More and more the Duma came into conflict with the cabinet and then with the Emperor personally, while meantime the popularity of Grand Duke Nicholas was constantly increasing. When in the fall of 1915 he was dismissed and the Czar took personal command of the armies, just as the economic strain was telling, and food was short in the cities of the north, the people began to talk openly of the German Empress, her adviser Rasputin and their sinister influence on the Czar. This was fertile ground again for radical propaganda, directed in part by Lenin, Martov and Chernov from Switzerland.

Paradoxically the military situation improved during 1916 while the political situation got worse. The Russian victories on the Austro-Hungarian front relieved the pressure on the Italians, but the conflict between the Czar and Duma was intensified. Ministers were changed constantly and the whole administration of the country *became* more and more confused. Finally in November Miliukov, leader of the Kadet party, made a violent attack against the Empress' interference, and on November 30th Rasputin was assassinated. But still the Imperial policies did not change and at the end of February industrial workers struck in Petrograd and the soldiers of the garrison joined the demonstrations against the government. The Czar finally replied to Rodzianko's demand that the Duma be permitted to deal with the situation by a ukase dissolving the Duma. The latter refused to obey and the revolution was on! After a little bloodshed a provisional government was organized headed by Prince Lvov and three days later Nicholas abdicated in favor of Grand Duke Michael who immediately abdicated in favor of the provisional government, and thus the provisional government was legalized by the dying monarchy. Meanwhile a soviet of workers and soldiers deputies was organized in Petrograd and it wasn't long before the irreconcilable conflict between the soviet which wanted to end the war and the Government, supported by the Duma, which wanted to continue the war became evident. With discipline already disintegrating, on May 7th Miliukov issued a ringing statement that Russia must fight to a victorious end. Instantly the soviet from its headquarters in the Smolny Institute issued its formula, "Peace without annexations or indemnities." Huge street demonstrations for and against the government followed; Miliukov resigned, socialists were included in the cabinet and Alexander Kerensky, the hero of the bourgeoisie, emerged as the leader.

In April Lenin arrived; in May, Trotsky, and in June the first Congress of Soviets met in Petrograd. The Bolsheviks were in the minority, but they were better organized, more energetic, their leadership incomparable and their demand to stop the war popular among the workers and the soldiers weary of the fighting. Disregarding the rapid spread of Bolshevist sympathy, the government decided on a new offensive and Kerensky made a tour of exhortation through the army. The offensive started on July 1st and the disorganized army was soon in disastrous retreat. The Bolsheviks attempted prematurely to seize the power in Petrograd, at the last minute lost their nerve and the government with the help of a cavalry division summoned from the front soon had the situation under control. The Bolshevists were charged with German support, Trotsky was arrested, Lenin fled to Finland and the Bolshevists for the moment were in popular disfavor. The government was reorganized with Kerensky as premier and the Executive Committee of the Soviets pledged support. In an effort to restore some discipline in the army General Kornilov was appointed commander-in-chief with wide powers. Influenced by some conservative politicians, army headquarters soon became the center of a rightest conspiracy against the socialist government. The end of August Kerensky dismissed Kornilov as a traitor; but he refused to obey and ordered the 3rd Caval[r]y Corps to march against Petrograd. This was the turning point. The rebellion was a blessing for the Bolshevists; Kerensky had to appeal to all parties for support; Trotsky was released from prison; the workers now mostly Bolshevist sympathizers were issued guns and allowed to form detachments of Red guards, and the Kornilov rebellion was crushed.

The Bolsheviks emerged from the rebellion as the only party with a simple, workable program — Stop the war, divide the estates among the peasants and introduce worker control over industry. In September they won a majority of the votes in the municipal elections in Petrograd and Moscow; in October a majority of the seats in the Petrograd Soviet and Trotsky was elected chairman. The only hope for the government and the moderate socialists now was the elections for the Constituent Assembly set for November 25th. But the Bolsheviks didn't wait; on *October 25th*, by the Russian calendar, supported by the Petrograd garrison, the sailors from Kronstadt and the workers of the Red Guards, they seized most of the government offices, penetrated the Winter Palace with little resistance and arrested most of the cabinet, but Kerensky escaped.

Troubles multiplied with amazing rapidity in every direction, near and far; Gen. Krasnov's Cossacks led an attack by Kerensky, the military cadets in Petrograd and Moscow rebelled, the civil servants struck, an independence movement swept the Ukraine, civil war broke out in the Don and Kuban areas. On December 5th an armistice was signed with Germany; on December 25th the political police which Kerensky had

[387]

dissolved was re-established as the Cheka. There followed the long negotiations at Brest-Litovsk and, in March 1918, the disastrous peace treaty with Germany, while things were getting worse and worse — civil disorders, German occupation of the Ukraine, seizure of the Eastern territories by the Czecho-Slovaks prisoners, food levies and civil war in the villages, mutiny in the Red Army on the Volga, revolt of the left wing Social Revolutionaries, then the right wing, and then the attempted assassination of Lenin in August which commenced the Red terror in earnest. The Japanese occupied Vladivostok; Admiral Kolchak proclaimed himself supreme ruler of Russia in Siberia, and then a period of civil war and intervention from every direction that lasted almost two years on fourteen different fronts, which the Soviet government could probably have never survived had it not been that with the collapse of Germany in November 1918 it was no longer necessary to maintain an eastern front and the allies rapidly lost interest in supporting a war party in Russia.

An impartial study of the turbulent confusion of these times can leave little doubt that Lenin and Trotsky were remarkable organizers and inspired leaders — one of those strange coincidences which make history, and also that without adroit propaganda and a simple slogan that the simplest peasant could understand — "bread, peace and liberty" — they might never have surmounted their fantastic difficulties.

I hope you will enjoy the movie and will consider the educational implications for the future in *adjustable* history by picture for the multitudes that enjoy *exciting* movies more than *dull* history books.

Dr. Parker C. Hardin, Stevenson's cousin, wrote Stevenson expressing sympathy over the loss of the Libertyville home. He expressed the hope that Grandfather Adlai E. Stevenson's papers had not been destroyed and added: "The rest of us look to you to keep alive the traditions of the past." He also described his work as a medical doctor in Monroe, North Carolina, and enclosed two papers he had written.

To Dr. Parker C. Hardin

February 18, 1938

Dear Parker:

You were kind to think of us in our sorrow and I appreciate not only your sympathy but the fine clinical report on the family, which just about brings me up to date. Ellen also had a sweet and comforting letter from Aunt Julia.[109]

[109] Mrs. Martin Hardin.

The loss of the new house was a bitter blow and the contents even worse. Much of the latter could have been saved had we been there, but, of course, every one lost their heads and little of any value was rescued except some of the library, including some precious family books, Bibles, etc. The electoral vote box, some photographs, two Cleveland-Stevenson silk handkerchiefs and a campaign pitcher which Ellen bought some years ago were destroyed. I had a lot of interesting old documents, correspondence, pictures and furniture of the Fell and Davis families that were all destroyed.

I am glad to hear that you are so happy and contented in Monroe, which sounds all the nicer as I look out the window at the damp fog.

. . . My three boys seem to flourish in spite of colds and they have had a great time with Buffy's boy Tim this winter. She has been staying in Bloomington since December and has been up here occasionally. Early next month she goes to Belfast, where her husband is now stationed.

And all the while I try to act like a lawyer with moderate success!

Many thanks again for your good letter and best wishes to you both.

Yours,

P.S. I am not a little impressed with those surgical papers!

In January, 1938, President Roosevelt in a special message to Congress said that since other nations were arming at an "alarming rate," national defenses had to be increased. By February, 1938, Japan was pushing ahead with its invasion of North China and Hitler was threatening to invade Austria. The following month German troops seized the country.

Professor William E. Dodd of the University of Chicago, who had been ambassador to Germany since 1933, had recently resigned his post. Stevenson introduced Ambassador Dodd to the Chicago Council on Foreign Relations on February 28, 1938.

In the absence of your President I have been assigned the privilege of presiding at this significant meeting of the Council. Tho both you and the speaker deserved something better.

I am asked to announce that on Friday of this week Graham Hutton, assistant Editor of the London Economist will discuss the recent sensational rever[s]als of British foreign policy.

I said this was a significant meeting of the council. The last fortnight has witnessed events that may prove the most significant in a decade. And hardly has Hitler's voice subsided, hardly has the deal with Austria been announced and renounced, hardly has England turned around, and the Council presents Dr Dodd. Having relinquished responsibility, with unanimous approval, this perfect timing and the continued efficiency of the council is all the more surprising to me. But not only is it timely — it is also in some measure a public reception for a distinguished fellow citizen lately returned from the wars — or perhaps I should say lately returned from the discharge of a formidable public service. And if your experiences here and elsewhere with ambassadors as public speakers have occasioned any misgivings as to their candor your attendance here today in such numbers is evidence of the fact that Professor Dodd enjoys a unique reputation as a non conformist in this respect.

I donot know whether to call him Professor, Doctor, Excellency[,] Ambassador or Honorable. His implacable championship of his political [word missing] have, I suspect, caused him to be called many other things less flattering and perhaps it will suffice if I present the Ex Ambassador to Germany and Emeritus Professor of American History at the University of Chicago merely as Dr. Dodd, spokesman of democracy.

To John T. Pirie, Jr.[110]

March 1, 1938

Dear John:

Clifford C. Morrison, 1529 West Congress Street, Haymarket 1597, comes from Bloomington where at one time he was employed by my mother as a chauffeur. His father-in-law was her gardener. I have known him well for many years. He has a wife and four children and for some time has been living here in Chicago employed as a fireman on the Alton Railroad. He tells me he has just been laid off with a lot of other men by the Railroad, due to lack of business. He has applied for a position at the employment office of Carson, Pirie, Scott & Co. and talked with the Chief Engineer and a Mr. Lang at the wholesale. They suggested that he keep in touch with them.

I merely want to pass on a good word for him and trust you will send on this letter to the proper place. He has had a lot of mechanical experience, including truck driving, and is an honest, industrious and competent workman. I hope that they can use him in some capacity.

Please forgive me for sending this to you and don't bother to acknowledge it.

Sincerely yours,

[110] Chairman of the board of Carson, Pirie, Scott & Company and husband of Ellen Stevenson's sister, Betty.

To John T. Pirie, Jr.

March 7, 1938

Dear John:

I will take a bet that the happiest man in Chicago is Clifford Morrison, who reported to me Saturday that he had gone to work for Carson, Pirie, Scott & Co. It was more than kind of you to befriend him and I am confident that he will turn in a good record.

Sincerely yours,

To Harmon A. Nixon

March 14, 1938

Dear Mr. Nixon:

I have your letter of March 10th.[111] Perhaps as good a title as any for my desultory remarks on international politics is "What's next?". Of course, I do not know what is next but I could speculate on alternatives and suggest some of the considerations. But after seeing the Ad-Poster and all the talking about foreign affairs you are having, I wonder why you want me at all!

As for other information, I am a lawyer and my only excuse for talking about foreign affairs is that it is my hobby. I have traveled a good bit and was President of the Chicago Council on Foreign Relations for two years.

Sincerely yours,

Benjamin S. Adamowski was opposed by the Kelly-Nash machine for reelection in the Democratic primary to the Illinois General Assembly. He was allied politically with Governor Henry Horner and the state's attorney for Cook County, Thomas J. Courtney.

To Benjamin S. Adamowski

March 15, 1938

Dear Ben:

I have your letter of March 14th and wish you would send me about twenty-five of your campaign cards, which I think I can use to good advantage in your district.

---

[111] Mr. Nixon had asked Stevenson to speak to the Advertising Men's Post No. 38 of the American Legion.

I am also enclosing a personal contribution. I wish it were more! Best wishes.

Sincerely yours,

To Jerome N. Frank [112]

April 5, 1938

Dear Jerome:

My friend, John B. Chamberlin, is the son of Colonel Henry Barrett Chamberlin, director of the Chicago Crime Commission, a well known and highly respected citizen of Chicago, whom you probably remember.

I am taking the liberty of giving John this letter of introduction to you, as he is anxious to go into government service, and I suspect that your interest in legal personnel is as active as ever!

John graduated from Northwestern University Law School in 1934 and then went to Yale Law School on a Sterling fellowship. His academic record was superlative and I have had some opportunity to observe his work. Though his manner is complacent, he is a quick, willing and "productive" workman. He has considerable maturity and with direction will prove a very useful man, I am sure. His experience has been conventional for a young lawyer, with major emphasis on corporation work.

I wish he could stay here, but, what with the evaporation of a lot of our financial work, it is no longer possible to keep him busy and he is getting restless. Moreover, he has a taste for public affairs and I have urged him to have a try at government work with the thought that temper[a]mentally he is well adapted and might make it a career.

I am sure any suggestions or advice that you can give him will be helpful and he will have no trouble politically.

I hope you will forgive me for trespassing on your meagre time; and I have not forgotten that a couple of years ago at the Chicago Club one night you said you were going to let me know when you were in Chicago. I am still waiting!

With best wishes, I am

Sincerely yours,

On April 11, 1938, Stevenson spoke to the Advertising Men's Post of the American Legion in Chicago.

I read articles and books and go to lectures on foreign affairs all of the time and constantly resent the way most speakers seem to presup-

[112] Commissioner of the Securities and Exchange Commission.

pose that I don't know any thing and insist on reviewing a lot of familiar ground before they start — so I will do the same to you! — by reminding you that because the U.S. would not join Br[itain]. and F[rance]. in the tripartite treaty of mutual guaranty afer the war, F., foreseeing the traditional Br[itish], isolation in Europe, was intent on protecting herself by dismembering Gr.[Germany], establishing and preserving a system of collective security and surrounding Gr. with states allied to F. and, not content with that, arming her frontier with impregnable defenses. One cannot blame the Fr[ench]. after the experiences of 1870 and 1914, though we see now all too clearly that a humiliated, impoverished and diminished Gr. was the inevitable instrument of complete destruction of all the complicated post war machinery to insure peace and we see now that one doesn't win wars any more — and that, paradoxically, the best insurance of peace is for the victor to rehabilitate the vanquished — but, of course, when the next war comes we will forget that lesson of history again!

The trouble started on the heels of the financial catastrophe of 1931, when Japan invaded Ma[n]churia and E.'s [England's] Sir John Simon declined to join the U.S. in representations to Japan. And thus commenced the collapse of the post war settlement and after the failure of the disarmamant conference in 1932, the successive steps unfolded themselves with inexorable certainty. G[ermany]. tore up the V[ersailles]. treaty and started to rearm — started to reassert her dignity and greatness as a nation in a way that was congenial to a people of strong tribal instincts and a congenital taste for discipline and strong medicine. The Nazi conquest of G. was swift and complete and H[itler] tore up the Wiemar constitution which as chancellor he had sworn to obey. The start of things was slow, tentative, exploratory but finding the demo[cracie]s. vacillating and uncertain the progress accelerated. The Nazification of "free" Danzig; then M[ussolini]. decided in the fall of 1935 to proceed with his Roman Empire and attacked Ethiopia, a member of the League. But this time the British did something, they invoked sanctions under the League covenant with immediate response from 49 nations; only to unilaterally abandon them and jerk her ships out of the Med[iterranean]. when M. made faces. This was all H. wanted to know and a few months later in March 1936, when it seemed apparent that the demos. were paralyzed and would not support their scheme of collective security, it was H's turn to take a chance and he reoccupied the Rhineland with nothing but protests and an acute case of nerves in Paris. Now it was Italy's turn again and she invaded Republican Spain, promptly supported by G. Seeing that all was well, Japan's military launched their gigantic exploit to conqure most of China and finally Austria was absorbed into the G[erman]. Reich.

Perhaps it is worth a moment to take an inventory in the most general terms of the present state of affairs.

Briefly our inventory discloses that in the short space of five or six years, Japan has taken by *force* a vast territory from China on the Asiatic mainland, Italy has taken by *force* a vast territory in Africa, Germany has broken her bonds and swallowed Austria, and Germany and Italy have jointly invested the Spanish peninsula. It reveals that *German guns* are trained on Gibraltar from behind on the Spanish mainland, and from Ceuta across the straits in Spanish Morocco; that the *British Mediterranean Base* on the Island of Malta is no longer defensible against Italian airplanes, that the *Arabs* are in a state of insurrection against Britain in the Near East, that Italy's African Empire *menaces Egypt* from both sides, and the *approaches to the Suez* Canal in both directions; that Italy's position in the *Balearic Islands* is directly athwart the French line of communications to her man power and food supply in North Africa, and that, when the Spanish tragedy is ended, *France* will be completely *surrounded* by Fa[s]cism. In short, the balance sheet at the end of the *first quarter* of 1938 looks pretty bad; but it is *worse* than that, for it also shows that *German political and economic mastery* is spreading out and down the Danube basin toward the wheat fields and the oil fields of Eastern Europe on the line of the old Imperial Berlin-Bagdad dreams of Kaiser Wilhelm. But it is STILL worse than that, — for it reveals that in a few short years States ruled by warrior castes, bent on conquest, by the most ruthless and inhuman force the world has ever seen, can create Asiatic, Roman and Germanic Empires out of the ashes of all the post-war idealism; that imperialism and power politics which plunged the world into the last war — (which you Legionnaires may recall) — has triumphed again!

So the balance sheet presents a gloomy picture and perhaps the gloomiest thing of all I haven't even mentioned. It is the fact that there are now maybe *three hundred million* people in the world today who are living under authoritarian governments and glorying in their success. The new ideology, the antithesis of liberalism and individual freedom, has spread throughout the world like wild fire. There is an emotionalism, a tribal emotionalism about it, a spartan discipline and intolerance of the bungling inefficiency and disorder of democracy that must make it infectiously attractive to young people. The marching millions of the youth battalions suggest a new generation bred in this new philosophy which some day must collide with those other millions bred in the liberal democratic tradition.

But I am ahead of myself; it is hard enough to speculate about the present, let alone the future! The inventory discloses, as we have seen, an uninterrupted series of successes at the expense of the post war order of things and to the great discomfiture of all the rest of us. There are those who say that the great liberal democracies, England and France, have lost the will to defend their historical position in the world, that Hitler and Mussolini have maneuvered them into a state of impotence, and will gradually pick them to pieces. In short, that the democracies are decadent and the new ideology is destined to rule the world. Only last week Goebbels, speaking in Vienna, said:

"Our critics are morbid, degenerate, democratic intellectuals — relics of the 19th century! They are dead, they are unable to act!"

If they are dead, and if the new ideology has won the day, then the future of the old world, and perhaps the new, is once more in the hands of the medieval warrior castes and the civilized era that began with the Renaissance is concluded.

Perhaps they are dead or dying and with France divided and torn with factional strife, with England wobbling around and this country "receding," the champions of liberty are certainly making a spectacle of themselves.

But let's examine the current position of the Dictators after all these successes. Here is G. strong and self reliant again — the winner in 1938 of the war she lost in 1918 — She has alienated the *Poles* from the French, she has absorbed *Austria,* she has purchased the entire food crop of *Hungary* and Hungarian economy is focused in Germany, and it is only a step from there to political control; the same thing is going on in Jugo Slavia. The Czecho[slovakian] position is already almost intolerable. Bismar[c]k said "He who rules Bohemia, dominates Europe." Czecho[slovakia] must capitulate in one form or another. Rumania cannot long survive the pressure and the conviction of the inevitability of Nazi domination is creeping throughout central and eastern Europe. But will she push on to these further triumphs at the risk of war with the decadent demos? I shouldn't think so — at least not for the present. Dictatorship lives on success — economic success and military glory — and I suggest that the economic success has been so indifferent to date that H. was sorely in need of a diversion this winter. The Spanish adventure had not gone too well, the peasants have been grumbling about the rigid regimentation of everything — the subordination of everything to the armament program. Industry has been complaining about the four year self-sufficiency program — the program of make something out of nothing — instead of nothing out of something as we do — the rigid controls of production, prices, wages, capital investment, in the interests of the state. I understand that economic dissatisfaction has been general this winter. Besides there was no more Jew fighting — no fighting of any kind! So H. had to do something — hence the ultimatum to Shusnigg [113] and the absorption of Austria when the opportunity came, with nothing but a post facto notice to partner M. that henceforth the G. army would garrison the Brenner pass. But now G. has several hundred millions of foreign exchange and 6 millions of population — easy going, low wage laborers, which G has needed so badly, and 70 or 80 millions of dollars of debts which can now be paid in paper marks instead of good Austrian shillings. So it seems likely that H. will enjoy the thunderous appluase of yesterday's "free" plebiscite for aw[h]ile and push ahead with his economic subjugation of eastern Europe & his countless domestic problems. But when the people begin the grumble about the tedium of slavery again and the Nazis get restless for another victory, then it will be another story.

Now let us take a look at the other partner Italy, a sad picture indeed. Italy has been called a "bluffer state" — a gold reserve of 120,000 millions or none at all. No resources, a low standard of living, getting lower; dependent on the united front with G, which has declared that it intends to incorporate all Germans in the Reich, which probably means that the Tyrol is doomed and then the important port of Trieste, and all of Italy's winnings in the world war are gone! Her African empire is a costly white elephant. But she has a foothold in the Med. and in Spain, (if she can ever lick the Republican army), and these constitute strong bargaining bases, but the time is short! For though the Rome-Berlin axis is ostensibly strong now, it is fundamentally weak. Italy today is the slave of G.; with one last hope that by aggressive behavior she can wrest concessions from E. before it is too late. It is said by some that Italy, if free, would gladly revert to the system of collective security. Her alternatives seem to be a deal with F and E which probably mean the abandonment of M's grandiose plans for a Roman Empire in the Med. region. Another alternative is to start a war — Chinese proverb.

So we see G emerging as a great power again and Italy gesticulating wildly in the hope of preserving something from the wreckage of her grandiose schemes, and both of them squandering their meagre substance on armaments, which every one else has to match in a world ruled by force.

On the other side of the poker table sit the *two demos*. F. with still the finest army in Europe and with her traditional singleness of purpose as to Germany, but in turmoil internally and reluctant to move un-

[113] Austrian Chancellor Kurt von Schuschnigg.

til E. has made up her mind. Then there is Britain whose power and prestige has kept the peace of Europe from Waterloo to the Marne. Historians generally agree now that if E. had made it quite clear where she stood well in advance, the Marne could have been avoided and Her vacillation now may be leading us all in exactly the same way again.[114] Since the reoccupation of the Rhineland two years [ago], when Louis Barthou, the Fr. foreign minister, wanted to intervene and was promptly assassinated, F. has daily been beseeching E. to take a strong position. But E., you know, is a clumsy, delibertate democracy, composed of diverse classes and peoples. (Tell story).[115] For a generation Britian has been ruled by conservatives — men of property from an exceedingly narrow social and economic strata, whose single concentration has been the menace of Bolshevism — hence the uncertainty as to what to do about Spain — hence for several years the open sympathy for Nazi Germany among powerful conservative leaders. Since the war British policy has been formulated on these principles:

1. Isolation — keep out of quarrels of that collection of petty warring states in which British intervention at the last minute can always be decisive.

2. Reconciliation — let us make friend[s] with our former enemies. It is good for business.

3. Peace — we are disarmed and because of the awful progress of the technique of war we must let Europe readjust its map peac[e]ably if possible, and

4. Communism —

So Britain under its Tory conservative leadership has wobbled along from one wishful gesture to another and has seen the *V. treaty* and the *Locarno* Pacts destroyed, the *L*[eague]. of *N*[ations]. emasculated, its *Med. supremacy* seriously threatened its *ally F.* isolated, its vast *Asiatic interests* imperiled, and its *prestige* shrunken. And now, and most of all, it sees the rebirth of a more powerful German empire than the one that challenged it in 1914!

It seems incr[e]dible to us that Ribbentrop [116] could have been reassuring Chamberlain [117] at lunch about German intentions in Austria at the very moment German troops 300,000 strong were crossing the Austrian frontier; that Lord Halifax, the foreign minister could have muttered — Horrible, horrible, I never thought they would do it. — But

---

[114] For a discussion of events immediately preceding the outbreak of World War I, see Barbara Tuchman, *The Guns of August* (New York: Macmillan, 1962).
[115] Not included in the manuscript.
[116] Joachim von Ribbentrop, German ambassador to Great Britain.
[117] British Prime Minister Neville Chamberlain.

it is all too apparent now that the elderly gentlemen who have ruled B[ritain]. for so long have only within recent months become fully conscious of the danger — only recently have the British upper classes generally come to realize that fa[s]cism not communism is the present danger. In short, the developments have been imperfectly perceived in E. But that is all *changing* now — rapidly I think — Italy's constant *perfidy* about Spain was a shock to the masses, *Eden's* resignation was a shock to every one,[118] Austria another, the chaos in France is disquieting — for every Englishman knows that E.'s frontier is on the Rhine — and this last week the first electoral test of the Chamberlain foreign policy resulted in an impressive victory for the opposition when a woman labor candidate beat the conservative candidate in the West Fulhan [Fulham] district of London. So Britain may be waking up and it can't be very long before the pre-war generation — Baldwin was 70 when he retired in favor of a younger man, Chamberlain, who was 68 — will have to relinquish control of the conservative party to the remnants of the generation of Englishmen that was lost in the war and to the post war younger generation. When that happens there is little doubt that Britain, rearmed and reborn, will prove again the truth of the old French maxim that Britain loses all the battles but the last one. Even the London Times may learn the difference between what it calls cool heads and cold feet.

This isn't speculation — this transition of England is in rapid progress — and the show down must follow. If it brings war the cards — economic and military — will be stacked against the dictators, and it is my guess that they know it and will act accordingly. But the long range consideration is the solemn one — there is hardly room in our small world for an aggressive antagonistic philosophy like facism and democracy at the same time and unless one retreats there must ultimately be a collision — a collision reminiscent of the impact of the Fr. revolution on the 19th cent[u]ry; the Napoleonic wars commenced as a holy crusade for the principle of individual liberty. My hope and my guess is that before it is too late the liberal democracies will realize that there is something worse than war — slavery! — and that fa[s]cism will retreat into history before their united front as a temporary and perhaps useful device for remaking maps and that the 20th century will be saved!

[118] Foreign Minister Anthony Eden opposed Prime Minister Chamberlain's policy of appeasing Hitler and Mussolini. Eden resigned on February 20, 1938, in protest over Chamberlain's determination to open negotiations with Italy. Eden insisted Italian troops should be withdrawn from Spain before the conversations began.

Stevenson gave John B. Chamberlin a letter of introduction to Thomas M. Woodward of the U.S. Maritime Commission. In his response Woodward expressed the hope that the results of the Illinois Democratic primary pleased him. Stevenson had joined the Illinois Lawyers' Non-Partisan Committee Endorsing Michael L. Igoe for United States Senator. Scott Lucas won the primary and was elected to the Senate that November.

To Thomas M. Woodward

April 15, 1938

Dear Tom:

Thank you for your note of April 13th. You were very kind to take time to interview Mr. Chamberlin personally. I appreciate perfectly that the tide of employment in the legal divisions down there has subsided.

The outcome of our primary was satisfactory in a large measure, though I was disappointed that Michael Igoe, the present District Attorney, was not nominated for United States Senator. He is a good tough independent Irishman, the type which you would approve. However, the successful candidate seems reasonably well qualified and I think will acquit himself well if he can get elected.

Best regards and many thanks.

Sincerely yours,

Chalmer C. Taylor wrote Stevenson on April 15, 1938, and asked for Stevenson's help in securing the support of the Horner administration for his proposed campaign for the Illinois Supreme Court.

To Henry Horner

April 18, 1938

Dear Governor:

I have just heard that my old friend, Chalmer C. Taylor, Circuit Court Judge at Bloomington, is a candidate for Lott Herrick's seat on the Supreme Court for the Third Judicial District. Although I suppose you do not intervene in judicial contests, I do want to tell you that he is a most exceptional young man — an excellent, thorough lawyer, with an unusual judicial temperament and a figure of great popularity and respect around Bloomington.

I hardly need say that the primary was gratifying in the extreme and I had hoped for an opportunity to congratulate you in person before this.

Faithfully yours,

Louise Wright, the wife of University of Chicago Professor Quincy Wright (and later executive director of the Chicago Council on Foreign Relations, 1942–1952) persuaded Stevenson to speak to the annual banquet of the Illinois League of Women Voters on the subject "Democratic Government in Illinois."

To Mrs. Matthew P. Gaffney [119]

April 25, 1938

Dear Mrs. Gaffney:

I have your letter of April 22nd. As I told Louise Wright, I do not think I am qualified to address your banquet, because — (1) your membership knows more about these things than I do, — (2) I am not very familiar with the state and local conflicts, and — (3) I am so busy at present that I will have no time to prepare anything worthwhile.

But if you still want me, I will talk about the legislature, and as good a title as any would be "Legislating for the Whole State." I am very much flattered about this invitation and only regret that it comes at a most inconvenient time for me.

Faithfully yours,

On May 21, 1938, Mayor Edward J. Kelly invited Stevenson to be a member of Chicago's New Century Committee designed to "herald our city's entrance into its second century and keep before the world the advantages which Chicago offers commercially and culturally."

To Edward J. Kelly

May 24, 1938

My dear Mayor:

I have your letter of May 21st and it will give me great pleasure to serve as a member of "Chicago's New Century Committee." The project sounds useful and interesting and I am flattered to be included as a member.

Sincerely yours,

[119] President of the Illinois League of Women Voters.

On May 26, 1938, Frank A. Rakouska of the Debate Society of the Chicago Chapter of the American Institute of Banking wrote Stevenson asking him for his definition of "Exclusive concern with the home market," "No guaranty of protection to American Nationals carrying on trade abroad," and "Defense of the Continental United States and its national possessions only."

To Frank A. Rakouska

May 31, 1938

Dear Mr. Rakouska:

Replying to your letter of May 26. I would interpret "Exclusive concern with the home market" to mean disinterest in the reciprocal trade agreements program of the administration, opposition to tariff adjustments and an effort to stimulate international trade and doubtless subsidies for domestic export industries which would suffer from "Exclusive concern with the home market." I take it that "No guarantee of protection to American Nationals carrying on trade abroad" refers to the revision of our foreign policy with respect to insistence upon equal commercial rights for American Nationals and the withdrawal of military protection in emergencies — a policy which, as you know, has been advocated by peace groups. As to "Defense of the continental United States and its national possessions only" I am confused on this point. Perhaps it means that our naval establishment shall not be larger than necessary to "defend" the United States, Alaska and the insular possessions. I am not aware that anybody knows what "defend" means in modern warfare but I presume the intent is to distinguish it from offensive forces.

I am sorry I have not had time to give your letter a little reflection, and the foregoing is very hasty dictation.

Very truly yours,

To Robert J. Dunham [120]

July 6, 1938

Dear Mr. Dunham:

My old friend, LeRoy A. Whitmore, star No. 104, who has been on the Park District police force for more than ten years, tells me that he is going to take the examinations for sergeant on July 12th.

I have known LeRoy for twenty-five years and went to school with him as a boy down in Bloomington. I believe he has a good efficiency

[120] President of the Chicago Park District.

record and certainly his character and education are exceptional. He had two years of college at Illinois Wesleyan before he left to attend the Naval Officers Training School at Pelham, New York. After the war he worked at Marshall Field & Co. for a number of years and then he joined the police force. His habits are good and I am confident that he is scrupulously honest.

I hope it will be possible for him to receive every consideration from the authorities, as I feel sure that he is not only deserving of promotion but that public respect for and confidence in the police is enhanced by this type of man. I would be more than glad to come over and talk to some one about him if you think it would serve any purpose.

With kindest personal regards, I am

Cordially yours,

To Henry Horner

September 23, 1938

Dear Governor:

I have your kind letter of September 21st reappointing me to the Committee on Child Welfare.

I accept with pleasure, and with sincerest personal regards, I am

Faithfully yours,

To William M. Spencer [121]

September 28, 1938

Dear Mr. Spencer:

I have rented my house in town and we have decided to spend the winter in the country. Accordingly my two boys will not be attending the Latin School this winter.

When John Winterbotham [122] asked me to accept appointment to the Board of Trustees of the Latin School and election as Vice-President, I told him I might be leaving the city but I thought that probably we would be in town this winter.

In the circumstances, I feel that my continuing as Trustee and Vice-President can serve no useful purpose and that some one in active contact with the School should take my place. Accordingly, please

[121] Chairman of the board of the Chicago Latin School.
[122] A member of the Latin School's board, and Mr. Spencer's predecessor as its chairman.

present to the Trustees my resignation both as Trustee and Vice-President.

I need not tell you that I have looked forward to my association with you, Mr. Wood [123] and the other people interested in this important enterprise, and I regret that I will not be able to participate in your work.

Cordially yours,

Stevenson served on a nationwide committee to welcome the Duchess of Atholl to the United States. She had resigned as the Conservative party whip because of her disagreement with the appeasement policy of the Chamberlain government. Stevenson arranged for her to speak at a dinner meeting of the Chicago Council on Foreign Relations, October 15, 1938, and introduced her.

I have made some inquiry of the ladies who have arranged this dinner, Mrs [Paul S.] Mowrer and Mrs [Quincy] Wright, as to why I was accorded the privilege of introducing our distinguished guest. The answers were a bit evasive but I suspect that it was in the interest of pure impartiality — at least I couldn't be charged with partiality for Duchesses until very recently because I never met one before and my recollections are all too vivid of the stern creature in Alice in Wonderland who spoke roughly to her boy and beat him when he sneezed. But my initial experience has been very reassuring — the pepper remains undisturbed and her grace has neither spoken roughly to me or beat me when I sneezed.

Indeed I have met a great lady — You recall that some people are born great, some have greatness thrust upon them and some achieve greatness, and one seldom meets all 3 in one, but her grace qualifies as the daughter [of] the distinguished scholar, Sir James Ramsay, as the wife of a great Scotch peer — the 8th Duke of Atholl; and finally by her own memorable achievements she has climbed the ladder right by right and not wrong by wrong as some celebrated women have.

For many years she has interested herself in Education, Public health, civil service and peace & for 15 years she has represented her district in Parliament. Where she has found time in an extravagantly busy life to write, of all things, a military history of Perthshire, Women in Politics and Conscription of a People and to publish music I don't know!

[123] James Wood, headmaster of the school.

Her scholarship, public service and great humanitarianism have been recognized thruout the English Speaking World and have been rewarded by the Order of the British Empire and the highest honorary degrees from the universities of Manchester, Leeds, Glasgow, Durham, McGill, Oxford and Columbia.

Last year she went to Spain to investigate the civil war for herself. Recently she has published a book — Searchlight on Spain — which has had wide circulation in England & which I recommend to anyone who is still on the fence — if there is a fence or anyone still on it. This spring she resigned as a conservative party whip in the House of Commons because of disagreement with the government's foreign policy — which doesn't precisely tarnish her record for some people. As chairman of the National Joint Committee on Spanish Relief she has come to this country for a brief visit and it is about Spain that she will speak this evening — Her Grace, the Duchess of Atholl.

On October 31, 1938, Governor Horner sent Stevenson an autographed photograph of Vice President Stevenson which the Governor had recently acquired.

To Henry Horner

November 1, 1938

Dear Governor:

I have your letter of October 31st enclosing the photograph of my grandfather. I cannot thank you enough for your courtesy and thoughtfulness. In the fire which destroyed my house a year ago, I lost the larger part of my collection and additions of this kind are valuable indeed.

I hope to have an opportunity to thank you in person before long. Meanwhile accept my sincere thanks and believe me

Most cordially yours,

At the Munich Conference, September 29–30, 1938, Britain, France, Germany, and Italy agreed to the cession to Germany of the Sudetenland in Czechoslovakia. Although Prime Minister Neville Chamberlain announced that "peace for our time" had been achieved, Hitler desired to eliminate Czechoslovakia. On October 5, 1938, President Eduard Beneš fled the country. Hitler encouraged Poland and Hungary to chip off portions of the country and supported the Slovaks and Ruthenians in their demands for autonomy from the Czechs. Finally in March, 1939, Hitler swallowed Bohemia and Moravia and made Slovakia a "protectorate" of Greater Germany.

Stevenson introduced Edward R. Murrow to the Chicago Council on Foreign Relations on November 3, 1938.

In the absence of your President I have been resurrected from my tranquil tomb back there and accorded the privilege of introducing the speaker today — a role with which I was not unfamiliar in the days when the average attendance at these intimate and learned luncheons was a mere thousand — eight hundred ladies and two hundred gentlemen. But, thanks to the enterprise of our foreign agents, Hitler and Mussolini, things have now reached such a pass that I should think we could sell 5 minute appearances on this platform to candidates for public office and soon have enough money to endow the Council permanently.

I am asked to announce that the next meeting or rather mobilization of the Council will take place next Monday. The speaker will be John T. Whitaker, Prague representative of the Chicago Daily News and a foreign correspondent of wide experience, who will give us an eye witness account of the last illness and death of a democracy — Czechoslovakia.

Contrary to the prevailing impression there were two triumphs at Munich — Hitler's and Columbia Broadcastings and, tho the former is not represented, we have the chief of staff of the latter here today. It was Mr Murrow's ingenuity and indefatigable efforts that recreated the historic drama of those fateful September days and brought to America the voices of the principal actors Hitler, Mussolini, Chamberlain, Daladier, Beneš, Eden and others. And it was Mr Murrow who also reported the conquest of Austria last March from Vienna, Berlin and Warsaw.

But more important than these spectacular demonstrations of the reportorial possibilities of radio are the implications in radio propaganda — the weapon of the twentieth century which knows no frontiers, no obstacles in time space and expense; which has been used with such telling effect already and is destined to play such a significant part in the world of tomorrow. For two years Mr Murrow has been chief foreign correspondent of the Columbia Broadcasting System and probably no American is more familiar with the techniques of radio propaganda. It is about Radio propaganda in international affairs — the air raid of ideas — that he will speak today. Mr. Murrow

Stevenson introduced Bertrand Russell to the Chicago Council on Foreign Relations on December 10, 1938.

When Anthony Eden recently announced that he was coming to N.Y. to make a speech the council, determined as always to render super service to its faithful legions, and unwilling to trust the wires and the mails, promptly dispatched its President, at his own expense, to England to remind Mr. Eden that the center of enlightened interest in foreign affairs in the United States had gone west and that the Chicago Council on Foreign Relations is the goal of all men with messages. But tho his effort to keep the center of gravity in Chicago maybe unsuccessful he will soon be home and and I hope you will no longer have to acom[m]odate yourselves to strange or even unfamiliar faces on your presiding officer.

It is now more than two months since Munich — Two months in which we've seen the virtual obliteration of Czecho-Slovakia as an independent state; bitter bickerings over Ruthenia; France tightening her belt; invigoration of the rebels in Spain; savage renewal of Jewish persecution in Germany; a hasty trip to London by King Carol [of Rumania]; enlarged Japanese activity in China; sudden clamor for French territory in Italy; and finally this week the signature of a Franco-German no-war pact just as France & Britain are making frantic efforts to redouble their armaments. Certainly the path of appeasement is thorny & rugged. But whether Munich was a divine blessing or a dreadful catastrophe[,] whether it was the greater or the lesser of two evils we cannot know and may never know. But we all have our opinions — for the most part righteous indignant opinion formed (at a safe distance) on the basis of what we feel, what we read and hear. And because you have heard a series of bitter denunciations of the Munich settlement from this platform we have asked Lord Russell to defend it.

Bertrand Russell as you know is in Chicago temporarily, lecturing at the Univ. of Chicago and perhaps never before has the council had an intellectually more distinguished or versatile guest. His writings in the fields of mathematics, education, philosophy and politics are major contributions to learning. And finally the espousal of unpopular causes is by no means an unfamiliar role for him. For the better part of a generation he has off & on been swimming upstream against the current and I think you will agree that for the fibre of mind and character there is no better or more courageous exercise. Lord Russell.

Former Vice President Charles G. Dawes spoke at a meeting in Chicago urging peace in Europe and observing that injustices arising from the Versailles Treaty needed to be corrected. Mr. Dawes empha- sized that the economic well-being of nations was essential to peace.

To Charles G. Dawes

January 18, 1939

Dear General:

After the meeting today I did not have the opportunity to thank you for inviting me or to thank you for the privilege of hearing your great and wholesome speech. I think you served the cause of peace well; and I agree with you that the memory of the last war in the democracies was decisive at Munich, but I wonder if the glorification of force and nationalism — the marching millions of the youth bat- talions — has not almost neutralized those memories in the dictator- ships. I suspect we may be dealing with a new generation which does not share our dread, which is not afraid of war and which is ap- plauding the daily triumphs of force.

I agree with you again the economic health is the best insurance of peace and human rights and that the injustices of the past must be corrected, much as we deplore settlement by threat and breach of contract. But I wonder how far the demands will go — how reason- able the aggressors will be. If they overreach, I believe you will agree that the clash of self-interest must come and that the instinct to fight a bully is still as strong in the mass man as the love of peace. I see little cause for confidence that the dictators will be reasonable, or, for that matter, that they could be even if they wanted to. History seems to indicate that deified mortals who use the implements of force often go too far.

However, I am much impressed with your optimism and I agree that we need more tolerance — more light and less heat! Forgive these gratuitous reflections on your fine and comforting speech.

Sincerely yours,

For Adlai E. Stevenson's thirty-ninth birthday, his close friend Her- mon Dunlap Smith sent him a letter written by Vice President Steven- son.

To Hermon D. Smith

February 6, 1939

Dear Dutch:

A thousand thanks for my best birthday present! In fact, there was hardly any competition.

If I am not mistaken, the John C. Black, the Commissioner of Pensions, to whom the letter was addressed, was the father of John D. Black whom you doubtless know. I do not recall the whole story but I think this John Black was General of the Illinois National Guard and was one of the several Generals in the Illinois Republican primary for Governor in about 1880 or 1890. You will recall that Joe Fifer [124] of Bloomington shrewdly ran and won in that primary as "Private Joe."

Yours,

The editor of the Advocate, *a Jewish weekly newspaper, asked Stevenson to state his sentiments on brotherhood and include with his statement a cut or mat of himself.*

To Sidney J. Jacobs

February 17, 1939

Dear Mr. Jacobs:

I am sorry not to have had an opportunity to answer your letter of February 9th before and that I cannot furnish you with a cut.

It seems to me that "brotherhood" rests upon the ancient concept of the essential dignity of man. Today the philosophies of half the earth treat man as a thing. But if man is not a soul — responsible, rational and free, there can be no brotherly sentiment, no fellowship of man with man. The word "brotherhood" reminds us again that in the great pendular swings of history, this simple concept of man as inviolable and free has been often challenged as it is today — but never crushed.

Sincerely yours,

To Arthur Krock [125]

February 21, 1939

Dear Arthur:

Perhaps you have heard about the Chicago Council on Foreign Re-

124 Joseph W. Fifer, governor of Illinois, 1890–1892.
125 Washington correspondent of the New York *Times.*

[408]

lations, of which I was President for several years and in which I am still interested. It is similar to the Foreign Policy Association in New York and in recent years has grown to huge proportions. Attendance at luncheons ranges from 1,000 to 2,500 once a week from October to June! At a meeting of the Executive Committee yesterday I was commissioned to see if I could persuade you to address a meeting at your convenience on our foreign policy — neutrality legislation and the then state of affairs in Congress.[126] Perhaps you read [Herbert] Hoover's speech before the Council a couple of weeks ago, in which he took the administration to task.

You can just about write your own ticket on a fee — so long as it is reasonable! — and I do hope you can be persuaded to come. Incidentally, it will give Ellen and me an opportunity which has become too infrequent!

Yours,

Stevenson introduced Eduard Beneš to the Chicago Council on Foreign Relations on February 25, 1939.

Members of the Council: Your president, Mr. [Laird] Bell, has been called out of town and has commissioned me to express his profound regret that he cannot be here to welcome our most distinguished guest. At the conclusion of his address Dr. Benes will respond to a few questions. Because of the necessity for meticulous accuracy in his answers I think it would be best if your questions were presented in writing and delivered to me by the ushers as soon as possible. For your convenience question blanks will be distributed by the ushers. I should also like to add that for reasons which are self evident I must ask you to confine your questions to principles and avoid personalities.

Like you I have attended number less lectures here and elsewhere and have heard a great deal of introductory [recital?] of familiar facts and as some of you know, I have practiced elocution at your expense from this platform altogether too often. Reflecting on my sins and your long suffering and Dr. Benes friendly good humor, I am prompted to risk an experiment and instead of devoting my brief moment of painful exposure to telling you that Dr. Benes was the great

[126] In January, 1939, President Roosevelt asked Congress to repeal the embargo on arms to belligerent nations. He said: "We have learned that when we deliberately try to legislate neutrality, our neutrality laws may operate unevenly and unfairly — may actually give aid to an aggressor and deny it to a victim." Congress failed to act until November, 1939, after World War II had started.

[Thomas] Masaryk's first assistant surgeon at the birth of a great nation, was co-founder of the Little Entente, perpetual foreign minister & pilot of C.S. [Czechoslovakia] until he became its President, and other facts that you already know, I am with the help of the Library of International Relations, going to tell you some dreadful, secret things about this famous personage. He was born of humble parents in Kozlany, Bohemia; he has supported himself since he was 15; as a boy he disliked the Hapsburgs and every day in school when the children sang the Austrian anthem he opened his mouth wide but never emitted a sound — unless the teacher was nearby; he escaped military service in the Austrian army — how — by injury in a soccer game fighting for the University of dear old Dijon!, when the war broke out he formed a secret society for Czech independence with the sinister name of Maffie and in 1915 had to flee from Austria; in 1918, after crawling across almost every frontier in Europe, he was arrested in England for travelling on a forged passport & in a few months was officially signing passports!

This my friends is the type of man he really is; the man that at Versailles opposed the wide frontiers that helped to bring about Munich; the man that worked ceaselessly to bring post war Germany into the league [of Nations] and back into the community of nations, the man that was known to every chancell[e]ry as the smartest statesman in Europe, the great political philosopher, the world's foremost authority on disarmament and collective security and the instrument of one of the epochal decisions of history. We welcome you Dr. Benes as a great advocate of great principles, grown greater in adversity. Ladies & gentlemen, the late President of Czechoslovakia, Eduard Benes!

Adlai E. Stevenson served as chairman of the Committee on Civil Rights of the Chicago Bar Association. He wrote the following report published in the Chicago Bar Record, *Vol. XX, No. 3, January–February, 1939.*

REPORT OF COMMITTEE ON CIVIL RIGHTS

The committee believes that its field is divided into three types of activity, namely:

1. Defending, or aiding in the defense of, the civil rights of persons in appropriate cases of violation of such rights.
2. Recommending changes in present law and practice with the

hope of preventing or reducing violation of civil rights; and attempting to get the recommendations adopted.

3. Education of the public in the meaning and value of civil rights.

---

1. Defending, or aiding in the defense of, the civil rights of persons in appropriate cases of violation of such rights.

This work is necessary because no amount of education and recommendation will ever be a substitute for action in defense of civil rights which are threatened or which are being or have been violated. It is necessary to take such action, on a proper occasion in behalf even of persons who might be able to defend their rights for themselves or enlist the aid of others. In no other way will the public realize that the civil and constitutional rights of individuals are the concern of the organized bar and not something to be regarded as primarily the concern of organizations specializing in this field.

The work which the Association should do under this heading is somewhat analogous to that of the Committee on Grievances and on Inquiry. It will be necessary for the staff of the Association to interview persons bringing complaints in order to sift out those which are clearly baseless or which the Association would clearly not be able to handle to advantage. The staff of the Association should not be increased; but the present staff should make a rigorous and even summary selection of cases in order to prevent the work becoming a burden, certainly until the committee has had a chance to feel its way. Ultimately these complaints might be heard by a subcommittee, as is done by the Grievance Committee and the Committee on Inquiry; but at first any case selected by the staff as suitable for further consideration should be heard by the full committee, and its decision submitted to the Board of Managers. This will enable the full committee to pass upon the selection of those cases which are deemed appropriate for action by the Association and to function on the formulation of the policy to be pursued. Originally, the Grievance Committee met in full to hear complaints, instead of in sections.

2. Recommending changes in present law and practice with the hope of preventing or reducing violations of civil rights; and attempting to get the recommendations adopted.

There are certain situations in which violation of civil rights is more likely to occur than elsewhere. Instead of merely taking action after the violation has occurred, the constructive approach is to see what procedures can be changed or what measures can be taken in advance in order to prevent the violation from arising. This is analagous to the procedure employed by our Committee on Unauthorized Practice. Not only does this committee prosecute persons engaged in unauthorized practice, but it has studied certain fields in which unauthorized practice is likely to occur, such as in the activities of collection agencies, and has worked out with representatives of the collection agencies a practical code which such representatives have agreed to, and which is expected to result in the elimination of such unauthorized practice. The Committee on Unauthorized Practice has done this part of its work through subcommittees, such as a Subcommittee on Collection Agencies, a Subcommittee on Banks and Trust Companies, a Subcommittee on Realtors, etc.

Among the areas in which violation of civil rights has frequently occurred are the activities of the police in connection with labor disputes, and attempting to obtain confessions and other evidence, as well as illegal searches and seizures in connection with the suppression of gambling. The censorship of books, magazines, movies, radio and theatrical performances is another conspicuous field.

In the first instance a subcommittee should be created on Improved Police Procedures with respect to Civil Rights. This committee would deal with the question of arrests and searches without warrant, the rubber hose, the role of scientific crime detection, etc.; and would consider improved police procedures with reference to the handling of labor disputes, such as those aimed to make the police neutral protectors of persons and property against disorder and violence, and respected as such.

Other subcommittees can doubtless be advantageously added from time to time, but the foregoing, because of its importance, is suggested to begin with. Any violation of law on the part of police or other persons whose duty it is to enforce the law has an especially serious tendency to undermine respect for law. On the other hand, law-enforcing officers cannot successfully enforce the law unless the procedure they must follow is not only legal but practical. It is believed that police methods can be practically effective in the detection and apprehension of law violators, but at the same time can be carried on so as not to violate the civil rights of anybody, and that the committee may have an important sphere of helpfulness in studying and working on the improvement of present police methods and procedures.

Before making efforts to get recommendations carried out, subcommittees should report back to the full committee to obtain its approval and that of the Board of Managers.

3. *Education of the public in the meaning and value of civil rights.*

A large part of the public is not aware of the value of the civil rights of the individual and of the centuries of struggle which lie behind them. People tend to favor free speech for themselves but not for the other fellow, without realizing their own free speech is unsafe unless it is also assured to others. Many people believe that law and order can be provided for themselves and their possessions by treating criminals and communists in an illegal and disorderly manner. Administrative agencies of a popular government also should not be permitted to use procedures which disregard the civil rights of individuals.

Educational work is complementary to the work in individual cases referred to in paragraph 1. Education is necessary to give meaning to the individual case, and the individual case is necessary to dramatize and give force to the educational activity.

A subcommittee on Education should be created for the purpose of studying and making recommendations as to the manner in which the Bar Association can best enlighten the public with reference to civil rights; and after approval of the program by the full committee and the Board of Managers, to make efforts to have the recommendations carried out.

ADLAI E. STEVENSON,
Chairman.

Stevenson was a member of a Chicago group called Stop Arming Japan. His friend Mrs. John P. Welling was secretary of the group. He wrote the following letter to the two Illinois senators and the two representatives at large.

March 2, 1939

Dear Sir:

May I urge that you do all in your power to bring about an embargo on the export of all war materials to Japan?

Aside from questions of international good faith and humanitarian considerations, I can no longer see any justification for affirmatively assisting Japan to destroy our influence and commerce in China. And now Congress declines to fortify the harbor at Guam because it would offend Japan!

It is also difficult to reconcile official loans to China to resist the aggression which we largely make possible.

Sincerely yours,

Mrs. James Hamilton Lewis replied to this letter of condolence over the death of her husband that Senator Lewis "had ever taken especial interest in your career and had rather hoped that you would want to be returning again to Washington where he felt there was much here for you to do."

To Mrs. James Hamilton Lewis

April 10, 1939

Dear Mrs. Lewis:

I can not tell you how distressed I am. As you know, Senator Lewis was a close friend of my family for three generations. He has always manifested a flattering and encouraging interest in my career, and I feel that I have lost my most distinguished friend.

Ellen joins me in this poor and hasty expression of our sympathy and affectionate regard.

Faithfully yours,

To Henry Horner

April 12, 1939

Dear Governor:

I hardly need say how pleased and relieved I am that you are again well enough to resume your work. I only hope that an opportunity to greet you in person presents itself before long.

Permit me to say that from my acquaintance with him and observation, I am inclined to think that T. V. Smith is qualified for the critical seat left vacant by the lamentable death of Senator Lewis.[127]

With sincerest personal regards, I am

Faithfully yours,

[127] Illinois Congressman at Large T. V. Smith had served in the state senate and was a professor of philosophy at the University of Chicago. He was not appointed to the U.S. Senate.

To Thomas M. Woodward

April 28, 1939

Dear Tom:

Fate has treated me badly this winter and I have not been in Washington for months; otherwise you would have found me on your doorstep long ago. Ellen and I are leaving tomorrow for a long delayed vacation abroad and I am writing this letter of introduction as the bearer, Mr. Joseph McCormack, may want to call upon you before I return.

I have known Mr. McCormack for a number of years and have been engaged in one prolonged professional matter with him. He is a lawyer of extensive experience and enjoys a position of the highest regard here in Chicago. His firm, Peabody, Westbrook, Watson & Stephenson, is old and distinguished. Besides all that, he is a swell guy! I am sure you will enjoy meeting him as he is a veteran of the early days of the Shipping Board.

I get more and more sentimental about Washington, and if and when the great day comes in Europe I expect to be in the vanguard of the migration to the Capitol.

Ellen joins me in best regards to you both.

Sincerely yours,

For six weeks in May and June, 1939, Adlai and Ellen Stevenson visited Ireland, Scotland and England. Before they left, the Stevensons bought a Dalmatian dog from Walter Paepcke, president of the Container Corporation of America. On May 5, 1939, Mr. Paepcke sent the pedigree of the dog the Stevensons had named Merlin.

To Walter Paepcke

June 13, 1939

Dear Walter:

We returned yesterday after taking the British pulse, and I find your entertaining letter of May 5th and the very impressive pedigree — I wish mine was as good.

Merlin has been weaned away from us by the gardener, and I shall devote the summer to reinstating myself in his discriminating and aristocratic affections.

Yours,

Chicago architect John A. Holabird sent Stevenson a medallion of the reception committee at the inauguration of President Grover Cleveland and Vice President Adlai E. Stevenson in March, 1893.

To John A. Holabird

June 13, 1939

Dear John:

I returned yesterday after taking the British pulse for six weeks, which, incidentally, was quite firm — and find your note of May 3rd and the inauguration badge.

I can not thank you enough! I have never seen this badge before. My grandfather's huge collection of trinkets was practically all stolen twenty-five years ago from his home in Bloomington, and many of the things I had were destroyed when our house in Libertyville burned down some time ago. So you will appreciate how precious such things are to me.

It was more than good of you to go to the trouble and I am really grateful.

Sincerely yours,

While he was abroad, Stevenson was elected a member of Chicago's Commercial Club. He received letters of congratulation from such prominent Chicagoans as R. Douglas Stuart, Edward L. Ryerson, Jr., Philip D. Armour, Clarence Randall, Paul S. Russell, and Laird Bell.

To Laird Bell

June 13, 1939

Dear Laird:

Many thanks for your kind note about the Commercial Club. I am, of course, pleased and flattered. We returned only yesterday from our trip or I would have acknowledged it long before.

Ellen talked with Helen [128] on the telephone in London and she seemed in fine form. Unfortunately we did not get to see her. . . . Incidentally, I found the British pulse very firm and the appeasers are not in evidence!

Sincerely yours,

[128] The Bells' daughter.

To Mrs. Martin D. Hardin

June 14, 1939

Dear Aunt Julia:

A nice old gentleman, Mr. Ulysses Gordon, who was evidently once well known in public life in Chicago, is engaged in preparing a biography of the neglected Vice-President!

A year or more ago he came to me and I gave him grandfather's book and various other books, clippings, etc. — indeed, substantially all I had, which is very little. He has made such use of these meagre materials as he can and some months ago left the enclosed memorandum with me.

I have neglected it shamefully but have added such nubbings of information as I can and am sending it on to you in the hope that you and Aunt Letitia [Stevenson] can supply the missing information. I am sure I have some of it, but I can not put my hands on it readily. I hope this is not an imposition — I suspect you are as busy as I am!

After the good start we made at Ephraim, I was hoping that we would see more of each other as time went on, but our paths seem to be as divergent as ever. I seldom get to New York any more and when Adlai [129] was in Chicago last year for a moment, I only had a telephone talk with him. When you write, please give me Julia's [130] married name and address. I believe she is not far away and perhaps we can arrange a meeting with her some time.

Buffy and her husband have been stationed in Belfast for the past year and a half. She is planning to come back this summer and I suspect will go to Charlevoix — such is the force of ancient habit!

Please give my best love to Aunt Letitia.

Affectionately yours,

To Eloise ReQua [131]

June 23, 1939

Dear Eloise:

We returned last week after a delightful trip — 10 days in Ireland, a week in London, and a week motoring in Scotland. We were no more than home when I was obliged to go East on business, and now

[129] Adlai S. Hardin, her son.
[130] Her daughter.
[131] Director of the Library of International Relations, Chicago.

have in prospect spending an indefinite period in Omaha — that celebrated summer resort! Accordingly, I suspect it will be some time before I see you or the library.

I enjoyed your letter immensely, and it even squeezed out of me the additional $10 enclosed herewith — something that in my circumstances happens very seldom! I have commenced negotiations with the Irish Free State Government about books but they are so poor that I doubt if they will give us anything to speak of. Gifts have to be approved by the Ministry of the Treasury and it is evidently a tedious procedure. I suspect the ones you received should be acknowledged and it may be that something else will be forthcoming later in response to a letter I wrote to a friend in the Irish Parliament shortly after I returned last week.

Sincerely yours,

Stevenson introduced Professor Samuel N. Harper to the Chicago Council on Foreign Relations on July 14, 1939.

Members of the Council — I was going to say that the only explanation for your attendance in such numbers in the middle of July was our fellow member, long time benefactor and biannual reporter on Russia, Prof Samuel N. Harper — the sage of Chicago. But in tender consideration for his hypersensitive feelings and modesty I will spare him embarrassment and say that your presence here is attributable to the critical currency of his subject — Russia — which may be holding the destiny of the world in her hands.[132]

Forseeing the critical situation which would develop in mid summer we dispatched Sam Harper, at his own expense, to Russia[,] Poland[,] The corridor[,] & Danzig (a quarter of the world he knows better than I know this Red Lacquer Room) — to insure you a first hand and expert, timely analysis of the situation. Meanwhile I dispatched myself, also at my own expense, to England to cover that front for you. But unfortunately I didn't learn much about the crisis — tho I am prepared to address a meeting at any time on the "Darby at Epsom Downs and How to pick the winner"!

Accordingly, having nothing to say myself, I seized this opportunity

[132] On August 23, 1939, Russia signed a treaty with Germany in which Germany recognized Finland, Latvia, and Estonia as being part of Russia's sphere of influence and agreed on a demarcation line between the Russian and German spheres in Poland, should Poland be partitioned. In September, Poland was defeated and divided between the two countries.

to introduce Prof Harper — a role which I have enjoyed before and as my prior introductions of Sam Harper are doubtless still fresh in your mind, it is apparent that I can't tell you anything about him you don't already know.

But it is just possible that some of you have been living in outer darkness and do not know that he returned only last week from his sixth survey of the Soviet Union and spent considerable time in Poland and watched developments in Danzig and the corridor at first hand. This is his sixth or seventh address before the Council. For my part I've never heard him enough and never wanted to hear him more. Our fellow member S N H, & one of the western worlds outstanding Russian scholars.

To John P. Brown

August 21, 1939

Dear John:

The Bar Association is after me to make a little talk on lawyers in the government service. Ever since my Washington experience, I have been impressed with the large number of young lawyers who have gone into government service, many of whom will probably continue as a career. It seems to me that unconsciously we have been developing an educated civil service due to overcrowding and unsatisfactory economic conditions in the profession.

I wonder if any statistics on the growth of this trend are available. With all of you bright guys thinking of things to do down there, someone must have worked up something or published something on this development of the last few years, and if you can give me any clues or give me any suggestions, I would much appreciate it.

I got my Order from the SEC [Securities and Exchange Commission] promptly and that miserable job is all but finished.

Yours,

To Tappan Gregory [133]

September 16, 1939

Dear Mr. Gregory:

Thanks for your kind letter about my talk at the Bar Association. I find I am obliged to keep a long deferred engagement to speak at The Law Club meeting on the following Friday and, being abnormally languid, I would like to use the same material at both places. The Law

[133] President of the Chicago Bar Association.

Club people feel that there is little conflict in the attendance and have no objection to the repetition. If you feel otherwise, I will try to work up something else.

I have had in mind a talk on the enlarging employment of lawyers in government service and the implications in the development of a considerable body of legal "civil servants." However, I find that there is but little statistical information available in this field and it may be that I will not be able to get enough together by that time to support a worthwhile talk. In that event, I should like to talk briefly on the use of factual motion pictures in propoganda, and illustrate it with a very interesting collection of old pictures taken in Russia at the time of the revolution. I doubt very much if many members of the Bar Association have seen this film — "From Czar to Lenin." It has been shown in Chicago only a few times to private gatherings and illustrates my feelings very well.

I am sending a copy of this letter to Stephen Hurley [134] and I hope that you or he will let me know if you have any objection to my resorting to this sort of thing in the event I cannot collect sufficient data on the other subject in time.

Sincerely yours,

To James L. Houghteling [135]

September 16, 1939

Dear Lawrence:

I must tell you again how much I enjoyed your visit Tuesday. I envy you being in Washington and doing such interesting and important work in these critical times.

Let me remind you that The Chicago Bar Association and The Law Club have asked me to speak about lawyers in the government service. It is my impression that with the latter day growth of government employment, lawyers have more than kept their relative position numerically; that large numbers of young lawyers have found employment in the government and that many important government positions (both legal and non-legal) are now occupied by lawyers. Moreover, I think that a good many of the younger men will continue in government service as a career and that we may be developing a considerable body of legal "Civil Servants" (in the English sense) with manifestly desirable implications.

Through John P. Brown I have already communicated with the Civil

[134] Member of the Civil Service Commission and later its president, 1947–1955.
[135] Commissioner of Immigration and Naturalization.

Service Commission, National Emergency Council, Federal Bar Association and District Bar Association, with little result, though the Civil Service Commission has given me some statistical information and I may be able to get a little more information from them. To do the thing properly would mean contacting each government department and agency to get figures, which, of course, is out of the question for me.

I doubt if the government has done much research in this field or if there is any published literature on it. But I should much appreciate a check through your friends, particularly Mr. [Robert] Jackson and Mr. [Thurman] Arnold, before I abandon the project and revert to my usual and thread-bare field of foreign affairs for public addresses! It may be that they will know of someone who has interested himself in this development and has accumulated some information.

Many, many thanks for your help, and best wishes.

Sincerely yours,

P.S. I enclose a couple of copies of this letter for whatever purpose they may serve.

A.E.S.

Francis Plimpton wrote Stevenson on September 20, 1939, a description of their pack trip in Canada, visit to Glacier National Park, and their climb of Long's Peak.

He also mentioned that Carl McGowan had just left their firm to join the faculty of the Northwestern University Law School. Plimpton praised McGowan highly and suggested that in time he might be lured back to private law practice. (In 1949 McGowan became legislative assistant to Governor Stevenson.)

To Francis T. P. Plimpton

September 23, 1939

Dear Francis:

I was not a little relieved to hear that you New Yorkers had emerged from the bush without untoward incident and that whooping cough was not an obstacle to your thorough survey of the Western provinces. I marvel at the ascent of Long's Peak — at least your participation in it. Did the boys carry you?

. . . I wish we could get down there this fall to take advantage of your hospitality. Having spent most of the summer in New York I have no appetite for more — including the [World's] Fair — but, of course, the Plimptons and their wooded highland is another thing.

I am writing McGowan and hope to have him for lunch soon. He sounds excellent, though I would be the last person to induce a scholar to leave his cloister for the practice. I believe he is taking the place of a man who used to be with us and is leaving Northwestern for Yale this fall. I will also have McGowan meet Kenneth Burgess, who is the President of the Board of Trustees of Northwestern.

Thanks again for your good letter, and don't be surprised if we turn up on a couple of minutes notice — perhaps before or after a football game at Princeton. . . .

Love to Pauline.[136]

Yours,

On September 1, 1939, German airplanes and armored units had attacked Poland and World War II was on. Two weeks later President Roosevelt called Congress into a special session and asked it to repeal the arms embargo on nations at war. Instead of the embargo, the President proposed that belligerent nations be permitted to buy arms with cash and transport them in their own ships. In November, 1939, Congress substituted cash and carry for the arms embargo.

To Loring C. Merwin

September 25, 1939

Dear Bud:

. . . I was disappointed that the Pantagraph took an editorial position against repeal of the arms embargo on Saturday. Not only do I think the position wrong and that we will ultimately reverse ourselves, but that the reason assigned (the best thing to do for the present) is quite invalid. We cannot shift our ground and hope to remain neutral. To reaffirm the embargo now, only to change it later if necessity arises, as the editorial implies, would be far more unneutral than to change it now at the outset. Moreover, any such course of action would be subject to far more criticism of the same kind that is being advanced now — changing the rules after the game has started; reasoning which the editorial approves. I shall not labor the apparent contradiction. And at all events, it might have been a better editorial service to at least await the development of the debate before stating a conclusion.

Yours,

[136] Mrs. Plimpton.

Mrs. Clifton Utley wrote Stevenson on October 11, 1939, urging him to make a financial contribution to the expanded work of the League of Women Voters. She pointed out that the League shared his "interest and concern" for "good government — local, state and nation."

To Mrs. Clifton M. Utley

October 12, 1939

Dear Frayn:

At the outset let me say you are the most persuasive beggar I have ever read. Your good work deserves better from me, and it hurts to say no. My contribution problem is no different from the rest, except for one circumstance. The Legislative Voters League, in which I have long been interested and which, as you know, performs a function in one narrow field much like yours, has had very hard going this year, with the result that I have felt obliged to double my contribution. Its poverty, I hope, is only temporary, but meanwhile I am sure you will understand that I feel it is my first responsibility for support in work of this kind.

This probably makes no sense, and if it does not please forgive me. I know the League of Women Voters and its splendid record well. I should like to help, but what can I do when my own babies are crying and there isn't enough to go around? [137]

Yours,

P.S. When you are back to doing one thing at a time we hope to see you in Libertyville.

Stevenson, as president of the board of governors of International House on the campus of the University of Chicago, welcomed the new residents and introduced the director of International House and the head of the Student Council in the following remarks on October 15, 1939.

Yesterday I attended a football game, or something of that kind, at a very nearby and very great university. Afterward on my way home I drove past international house — a sight which generally fills me with

[137] Mrs. Utley replied on October 16, 1939: "I'm glad that most people haven't your ability to turn them down and make them like it — and I'm specially conscious of the fact that your genius with the English language is not limited to the introduction of speakers."

elation but yesterday it reminded me of this evening and my participation in this first Sunday night supper of the new year. I could not help remembering an incident that happened long ago. I was walking along the street in N. Y. with a classmate of mine in college who had become an actor & a very good one. We passed a restaurant & he stopped abruptly. In the window were a lot of fish, dead glassy eyed fish lying on ice. One monster in the middle [had] peculiarly cold, humorless eyes. My friend looked at it a moment transfixed & then exclaimed — Ye Gods that reminds me; I have a matinee this afternoon!

I don't find you exactly "fishy["] but all the same I might as well ack[nowledge] that I don't really relish this exposure and I enjoy talking with you rather than at you. Furthermore I am app[alled] that I may not be an adequate rep[resentative] of the B[oard] of Gov [ernors]. Reflecting on that thought and the remarkable & cruelly decisive football game I had just witnessed I was reminded that football after all bears the same relation to culture as bull fighting does to agriculture; and then it occurred to me by the same devious & careful reasoning, for which I have infinite capacity, that my function here tonight, as Pres of the Bd of Gov, have some resemblance to the Bull!

However all that may be, I do want to extend on behalf of the Bd of Gov a warm welcome to Int House to the new & old members alike. The world has not visibly improved since this house opened 7 years ago this fall. But the house endures & probably the world will too and — in the travail of the future — our function and purpose becomes even more important to the survival and continuity of civilization.

Noone knows better, feels more deeply, and is more steadfast in faith in the ideals & purposes of this inst[it]ution than it[s] distinguished director. The Gov [board of governors] think it peculiarly fitting that their respected and trusted friend who has contributed so much to the furtherance of the ideal for which this bldg stands should speak to you & to us on Int House looks forward at this first Sunday Supper in a troubled critical year, Ernest B Price, Director of Int House.

I hope you will remember the Directors words — together, together we will build well a structure of humanity, faith courage & vision. *"Together"*

I am advised that there will now follow the organization of the new student council. If I can trespass on your splendid good nature another moment I should like to say in this connection that the texture & content of House activities have been builded in the past very largely on ideas emanating from the membership. Thru the medium of the student council these ideas can be drawn together, studied, & passed on to the administrative depts of the House. The variety of our membership is large — hence the variety of ideas is large — few can be chosen & but those that have sufficient backing are likely to be given a trial. The activities are your activities — your interest and ingenuity will make more & more things possible to the end that your experience here is richer and richer. Now let me introduce Mr Juan Castillo, Pres of the student council.

Stevenson spoke at ceremonies marking the eightieth anniversary of the Unitarian Church of Bloomington, Illinois, on October 22, 1939.

During the 80 years' life of this church, our institutions have weathered several crises with little impairment, and we have enjoyed the blessings of freedom, peace and prosperity. But recently things have happened; our freedom has diminished; prosperity has declined; and our old age is troubled. More than half the peoples of the world are celebrating by war the 25th anniversary of "the war to end wars." The anniversary of "the war to make the world safe for democracy" finds dictators enthroned throughout much of the world and democracy struggling for survival, and, paradoxically, deliberately shackling itself to save itself. It is a noteworthy phenomenon that freedom always has to be suppressed in a crisis to save it for later enjoyment. But the question this time is whether freedom *can* be saved or whether the movement of the close-knit world is irresistible; whether the lights are doomed to go out one by one; and whether the darkness is the destiny of man, as it has been before. If our system *is* failing and if intellectual and cultural freedom *are* being abandoned and suppressed throughout the world, then we in America find ourselves in the position of complacent witnesses of one of the greatest tragedies in the history of the human race.

I suppose it is orthodox to start one of these ponderous dissertations on the prospects for democracy by defining democracy — by stating in concrete terms what it is we want to preserve as a bulwark against the shadows. There are countless definitions. Every political philosopher has produced at least one, and so far as I know they are all good, but I won't quote any of them! Rather let me remind you of a prevalent misconception and confusion of terms. What we commonly understand by democracy is not *only* a system of popular government, but also the individual liberties embodied in our Bill of Rights — freedom of worship, speech, press, assembly, trial by jury, due process of law, etc. — liberties which have flourished only in democratic soil. So let me suggest that what we really *want* is individual freedom, and what we *talk* about is democracy. And so will I!

But faith in democracy is ebbing throughout the world; it may even now be locked in a death struggle in Europe, and in spite of what you and I think about it, there are manifest doubts as to its survival even here. Why? And is our system no longer able to do the job? If so, it will have to go voluntarily or by force, for no human scheme of things is static, and man will mold his institutions to fit his needs and desires. What are our needs and desires? These questions suggest the problems that we must analyze and answer — not rhetorically and sentimentally — but realistically and critically. What do we really want most of all, and what sacrifices are we prepared to make for it? It seems to me that as a people who have enjoyed democracy, relative freedom and relative prosperity for 150 years we have come dangerously close to taking for granted the inheritance of the liberal age as the inalienable property of our civilization. Yet freedom and democracy are not free gifts which will remain with us only if we wish it.

Actually democracy is the most difficult and most dangerous form of government. It achieves progress the hardest way in the belief that the process is as important as the result. In normal times the state waits upon the voluntary activity of its citizens to shape its policies and solve its hardest problems. The result, of course, is clumsy, inefficient, extravagant, undisciplined, unstable, and permits gross inequalities in wealth. Let me particularize by reminding you of a few of our many dilemmas.

To endure, any nation must take action adapted to meet effectively the conditions of its environment and the acts of the individuals must conform to these requirements. The contrast between coordinated effort and democratic decision is striking; for whereas cooperation means approximate unanimity of will, the democratic process means decision by division — by majorities, sometimes small ones. Such determinations can become wholly effective only as faith in the democratic process leads to their acceptance as controlling, notwithstanding individual dissent (which reminds one of Theodore Parker's remark that democracy means not "I'm as good as you are," but "you're as good as I am"). But such faith, such conformance, does not in fact exist in all cases. Prohibition was an illustration.

Another clearly related difficulty is the abstract character of most decisions at the time they are made. All general decision is abstract and relates to the future and the enormous detailed action covered by a general decision is beyond the comprehension and imagination of most men. So one often finds a conflict between general decision which is approved and concrete action thereunder which is disapproved. But democratic decision is difficult to reverse promptly so we avoid such conflicts by disregarding the decision. Hence, the tendency to create illegality and thus destroy the democratic process. (But of course this is a field so important to the welfare of the legal profession that nothing can or should be done about it!)

One of the worst difficulties is the slowness inherent in the democratic process. There is (1) delay in recognizing the need for decision, (2) time required for making it, and (3) time necessary to promulgate and execute it. Sometimes in emergencies courageous leaders have circumvented the democratic process. Such solutions are usually illegal, however, and require an assumption of responsibility from which most men will shrink. Not only is effective timing often impossible in our system, but delay and indecision depress the initiative and enthusiasm required for proper execution of decisions.

And then there is the political obstacle — the competition between parties and groups for public favor. We are all too familiar with the techniques of political tactics — the imputing of false motives and the everlasting drawing of "red herrings." Avoidance of political conflict and disruption of organization frequently make it necessary to resort to weak compromises or result in failure to make any decision at all.

Again there is the turnover in leadership occasioned by the party system, with the result that our process either affords no stability of direction or requires a larger quantity of qualified leaders than would otherwise be sufficient. Added to this is the system of selection, which, being political and partisan, rewards political abilities rather than abilities for the job. In short, it is apparent that democracy requires leadership of the highest order, yet the system is by no means designed to furnish it. And the quality of men who are risking private peace and security for public ingratitude and insecurity is probably decreasing. To me it has always been a marvel that an unchristian thirst for power and prestige has supplied as good leadership as it has.

But it serves no purpose to multiply the counts in the indictment of democracy. We can readily admit her deficiencies; we can readily admit that she is at a disadvantage in competition with streamlined totalitarian idealogy. We cannot expect democracies managed by millions to maneuver with the agility of governments managed by a corporal, or even a corporal's guard!

So, acknowledging our technical handicaps, let us also acknowledge that within every country enemies are bred by discontent and the marching millions of the unemployed in Britain, France and America have been a grave danger to democracy *at home* and is perhaps the most effective propaganda against democracy *abroad.* The right and the duty of earning our daily bread are fundamental to normal human beings. A "hand-out" by whatever name it may be called will feed the body but it starves self respect. The foundation of the success of Nazism, Fascism and Communism is the simple proposition that under modern conditions men cannot have both work and freedom. The war may temporarily relieve the *pressure* of materiall *ill* being on spiritual *well* being, but when the hurricane is spent I wonder if the same old question won't be there again clamoring for solution. My guess is that the seductions of Marxist dogma which traces all evil to the imperfections of the economic system will arise to plague us again; that democracy will still be confronted with the *only* idea common to 19th century liberalism and present day socialism; the belief that the consummation of individual freedom can only be achieved if we break the "despotism of physical want."

I have tried to sketch crudely some of the perils and the problems. I can suggest no remedies. But of one thing I'm sure; that it's not too late or too soon to commence preparation for the defense of democracy. For democracy can only survive if the people want it, and to want it badly enough to defend it they must understand it. So our defense is education — education in its meaning and its relative worth. I can suggest some broad essentials to wisdom as a basis for such education in defense of democracy. The first is perspective. Perspective is attained by broadening and lengthening experience far beyond the boundaries, either in time or space, of the life span of an individual. It is perfectly evident that the shock and terror of incidents decline if it is realized that the same sort of thing has happened many times before, and that the world has survived. The thinking of Plato and Aristotle regarding democracy is as real, as valid, as informing as ever it was; and mere nearness in time does not make the views of lesser minds more important. The history of tyranny is long — even longer than the history of democracy. Its transient character, the manner in which it has always nurtured the seeds of its own destruction make it desirable to follow its record whenever and wherever it has appeared in human history.

Henry Wriston, President of Brown University, said not long ago: "It will be helpful to perspective in these days of doubt regarding democracy to realize that democracy is not some fresh and untried invention, that it is a sturdy growth maturing through the centuries, that in Britain and America, at least, its roots have struck deep into the soil.

Where there was a mere veneer of democracy, the intense heat of the World War and its aftermath has blistered it and destroyed its finish. Where democracy was grafted onto an alien stock, the graft in some cases, has parted and the bough withered. But those events, unhappy and unfortunate as they are, do not affect the validity of its principles or the sturdiness of its growth."

The second essential of wisdom as a basis for education in democracy is disciplined emotion, or response to values. Our emotions have no depth, no warmth. The age is cynical. We are more afraid of sentimentality than slavery. The accent in art is on ugliness. We call it "honesty" or "realism." Popular books are written debunking George Washington. The Constitution has been interpreted as an effort of speculators to make good their gamble. The emphasis has shifted from triumphs and advances to shortcomings and failure. We talk of the "tragedy of youth" and the "lost generation." Spiritual achievement is interpreted in materialistic terms. The story of the race has been robbed of the sense of victory and achievement, and all too often is interpreted as a record of exploitation, frustration and perfidy. Science is the only success story now, and with even hand it serves destruction as well as construction. We talk too much of security, of safety. But democracy is dangerous! We give its enemies great freedom; we guarantee freedom of expression to thoughts we hate. Safety first is an idea corrosive of democracy, for democracy is a great human adventure, and the sense of adventure is emotional.

Don't misunderstand me. I am not counseling an emotional upheaval. The asylums are already overcrowded with intense, well-meaning people. What I am suggesting is eager minds and warm hearts and a sense of values. We can't have what we want unless we know what we want and want it hard enough. Loring Merwin sent me the other day some clippings from the Pantagraph on the occasion of the celebration of the 50th anniversary of this church in 1909. I was struck by this passage from a sermon by Rev. S. A. Eliot: "After all, the controlling powers in human life are not intellectual but emotional. Faith, hope and love are functions of the heart, not the head. The noblest intellect is that which is shot through with passion. Reason must be *lifted* on the shoulders of a great emotion before its beacon can enlighten weary and distressed humanity." That sounds intemperate to us nowadays. Perhaps it is. But it suggests what I'm trying to say. We have to select our values, separate the gods from the half gods, and then enthrone them with our hearts as well as our minds.

Patience and industry are other constituents of wisdom because our education for democracy is an education in ideas and ideas are harder to grasp than facts. The pursuit of truth is easy now. Books are plentiful, communication constant and the daily newspaper in one day gives you more comprehensive information about the world near and far than you could get in months when this church was founded. But learning is hard work, and in a sense we seem to have neutralized the advantages our times offer to education. The schools furnish buses, books, materials and teachers that were once hard to acquire. But the emphasis seems to be vocational and materialistic; the motive of gain has replaced the motive of service and materialism has replaced idealism. As everywhere else in our social organism one detects that security is the ideal — that youth is seldom animated by the will to know for the sake of the freedom that is in knowledge. A short cut to a salary is the purpose and end of education. This is *not* the best education for democracy.

Democracy seeks to fulfill an ancient idea: "The multitude of the wise is the welfare of the world." Democracy is ill adapted to illiteracy, but in the hands of the wise it affords the best insurance for the realization of man's immemorial aspirations. With better perspective, better values, patience and industry democracy can and will become a more efficient instrument. Meanwhile history has taught us that justice is the best thing in life — it is well to remember that Greece and Rome loved *peace* more than justice! and when we get impatient with democracy it is also well to recall that the history of today, as yesterday, teaches us that the price of efficiency is often tyranny and the surrender of those vital human values, those liberties, which distinguish the free man from the slave, which exhalt the dignity of the individual as an inviolable, rational soul and not merely the creature of the state. When in doubt let us remember that "the things which are seen are temporal; the things which are not seen are eternal."

Dictatorship rejects the concept of individual freedom and the inner life of man for which he is responsible to God alone. It lays claim to the whole of him for the society of which he is an insignificant part. This concept in essence is anti-religious. If man has no freedom of choice for thought, expression or action how can we have any religious faith? Let me recall some words of President Roosevelt which cannot be repeated too often:

"Storms from abroad directly challenge three institutions indispensable to Americans, now as always. The first is religion. It is the source of the other two — democracy and international good faith.

"Religion, by teaching man his relationship to God, gives the individual a sense of his own dignity and teaches him to respect himself by respecting his neighbors.

"In a modern civilization, all three — religion, democracy and international good faith — complement each other.

"An ordering of society which relegates religion, democracy and good faith among nations to the background can find no place within the ideals of the Prince of Peace."

So we retain our ancient faith in democracy and continue to believe, to borrow a phrase from Tall[e]yrand, that "the only thing wiser than anyone is everyone." We shall not forget that the course of human progress has suffered tragic reverses in the past. It may again in the future. It has lost many a battle. It can never be ultimately defeated. We in America *can* save individual liberty. We *can,* in Lincoln's words, "Nobly save this last best hope of earth!"

To Mrs. Edward Erickson [138]

October 24, 1939

Dear Mrs. Erickson:

You will probably not remember me, but I am the grandson of Adlai E. Stevenson, of Bloomington. My old friend, Jacob L. Hasbrouck,[139] told me this weekend in Bloomington that you had a Bible which my Aunt Letitia Stevenson gave to you at the time of my grandfather's death, and which evidently had belonged to my great-grandmother [Mrs. Lewis Warner] Green.

If it is not too inconvenient for you, I should like very much to have an opportunity to look at this book, as I have few remnants of the Green family. I shall, of course, return it to you promptly. If it is any trouble I am sure Mr. Hasbrouck would be glad to take it down to the office and have it wrapped up and sent to me.

With very best regards, I am

Sincerely yours,

At the Wayfarers Club, February 15, 1938, Stevenson had introduced the film From Czar to Lenin. *On October 28, 1939, he introduced the film at the Chicago Bar Association in quite a different fashion. (The* Chicago Bar Record, *Vol. XXI, No. 2, November, 1939, pp. 52–54, published a condensed version of the speech. We use the complete version.)*

138 A longtime resident of Normal, Illinois.
139 Editor of the *Daily Pantagraph.*

PROPAGANDA, HISTORY AND MOTION PICTURES

The reasons I have chosen this eccentric topic are four. In the first place preparation has been manifestly easy, which you will agree, is always an important consideration; secondly, Russia interests me and I travelled there extensively in the early days of the revolution. In the third place, the present re-emergence of Russia as a dominant factor in Western Europe lends new interest to the origins of an ominously stable political organization, and, finally, the extraordinary development of the techniques of propaganda present, it seems to me, some incidental and thought worthy considerations.

We all know that propaganda is as old as oratory. But in the last few years we have witnessed the exaltation of this ancient art to the dignity of state ministerships and the constant employment of this mighty weapon as an instrument of national policy. The story has been often told: In *March* 1935 he [Hitler] reintroduced universal military service; in *March* 1936 his troops occupied the demilitarized Rhineland; in *March* 1938 his troops occupied Austria; in *March* 1939 his troops occupied Prague and Memel (in *March* Caesar was stabbed, but the English and French evidently had no Calpernius). Each step was accompanied by peaceful reassurances, illustrating Adolph Hitler's audacious propaganda principle: "The lie is almost always more effective as propaganda than the truth. The larger the lie, the more effective." On September 1, 1939, his troops entered Poland and he issued a proclamation charging, among other things, that "the Poles were no longer willing to respect the German frontier" and that he had no choice but "to meet force with force," thus illustrating another propaganda principle he has always applied: "As soon as by one's own propaganda even a glimpse of right on the other side is admitted the cause for doubting one's own right is laid." (A principle, incidentally, which I believe is deemed effective by some advocates.) Or, as the late Texas Guinan put it, "Never give a sucker an even break."

In the day of mercenary armies, war was a payroll, not a propaganda, problem. But in our age when the bludgeon of war falls on whole populations and the difference between soldier and civilian is imperceptible from a bombing plane, propaganda can be as important as petroleum. In the current war we won't hear the rattle of the machine guns, but a battle for the mastery of our public opinion, a battle more constant and no less bitter, will be waged by the combatants on *our* soil.

However, it is not of this dramatic international propaganda with which we are all too familiar that I want to speak. I think we are rapidly developing in America an immunity or at least some power of discrimination as a result of long exposure and experience with the brazen and arrogant technique which Herr Hitler has used so effectively. From the less transparent forms of propaganda we are also probably learning that to be literate is not enough; that to literacy must be added insight into the forces that are trying to shape public opinion. But there is another aspect of the enormous problem of propaganda with which we are all familiar and which seems to me subtle and of far-reaching and enduring effect — education in history.

In every country education is a domestic commodity not intended for export. Generally it represents a gradual accretion of national traditions, popular hopes and hates; sometimes it is consciously used by special groups for special purposes. Recently it has, we know, been widely used in Europe by government itself for chauvenistic propaganda. In any case, as Professor Schlesinger [140] of Harvard has said, "Historical education occupies a central position with reference to all other provocations to war, for in so far as it embodies dangerous nationalistic prejudices, it is the means of disseminating them constantly to all the people. It is a seedbed of international discord for both present and future generations."

Broadly speaking, the term education embraces all the agencies that influence opinion: not only the school, the high school and the college, but also the printing press, the public library, the pulpit, the stage, the radio, and the screen. And it is to the screen that I want to call your attention; particularly to its use and influence as a medium for the teaching of history. For within their limitations historical teaching pictures have possibilities that have hardly been explored.

History has been defined as philosophy teaching by example. It is difficult to imagine a more effective medium than the film for the portrayal of that example. Pictures will always give a different and more vivid impression from that conveyed by the written word, particularly to the young. In the matter of contemporary history it is well known that many country people of school age know little of life in a great city. Many know nothing of the organization of modern industry and commerce. Teachers for the most part are in a similar predicament. Not even many historians have taken an active part in political and economic life. Moreover, we must not forget that even in our enlightened country the great mass of the people have little more

[140] Arthur M. Schlesinger, professor of American history, Harvard University.

than grammar school education. The documentary film can do much to reveal the interconnection of the laboratory and the factory; activities of government; relationship of class and class, nation and nation. It is not surprising that documentary films are being used more and more to teach contemporary history both here and abroad.

But I am more concerned with the familiar historical entertainment film which is teaching so-called "history" to more old and young than all the history teachers combined. The main concern of these pictures (and of much historical writing, by the way) has been with people and not with peoples; with kings and not with commoners; with governments and not with the governed. Chesterton called history gossip about kings. Of the employment, living conditions, food, clothes, social habits and other particulars of daily life of the people contemporary with these films we generally learn nothing. Moreover, stories bearing almost no relation to historical events are dramatized and shown to thousands as "history." For the most part they are good films but bad history. Yet the historical entertainment picture is packed with human interest and puts *no* strain on the intellect — it is vivid, exciting, and the historical flavor comforts the mind with the sense of painlessly learning something. Even though the spectator knows that the story has been produced in a studio, it will be difficult not to attribute to it a certain degree of reality. Furthermore, visual impression retains its hold over the processes of memory long after the impression was first received. In short, motion pictures, like newspaper photographs, have great prestige with the people and their influence is lasting.

Someone has said that to have propaganda you must have proper geese. So consider for a moment the effect on millions of movie conditioned people of *actual* history — not the sense of reality, not make believe, but reality! There can be no doubt that the development of photography in recent years and its extensive use in news gathering will make the pictorial history of our times available to the future, not by the image masquerading as the fact in the old fashioned way, but by the fact itself! Great events are sometimes not identified until time has had an opportunity to assign them proper roles. But when that time comes history will unfold not in books for the *few* to read but on the screen for the *millions* to see *and* hear — to see and hear not actors in Hollywood, but the real people, enacting the real events, saying the real words, in the real places!

No amount of books, pamphlets or periodicals can undo the graphic fidelity of the camera and the effect it produces on the human eye.

It requires scant literacy. It can ridicule a character or a whole movement. It can stimulate the emotions of more people, more quickly and with more lasting effect than any other medium of communication. Once remove the atmosphere of make believe and replace it with the authentic sounds and scenes of great events and here is an educational instrument of incalculable power and incalculable danger! Here is history unadulterated by historians and by national prejudices. *But* — and this is what I want you to consider — distort the emphasis slightly, omit a little something, alter the sequence a little, and we have the subtlest, most penetrating, propaganda — respected by millions as history!

Now the picture I am going to show you is interesting, to me at least, as perhaps the first crude experiment with *factual historical* propaganda. The picture was shown publicly in New York a couple of years ago and was promptly picketed by Communists because there is too much Trotsky and not enough Stalin. (Actually this is quite accurate, as Stalin was, of course, relatively obscure at the beginning of the Bolshevist revolution.) Since then it has been shown only privately. A man named Herman Axelbank spent some 13 years assembling these fragments of film. Some were taken by the Czar himself who evidently was a very early home movie addict, and were found in his private apartments in the Winter Palace; some were taken by his personal photographers; some were propaganda for the White armies, others for the Red; some are the work of news photographers and many were found in the archives of the French, English, German and Japanese armies of occupation and in private film libraries in Europe and America.

That a record as complete as this could be assembled is the more remarkable when one recalls that the motion picture camera was a rarity 25 years ago. The film commences in 1912 with pictures of the Czar, the royal family, the impressive Grand Duke Nicholas, and from that time on you have a glimpse of almost every important figure in the following decade of Russian history. The picture ends with a remarkable intimate study of Lenin in the animation of earnest speech that gives one some visual comprehension of his magnetism and energy.

I hope you enjoy it and that it will compensate you for my tiresome introductory transgressions.

To Mrs. Edward Erickson

October 31, 1939

Dear Mrs. Erickson:

I have received the Bible and your good letter.[141] I cannot thank you enough. This is the only thing I have of any kind that belonged to my great-grandmother Green. I am placing your letter in the flyleaf so there will always be a record of the book's history.

With sincerest good wishes and many, many thanks, I am

Yours always,

On November 3, 1939, Stevenson gave essentially the same talk he had given on October 28, 1939, and then showed the movie From Czar to Lenin *to the Law Club of Chicago. Silas H. Strawn, prominent Chicago lawyer, wrote Stevenson the following day that it was always a pleasure to hear him speak because of his "unusual facility of expression" and his "apt language."*

To Silas H. Strawn

November 6, 1939

Dear Mr. Strawn:

Thanks very much for your note. I appreciate it more than I can tell you. My speech was none too good anyway, and what with my wretched voice and cold I felt a little dismal about it.

Faithfully yours,

On November 21, 1939, James L. Houghteling wrote Stevenson that he had been so busy drafting an amendment to the Neutrality Act that he had not been able to gather any information for him about the employment of young lawyers in the government service.

To James L. Houghteling

November 24, 1939

Dear Lawrence:

A thousand thanks for your delightful letter. Please feel no remorse about my speaking project on the subject of lawyers in the government

---

[141] Mrs. Erickson had made Stevenson a present of the Bible mentioned in his letter of October 24, 1939, above.

service. I made a number of inquiries and found little information available — not enough to support a speech without a lot of independent research. My speeches have already been made and my subject was "Propaganda, History and Motion Pictures"! So you see I abandoned the original idea completely. Many thanks for your efforts all the same — as a subject of interest to lawyers it really has great possibilities.

Your recent activities fill me with envy — while you were amending the Neutrality Act I was amending a trust! It all makes me very unhappy with my lot.

My best to Laura [Mrs. Houghteling] and your kind self.

Sincerely yours,

To Mrs. John W. Stephan [142]

December 12, 1939

Dear Ruth:

I have just read of your father's death and want you to know how sorry I am. Both of my parents died years ago and I know how few the comforts are in these dreadful moments. But you can find, I am sure, some comfort in the recollection that he was an extraordinary product of our civilization and made extraordinary contributions to it.

Sincerely yours,

To Thomas Furness [143]

December 21, 1939

Dear Tom:

Looking through some old clothes the other night I ran across an evening scarf of yours which I think fell into my possession in some more or less honest fashion some ten years ago.

This being the Christmas season, and my heart overflowing with good will, it seemed not inappropriate to return it to you, which I am doing under separate cover. Had I thought of it, I might even have done this many years ago. But of course as you never go out in the evenings, I am sure you have not missed it, and the reunion will be the more affectionate after the long separation! I shall not attempt to apologize.

Yours,

[142] A family friend in Chicago.
[143] A friend from Lake Forest, Illinois, and a stockbroker and member of the Chicago Stock Exchange.

On January 3, 1940, James L. Houghteling wrote Stevenson that John Palenyi, Hungarian minister to the United States, wanted to meet some Chicago businessmen interested in foreign affairs. He mentioned that he was also writing Donald McPherson, the president of the Chicago Council on Foreign Relations, about Palenyi's visit, but "I should like to have him meet the equally distinguished ex-President of the Council."

To James L. Houghteling

January 5, 1940

Dear Lawrence:

This seems to be our open season on ambassadors, and very pleasant hunting it is, too. Last night we had Lord Lothian [British ambassador], who made a disarming speech and set a new high in ambassadorial candor! Our arms are now open for his Hungarian Excellency. If McPherson does not fix something up, I will; and thanks to you for giving me the opportunity — evidently you know my insatiable appetite for foreign goings-on. . . .

Yours,

p.s. Since dictating the enclosed I have talked with McPherson, and I wish you would ask Mr. Palenyi to notify me when he will be available for luncheon as far in advance as possible. I propose to arrange for a closed luncheon meeting of the Executive Committee of the Council on Foreign Relations at which he will be able to talk informally and with candor to twenty or thirty people, including some very well informed ones. I think you know what these meetings are like, and we have frequently had ministers and officials who did not care to speak publicly.

A.E.S.

On January 31, 1940, Stevenson addressed a Zionist mass meeting in Chicago.

I must confess at the outset that I hardly know why I am here, and I suspect that before I have finished my brief remarks, you will wish I wasn't here. I am not a Zionist and I am not distinguished in any way, but I *am* a practicing lawyer in Cook County and when your friend and my friend, Judge Harry Fisher,[144] suggests that I do some-

[144] Cook County Circuit Court Judge Harry M. Fisher wrote Stevenson the next day, "At lunch today you were the sole subject of conversation and everyone recalled

thing, I generally find it convenient to do it with alacrity! Moreover, I must admit that to have a part in this meeting is the most flattering thing that ever happened to me. Though, if I had foreseen my terror at this moment, Judge Fisher would have had to lock me up for contempt of court before I could get across the state line!

I said I was not a Zionist. I am a Gentile and what is worse, I am a Scotch Presbyterian — on my father's side. But on my mother's side I am a Unitarian. I shall never forget a conversation between my devout and aggressive grandparents. The Unitarian said acidly that the Scotch Presbyterians kept the ten commandments and everything else they could lay their hands on. The Scotch Presbyterian replied that he had made some study of the Unitarian faith and would be obliged if the Unitarian could enlighten him as to how it differed essentially from the Jewish! So I guess I cannot claim to be a religious pure-bred.

But I don't see why the Jews are so exclusive about their Zionism and in so far as it represents the aspiration for a national home, I am a Zionist; and you will have to accept me, gentlemen, even if you do not like to be adulterated with cross bred Protestants!

I said that to be here tonight was the most flattering thing that ever happened to me. I do not need to tell you why. Like everyone that has followed world events since the last war, I have known something of Dr. [Chaim] Weizmann [145] and his heroic work. Day before yesterday I saw and heard him for the first time at the Council on Foreign Relations — I saw and heard a great man! And for a moment I lost his words and thought of the quality of great leadership — of enduring greatness. I thought of an indomitable will to gain a great objective — not by hate, not by bigotry, not by ignorance, enslavement, brutality and blood, but by compromise and peace. Here, I thought, is no conqueror; here is a creator! Here is the imperishable quality of great historical leadership.

And just then I emerged from my reverie to marvel again at his tolerant understanding. With the humble, earthy good humor of many great men, he complained not of his adversaries, not of the Arabs and the British, but of the type of Jew who, as he put it, is delighted to get a seat in a crowded street car and even more delighted that you haven't got one! And then I lapsed into another reverie and thought of the afternoon in May last spring when I slipped into the galleries of the House of Commons to find the place packed, hushed, and tense. The Colonial Secretary was presenting the White Paper on Palestine and

some of the fine bits of humor or particularly excellent serious thoughts which so happily fitted the occasion."

[145] Leader of the international Zionist movement, a distinguished chemist, and in 1948 the first president of Israel.

gently but firmly reclaiming the seat in the crowded street car of the world which Lord Balfour had promised the Jews twenty odd years ago.[146] I stayed until Parliament adjourned and I went back the next day and the next and I heard the plan attacked and damned from every quarter of the House; I heard an eloquent, courageous and moving appeal for the Arabs, and I heard the name of Dr. Weizmann mentioned by everyone with something more than respect! And I never envied a man his job less than Malcolm MacDonald, the Colonial Secretary. Britain in that conflict of interest reminded me of that charming line in the Beggar's Opera when the girl, beset by two suitors, laments: "How happy I would be t'were either dear charmer away," — or more appropriately to our scheme of things, how nations, like politicians, sometimes find too many promises embarrassing. But I felt, as an ignorant, inexperienced outsider, that the heart of Britain was not perfidious, that for manifest reasons everything had not been said in the House of Commons and that with the world rushing to the crisis the Moslem East must be tranquil.

What was the crisis in May is now the war which is gradually creeping over Europe. Things must get worse before they get better and it may well be, as many have foreseen, that before the fury has spent itself, the fire of hate and fear and intolerance will engulf the Catholics and other groups as well as the Jews. Perhaps even we here in America are in for a period which will test our restraint and fidelity to our ancient ideals of tolerance and civil liberty on which the precious democratic tradition rests. At least one detects unpleasantly familiar symptoms — the restless unemployed, growing anti-semitism, red scares, intolerance and a quickening nationalist feeling — all in the name of Americanism.

But I cannot help but feel that the civilization of our times is destined to survive the present challenge; that the basis for this wave of oppression, bitterness and bloodshed is insufficient to support it long

---

[146] In 1917 the British Minister of Foreign Affairs, Arthur Balfour, stated that his government looked favorably upon the proposal to establish in Palestine a national home for the Jews provided the civil and religious rights of non-Jews already there were protected. Britain ruled Palestine under a League of Nations mandate from 1920 to 1948. In 1929 local Arabs launched their first large-scale attack on Jews. The next year the British placed restrictions on Jewish immigration. During the next few years there was considerable bloodshed and terrorism. In May, 1939, the British Parliament approved a plan for an independent Palestine in ten years. Jewish immigration was to cease in five years unless the Arabs agreed to its continuance. During the five years, 75,000 Jews could be admitted, making the Jews one-third of the population by 1944. The plan was widely denounced by Jews and Arabs alike.

enough to wreck our world. A demonaic ambition for world mastery sustained by a loyalty which is bred of falsehood and force cannot, I believe, ultimately prevail! You remember the old wisecrack — that God gave Germany three gifts: Intelligence, honesty and national socialism, provided that they could not use more than two of them at the same time!

So, as long as prophecy is free and I am not running for public office, I foresee that the garden the Jews have wrested from the wasted sands of Palestine must and will flourish; and in large part because inscrutable Providence has given them a great leader in this dreadful hour of trial. And perhaps some time when the Hebrew scholars and scribes of latter days continue the chronicle of their imperishable race, they will find an illumined page for the man who, after two thousand years of troubled wandering, led them back to their promised land — led them back with an example and an ancient admonition: "To do justice and to love kindness and to walk humbly with thy God."

To Hermon D. Smith

February 5, 1940

Dear Dutch:

"Illinois Democracy from 1818 to 1899" [147] has just landed on my desk, and I have already squandered on it some precious moments which could have been more profitably and less pleasantly spent. This is the best thing that happened to me on my birthday — or any birthday for that matter, and I am again beholden to you, and your genius for penetrating the dustiest corners of old bookshops.

I must also add that I marvel again at the commercial ingenuity of man — think how many poor but honest Democrats had to pay $10 the copy for this great historical work, and how many proud families pay God knows what for a permanent biography of dear old Dad, who rose from precinct captain to the dizzy heights of State Senator!

Many, many thanks, and pretty soon I'll ask you to tell me something about my grandfather — I am sure by this time that you know more about him than I.

Yours,

[147] *Illinois Democracy, 1818–1899: A Brief History of the Rise and Progress of the Democratic Party in Illinois. Biographical Sketches of Well-Known Democratic Leaders Together with Portrait Likenesses of Many Familiar Faces* (Chicago: Democrat Publishing Company, 1899).

To John D. Black

February 6, 1940

Dear Mr. Black:

I am in receipt of an elaborate announcement of an entertainment at the Chicago Club for which I apparently am in part responsible, and in which I am evidently expected to participate. In association with you I gladly accept the responsibility, but as for the participation, I would hesitate even if it were possible for me to be there. Imagine my debating such a ponderous question as whether to debate whether liquor should be served in the clubhouse.

Consider for a moment the serious implications; what if you were assigned the affirmative, and having prevailed, it then became necessary to debate not whether to debate but whether liquor *should* be served in the clubhouse! Assume again that your reasoning powers and eloquence overcame the judges — and it is not improbable that they would be easy to overcome by that time! What a dreadful predicament! — you have won your debate and ruined our club! No, Mr. Black, it is too solemn a responsibility, and I tremble at the thought of the everlasting damage you may be about to do — all unwittingly — with that sweet voice and persuasive tongue. No, Mr. Black! Liquor has been too good a friend and too honorable a member of that club to ever risk its fate in such unequal encounter — besides I have to go out of town! [148]

Yours, etc.

To Henry Horner

February 13, 1940

Dear Governor:

I cannot resist expressing to you my deep personal disappointment that you have found it necessary to withdraw.[149] I know you have taken this decision with the greatest reluctance and only in view of compelling considerations.

Though I find little political satisfaction in this situation, I can take

[148] Mr. Black replied the next day: "If my hat were not at the cleaners I would be tempted to put it on and rush over at once to wring the hand of a man of such principle. We shall miss your eloquence."

[149] A serious illness forced Henry Horner to announce that he would not seek renomination for governor. (He died before the end of his term.) He replied to Stevenson on February 27, 1940: "Your generous words touch me deeply and tend to make me feel that I have not striven in vain to contribute to the progress and welfare of Illinois."

no small comfort in the thought once back in Chicago I may have the good fortune to see you more frequently.

With sincerest regards and best wishes, I am

Faithfully yours,

To Robert M. Hutchins

February 19, 1940

Sir:

Not only do I work, but I do practically nothing else — a condition of which I am not proud. Albeit, I still occasionally eat and, as you know, I have no pride of companionship. So let me know when you are available.[150]

Yours,

Town Meeting of the Air, *one of the important discussion programs on network radio, originated a program from Chicago. The following day, February 23, 1940, its director, George Vernon Denny, Jr., met with a group of Chicagoans to discuss adult education. Adlai E. Stevenson was one of the speakers.*

An amateur speaker should never have such a good introduction and Mr. Saltiel's [151] flattering remarks have left me in a state of acute nervous disorder and oratorical impotence. I had thought of a few simple things to say here today but now they all seem trivial and unimportant and not worthy of a man of the proportions which Mr. Saltiel has assigned to me. I feel like that wretched little man in the New England village who was a candidate for selectman. His neighbor told him he hadn't much chance of election because people were saying that he didn't think enough. Why, he replied, that's not true — I'm thinking about something *practically* all the time!

I am happy to pay my respects to Mr. Denny in person. As one of the countless confused Americans, I have thanked him fervently on a good many Thursday nights after the Town Meeting of the Air suddenly became a torrid tango from the Argentine or one of the other equally uplifting aerial vitamins that seem to sustain the larger part

[150] Hutchins replied on February 24, 1940: "On receipt of your letter I left town in order to avoid seeing you and shall remain away as long as possible. When I get back you may hear from me." These letters are in the Hutchins papers, University of Chicago Library.

[151] Unable to identify.

of the American body politic. Not only have my thanks to Mr. Denny on Thursday nights mingled with the gentle melody of the trombones, but I've also startled my wife and my radio by deferential bows of appreciation for his art and decision as a presiding officer. Having, as the chairman indicated, had some slight experience with that business in the Chicago Council on Foreign Relations, I am not wholly unfamiliar with its perplexities, and I've developed a *fine* appreciation of the more civilized techniques for persuading people briefly and decisively to sit down and shut up. I want you to take my word as one who knows that Mr. Denny's genius is not only making a major contribution to American adult education but that he has also developed the obscure art of animal training to its highest perfection — and with the most difficult of all animals! There are the smug, complacent, well fed ones that need constant stirring up, and then there are the even worse offenders who are so stirred up that they can't relax. But, as Mr. Denny can testify, that kind sometimes go flat after being exposed to the air for awhile, like champagne. However, I suspect that your chairman, Mr. Brightman, did not ask me to come here to discuss Mr. Denny's less familiar talents as an animal trainer!

My job is an assessment of the town meeting idea, and I suppose that means what it's worth educationally. I think I will start by reminding you, yesterday being Washington's birthday, that Washington had very little formal education. Neither did Lincoln. But they both had great wisdom. They both knew, to borrow a phrase from Tall[e]y-rand, that "the only thing wiser than any one is every one." Unless we too believe that everyone is wiser than anyone, we cannot believe in the survival of popular sovereignty. On the contrary we must believe that the wisest should rule us, and because mankind has seldom been wise enough to select the wisest or because the wisest is not always the best, we look back across a history of tyranny that is longer than the history of democracy. Actually self government is the most difficult and most dangerous form of government. It achieves progress the hardest, slowest way in the belief that the process is as important as the result. In normal times the state waits upon the voluntary activity of its citizens to shape its policies and solve its hardest problems.

And there, it seems to me, is where the town meeting idea comes in. If, as time goes on, the wisdom of the plain, humble people of our country is not sufficient to solve our hardest problems, or if the traditional deliberate, clumsy, inefficient process of solution proves too slow and too costly, we may abruptly discover, as other peoples have, that we have substituted a streamlined, modern, efficient system — at the price of our freedom! So as the problems get harder to solve, and they are going to get harder and not easier, it becomes more and more apparent that the people need more and more enlightenment to solve them. We have the freest press and the freest radio in the world; we have an enormously powerful and effective educational medium in the movies. With all these devices at work we should be able to develop and maintain the informed public opinion on which the ultimate success of popular sovereignty depends.

But it is said, and I suspect it is true in part, that we don't as a people want to be bothered with these vexatious questions. The intensified struggle for existence; the ponderous complexity of it all, the discordant babble of voices mouthing half truths, and all of them making use of these quick, efficient, modern means of inter-communication, have conspired to develop a sombre cynicism or a light-hearted indifference, depending whether you are over or under 40, I suppose. Don't misunderstand me. Everyone is interested to some extent in current problems which touch his person or his purse directly and visibly. But for the most part the attitude is one of laissez-fair[e], both as to men and measures. As an Englishman said — Your public servants serve you right!

Only yesterday I heard a distinguished journalist complaining that people want what's easy and painless and *not* what's disagreeable or disturbing to our firmly established racial fixations even if it's true. I can illustrate, I think, by reminding you of the prevalent attitude in this country that Europe is a nest of decadent, jealous, quarrelling rascals and that it's a pity they can't take advantage of our peaceful, prosperous example. But since that warm July day in 1776 when we declared our independence from Great Britain, of the five great powers, Russia, Spain, France, Great Britain and ourselves, that have been great powers continuously ever since, we have been engaged in more wars than any of them, with the possible exception of France, depending on whether or not you include her intervention in the Italian wars. And in one of them, the Mexican War, we deliberately took an empire about as large, I think, as Germany and France, and in another, the Spanish War, we were so determined to have it that President McKinley declared war 24 hours after our minister in Madrid had advised him that Spain had capitulated on all points — a message which was not disclosed for some 15 years afterward, I think.[152]

Well it may be that as a people we are too busy to be bothered with adult education and that, as someone said, we don't think, we

[152] This point of view was commonly held, but the Spanish government did not accept all of President McKinley's terms. Ernest R. May, *Imperial Democracy* (New York: Harcourt, Brace & World, 1961), p. 153.

merely occasionally rearrange our prejudices. But granted that every-one can't or won't be educated or, for that matter, that even a large por-tion of the people can't be reached, still, as Mr. Denny, I believe, has pointed out, the balance of power in this country rests with only about 20% of the voters. It's the small minority of independent voters that oscillates back and forth between the inert masses of partisanship and prejudice that determines the broad course of events. And if this group can be educated, can be made to think their way through the prob-lems of our times, and can be enlarged, we will have, I think, some sound cause for confidence.

And fortunately this is the point of import of the Town Meeting of the Air. These are the millions who are reacting so energetically, so appreciatively to this experiment in mass adult education; these are the people who want to know, who want to know so badly that they have voluntarily and spontaneously organized more than 1400 listen-ing and discussion groups throughout the land. I don't need to tell you about the vitality and sincerity of the interest of this vast section of the American people; nor of the physics of light and how it spreads wide and travels far. Mr. Denny has divided adult education into two broad classes, the area of stimulation and the area of information and clarification. Your presence here today and the throng at the broadcast in Chicago last night are the best evidence of the success of the Town Meeting idea in both areas of adult education.

In conclusion let me remind you that arrogance of opinion; the temptation to read, hear and discuss only what's sympathetic are the enemies of electoral literacy. But free discussion, free combat of ideas with the people as the jury is the essence of our scheme of things. "The multitude of the wise is the welfare of the world" is an ancient adage. If you can give a little light the people will find their way and we will, in Lincoln's immortal words, "Nobly save this last best hope of earth."

To the Chicago Council on Foreign Relations

March 8, 1940

Attention: Miss Armstrong
Dear Miss Armstrong:

My conscience has been troubling me, and I finally discovered why! I am enclosing a check for $15 in payment of tickets for the [Lord] Lothian dinner, which I never purchased, and also for credit on the very considerable deficit which I understands exists!

Sincerely yours,

To Jacob L. Hasbrouck

April 2, 1940

Dear Jake:

I do not know what you are planning to do about recommendations for the principal offices in the primary. But I want to give you my preferences, as I have not seen Bud [Loring Merwin] lately, and I know most of the candidates — some of them quite well; well enough in some cases to be against them!

For Governor — Republican — I think Green is better qualified than Lyons. As for the Democrats, I am opposed to Stelle and will vote for Hershey.[153]

For Senator — Republican — Church is infinitely better qualified than Brooks, with whom I went to school, though Church has little chance of winning, I am afraid.[154] Among the Democrats I have great respect and admiration for Adamowski;[155] in spite of his youth he is one of the infrequent opportunities that our politics affords the voters. Though again I doubt if he can win with that name and against the organization.

For the other jobs I have no strong preferences, except that T. V. Smith should be kept in Congress.[156] You know all about him.

Best regards,

Sincerely yours,

To Benjamin S. Adamowski

April 2, 1940

Dear Ben:

Thank you for the impressive announcement of your new firm. I am sure it is destined to flourish.

I need not tell you that I am rooting for you in the primary. I am taking the liberty of enclosing a "token" contribution to *your* campaign expenses.

[153] Dwight Green defeated Richard J. Lyons in the Republican gubernatorial primary. Harry Hershey defeated Lieutenant Governor John Stelle in the Democratic gubernatorial primary. That fall Green won the governorship and held it until Stevenson defeated him in 1948.

[154] C. Wayland Brooks defeated Ralph Church in the Republican primary and won the U.S. Senate seat that fall.

[155] Benjamin Adamowski lost in the Democratic senatorial primary to Harry Slattery.

[156] Congressman at Large T. V. Smith was defeated that fall by Republican William G. Stratton.

When the primary is over and you can breathe again, I hope you will have lunch with me some day and tell me all about it.

Sincerely yours,

Mr. Hasbrouck replied to Stevenson's letter of April 2, 1940, that the Daily Pantagraph was supporting the candidates he favored, except that the paper preferred C. Wayland Brooks to Ralph Church.

To Jacob L. Hasbrouck

April 4, 1940

Dear Jake:

Many thanks for your letter. I am sorry the paper picked Brooks instead of Church, as he has almost no qualifications, so far as I have been able to discover — but he is sure to win!

At your convenience let me have Ted's [157] address in Chicago. I want to look him up.

Yours,

Harold H. Swift, chairman of the board of trustees of the University of Chicago, called a meeting of prominent Chicago citizens to announce plans for celebrating the fiftieth anniversary of the University. Each person who attended was sent a publication entitled The First Fifty Years.

To Harold H. Swift

May 2, 1940

Dear Harold:

I look forward to "The First Fifty Years" eagerly, and you may rest assured that I will read it and circulate it!

Let me take this opportunity to thank you for the delightful evening at the Chicago Club. It was dignified, impressive and also very pleasant, and your own part was by no means the least of it. I only hope that the future will leave no doubt that Chicago citizens of today have the same vision as those of fifty years ago.

Sincerely yours,

[157] Mr. Hasbrouck's son.

To H. J. MacFarland [158]

May 29, 1940

Dear Sir:

Several people have called to my attention a brief article in your edition of May 28 bearing a New York date line and reporting some remarks on academic freedom by a lawyer named A. E. Stevenson.

I take this means of resolving any doubt as to the identity of the author of these remarks. I did not make them.[159]

Sincerely yours,

---

[158] Editor of the *Chicago Daily Law Bulletin*.

[159] The A. E. Stevenson who spoke in New York City denounced academic freedom as placing a "Fifth Column" in the public schools. He also criticized the views of Mrs. Franklin D. Roosevelt, John Dewey, and Bertrand Russell. *Chicago Daily Law Bulletin*, May 28, 1940.

Part Ten

Aid to the Allies
1940–1941

*L*ate in September, 1939, William Allen White, editor of the Emporia, Kansas, Gazette, and Clark Eichelberger, director of the League of Nations Association and the Union for Concerted Peace Efforts, organized the Non-partisan Committee for Peace Through the Revision of the Neutrality Law. This committee focused pressure on Congress to support President Roosevelt's request that the Neutrality Law be revised and cash and carry be substituted for the arms embargo.

After Congress adopted the cash and carry legislation in November, 1939, the White Committee temporarily suspended its activities. In April, 1940, after Germany smashed into Norway and Denmark, White and Eichelberger started to organize the Committee to Defend America by Aiding the Allies.

On May 10, 1940, German divisions invaded Belgium and the Netherlands and mounted a massive assault on the French. Five days later, German mechanized divisions sliced through the French line at Sedan. Within a week, they cut off French and British forces in Flanders. On May 28 King Leopold of Belgium surrendered. During the next week, the British pressed all types of boats into action and evacuated French and British forces from the beaches at Dunkirk.

On June 5, Germany launched an assault to crush France. Five days later Italy joined the war. And on June 22, France surrendered.

During these hectic weeks William Allen White and Clark Eichelberger expanded the membership of their committee to rally support for aid to the allies. The national committee, with headquarters in New York City, had on its executive committee among others Lewis W. Douglas, Thomas K. Finletter, and Mrs. Emmons Blaine. By July 1, 1940, the committee had organized three hundred local chapters.[1]

In Chicago, Professor Quincy Wright and Professor Paul H. Douglas

[1] Walter Johnson, *The Battle Against Isolation* (Chicago: University of Chicago Press, 1944).

of the University of Chicago, and Clifton Utley, executive director of the Chicago Council on Foreign Relations, recommended to William Allen White that Adlai E. Stevenson be asked to be chairman of the Chicago chapter. White phoned Stevenson and he accepted after consulting with his law partners.

Over the next months Stevenson plunged into the most important public activity he had ever been engaged in. Members had to be recruited, money raised, and speeches made to present the committee's case to the public. As head of this highly controversial committee he broadened his friendships and became acquainted with a wider variety of people, including trade union leaders, than in the past. But many of his old friends drawn from Chicago's wealthy circles denounced him and some accused him of being a warmonger.[2] Many of them joined the America First Committee, headed by General Robert E. Wood and R. Douglas Stuart, Jr., with national headquarters in Chicago.[3]

Years later Stevenson observed that as chairman of the White Committee he sharpened his writing style. Since the committee was under constant attack, particularly from the Chicago Tribune and many of his old social friends, he wanted everything he said to be precise in order that it could not be quoted out of context.[4] He also remarked that his experience with the White Committee sharpened his determination to be more active in public life.

The letters and speeches published in Part Ten are in the Adlai E. Stevenson collection, Princeton University Library, unless otherwise indicated. Stevenson's papers during his activities with the Committee to Defend America by Aiding the Allies are voluminous and we have, as a result, been more selective than in the earlier parts of this volume. Stevenson's idiosyncrasies of spelling and style have been retained as he wrote them.

[2] See Harriet Welling, "Friend of the Family," in As We Knew Adlai, edited and with preface by Edward P. Doyle, foreword by Adlai E. Stevenson III (New York: Harper & Row, 1966), p. 44. See also some of the letters (in the papers at Princeton University) Stevenson received when he invited some old friends to join the White Committee.

[3] See Wayne C. Cole, America First (Madison: University of Wisconsin Press, 1953).

[4] Stuart Gerry Brown, letter to Walter Johnson, December 9, 1966.

To Frank C. Rathje [5]

June 27, 1940

Dear Mr. Rathje:

I received your check for $100 yesterday morning and deposited it in the little account which we have opened for the Chicago Committee. Our plans are progressing and I am sure you realize how comforting it is to find such ready support and good will and I appreciate it more than I can tell you.

I shall undoubtedly take the liberty of communicating with you further as the plans for our activity develop.

With sincere thanks and kindest regards, I am

Faithfully yours,

To Mrs. John Alden Carpenter

June 27, 1940

Dear Tonnie:

Your secretary has called me about the bona fides of the British Relief Commission in Chicago. I think it is the organization that Mrs. [Edward] Bernays spoke to me about the other day and that it is entirely o.k., but I am not sure.

After doing a lot of work for the American Volunteer Ambulance Corps, I have now turned my attention (reluctantly) to streamlining the activity of the Chicago William Allen White Committee to Defend America by Aiding the Allies. I am convinced that it is our interest to help Britain stop or hold Hitler and that a rising tide of sentiment in the next few weeks could be decisive or could at least bring about ultimately a negotiated peace of which we could be a major beneficiary. I don't believe our economy or standard of living can long endure the burdens in prospect if we are really going to do the job.

This is not a solicitation for funds, and I do not write to compete with the British Relief Committee. But if you have any spare money, we could use a little in our work here. We have made no attempt to get any large money yet and what we propose to do will require very little.

Ellen and the children are fine. Buffy and Ernest spent last night with us and are going down to Bloomington today for a month before going to Charlevoix.

Love,

[5] President of the Chicago City Bank and Trust Company.

On June 28, 1940, Stevenson sent the following letter and statement to the Chicago White Committee's informal executive committee consisting of among others Colonel Frank Knox, publisher of the Chicago Daily News; Clarence B. Randall of the Inland Steel Corporation; Mrs. Emmons Blaine, philanthropist; Rabbi Solomon Goldman; Walter Dill Scott, president of Northwestern University; Stevenson's Princeton classmate William B. Hale; Clifton M. Utley; Professor Quincy Wright; Professor Bernadotte E. Schmitt, and Professor Walter H. C. Laves.

Among the new names that signed the statement were Joseph D. Keenan, Secretary of the Chicago Federation of Labor; Samuel Levin, manager of the Chicago joint board, Amalgamated Clothing Workers of America; Stevenson's law partner William P. Sidley; H. T. Heald, president of the Armour Institute; Dean Leon Greene of the Northwestern University Law School; Alderman Earl B. Dickinson; and Max Epstein, Chicago businessman.

To the Chicago Committee to Defend America by Aiding the Allies

June 28, 1940

I enclose a statement which we propose to release to the newspapers on behalf of our Committee. We have prepared a list of names of people from whom we hope to get endorsements of this statement. As the endorsements come in (if they do!) we can make a series of newspaper stories out of them. The list is merely preliminary and is designed to appeal to labor, etc. — "the common people."

Any suggestions you have of possible endorsers whose names would be effective among any group will be helpful. Please communicate with Miss [Lucy] McCoy, our secretary, at Randolph 0674. Also please let her have your suggestions as to what we can do to increase pressure on Congress for more aid to Britain, bearing in mind that our funds are meager.

At the moment, I cannot give the time to organizing this work which it should have. If you know of any experienced person who could help for a few weeks, please let me know. If we are going to accomplish anything, we must get to work at once.

Very truly yours,

STATEMENT OF CHICAGO COMMITTEE
TO DEFEND AMERICA BY AIDING THE ALLIES

89 East Randolph Street, Chicago, Illinois

Hitler and Mussolini detest democracy. They have said so. They are our envious enemies.

We believe that "isolation" is impossible; that a triumphant Nazism will make repeated inroads in the Americas. With or without military invasion, our security, our economy, our way of life is in deadly peril from an unappeasable, dynamic, ruthless and victorious foe.

The collapse of France has seriously imperiled a democratic resistance to Hitler's quest for world dominion. But England fights on — on the last line of defense in Europe and first line of defense in America.

We believe that England can win — with our help! If she can, it is our manifest interest to give her the substantial and immediate help which we can.

But even if she cannot win, we must recognize that every day, every week that she continues to fight helps us in two ways. It weakens Hitler. It puts off the time when aggressive pressure — military or political — will commence in the Americas in earnest. It gives us what we need most — time to prepare, organize, educate!

Therefore, whatever Britain's chances of winning may be, we believe that American national interests will be served by resistance before the enemy is even bigger, even stronger and before we are alone in the world.

Britain is the first line of defense. Let us help her in every possible way to stop Hitler now. Urge your Congressmen to act — before it is too late!

To Walter J. Cummings

July 3, 1940

Dear Mr. Cummings:

I do not know to whom or when to apply for tickets to the Democratic Convention. Accordingly I am writing you — like altogether too many others, I suspect! Please forgive me, and rest assured that I shall much appreciate your suggestions.

I do not believe I need give you a Democratic character reference, or to remind you that I participated actively in the last two national campaigns.

Sincerely yours,

To Stanley Field [6]

July 3, 1940

Dear Mr. Field:

The Chicago William Allen White Committee to defend America by aiding the Allies has been relatively inactive since its organization a few weeks ago, and the newspaper advertising which you probably saw.

In the East and far West the Committee has been very active and very effective. It now seems evident that if our help to Britain is to be largely expanded now — when it can do some good — the pressure on Congress must come from the Middle West, where the isolationist sentiment is still strongest.

Hence, we plan to enlarge the activity of the local Committee. We do not plan to do anything that requires much money at the moment, and we should be able to accomplish something effective with not more than $5,000 and the considerable volunteer help which has been offered. When the attack on England commences in earnest, the response and sentiment for more help will doubtless accelerate. But we must be ready for it. That means immediate organization and preparation, and I hope to get enough money from a few people to see the thing well started without expending much time or effort raising money.

I suspect you are in sympathy with this aspect of our defense, and I hope you will find it possible to help finance the local activities. I should be glad to see you and to give you more detailed information about any aspect of the work.

Sincerely yours,

P.S. I am enclosing a statement which we are releasing next week, and for which we hope to get endorsements from all sorts of prominent people. I hope you will endorse it and give me permission to use your name. The response so far has been most gratifying. [7]

A.E.S.

President Roosevelt nominated Frank Knox, publisher of the Chicago Daily News *and 1936 Republican Vice Presidential candidate, to be Secretary of the Navy. After Colonel Knox testified before the Senate Naval Affairs Committee, his appointment was approved.*

[6] President of the Field Museum of Natural History.

[7] In general they were, except for an occasional refusal which asked, "Are you personally available for, and would you make good cannon fodder?"

To Frank Knox

July 5, 1940

Dear Colonel:

May we use your name as honorary chairman of the Chicago chapter of the William Allen White Committee? I am sure it would be very helpful to us.

Apparently you dissolved the opposition in the Naval Affairs Committee, and I congratulate you.

With kindest regards and sincerest best wishes, I am

Faithfully yours,

Edward L. Ryerson, Jr., president of the Inland Steel Corporation, asked Stevenson to clarify such phrases as isolation and non-intervention before he could sign the statement of the Aid the Allies Committee.

To Edward L. Ryerson, Jr.

July 8, 1940

Dear Ed:

Thanks for your good note. I agree with you that something should be done to clear up the confusion between "isolation" and "non-intervention." The William Allen White Committee is non-isolationist and non-interventionist. It believes that as long as Britain has a fair chance of holding Hitler off until winter we should do everything we can by material assistance to insure that result. The best chance we have of avoiding the economic risks of huge military expenditures for years is a negotiated peace — and another winter under the blockade might make that possible. Alternately, one must contemplate that England, if crushed, may go Fascist, too — as France has — and perhaps the component parts of the Empire will have to follow suit.

Briefly, it seems clear to me that it is in our manifest interest to help Britain to stop Hitler now. It can properly be said that such help is only a half way measure and that if we believe in the premise we should go to war now. My only answer to that is the reality of the situation. In the present state of public mind, we cannot go to war. Therefore we shall do the next best thing and sell them the planes, munitions and ships they need now — while they can do some good.

We are planning to run some newspaper stories about the statement I sent you carrying the endorsements of prominent Chicagoans. Our purpose is to develop some pressure on Congress from the Middle West, which has been the principal obstacle to more help, I understand.

I hope this letter makes some sense to you and that you will endorse the statement, which is necessarily brief and not adequately argued.

Sincerely yours,

Colonel Knox explained to Stevenson that, since he would be Secretary of the Navy, it was better that he not be honorary chairman of the White Committee. He added that the committee had his complete approval.

To Frank Knox

July 8, 1940

Dear Colonel:

Thank you for your good letter. I appreciate your position and am gratified that with your access to all the facts you are still confident that more aid to Britain and the William Allen White Committee are on the right track. My satisfaction with your confirmation is diluted by the consideration that your influence on local thought along this line cannot be replaced.

Sincerely yours,

To Robert M. Hutchins [8]

July 12, 1940

Dear Bob:

We are having a small informal buffet supper party for Charles Michelson and Jim Farley and his daughters on Sunday evening.[9] I hope you and Maude can join us at any time after 7:30 at Mrs. [John Alden] Carpenter's house — 1020 Lake Shore Drive.

Yours,

P.S. It would do you good to brush shoulders with the 'polls' —

William Allen White and other leading members of his committee worked to influence the platform-makers of both political parties to endorse aid to the allies. The nomination of Wendell L. Willkie by

[8] This letter with the handwritten postscript is in the Hutchins papers, University of Chicago Library.
[9] James Farley was chairman of the Democratic National Committee and Charles Michelson was publicity director.

the Republicans insured that both candidates favored such aid. Stevenson testified on July 14, 1940, to the Democratic platform committee.

The Democratic party reaffirms its faith in the principles of individual freedom, equal justice and the dignity of man on which our nation was founded and has endured the envy of the world. We believe that peace is the only assurance of the preservation of these principles. We pledge ourselves anew, therefore, to furtherance of the Democratic party's traditional and constant effort to prevent war and to organize peace by cooperation with all nations similarly disposed; we applaud and reaffirm our faith in the good neighbor policy in our international relations.

We believe that influences in the world which exalt force and deny the validity of the democratic principles on which our government and our way of life depend, endanger not only the liberties of free peoples, but also the standard of living and the prosperity of the American people. We must, therefore, and we do, recognize that in a world so constituted preparedness is the path to peace. Mindful of the sacrifices by all the people which such a program entails, we dedicate ourselves to the immediate organization and building of an invincible defense on land and sea and in the air — a defense adequate not only for our own territory but also to discharge if necessary our historical responsibilities.

We believe that no American *wants* war; we believe that the Democratic party expresses a unanimous national sentiment in declaring unequivocally, as we do, that our armed forces shall not be used for aggression anywhere, and that our soldiers shall fight only for our defense and not in Europe.

We recognize that qualified opinion may differ as to our true defense; we recognize that the freedom, security and prosperity of our people is closely associated with the fortunes of those nations that are fighting for their survival. Moreover, it has not been the historical role of the United States to view with indifference the tyrannical subjugation and suppression of freedom. Hence we believe that it is compatible with our traditions and in our manifest national interest to extend to Great Britain in this hour of peril to her democracy and to ours all possible material aid and comfort.

Finally, we believe it is the part of forthright leadership not to minimize the menace to our country, our civil liberties and the economic order on which our civilization rests in the triumph of aggressive force. What lies ahead is obscure. America must meet it with unity, conviction and courage!

To Lucy McCoy [10]

July 17, 1940

Dear Miss McCoy:

I enclose a very good endorsement of our statement from Dr. John Timothy Stone, who was for many years pastor of the Fourth Presbyterian Church and is now, I believe, president of the McCormick Theological Seminary.

Mr. Samuel Laderman, Manager of the Chicago Leather Workers Joint Board, 417 South Dearborn Street, Harrison 9083, wants the Committee to write him a formal letter stating that we are including his name as a member of the Chicago Committee, asking his union to endorse the movement, and asking for a contribution. I believe you have already sent him some petitions, and he might be very useful in assisting with the organizing work among labor.

His union is having meetings on Monday, Tuesday and Thursday evenings of next week, and he would like very much for Alderman Paul Douglas to address their union on the subject of aid to Britain for ten or fifteen minutes on Tuesday evening. Will you communicate with Mr. Douglas and ask him to notify Mr. Laderman if he can do so. I believe the hour is six o'clock.

Very truly yours,

Stevenson's old friend Laird Bell, prominent Chicago lawyer, in joining the Aid the Allies Committee wrote: "I am full of admiration of the good works which you seem to find time to do and your efficiency in performing them."

To Laird Bell

July 19, 1940

Dear Laird:

I am delighted that you have decided to "sign up" with the White Committee, and, of course, your contribution is a major incident in our progress. Money will become increasingly important, and a man is pretty much at a loss as to where to turn for support, having worn out my welcome pretty generally. If you can enlist the support of anyone else, either financially or otherwise, it will be a great help, as we need volunteer workers to circulate petitions, etc., as well as money.

[10] Secretary of the William Allen White Committee.

Many, many thanks for your help — and your kind remarks. I suspect my partners are beginning to wonder how I find time to do some of these things, too!

Sincerely yours,

Stevenson wrote his friend Chauncey McCormick on July 10 asking for office space for the William Allen White Committee in a building owned by Mr. McCormick.

William McCormick Blair, Jr., by now twenty-three years old, was a full-time volunteer worker for the committee He had just returned to Chicago from his graduation at Stanford University. Blair's father was a first cousin of Robert R. McCormick, publisher of the Chicago Tribune, *who was a vitriolic foe of the White Committee. It was in the summer of 1940 that Blair began his close association with Stevenson.*

To Chauncey McCormick

July 23, 1940

Dear Chauncey:

A thousand thanks for your letter of July 22nd. This is very good news to us, and I am asking Bill Blair, Jr., who is doing volunteer work for the William Allen White Committee, to get in touch with Mr. [William] Pick [11] at once.

I felt confident that you would be in sympathy with this movement, and I only hope it will be possible for us to accomplish something in this neighborhood while there is still time. The Great Lakes area seems to be the most obtuse and the most hesitant about doing anything further to aid Britain.

Sincerely yours,

To Andrew R. Montgomery

July 24, 1940

Dear Mr. Montgomery:

I am the chairman of the Chicago Chapter of the William Allen White Committee, and at Gilbert Scribner's suggestion, I have taken the liberty of instructing our office to notify some people in Milwaukee who have been interested in forming a chapter of the Committee to get in touch with you.

We sent a representative of our office up to Milwaukee a couple of

[11] In charge of managing the building owned by McCormick.

weeks ago, and I have the impression that there is a small group trying to get organized which needs leadership. I hope very much that you will be able to help them, and, of course, our office here in Chicago will be delighted to give you any information we can.

With kindest regards, I am

Sincerely yours,

On June 29, 1940, President Roosevelt discussed with William Allen White the possible exchange of World War I destroyers for naval and air bases in British possessions in the Western Hemisphere. During much of the summer, the Aid the Allies Committee organized sentiment to demonstrate to Roosevelt that the public supported the exchange. A Gallup poll in mid-August reported that a majority of those polled favored the release of destroyers to Britain.[12]

To Franklin D. Roosevelt [13]

July 25, 1940

MANY CHICAGOANS JOIN ME IN URGING IMMEDIATE SALE TO BRITAIN OF 50 OR 60 OF OUR OVER AGE RECONDITIONED DESTROYERS. SINCERELY HOPE THIS MAY SOON BECOME POSSIBLE UNDER YOUR COURAGEOUS LEADERSHIP.

To George A. Richardson [14]

July 26, 1940

Dear George:

I am sure you know all about the William Allen White Committee, and I suspect that you and Marshall Field are both in sympathy with our aid to Britain — now. If you are, and if you would let the Chicago Committee set up a desk somewhere in the lobby in the Field Building for a few days to distribute literature and petitions, it would be enormously helpful to us.

But if I have suggested something quite impossible, just credit it to my simplicity!

Sincerely yours,

[12] Johnson, *The Battle Against Isolation*, p. 111.
[13] A telegram.
[14] He worked for the Marshall Field Estate which owned the Field Building.

To Charles R. Walgreen, Jr.[15]

July 26, 1940

Dear Chuck:

I am the chairman of the Chicago William Allen White Committee, with which you are probably familiar. According to the Gallup polls, etc., public sentiment for more aid to Britain has been mounting rapidly all over the country, but this area is still behind the rest of the country, or at least is less articulate.

I enclose some things which will give you an indication of what this Committee stands for, and I am asking our office to send you a copy of our local poster. If we could put one of these posters in a conspicuous place in each of the Walgreen stores, it would be tremendously helpful.

I hope you are in sympathy with this program, but if you disapprove of the White Committee or my suggestion is against the Company's policy, please drop me a note, and forgive me for bothering you.

Sincerely yours,

To Thomas A. Connors[16]

July 29, 1940

Dear Tom:

This is a touch. I suspect you feel as strongly as I do about more aid to Britain as the best and cheapest defense to America and our idea of a world economy.

I have been struggling for several weeks to spread a little light locally on this subject as chairman of the Chicago William Allen White Committee, with which you are doubtless familiar. The Great Lakes area is the most isolationist section of the country, and our job is a big one. We have some good volunteer workers, lots of splendid literature, and have had excellent cooperation from some of the newspapers and several large labor organizations. But we need money and help of all kinds.

If you could find me some money it would be very helpful, and if you could use any of our literature, posters, petitions, etc., I will send them along, and welcome your suggestions of any kind.

Sincerely yours,

[15] Owner of the Walgreen Drugstores.
[16] A Chicago executive of the Great Atlantic and Pacific Tea Company.

Senator Claude Pepper wrote Stevenson on July 23, 1940, thanking him for entertaining him at dinner and for assisting him in "our [Democratic] platform efforts, and for the generous time you gave me when we were considering the possibility of a [convention] floor fight on the platform."

To Claude Pepper

July 29, 1940

Dear Claude:

Just this morning I was reading in the paper about your transatlantic conversation with Ambassador [Joseph P.] Kennedy. How you find time to write personal letters I can't understand. Our encounter in Chicago with you and Mrs. Pepper was a delight for both of us, and I only hope it is the beginning of more frequent meetings.

My participation — thanks to you — on the fringes of high political strategy was intoxicating, and I would be tempted to run for County Commissioner if I didn't live in such a nest of Republicans!

I hope you can keep up the good work in spite of the heat. Ellen joins me in best regards to you both.

Sincerely yours,

To Claude Pepper

August 12, 1940

Dear Claude:

Thanks for your letter and the copy of your speech at Harvard, which I shall read with the greatest interest and applause, I am sure. I still marvel how you find time to do all these things.

As you doubtless have heard, the stadium meeting a week ago Sunday was a dismal failure.[17] The attendance was estimated in the Tribune at 40,000 and in the Times at 10,000. The truth is somewhere in between, and of course it looked very meager in that vast amphitheater. There was reported to have been a serious dispute just before the thing started, arising from the fact that Senator [Pat] McCarran was not on the air as he had anticipated, which aroused the senatorial indignation. The meeting was sponsored by all of the pacifist and antiwar organizations and of course largely publicized by the Chicago Tribune. The principal instigator seems to have been a Republican candidate for municipal court judge, who is an important functionary in the Veterans of Foreign

[17] A rally opposed to the White Committee's request for the release of destroyers to Great Britain.

Wars.[18] Many of the leaders of the latter publicly disavowed in the Daily News any support for or interest in the meeting, and when all was said and done, one got the impression, which I have not been able to confirm definitely anywhere, that the inspiration and financial backing was largely the Chicago Tribune.

I was in Washington last week and had a long visit with Frank Knox, which was moderately reassuring about the destroyer situation. We are redoubling our efforts locally to bring more pressure on Congress and if you have any suggestions for me, I will of course welcome them as always.

Cordially yours,

After hearing Stevenson speak on the need of aid to the British, Frank D. Graham [19] *wrote him that in view of the enormity of the crisis the work of the White Committee was pitifully inadequate. "Why fool ourselves with talk of 'aid short of war,'" he wrote. If it came to a showdown, the United States would have to go to war, he added. He then suggested that the White Committee persuade President Roosevelt and Wendell L. Willkie to issue a statement that they would not see Great Britain conquered. If this became imminent, they would urge Congress to declare war.*

To Frank D. Graham

August 19, 1940

Dear Mr. Graham:

Thank you very much indeed for your letter of August 9. I apologize for my failure to reply sooner, but I have been out of town.

As you know, it is difficult enough to accomplish our immediate objectives in view of all the obstacles. To take the position that you suggest would, I am afraid, impair what usefulness we have as we are constantly confronted with the "interventionist" accusation.

I should strongly recommend that you express your views in a letter to the Daily News or the Tribune and if it were published, I believe it would be highly desirable to send clippings to our Congressional representatives — and also yours from New Jersey.

I hope you have not forgotten your promise to let me know when you were in the loop some day. I should like to see you again and perhaps we could have lunch.

Sincerely yours,

[18] Unable to identify.
[19] Professor of Economics, Princeton University.

In addition to his chairmanship of the Chicago committee, Stevenson stimulated the founding of chapters in other parts of Illinois.

To Loring C. Merwin

August 22, 1940

Dear Bud:

I suspect there are some people down there who feel strongly about more aid to Britain and we have had so much success in organizing committees in towns around Chicago that I am making bold to inquire if you think you could get a dozen or so people together for a meeting in the evening to discuss organization of a "William Allen White" branch in Bloomington. If you can, and will set a date, I wish you would notify Miss Lucy McCoy, Chicago Committee to Defend America by Aiding the Allies, 86 East Randolph Street, Chicago, and she will send you a speaker who could explain the organization and objectives of the Committee and bring with him a supply of literature, etc. I should like very much to come myself but I am leaving town today and will not be back until early in September. . . .

In several instances up here in the last few weeks meetings have been held in someone's house, commencing about eight or eight-thirty and after a short explanation of the current situation and the White Committee work and purpose, officers were elected and an executive committee appointed and thereafter the results have been surprising.

I hesitate to impose upon you and if you do not like the idea perhaps you could pass this letter on to someone else who might feel disposed to try it.

With best regards,

Sincerely yours,

Colonel Frank Knox, after becoming Secretary of the Navy in June, 1940, talked a number of times to Stevenson about joining him in Washington. They both agreed, however, that for the time being Stevenson's work as chairman of the Chicago Committee to Defend America by Aiding the Allies was more important. During the next few months Knox and Stevenson conferred a number of times either in Washington or Chicago about the work of the committee and of developments in the defense effort in Washington. In May, 1940, President Roosevelt created the National Defense Advisory Commission to spur defense production.

To John O'Keefe [20]

August 22, 1940

Dear John:

Yesterday I had a long talk with Harry Hopkins [21] about the committee. He has some ideas which he is going to discuss with Colonel Knox. Meanwhile, I am leaving tomorrow to visit William Burry, Jr. [22] at Desbarats, Ontario, over Labor Day. Harry Hopkins had no objection but if Colonel Knox wants to get in touch with me, that will be my address. They live on an island and have no phone! I shall be back in Chicago on September 3 or 4.

I have just run into an old friend of mine, John Paulding Brown (1911 R Street, N.W., Washington), who tells me that he has just resigned his post in the Federal Alcohol Administration, which has been taken over by the Alcohol Tax Unit of the Bureau of Internal Revenue. Brown is an exceptionally able and experienced lawyer about forty-six years old. He tells me he is anxious to get into some of the defense work with the Defense Commission or the navy or army, and if he does not succeed he will return to private practice.

From my experience in government service in Washington, I am confident that Brown should not be lost. His talents, maturity and judgment are in marked contrast to the usual run of government lawyers. He knows a lot of people: William Hasset [23] and Jim Rowe of the White House staff, [William] Youngman, General Counsel of the Federal Power Commission, Tom Woodward of the Maritime Commission, etc. I suppose they will try to find something for him, but I am writing you thinking that Colonel Knox might be able to make good use of him or might pass him on to the Defense Commission. I should hate to see Brown leave government service just as things are warming up again and as good men will be in increasing demand.

Use your own good judgment about him and, believe me, I am not trying to fix him up with a job so much as to recommend him to you as a very useful man.

Sincerely yours,

---

[20] Secretary to Colonel Knox.
[21] By 1940 Hopkins was President Roosevelt's principal adviser.
[22] A Chicago friend who had a summer home in Canada.
[23] Assistant press secretary to President Franklin D. Roosevelt.

To John Paulding Brown

August 22, 1940

Dear John:

Your letter arrives in the midst of a lot of confusion just as I am leaving town. I am writing a letter to John O'Keefe, Colonel Knox's secretary, about something else and am including a long recital about you, along the lines you suggest — i.e., importance of keeping you in government service, etc., etc. I have reason to think that writing O'Keefe is, if anything, better than writing or talking to Knox by telephone as I know his present situation is frenzied. He depends very largely on O'Keefe for much detail work and, I suspect, uses him on personnel things too. I know nothing about his legal requirements or whether there is any prospect of anything in that direction but I have suggested that he pass you on to the Defense Commission if he does not have anything.

I think you made the right decision and I hope that something suitable will develop soon. I shall be back after Labor Day and if you can drop me a note as to how things are going I shall appreciate it.

Yours,

Harry Hopkins resigned as Secretary of Commerce on August 22, 1940. Although in poor health, he played an active role in the 1940 presidential campaign and lived in the White House throughout the war, serving Roosevelt as a confidant and valuable aide.

To Harry Hopkins

August 22, 1940

Dear Mr. Secretary:

If you decide to have a "family party" to discuss the project,[24] it occurs to me that possibly some one from the active armed forces, like General [George C.] Marshall or Admiral [Harold R.] Stark, might well be there. I have a feeling that there is a latent suspicion of disorderly and confused civilian activity among the "professionals." But, of course, you know best.

I enjoyed meeting you — at last!

Sincerely yours,

[24] Possibly Stevenson refers to the White Committee's request for the release of destroyers to Great Britain.

On September 3, 1940, President Roosevelt announced that fifty over-aged destroyers had been turned over to the British in return for bases in British possessions in the Americas. With this transaction completed, the Committee to Defend America by Aiding the Allies urged the government to release bombers, fighter planes, and mosquito boats to their manufacturers for sale to Great Britain.

Day after day in late August, German airplanes bombed Great Britain. On September 7 several hundred bombers attacked London. To stimulate public opinion to put pressure on Washington for the release of airplanes and ships to the British, the Chicago William Allen White Committee sponsored a mass meeting on September 18.

Throughout the summer, William McCormick Blair, Jr., worked as a volunteer in the committee's office helping the secretary, Lucy McCoy.

To William McCormick Blair, Jr.

September 4, 1940

Dear Bill:

I was delighted to have your letter. Things are moving apace and we are committed to the mass meeting on the 18th. We have assurances that Dorothy Thompson [25] and Maury Maverick [26] will be here. Meanwhile we are attempting to get a couple of others — preferably Charles Taft [27] and Admiral Harry Yarnell.

Mr. White has been here today and we have just finished a most successful luncheon party at the Chicago Club which netted us just under $2,000 in subscriptions on the premises.

. . . I had a long talk with Harry Hopkins here in Chicago ten days ago and suspect that when Colonel Knox gets back from Hawaii I will have another summons to discuss the thing [28] in Washington. It all sounds very nebulous but very interesting and a little too large for my comfort or self-confidence.

I can imagine nothing that would be more congenial to me than to enlist you as a partner if this enterprise should develop, but it does not seem likely that it will attain concrete form soon — if ever! Accordingly, I suspect your best bet is law school, and don't be surprised if I make seductive advances later on.

We miss you more than I can tell you, and poor Lucy [McCoy] has

[25] The syndicated columnist.
[26] Mayor of San Antonio, Texas.
[27] Son of former President William Howard Taft.
[28] A possible job in Washington.

had no fun since you left — indeed, she fell seriously ill and was out of commission several days last week. See what you did!

Yours,

The Committee to Defend America by Aiding the Allies was officially nonpartisan in the presidential campaign. William Allen White supported Republican nominee Wendell L. Willkie. The national director of the committee, Clark M. Eichelberger, supported President Roosevelt as did Adlai E. Stevenson. Stevenson wrote the following statement for the Chicago Herald-American, *September 4, 1940.*

WHY I'LL VOTE FOR ROOSEVELT

On the basis of his acceptance speech and what little I know of Mr. Willkie, he seems to me a sincere and forthright liberal. His record in business is one of manifest ability.

I am not impressed by the suggestion that he is a tool of sinister power interests or of that familiar political figure of speech: Wall Street. In short, I believe he is a fine product of our democratic system — an honest, enlightened, vigorous minded and courageous American businessman.

But I expect to vote for President Roosevelt.

In doing so I will not consider that I am voting against Mr. Willkie, because he might make a fine President. Rather I will feel that I am asking for more of a leadership which has, it seems to me, been in the main progressive and wholesome and which came to the American people none too soon.

I am no happier about our unemployment, our taxes, our debt than my Republican friends who still seem to think it is the nineteenth century, and I don't congratulate President Roosevelt on those scores any more than he congratulates himself. Indeed, I will concede that he has spent too much money and annoyed business too much. But even after charging President Roosevelt's account, justly or unjustly, with these and many other important things, the ledger seems to still balance heavily in his favor.

I shall not attempt to review the long familiar story of the last eight years or enumerate the progressive corrective legislation that has, at long last, come to pass. I agree with many scholars that, after due allowances for the contradictions, the extravagance, the demagog[u]ery, even the injustices, history will assign these years a prominent place in our annals. And I applaud Mr. Willkie's candid and specific endorsement of a large part of these reforms.

So, on the ground that under President Roosevelt's leadership democracy has made up much lost time and strengthened its position in the everlasting competition for man's allegiance, I suspect I would vote for him in any event.

But there is another compelling consideration. In the present situation it leaves me no choice, even if I were disposed to hand over the tools which Roosevelt has fashioned to Willkie and the less tender mercies of some of his supporters. What the world, and we as a large part of it, confront now is not merely a crisis — a critical temporary situation — but something which for convenience has been called a world revolution; a death struggle of ideals, of which armed conflict is only one manifestation.

How long this struggle will last no one can foretell. Thirty years, a generation, might not be an extravagant estimate. What will emerge as the dominant scheme of political organization, as democracy emerged in the nineteenth century, we cannot foresee. But we can hope, we can plan, we can prepare to resist the stealthy envelopment of another dark age. The richest and most powerful nation in the world can with unity, determination, foresight and courage largely influence the shape of things to come.

Destiny has assigned America a mighty role. There are many among us who don't like the role and think, by refusing to play, the show won't go on and everything will be all right. They persuaded us not to play our part after the last war and there was no peace. And now they urge us to be strong but they oppose conscription; they condemn aggression but they oppose aid to Britain.

I don't number Mr. Willkie among these. On the contrary, he has clearly shown his awareness of our peril and determination to combat it. But in doing so he has fallen into error. He decries the President's "inflammatory statements" and then goes him one better. His criticism of the President's conduct of our foreign affairs seems to me both inconsistent and naive.

Moreover, the record of Mr. Willkie's adopted party does not inspire confidence that it either understands what is going on in the world or that it appreciates the implicit menace to us; or, if it does, that it is prepared to reverse its traditional policy of isolation to deal with that menace. It is well to remember the progress that has been made in the last eight years in combating hostile trends in foreign affairs by the present enlightened leadership.

Feeling as I do that our political and economic future must be largely influenced by external events, I am thankful to be able to turn to President Roosevelt and his great Secretary of State [29] to lead us through the first of the perilous years that lie ahead, boldly and with an uncompromising passion for our principles: This is democracy's trial — if we hesitate, if we equivocate, if we divide, we are lost!

The sea is rough and I think I will stick to the old skipper.

To William Allen White

September 5, 1940

Dear Mr. White:

I enclose an interesting little piece that a client of mine, Mrs. Ada W. Dickerson, of Oregon, Illinois, has written and sent to me. I believe you will like it.

I am also taking the liberty of enclosing something I wrote the other day at the request of the Herald-American. I am sure you can agree with me on at least part of it!

Let me renew the thanks of all of us for what you did for us yesterday. I hope this will not be my last visit with you when you pass this way.

Do not bother to acknowledge this letter.

Faithfully yours,

To Logan Hay [30]

September 6, 1940

Dear Mr. Hay:

I saw Vincent Dallman [31] at a meeting here in Chicago the other day and he brought me most reassuring reports on the development of your Committee in Springfield. I was gratified but not surprised to hear that you were, as usual, in the lead on this important project and I hope you will let me know if there is anything that our Committee up here can do to help you.

We are planning a large mass meeting at the Coliseum on September 18th and have already signed up Dorothy Thompson and Maury Mav-

[29] Cordell Hull.

[30] A prominent lawyer in Springfield, Lincoln scholar, and descendant of Lincoln's Secretary of State, John Hay.

[31] Editor of the *Illinois State Register.*

erick to speak. We expect to get some others equally good, and I believe it is going to be a fine show. I hope that some of you from down there may find it possible to come up.

With sincerest regards, I am

Faithfully yours,

To Harry M. Fisher

September 6, 1940

Dear Judge:

Do you think you could arrange with someone to send letters to the members of the Covenant and Standard Clubs calling their attention to the mass meeting at the Coliseum on September 18th and urging their attendance? If so, I will supply you with flyers for insertion in the envelopes. Let me know how many you will need. We feel it very important to insure a good crowd for the contrast value with the recent opposition group meetings.

Sincerely yours,

To John P. Brown

September 7, 1940

Dear John:

I returned the first of this week and found your note. I suppose Knox's trip to Hawaii and the terrific pressure he must be under make it unlikely for anything to develop in that direction presently, though I had a nice letter from John O'Keefe acknowledging mine and saying that he would look into the possibilities at the first opportunity. However, I note by the newspapers that he accompanied Colonel Knox on his trip.

. . . Just now I seem to be spending all of my time on the William Allen White Committee to Defend America by Aiding the Allies. I wish you would do something to finish off Hitler so I could go back to work.

Yours,

To Clark Eichelberger

September 10, 1940

Dear Clark:

My attendance at our telephone conference was interrupted by a bad connection, but I understand from John Morrison that in addition to [Maury] Maverick and [Dorothy] Thompson we can probably count on

Admirable Standlay [32] (to be confirmed by you promptly), and that Mr. White is telephoning Governor [Harold E.] Stassen in an effort to persuade him to participate. We all agree that he would be far better than Lewis Douglas, who is not only less well known among the mass of the people here but is also associated with the East. However, if Stassen is not available I think Douglas would serve our purpose.

I hope that these speakers have all been cautioned not to overreach or to talk about intervention or immediate participation in the war. The label of "interventionist" is, as you know, very dangerous in this community and we do not want to give the Tribune or the America First Committee any ammunition along that line. I also hope that at least one of the speakers can bring out the Midwest angle — the danger to this region, both economic and military. There is the Hudson Bay and St. Lawrence River aspects which might be mentioned as appropriate to this audience.

I am very hopeful that you can induce Douglas Fairbanks, Jr., and some important opera singer to participate. Names of this kind have, of course, the best box office appeal.

We are working diligently, and I am quite sanguine that it will be a most successful affair. We need material for press releases on which to hang stories about the mass meeting constantly, and any news of that kind that you can let us have by wire will be most helpful. I take it that the new objectives are not available yet. They would be the best sort of thing for publicity, and I hope something of this character is forthcoming soon.

Sincerely yours,

To Howard Vincent O'Brien

September 10, 1940

Dear Mr. O'Brien:

I read your column [33] (as usual!) last night with interest, profit and pleasure — also as usual.

However, permit me to remind you that the name of this Committee is not "Committee to Aid the Allies" but "Committee to Defend America by Aiding the Allies." I think the distinction in purpose is implicit in the name. As for the use of "Allies," the name was originally adopted when there still were "Allies" — other than members of the British commonwealth and the refugee governments of the occupied countries.

Sincerely yours,

---

[32] Admiral William H. Standley (Retired).
[33] In the Chicago Daily News.

To Mrs. Ernest L. Ives

September 11, 1940

Dear Buffy:

We have sent to Carl Vro[o]man some recent pieces of literature, bulletins and some leaflets about the mass meeting next week.

In addition to Dorothy Thompson and Maury Maverick we will have Douglas Fairbanks, Jr., either Governor [Harold E.] Stassen, of Minnesota, or Lewis W. Douglas, and possibly some others.

I have received the following telegram from Mr. White this morning, which is the only indication of our present objectives in view of the confused situation in England:

"Not necessary to tell you German bombings of London very serious and this may be most critical hour in modern history. Our policy remains the same; that everything that can be spared, especially planes, from our armed forces or from our factories should go immediately to Britain in this critical hour. Our urgent suggestion is telegrams, letters, editorials directed to President Roosevelt urging the Government to send everything possible, especially planes, now.
William Allen White"

If you will let me know approximately how many people from Bloomington or Springfield are coming to the mass meeting, I will make arrangements so that they can sit on the platform, which will be more comfortable and convenient.

Hastily,

To Mrs. Raymond Woodward

September 11, 1940

Dear Mrs. Woodward:

Douglas Fairbanks, Jr., will be on the program for our mass meeting next Wednesday night, and I am suggesting to him that perhaps he would like to read excerpts from Stephen Benet's poem which you so kindly brought to my attention.[34] This follows your suggestion, which I think is admirable — assuming he cares to do it and can read well!

Cordially yours,

[34] Probably refers to "Nightmare at Noon," *New York Times Magazine*, June 23, 1940, p. 7.

To Maury Maverick

September 11, 1940

Dear Mr. Maverick:

I am returning your speech. It is splendid! I have nothing to suggest, unless possibly a note of warning toward the end against the influence of defeatists, isolationists and appeasers in Chicago and elsewhere who, well intentioned or otherwise, would have us fiddle while freedom dies. However, I suspect that some of the other speakers will cover that point and it may be just as well for you to omit it, if you wish. I like particularly your emphasis on the economic implications which seem to be imperfectly perceived.

In addition to you and Dorothy Thompson, we expect to have Douglas Fairbanks, Jr., Admiral [William H.] Standley and Lewis Douglas or Governor [Harold E.] Stassen. I think these will give us a good balance, and I feel reasonably confident that we will have a "crowd."

We think your suggestions about God Bless America and the hymn are excellent, and I hope we can work it out just as you suggest.

If convenient, I would like a copy of your speech in final form for press release as far in advance as possible. Also I hope you will let me know, in advance if you wish, about your expenses. My appeals for support have met with fair success and we are "in funds," so don't be modest.

Sincerely yours,

To Wilbur E. McFarlane [35]

September 13, 1940

Dear Mr. McFarlane:

As you undoubtedly have noticed in the newspapers, a mass meeting sponsored by the Chicago chapter of the William Allen White Committee to Defend America by Aiding the Allies will be held at the Chicago Coliseum next Wednesday night, September 18, at 7:30 o'clock. Among the speakers will be Dorothy Thompson, author; the Honorable Maury Maverick, former Congressman from Texas and Mayor of San Antonio; Douglas Fairbanks, Jr.; and Admiral Standley.

Knowing that in matters of vital interest to the American public the Mutual Broadcasting System attempts to present all important viewpoints, we request that the Wednesday night mass meeting be broad-

[35] President of the Mutual Broadcasting System.

cast by WGN [36] and the Mutual Broadcasting System. Recently Mutual broadcast the proceedings of the Lindbergh gathering at Soldier Field.[37] At that meeting one viewpoint on national defense was presented. At the Coliseum another opinion on defending America will be the fundamental topic.

We shall appreciate your favorable consideration of this request.

Sincerely yours,

Colonel McCormick's Chicago Tribune *was a vitriolic foe of the Committee to Defend America by Aiding the Allies. It charged, among other things, that William Allen White was "simple" for not understanding that measures short of war led to war. On September 5, a* Tribune *editorial noted that the White Committee kept repeating the statement that "the British fleet is our present chief defense." "That is a monotonously chorused untruth," the* Tribune *stated.*

William Allen White refused to answer Tribune *attacks, saying, "I would be surprised and deeply shocked if the Chicago Tribune would ever agree with me."* [38]

Adlai E. Stevenson, however, did answer one attack for the Chicago chapter. On September 7, the Tribune *denounced members of the White Committee as "cookie pushers" and insinuated that they were unpatriotic. On September 14, the* Tribune *published the following letter from Stevenson and captioned it "From America Second."*

Chicago, Sept. 9 — The America First Committee, including a few respected Chicagoans, has for its only significant purpose opposition to aid to Britain. Enthusiastically indorsing this committee, the Chicago Tribune characterizes the committee to defend America by aiding the allies as "war mongers," "cookie pushers," and "professional bleeding hearts." These are colorful descriptions, even for the Tribune, of many outstanding Americans.

But we "professional bleeding hearts" constitute a decisive majority of the population, and perhaps we can afford to resist the temptation to exchange familiar epithets. Indeed, perhaps most Americans would agree that the importance of the controversy warrants more sobriety. So we "cookie pushers" and "war mongers" might, in the interest of

[36] The Chicago *Tribune*'s radio station.
[37] Flyer Charles A. Lindbergh was a featured speaker for the America First Committee.
[38] Johnson, *The Battle Against Isolation*, p. 155.

general enlightenment, ask the America First gentlemen and the Tribune a couple of elementary questions.

(1) Do you think a Hitler victory over Britain would constitute a menace, economic and or military, to the United States?

(2) If so, is Britain now resisting that menace?

I suspect the answer will be "yes" to both questions. But the Tribune says even if Hitler is a menace to us and Britain is fighting that menace we should not help her. The position of the Committee to Defend America by Aiding the Allies is the reverse. We think that Hitler is a menace and detests democracy; he has said so. We think Britain is engaged in a death struggle to stop that menace. We think that with our help she can succeed; or, if not, that prolonged resistance will weaken Hitler and give us more time to get ready. We think, in short, that to withhold aid to Britain may hasten the day when we are alone in the world struggling to preserve defeated and discredited principles. We know that no more aid for Britain would be great news in Berlin — and evidently in some quarters in our country.

But say the America First gentlemen and the Tribune, aiding Britain may involve us in the war. We heard that one during the debate on the repeal of the arms embargo almost a year ago. We heard it when we began to sell airplanes and ammunition to the Allies. I suppose we will have to hear it again and again. "Cookie pushers" and "bleeding hearts" should not have to tell great newspapers and great patriots that it takes two to make a war, that Hitler is well occupied just now; that he will not declare war and add our air and sea forces to Britain's defense. No, he will wait until he conquers Britain, if he can, and then he will make war, as he always has, when and where he pleases and without regard to previous provocations or appeasements!

To Loring C. Merwin

September 14, 1940

Dear Bud:

I have no objection to the endorsement of Willkie, but I do have strenuous objection to endorsement without my knowledge and in advance of the usual time. As you know, matters of policy are usually decided by directors — not officers, and that has always been our practice.

It has been our policy for many years to analyze issues and candidates during campaigns and reach our conclusions during the end of the period. Perhaps in some cases it may be wise to depart from this practice. If you think so, the directors should be consulted.

Yours,

On September 10, 1940, S. S. Spivack, of the Columbia Broadcasting System, an old friend from Washington days in 1933 and 1934, wrote Stevenson urging him to take an active role in the Roosevelt campaign in Illinois. Stevenson enclosed with his reply an announcement of the White Committee's mass meeting.

To S. S. Spivack

September 16, 1940

Dear Spiv:

Your letter astonishes me. I am surprised you have not read the enclosed. Can it be that momentous pronouncements of this character are escaping your attention?

I did a large part of the Illinois financial work myself last time — but not this time! The cause represented by this letterhead has practically deprived me of my senses for the last two months — and certainly of my spare time!

Yours,

To John Gutnecht [39]

September 16, 1940

Dear Judge:

I am counting on you to introduce Maury Maverick at the rally Wednesday night. The meeting is set for 7:30, and we hope to start the program not later than 8:00 o'clock. We expect to have radio time for one of the speakers and it is imperative that the program move on schedule. At the present we expect that Mr. Maverick will be the last speaker, and we should reach him very shortly after 9:00 o'clock.

I will introduce you in just one sentence, and your introduction of Mr. Maverick should not exceed about two minutes. I think you should bear in mind that in an audience of this kind there will probably be thousands who never heard of Maverick.

I am enclosing a little biographical material about him which may be helpful. I presume you will want to advert to your German descent. My purpose in asking you and other leaders of European ancestry to participate is to indicate that the Committee is American and not English or anything else.

We appreciate your participation in this meeting more than I can tell you.

[39] The judge was prominent in Democratic party affairs and an American of German ancestry.

Please present this letter to the attendant at the South Annex door of the Coliseum, and meet me on the small dais on the platform as soon as you can get there.

Sincerely yours,

Loring Merwin replied to Stevenson's letter of September 14, 1940, that during the five years he had been with the Daily Pantagraph *editorial policy had been made at conferences by the editor, the managing editor, the general manager and himself as president. But, if the system was wrong, he was willing to have it discussed and modified.*

To Loring C. Merwin

September 17, 1940

Dear Bud:

Thanks for your letter. I understand perfectly about the editorial conference and I agree that matters of daily conduct of the paper should be disposed of by the management in this manner. These departmental conferences were, as you know, instituted long ago, and I think you have improved on the former arrangement immensely.

My point is, however, that matters of major policy, and politics is always one in a newspaper, are, like matters of major policy in any business, determined by the directors.

I have heretofore felt that our policy of analysis and discussion and postponement of recommendations was a sound one for an independent newspaper and afforded the electorate the most help. There are, it seems to me, altogether too few papers which approach public questions in this manner. For that reason I do not like to see us depart at a time when I think the former system is particularly desirable. Let's talk it over some time.

I was delighted to read about the formation of the committee [40] in Bloomington and it sounds to me like an excellent start.

Sincerely yours,

Stevenson received many letters critical of the Committee to Defend America by Aiding the Allies. One charged that Stevenson and other committee members were pro-British because of their ancestry and that the committee was hostile to Americans of German ancestry.

[40] The William Allen White Committee.

To W. M. Uphaus

September 18, 1940

Dear Mr. Uphaus:

Thank you for your letter. I appreciate its full explanation of your views. May I suggest that it would be quite as easy for me to reply by saying that your race consciousness dominates your love of America as it is for you to say the same of me and the members of the William Allen White Committee. I believe that neither is true and that we are both Americans approaching a problem of equal concern and debating it publicly in the democratic way.

I have never heard it said that Americans of German ancestry love their fatherland better than America. I should be glad to have you point out to me where you find this statement in any of our literature or in any speeches.

I hope that you will be at the mass meeting tonight, in which representatives of many foreign-born groups, including the Germans, will participate.

Sincerely yours,

P.S. It may interest you to know that my ancestors came to this country in the 17th century, and possibly my British sympathy is even more diluted than your German sympathy.

Some 16,000 people attended the September 18 mass meeting at the Chicago Coliseum and several thousand more were turned away. Adlai E. Stevenson presided. The speakers were motion picture actor Douglas Fairbanks, Jr.; columnist Dorothy Thompson; Admiral William H. Standley (retired); and the mayor of San Antonio, Maury Maverick.

STEVENSON'S REMARKS AS PRESIDING OFFICER

The Right Reverend Monsignor Thomas V. Shannon of St. Thomas' The Apostle Church will pronounce the invocation.

Mr. George Chaplicki, a distinguished member of the Chicago Opera Company, has kindly consented to sing that popular and moving song "God Bless America."

Mr. Chaplicki, Ladies and Gentlemen: I welcome you on behalf of the Chicago Committee to Defend America by Aiding the Allies. (I am sorry we could not *afford* to hire a larger hall to accommodate the thousands that have been turned away.) Your presence in such large numbers is most reassuring and we will fill the Grant Park Stadium next time — I believe you could do a better job of filling it than Col. [Charles A.] Lindbergh did last month!

I am thankful that you *are* here in such large numbers; for the opinion is freely expressed throughout our land that Chicago and the Great Lakes Region is the citadel, the stronghold of pacifism, isolationism and appeasement — that aid for Britain has been and is being retarded by adverse public opinion in this area. The polls reveal that the country *as a whole* is overwhelmingly in favor of aid to Britain. We who have arranged this meeting feel confident that the vast majority of the citizens of Chicago likewise realize the significance of the *deadly struggle* that is going on over London tonight; that Chicago likewise shares the opinion of that wise and humble patriarch, William Allen White, and the tens of thousands of Americans of all stations, great and small, rich and poor, who have spontaneously joined his cause in more than seven hundred communities from coast to coast; who all believe that the best, the surest and the cheapest defense of our democracy, and of our economic security, is to give Britain all possible material help — short of war — in this critical hour in the lives of all free men.

For this *is* the most critical moment in our lives — perhaps in modern history! Man's destiny hangs in the balance while the two greatest powers on earth are fighting to the *death.*

We are glad you have come tonight to hear some of the most respected leaders of American thought say why they believe that aid to Britain is our best policy. Your presence confirms our *conviction* that Chicago can and will, with *your* help, give a resounding, decisive answer to the vocal minority, — to the pacifists, the isolationists, the defeatists and the appeasers — well-intentioned and otherwise!

Americans, be they of English, Irish, Scandinavian, Polish, Bohemian, German or some other descent, are all Americans, and it is *as* Americans that they are supporting this Committee's efforts to help Britain stop Hitler now! Outstanding *Americans* of *many* national origins have helped us arrange this meeting. To evidence our unity I have asked some of them to assist me tonight. I felt it would also be desirable if you did not have to look at me any more than necessary.

Mr. J. J. Zmrhal, District Superintendent of Schools and President of the Czechoslovak National League, will introduce the first speaker. Mr. Zmrhal.

[Mr. Zmrhal introduced Douglas Fairbanks, Jr.] . . .

We have asked another distinguished Chicagoan known to all of you, to introduce the next speaker — Anthony Czarnecki, of the Chicago Daily News and former Collector of Customs for Chicago. Mr. Czarnecki.

[Mr. Czarnecki introduced Dorothy Thompson.] . . .

Judge John J. Sonsteby, whose ancestors came from Scandinavia, is Chief Justice of the Municipal Court and an outstanding leader in Chicago. Judge Sonsteby will present the next speaker.

[Judge Sonsteby introduced Admiral Standley.]. . .

Judge Gutnecht's vigorous crusade for safety in the streets of Chicago has attracted national applause. (I am glad the police have not *yet* requested my attendance in his courtroom.) I do not need to tell you that this distinguished American's father came from Germany. Judge Gutnecht.

[Judge Gutnecht introduced Maury Maverick.] . . .

Sonia Sharnova of the Chicago Opera Company has most generously agreed to sing you a song precious to all of us — "America the Beautiful." Madame Sharnova.

Before we conclude with a prayer and our national anthem, let me say one more word — America *is* beautiful, but her beauty is not alone what you can see and touch. Her beauty is something of the spirit — the spirit of free men resolved to *defend* their heritage! Liberty is like air. You do not notice it until it is gone. *We* — all of us for whom America is something more than a word — must rekindle our national passion for liberty which was *won* in danger and sacrifice and will be *preserved* in danger and sacrifice! You have heard the testimony of these distinguished and highly qualified witnesses: Douglas Fairbanks, Dorothy Thompson, Admiral Standley and Maury Maverick — who along with countless other great Americans are supporting the purposes of the William Allen White Committee to Defend America by Aiding the Allies. With your indulgence, I should like to read you those purposes:

1. To supply Great Britain with such planes, guns and ships as she may legally acquire from our armed forces as soon as possible and in the greatest possible quantities without injuring our national defense.
2. To make available to Great Britain our surplus food supplies.
3. To expand our preparedness program so that we may safely aid Great Britain in every legal way possible and quickly, as the by-product of that expansion.

4. To assist in bringing mothers, children and old people from the British Isles to the Western hemisphere.
5. To remove difficulties prohibiting Americans from volunteering in the British armies anywhere.
6. To guard against war materials reaching aggressor nations either directly or through neutral powers.

This policy of aid to Britain and her allies is, we think, best calculated to keep America out of war by keeping the war out of America! We think it is the best way to save America from the menace of economic competition with slave labor — in other words, to save your job and mine, and the highest standard of living in the world! We want to enlist everyone of you in our campaign. To organize public opinion in a mighty city like Chicago is an enormous and expensive undertaking. We want your help and we need ammunition, and ammunition is money. The headquarters of our Chicago committee is 86 East Randolph Street. We also have an office and literature display at 64 East Adams Street. There are active committees in Evanston, Winnetka, Highland Park, Gary and DuPage County. We hope regional branch committees throughout Chicago and in all the surrounding towns will be formed and that there will soon be no doubt where Chicago stands on this question.

We thank you for coming tonight. We thank Mr. Fairbanks, Miss Thompson, Mayor Maverick and Admiral Standley, who have come from all over the country to speak here. We thank the press of Chicago — that is, the best part of it — for all it has done to make this meeting a success; and now let me read you a resolution that has been proposed and which gives point to our meeting tonight while London is withstanding her twelfth night of incessant and ruthless bombing:

WHEREAS, our security and the things in which we believe are threatened as never before; and

WHEREAS, each week that Britain holds out is time gained to prepare the defenses of the New World against that threat; and

WHEREAS, each gun, ship, airplane or tank used to fight aggression across the Atlantic weakens the forces which endanger us and aids our defense;

THEREFORE, BE IT RESOLVED, that the United States extend to Britain all possible aid, compatible with our defense requirements, to sustain her gallant resistance against Naziism and Fascism, and be it specifically urged that 25 "flying fortresses," as many other combat planes as can be safely released, and 20 mosquito boats be made available to Britain immediately.

All those in favor of the resolution will stand up. The resolution is unanimously adopted and you are urged to make your views on these specific things which Britain needs so desperately known to the President and your Senators and Congressmen by wires or letters at once.

And now in the spirit of this solemn hour in man's history, the Reverend John Timothy Stone, for many years Minister of the Fourth Presbyterian Church and President Emeritus of the Presbyterian Theological Seminary, will lead us in Prayer. Dr. Stone.

Madame Sharnova and Mr. Chaplicki will lead us in the national anthem.

The meeting is adjourned.

To Douglas Fairbanks, Jr.

September 19, 1940

Dear Mr. Fairbanks:

I want to say once more how much we appreciate all you did for us last night. I think your destiny is the United States Senate — at least I hope so.

They will send you fifty copies of the speech and look into the record matter.

Please don't forget that we are looking forward to a glimpse of you and your charming wife when you pass this way again.

Sincerely yours,

To Maury Maverick

September 19, 1940

Dear Maury:

I want to say again how much we appreciate what you did for us last night. We were all more than disappointed that you could not celebrate with us afterward. Poor Fairbanks fell ill and had to be put to bed at the Blackstone [Hotel] with a doctor in attendance, but Dorothy Thompson entertained us until a quarter after two this morning! And kept lamenting the fact that you weren't there to exchange blows with her.

You did a superb job and the meeting, from all accounts, was a huge success. I hope and trust that it won't be long before you pass this way again and that when you do you will let me know and share a little of your inspiration with me!

Cordially yours,

Stevenson sent his friend Barrett Scudder a copy of his article "Why I'll Vote for Roosevelt" and policy statements of the White Committee. Mr. Scudder replied that he was no longer an isolationist and agreed with the White Committee but intended, despite Stevenson's article, to vote for Wendell Willkie.

To Barrett Scudder

September 20, 1940

Dear Barrett:

Thanks for your note. I am glad that you are at least half way redeemed from darkness! At this stage in one's conversion it is usually appropriate to ask for a contribution.

Sincerely yours,

Leaders of the White Committee were not only sensitive to the charge that they actually were for intervention in the war but that they were dominated by Jews.

To John Morrison [41]

September 20, 1940

Dear John:

I am returning some telegrams which I found in my pockets. I had some others, which disappeared from the rostrum at the mass meeting. I feel that you should send a letter of thanks to each of these people on my behalf.

Dr. Edwin P. Jordon, of the Winnetka Committee, urges that we include Mrs. John F. Fenn on our Committee. She has been very diligent and I think we should do so, and probably Denison B. Hull also. You might talk with Lucy [McCoy] and I am not sure but what Mrs. [Beatrice] Biggert should be "rewarded" in a similar manner.

John Paul Welling asks that his name be stricken off the Committee

[41] Executive director of the Chicago Committee to Defend America by Aiding the Allies.

list. Please attend to this as he is very touchy; I probably put it on without getting his permission. He is, of course, in sympathy and a contributor.

A Mrs. Bernice Herman, Lorel Avenue, Niles Center (telephone Niles Center 1267), has volunteered to work a couple of days a week in any capacity that you can use her. It occurs to me that this sort of person might be disposed to help us form a committee in that area. I have not seen her. She may be a Jewess, so tell Lucy [McCoy] to be a little cautious.

Sincerely yours,

The Reverend Mr. Stone wrote Stevenson, September 19, 1940, and praised his running of the mass meeting as "superb."

To the Reverend John Timothy Stone

September 20, 1940

Dear Dr. Stone:

You were more than kind to write me. The meeting was so interminably long that I was obliged to delete a large part of it toward the end, and I am afraid it got a little confused. Some of our speakers, as you can imagine, overstepped their time allowances considerably.

On behalf of all of us I want to thank you again for your participation. Many people have commented on your beautiful prayer and the solemnity of our conclusion — thanks to you.

Faithfully yours,

To Scott W. Lucas

September 21, 1940

Dear Senator:

Your letter from Washington dated August 24th for some curious reason was misplaced while I was out of the city and has just come to my attention.

I should be glad to talk with you at any time about the campaign but I am afraid I cannot be much help as I have been devoting practically all of my time to the Committee to Defend America by Aiding the Allies, for which I am the Chicago chairman. It's been an enormous job and I can't see how I can very well get out of at this critical stage.

Sincerely yours,

To Dorothy Thompson

September 21, 1940

Dear Miss Thompson:

Chicago is still buzzing with enthusiasm about our meeting the other night and your magnificent speech. We have had countless requests for copies.

I feel that in the confusion I did not properly express our thanks to you. Let me do so now. Do you remember Newton Baker's speech on the League of Nations plank at the Democratic Convention of 1924? I have heard nothing since that moved me as much as you did.

I hope we will catch a glimpse of you when you pass this way again.

Sincerely yours,

To William McCormick Blair, Jr.

September 23, 1940

Dear Bill:

I was delighted to have your note and am not surprised that you find the law a little baffling at this stage.[42] Indeed I won't be surprised if you find it somewhat baffling for the rest of your life!

The meeting was a fantastic success and I wish you could have been here to see the cynical pleasure of the Tribune photographer who whispered to me that he had been sent down to photograph the "empty seats." The crowd was estimated at 18,000 — the largest that has been in the Coliseum since the night [Warren G.] Harding was nominated in 1920, and it was jammed to the walls and many were turned away.

It was a great deal of work but you were entirely right and I am delighted that we did it now. [Clark] Eichelberger wants to establish a midwest office here in Chicago, and I have John Morrison signed up to stay with us until at least the end of the year. He has done excellent work and our problem now is what to do with the numerous "volunteers." I have become more and more skeptical of the value of part-time volunteer work, but I think we are developing a "permanent" staff which can do an efficient sustaining job.

There have been no developments with regard to the other matter [43] which I discussed with you, and you may rest assured that if anything turns up I shall be in touch with you.

Sincerely yours,

[42] Mr. Blair was attending the University of Virginia Law School.
[43] A possible job in Washington.

To Douglas Fairbanks, Jr.

September 23, 1940

Dear Mr. Fairbanks:

Mr. [John] Morrison reminds me that we neglected to get from you a statement of your travel expenses, for which we should like to reimburse you. Miss [Lucy] McCoy tells me that she has already attended to the Blackstone account.

I think you need have no misgiving about your leaving the platform the other night, as a number of people have commented that they assumed you had to leave to catch a train.

I understand from Mr. Morrison that you are spending the weekend at Hyde Park, and I hope you will have an opportunity to tell the President that Chicago is not altogether apathetic! [44]

With kindest regards and renewed thanks, I am

Sincerely yours,

To Edison Dick

September 26, 1940

Dear Eddie:

As I recall, when I spoke to you in June about helping to get this Committee started you expressed disapproval. Hence I was most interested in your attitude "beneath the searchlights" last night. I assume the greater includes the lesser, and if you believe in actual belligerency you also favor aid to Britain, short of war, which this Committee has been frantically promoting since last May throughout the country.

Although our efforts to raise funds to promote the work in this area have been reasonably successful and at the moment we are not pressed, we *will* need a lot more to see us through the year effectively. I have not checked the figures recently but I suspect our contributors exceed a thousand in number and the amounts range from 10¢ to more than $500, including, recently, a number of substantial corporate gifts.

If you feel disposed to help us I should like very much to talk with you about it, and I hope you will forgive me for jumping on you with such alacrity. If you are not interested please disregard this letter and my impertinence.

Sincerely yours,

[44] Mr. Fairbanks replied on September 25 that President Roosevelt was "very pleased about the Chicago meeting."

Time *magazine's issue of September 23, 1940, ignored the Chicago mass meeting. Stevenson wrote to his Princeton classmate this letter of protest.*

To Thomas S. Matthews

September 27, 1940

Dear Tom:

I am not a grouser, but I *had* hoped for more than this — first because it was a sensational meeting, particularly for this fortress of isolationism and, second, because we had not only [Admiral] Standley but also Maury Maverick, Douglas Fairbanks, Jr., and Dorothy Thompson. The latter made one of the best speeches I have ever heard. It was the largest crowd that has jammed the Coliseum since the night [Warren G.] Harding was nominated in 1920 and a riotous answer to the Chicago Tribune and its America First Committee.

I even persuaded the Archbishop to permit a member of the high Catholic hierarchy to pronounce the invocation, and ended with a bellicose prayer by the dean of all the Protestant pastors hereabouts. In short, it was really something and in eloquent contrast to the thin show the Tribune worked up for [Charles A.] Lindbergh last month. However, I know your space problem and perhaps the balance was O.K.; so don't think ill of me for this impetuous note.

Yours,

To Edward E. Brown [45]

September 30, 1940

Dear Ned:

From some remarks at lunch today I suspect you are arriving at the same conclusion I have and by somewhat the same process. This is gratifying to me, as people seldom share my views about everything, and almost never by the same reasoning!

Hence I thought you might be interested in glancing at the enclosure, which I wrote at the behest of the Herald-American some time ago. The performances since then — the vote on conscription — encourage me to think I may be right in my distrust of Republican congressional leadership in foreign affairs.[46]

[45] Chairman of the board of the First National Bank of Chicago.
[46] On September 16, 1940, Congress passed the Selective Training and Service Act (Burke-Wadsworth Bill). The votes against it were cast predominantly by Republicans.

Do not bother to acknowledge this. Just put the piece in the enclosed envelope and mail it, as it is the only one I have.

Sincerely yours,

C. Wayland Brooks, Republican candidate for the United States Senate, was a consistent advocate of the Chicago Tribune's *position on domestic and international affairs. Harry Slattery was the Democratic candidate. The* Daily Pantagraph *endorsed Brooks, who won the election.*

To Loring C. Merwin

October 21, 1940

Dear Bud:

I have been hoping to see you before this to make only one suggestion with regard to the political endorsements which you and the others agree upon. I refer to Brooks, whose violently isolationist stand is, as you can imagine, highly objectionable to me. Moreover, his gymnastics in "standing 100% behind Willkie's foreign policy" and his constant isolationist preachments seem to me to conclusively confirm the impression that I have had for a long time, that he lacks intellectual integrity. Moreover, the mortgage of the Chicago Tribune could only be more notorious if it was recorded in the county recorder's office!

The above is but a brief and hurried suggestion of a lot more I could say, but I think it gives you the idea. It also is not to be construed as evidence of any love for Slattery — but at least he goes along with the more enlightened leadership in this critical field.

Hastily yours,

Clay Judson, a prominent Chicago lawyer and a former president of the Chicago Council on Foreign Relations, was a leading speaker for the America First Committee. On October 4, 1940, in introducing General Robert E. Wood, national chairman of the America First Committee, Mr. Judson said: "America's destiny is the preservation of peace for its people; abstention on any account, and no matter how emotional the appeal, from European and Asiatic wars." Arthur Krock in the New York Times, *October 30, 1940, described the struggle in Chicago between the America First Committee and the Committee to Defend America by Aiding the Allies. On October 14, 1940, Stevenson debated Judson before a meeting of the League of Women Voters.*

I apologize for using a hastily prepared manuscript — but the League of Women Voters does not have a good reputation among careless, extemporaneous ad libbers!

Much as I dislike to contradict the omniscient Chicago Tribune or Mr. Judson, I must, at the outset, challenge the constant imputation of a dishonest motive to the Committee to Defend America by Aiding the Allies. It is *not* trying to get us into war by the back door, the front door or even the cellar door. Although 17% of the people favor immediate participation in the war, the White Committee does not. On the contrary it confidently believes that aid to Britain is best calculated to keep us out of war. It believes, in short, that the best way, the only way, to keep America out of war is to keep the war out of America — be it military or economic war.

I am going to tell you as briefly and simply as I can why I favor all possible aid to Britain short of war; why, according to the most recent poll, a majority of all Americans support the principal objective of the Committee to Defend America by Aiding the Allies — all possible aid short of war — and, if you will, even at the risk of war.

Why do I believe in this program; why do both candidates for the presidency; why does almost every scholar with distinguished qualifications in the field of international relations who has publicly expressed an opinion; and why do more than *half* the American people favor this program?

The answer is that they believe:

1. That Hitler is a menace to the United States;
2. That Britain is resisting that menace; and
3. That, therefore, in helping Britain the United States is helping itself.

These propositions seem simple and self-evident, but you have just heard a contrary point of view expressed by another American whose motives are certainly as good as mine and who, like many other citizens of unimpeachable patriotism, believe that our mutual purpose of preserving our institutions and economy intact as long as possible can best be served by either no aid to Britain whatever, or no aid except private aid. To determine which of these two points of view is correct one must examine the assumptions underlying them.

We think that Hitler is a menace to us. The record is clear. You can *never* believe Hitler when he says anything reassuring; but his record for fulfillment of what we thought were fantastic, chauvinistic threats is fearful! A world revolution started in 1914 and is still going on. Its objective is *world domination,* and there is no secret about it. The superior race heresy did not start with the Versailles Treaty. It has been going on for three generations. In 1868 Professor Lasson, of the University of

Berlin, said that the state could reach the full fruition of its destiny only through the destruction of other states. In 1895 a German wrote: "Germans alone will govern . . . Let no man say every people has a right to existence. They may live only as long as they do not stand in the way of a mightier one. If they stand in our way to spare them would be folly." Bismarck labeled the Monroe Doctrine as an international impertinence. A member of the German Center Party, in 1897, said that the task of the new German navy would be to *end* the Monroe Doctrine. Thereafter, surveys were made of the American coastline and much was written about the prospects for successful invasion. In 1900 Von Schlieffen, of whom you have heard so much, was indignant not because the Von Edelsheim plan for conquest of the United States was *prepared* but because it was *published*. The Kaiser told King Edward that the German navy was aimed not at England but at the United States. Early in this century Theodore Roosevelt, writing to Senator Lodge, said that Germany was "the only power which may be a menace to us in anything like the immediate future." It serves no purpose to multiply quotations. As recently as 1938 the New York Times published a report of a survey made by German engineers, naval and air officers of Anticosti Island at the mouth of the Gulf of St. Lawrence.

But let us see what the dictators have said more recently. Mussolini has frequently expressed his contempt for democracy. His favorite metaphor is something about Fascism trampling on the putrid corpse of individual freedom; and more recently, speaking of the aims of the Axis, he said that the pluto-democracies must and would be destroyed. Which democracy was or is the most "pluto"?

Raushnigg [47] quotes Hitler as saying:

> "The present government of the United States . . . is the last disgusting death-rattle of a corrupt and outworn system which is a blot on the history of this people. Since the Civil War . . . the Americans have been in a condition of political and popular decay.
>
> "We shall soon have storm troopers in America. We shall train our youth. We shall have men which degenerate Yankeedom will not be able to challenge. National Socialism alone is destined to liberate the American people from their ruling clique and give them back the means of becoming a great nation."
>
> "I shall undertake this task simultaneously with the restoration of Germany to her leading position in America . . . The German component of the American people will be the source of its political and mental resurrection."

[47] Herman Rauschning, anti-Nazi politician and writer.

"I guarantee that at the right moment a new America will exist as our strongest supporter when we are ready to take the stride into overseas space. We have the means of awakening this nation in good time. There will be no new Wilson arising to stir up America against us."

And Hitler *wrote* these words, of dreadful and prophetic accuracy, in Mein Kampf: "Each country will imagine that it alone will escape. I shall not even need to destroy them one by one. Selfishness and lack of foresight will prevent each fighting until it is too late." Raushnigg adds, "In the National Socialist view the political situation in America is unstable and can be developed into an outright revolution; to do this is both a tactic[al] aim of National Socialists, in order to hold America aloof from Europe, and a political one, in order to bring both North and South America into the new order. National Socialism is preparing to occupy the key possessions for colonial domination; for domination of the great sea routes, and for the domination of America and the Pacific."

Yes, I believe Hitler *is* a menace, though perhaps the destroyer trade for British bases in the Atlantic has, at least in part, forestalled this last mentioned intention. And I remind you that the isolationists in and out of Congress opposed the destroyer deal — including, I believe, General [Hugh] Johnson, the first radio sponsor for Mr. Judson's America First Committee. In this connection I must add that it is now abundantly clear that if the Embargo Act had not been repealed last November, six months after the President asked for it, Britain might have been defeated already. The isolationists vigorously opposed *that* also.

But perhaps the Tribune is right and I am just a "cookie-pusher," a "war monger," and a "professional bleeding heart" to believe any of these boastful things that the dictators say. But I do believe them. I do believe that if Britain and her navy fall, somewhere, sometime, we cannot escape a frontal impact with the triumphant National Socialism. I do not think that the centrifugal dynamism of dictatorship *can* stop, even if it wanted to. I do not think there are any limits to Hitler's ambition short of world conquest, just as there were no limits to the ambitions of Napoleon, Caesar and Alexander. I do not think a world that has obliterated time and space can exist half slave and half free. I do not think that tyranny in four-fifths of the world and freedom in one-fifth can endure.

But you will say these are mere surmises, and General [Robert E.] Wood and others have confidently assured us that the British fleet cannot be destroyed, though in the same breath they seem to admit the possibility because they propose an impregnable defense for America and endorse the appropriation of more than 12 billion dollars in a single session of Congress to commence militarization of this country and the building of a two-ocean navy; which can only be necessary if Britain *is* defeated. Some of us who never shared the pathetic faith in the Maginot Line feel the same about the British navy. We do not think it will surrender, but we *cannot* be sure. We know that Britain confronts a mighty drive on Suez, on Haifa, and the Near East oil fields and on Gibraltar. The Mediterranean may be closed. The battle of Britain is not over. With Europe and North Africa consolidated Britain may yet be defeated, and how can we be sure that the British fleet will not follow the French. Threats of brutal reprisal and extermination of the families of soldiers and sailors is an ancient device. It has worked before. It may work again. If the opportunity comes no one can seriously believe that humane considerations will deter the author of concentration camps, pogroms and Polish slavery from trying it.

In short, with the multiple lessons of the past so fresh, we must not let over-confidence and complacency suddenly confront us with the horrifying spectacle of a Nazi Britain. A year ago few of us foresaw a Nazi France. I'm sure Mr. Judson didn't. Responsible men are constantly reminding us in General M[a]cArthur's tragic words "too little and too late"; [48] that if we don't *help* Britain enough we may have to *fight* Britain, as well as Germany, Italy and Japan.

Another assumption that deserves scrutiny is that even if Britain falls we are in no danger of attack, that German difficulty with the English Channel multiplied 100 times is the short answer; that when this phase is over Germany will be exhausted, her allies even more so, and all this talk of possible invasion is "fantastic hysteria" — to borrow General Woods' words or "impossible" in Mr Judsons. If it is fantastic hysteria, then it is even more fantastic to be spending 12 billion dollars to merely *commence* preparation for the defense of this continent and this hemisphere against such an attack. There is something tragically inconsistent about all this.

But the paradox is easily explained; for *if* Britain falls the Axis' naval power will at once outclass us, and if the British fleet falls into their hands — as the French navy has in part, and would have in whole had it not been for Britain's decisive action — they will outclass us 2 to 1, and in addition to that they will have naval shipbuilding facilities exceeding ours from 5 to 8 times! Will they stand by like good sportsmen

[48] General Douglas MacArthur issued a statement in September, 1940, supporting the William Allen White Committee's program of releasing bombers, fighter planes, and mosquito boats to the British. Among other things he warned the U.S. not to be "too late" in aiding Great Britain. Johnson, *The Battle Against Isolation*, pp. 130–131.

and give us the necessary five years to double our naval strength? *Of course* a successful invasion requires bases; but the answer to bases is sea power, and there is, as I have said, a real possibility of predominant Axis sea power if the British navy is surrendered or even destroyed. But, notwithstanding, the isolationists say, to use General Woods' words, "There is absolutely *no* danger of an invasion of the United States even if Germany is completely victorious."

I am disposed to agree that an immediate invasion of our continental area is quite unlikely. But how about South America and our outposts where we would be as far from home as they are? It is only 1600 miles from Africa to the bulge of Brazil; it is 3400 miles from the United States. And General Wood also says, "I would unhesitatingly throw everything we have into a war to defend the North American continent and part, if not all, of the South American continent." Now consider this problem of hemisphere defense a moment. With our fleet divided in the Atlantic and the Pacific, with Japan pressing from the west and superior naval forces from the east, with the Panama Canal threatened from both sides, and perhaps from Nazi air fields in Latin America; with no absolute certainty that Canada will not follow the mother country into the Nazi orbit; with no certainty that Hitler cannot do what Napoleon III did in Mexico and do it better; with no certainty that there will be time to get ready to defend *ourselves,* let alone the Monroe Doctrine, I cannot share their confidence that military danger can be dismissed. Two million Americans crossed the same ocean in 1918; perhaps Germans and Italians can cross it too. At all events we are, with almost undivided national approval, preparing feverishly against that very possibility. And every day that Britain holds out on the island and in the Mediterranean gives us that much more time to get ready. Furthermore, I have yet to hear any military expert say that partial defense of South America is practical. Maybe it is, but when the time comes I suspect we will try to defend all or none of it. Let us not forget, moreover, that the coastline of this hemisphere is 43,000 miles; that there are some three million Germans in Brazil, Uruguay [and] the Argentine; that the cultural affinities of South America are European; that the percentage of literacy is not high, and that the mass of people share but little of our heritage of individual liberty and democracy.

But let us adopt the assumption that there is *no* military threat to this hemisphere. The export trade of South America outside the United States was 1¼ billion dollars in 1937 and vital to the economy of Chile, Argentina, Uruguay and Brazil. If the British blockade is broken and these countries want to trade with Hitler's Europe, as they must, what are we going to do? If we permit it, have you any doubt that Nazi political control will follow Nazi economic control attained by the barter system? Suppose we decide that we will have to wage economic war to defend the Monroe Doctrine which we have considered essential to our security for 100 years. How can we do it? We can buy up their export surpluses. That will cost us about a billion a year, which can be added to our own foreign trade loss outside the American continent of three quarters of a billion. What will our farmers say about buying all this wheat and meat, etc. We may find it too expensive or politically impossible. The other alternative is to *enforce* South American coopera- tion — enforce economic misery in S. A. When that time comes, do you think we will be any more eager to risk our boys' lives in the jungles of Brazil or the pampas of the Argentine than we are in Europe? There is still another consideration which seems to be imperfectly understood. If this war ends in a stalemate with the domination of all Europe Hitler will still lack four essential raw materials — petroleum, grain, cotton and copper. But if he subjugates the Near East, the petroleum shortage is eliminated; if the Axis squeezes Britain out of the Mediterranean and takes Africa, the copper shortage is eliminated. Africa and a reluctant Russia will in time fill the grain and cotton shortages. With this pros- pect do you doubt for a moment that South America, producing sur- pluses that we can't use and won't buy, will not be begging to trade with Europe? Of course she will, and probably we will, too!

And that brings me to the most important reason for supporting Brit- ain. Have the dictators still another weapon? I think so. I refer to the dislocations and readjustments that we will suffer in this country as the result of a Hitler victory. If the Nazi system is a menace to our way of life, it is a menace after, as well as before, the killing stops in Europe. So what will our military expenditures have to be? Possibly one-quarter of our national income. Will we be economically blockaded? Will we have to ration strategic materials like rubber and tin? Will Germany reverse the tables and will we be forced to develop substitutes at great cost and inconvenience? Will conscription become permanent and after 150 years of blessed peace will we become an armed camp like Europe? What happens to our civil liberties? Much is being written and said on that score and it is not reassuring. I have already suggested some of the problems that will arise in preventing Nazi eco- nomic penetration in South America. Walther Funk, the Reich Minister of Economics, tells us that Germany will organize the economy of all Europe on a continental monopoly basis, and insolently adds that it will not deal with any other unit similarly organized. How can our in- dividual competitive system compete economically with totalitarian Eu- rope on one side and totalitarian Asia on the other? What happens to the little independent in a chain store town? Will we be able to sell outside Canada and the Caribbean precisely what the masters want us to and no more? After their temporary deficiencies are satisfied *we* will still have to get many important raw materials from the totalitarian monopolists. On whose terms — theirs or ours? To wage economic war against not merely government but continental monopoly will we have to adopt similar controls? Will all our foreign trade inevitably pass under government control, or, perhaps, "pass out?" What happens to the standard of living as foreign trade contracts and more and more production goes not into goods, but arms? What has happened to the standard of living in Germany in the seven years of her great effort for guns instead of butter? And how will we make our arms pay dividends as she has? How do we finance coincident arms expansion and trade contraction? How much debt can we stand before inflation and repudiation begin? — And when in this process will we begin to hear demands for "a strong man?" When will people begin to ask, "Can't we get along with this new order in Europe, in Asia?" When will someone suggest a halt to the defense spending? And will others say, "No, we can't play with Hitler and survive?" In a two-party system will one inevitably become the party of appeasement? Where then is our unity, our faith in the American way of life, our passion for freedom, truth and justice?

Pragmatism is central to our philosophy: we believe in what works. The derogation of values which has characterized the age of applied science and industrial society has established performance as the criterion. The values of American life have, I'm afraid, only a modified appeal to many people in various groups: pragmatic industry, cynical youth, those to whom property outranks principle, and, conversely, the unemployed. Combine the prestige of Nazi success with the prestige of Nazi technique, and how many of these people will conclude that Nazi society cannot be so bad after all?

Frankly, if Britain falls, it is the development of this tolerant attitude nourished by economic pressures and the 5th column from within (and one can detect signs of it already), that concerns me most.

I think this is the most critical moment in our history. I think we are witnessing a death-struggle for control of the western world, a death-struggle between our traditions and pagan traditions never disciplined by the Roman Empire in the West or Christendom in the East. It is only as we believe the western tradition worth preserving, *at any price,* that we will as a nation have the counterdynamic required to meet and defeat the Nazi outthrust if Britain falls. Division, cupidity and treachery are Hitler's deadliest weapons. He has said so! He may be right.

We cannot be sure that the economic and social controls which must follow British collapse will not themselves ultimately betray us. We cannot be sure that in trying to save freedom we will not embrace slavery, either in or out of war.

I have attempted to suggest the shape of things to come and why Britain plays a strategic role in our defense, both military and economic, — why if Britain falls we face incalculable dangers from within and without — why there is everything to gain and little to lose by helping Britain to stop Hitler now! I have said nothing about our racial and lingual heritage, our common traditions, our 100 years of peace and prosperity and unarmed security, thanks to the British navy. Nor have I mentioned the moral effect of American aid on the British Dominions against the day when we may desperately need friends. I have in short said why, in America's self-interest alone, we should help Britain; why, if you will, we should defend America to the last Englishman!

And now in conclusion let me read you some prophetic words of Winston Churchill to the House of Commons on February 22, 1938, — seven months before Munich: "I predict the day will come when at some point or other, on some issue or other, we will have to make a stand, and I pray God that when that day comes we may not find that through an unwise policy we are left to make that stand alone." We too can pray God that through an unwise policy we may not be left to suffer or to fight, alone!

William C. Bullitt, who had been ambassador to France when it surrendered to Germany, spoke before the Chicago Council on Foreign Relations and met a number of prominent Chicagoans at the Stevensons' home. Years later Stevenson recalled: "It was an exciting time. . . . The Tribune *used to send photographers to photograph all empty seats, if any, in halls where we presented programs — and the* News *photographers photographed all the full ones. I'd be a dirty dog in the* Tribune *in the morning, and a shining hero in the* News *at night."* [49]

To Franklin D. Roosevelt

October 22, 1940

Dear Mr. President:

I cannot resist the temptation to thank you personally for permitting Ambassador Bullitt to speak before the Chicago Council on Foreign Re-

[49] Kenneth S. Davis, *The Politics of Honor: A Biography of Adlai E. Stevenson* (New York: Putnam, 1967), pp. 132–133.

lations last night. Not only did he make a splendid, forthright and vigorous speech, but he also made a personal impression on a large number of influential Chicago people, which did the Administration and our foreign policy no little credit. And you know how important that is in this section of the country.[50]

With sincerest respect and best wishes, I am

Faithfully yours,

To William C. Bullitt

October 22, 1940

Dear Mr. Bullitt:

I want to thank you again not only for your magnificent address but also for your patience and courtesy in talking with our guests last evening. The fine personal impression you made on the audience and the people at the house will have a wholesome effect in several directions.

I enclose draft of a recent talk, in which I attempted in a clumsy, inadequate, and perhaps inaccurate way, to comment on some of the economic implications. As I said, I feel that this aspect has been a little neglected in favor of the military threat, to which there are so many plausible answers.

With renewed thanks and best wishes, I am

Faithfully yours,

To Edward J. Kelly

October 22, 1940

Dear Mr. Mayor:

I enclose a small campaign contribution. I wish it could be more, but I am also contributing to the State Central Committee, the National Committee and the Norris-LaGuardia Independent Committee, in which I am active.

With kind regards,

Sincerely yours,

On October 25, 1940, Stevenson presided at a meeting of the Norris-LaGuardia Committee of Independent Voters for Roosevelt in the northern suburb of Skokie, Illinois.

[50] On October 26, 1940, the President wrote: "Dear Adlai. I appreciated much your nice note of October twenty-second. . . . It is good to have your favorable opinion on Bill's presentation."

Madam Chairman, ladies and gentlemen; or perhaps I should say, "independent ladies and gentlemen"; and distinguished guests. I believe those are the customary salutations, though I must acknowledge my unfamiliarity with current political fashions.

Indeed I had not expected to be called upon to speak in a political campaign again. I wound up the last one in 1936 with a masterful address in the chapel at Carl[e]ton College in Minnesota. It was a carefully prepared speech designed for a high order of intelligence and discrimination. First, I told at length what I thought was wrong with the "New Deal" and then gradually developed an overwhelming mass of evidence in President Roosevelt's favor, leaving no possible doubt where I stood. In short, it was the perfect speech for a college community. I was much pleased with my scholarly and well-reasoned performance and — not to mention my major contribution to President Roosevelt's campaign. Emerging from the side door with the president of the college, we passed behind two students. I overheard one of them say, "Sure it was O.K.; but who was he for — Landon?"

From the solid phalanx of Willkie buttons on the North Shore commutation trains these days I had about concluded that the campaign was about all over in this neighborhood. So I am delighted that there are evidently still a lot of people hereabouts who have not made up their minds. I congratulate you as fellow veterans of the most incessant and relentless bombardment by air and by newspaper of all time. Up in Lake Forest where I live the mortality has been terrific — though most of them seem to have died about eight years ago. Some of my friends remind me of that famous epitaph that a great educator is reputed to have suggested for a reactionary colleague — "He died at 30 and was buried at 70."

I say I am glad you have come tonight for two reasons, one, because the largest proportion of independent voters should be found in privileged communities like this and, two, because the independent vote might win this election — an election which may well be the most important in which any of you have ever or will ever vote. We cannot foretell the shape of things to come. The world is in violent revolution. Tyranny, a form of government much older than democracy, is once more competing for mastery of man's destiny. Mighty forces are at work in the world — forces which I am afraid are neither perceived nor understood by many of us, including certain candidates for public office. We will need great leadership — great understanding, great vision, and great courage. America has come a long way in a few years, thanks to that kind of leadership. She must not retreat, she need not retreat now! And now some distinguished, respected and independent Chicagoans will tell you why.

The first speaker is Miss Charlotte Carr, director of Hull House, a woman known and honored wherever people know and honor service to humanity — to the meek, to the lowly. There is no more distinguished name in the field of social service than Charlotte Carr, who is carrying on the great work commenced by Chicago's once foremost citizen — Jane Addams. Miss Carr will discuss "Social Welfare in a Democratic State." — Miss Carr.

Professor Jerome G. Kerwin, as many of you know, is not only a distinguished scholar, professor and dean of social sciences at the University of Chicago, but also a widely recognized authority on problems of city government. Many civic reform movements have enjoyed the benefit of his participation and direction. Dr. Kerwin's subject is, "Roosevelt — Symbol of Progress."

Professor A. R. Hatton, like Mr. Kerwin, is also a political scientist and was formerly chairman of that department at Northwestern University. Professor Hatton is the author of the city charter of Cleveland, and is one of the country's foremost authorities on city government. — Professor Hatton.

Our last speaker is a lawyer. However, in extenuation you should know that Mr. Megan started life as an honest man — he was an educator; in fact, he was Assistant Superintendent of Schools in Chicago from 1902 to 1912. Why he then took up the law I don't know, but he evidently knew what he was doing for he has made signal contributions to the profession and has been signally honored by it. Mr. Megan has been president not only of the Chicago Bar Association but also of the Illinois State Bar Association, and there is no more accomplished, scholarly and respected lawyer in Chicago than Charles P. Megan. — Mr. Megan.

To Niblack Thorne [51]

October 28, 1940

Dear Niblack:

I am sorry you "resent" my being for Roosevelt. I don't "resent" in the least your being for Willkie, as I presume you are. Moreover, I don't "resent" the fliers advertising Republican meetings I find in my mail box and car. And I am delighted that you are taking an active interest in better government — I have for about fifteen years.

Sincerely yours,

[51] An acquaintance from Glenview, Illinois.

Loring Merwin explained to Stevenson the Pantagraph's *endorsement of Republican senatorial candidate C. Wayland Brooks. He wrote: "I do not believe that being non-isolationist ourselves and supporting a candidate for senator with isolationist views is necessarily inconsistent." Later in the letter, he said: "During this present campaign, for instance, you feel — and I am sure with perfect honesty — that we are being partisan. With equal honesty, we feel that you are partisan — and not at all because you intend to be."*

To Loring C. Merwin

October 31, 1940

Dear Bud:

I am sorry my letter made you angry. It was not written in anger but in a state of extreme disappointment at the way the independent Pantagraph has handled the men and the issues.

And now I read that you are endorsing [William] Stratton for congressman at large — 26 years old and without experience of any kind — in lieu of [Professor T. V.] Smith, a distinguished scholar, experienced in politics, notoriously independent, and an incumbent with perhaps the best first term record in the entire House, on the ground that "under present conditions Illinois should have a larger minority representation."

On September 16th you wrote me, "We will attempt to endorse each candidate on his merits as the time comes, and will avoid any specious reasoning about filling the legislative branch with Republicans in the interest of unity." I confess it's all too much for me, and I can see no escape, in this case, from the conclusion that you deem, as the editorial says, party affiliation more important than qualification or record. This seems to me hardly an intelligent or independent approach to one of the most critical elections in our history. Did you know, by the way, that Stratton has refused to endorse Willkie's position on aid to Britain?

Yours,

P.S. I have just read the editorial on [Congressman Leslie] Arends. Please understand that I know nothing about him or his record or for what he stands. But I note that you state, with apparent approval, "such occasions were Mr. Arends' vote to retain the arms embargo and against the revision of the Neutrality Act; his vote against the draft law (in the belief that enlistments would provide an adequate army), and his vote for a 60-day delay in putting the draft into effect." Is this consistent with the position of the paper? I am confounded! Perhaps there were some other good reasons for endorsing Arends in spite of his record — if so, it seems to me they should have been stated with great vigor.

A.E.S.

Arthur Krock in discussing the conflict between the America First Committee and the Committee to Defend America by Aiding the Allies in his New York Times *column, October 30, 1940, wrote: "The high type of the White Committee membership is identified by the fact that its chairman is Adlai E. Stevenson."*

To Arthur Krock

October 31, 1940

Dear Arthur:

I have just read your column of Wednesday and hasten to thank my benefactor for the gracious and accurate advertising. You are quite right about the unfortunate "appeaser" versus "interventionism" labels we have pinned on each other. I wish I had known you were going to write the piece, as there is much to be said about this and the aggressive manner in which the Tribune set the pace out here. Even your humble friend Stevenson has drawn such published epithets as "cookie pusher", "war monger" and "professional bleeding heart"!

Of course the debate should be on the ground of "what is the best way to defend America." But they won't leave it on that basis, because they insist that "aid short of war" is disingenuous; that we are insincere and secretly want to intervene; and that the U. S. has everything to lose and nothing to gain from war. Frankly, it seems to me that their argument ultimately comes out somewhere very close to your excellent defense of an "appeaser."

Again many thanks, and let me know next time what you are up to!

Yours,

To Mrs. William G. Hibbard [52]

November 1, 1940

Dear Mrs. Hibbard:

I have taken several oaths that I would *never, never, never* ask you for help again. And here I am!

[52] Mrs. Hibbard, of Winnetka, Illinois, was prominent in the League of Women Voters.

Charlotte Car[r] just called to tell me about the Sunday broadcast in which you and Mrs. Blaine [53] are going to participate. My instantaneous and unworthy reaction was this letter.

I have been working, speaking and soliciting for the National Committee of Independent Voters (Norris and LaGuardia), along with Charlotte Carr, Paul Douglas, et al. We put on a magnificent show at the Stadium for LaGuardia this week and are approaching the end of our activities with some important radio time and down-state newspaper advertising contracted for, and no money! Our work, we hear from all sides, has been most effective and we want to carry on to the end, if possible.

I shall not say more — if you can do anything please telephone me. If you can't you will be like most of us Democrats.

Faithfully yours,

To Paul Scott Mowrer [54]

November 2, 1940

Dear Paul:

The William Allen White Committee ran an ad in Friday's paper which was placed on page 40. An America First Committee ad was on page 6. I am not complaining, as I understand perfectly all the problems involved.

However, we are sending you copy for another ad for Monday's paper, and I hope you will see that it gets the best available space.

Yours,

On November 1, 1940, Hermon Dunlap Smith, Stevenson's close friend, wrote him that he was puzzled to see his name on an advertisement of the Norris-LaGuardia Independent Committee for Roosevelt entitled "Sorry Mr. Willkie, This Is Where We Get off the Fence." Smith wrote: "To get off a fence which you were never on, is a piece of gymnastics which I am unable to explain." He added that he had the greatest confidence in Stevenson's integrity.

[53] Mrs. Emmons (Anita McCormick) Blaine, a prominent Chicago philanthropist, was on the national board of the Committee to Defend America by Aiding the Allies.
[54] Editor of the Chicago *Daily News.*

To Hermon Dunlap Smith

November 4, 1940

Dear Dutch:

1. I did not see the advertisement or know anything about it.

2. However, I see no "gymnastics" in stating that I am off the fence — unless you *assume* that I have no independent judgment on political candidates. I did not decide to vote for Roosevelt until after the Elwood speech when Willkie endorsed the New Deal, both domestic and foreign, and then ridiculed the conduct of foreign affairs in what seemed to me a foolishly contradictory way.

3. That I have generally supported Roosevelt in the past, does not seem to preclude me from having any independent judgment now. If it does, then you should ask a lot of "No Third Term Democrats" who have never supported him about *their* gymnastics — and I can give you their names.

4. I don't understand your use of the words "integrity" and "judgment," unless you deem me dishonest for stating that I have decided to vote for Roosevelt.

5. I agree with you on one thing — that traditional partisans should not identify themselves with "independent" committees. Perhaps I am such a partisan, though I had never so considered myself, and should not have helped this committee even in the meager way I have.

But let me ask you this: If mine was not a Democratic "name," would you have written that letter? I am afraid my "integrity" suffers from my ancestry! [55]

Yours,

On November 11, 1940, Stevenson presided at a fund-raising luncheon. William Allen White was one of the speakers.

I need not remind you that this is the anniversary of Armistice Day. November 11 — 22 years ago, was a day of promise for a new world. We can't foretell when there will be another armistice day. But we do know that sometime, somehow the war will stop, or at least suspend. And we know that the United States cannot escape the implications of that day.

We who march with Mr. White cannot view those implications with

[55] Mr. Smith replied: "I do not need to tell you that I rate your integrity 1000%⁺. As for your judgment, I have so much confidence in it, that if you say the ad was all right, I am willing to accept your opinion fully."

indifference or composure. It will be a sad, sick world whoever is the winner on that next armistice day. But can there be any doubt what it will mean to us in America if Britain triumphs that day? There will be such national relief and rejoicing as our country has never known before. But what if Hitler is the master of that day? I don't know and neither do any of you, but tens of thousands of thinking people from coast to coast share our sinister forebodings and, through William Allen White's Committee to Defend America by Aiding the Allies, have translated their foreboding into action.

I feel that as a brief prelude to this meeting I owe you who have participated in and supported our work here in Chicago an account of our stewardship. Because our luncheon program is so full I can give you merely the barest bones of an interim report.

We started as a dozen people who shared the views on the necessity for aid to Britain in our own self-interest, which Mr. White so eloquently expressed last May. In June we met and talked, and because I was out of town of course I was elected chairman and assigned the modest task of obliterating isolation in Chicago! We got Lucy McCoy, thank God; we got office space; we got a little money and a lot of encouragement. Clifton Utley and I wrote a statement (a splendid statement!), a confession of faith for the Chicago William Allen White Committee — which didn't exist — and we got a lot of prominent people to endorse it. And then we had a committee. We gave it to the newspapers. The Tribune ignored it but the News and Times published it and we had some publicity. Speakers volunteered and speaking opportunities developed. Robert Sherwood's "Stop Hitler Now" advertisement was published in Chicago — with money from New York. Then came the Democratic convention. Volunteers were turning up. We opened an office in the Stevens Hotel and harried the delegates with literature, questionnaires and good advice. Mr. [Clark] Eichelberger addressed the platform committee — funny how important platforms seem at convention time! More advertising appeared; the isolationists began to single us out for abuse. We had arrived!

Professor Colegrove [56] started a committee in Evanston. We borrowed a store on Adams Street and opened a display room — and stopped the traffic for a couple of days. We had fights and bombing threats and saw to it that it got in the paper. Our North Shore friends got committees under way in Winnetka and Highland Park — another was organized in DuPage County, another in Gary. We were causing literally thousands of petitions and messages to be sent to Washington during the destroyer ordeal.

Then I left town for a week. While I was gone they all lost their

[56] Kenneth Colegrove, professor of political science, Northwestern University.

wits and decided to put on a massmeeting — a massmeeting in the capital of isolation and under the very nose of the Tribune! And we were broke! But Mr. White and Mr. Eichelberger and the National Committee in New York came to our rescue and we passed the hat and *you* came to our rescue. In spite of me the mass meeting came off and packed the largest crowd into the Coliseum since the night Harding was nominated in 1920. It left us a little dizzy and so did the campaign, as both candidates out-did each other in pledging more aid to Britain. But meanwhile we have not gone to sleep; we have perfected our organization and met on every opportunity by speeches and advertisements the challenge of the "America First Committee," which seems to be in favor of some aid to Britain, — just how much I have not been able to discover.

And now the elections are over and the fever is subsiding, I hope. It is the morning after; it is armistice day and we are confronted with the cold, stark realities of Britain's plight. There is work to be done. Much work. Today we are having a regional conference here in Chicago of representatives from various White Committees in this area to discuss our manifold problems. But before Mr. White tells us something of what's ahead, I have asked Mr. Boardman, our treasurer, to give you a brief report of what we have done with your money. Money seems to be always about the starkest of realities to a chairman! — Mr. Boardman

---

I shall not waste your time, his or mine introducing Mr. White. Ladies and gentlemen — the father of this movement, a great American philosopher, patriarch and patriot — William Allen White.

Like most, I was going to say like all, Americans who know from long personal experience something about the influences that are at work in Europe today, Miss Elsa Maxwell has been fighting for our purposes from the start. She happened to be in Chicago today and has kindly agreed to speak to you for a few minutes. — Miss Maxwell.

Do you remember that just a year ago people were saying that this was "phoney" war. Poland had been conquered in 3 weeks and then nothing much happened until the British mined the port of Narvik. Then the real war commenced for us. Narvik was for days the most active theatre of war in the whole world. The greatest sea battle of the war took place in Narvik harbor. The siege lasted some two months and I have never read or heard a first-hand account of what happened there.

Our great Theodore Brock is the son of the last minister of war of the independent Norwegian government. For the last six years he was mayor of Narvik. The story of his arrest, his sentence to execution, his reprieve, his administration of the city during the siege, his rearrest and his escape through Sweden and Russia to this country is better than fiction. — Mr. Brock.

On November 13, 1940, V. Y. Dallman praised Stevenson's leadership of the Committee to Defend America by Aiding the Allies in his column in the Springfield Illinois State Register.

To Vincent Y. Dallman

November 15, 1940

Dear Mr. Dallman:

It was good of you to send me the clippings, and I could not overlook your flattering adjective about me — I am blushing! The buoyant, photographic style of your column always charms me.

I am glad you liked the luncheon. The pictures at the end were a sad mistake, and I did not even know they were coming, but the luncheon at least served the purpose of reviving a little interest, now that the election is out of the way, and that was all I had in mind to do.

Logan Hay was most interested and participated actively in the discussion. I am so glad the Springfield chapter is really under way — thanks to your constant plugging. It is too bad we cannot have an enlightened, aggressive editor supporting us in every city. I spoke in Milwaukee last night. The newspaper situation there is most disheartening, as you can well imagine.

Faithfully yours,

P.S. I was disappointed not to have a little talk with you. I looked for you after lunch but evidently you were obliged to leave. I hope there will be another opportunity soon.

A.E.S.

On November 20, 1940, Stevenson spoke to the Wayfarers Club of Chicago, describing the Irish portion of the trip that he and Ellen had made to the British Isles in May and June, 1939. The following copy of his remarks was transcribed from the handwritten text in 1959. The handwritten text has disappeared. The occasional blank spaces apparently are a result of the 1959 typist's inability to read Stevenson's handwriting. The same may be true of the misspellings.

Why your otherwise discreet secretary selected me to speak tonight I don't know. I've had no adventures worth mentioning this year and I told him so. But somehow he recalled that I had been abroad the previous summer and as the Wayfarers evidently are doing little wayfaring he insisted that I go back a full year and a half and tell you something of a trip to Ireland, England and Scotland. I feel a little foolish traveloging about Ireland when so many of you know much more about it than I. But I travelled about in Ireland for a couple of weeks so I guess I'm qualified.

We went abroad in May a year ago for two reasons — because somehow we knew the war was coming that summer and it might be a last chance at London and Edinburgh. I believe I was right about London and maybe about Edinburgh. — And because my sister and brother-in-law were living in Belfast where he was our consul general. We landed at Cobh. Queenstown has been called Ireland's wound. In the last 30 years about a million young Irish men and women have migrated, mostly to America, from this part. For more than [a] hundred years it has been an unstanched wound of Ireland's best and youngest blood. The harbor is faded and quiet now. We docked late. The consul from Cork met us and took us to dinner with some sprightly "Corkers" in the saddest Club in the world — the Royal Cork Yacht Club — a beautiful and dingy, moth-eaten old building on the quayside. It was built in 1740 and is the oldest yacht club in the world; the walls were hung with paintings, prints and old photographs of brave yachts and gallant yachtsmen of better days in Queenstown. But there are no yachts in her harbor any more. That all ended with the last war and the trouble, as the Anglo-Irish so eloquently refer to disorders and final independence of the Free State. Only rising now are a few little catboats and the tugs of the Hamburg-American and Cunard Lines.

My sister had sent her car and chauffeur down from Belfast to motor us north in a leisurely way along the west coast, and had enjoined the chauffeur, a speechless Ulsterman named O'Donnel, to deliver us at Colebrack [Colebrook] on Saturday evening at 5 o'clock. We were off early on Tuesday morning after a noisy night in noisy Cork. We made short work of Bla[r]ney Castle. It was early May, but there on the languid almost tropical south coast the trees were in full leaf, the fields were green and the yellow gorse on the Waugh hills more beautiful than anything I have seen. At Mackram [Macroom] we passed the first great ruined castle — a sight that was to become familiar. And a watch tower which served in wars forgotten a century ago. You remember Terance McSweeney, the Mayor of Cork, who died of starvation after eighty dreadful days back in the black and tan days. I'm told that perhaps nothing did more to impress the Irish in America than Mc-Sweeney. His is not a Munster name. His clan came from Donegal in the north and long ago they were professional soldiers, like the Condottieri of the Continent. They were hired to fight in Munster and built the old town at Macraam [Macroom].

A bit further you pass a picturesque castle, Bridge Crag, on a rock in the middle of the river Lee. In the old days there was no bridge. Cornwall's [Cromwell's] troops built the bridge when they were besieging the castle and there is a fine story of the Bishop of Bass.

Glengariff beyond the wild high pass of Remligh at the head of Bantry Bay some of you will remember — I suspect no one can forget it and Garinish island where Lady Bryce built her fabulously beautiful Italian garden which, like most everything, you can see for a fee. There's something langourous about the Kerry coast and you have small wonder that the Kerryman can never get anything done. Subtropical plants are everywhere and fushia grows in endless dripping hedges. I'm going back there and sleep for two weeks sometime — maybe I'll talk to the old men and children along the road-side who never seem to have anything much to do. Then Dingle Bay and Dallywane — and all the other wonderful names that remind you of the richness of Irish literature.

We stopped long enough to marvel at Muckrass Abbey and the mighty trees in the beautiful grounds. Muckrass belonged until recently to ——— Vincent of Boston, who couldn't keep it up any longer and has now given it to Killarney as a park. The scenery is wild and beautiful, I suppose, but the lakes disappointed me — it seemed to me there are finer ones in the north, and in Scotland. No first generation Kerrymen here. But certainly more fascinating country, past and present, than the country round about the Lakes of Killarney.

The road passes thru Kenmore, and by the vast bruised mansion of the Earl of Kenmore. We spent a night at Adair, the seat of the Earl of Dunraven whose ancestors built one of the most colossal and hideous manor houses in the most beautiful setting I've seen. A famous trout stream, a tributary of the Shannon, runs thru the great park and he's built a golf course on which the town — and I think its the only ——— happy ——— in Ireland — can play. The principal obstacles on this golf course are a well preserved castle of the Geraldine Earls of Kildare who with their cousins, the Geraldine Earls of Desmond, came to subdue Ireland soon after the conquest; became more Irish than English and engaged in everlasting bloody quarrels with the King and were finally destroyed by Elizabeth, I think. But the golf course also boasts a 12th and 13th century abbey and church. The walk thru these ghastly ruins on soft turf under gigantic trees, by the quiet river in the long spring evening is worth an awful lot of vile Irish food.

This is the Limerick country; it's rich soft dairyland and good horse country and quite a contrast to Kerry. Outside is the stud farm of Lord Adair, Dunraven's son. There it was that Man of War was sent some years ago when he lost his interest in mares. The Irish grass did the anamnesis, etc.

There is little of interest in modern Limerick except the great hydro-electric development on the Shannon. But the past is full of great deeds and lost causes, like most of Ireland. What Ireland needs is a Walter Scott. The heroes of Scotland are familiar to every American school boy — Wallace, Bruce, Douglas, John Knox, Mary Stuart, Montrose and Bonnie Prince Charlie. But few of us know anything of the countless heroes of Ireland's everlasting travails. The story of Patrick Sarsfield and the siege of Limerick and the ———— stone at the Shannon bridgehead where you cross over from Irish and down to English town is a good illustration. I could hardly remember what it was all about so I looked it up in a book. Perhaps you would like to hear a little about the siege of Limerick in these peaceful, tranquil days. (Read)

We came over the rugged highlands of Clare to the gray city of Galway. The curse of Cornwall [Cromwell] lies heavy on Galway as it does most everywhere in Ireland and Scotland. It was called Galway of the Tribes and for centuries was dominated by fourteen Anglo-Norman families. It did a flourishing business with Spain but Cornwall [Cromwell] had his way with it because of its loyalty to [King] Charles, and it's never recovered. Even 100 years ago it had a population of 40,000, and now its 14 or 15. Under the bridge over Galway river at a certain season the salmon lie back to back — a solid mass of them — waiting to get up the narrow channel to the 1,200 miles of lakes beyond.

The Claddagh village, which some of you have seen, is fast disappearing — this is the ancient Irish town that grew up outside each of the Anglo-Norman towns. It's a fishing village and until recent times had its King who administered an unwritten law. His verdicts were never questioned. The houses are the white thatched cottages of the picture books except they are fabulously old — many 14th and 15th century, and they are set about with no sense of order or arrangement, just as though they had been scattered there by some giant long ago. But it's fast disappearing; the authorities are insisting on better sanitation, fire protection, etc., and lovely little square boxes of concrete block and corrugated iron roofing are taking the place of the old cottage — and they tell me that the Claddagh people are fading out — the girls are marrying Galway boys and the pure Spanish — or primitive Gallic — strain is disappearing rapidly.

The motor ride north across Connemara is an endless vista of gray stone walls, peat bogs and an occasional cottage. The fields are sometimes no larger than carpets. There's hardly a plow in Connemara, I'm told, and seaweed is laboriously dragged up from the sea shore to fertilize the stony soil. It's a wild, treeless, desolate region and very poor. There's hardly a family in Connemara that doesn't eke out its living in part by remittances from America. The real capital of Connemara is New York and London is only an abstraction. They're a strong, sturdy people and probably the descendants of the ———, the early Irish which were driven back to their wild inhospitable country by the successive invasions from the N[orth] and E[ast]. They say little can be done for Connemara — the young have their eyes on America and the old on heaven.

It was in Clew Bay on the Connemara coast that Grania Sean O'Malley, the woman free-booter who harried western Ireland on land and sea for years, had her headquarters. The coast is dotted with the ruins of her strongholds. In her old age she decided to go straight. She visited [Queen] Elizabeth and the two remarkable old women had some hard words, but she got her pardon and in her own words "gave over her former trade of maintenance by sea and land." It seems to me that maintenance is a charming word for piracy.

Beyond the sharp steep little mountain called Cragh Patrick facing into the open sea by a wooded lake in a beautiful ravine is Kyhonar Castle, now the home of nuns who fled from Ypres during the last war. Thousands of devout Irishmen climb the 2,500 feet to the summit of Cragh Patrick each year, and cross the summit on their knees to do homage to their patron saint. Here it was that Patrick is said to have driven the venomous things of Ireland into the sea with a tinkle of his bell. We spent a night by the Killary at a fine inn called Reynvale House, and I saw down the coast a mile or so at the little village some of the coracles, exactly the same as those used by the ancient Britains [Britons] when Caesar came.

Here in Connemara the Gallic [Gaelic] is still the common language of the people and though the compulsory revival of the language by the Eire government seems to make little sense in this day and age it is interesting to note that it is a very rich language.

"It has been said," writes Padraic Colum in THE ROAD ROUND IRELAND, "that in England the country people have a vocabulary

[515]

of from 300 to 500 words. Doctor Pedersen took down 2,500 words of the vocabulary of Irish speakers in the Aran Islands. Doctor Douglas Hyde wrote down a vocabulary of 3,000 words from people in Roscommon who could neither read nor write, and he thinks he fell short by 1,000 words of the vocabulary in actual use. He suggests that in Munster — especially in Kerry — the average vocabulary in use amongst Irish speakers is probably between 5,000 and 6,000 words."

In short, the Irish speakers are using a vocabulary from five to ten times as large as the country people of England.

Well I must get along with this. In Donegal we visited Glenreigh Castle which used to belong to my wife's uncle — Kingsley Porter of Harvard, who wrote volumes on Irish ———.[57] It sits by a little lake in a dark ravine in the remote county surrounded by 20,000 acres of deer forest — a deer forest, you know, is rugged, stony highland and utterly treeless. Kingsley Porter knew Ireland and the Irish like few Americans. He had a little island and stone cottage off the coast where he used to go to write. He disappeared one morning some five or six years ago and has never been seen since. The peasants loved him dearly in that region; he had done much to alleviate their condition — but his disappearance has never been explained and the peasants say he may have known too much about the little people that inhabit the dangerous, obscure nooks and crannies of the wild ancient country.

We stayed a night at Holy Hill, a fine 18th century manor house at the ford of Strabane, which has seen some of the bloodiest clan warfare of ancient Ireland. Mrs. Sinclair, the owner, told us of an incident at Glenreigh a few years ago during the annual theatricals the Porters used to put on. She said without conscious embarrassment that a long line of ladies were lined up before the door to the toilet on the ground floor of the castle and as one emerged in front of her she exclaimed with "my dear a perfect flush." Yes, most of the plumbing in those great houses has had little attention since the last war and the succeeding troubles which ruined so many of the great Anglo-Irish families.

I haven't mentioned Lac Sill at Sligo, which to me was the most beautiful part of Ireland.

Crossing the frontier we entered Ulster near Ballyshannon in Fer-

---

[57] Kingsley Porter wrote *Romanesque Sculpture of the Pilgrimage Roads* (1923); *The Virgin and the Clerk* (a play; 1929); *Spanish Romanesque Sculpture* (1929); *Crosses and Culture of Ireland* (1931). He died in Ireland in 1933.

naugh [County Fermanagh] and at exactly 5 o'clock, the appointed hour, past the gatekeeper and drove up the long drive thru the Park to Colebrack [Colbrooke], a great Georgian house with mighty columns. This is the ancestral home of Sir Basil Brooke whose ancestors came with William of Orange and received for the prowess this estate.[58]

To the Editor, Chicago Tribune

November 22, 1940

Dear Sir:

In the Sunday Tribune, November 17, 1940, an article bearing a New York date line states that the Committee to Defend America by Aiding the Allies is, now that the election is over, "urging an outright declaration of war against Germany by the United States immediately." The article goes on to state, "This call to arms is sounded in the new pamphlet, 'Battle of America — How We Can Avoid It,' by Livingston Hartley, well known interventionist author." You have made a surprising mistake.

Summing up his argument for aid to Britain, the author of this pamphlet, on page 18, states, "We do not want to go into this war. We want to avoid both this war and a Battle of America against Germany later alone. We wish to preserve peace for America," and then says that the way to preserve peace for America is to aid Britain to hold out and to defeat Nazi Germany.

Your correspondent's inaccuracy cannot be explained by his failure to read the pamphlet he was writing about, because the article contains several quotations therefrom. I can only conclude, therefore, that this flagrant misstatement was deliberate. Why?

Very truly yours,

On November 16, 1940, Walter P. Paepcke, president of the Container Corporation of America, wrote Stevenson that he was returning the pair of socks that Stevenson had loaned him to play tennis. He expressed the hope that they would last for the next four years since the Roosevelt Administration had already "cost us our shirts" and it was likely to "cost us socks" as well.

---

[58] The Stevensons visited with Sir Basil and Lady Brooke before staying with Mr. and Mrs. Ernest L. Ives in Belfast. Sir Basil Brooke later became Prime Minister of Northern Ireland. The copy of the speech available ends with this abrupt statement.

To Walter P. Paepcke

November 25, 1940

Dear Walter:

My wife has finally come across with your letter of November 16. Your thoughtfulness astounds me — and your credit is now good for another pair of socks, or even that shirt which "my friends" have taken from you.

Thanks, incidentally, for that last Container dividend.

Yours,

Stevenson debated Clay Judson before the Chicago Bar Association, November 29, 1940. A good deal of the speech was similar to what he said to the League of Women Voters on October 14, 1940. Therefore, only what is new in the Bar Association speech is included here.

The audience was basically hostile to Stevenson's position. Carl Mc-Gowan recalled that in the question period that followed the prepared speech, Stevenson "handled himself extraordinarily well." Up to this point, McGowan had known Stevenson only as a pleasant person. But McGowan left the debate deeply impressed by Stevenson's intellectual ability and his style.[59]

I notice that the title of this discussion is "Should We Help England and How." The "and How" with the proper vernacular emphasis states my position; and my job here today is to tell you *why* I think we should help England — and how!

On Tuesday of this week the Gallup Poll reported that in response to this question: "Which is the more important for the United States to try to do — to keep out of the war ourselves or to help England win, even at the risk of getting into the war," the response was 50% for staying out and 50% for helping England even at the risk of war. This, I take it, is the issue; this is the decision the American people must make, not deliberately in our traditional way, but soon, very soon, and not 50–50 but by a preponderant public sentiment. It is my conviction that we have not been confronted with a more vital, a more inescapable decision in our national history.

Now the policy of aid to Britain is our national policy — and is not the issue. The issue is *how much* aid to Britain. Mr. Judson's view is

[59] Interview with Walter Johnson, January 26, 1967.

that we must not get involved in war and we should extend to Britain only such aid as is not likely to involve us in war — in other words, that the policy of aid to Britain should be governed *not* by the likelihood of insuring British victory, but by the likelihood of involving us in war. He and those who share his views apparently draw the line of safety between private and public aid; apparently they deem the aid available under our neutrality laws to any customer of private industry safe, but direct or indirect aid from our government unsafe. Now this distinction makes little sense to me. In the first place, not a plane or a shell could go to Britain unless the government permitted it. Britain is not just merely a customer in our stores; everything that she gets is necessarily at the expense of our own rearmament and with our government's acquiescence. Secondly, distinguishing between public and private aid seems to overlook the whole purpose of any aid. A little aid is worse than no aid. It won't save Britain and takes the material away from us. The real question is whether it is best for us or not best for us for Britain to stop Hitler at the English Channel. If it is best for us to stop Hitler now, then our only consideration should be what kind and how much aid can we afford to sell or give — not where does it come from, government armories or private factories. To say that arms from one source is fine and from another bad is about on a par with Lindbergh's brilliant proposal just a year ago that we embargo *off*ensive arms and sell *de*fensive arms.

Nor is the issue between Mr. Judson and me one of involvement in war. I am no more anxious to actively intervene in this war than he is and I think we can all foresee some possible consequences from intervention which I suspect he will talk about. Moreover, I am not in the least impressed with arguments about the danger of aid which is violative of the letter or spirit of our neutrality legislation. In the first place, the United States is not neutral and has not been — 80 or 90% of us are praying for British victory because we sense, if we don't clearly perceive, the sinister implications in a Nazi victory. We are not neutral; we are merely non-belligerent, and that's the way we want to stay if possible. Moreover, my impression is that the neutrality acts were adopted by our Congress for *our* benefit (mistakenly I thought then and think now); they were not imposed upon us by God Almighty or even by Germany. There is nothing sacred about them and if they don't *serve* us they should be repealed, and we should not continue to *serve* *them* in any fanciful hope that by doing so we can escape, because we all know, I hope, that you don't escape the Nazis by being good and that Hitler moves exactly when and where he pleases, and without regard to previous provocations or *appeasements!* The only obstacle he recognizes is not law or good behavior or promises or anything but — force!

No, the issue between Mr. Judson and me, or the America First Committee and the William Allen White Committee, is not peace or war for the United States; for he wants to avoid war for us no more than I. The issue really is; what is best for America — to give Britain some aid (I'm not sure how much), or all possible aid, even at the risk of somehow getting involved in the war ourselves.

Frankly, I feel a little foolish telling this audience why we should, why we must, give Britain all possible aid and let the chips fall where they may. You all know the arguments, probably better than I do. . . .

I have one more thought I want to suggest. England, Germany or Russia will win this war and will dominate Europe and a large part of the world for generations to come. If it's a long war, Stalin may win. There is, what Sir Norman Angell calls, a "brooding Stalinism" at the bottom of world society. Prolonged misery of the masses breeds Bolshevism, and Russia may be the victor whoever wins the battles.

Today Germany commands the land, Britain the seas, and whoever commands the skies will win the war. Both Britain and Germany can bomb each other's factories, but only Britain can import planes and food from us. Britain *can* win. But I am not sure she *will*. It is up to us. If she wins we are safe, our problems are almost simple. If she loses now — Naziism, later — Bolshevism. Take your choice.

I think freedom has a last chance. We can save it if we will. If we don't, those tragic words — "too little and too late" — will be the epitaph again.

On December 4, 1940, advertising executive Howard Mayer wrote Stevenson urging positive efforts to counteract adverse publicity that the Committee to Defend America by Aiding the Allies really favored intervention in the war.

To Howard Mayer

December 5, 1940

Dear Howard:

I agree that we should combat the recent unfavorable publicity. But how? We are, as you know, filling many speaking engagements; enlarging our organization; having a dinner meeting on December 16 to stimulate interest and activity; planning to inaugurate, after January 1, a series of little narrative advertisements in the Tribune like the ones

[Marshall] Field's used to use; and, finally, [John] Morrison is working constantly on Committee expansion in this area.

Frankly, I don't know what to do next, and I would welcome your suggestions. I am worried about the hypocrisy accusation, which seems to be growing (that we really want to intervene and that we're afraid to say so); and the trouble with it is that many of the White Committee people around the country are sounding off in that direction.

Couldn't we get together for lunch some day next week?

Sincerely yours,

Stevenson introduced Edgar Ansel Mowrer to a meeting of the Bloomington, Illinois, chapter of the Committee to Defend America by Aiding the Allies, December 5, 1940.

About 25 years ago, (I believe the orators call it a quarter of a century) a boy in Bloomington sneaked out of his house one evening and met some of his more disreputable playmates. I hope some of them are here tonight. Their sinister purpose was to explore the bright lights, and they were soon cowering self-consciously in this gilded palace of pleasure — waiting for the vaudeville to commence. I was the boy and I haven't forgotten some of the wondrous things I saw that night. Particularly the trick bicycle rider who did incredible feats on this little stage — it was larger then in the vaudeville days. Perhaps I remember even better his assistant — a bewitching girl in a short ballet skirt and pink tights who did a little curtsy each time the rider finished a stunt. I've thought a good deal about her and I'm still wondering how her hair could have been so golden. I even tried a little trick bicycle riding myself, but it didn't work out very well and a golden-haired girl in pink tights never materialized on East Washington Street.

Ever since that night, I think it was about 1915, the Majestic has had a peculiar fascination for me and now I'm in it again, and somehow, all of a sudden, I can't seem to forget the chastisement I got that night when I sneaked up the back stairs at home and tripped over the cat in the dark.

On that epic evening at the Majestic the world was in flames, but somehow the bicycle rider (or the girl in pink tights!) seemed a lot more important to me than the war. Tonight the world is in flames again and I wish I could feel about it now the way I did then. It would be nice to be complacent in the shadow of an awful catastrophe; to be indifferent to the relentless march of men and machines over Europe,

Africa and Asia; to be indifferent to the triumph of a philosophy of life that denies the validity of every single principle we Americans hold dear; to be undisturbed while tyranny engulfs free peoples everywhere; to be light-hearted when we *know* we can't escape; when we *know* that a world that has obliterated time and space can't exist part slave and part free; when we know that tyranny in ⅘ths of the world and freedom in ⅕th can't endure; when we know, in short, that America is on the brink of a long ordeal, military, economic and spiritual, with mighty forces bent on world dominion — unless — and thank God — there is an unless — unless Britain wins! For if Britain wins, America can escape a trial, within and without, of a magnitude, character and duration that no man can foretell.

That's why I have been devoting most of my time for the last 6 months, that's why thousands of people from coast to coast have followed William Allen White and organized more than 750 of these local committees to Defend America by Aiding the Allies — to crystallize, to make articulate, a public opinion that senses the deadly implications in a Nazi victory. That's why both candidates for the Presidency and almost every single person in America (with only two exceptions that I can think of), who has acknowledged qualifications as an expert or a student of foreign affairs, is beseeching this country to wake up, to realize what the collapse of Britain will mean to us — before it is *too* late!

That's why Edgar Mowrer has come back to his birthplace tonight. And Edgar Mowrer, I must remind any of you who don't know, has been talking, traveling, reading, and writing all over the world continuously for almost 30 years. He's the spark-plug of the greatest staff of foreign correspondents of an American newspaper — the Chicago Daily News, of which another equally famous Bloomington boy is editor — his brother, Paul Scott Mowrer. For years Edgar Mowrer has been telling the American people what was coming and from where. He has watched the birth and growth of Naziism and Fa[s]cism from their cradles. In 1932 he was awarded the Pulitzer Prize for the best foreign correspondence, and in 1933 the Nazis kicked him out of Germany because his book "Germany Puts the Clock Back" was too clairvoyant. For his pains he has often been called an alarmist and a war-monger by many complacent people here and abroad — but somehow what he foretold most always happened! It's curious how man throughout history has rejected his prophets when he doesn't like their prophecies. Pray God that we in America will listen to our prophets before it is too late!

I know no one in or from Bloomington who has earned the pride and respect of Bloomingtonians more than Edgar Mowrer — except for one sad fact; as a boy he lived on East Grove and out on East Washington we didn't care much for those Grove Street mugs! Mr Chairman I appreciate the privelege of introducing Edgar Ansell Mowrer to our home town — Mr Mowrer.

To Clark M. Eichelberger

December 6, 1940

Dear Clark:

Mrs. John Alden Carpenter, 1020 Lake Shore Drive, who heads the Chicago British Relief, saw the poster exhibit at 400 Park Avenue in New York last week. She is anxious to get as many of these posters as possible for display here and elsewhere. She may want to have some of the best ones printed for wider distribution through the British Relief organizations. In short, she would like to keep as many of the originals as possible, and will return, as soon as you direct, those you want back.

Mrs. Carpenter tells me that she talked with someone in your organization about this and he felt confident she could have some of them. Hence, I write merely to add my voice to her request. I think she could make good use of them, and, if it has your approval, I hope you will pass this letter along to the right person.

Edgar Mowrer and I spoke in Bloomington last night to a capacity theatre crowd of about 1400. I am broadcasting tomorrow evening over Columbia [Broadcasting System] on Dr. [Lyman] Bryson's People's Platform program on "Financial Aid to Britain." Don't worry — Jake Viner [60] is going to implement me beforehand!

Sincerely yours,

On December 13, 1940, Ernest B. Price, director of Chicago's International House, wrote Stevenson thanking him for the work and thought he had given to International House as president of the board of directors the past two years.

To Ernest B. Price

December 14, 1940

Dear Ernest:

I appreciate your thoughtful letter more than I can tell you. I feel that the thanks are rather due from me to you for making my job so

[60] Professor Jacob Viner of the University of Chicago.

easy. Some day I am going to do just what you suggest — review the quarterly reports for several years. I feel confident that the experiment is shaping up gradually and that the potential usefulness of these Houses for the future is great — thanks, in our case, to your vision and patience.

I suspect that our contact will little diminish in the future — I hope so. Meanwhile, many thanks for your kind letter.

Sincerely yours,

To Mrs. Martin D. Hardin and Miss Letitia Stevenson

December 14, 1940

Dear Aunt Julia and Aunt Letitia:

I did not expect any fan mail after that broadcast with Dr. Bryson — let alone from my own dear aunts. Moreover, I confess, I never had any doubt that we all saw alike in this dreadful hour. It was sweet of you both to write me.

You are quite right that we have to be careful to respect the views of the multitudes that disagree with us. After all, it is that very right to disagree that we are trying to preserve. But, like you, my patience can barely withstand the everlasting yammering about war and the confused optimism of these highminded — and rich! — isolationists. But there I am, off base again!

We had a too brief visit with Parker and Catherine [61] not long ago; but it served to bring Judy and her fine husband [62] back into our lives, and Bill followed up a couple of weeks later by landing his plane in an adjoining field! We only hope they will be flying in to see us with some regularity from now on.

It was good to have word from you but a visit would be better!

With love to you both,

Affectionately,

Some clients who were bitterly hostile to Stevenson's activities as chairman of the Chicago Chapter of the Committee to Defend America by Aiding the Allies withdrew business from Stevenson's law firm. Several members of the firm complained about this and the amount of time Stevenson spent on committee matters. Stevenson thought some of the criticism was justified and offered to take a reduced share of the profits.

[61] Mrs. Hardin's son and daughter-in-law.

[62] Mrs. Hardin's daughter and her husband, William (Bill) Foote. (After his death she married Dr. Walter Baumgarten, Jr.)

Senior partner William Pratt Sidley refused the offer. Mrs. Stanley Mc-
Cormick wrote Stevenson praising him for his leadership of the Chicago
chapter.

To Mrs. Stanley McCormick

December 17, 1940

Dear Mrs. McCormick:

Yours was the kindest letter I think I have ever received. I have never really felt that I was doing or had done in the past more than what I thought my simple duty as a citizen with some convictions. But recently, in connection with this White Committee work, I find that there has been considerable pressure brought to bear on my firm. I think suppression of thought by indirect commercial coercion is despicable, but of course I must consider not only myself but the others that may be injured by what I do. It is all very unpleasant, and your letter makes me feel much better. Your reference to my parents touched me deeply.

I hope some time while you are still here I may have an opportunity to talk with you again. Could we have lunch together at the Palmer House some day? Just telephone me at your convenience and set the day.

Faithfully yours,

On December 16, 1940, the Committee to Defend America by Aiding
the Allies sponsored a meeting with Louisville Courier-Journal *editor*
Herbert Agar as the speaker. William B. Hale, a law partner of Clay
Judson, praised the speech but in a letter to Stevenson on December 17,
1940, expressed concern over the number of Jewish people at the speak-
er's table. He felt that the committee's work would be ruined if people
thought that the White Committee was supported by Jews who wanted
to force the United States into war because of the persecution of Jews
in Germany.

To William B. Hale

December 18, 1940

Dear Mr. Hale:

Thanks for your letter. You are quite right about the conspicuous number of Jews the other night. This is the sort of thing that is always happening, but I just cannot find time to attend to every detail. I have talked with many, many Jews of all classes the last few months, and they are uniformly adverse to taking any aggressive or conspicuous position — though as you know they account for a substantial part of our funds. I have felt that we should try to keep a little balance and not obscure them altogether, which would be too transparent. . . .

I appreciate your continued interest and good will more than I can tell you.

Sincerely yours,

To the Editor, Chicago Daily News

December 23, 1940

Dear Sir:

In your splendid front page editorial, "United We Stand," on December 20, you called attention to the lamentable fact that our defense program is lagging. You suggested that whatever their differences on the question of aid to Britain, there were no differences between the Committee to Defend America by Aiding the Allies and the America First Committee on the absolute and immediate necessity for a strong national defense.

I believe you are correct. Certainly the Committee to Defend America by Aiding the Allies has been aware for some time of our inadequate defense effort, and in the statement of its present objectives, widely published in November, urged "the mobilization at once of all the industrial resources of the nation for maximum production." We welcome the suggestion in your editorial and we are eager to join forces with all Americans similarly disposed in a common effort to arouse public opinion to that end. Whether the objective is defense here in the United States, in the western hemisphere, in Britain, there is no time to lose. America must rise to this emergency united in purpose and determination.

But this is not all that must be done. We have another decision to make — not deliberately, but very soon! Is our first purpose to keep out of this war, or is it to supply Britain with what she needs and must have to stop Hitler at the English Channel? America does not want war, nor does it want Britain defeated. But Britain cannot win without our help on a tremendous scale. So we must decide in the critical weeks ahead how far we are going to help her, what risks we are willing to take.

I hope and pray that this issue can and will be presented to the people henceforth with the restraint and responsibility it deserves. Sincere, patriotic Americans can honestly disagree on this issue. Because we view with profound concern British defeat and Nazi domination of most of the world, must we be "war-mongers," "interventionists" and "hypocrites" conspiring to get our "defenseless" country into war? Because others view the danger of involvement through aid to Britain with equal apprehension must they be "appeasers," "defeatists" and "fifth columnists"?

There has been too much suspicion, too many epithets, too little reason. The decisions which we must and will make this winter will affect our future for years, perhaps generations. Let us approach them in our best, not our worst, national tradition.

Sincerely yours,

In a "fireside chat" on December 29, 1940, President Roosevelt stated that "business as usual" had to go. "We must be the great arsenal of democracy. For this is an emergency as serious as war itself." He added: "I make the direct statement to the American people that there is far less chance of the United States getting into war, if we do all we can now to support the nations defending themselves against attack by the Axis than if we acquiesce in their defeat, submit tamely to an Axis victory, and wait our turn to be the object of attack in another war later on." The following day, Stevenson sent a telegram to President Roosevelt encouraging his stand.

To Franklin D. Roosevelt

December 30, 1940

THE CHICAGO CHAPTER COMMITTEE TO DEFEND AMERICA BY AIDING THE ALLIES IS PROFOUNDLY GRATEFUL FOR YOUR GREAT APPEAL TO US AMERICANS AND TO FREE MEN EVERYWHERE. I BELIEVE THAT YOUR CLEAR STATEMENT OF THE IRRECONCILABLE CONFLICT IN THE WORLD WILL MARK BEGINNING OF REVIVAL OF DEMOCRACY AS A FAITH AND THE END OF TYRANNY'S LATEST CHALLENGE.

On November 11, 1940, Stevenson and other Midwestern leaders of the Committee to Defend America by Aiding the Allies had met with William Allen White to discuss future policy. Stevenson was particularly concerned over the sinking of British merchant ships by German submarines. He favored the convoying of such ships by the U.S. Navy. Mr. White was reluctant to endorse this step.

On November 26, 1940, however, Mr. White and the National Committee issued a new policy statement. It did not specifically call for convoys but it stated: "The life line between Great Britain and the United States is the sea route to the Western Hemisphere. Under no circumstances must this line be cut and the United States must be prepared to maintain it." The statement also called for "the revision of our international policy" which "would include a repeal or modification of restrictive statutes which hamper this nation." Although the statement did not explicitly refer to the Neutrality Act, everyone present at the policy meeting knew that this phrase meant the Neutrality Act.

Although William Allen White had agreed to the November 26 policy statement, when he returned to Emporia, Kansas, he worried and worried over the charge that he was head of a committee that was leading the United States into war. On December 20, when he learned that the Scripps-Howard newspapers were going to launch an attack on his committee, he wrote Roy Howard and denied that his committee favored convoys and the repeal of the Neutrality Act.

Immediately White's position was praised by the America First Committee and attacked by many members of the Committee to Defend America by Aiding the Allies. On December 26, 1940, White resigned as chairman. Despite phone calls from Adlai E. Stevenson, Clifton Utley and others, White would not withdraw his resignation. Lewis W. Douglas, as chairman of the executive committee of the White Committee, was in charge of finding a new chairman.

To Lewis W. Douglas

January 4, 1941

Dear Lewis:

Confirming our telephone conversation, let me say that we have given Mr. White's successor considerable thought and have consulted the chairmen of several other chapters in the middle west — Detroit, Milwaukee, Minneapolis, St. Louis, Springfield, etc.

We feel strongly that a man from the middle west or far west would be better than one from the east. We think the Committee's influence and integrity would be best preserved out here where the suspicion and antagonism are greatest, if the leader was a western man — preferably a Republican. Let me repeat the names which have been suggested, and please bear in mind that I know nothing about the availability of any of them: [Wendell] Willkie, [Alf M.] Landon, Dr. Robert A. Millikan,[63]

[63] President of the California Institute of Technology.

Charlie Taft, Chester Rowell,[64] Governor Lloyd Stark,[65] ex-Senator King.[66] If for reasons sufficient to you an outstanding western man cannot be found, we would prefer yourself or Jim Conant. I have personally felt that an outstanding "holy man" — preferably Irish Catholic — might be worth considering, someone like Monsignor [John] Ryan. In connection with the Irish angle, Jim Farley has been mentioned. The names of Cyrus Eaton [67] and Guy Stanton Ford, who is about to retire as president of the University of Minnesota, have also been mentioned.

While I am at it, let me suggest again, as I have before, that the middle west is the battleground and that the national headquarters should be here. It would also serve the useful purpose of disassociating the national organization from the New York chapter.

Please forgive me for bothering you personally about all this. I felt that you were probably most aware of the growing intensity of the isolationist and appeasement pressure in this area. We do not care about the method of selection of the chairman so long as we know that he is being chosen with a realistic understanding that the thinking out here is behind the procession and must be brought along in an honest but moderate and orderly way.

Sincerely yours,

P.S. I would like to arrange a large mass meeting for Willkie to speak here, if he would do it. It could be entirely divorced from the White Committee, but of course would help us enormously and pull the teeth of a lot of the rich, the apathetic and the appeasers. I had in mind getting an outstanding labor leader to speak with him. I hope you will use your influence to persuade him to do this. I am sure you agree that there would be no better place for him to take his stand than here.

A.E.S.

A Princeton classmate of Stevenson's wrote him that the fundamental trouble behind the war was that Germany did not have enough territory for its population. He asked whether it was not possible to assign Germany areas held by the British Empire, parts of Latin America, and Russia.

[64] A California newspaperman and progressive Republican.
[65] Former Democratic governor of Missouri.
[66] Former Senator William H. King of Utah.
[67] A Cleveland industrialist and financier.

To Webster B. Todd

January 7, 1941

Dear Web:

Thanks for your Christmas letter! Come now. You haven't fallen for the old lebensraum stuff? Your figures are all just dandy, as far as I know, but if 363 people per square mile in Germany, or even more in Italy and still more in Japan, means that those peoples should take over the rest of the world, then what about the Belgians with some 700+ per square mile, the Dutch with more than 600, England with more than Germany, and so forth and so forth? There is only one world for us to live in.

My recollection is a little vague (you know how dizzy I am!) but I think that you will find that only about 15,000 Germans colonized an empire in East Africa, several times larger than Germany, in about thirty years — and it included some of the best parts of Africa, too.

If they just want the colonies back again, why doesn't Hitler say so? If they just want some more elbow room on the continent, why don't they take it from Russia, as they easily could?

You better come out here and let me resume your education. Evidently I let you get away from me too soon!

Sincerely,

P.S. And where do you get that stuff about my trying to get us into war? I am trying to get the British to win it so we won't have to. And remember that total war involves not only military operations but some economic and moral weapons that we may find very uncomfortable.

P.P.S. This is more letter than I generally write. Please wire me at once that you are convinced and take it all back — or send me a three-cent stamp — you old lebensraumer!

On January 10, 1941, President Roosevelt asked Congress for legislation allowing the country to "sell, transfer, lease, lend, exchange or otherwise dispose of" articles of defense to the allies. The Committee to Defend America by Aiding the Allies gave powerful support to the passage of "Lend-Lease." Wendell Willkie made speeches and testified before the Senate Foreign Relations Committee in support of the bill.

The White Committee, shortly after the following letter, made former Republican Senator Ernest Gibson of Vermont chairman of the commit-

tee. Lewis W. Douglas was made chairman of the national board of the committee. Stevenson had urged the New York leaders of the committee to select a Midwesterner or Westerner as chairman.

To Lewis W. Douglas

January 11, 1941

Dear Lew:

I am just back from Washington and find your letter of January 7. I am sure you realize that the fuss we made at the meeting Thursday was not captious or due to any personal misgivings about Senator Gibson. I was doing what I believed the groups here and elsewhere in the West wanted done, and, as I implied, the White House had reacted with surprising enthusiasm. However, in view of what I heard there about the uncertainty of his position, I am more than reconciled, — particularly in view of the fact that you will figure more prominently in Committee news henceforth.

Yesterday in Washington it was suggested that if Willkie would come forward now in support of the lend lease bill it would be enormously helpful. I am afraid they are getting a little overconfident in the administration and that the bill goes too far for this stage of thinking at the Capitol. But of course if they can get away with it, much painful delay will be avoided in the future, and sometime, if Willkie was as sincere as people thought him during the campaign, he could do us a great service — at least out here.

I do not know how to approach him. His few close personal friends here are either against us or badly confused and unconvinced. I hope there may be some way for you people down there to impress on him the importance of taking a forthright position on top of the wave soon.

Please forgive me for my misbehavior. I am sure you understood my motives and duty.

Sincerely yours,

Senior partner William Pratt Sidley refused the following request.

Memorandum to Mr. Sidley

January 16, 1941

For the last two years I have been a director of Industrial National Bank (formerly Personal Loan & Savings Bank). During that period my director's fees have been deposited in a savings account at the Bank and I am today advised that the total, plus interest, in the account is now $651.87.

As you know, I have engaged in sundry activities which have required some "office time," use of stenographers, etc. As I have told you, my trespasses have embarrassed me. Attendance at these Board meetings have been on office time and as I have received some compensation for them, I feel that it properly belongs to the firm. Accordingly, I want you to accept the attached check. It is little enough and I would REALLY feel much better about it.

A.E.S.

P.S. Mr Sidley — Please understand that I have long planned to do this with these directors' fees & that it bears no relation to the White Committee matter.

To Ralph C. De Mange [68]

January 25, 1941

Dear Ralph:

I was delighted to have your letter and the enclosure. I know the Trustees of the Princeton Club Scholarship Fund, and I used to be President of the Club. I shall talk with them at once, and file with them a letter about Ewing [69] who seems to me more entitled to a scholarship than any candidate they have had for years. The only trouble is that the Trustees of the Scholarship Fund have been disposed to confine the scholarships to boys living in the Chicago area. Rest assured that I will do what I can to ensure the most favorable possible consideration of Ewing's application.

I suppose you know that last year Mrs. Adele Harris Whiting established a thousand dollar scholarship in memory of her son, Bradford Hill Whiting, of the class of 1934. This scholarship is available for award to a student entering Princeton as a Freshman in 1941. Preference in awarding a scholarship will be given, first, to residents of Chicago and its suburbs, and second, to residents of the State of Illinois. The scholarship is awarded by the Princeton University Committee on Scholarships, and application should be made to the *Secretary of the University Committee on Scholarships, Nine Nassau Street, Princeton, New Jersey*, before March 1, 1941. I think you should write for information about this

[68] A family friend from Bloomington, Illinois.
[69] Mr. De Mange's son.

scholarship, and, if he has not done so, Ewing should make application for this one at once. It seems to me he has superb qualifications for this particular scholarship, which is granted on the general principles of the Rhodes Scholarship plan.

I hope you will keep me advised of developments in this connection, as Ewing is entitled to, and certainly can get, a scholarship of some kind if the matter is handled properly. I shall let you know the attitude of the Trustees of our Scholarship Fund here.

With best regards,

The Chicago chapter of the White Committee was planning a rally to stimulate support of Lend-Lease. Professor Paul H. Douglas of the University of Chicago recommended that Philip Murray, head of the Congress of Industrial Organizations, and William Green, head of the American Federation of Labor, be two of the speakers.

To Frank Knox

January 31, 1941

Dear Colonel:

I was disappointed not to see you yesterday before you left. There were two things in particular I wanted to suggest. Paul Douglas thinks we might be able to induce both Murray and Green to speak on behalf of the bill, national unity, etc. If we could persuade Willkie to speak with them shortly after his return, it would have a manifestly wholesome effect in this benighted area. Hence, if there is any influence you can exercise on him after he returns, I hope you will do so. We can arrange a big meeting, I think, which need not appear to be under the auspices of the White Committee.

In the second place, I wanted to ask you to urge Clarence Randall [70] to assume the chairmanship of the White Committee. I can no longer take the leadership and we need a new and better leader badly! He is quite disposed to do it, but is apprehensive that it may affect his close friendship with Ed Ryerson. [71] Possibly a little encouragement from you would do the trick if you could drop him a note. Of course, I would rather he did not know I had asked you to do it.

[70] President of the Inland Steel Corporation.
[71] Chairman of the board of the Inland Steel Corporation. He was opposed to the White Committee.

The opposition has us on the run here and your splendid speeches were the best stimulant we have had for a long while. I am going to see if [Governor] Dwight Green cannot be persuaded to make some kind of a statement.

Faithfully,

P.S. — I have enthusiastic reports today on a speech Edgar Mowrer made for us in Minneapolis Wednesday night. He has been remarkably effective everywhere.

To Thomas K. Finletter

February 3, 1941

Dear Mr. Finletter:

I have your letter of January 24 and wish it were possible for us to be of some help to the National Committee. I appreciate perfectly your position; on the other hand, we are just now embarking on a large mailing project which will cost some $10,000, the larger part of which we will have to raise at once. I am sure that Victor Elting is entirely familiar with our circumstances and problem here, and that he can explain it to you in detail.

Solicitation of funds by the National Committee from people in Chicago has caused us constant embarrassment and caused them constant confusion. Only last week, one of my partners had a letter from Mrs. Kermit Roosevelt asking him to contribute when he was attempting to get money to meet our local needs. We have had a great many inquiries from people who have contributed to us who have been solicited by New York, and I wish it were possible to let us have this field to ourselves, and if and when we can find any surplus funds, they will of course be available to you.

With kind regards, I am

Sincerely yours,

To C. F. Childs [72]

February 3, 1941

Dear Mr. Childs:

Thank you very much indeed for sending me a copy of your splendid letter to Senator [C. Wayland] Brooks.

We are told that the mail down there is running against us from 5–8 to 1. We must, therefore, take some immediate measures to counteract

[72] Unable to identify.

this and to that end we have in contemplation a very large mailing, perhaps 500,000. I hope you will keep after your Congressman and the Senators and if you can give or get us any help against the expense of the mailing, which will be about $10,000, it would be most welcome. I hate to beg!

Sincerely yours,

P.S. — Checks should be made payable to Chicago Committee to Defend America by Aiding the Allies, and can be sent to me or to the Committee office, Room 827 First National Bank Building.

To Mrs. Paul B. Magnuson [73]

February 3, 1941

Dear Laura:

I hesitate to ask you for help and am assuming that you are in favor of the White Committee's efforts for all possible aid to Britain. We find we are in a critical situation at the moment on the "Lend-Lease Bill" and that the mail in Washington is running adversely by a large proportion. Accordingly, we are obliged to make some heroic efforts to counteract the adverse effect on Congress in this region. We have in contemplation a letter to about half a million people throughout this area, which will cost us some $10,000. As our funds are low and we have already tapped the same sources over and over again, I am writing you and a few others in the hope that you will be able to make a contribution to defray the expense of this work.

Sincerely yours,

P.S. — Check should be made payable to Chicago Committee to Defend America by Aiding the Allies, and can be sent to me.

Stevenson introduced Sigrid Schultz to the Chicago Council on Foreign Relations on February 4, 1941.

In the absence of your President the Director has dusted me off and asked me to resume my ancient activities on this platform. I am much flattered and also a little confused. I can't remember whether the customary greeting is members of the Council and Ladies & Gentlemen or

---

[73] Dr. and Mrs. Paul B. Magnuson were close friends. In later years after they moved to Washington, D.C., Stevenson stayed with them regularly on his visits to the capital.

Ladies and Gentlemen and members of the Council. Somehow neither sounds quite [right] and I'm almost tempted to say My Friends.

You all know that ours is a large and prosperous organization. If it wasn't large and prosperous it couldn't provide you with the program it does; and it is your responsibility to keep it large and prosperous and thereby effective! So when I tell you that in the last two years the Council's total membership has actually declined a little, I know you will go right to work to remedy this deplorable situation — having no other causes to support and no other demands on your time, energy and good will in these tranquil days!

Because the Council has, I understand, been criticized for partiality to correspondents of a certain evening paper we are all the more pleased to have a distinguished correspondent of a certain morning paper. I hope the Council won't be charged with more gratuitous advertising if I tell you in confidence that the "certain morning paper" is the Tribune! Sigrid Schultz is a Chicagoan by birth whom we see altogether too seldom! She was educated in Paris and Berlin and after the last war joined the Tribune staff in Berlin under the well loved and lamented Richard Henry Little. She has lived in Germany continuously since 1919 and is now the dean of all foreign correspondents in the Nazi capital.

Sigrid Schultz saw the post war disorders in Germany, the inflation, the rise and fall of the Weimar Republic and the rise of national socialism and its prophet, Adolph Hitler. But she has seen much more. She has seen the procession of the fateful months of March. In 1936 Hitler reoccupied the Rhineland while we debated the merits of the first New Deal; in March 1938 he rode into Vienna while we debated whether the recession was due to too much spending or not enough. In March 1939 he rode into Prague, while we debated whether to spend a little money on the Navy. In March 1940 it was too foggy in Norway so he waited until April, while we warmed up for the quarennial [quadrennial] Presidential debate.

And now it is March again and Berlin is the capital of all Europe from Spitzbergen to Sicily — and of course we are — debating!

Sigrid Schultz has watched these fateful years unfold and reported them from Berlin — from the cradle and incubator of the new world order — from behind the German lines. We welcome our distinguished fellow townsman to the Council for the first time. Miss Sigrid Schultz.

Stevenson's old friend Robert M. Hutchins, president of the Uni-

versity of Chicago, opposed the passage of the Lend-Lease bill. After Hutchins made a radio speech against it, Stevenson issued the following statement.

I agree with Dr. Hutchins that our democracy is far, far from perfect and that we must build a new moral order for America. But I do not see what that has to do with the immediate issue of defense of our democracy, imperfect as it may be.

Does Dr. Hutchins think that we will be able to make much progress toward a new moral order for America if Britain falls and America becomes a lonely, armed camp surrounded by gigantic, hostile forces pledged to destroy our way of life? Does Dr. Hutchins think that we alone can be free and freer while rigidity and bondage envelop the shrinking world around us?

No one wants war; everyone wants peace. But peace and freedom are not had for the asking in this world. Any course we take is full of risks. We must decide what risks we are willing to take and when. President Hutchins is for no risks now. I think we must take some risks now or far greater risks later.

I do not believe there can ever be a new moral order in America if there is a new unmoral order in the rest of the world. I cannot view the economic, moral, and military implications of Nazi mastery with the complacence of Dr. Hutchins and Col. [Charles A.] Lindbergh. I wish I could!

To Mrs. John Stuart [74]

February 7, 1941

Dear Mrs. Stuart:

A thousand thanks for the editorial. It is splendid!

I have personally felt and preached for a year or more the menace from within; our apathy, ignorance, and indifference. I am sure it is Hitler's most deadly weapon and unless we can rekindle some fighting faith in freedom, Britain will go down and then in time, we too will be confronted with terrific pressures from without and will conform to the new world pattern — unless we are prepared to make greater sacrifices than we are now.

Sincerely yours,

[74] Mrs. Stuart, of Hubbard Woods, Illinois, sent Stevenson an editorial supporting aid to the Allies.

To Milton J. Krensky [75]

February 10, 1941

Dear Mr. Krensky:

We hear some disturbing reports on the progress of the Lend-Lease Bill in the Senate and propose to make a large scale effort by mail to promote favorable messages from this area.

I hesitate to ask you for help and I am writing merely to advise you that if you know of any funds that are readily available, they would be most welcome to meet our "emergency."

Sincerely yours,

On February 12, 1941, Mrs. Kermit Roosevelt wrote Stevenson a letter explaining how much she had enjoyed meeting him at Victor Elting's apartment in New York City.

To Mrs. Kermit Roosevelt

February 14, 1941

Dear Mrs. Roosevelt:

Thanks for your nice note! You abruptly changed my opinions about the Oyster Bay Roosevelts — though your heroic husband had long seemed a swell "maverick" to me!

I hope that the good hour at Victor's was only the first encounter, and that when you pass this way the Stevensons will not be overlooked, though my partner, Donald McPherson, says I will have to do battle with him!

Cordially yours,

To Ira Nelson Morris

February 14, 1941

My dear Ira:

You have done a very fine and gracious thing.[76] I have sent your generous check and a copy of your letter to Ernest Price. As you know, this student's predicament is desperate. To make possible the realization of a gifted scholar's ambition for education will, I know, give you deep satisfaction and comfort.

[75] A prominent Chicago businessman and a leader of the American-Jewish Congress.

[76] At the urging of Stevenson, Mr. Morris, who was vacationing in Arizona, had sent a check to enable a student at International House to continue his studies.

[538]

We are all well and look forward to seeing you in the country when you get back to this inhospitable climate.

Ellen joins me in affectionate regards.

Yours,

To C. Wayland Brooks

February 17, 1941

Dear Senator:

I am aware of your opposition to the Administration's foreign policy and the Lend-Lease Bill in particular. However, I take the liberty of reminding you that the Republican Congressional leadership you are following has been continuously wrong in this field for years. You recall that they opposed the Naval Expansion Bill in 1938, the Repeal of the Embargo Act in May, 1938, Repeal of the Embargo Act in October, 1939, conscription in August, and now the Lend-Lease Bill.

They now acknowledge their prior errors, at least some of them, by approving all defense expenditures and even some aid to Britain, short of effectiveness. Had their earlier judgment prevailed, our own defenses would have been much retarded and Britain would have fallen.

I make bold enough to suggest that you would be well advised not to follow an obstructive leadership with such a perfect record of bad judgment and myopic statesmanship.

Very truly yours,

To Scott W. Lucas

February 17, 1941

Dear Senator:

I enclose a letter to Brooks. The Chicago Committee to Defend America by Aiding the Allies is making a vigorous effort to increase his mail in support of the [Lend-Lease] Bill, not that it will do any good, but in the hope that it may tend to silence him and serve to indicate something better than a sorry division of opinion in this area.

Faithfully yours,

To Harry Hopkins

February 22, 1941

Dear Mr. Hopkins:

I hope you will remember me. We met in the Lehman Bros.' office here last Fall to discuss a committee which you and Frank Knox had in contemplation.

My work here as Chairman of the Committee to Defend America by Aiding the Allies is largely finished, and I am anxious to help in any other way I can. If your engagements permit, I would like very much to see you briefly when I am next in Washington and I shall take the liberty of telephoning you for an appointment, subject to your convenience.

Sincerely yours,

To Graham Aldis [77]

February 24, 1941

Dear Graham:

I know a good, reliable man, about fifty-four years old, who has had considerable experience as bookkeeper and accountant. Latterly he has been doing accounting on various receivership properties for the Muskegon Trust Company, Muskegon, Michigan. The receiverships are now all closed and he is out of a job and has come back to Chicago, where he used to live, to look for work. At his age it is not, as you know, easy to get a job. But his requirements are modest and even part time employment would be very helpful to him.

It occurred to me that he might be useful to someone like yourself as an accountant or bookkeeper on your buildings. His name is F. H. Duggan and I once did some work for a corporation of which he was secretary and bookkeeper. If you would be interested in seeing him, I will send him over. If not, please disregard this letter and accept my apologies for bothering you.

Sincerely yours,

To Mrs. Emmons Blaine

March 1, 1941

Dear Mrs. Blaine:

Senator [Ernest] Gibson and Mr. [Clark] Eichelberger report from Washington that they are much worried by the unsatisfactory progress of the Lend-Lease Bill and the apparent adverse effect on public sentiment that the prolonged isolationist opposition is having.

Next week they want to run all over the country advertisements entitled "The Truth about the Lend-Lease Bill," using copies substantially like the enclosed yellow hand-bill. A quarter page in the [Chicago Daily] News and a half page in the [Chicago] Times would cost us here in Chicago about $650 net after repayment to us by a friendly advertising agency of the agency's commission of 15 per cent.

[77] Head of Aldis & Company, real estate managers.

We have just finished a drive for funds to pay for our large mail campaign in support of the Bill and our money is very low, with little prospect of getting more for the present. Do you feel strongly enough about the desirability of such an advertisement to help us finance it? If not, please do not hesitate to say so. Frankly, I have some misgivings about its usefulness at this late date. On the other hand, the filibustering tactics of the opposition are largely supported by hostile or indifferent public sentiment in this area and I suppose it is our job to keep everlastingly at it.

Please let me hear from you promptly as we should run this ad at once to get the maximum benefit. I hesitate to ask you for help after all your generosity, but we have recently tapped again most of our other friends.

Sincerely yours,

P.S. — During the last week, we have distributed thousands of handbills like the other one which I am enclosing.

A.E.S.

On the day Stevenson wrote to the chairman of the Committee to Defend America by Aiding the Allies, the Senate passed the Lend-Lease bill. After passage, the America First Committee concentrated on the question of peace or war for the United States and accused President Roosevelt and the Aid the Allies Committee of actually favoring intervention in the war.

To Ernest W. Gibson

March 8, 1941

Dear Ernest:

I thank you for your letter of March 6 and the enclosed editorial from the Herald-Tribune. I am sending it to the Chicago Daily News and stating they may be able to make some use of it.

Last night I exchanged a few words with my old friend, Mrs. Kellogg Fairbank, who is the active leader of the America First Committee in Chicago. Their National Executive Committee had just completed an all-day meeting and I got the impression from her that they propose to continue their activity "resisting the trend toward war" after the passage of the Bill. She talked vaguely of using their many chapters for organization of "discussion groups."

Thank God the news indicates that the Bill will soon be out of the way and we can get started at last.

Faithfully yours,

In addition to writing Harry Hopkins on February 22, 1941, Stevenson also wrote Wayne Chatfield-Taylor expressing his desire for a position in Washington. On March 10, Mr. Taylor wrote: "I think some progress has been made in bringing your name to the attention of the powers that be."

To Wayne Chatfield-Taylor

March 12, 1941

Dear Wayne:

Thanks for your letter. My patience is more than adequate! About a month ago I wrote Harry Hopkins that if convenient for him I would like to stop in on my next trip to Washington. My thought was merely to tell him that I wanted to help in any way, either here or there. I enclose copy of his reply. Meanwhile, the anticipated business trip to Washington has become unnecessary — and on Friday we are off to Jokake Inn at Phoenix for a couple of weeks — my first winter vacation.

I may be going down to Washington shortly after I get back, around the first of April. I will look in on you and if you think well of it, I will also call on Hopkins, although my acquaintance with him is very slight.

Yours,

P.S. — Last night Ellen heard . . . that Adelaide [78] was going to be married soon. The surge of time gets me down! — I think of her as a schoolgirl still.

Mrs. Robert Biggert suggested on March 12, 1941, that a petition be circulated to secure the signatures of those who favored a morning newspaper in Chicago to compete with the Tribune.

To Mrs. Robert Biggert

March 14, 1941

Dear Bee:

Thank you for your letter of March 12 which I am answering hastily as I am about to catch a train. The exploration of the possibility for a new morning paper in Chicago has been going on for years and all of the suggestions you mention have been explored. I have no doubt that ultimately something will develop but I am afraid it will take an enormous financial backing which does not seem to be forthcoming yet.[79]

Yours,

[78] The Taylors' daughter.
[79] In December, 1941, Marshall Field launched the Chicago *Sun.*

To Leo S. Samuels [80]

April 7, 1941

Dear Mr. Samuels:

I was delighted to have your letter of April 5 and the most welcome check. Your generosity is more than kind and particularly helpful now that interest in our work is declining. At the present we are "coasting," awaiting the development of more concrete issues and also with the thought that silence gives the America First Committee less to fight and therefore less on which to support its huge organizing program.

I did not overlook your generous suggestion of further contributions and I hope it will not be necessary to call upon you.

Very truly yours,

To Clark Eichelberger

April 8, 1941

Dear Clark:

I am arranging a meeting for next Monday noon and am asking approximately twenty of our more active people, of whom more than half will doubtless attend. A note from John Morrison this morning tells me that he will be back on Thursday of this week.

I propose that we discuss and reach some conclusion at this meeting

(1) as to the present policy of the Committee,
(2) as to whether it should be reorganized with a view either to immediate activity or "coasting," whichever is decided upon, and
(3) if reorganization is deemed desirable, the selection of a new chairman and director if John wishes to withdraw after the first of May.

The only purpose that Mr. Blaisdell [81] would serve by being here would be to give us last-minute information as to the state of affairs in Washington and the organization of activities. I think the latter has already been covered in Mr. [Ernest] Gibson's recent memorandum. However, if you think it would be helpful to us for Blaisdell to be here, send him by all means.

With best regards,

Sincerely yours,

[80] Unable to identify.
[81] It had been suggested that Donald C. Blaisdell, who was on the Washington, D.C., staff of the Committee to Defend America by Aiding the Allies, join the Chicago office.

To Dean Acheson [82]

April 12, 1941

Dear Dean:

Yesterday Colonel Donovan [83] told me that the Minister of War in the Eire Government was in America and that you were in touch with him — and probably "working on him." [84] For some time I have been exploring the possibility of doing something with Irish-American opinion here and if this man is coming to Chicago, I would like to know it. Possibly I could arrange something which would be helpful.

If I seem to be a little off balance, you will understand that I picked this fragment out of a talk with Donovan yesterday about other things and I may have misunderstood him.

With best regards,

Sincerely yours,

The director of Hull House, Miss Charlotte Carr, persuaded Stevenson to become a member of the board of trustees of the Hull House Association.

To Mrs. Joseph T. Bowen [85]

April 18, 1941

Dear Mrs. Bowen:

Thank you so much for your kind letter of April 17th. As I explained to Miss Carr, I am apprehensive that I will be of little use to Hull House, but I could not resist her blandishments and I shall attend the next directors' meeting on April 25th.

Cordially yours,

Essayist and raconteur Alexander Woollcott was a speaker at meetings for the Committee to Defend America by Aiding the Allies.

[82] Undersecretary of State.

[83] William Donovan, New York lawyer and soon to head the Office of Strategic Services.

[84] The Republic of Ireland refused to grant the British naval bases to assist the convoying of merchant shipping from the United States.

[85] Chairman of the board of directors of Hull House.

To Alexander Woollcott

April 19, 1941

Dear Mr. Woollcott:

It was good of you to ask me back to your apartment for a drink. I felt I had already taken full advantage of your hospitality. But when you pass this way next time my impertinence will be quite fresh again.

I will not forget your broadcast offer [86] and I hope it will not be long before we can take proper advantage of it.

Faithfully yours,

After the passage of the Lend-Lease legislation, the William Allen White Committee recommended that Allied naval vessels be repaired in American waters and American naval ships convoy Allied shipping "if need be." With the America First Committee increasing its efforts, the White Committee tried to sponsor rallies with prominent leaders as speakers.

To Wendell L. Willkie

April 24, 1941

Dear Mr. Willkie:

You were more than generous with Mr. [John] Morrison and myself last night. We feel that we imposed upon you ungraciously and I hope you — and Mrs. Willkie! — will forgive us.

Mr. [William Allen] White passed through town this morning. He was enthusiastic about the prospect of a meeting for you here and eagerly embraced the suggestion that he appear on the program — perhaps to introduce you.

Mr. Morrison has already suggested to Bell [87] and [Clark] Eichelberger that they let us have the May 7th date — subject to your approval, but I am afraid there would be much resistance from the New York people.

Thank you again for your courtesy.

Sincerely yours,

[86] Mr. Woollcott had offered to do a radio speech.
[87] Ulric Bell, formerly Washington correspondent for the Louisville *Courier-Journal,* was in the national office of the Committee to Defend America by Aiding the Allies.

To Lowell Mellett [88]

May 5, 1941

Dear Mr. Mellett:

It was very good of you to receive me last Friday. I have at least some conception of the pressure and know how unfair it is to impose on you.

I felt afterward that you might have misunderstood my inquiry as to what the President wanted or expected from us. As one of his most (I think) active supporters in Chicago in the last three campaigns, I did not intend to imply any criticism of a leadership that I respect and admire as much as anyone. But what I did want to convey to you was the feeling of many people in this area who share his views on the crisis that the state of public opinion is fairly satisfactory now, but that it may deteriorate in the present atmosphere. There is much latent defeatism hereabouts — "Britain is doomed, Hitler is unbeatable, perhaps we had better pull out while we can, etc." I am apprehensive that this can and will spread rapidly unless the President pulls the people up sharply, no one else can do it.

You have heard all this from a thousand better sources, I know. I merely wanted to add my testimony. Please forgive me.

I enjoyed meeting you and I hope some time you will afford me an opportunity to be of some service.

Cordially yours,

P.S. — I am also much interested in the possibility, as time goes on and things get worse, of the Government's making some organized use of the many groups that have sprung up through the country in the last year in support of the President's policy. It seems to me that it should be possible to turn these resources to some account in civilian mobilization.

A.E.S.

On April 19, 1941, Ulric Bell helped launch the Fight for Freedom Committee. The new committee felt that the White Committee was equivocating and failing to lead public opinion. The new committee

[88] Director of the Office of Government Reports, Washington, D.C.

favored a declaration of war against Germany. Stevenson himself by this time had become an interventionist.

To Ulric Bell

May 5, 1941

Dear Mr. Bell:

I was sorry to miss you in New York last week. My work downtown kept me busy until after five. I spent Friday in Washington seeing as many people as I could, including Lowell Mellett. As to the President's apparent reluctance to assume more vigorous leadership, I was able to find out little, except possibly that he does not want to participate in a public controversy now on some incidental issue like convoys — which will not be enough.

I wanted to tell you how much I appreciate being included in your mailing list, and to express my conviction that the distribution of selective material of this kind is most effective. I had a number of other things I wanted to discuss with you, and I hope there will be another opportunity before long.

Sincerely yours,

P.S. — I enclose form of petition which I wrote and which our "White Committee" has been distributing throughout Chicago for the last few weeks.

A.E.S.

Although by the time of this letter, Stevenson had resigned as chairman of the Chicago chapter of the White Committee, he remained on the executive committee.

To Albert A. Sprague

May 6, 1941

Dear Colonel:

As you know, there is an appalling lack of awareness here in Chicago of the seriousness of the emergency confronting the nation. There is no doubt that the defeatism of the *Chicago Tribune* — to give it no worse a name — and the America First crowd is creating a dangerous division and confusion here which must be combatted.

For some time our Committee has been working on plans for another large mass meeting like the one we staged at the Coliseum last September. We have been in touch with Mr. Willkie and he has expressed anxiety to speak here when the time seemed ripe. Matters were brought to a head by a reliable report that the America First Committee planned a meeting at Soldiers Field on Memorial Day. I suggested to our director, John Morrison, that he get in touch with you in regard to an application for Soldiers Field for that day. Morrison tells me he talked with you over the phone, and that you put him in touch with Donoghue [89] of the Park Board.

Donoghue pointed out that with Memorial Day coming on Friday this year, it would be difficult to fill the stadium on account of the number of people who will be out of town. He also pointed out that the Memorial Day parade on Michigan Avenue would preclude the use of the field until evening.

However, Morrison has talked with a number of people familiar with these affairs, and there seems to be a feeling that if the Memorial Day parade could wind up in Soldiers Field with a "National Unity" or "National Defense" mass meeting sponsored by a non-partisan committee, highlighted by speeches by national figures like Willkie, bands from Great Lakes and Fort Sheridan,[90] and possibly by a flight of bombers en route from California to Britain, we could turn out a large crowd. We have close contacts with the Polish, Czechoslovak, Yugoslav and Greek groups, who, as you know, will turn out for these affairs when properly urged.

The crux of the problem is to get the Memorial Day parade to wind up in Soldiers Field. Morrison tells me that the parade is put on by the G.A.R. Memorial Association of Cook County and that the man in active charge is Carlin H. Woodridge of the American Legion.

We need your advice at the earliest possible date on whether we should attempt such a meeting at all and on how best to secure the cooperation of the parade group and the city authorities, since we envisage this meeting as a demonstration of Chicago's support for the national defense policy. Would it be possible for Harland Allen, our new chairman, Morrison and myself to discuss this with you at your early convenience, say tomorrow at lunch?

If we are going to put on this show we will need to start very promptly. We can count on the wholehearted support of the News and the Times.

Sincerely yours,

[89] George T. Donoghue, superintendent of the Chicago Park District.
[90] Navy and Army bases in the Chicago area.

To Robert A. Gardner [91]

May 9, 1941

Dear Bob:

Last night I noticed the name of Adlai Ewing Stevenson among the members of The Commercial Club and almost at once identified it. But it gave me a feeling of, shall I say, uncomfortable distention, and if it does not occasion you or your secretary too much trouble, I believe I would prefer to replace the musical "Ewing" with the vowelish "E."

Yours,

P.S. — It was a great show last night and warming to a "warmonger's" heart!

A.E.S.

To Fowler McCormick

May 13, 1941

Dear Fowler:

I do not want to be the last to congratulate you.[92] I am delighted by this splendid recognition of your talents and industry, though I hardly envy you the enormous responsibility!

It is comforting to see a great American enterprise that can still find competent leadership on the genealogical tree!

Sincerely yours,

P.S. — I just had a wire from Buffy reporting that all her possessions were destroyed in the bombing of Belfast last week — but I am sure it won't make her more belligerent than she was already!

A.E.S.

Mrs. Harry Bestow sent a telegram to Stevenson on May 9, 1941, stating that she was a mother of five children and favored aid to the British.

[91] Secretary of the Commercial Club of Chicago.
[92] He had just been made president of International Harvester Company.

To Mrs. Harry Bestow

May 13, 1941

Dear Mrs. Bestow:

My wife was much gratified by your telegram. We who have been working in support of the national policy of aid to Britain in defense of America sometimes get discouraged by the pacifism and apparent indifference of some mothers to the implications of a Hitler victory. It is therefore the more comforting to find a mother of five with the vision that you have.

Thank you again for your good wire.

Sincerely yours,

In view of the dangerous situation abroad, Stevenson's Princeton class decided to hold their twentieth reunion in 1941 instead of 1942.

To Charles Shipway [93]

May 16, 1941

Dear Charlie:

Your letter arrived along with one from Dick Stevens [94] and a circular from Ed DeLong.[95] I think it is a splendid idea — what with the uncertainty of next year. I wish I could say yes without equivocation, but I can't and may not know until the last moment. However, I suppose it will be possible to find some place to stay even then. So, God willing, you may have the unfathomable pleasure of inspecting my sparse thatch and ample girth. And, let me add, it will give me incontinent satisfaction to have a look at you and certain other disreputable personages.

Thanks again!

Sincerely yours,

Former President Herbert Hoover proposed a plan to supply food to the peoples in the nations captured by Germany. Many leaders of the William Allen White Committee opposed the idea on the basis that it would strengthen Germany.

[93] Of Stevenson's Princeton class.
[94] Of Stevenson's Princeton class.
[95] Secretary of the Princeton Alumni Association.

To the Reverend Henry P. Van Dusen [96]

May 19, 1941

Dear Pit:

Ulric Bell sent me a reprint of your article on "Food for Europe" from Christianity and Crisis. I have read it with great pleasure and profit. It is the best concise presentation of the matter I have seen. But I can, happily, take issue with you on Hoover's "immense political influence." It was a courteous, gracious thing to say, but I am confident that his influence is meager at best. His last curious speech seems to have evoked little public reaction, even in this benighted area.

Sincerely yours,

To George Gillespie [97]

May 19, 1941

Dear George:

This will introduce to you Edwin Clough, who was for several years librarian of the Library of International Relations and more recently has been director of the World Citizens' Association, an interesting and ambitious project sponsored by Mrs. Emmons Blaine. Mr. Clough is a scholar of standing in the field of international relations and incidentally a "good guy."

I understand that his wife is obliged to live in the Southwest and that he must now resign his position and move out there too. He will have to find some employment and he has no acquaintances. So far as I know, you are Phoenix's most enterprising citizen and hence I am presuming to send him to you for advice. Though an "intellectual," he is not proud and will welcome any suggestions you can give him, I am sure.

Incidentally, he tells me his wife met you and Kay at some ranch this winter, which in turn causes me to inquire whether you still find calf-roping easier in blackface and a dinner coat!

Ellen joins me in best wishes to you both.

Sincerely yours,

An All-Chicago Citizens' Committee on America's Crisis sponsored a large rally with Wendell L. Willkie as the featured speaker. The execu-

[96] President of Union Theological Seminary.
[97] A friend of Stevenson's who lived in Phoenix, Arizona.

tive committee was composed of Clifford W. Barnes, chairman; Laird Bell; James H. Douglas, Jr.; James B. Forgan; Albert S. Long; Charles P. Megan; Clarence B. Randall; A. A. Sprague; Adlai E. Stevenson; and John Stuart.

To Wendell L. Willkie

May 20, 1941

Dear Mr. Willkie:

I am delighted that you are going to speak here on June 6th. Yesterday Carl Sandburg also agreed to speak, though we are withholding publicity on him for the present. We are at work on the organization of a Citizens' Committee to sponsor the meeting, and, except for the inevitable coincidence of some names, it will have no connection with my Chicago Committee to Defend America.

As we told you in Rushville, I am confident that your speech here will be a most effective contribution to "the cause" and we are all deeply grateful to you.

Cordially yours,

On May 20, 1941, President Roosevelt appointed the mayor of New York as head of the new Office of Civilian Defense.

To Fiorello H. LaGuardia

May 21, 1941

Dear Mr. LaGuardia:

For the last year I have been Chairman of the Chicago Committee to Defend America by Aiding the Allies. For some time I have been following the plans in Washington for the organization of the Office of Civilian Defense announced yesterday, and I should like to volunteer for service either in Washington or here.

I would be glad to give you any information you wish or come to Washington or New York to see you or your assistants.

Sincerely yours,

P.S. — I know David Rockefeller, whom I believe is in your New York office, and I had the pleasure of meeting you here last fall at our "Norris-LaGuardia" massmeeting.

A.E.S.

The Citizens Board of the University of Chicago was raising funds to commemorate the fiftieth anniversary of the University and Stevenson was one of the fund-raisers for the board.

To Edwin W. Winter [98]

May 22, 1941

Dear Eddie:

I enclose contribution of $10 from Steve Hord, which was extracted with the utmost mutual pain, and which he wishes you to realize is accompanied by no inference that it is sustaining in character.

I also enclose a contribution from myself, which, added to a recent contribution to the Linn Scholarship Fund, will immediately diminish the diet of my children.

I am making practically no progress on my other cards, as I haven't had a luncheon hour off in the last two or three weeks. However, do not lose all faith in me.

Yours,

On May 27, 1941, President Roosevelt proclaimed an unlimited state of national emergency. After pointing out that German submarines were sinking merchant ships more rapidly than they could be replaced, he stated: "Our patrols are helping now to insure delivery of the needed supplies to Britain."

At Stevenson's urging, Mayor Kelly issued a proclamation calling for unity and support for the June 6 rally of the All-Chicago Citizen's Committee on America's Crisis.

To Edward J. Kelly

May 28, 1941

Dear Mr. Mayor:

The proclamation is splendid. We are releasing it today. Many, many thanks!

We have given much thought to the problem of filling the Stadium and after consulting many interested people, have decided to go ahead. Of course, the President's great speech last night fortified our resolve to risk it.

Accordingly, if you see fit to speak to Mr. Wertz or Mr. Norris [99]

[98] Executive vice chairman of the Citizens Board of the University of Chicago.
[99] Owners of the Chicago Stadium.

about the expense, it would, I am sure, be enormously helpful. We have not forgotten your own generous proposal but we do not want to impose on you if we can avoid it.

We have been trying to induce Bishop Shiel [100] to pronounce an invocation or benediction at the meeting but with little success so far. After last night's speech, it seems all the more appropriate for him to participate in our appeal for unity.

Sincerely yours,

On May 26, 1941, Thomas Woodward of the United States Maritime Commission wrote Stevenson that he should be in government and asked if he had any particular position in mind.

To Thomas M. Woodward

June 4, 1941

Dear Tom:

What with a lawsuit and a big Unity Rally on Friday which I instigated, I have neglected your good letter. I do not know where the manpower shortages are down there, if any, and I have nothing particularly in mind. The economic warfare business interests me and of course your shipping problems seem to me the critical corner.

Just bear it in mind and if anything turns up that seems promising, I will hop down for a look.

Yours,

J. Lionberger Davis, chairman of the board of the Security National Bank of St. Louis, Missouri, wrote Stevenson on June 11, 1941, that he had heard a good deal about his work with the William Allen White Committee and wanted to meet him.

To J. Lionberger Davis

June 14, 1941

Dear Mr. Davis:

I was delighted to have your letter and the enclosed copy of the St. Louisan, which (if I finish a lawsuit I am in at the present alive) I shall read with great pleasure — and because I know you better than you know me — profit!

100 Bernard J. Shiel, Roman Catholic Bishop of Chicago.

I have felt for a long time that if a few men like yourself, who have the confidence of business and the Roosevelt haters, would organize properly you could effectively counteract the apathy and isolation which has been so prevalent in that class of people. I hope you agree, however, that things are moving now and that our friends are coming around at last — God knows it has taken a long time for them to "read the book."

I shall be more than disappointed if we do not have an opportunity to meet this summer.

Yours,

P.S. — John Stuart has been a stalwart in an awkward situation.

A.E.S.

Every time Secretary of the Navy Frank Knox had visited Chicago, he had conferred with Stevenson and discussed the possibility of his taking a post in Washington. In June, 1941, Colonel Knox asked Stevenson to come to Washington. Stevenson recalled later that Knox said: "I go to all these meetings. Every day, important meetings with important people. There sit [Sidney] Hillman and [William] Knudson and [Henry L.] Stimson, and the others — and every one of 'em has his own personal lawyer. Even Jim Forrestal [101] has his own lawyer and I don't have one. Why don't you plan to come down here and be my lawyer, so I won't feel so defenseless?" [102]

While in Washington, Stevenson explored other possible positions with the government. He returned to Chicago late in June to complete some work at the law firm.

To Oscar Cox [103]

June 27, 1941

Dear Mr. Cox:

I have searched my soul and find it irresponsible as usual. I have also taken counsel of several people of better judgment and have perversely disregarded their advice. In short, I am taking the job with Colonel Knox, instead of a far more adventurous and engaging station with you at better pay! It does not make sense.

The only explanation is that I think Colonel Knox and Mr. Bard [104] really need some help — even mine. I reached my decision with great

[101] James Forrestal, Undersecretary of the Navy.
[102] Davis, *The Politics of Honor*, p. 141.
[103] Director of the Office of Emergency Management, Washington, D.C.
[104] Ralph Bard, Assistant Secretary of the Navy.

reluctance and I earnestly hope that somehow I will find opportunities for conspiracies with you.

You were very kind to me and I shall not soon forget it.

Sincerely yours,

To Herbert Emmerich [105]

June 27, 1941

Dear Mr. Emmerich:

You were more than kind to arrange the appointments with Judge O'Brian [106] and Mr. Oscar Cox for me, and I was disappointed not to meet you. Colonel Knox seems at last to want a lawyer around, and I am expecting to come down to join him in a few weeks. I will look for another opportunity to meet you at that time.

Judge O'Brian was most cordial and generous with his time and I had an illuminating talk about OPM with Mr. Eaton and Mr. Smith.[107] Mr. Oscar Cox suggested a position in his "shop," which I was probably a fool not to accept. I think he is close to the nerve center of the whole defense organization, and I cannot imagine more engaging work or a more congenial association from the little I saw of him and the much I have heard about him. Moreover, the compensation was much larger!

But candidly I feel that Colonel Knox and Ralph Bard need some help, even of my modest quality, far more than Mr. Cox. Hence, my reluctant decision — and I only hope my native [naval] work will afford me an opportunity to see something of you and of him.

Sincerely yours,

To John Lord O'Brian

June 27, 1941

Dear Judge O'Brian:

Following our conversation on Monday, I had a very enlightening talk with Mr. Eaton and Mr. Smith. I promised to give them full information about myself and they were good enough to suggest that, subject to a satisfactory check, it was not unlikely one of them might use me in his division.

Meanwhile, Colonel Knox seems to be going the way of all govern-

---

[105] On the staff of the Office of Production Management.
[106] John Lord O'Brian, general counsel of the Office of Production Management.
[107] Frederick Eaton and Geoffrey S. Smith were on the staff of the Office of Production Management.

ment flesh and has asked me to come into his office as his legal advisor; it seems a poor reward for an unright [upright] man who has for a year been uncorrupted by us lawyers! But you will understand my anxiety not to let him escape now that he has capitulated.

I am most grateful for the precious time you wasted on me, and I will look forward to further encounters when I return to Washington in a few weeks.

Sincerely yours,

To Frederick Eaton

June 27, 1941

Dear Mr. Eaton:

I am enclosing a copy of a letter to Judge O'Brian. From something you said while I spoiled a large part of a precious morning for you, I suspect you will feel that I have made a proper decision. Moreover, Colonel Knox does need some so-called "legal" help badly, and I flatter myself that I may be of some use to him — at least he has no one else!

I will look forward to seeing you again when I am a sailor and I will apologize for my trespasses.

Sincerely yours,

Colonel Knox replied to the following letter on July 2, 1941, "I am tremendously pleased over the contents of your letter . . . You tell your partners that I have no doubt whatever about my judgment in this particular matter."

To Frank Knox

June 30, 1941

Dear Mr. Secretary:

I signed my oath, etc. and sent the papers to Mr. Piozit [108] last Friday. I trust they were in his hands in ample time to avoid any conflict with the Ramspeck Bill. [109]

I have talked with my partners at length and they were glad to give me a leave of absence until October, at which time we can all look the situation over again. They were as much surprised and flattered as

---

[108] Charles Piozit, director of personnel in the Secretary's office.
[109] The Ramspeck Act, November 29, 1940, altered some classifications in the Civil Service. 54 Stat. 1211; S.U.S.C. 631a.

I was — and doubtless somewhat shocked by your doubtful judgment!

I have told Ralph [Bard] that I expect to get my desk cleaned up sometime between the 16th and 23rd of July and will report at once thereafter. I only wish it could be sooner, but I seem to have a myriad of things to liquidate. I have also undertaken to help the Treasury find a suitable administrator for Illinois for the War Savings Bonds sales campaign.

Faithfully yours,

p.s. Should you think better of your invitation before I leave, I should not be in the least surprised!

A.E.S.

To James H. Douglas, Jr.

July 12, 1941

Dear Jim:

I don't know where I have been the last couple of weeks, but only yesterday I heard about your election to the Board of the Metropolitan [Life Insurance Company].

This is an honor of such magnitude that it calls for no ordinary congratulations — particularly tardy ones like this! I take a personal satisfaction in the thought that this great institution has recognized the midwest not by a greybeard but by a member of my generation — and I can think of no better representative! Forgive me for my last row place in the congratulatory chorus.

Yours,

To William P. Sidley

July 15, 1941

Dear Mr. Sidley:

I plan to leave the office the end of this week and report for duty in Washington as assistant to the Secretary of the Navy on Monday, July 21st. As I have told you I have accepted Secretary Knox' invitation on a temporary basis and have agreed to stay not less than three months. In short, I expect to be "at large" at the expiration of that period. However, in the present critical circumstances I cannot, of course, be sure that my service will terminate at that time.

In any event I feel that in fairness to the firm and to avoid any possible inconsistency in my position with the government I should terminate my partnership as of July 21st. I need not tell you with what reluctance and misgivings I have come to this decision!

With sincerest personal regards to you all and best wishes for the continued prosperity of the firm, I am,

Faithfully yours,

To Kenneth F. Burgess [110]

July 17, 1941

Dear Kenneth:

I have just finished reading the petition.[111] It is splendid and I am utterly persuaded! Before I go I want to thank you again for taking so much of your precious time to work on this thing, and to put it in such effective shape. It was another one of those gratuitous things you always seem to do for me in a pinch, and I appreciate it more than I can ever tell you.

I should like to add something about how sensitive I am to one who seems to understand my depth of conviction about the war and my restless anxiety to help in some way. Your prompt approval of this adventure did not surprise me — but it did reassure and comfort me enormously. This kind of stuff is hard to say, but I am sure you know what I mean and feel about your generosity and your patient, tolerant understanding of my eccentricities.

Please give your lady my best regards, and I assume it won't be long before I see you in Washington.

Yours,

P.S. I hope to study a little navigation — along the Potomac — with Kenneth.[112]

Stevenson received a large number of letters congratulating him on his new post in Washington. Only a few of his replies to these are included. His friend Arthur J. Goldberg reminded him that when President Roosevelt asked Mr. Justice Holmes for advice in 1933, Holmes said: "Mr. President, I have been in a war; you are in a war. When you are in a war, you form your battalions and carry the fight to the enemy."

[110] Mr. Burgess, a senior member of Stevenson's law firm, was on a vacation at Green Lake, Wisconsin.

[111] Not clear to what this refers.

[112] Mr. Burgess's son, who lived in Washington, D.C.

To Arthur J. Goldberg

July 18, 1941

Dear Arthur:

I have received a lot of letters in the last few days, but your reminder of Holmes' words fortifies me most of all.

I trust you are not going to forget that you have promised to let me know when you are in Washington. I am still enjoying occasional glimpses from the dizzy mountain top to which you led me the other day! [113]

Sincerely yours,

To General Edwin B. Watson [114]

July 18, 1941

Dear General Watson:

I have your telegram of July 18th inviting me to become a member of the Volunteer Participation Committee in the office of Civilian Defense. I should be delighted to accept this appointment and be of any possible service. However, I am leaving Chicago tomorrow and on Monday, July 21st, will commence work as Assistant to the Secretary of Navy in Washington.

In these circumstances, I presume you will wish to designate some one else from this area. Please rest assured that I appreciate immensely the President's confidence and courtesy.

Faithfully yours,

Judge Harry M. Fisher, of the Circuit Court of Cook County, wrote Stevenson on July 17, 1941, "It is a brilliant choice . . . You will . . . find ample compensation and joy in doing the things which are so close to your heart."

[113] Mr. Goldberg, in a letter to Walter Johnson dated September 16, 1968, explained: "The 'dizzy mountain top' to which I led Governor Stevenson in 1941 was my suggestion that he run for public office and specifically the United States Senate. In my conversation with him I discovered that he had never met the labor group in Chicago and arranged a meeting at the Amalgamated Bank with the members of the State CIO to promote this idea of mine that Adlai would make an outstanding public servant. As you can see, my faith in him proved to be justified."

[114] A military aide to President Roosevelt.

To Harry M. Fisher

July 18, 1941

Dear Judge:

I appreciate immensely your kind and thoughtful letter. I suspect I will be of little help, but you put your finger on it when you said I would at least have the personal satisfaction of feeling that I am doing my bit.

With kindest personal regards, I am,

Sincerely yours,

Mrs. Mitchell [Julia] Follansbee wrote from her summer home at Traverse City, Michigan, that Stevenson was one of her favorite young men and "Mrs. Carroll Sudler and I have agreed that you are good 'presidential timber' and isn't this exactly the way both Roosevelts got their start?" [115]

To Mrs. Mitchell Follansbee

July 21, 1941

Dear Mrs. Follansbee:

Your letter was more than kind and thoughtful and I appreciate it immensely, but I thought you and Mrs. Sudler were much better judges of "timber" — what have you been doing up there in the forests of Michigan all these years?

Faithfully yours,

Gardner Cowles, Jr., of the Register and Tribune, *Des Moines, Iowa, congratulated Stevenson on his job with Colonel Knox and added, "If at any time there is anything* The Register and Tribune *can do to help, just let me know."*

To Gardner Cowles, Jr.

July 21, 1941

Dear Mike:

Many thanks for your note, which awaited me on my arrival for duty

[115] Mrs. Follansbee and Mrs. Sudler were older members of the same social group in Chicago to which the Stevensons belonged.

this morning. I hope you will find a moment for me when you pass this way. It was thoughtful of you to write, and I appreciate it.

Sincerely yours,

The mayor of Chicago wrote Stevenson on July 23, 1941, that, "I am confident that your exceptional qualifications will enable you to render valuable service to your country in this capacity. . . . The patriotism which prompts you.to devote your time and ability to the needs of the nation in this crucial period is worthy of the highest commendation and will be gratefully remembered by your fellow citizens."

To Edward J. Kelly

July 25, 1941

My dear Mayor Kelly:

It was more than kind of you to write me and I appreciate your thoughtfulness immensely.

I know you share my feeling about the emergency, and can understand my anxiety to be of any possible help.

I shall not soon forget the enthusiastic comfort and support you gave our Stadium meeting last month. I am still feeling gratifying repercussions and our success was the incentive for similar meetings in Los Angeles and San Francisco this week.

Faithfully yours,

When, near the end of his life, Adlai E. Stevenson was honored at the Third Annual Eleanor Roosevelt Memorial Award Dinner on April 12, 1965, Mrs. Danny Kaye produced a show based on the television program This Is Your Life. *A number of people took part, all of whom were concealed behind a curtain and who first spoke without appearing on the stage. Stevenson was asked by the master of ceremonies, Steve Allen, to identify the voices.*

Edward D. McDougal, Jr., who had been a partner in the firm of Sidley, McPherson, Austin, and Burgess at the same time as Stevenson, prepared a skit about Stevenson's requests in 1933, 1941, and 1947 for leaves of absence from the law firm. Steve Allen took the part of Adlai and McDougal the part of senior partner William P. Sidley. The second part of the skit, which follows, describes what occurred when Adlai asked Mr. Sidley for a leave of absence in 1941.[116]

[116] "I must confess that a great deal of the material in my skit is apocryphal,"

Head of the firm at his desk. Enter a junior partner, on the run, pursuant to appointment.

HEAD OF THE FIRM: "Good morning, Adlai."

ADLAI: "Good morning, sir. I greatly appreciate your taking time to consider my problem. I respectfully request a leave of absence. Mr. Frank Knox, Secretary of the Navy, has asked me to go to Washington as his assistant. I served as an apprentice seaman in the late war and he believes my know-how will help him in his duties by giving him the viewpoint of the man before the mast. I will gain valuable experience which will enable me, on my return, to represent with greater competence the firm's distinguished clients who pursue shipping."

HEAD OF THE FIRM: "Adlai, you have done excellent work since your return from Washington in 1934. Our clients are well pleased. The treasurer of Commonwealth Edison has expressed great satisfaction with your work on the prospectus and mortgage indenture for the company's recent bond issue. He tells me your style plainly showed the influence of Macaulay and Ogden Nash, and accounts, he believes, for the extra ⅛th point bid by the underwriters. Your argument in the Rialto real estate case was in the best tradition of Winston Churchill. It's a pity you lost the case. But your drafting of the future interest provisions in the Clifford Jones' will evidenced a firm grasp of the Rule in Shelley's Case.

"We have recognized your accomplishments and made you a partner. You are moving onward and upward. But, my boy, remember, a rolling stone gathers no moss. Do not interrupt the continuity of your progress here for a life on (or near) the ocean wave. There can be no assurance, if you leave us, that there will be an opening on your return."

ADLAI: "Thank you sir. Your remarks are to the point, but I feel I must go."

Mr. McDougal wrote, "but the interviews actually took place and the attitude of the head of the firm was about as outlined." Letter to Walter Johnson, November 15, 1967. The first part of the skit appears at the close of Part Six of this volume.

Acknowledgments
and Index

Acknowledgments

We are most grateful to Governor Stevenson's sister, Mrs. Ernest L. Ives, for her infinite patience and her considerate help at all stages in the preparation of this Volume, including the excellent photographs she provided. In addition to Mrs. Ives, Professor Stuart Gerry Brown and Kenneth S. Davis read the entire manuscript, and the entire manuscript was submitted to the members of the Advisory Committee to *The Papers of Adlai E. Stevenson;* and their suggestions have been most valuable. Edward D. McDougal, Jr., and Mrs. Edison Dick read Parts VII, IX, and X. Edmund S. DeLong read Part III, Francis T. P. Plimpton read Part IV, Loring C. Merwin read Part V. Their help is deeply appreciated. We are also deeply grateful to Adlai E. Stevenson III and his brothers, John Fell Stevenson and Borden Stevenson, for their help and cooperation.

Little, Brown and Company, Mrs. Eugene Meyer, Mrs. Marshall Field III and the Field Foundation, Mrs. John French, Mr. and Mrs. Harold Hochschild, Arnold M. Picker, Robert Benjamin, Newton N. Minow, James F. Oates, Jr., Francis T. P. Plimpton, Benjamin Swig, Philip M. Klutznick, Mrs. John Paul Welling, William McC. Blair, R. Keith Kane, Simon H. Rifkind, Wilson W. Wyatt, William Benton, Daggett Harvey, Mr. and Mrs. Edison Dick, William McCormick Blair, Jr., Lloyd K. Garrison, J. M. Kaplan, Jerrold Loebl, Hermon D. Smith, Edward D. McDougal, Jr., Glen A. Lloyd, Mr. and Mrs. Gilbert Harrison, Irving B. Harris, Edwin C. Austin, Archibald Alexander, Jacob M. Arvey, Paul Ziffren, Frank Karelsen, George W. Ball, C. K. McClatchey, Maurice Templesman, Barnet Hodes, and Scott Hodes generously provided funds to defray the editorial expense of these volumes. The University of Hawaii kindly assisted us in defraying the cost of typing the manuscript.

We are grateful to Roger Shugg, of the University of New Mexico Press; Larned Bradford, of Little, Brown and Company; and Ivan von Auw, of Harold Ober Associates, for their encouragement and support.

[567]

William S. Dix, Alexander P. Clark, and Mrs. Nancy Bressler, of the Princeton University Library; and Paul Spence, of the Illinois State Historical Library, have been most cooperative. John Bartlow Martin, Francis Nipp, Phyllis Gustafson, Roxane Eberlein, Glen Holt, Eric Sears, Karen Ching, Evelyn Elliott, and Robert Carden have helped us in many ways. Jo Ann Jay typed the manuscript with great care.

WALTER JOHNSON
CAROL EVANS

Index

INDEX

Howard, Roy, 528
Howe, Sheldon J., 104
Hubbard, C. J., 141
Hubbard, Janet, 148
Hull, Cordell, 301, 307, 310, 474; letters to, 307-308, 316-317
Hull, Denison, 488
Hull House, Chicago, 210, 284; AES joins board of trustees of, 544
Hurley, Stephen, 420
Hutchins, Maude (Mrs. Robert M.), 359
Hutchins, Robert M., 211, 226, 359, 443n; letters to, 227, 286, 287, 443, 460; quoted, 284; opposition to Lend-Lease bill, 536-537
Hutton, Graham, 389

Ickes, Harold L., 27, 238, 239, 307, 310; letters to, 292-293, 294, 307
Igoe, Michael L., 293, 399
Illinois Children's Home and Aid Society, 284-285
Illinois Lawyers' Non-Partisan Committee, 399
Immigrants' Protective League, Chicago, 284
Insull, Samuel, Jr., 227, 299
International House, University of Chicago, 423-425, 538n
International News Service, 167, 168
International Typographical Union (I.T.U.), 230
Ipswich, Mass., 263-264
Ireland, 354, 359, 368, 415, 417-418; Stevensons' vacation described, 511-517
Irons, Dr. Ernest, 288-289
Israels, Joseph, 315
Italy, 11, 167; AES stories in *Pantagraph* on, 169-175
Ives, Elizabeth (Buffie) Stevenson (Mrs. Ernest): mentioned, 4, 8, 13, 14, 17, 19, 21, 36-39, 41, 45, 47, 48, 56, 68, 72, 73, 75, 76, 81, 104, 106, 114, 124, 125, 126, 127, 129-130, 132, 139, 142, 144-145, 147, 191, 199, 204, 213, 214, 217, 218, 219, 231, 232, 236, 248, 254, 257, 258, 259-260, 261, 370, 455; letters to, 20, 22-23, 101-102, 104, 124, 221, 260, 261, 345-346, 347-348, 350-352, 353-354, 358-359, 362-364, 365-366, 368-369, 477; in Europe, (1920) 85, 89, 92, 93, 94, 98, (1923) 131, 133, 134-135; visits her brother at Harvard, 116-120 *passim;* recalls Christmas 1922, 122; her New York apartment, 180, 181; mar-

riage, 202, 211, 212n; her move to Copenhagen, 216-217, 221; in South Africa, 221, 224, 232; in Washington, D.C., 236-237, 240; in Algiers, 251, 252; in Manchester, Mass. (1934), 260, 264; her move to Stockholm, 345-346, 350, 351, 353; her move to Belfast, 389, 417, 512, 549
  QUOTED, 75n; on Grandfather Davis, 5; on AES's love of travel, 8-9; on Adlai's first visit to Windsor Castle, 11; on Adlai's literary ability, 13, 89n; on family's life in Springfield, Illinois, 17-18; on Adlai's love of sports, 20; on their mother, 22, 77-78; on 1916 political conventions, 27; on her brother's introduction to Washington society, 42; on her brother's smoking, 70n; on their mother's taking a house in Princeton, 77-78; on her brother's knowledge of Paris (1920), 92; on Adlai as traveling companion, 92, 93; on Adlai's maturation at Princeton, 107; on Adlai's joining the *Pantagraph*, 153-154; on Adlai's hatred for Italian Fascism, 167; on her brother's beginning his legal career, 209; on first AES-FDR meeting, 228
Ives, Ernest L., 211, 212n, 216-217, 218, 221, 232, 236, 252, 254, 351, 352, 364, 376, 455; AES's letters to Buff and, 221, 223-225, 347-348; diplomatic post in Turkey, 202, 211, 212n; in Copenhagen, 216-217, 221; in South Africa, 221, 224; in Washington at State Department, 236n, 237, 239-240; Adlai stays with in Washington (1933), 248, 250; Algiers post, 264; Stockholm post, 346; Belfast post, 370, 371, 389, 417, 512
Ives, Timothy Read, 202-203, 205, 214, 216, 218, 223, 224, 231, 248, 351, 353, 362, 365, 368, 389; AES's description of, 204; summer in Manchester, Mass. (1934), 258, 260n, 263, 265

Jackson, Eleanor, 146
Jackson, Robert, 421
Jackson, Schuyler, 104
Jacobs, Sidney J.: letter to, 408
Jaffrey, New Hampshire, 123, 125
Jencke, Marcien, 131
Jenkins, Newton: letter to, 303
Jessup, Philip C., 311-312
Jews, 248-249, 438-441; and White Committee, 488-489, 525-526

member of the executive committee, 547

AND INTERNATIONAL AFFAIRS: stories on Fascist Italy (1926), 169-175, 200; speeches on, 375-382, 383-388, 391, 392-398, 493-501; foreign policy debates with Judson, 493-501, 518-520; and All-Chicago Citizens' Committee on America's Crisis, 551-552. *See also* Chicago Council on Foreign Relations; Committee to Defend America by Aiding the Allies, *above*

AND JOURNALISM, 111, 167, 184, 192; at Choate, 29-31, 39-45, 50-52, 56, 67; at Princeton, 60, 74-76, 78, 98-100, 102, 104; and the *Daily Pantagraph*, 114n, 153-175, 186, 225-226, 255, 256, 262, 312-313; eyewitness stories on Carbondale tornado, 155-160, 186; Scopes trial editorials, 161-167; stories on Fascist Italy (1926), 169-175, 200; his "Why I'll Vote for Roosevelt" in Chicago *Herald-American*, 472-475, 488; Letters to the Editor, 517 (Chicago *Tribune*), 526-527 (Chicago *Daily News*)

AND THE LAW: decision to enter, 154; young lawyer in Chicago, 199-200, 202, 209-241; quoted on, as a profession, 202; leave of absence from Cutting, Moore & Sidley (1933), 240-241; quoted on his frequent boredom with, 284; seeks post of U.S. District Attorney, 291-295, 313; seeks appointment as special counsel for RFC, 294-298, 300

PERSONAL LIFE: religion, 3-5, 41, 52, 54, 59; family background, 3-5, 111, 358, 371-372; parental constraints, 4, 13, 29-30, 60, 77-78, 93, 106; education, 13, 27-56 (Choate), 59-107 (Princeton), 111-150 (Harvard Law School), 154 (Northwestern); nicknamed "Rabbit" at Princeton, 78; European vacation, (summer 1920) 79-98, (summer 1921) 102-103; and Claire Birge, 179-206; and Buffie's marriage, 211; his engagement to Ellen Borden, 205-206, 212, 214, 215, 216; his marriage, 216-218; his father's death, 218; decides to return to Chicago (1934), 258-259; honored at Third Annual Eleanor Roosevelt Memorial Award Dinner, 240n; his mother's death, 288, 351; fire at his Libertyville home, 382, 388-389, 416; his memorabilia of his grandfather, 352, 404, 407, 416, 431;

his own sons' education, 402; decides to return to wartime Washington, 539-540, 552, 554, 555-556, 557-563; congratulated on position with Knox, 559-562

POLITICAL AND PUBLIC LIFE, 27, 28, 97, 149-150, 325, 375, 399, 457, 460; fascination with public affairs, 3-5, 111, 358, 371-372; investigates diplomatic service, 188, 190; decisions concerning a political career, 218-219, 220; and FDR, 218, 237, 330-331, 333, 337, 351, 472, 481, 508, 527; and 1932 Illinois gubernatorial campaign, 228-231; and New Deal, 237, 238, 245-279; and Agricultural Adjustment Administration, 246-252; and FACA, 252; seeks post of U.S. District Attorney, 291-295, 313; first political endorsement (for Mayor Kelly of Chicago), 294; seeks appointment as special counsel for RFC, 294-298, 300; and Cook County Democratic party, 319; and Democratic National Committee, 331; first "political speech" (Carleton College, 1936), 337-342, 503; and 1936 presidential election, 343; chairman of President's Birthday Ball (1937), 347; suggested for post of Commissioner of Immigration and Naturalization, 357-358; suggested for appointment as assistant Attorney General (1937), 362; called leader of Young Democracy in Chicago, 366; and 1940 Illinois primaries, 447-448, 502; and Norris-LaGuardia Committee of Independent Voters for Roosevelt, 502-504, 507-508; decides to return to wartime Washington, 539-540, 552, 554, 555-556, 557-558, 563; congratulated on position with Knox, 559-562

QUOTED: on mood of 1920, 97; on 1924 Democratic convention, 149; on atmosphere of 1926 Moscow, 168; on the law as a profession, 202; on his view of his life, 203; on his discomfort with public speaking, 283; on his frequent boredom with the law, 284; on definition of brotherhood, 408

SOCIAL LIFE: at Harvard Law, 117, 119, 126, 130-150 *passim;* in Chicago (1928-1933), 202, 210, 217; Washington, 253

SPEECHES AND ORATORY, 70n-72n, 283, 287, 317, 419-420; at Choate alumni meeting, Chicago 1936, 28-29; at Princeton 1954 senior class